MONTY

MONTY

*The Battles of Field Marshal
Bernard Montgomery*

Nigel Hamilton

Hodder & Stoughton

Copyright © 1981, 1984, 1986, 1994 by Nigel Hamilton

The right of Nigel Hamilton to be identified as the Author of
the Work has been asserted by him in accordance with the
Copyright, Designs and Patents Act 1988.

First published in Great Britain in 1994
by Hodder and Stoughton
a division of Hodder Headline PLC
Trade Paperback edition 1995

10 9 8 7 6 5 4 3 2 1

British Library Cataloguing in Publication Data

A CIP catalogue record for this title is available from
the British Library

ISBN 0 340 64692 6

Printed and bound in Great Britain by
Mackays of Chatham PLC, Chatham, Kent

Hodder and Stoughton
A division of Hodder Headline PLC
338 Euston Road
London NW1 3BH

In memoriam
General Sir Charles Richardson
1908–1994

Preface

The contribution of Field Marshal Bernard Montgomery to Allied victory in World War II can never be overstated—though "Monty" (as he became known the world over) often overstated his genius for battle. Lacking the opportunistic flair of Rommel or George S. Patton, he nevertheless possessed qualities that would prove far more important in the history of the democratic world at war.

As I have tried to show in my *Monty* trilogy,* Bernard Montgomery's military success was not accidental. Nor was it due to simple preponderance of arms. On the eve of the Second World War he was an unemployed major general. He finished it a field marshal and the most famous soldier of Europe.

His legacy to the Allied armies endures today: training, rehearsal, and professionalism in the handling of men and women in a democratic cause—guided by the demand for simplicity, clear aims, frontline leadership and care among commanders to preserve human life as far as is possible.

Yet Monty's reputation, among historians, particularly in America, has not fared so well. Often on the border of madness in his determination to see the right military decision prevail, he was venerated by his troops but often maligned by his allies, and had a hard time under the postwar scalpel of historical pathologists. Arrogant, vain, boastful, boorish and bigoted, he wanted to win, in his subsequent celebrity, all the battles he had lost as a child. Lacking magnanimity, he went to his grave embattled, lonely and haunted, for all his greatness.

Monty: The Making of a General (London: Hamish Hamilton, 1981); *Monty: Master of the Battlefield* (London: Hamish Hamilton, 1983); *Monty: The Field-Marshal* (London: Hamish Hamilton, 1986).

Yet for all his failings as a man he was a great soldier, and without him, General Eisenhower once mused, it remains questionable whether the Allied landings in Normandy on D-Day, 6 June 1944, could have succeeded.

However awkward his character, however infuriating his ego, we are doing history a disservice if we ever forget or denigrate what, at a critical moment in the history of the democratic cause, Monty did. The full narrative of his life, complete with footnotes, sources and documentation, can be found in my original trilogy. But on this, the fiftieth anniversary of the D-Day landings and the Allied campaign in northwest Europe, I wanted simply to record Monty in his most historic role: first as the man who turned defeat into victory for the British Eighth Army, then, as Commander-in-Chief of the American, British and Canadian armies, the man who mounted the greatest seaborne invasion that history has ever known: an invasion whose prize, after eleven months of bitter fighting, was the conquest of Nazi Germany.

Nigel Hamilton
John W. McCormack Institute
University of Massachusetts at Boston

Contents

List of Maps

Prelude

Monty, his wife, Betty, with Monty's stepson
Dick and son, David, India, 1934.

I

Bernard Law Montgomery was born on 17 November 1887 in Kennington, South London. In many ways, he later wrote, his whole life was to be a series of battles: with his mother, his teachers, his army superiors; with the grim reaper who robbed him of the love of his life, his wife, Betty; with his allies; and, above all, with the enemy in two world wars.

Bernard Montgomery's father was an Anglican vicar; his mother the daughter of a famous Victorian preacher. By the age of two Bernard was on his way to Australia, where his father had been appointed Bishop of Tasmania.

Bernard, however, was not destined to take holy orders, but to disobey them. As third son and fourth child in a family of nine children he grew up a sort of misfit: too smart, too spirited, too mean for his own good. He adored his father, but his father was seldom at home, since the Bishop took his new job to be that of a missionary, converting aborigines and islanders with tireless energy and unwavering faith. Bernard's handsome mother, Maud, had become engaged at fourteen and had married at sixteen. In the absence of her husband she began to rule the home in Hobart with a rod of iron, beating her children for any infraction of her domestic rules—especially Bernard, who rapidly became a rebel. "Go and find out what Bernard is doing and tell him to stop it!" became her stock saying. "He was the bad boy of the family, mischievous by nature and individualist by character," Bernard's elder brother Donald described him.

Beyond the small town of Hobart there was an unspoiled hinterland where Bernard could hunt, fish, ride, swim and explore to his heart's content. His childhood thus followed a harsh passage between freedom and flagellation. He bullied other children, was beaten; he picked up an Australian accent and was forced to stand in front of the family intoning "correct" English. He chased a girl through the house brandishing a carving knife and was flogged. Often he would fling himself down in the long grass of the rambling garden crying, "What have I done? What have I done?"

Where Bernard Montgomery's life would have led had the Bishop remained in Tasmania is a matter of speculation, but at the age of fourteen Bernard returned with his family to London, where his father became secretary of the Society for the Propagation of the Gospel, the Church of England's missionary organization. Bernard was sent to St. Paul's School. Treated as a "colonial," he soon decided he would join the army. In 1906 he passed into Sandhurst as an officer cadet and was quickly promoted to command of his company. However, the vicious, impetuous streak in his character inevitably drove him to excess. Leading a charge against another company, armed with pokers, he found and took a "prisoner," ordering his men to hold the cadet fast while he set fire to his regimental dinner-shirt from behind.

In the ensuing scandal—for the student was severely burned and had to be hospitalized—Bernard was demoted and sent home pending an inquiry. Only the intervention of his mother, Maud—who took the next train to Camberley and sought a private interview with the commandant—saved Bernard from expulsion.

It was a salutary experience. Bernard could not and would not change his bullying character; but he could, and did, attempt to harness his prodigious energy and initiative to his chosen profession: that of a professional soldier. Commissioned into a battalion of the Royal Warwickshire Regiment serving in India, he was soon asked to run a school for reconnaissance scouts. As sports officer of his battalion he refused to obey his colonel's order to field a second-rate soccer team to play the crew of the German battleship *Gneisenau*, which was paying a courtesy visit to Bombay with the German Crown Prince aboard. "Every single man of our first team was on the field," the colonel later recalled in chagrin, "and the result was a shambles—forty to nothing I think. To my remonstrations he replied: 'Oh! I was taking no risks with those bastards!' "

In 1912 the battalion returned to Britain. Bernard—by now known as "Monty" to all but his own family—passed out top in the army signaling exams and became assistant adjutant. He was twenty-six, a full lieutenant, and showing a belated interest in military history when, in the summer of 1914, Europe became engulfed by crisis. Mobilized, Monty's regiment was ordered to repel a possible German invasion of the eastern counties.

"The general opinion, which I share, is that Germany will get an awful hammering," Monty wrote his mother. "Austria will be pretty well occupied by Servia and the Balkan states who will probably come in; Italy is trying to remain neutral. So Germany will be left on her own to take on Russia & France, one on each side of her, and England. Germany couldn't possibly do this; the trouble is that she may realise this & back out of it. Then we would be as we were before. . . ."

Monty had much to learn.

II

The German Reichswehr, ignoring Belgium's neutrality, advanced through the Ardennes, broke through the French lines at Sedan and sought to outflank Paris. For a "scrap of paper"—Britain's guarantee of Belgian neutrality—Britain reluctantly but honorably declared war. The bulk of Britain's regular army in England was dispatched to France, and on 23 August 1914 Monty's battalion disembarked at Boulogne, just in time to see action during the retreat from Mons.

Little in Monty's training, whether in India or Britain, had prepared him for the reality of modern field warfare. With only a smattering of machine guns and light field artillery, the "flower of Britain's manhood" was mown down—indeed, Monty's life was saved only when he tripped on his sword strap, while leading his first, suicidal infantry charge against the enemy.

The days of fighting Zulus and Afghan warriors were over. This was war between "civilized" nations, each fighting the other with a barbarity and indifference to casualties that still chill the imagination. Leading his company in another charge at Meteren in October 1914, Monty stormed the village, earned the Distinguished Service Order— Britain's second-highest award for gallantry—and was shot through the chest and knee by a sniper. One soldier, attempting to bring him to safety, was killed and collapsed on top of him. For three hours, in pouring rain, Monty lay bleeding to death. A grave was dug, but somehow he survived, and by the following year was preparing again for combat—this time as a staff officer.

For Monty, this was to be the seminal experience of his entire life. Others might demonstrate equal courage, show greater military inventiveness or powers of charismatic leadership in the field, but few if any possessed the young Captain Montgomery's perception that the war on the Western Front would be won or lost not by guns or even, later, tanks, but by those nations able to raise fresh armies when the first flower wilted and fell, as it did in the spring of 1915. Such fresh armies would have to be created out of nonprofessional soldiers: volunteers and later conscripts, men without the remotest military experience, acting only out of patriotism or duty. To these men, as brigade major of the 105th Brigade, Monty recognized a sort of burning, evangelical mission that was akin to that of his father as a young vicar and bishop. Ideas of glory and wild courage were over. The task of a brigadier or general was to train his men and so command them in combat as to gain objectives with the minimum of casualties. While men like Field Marshal Haig butchered the British army in a series of bloody battles (at the Somme in 1916, some 57,000 British casualties were sustained in a single day), Monty learned the lessons that would, one day, help save the democratic world.

What can a responsible commander, concerned with human life, ask the men of a democracy to do? Does not a commander carry a responsibility to study his enemy, and train his officers and men *in advance of* battle, integrating artillery and infantry, pivoting both attack and defense upon positions of strength, and streamlining communications to ensure maximum cohesion? Clarity of purpose was imperative, but imaginative rehearsal—by the staff as well as the participating troops— was the secret of waging modern war, Monty became certain. By the summer of 1917 Monty had been promoted to become training officer of an entire British army corps. In its autumn offensive under General Plumer, 9 Corps was "entirely successful every time we attack," Monty wrote with pride to his father. "The attacks delivered on 20th Sept (Polygon Wood), 26th Sept (Menin Road), 4th Oct (Broodseinde), and today, are really masterpieces and could not have been better," he boasted—for his sixty-page training instructions and "full dress rehearsal of the attack in every detail," conducted under his own supervision in a special training area prior to the offensive, had kept casualties to a minimum. Officers and men were finally "learning many valuable lessons and there are few, if any, mistakes."

Once again, Haig misjudged the situation, ordering Plumer's model attacks to be extended into an unrehearsed battle for the Passchendaele Ridge. The bloodletting recommenced. By 11 November 1917 the Canadian Corps—which had joined the Ypres battle in late October—had lost 12,000 casualties. "The Canadians are a queer crowd," Monty confided to his mother. "At plain, straightforward fighting they are magnificent, but they are narrow-minded and lack soldierly instincts. . . . They forget that the whole art of war is to gain your objective with as little loss as possible."

Still only twenty-nine, Monty had, in the "fog of war," proved his courage, embarked upon a great mission, and seen its value proven in battle. The question now was whether he could, given his difficult character, master the art of command in battle himself.

III

Promoted to major and subsequently to temporary lieutenant colonel, Monty was charged in 1918 with operational planning in 9 Corps throughout the devastating defensive battles of the Lys and Chemin-des-Dames during Ludendorff's "Spring Offensive," then became chief of staff to the Commander of 47th (London) Division during the triumphant Allied counteroffensive in the summer and autumn, which culminated in German retreat, political collapse and a general armistice on 11 November.

Watching his commanding officer, Major General Gorringe, at close quarters, Monty was consumed with interest in the nature and conduct of generalship. The experience, however, lasted only four months—after which Monty cascaded down the ladder of the British army hierarchy. Though a student at the army's Staff College at Camberley, then brigade major during the "Troubles" in Ireland, and an instructor himself at Camberley in the mid-1920s, ten years after the end of World War I he was *still* only a major: admired by some for his energetic professionalism, but disliked by others who found him meddlesome, narrow-minded and insufferably sure of himself.

Dancing with a seventeen-year-old music student in Brittany, for example, Monty proposed to her. When she declined to marry him, he pursued her for the next eight months. When she declared, finally, that she would never marry him, he told her she was "the first thing I have failed to conquer."

The experience, however painful to Monty's *amour propre*, was crucial. People were not things, and could not always be molded according to the will and designs of a commanding officer. Humbled, he resigned himself to the life of an army bachelor, only to find himself falling in love with a woman his own age—he was approaching forty—whose husband had been killed at Gallipoli, and who had two teenage sons: Betty Carver.

Marriage to Betty, on 27 July 1927, was to provide Monty with the missing ingredient in his life. Ambitious, courageous, blessed with a sharp mind and a gift for simplifying the complicated, he had been fighting since childhood to assert himself, without ever winning love. In Betty Carver he found a woman, mature, artistic, maternal, humorous and loyal, who returned at last his affection. They became inseparable; she bore him a son, David; he took command of his Royal

Warwickshire battalion, and they traveled together to Palestine, Egypt and India. The most brilliant trainer in the British army was finally a full colonel, his mind and heart broadened by a quality of marital fulfillment he had never really believed would be his.

It was not to last, however. Recalled from India in 1937 to take command of an infantry brigade in England—usually the precursor to appointment to the rank of general—he flung himself into his new job with customary energy and a growing sense of confidence in himself as a leader of men. Commanding the brigade in summer maneuvers on Salisbury Plain, he left Betty with nine-year-old David at Burnham-on-Sea for a holiday. There, Betty was bitten by an insect on the sand. The wound became infected, and she was moved to a cottage hospital. Septicemia and gangrene set in, and despite amputation of her leg as a last resort, she passed away.

IV

Betty's death almost crushed Monty. He wrote to his stepson, Dick Carver, on 19 October 1937:

> I never left her for the last 24 hours and it was heart-breaking to watch her slowly dying. The final end was very peaceful, just one deep sigh; and she had no pain the last few days. She knew me up to about one hour before she died, after which she never opened her eyes or spoke. . . .
>
> I think she knew she could not live. This morning when the doctor had left the room she whispered to me to go after him and ask him what he thought. And later when he came in again she gasped "Is there any hope?" Poor darling—she had a ghastly time during the last 6 weeks and had fought most bravely to live. I used to tell her she must fight for our sakes. But it was too much for her.

Two days later he described Betty's funeral—which in his grief he only permitted four people to attend:

> The funeral is over and I am back at Ravelin House. It was a lovely day & brilliant sun. Dick Sheppard came and took the service most beautifully.
>
> I sat [. . .] in the room at the hospital until they came to screw the lid on the coffin. She looked too wonderful—utterly calm and peaceful. . . .
>
> I kissed her dear face for the last time just before the lid was put on. The room was full of the most lovely flowers sent by all our friends. All my battalions in the Bde sent wreaths, and I was very touched to see one

from the men of the Queens. I tried hard to bear up at the service and at the graveside. But I could not bear it and I am afraid I broke down utterly. Dick [Sheppard] was too wonderful & when everyone had gone away we knelt down together at the graveside and he said a very intimate family prayer, and we knelt there in silence. I said I could not believe it was God's will that she should have all that pain & suffering, and then die after it; surely if she had to die it should have been before all the pain. He said that God's ways of working are very mysterious, and I suppose that is true.

But, oh Dick, it is hard to bear and I am afraid I break into tears whenever I think of her. But I must try to bear up. I have come back alone to this big empty house for good now. And I get desperately lonely and sad. I suppose in time I shall get over it, but at present it seems that I never shall.

Yet Monty did—indeed he now threw himself back into his work as a missionary trainer of officers and men, propelled by certainty that there would be another war with Germany, and that the British army was ill equipped both in arms and in imagination to confront its coming challenge.

Betty Carver had ensured that, in terms of Monty's brilliant but awkward character, his rough edges had remained but edges. With Betty's death there was now no safety net. Though Monty organized the first British assault-landing rehearsal since the Great War, at Studland Bay in 1938, and prepared a remarkable special report to the War Office on the likely use and effect of gas attacks in a new war, he eventually fell foul of his enemies. Together with the mayor of Portsmouth he had rented out government property to raise £1,000 for his brigade's welfare fund (for soldiers' families in special need). As a result, he was told that "this incident had ruined my chances of promotion in the British army." The brigadier would remain a brigadier.

Destiny dictated otherwise. Though he had made himself thoroughly disliked in certain quarters, Monty was widely acknowledged to be an exceptional commanding officer. When the Arabs revolted in Palestine against Jewish immigration and the British mandate (granted at the Peace of Versailles), Monty was promoted to major general and asked, as Commander of the 8th Division, to "sort out the mess."

Monty did—and was rewarded, in the spring of 1939, with promised command of Britain's famous 3rd (Iron) Infantry Division, which was due to be reequipped as a motorized division.

At this crucial juncture in Monty's life, at age fifty-one, he suddenly and for the first time in his adult life fell seriously ill. Hospitalized in Haifa, he was diagnosed as having suspected tuberculosis: "evidence of tubercular infiltration in the mid-zone of the left lung, with minimal pleural effusion at the base." Carried on board the SS *Ranchi* at Port Said on a stretcher, he seemed past his soldiering days. "He'll never see action," predicted the ship's doctor.

Monty's sister Winsome traveled with him. She watched as, each day, the invalid set himself a new target. "I watched Bernard each day . . . being carried up on deck, unable to walk; then he'd get out of the chair and he'd walk. He'd walk say the length of this room, and the next day the length of the deck, and in no time at all he was walking around it. . . . It was just sheer guts, will power. He wasn't going to give in. There was the sea air, rest, good food. He had Betty's photographs in the cabin. . . . I've often wondered what the ship's doctor thought."

V

Given a clean bill of health by the Military Hospital, Millbank, in London, Monty prepared to take command of the 3rd (Iron) Division. In the meantime he was "placed on the unemployed list" by the Military Secretary at the War Office.

World events, however, shattered the thin veneer of "peace in our time" which Prime Minister Neville Chamberlain claimed to have won at Munich, when agreeing to Hitler's threatened rape of western Czechoslovakia. Though Chamberlain refused to mobilize the army, the Minister of War ordered partial mobilization—an order which, by War Office rules, canceled all pending appointments, including Monty's appointment to command the 3rd Infantry Division.

Like Churchill, Monty had predicted for years that this moment would come, and that Britain's defense forces must be ready. Unemployed, he now called every contact he had in the War Office. In the end, an accelerated position for the indolent and indifferent Commander of the 3rd Division was found as Governor of Bermuda. Monty thus took command of the division on 28 August 1939, only three days before Hitler's invasion of Poland, under an austere, bespectacled new corps commander, a man who was one day to play a cardinal role in Monty's meteoric rise to military renown: Lieutenant General A. F. Brooke.

Dispatched to France soon after the declaration of war on 3 September, Monty's division was part of the British Expeditionary Force, defending northwest France, as in 1914. The French, meanwhile, had put their faith in the Maginot Line. Their air force was weak, army morale low. To the north, Belgium clung tenaciously to a principle of neutrality that had been sundered in 1914; meanwhile it forbade discussions with the high commands of the democracies, or any reconnoitering of terrain by British or French officers in the event of a German invasion.

The military outlook for the democracies thus looked bleak. Jealousy, bigotry and bloody-mindedness characterized the senior French commanders, while Lord Gort's failure, as Commander-in-Chief of the British Expeditionary Force, to organize, train and rehearse his men would go down in history as the most feeble display of British military professionalism in the twentieth century.

In conformity with French plans, Lord Gort had given orders that the British army should leave its prepared defenses in France and invade Belgium from the southwest whenever the German offensive opened. Monty, having got to know Lord Gort and assembling a shrewd picture of French and Belgian unwillingness to fight, had no illusions about what would happen. Thus for six months before the German attack he trained and rehearsed his 3rd (Iron) Division in the art of *retreat:* fighting by day, withdrawing at night.

Monty's 1939–40 divisional exercises remain the most spectacular example of his genius for imaginative training, as—to furious protests from the civilian French authorities—he commandeered sixty miles of French territory to the rear of the British front line and practiced, again and again and again, the role he believed his division would have to play in the coming campaign.

As result, when on 10 May 1940 the German armies once again burst through the Ardennes and split the Anglo-French armies in two, Monty remained wholly unperturbed. Under Brooke's supervision, amidst scenes of utter panic and mass civilian flight, he brought his division almost unscathed back to Dunkirk, where—on Brooke's departure to safety in England—he became 2 Corps Commander.

The prospect looked hopeless to all except Monty—indeed, Brooke, a grown man, burst into tears when bidding Monty farewell on the beach at La Panne. Summoned to a conference with the departing Commander-in-Chief, Lord Gort, Monty listened with amazement as Gort ran over his plans for eventual surrender. "C-in-C very pathetic sight, a defeated and disappointed man," Monty noted in his diary that night, 31 May 1940—and proceeded, with General Alexander, the other corps commander, to ensure that, by maintaining a punishing artillery barrage on the German forward positions, a reasonably orderly evacuation of the entire remaining British and French forces was carried out.

Monty was himself taken off the mole, or harbor wall, at Dunkirk. Traveling by train to London on the afternoon of 1 June 1940, he demanded "a private interview" with General Sir John Dill, the CIGS (Chief of the Imperial General Staff, and thus head of the British army). The next morning, in Dill's office, "I gave it as my opinion that the BEF had never been 'commanded' since it was formed," he recorded in his diary, "and that for the next encounter we must have a new GHQ [general headquarters] and a new C-in-C. I said that the only man to be C-in-C was Brooke."

VI

Monty's remarks about Lord Gort spread like wildfire—and were not forgiven. Both Churchill—who had succeeded Neville Chamberlain as Prime Minister on 10 May—and General Brooke—who did indeed become C-in-C of Britain's Expeditionary Force and then CIGS—were men of extraordinary personal stature: thinkers as well as doers, and, above all, magnanimous towards their discredited predecessors.

Widowed, vengeful and driven by a reformer's zeal, Monty could not find in his heart any such magnanimity. Brave men—including his chief of staff, "Marino" Brown—had been killed as a result of Lord Gort's ineptitude; Britain's field army had been humiliated and forced to return to Britain, often in their underclothes. It was, Monty felt, a disgrace: predictable and wholly unnecessary. The Germans were *not* invincible; indeed, within a week of his return to England, Monty was issuing new training instructions to his division (to which he had been demoted), analyzing the lessons of the recent fighting, and on 17 June 1940 he assembled all 466 officers of the division for the first of his great wartime addresses—forbidding all smoking, coughing or talking while he outlined the story of the Dunkirk campaign, the combat techniques of the German army they had faced, and the proper way in which to defeat the Wehrmacht in battle.

From this time onward, Monty's reputation among his subordinates would grow and grow: a battlefield commander who possessed a razor-sharp ability to assess morale, technical ability and standards of training, as well as an infectious certainty that Britain's army could and would defeat its German foe in battle. However, his reputation among his superiors became as negative as it was positive to his subordinates. His corps commander, General Auchinleck, despised him for his cocksure bombast and his obsession with training exercises—which Auchinleck later considered to be "mostly rubbish." Worse still, in a Britain which might well have found political accommodation with Hitler after France's surrender in July 1940 had it not been for the spirit and leadership of Winston Churchill, Monty did not hit it off with the new Prime Minister.

The two men met for lunch on 2 July 1940 in Brighton—where the brunt of German invasion was expected to fall. Monty was full of himself, and boasted he would make mincemeat of any German invaders. He did not smoke (he had given up smoking after a brush with tuberculosis in 1938) and he did not drink (he had given up alcohol at the same time). As a result he was, he claimed, one hundred per cent fit.

Churchill eyed Monty for a while: this little man with a balding head, beaky nose and small mustache. Then, toying with his glass, the Prime Minister responded. "I drink," he acknowledged, "and I smoke," he added, taking a puff from his huge cigar. "And," he declared, bellowing out his immortal rebuke, "*I AM TWO HUNDRED PER CENT FIT!*"

"A little man on the make," Churchill sniffed to his staff after luncheon was over. Though Monty was eventually given a corps command, a further year and a half was to pass before he was given a higher command (as Commanding General, South-Eastern Command, which he instantly retitled "South-Eastern Army"), and always in Home Forces in England, while his contemporaries—such as Wavell, Alexander, O'Connor, Percival and Slim—were all sent abroad to fight.

Greece, Crete, Hong Kong, Singapore, Burma, Tobruk: week by week, month by month, disaster after disaster beset Britain's armies overseas. Yet still Monty, disliked by Churchill and resented by his military superiors, was consigned to the wings and denied the opportunity to fight. Thus condemned, he watched, frustrated and often appalled, while the catalogue of Churchillian bungling and British defeat in the field reached, by the summer of 1942, the level of lunacy.

Amidst the rumblings of parliamentary calls for his resignation, Churchill flew at last to North Africa to see for himself what was wrong, and to appoint, if need be, a new commander in the North African desert.

After a veritable lifetime of self-preparation, Monty's hour of trial was finally approaching. It was not, however, to come in the way he imagined.

Part One

ARRIVAL IN THE DESERT

Monty, photographed on his arrival in Cairo,
12 August 1942.

The Call to the Desert

"Early in August 1942 a large-scale exercise was to be held in
Scotland and General Paget, then Commander-in-Chief Home
Forces, suggested I should go up with him to see it. I was de-
lighted to have an opportunity to see what other troops were doing,"
Monty later recounted—having just organized his own eleven-day ex-
ercise involving over 100,000 armored and infantry troops in the Kent-
Sussex area.

Monty had also hoped to see his stepson, John Carver, serving in
Scotland. But the Scottish maneuvers had barely begun when, on 7
August 1942, Monty received a telephone call from the War Office,
appointing him to command the Northern Task Force in the Anglo-
American invasion of Morocco and Algeria, scheduled to take place in
October 1942: Operation Torch. Monty was not even the War Office's
first choice, for General Alexander, returning from the British retreat
in Burma, had been detailed for the operation, but had suddenly been
promoted to Commander-in-Chief, Middle East, in Cairo, following
Churchill's dismissal of General Auchinleck. Moreover, Monty's new
boss for Operation Torch would be an American, General Dwight D.
Eisenhower—who had never served in battle or commanded any combat unit above a company.

"I returned to London at once," Monty recalled, "and then went to
the War Office. I was there given more details and was told that the
first thing I must do was to get Eisenhower to make a plan for the operation; time was getting on and the Chiefs-of-Staff could not get Eisenhower to produce his plan. The whole thing did not sound good to
me; a big invasion operation in North Africa in three months' time,
and no plan yet. . . . I returned to my Headquarters at Reigate hoping
for the best."

Ironically the army commander beside whom Monty was to serve under Eisenhower was none other than General George S. Patton. At the American Desert Training Center, Patton had impressed all by his energy and ambition, as well as his flair for tactical exercises. Indeed, in many ways Patton's self-preparation for war was the counterpart of Montgomery's, and from this flowed a similar conviction of the rightness of his own military tenets and beliefs. Just as Monty in England insisted on changing the name of South-Eastern Command into South-Eastern Army, so Patton in America had bullied colleagues and seniors into seeing that standardization and matériel were but half the battle, and that there was a need for proper insignia and markings on all "trucks and vehicles showing the company, regiment, and division to which they pertain. . . . To die willingly, as many of us must," Patton warned the head of American Army Training, "we must have tremendous pride not only in our nation and in ourselves but in the unit in which we serve." Patton was certain he would one day be given the chance to fight against the Desert Fox and "just to keep my hand in for Marshal Rommel" he was in the habit of shooting at least a hare a day with his ivory-handled pistol.

Certainly there were many points of similarity between the two Allied army commanders: both considered brilliant by many, mad by some—and intolerable by others. Yet there was also an intriguing difference in their military philosophy already at this stage of the war, as they both prepared to serve under General Eisenhower on Torch—a difference that made them, despite all other similarities, as variant as chalk from cheese. For Patton believed that the exercise of command in battle was an art and "he who tries to define it closely is a fool"— whereas it was Montgomery's great belief that command could be defined, and ought to be; ought to be something so clear, so widely known among his subordinates, and so rehearsed that victory over "any enemy anywhere" was assured.

Both generals had now proved themselves as trainers and potential army commanders to the point where they had been simultaneously selected to lead their national forces in Operation Torch. Patton was to command the Western Task Force landing on the coast of Morocco, Montgomery the Northern Task Force landing inside the Mediterranean on the coast of Algeria.

On 7 August 1942, Patton reported to Eisenhower in London. The next day he and Monty were due to meet for the first time at a conference to decide the basic plan for Torch. Typically, Patton was afraid that Montgomery would be given the lion's share of the fighting— indeed, Patton's diary for 8 August records that he "said that Northern Task Force was being favored at expense of Western Task Force. Finally got some change. . . ."

The concession, however, was not at Monty's expense. Fate had thrown both men almost together—but not quite. For, as Monty shaved at his villa at Reigate early in the morning of 8 August, there was an urgent telephone call from the War Office in London. His orders regarding Torch were canceled. He was to fly immediately to the Middle East and assume command of the British Eighth Army at Alamein.

A Hasty Departure

M onty's relief was enormous. "Instead of carrying out an invasion of North Africa under a C-in-C whom I barely knew," he later wrote, "I was now to serve under a C-in-C [General Alexander] I knew well and to take command of an Army which was at grips with a German and Italian Army under the command of Rommel—of whom I had heard great things. This was much more to my liking and I felt I could handle that business, and Rommel. So it was with a light heart and great confidence that I made preparations for going to Africa." He added that his only anxiety concerned his thirteen-year-old son, David.

By good fortune, in an old tin trunk in Yorkshire, Monty's letters to Tom Reynolds, headmaster of David's preparatory school at Amesbury, and his wife, Phyllis Reynolds, would later be found to have survived—letters which gave a unique insight into Monty's personality on the eve of the greatest challenge of his life.

Already at the beginning of May 1942, David had left Amesbury School to go to Winchester College. Monty had taken him there by car, reporting to the Reynoldses afterwards: "We all had tea together with the Housemaster & Miss Robertson, and David seemed quite happy and not in the least upset or nervous."

Handing David over at the ancient public school—which Reynolds had recommended in preference to Monty's old school, St. Paul's—

had caused Monty to reflect on how much he already owed the Reynoldses: "I cannot thank you and Tom enough for what you have done for him. It has been the greatest relief to me to know that you were watching over him, and you have brought him on in a way that no one else could have done." Indeed, perhaps recognizing the extent of his neglect of David since 1937, Monty was prepared to see in the firm custodianship of the Amesbury Preparatory School headmaster and his wife a cause for emphatic, almost excessive gratitude: "He lost his Mother when he [was] 8 and the fact that he is now what he is, is due entirely to you and Tom. I am truly grateful to you both."

Monty's next letter, written three months later on the morning of 8 August, was of necessity more urgent. It was addressed to Tom Reynolds:

My dear Tom,
I have to leave England at very short notice to take charge in a very important place. My destination will appear in the papers in due course.

I have been given 8 hours in which to hand over, pack some clothes, and be off. I have not time to see David. He is with

> Mrs. John Carver
> Corner Cottage
> Littlewick Green
> Berkshire
> Tel: Littlewick Green 83

John Carver is on the Staff in Scotland, and may go anywhere. She (his wife) is not really capable of looking after David's affairs, though it is a very good place for him to go in the holidays whenever he likes.

This was somewhat patronizing, considering that Monty had for weeks left his dying wife in young Jocelyn Carver's care, and that David now went to stay with Jocelyn every holiday. However, this was as yet a mild form of Monty's almost pathological urge to reject his own family, after Betty died and he rose to great heights. "Will you and your lady wife take charge of David for me until I return?" he asked. "I would sooner leave him with you than with anyone I know. I am anticipating your acceptance of this task. There is really no one else who could do it. I am sure you will do this. I can never really repay you, but will do my best."

Monty then enclosed a copy of his will—leaving "everything I possess" to David—and £200 on account. "I would like you to pay his school bills, buy his clothes, and in fact be his guardian so long as I am out of England. Give him whatever pocket money you think right. Last term I sent him to Winchester with £2 and gave him another £1 halfway through the term."

Monty also enclosed David's latest school reports from Winchester—a half-term report from June, as well as the end-of-term report for July—which, in his haste, he wrote as "Xmas."

"There is one thing I want you to watch," Monty warned, however:

His Grandmother is Lady Montgomery, New Park, Moville, Co. Donegal. She is an old lady and quite unable to take charge of anyone. She will want David to go and stay in Ireland for his holidays.

On no account is he to go.

She is a menace with the young.

He can have very happy holidays with you, or the Blacklocks, or at Littlewick Green with Mrs. John Carver—this is 3 miles from Maidenhead on the Bath road.

The malevolence with which Monty referred to his mother raises many questions about Monty's state of mind in the summer of 1942. Whether it was the pressure of war or his dedication to what he increasingly saw as his historic military vocation, he now saw his elderly mother as a direct threat—and would increasingly do so as time went on. The tension which seemed to grip him after Dunkirk never relaxed—at least, not until Lady Montgomery was safely dead and old age began to mellow him. By then Monty had quarreled savagely at least once with almost everybody who had ever come to mean anything to him, had scandalized his family by his pretensions and his treatment of his mother, had "insulted and injured" colleagues, seniors, subordinates, friends—and even, in a final irony, turned against the very son David whose custodianship he had, in the summer of 1942 and afterwards, so jealously guarded and apportioned.

In the meantime, on 8 August, Monty begged the Reynoldses to "write and welcome" David as "a No. 2 son." He had himself written to David, who might be "rather upset when he gets my letter." David was "all I have left now," and he left him to the Reynoldses. He signed himself "Monty." Below this signature he added, somewhat indiscreetly:

For your special information and not to be spoken about for a day or two, my address will be:

HQ 8th Army,
Middle East Forces

In fact Monty's flight was canceled that night, owing to bad weather. The following day, 9 August 1942, Monty wrote again from Reigate to reiterate his almost manic determination that no member of his family be allowed power or even the right to advise over David:

> My dear Tom,
>   I am just off.
>   In case my letter (the long one) of yesterday did not make it clear, I want to say again that I put David in your complete and absolute charge. If any members of my family chip in and want to advise, see them right off. The sole authority in EVERYTHING connected with David is yourself; I want you in fact to be his official guardian as long as I am out of England.
>   If I am killed his legal guardian is then John Carver. But I shall not be killed.
>   Good-bye to you.
>
> Yrs ever
B. L. Montgomery

At Lyneham, weather conditions again delayed Monty's journey. Finally, on the evening of 10 August, Monty was able to leave England. He landed the next morning in Gibraltar, taking off in the evening for Cairo. "During the journey I pondered over the problems which lay ahead," he recalled later, "and reached some idea, at least in outline, of how I would set about the business."

The question of his son, insofar as Monty was concerned (he had deliberately not telephoned the Reynoldses lest they decline his request), had been resolved. Once again, as so often in his military life, he was taking over a military command upon which he hoped to imprint his own distinctive authority. This time, however, it was an historic undertaking, at what could become a turning point in the war.

Arrival in Cairo

Churchill had sacked General Auchinleck on 6 August 1942, not only as Eighth Army Commander but as Commander-in-Chief of all British forces in the Middle East.

To replace Auchinleck in Cairo, Churchill had decreed, General Alexander would take over as C-in-C, Middle East. But to face Rommel in the field of battle, as the fourth commander of the British Eighth Army to be appointed in nine months, Churchill had personally selected not Monty but a young, forty-three-year-old corps commander: Lieutenant General Richard Gott.

For all his genius as a statesman and strategist, Churchill was in reality a poor picker of men. General Gott was exhausted, having taken part in the British disaster at Gazala, the retreat to Alamein, and the desperate attempts to hold the line before Rommel brought up further supplies and tanks.

The day after his appointment, Gott had left the front for a brief rest in Cairo and a "proper bath." His plane, however, was shot down and Gott was burned alive in the wreckage. "All my plans were dislocated," Churchill later said of the dilemma for which he himself was responsible. "The removal of Auchinleck from the Supreme Command was to have been balanced by the appointment to Eighth Army of Gott, with all his Desert experience and prestige. . . . What was to happen now?"

Churchill had next favored, to become Eighth Army's *fifth* commander, General "Jumbo" Wilson, commanding the British Ninth Army in Palestine. However, the CIGS, General Sir Alan Brooke, had countered by recommending Monty.

Churchill, dictatorial and tormented by Britain's continuing failures in the field of battle, had balked at Brooke's suggestion. At South-Eastern Army, Monty had earned a reputation for aggressive behavior bordering on insanity. When commanding 12 Corps, for example, Monty had, in defiance of Churchill's instructions, ordered Britain's biggest coastal guns to be fired at Calais, across the English Channel. By chance this had killed a group of high-ranking German officers. As retaliation, the Germans had ordered a bombing raid on Dover the next night, which killed a number of British civilians. "Of course there's nothing wrong with Monty really," one War Office brigadier had said when posting a hapless young Intelligence officer to Monty's staff. "He's just a bit mad."

"Sometimes," the Intelligence officer later recalled, "one had the feeling that the Army commander might at any moment lead his army across the Channel in a personal campaign to liberate Europe."

In time Monty would do just that—indeed, had actually rehearsed such an invasion, involving army, RAF and naval units, in 1938, a year and a half before war broke out. "Mad is he? Then I wish he'd bite some of my generals!" King George II had once remarked of General James Wolfe, before appointing him to command the British army in the capture of Quebec. Similarly, while arousing deep skepticism as to his mental health, General Montgomery was feared and respected in a British army hidebound by tradition, given to much polo-playing and geared to ceremonial: a unique British commander, with a crusading vision not only of how men should be trained, but how modern battle should be conducted. Was he not the best man to pit against Rommel, the "Desert Fox"?

General Brooke felt so. He had taught with Monty at the Staff College, Camberley, in the late 1920s, had remained Monty's loyal friend and advocate over the years; had seen Monty's mettle in 1940 at Dunkirk. Finally, with the help of the South African Prime Minister, Field Marshal Smuts, Brooke persuaded Churchill to change his mind over "Jumbo" Wilson, and to summon, instead, Lieutenant General Montgomery from England.

The resistance to his appointment, fortunately, was concealed from Monty until publication of Brooke's diaries in 1957. To Monty, his promotion to command 8th Army had simply come as a godsend, and he had traveled out to Egypt knowing that he had been given, at last, the chance he had cherished: command of a modern army in the field of battle.

Early on the morning of 12 August 1942, Monty's plane touched down in Cairo: the day Churchill had informed the Cabinet in London that Alexander and Montgomery were to take over their respective new commands. As Monty was soon to discover, however, General Auchinleck had other ideas.

A Fateful Interview

Having bathed, breakfasted and sent his personal aide, Captain Spooner, to buy him some desert clothes, Monty was driven to GHQ to meet Auchinleck in person.

The resulting interview at 11 A.M. on 12 August 1942 was to be, for Monty, as fateful as his meeting with General Lord Gort, the Commander-in-Chief of Britain's army in France, had been on 30 May 1940. Just as Monty bore away from Dunkirk the impression of a defeated commander, bereft of hope, so now his piercing gray-blue eyes studied the face of the soldier he was to replace as Commander, Eighth Army.

He remembered how he had succeeded Auchinleck once already, as Commander of 5 Corps in July 1940; how on that occasion he had instantly reversed Auchinleck's policy of static beach defense; remembered the subsequent quarrels between them while Auchinleck remained GOC (Commanding General) Southern Command.

Since those difficult days in Home Forces, under threat of German invasion, Auchinleck's star had risen—and had fallen. He had failed in battle, and as a consequence had been dismissed. Instead of simply handing over Eighth Army to Monty with his blessing, however, he chose to brief Monty on his own plans for the army—whose commander, he began by announcing, he would remain, in defiance of Churchill's orders, until the end of the week.

Brushing away Monty's questions about current British plans for attack, Auchinleck explained the Eighth Army was refitting. It had suffered over 100,000 casualties during the past months, and there could be no question of an immediate British offensive. On the contrary, it was known from British secret intelligence that Rommel was building up huge stocks of petrol, ammunition, tanks, troops and supplies for another German offensive. If Rommel was successful, it was imperative the Eighth Army not be allowed to become fragmented and destroyed. As it was the only coherent, battle-worthy British army in the Middle East, contingency plans had therefore been made for part of the army to withdraw up the Nile, the other part into Palestine. These plans were being prepared personally by one of his subordinates, the Deputy Chief of the General Staff, Major General John Harding.

"I listened in amazement," Monty recounted in his *Memoirs*, "but I quickly saw that he resented any question directed to immediate changes in policy about which he had made up his mind." For once, Monty was speechless—but with anger at Auchinleck's defeatist stance.

Planning a Reserve Corps

Did Monty exaggerate Auchinleck's pessimistic briefing? There can be no doubt, as will be seen, that exaggeration was one of Monty's techniques in dealing with both human and military problems. As a caricaturist does, he would observe intently, sketch an outline in his mind containing all the essentials of the matter under review, and then bring forth an impression, brilliantly clear to all. Often that impression was distorted, even grotesquely so; but in the main it was frank, sincere—and always arrestingly simple.

Monty's "caricature" of Auchinleck on 12 August 1942 was, and would remain for the rest of his life, that of a toppled general, resentful of his fall and bankrupt of hope: an image typified by plans for British withdrawal.

If Auchinleck was besotted by contingency plans for withdrawal, Monty was obsessed with the idea of attack. From Auchinleck's office he therefore went to see his old companion-in-arms from Dunkirk, General Sir Harold Alexander:

During the journey out by air I had considered the problem very carefully. It was clear to me that what was wanted in Eighth Army was a reserve Corps, very powerful, very well equipped, and very well trained. This Corps must be an armored Corps; it must never hold static fronts; it would be the spearhead of all our offensives.

The Germans had always had such a reserve formation—the Panzer Army—which was always in reserve and was highly trained.

We had never had one; consequently we were never properly "balanced" and we had never been able to do any lasting good. I came to the conclusion that the formation, equipping, and training of such a reserve Corps must be begun at once and must be a priority commitment.

Immediately on arrival in Cairo on the morning of 12 August, I put the project to General ALEXANDER. He agreed, but we had to be very careful as he was not yet C-in-C. It was obviously useless to discuss the matter with General AUCHINLECK or the CGS [Chief of the General Staff], so I put the question, quietly and unofficially, to the DCGS (Gen. HARDING) and asked him to prepare a paper on the subject and to say definitely whether such a reserve Corps could be formed from existing resources. There were 300 new Sherman tanks due at Suez on 3 September, and these would provide the equipment for the Armoured Divisions.

Harding remembered the interview well. By 12 August rumors had begun to circulate about an imminent change in command, so that when, that afternoon, he was sent for by the Commander-in-Chief, Harding had asked, "Who *is* the C-in-C?"

No one seemed sure. In the forthcoming Middle East C-in-C's office Harding found "Monty sitting in the C-in-C's chair at the desk, and Alex sitting on the desk drumming his heels. Monty greeted me, introduced me to Alex and explained the posts they had been appointed to.

" 'Now you've been out here for some time, John,' Monty went on, 'You know all the people in these parts; I want you to tell me something about them, who's good and who's no good.' And for about an hour he put me through a long questionnaire about all the commanders and formations in the desert at that time down to the brigade level."

In his desert diary, Monty was candid, not only about Auchinleck ("very difficult to deal with"), but about Auchinleck's chief of staff ("quite useless") and vice chief of staff ("a menace"). However in Harding Monty found "a first-class officer who had been a student under me at the Staff College—Major-General HARDING. HARDING seemed to me to be the only officer at GHQ who talked sense, and who obviously knew what he was talking about. The DMO [Director of Military Operations] and DMI [Director of Military Intelligence] were, in my opinion, quite unfit for their jobs."

Harding talked a language Monty could understand: simple, direct English. As Harding later recalled, "nobody knew whether they were standing on their arse or their elbow. The army had got completely mucked up: I think the word bewildered describes it better than any other word I can think of. . . .

"The German advance had run out of steam. The 8th Army had come to rest where it had come to, and was in a defensive position—more or less on the Alamein position, but it was really more where it had come back to than any organisation of the Alamein defensive position as such. Very little had been done to fortify it, as far as I remember.

"As far as the atmosphere in Cairo was concerned . . . nobody was at all sure—I mean nobody was in any doubt that sooner or later Rommel would resume the offensive, and then it was a matter of conjecture whether the Alamein position would be held or not. And so the Auk decided to have plans prepared for a withdrawal. And these plans were duly prepared. I myself was involved, as DCGS, because I was given the job, in the event of withdrawal taking place, of trying to delay the German advance into the Delta by holding a series of canal lines and so on. I had a temporary staff, a small number of staff officers and DRs [messengers], on a very temporary and sketchy basis. The plan was that part of the army should withdraw into the delta and should make its escape into Sinai, and the other lot would go down south into the Sudan. . . . How far it was widely known I wouldn't like to say—but certainly I knew about it, and took it seriously, because personally I was quite uncertain that the 8th Army on the Alamein position could hold its own against a further offensive by Rommel."

Monty, however, wished to hear no more about withdrawal. "You see," Harding recounted, "one of Monty's great points in his teaching at the Staff College, Camberley, when I was a student there, was that the critical thing in war was to gain and keep the initiative. And I guessed he'd already made up his mind before he arrived on the scene that he would have to fight a major battle in order to get the initiative, and to keep it. And in order to do that he would have to reorganize and revitalize the 8th Army. Those were the things he'd probably made up his mind about; how to do it, he probably kept an open mind about. And this is why he wanted to hear from me personally about the state of the army, the confidence of the various commanders and how he could reorganize the army."

Harding was quite forthright about the state of the army. "I remember going through all the formations and telling him about them and about their commanders—that at brigade and divisional level they were very good and efficient and morale was very good. But as a total, no, they were disorganized and they were rattled. They had lost their confidence. And he then asked me, 'Well I want to form a Corps de Chasse in order to be able to carry out a major offensive and drive the German/Italian forces out of Egypt and Cyrenaica.' And he asked me, he'd got in mind having two armored divisions and a mobile infantry division and how could this be organized? I said: 'And I presume to hold the front at the same time?' And then I said, yes, I thought I could produce a plan to do this.

" 'Well, I've got to go now with the C-in-C, General Alexander, to see the Ambassador. Can you get on with it for me?' Monty asked. I said yes, if you don't mind it being in my own handwriting I can have it ready in an hour or so. So Monty went off with Alex and I went to my office, where I locked the door and got down to produce those two armored divisions and mobile infantry division as a main striking force to drive the Axis army out of the desert."

Ironically, Harding was now serving two masters. For General Auchinleck he had been charged with the preparation of plans for Eighth Army's withdrawal to the Delta, Khartoum and Sinai; for General Montgomery, plans for a *corps de chasse*!

Monty, having seen the Ambassador and "spent the afternoon buying clothes suitable for the desert in August," was delighted by Harding's secret list of units. "Harding produced a plan that looked good and we decided to adopt it," he noted in his diary. However, to plan such a reorganization and to put it into practice were two different things. It was now Wednesday. Auchinleck had stipulated that the hand-over of both commands was not to take place before the end of the week, a Saturday; moreover he had made clear that, although Montgomery might in the meantime visit Eighth Army, he *was to wait until Saturday before assuming command*. If Rommel attacked before then, Auchinleck had declared he would, himself, resume command of Eighth Army in the field.

In retrospect it was an amazing state of military affairs, in the midst of a world war: Churchill's newly appointed Middle East and Eighth Army commanders not only shackled, but driven to feel they could not openly suggest any change of plans or army reorganization to the outgoing British commander for a further four days.

Such appeared, however, to be the case. Harding was told to wait until Saturday 15 August before issuing any instructions relating to the formation of the new armored corps.

Meanwhile, Monty had asked Alexander's military assistant if he could recommend a second personal aide, or ADC. The recommendation was a young captain, John Poston, who had been ADC to Lieutenant General Gott, but had not been with him on his fatal flight back to Cairo. Monty interviewed Poston immediately, took him on, then set off to dine with the British Ambassador, Sir Miles Lampson, together with Alexander. Meanwhile he instructed Poston to have a car ready before dawn the next morning. It was time to see his new army—on the battlefield.

The "Meat-Safe"

From Cairo Monty's car took the road to Alexandria. There, at the crossroads outside the city where the road branched left to the desert, he was met by "Freddie" de Guingand, Brigadier General Staff (BGS) of Eighth Army, who had been detailed to accompany him to Eighth Army Headquarters, just behind the Ruweisat Ridge, ten miles south of Alamein.

It was now 7:30 A.M. De Guingand had prepared a paper to show the new commander-elect, but Monty, having asked de Guingand to join him in his car, characteristically pushed away the paper and insisted on a verbal précis.

The two men's paths had crossed often before: in southern Ireland in 1922; in York in 1924; and more important, when de Guingand served as Monty's brigade major during military maneuvers near Suez in 1932. Monty, impressed by de Guingand's staffwork, had been instrumental in getting de Guingand nominated as a student to the Staff College, Camberley, in 1935, but they had not met since de Guingand visited the 3rd Division as military assistant to the Secretary of State for War, Hore-Belisha, in December 1939.

In those intervening three years, both men had made their mark. While Monty had risen to corps and then army command, de Guingand had served as an instructor at the Middle East Staff College at Haifa, had acted as a planner in Greece under Wavell, then been made Director of Middle East Intelligence under Auchinleck, and finally chief of the operations staff, or BGS, of Eighth Army under Auchinleck at the end of July 1942.

Would Monty keep de Guingand? De Guingand was a man few could dislike, with tremendous *joie de vivre*, an immensely fertile mind—and a natural charm which Monty did not, himself, possess. However, in the same style as the German army, Monty always insisted on making his senior operational staff officer his chief of staff: responsible not only for all staffwork, both operational and administrative, but his absolute deputy in his absence. Was Brigadier de Guingand up to this?

Undoubtedly the best chief of staff Monty had had was "Simbo" Simpson at 9th Infantry Brigade, 5 Corps and 12 Corps in England. If the War Office would release him, Monty hoped to have Simpson sent out to Egypt; in the meantime de Guingand gave "a first-class review of the present situation and the causes of it—with nothing held back. . . . We sat close together with a map on our knees and he told me the story; the operational situation, the latest Intelligence about the enemy, the generals commanding in the various sectors, the existing orders of Auchinleck about future action, his own views about things. I let him talk on. Occasionally I asked a question but only to clarify some point. When he had done there was silence for a moment or two."

This was undoubtedly one of Monty's great gifts: the ability to listen. The next full moon was considered a likely date for Rommel's forthcoming offensive. Originally it had been thought he would attack in the north, along the coastal road, but the strength of British minefields and prepared positions now made this less likely—suggested, instead, an outflanking move to the south with a very mobile force, while feinting in the north. This, de Guingand explained, would be characteristic of Rommel, and give him tactical surprise, since he could assemble his force in the center-rear of his positions and withhold the direction of his assault until the final moment.

General Auchinleck's answer, de Guingand explained, had been to prepare a rehash of Eighth Army's defenses when defeated at Gazala in June: a system of lightly held Forward Defence Localities (FDLs), and behind them a string of "boxes" into which the army would retreat if heavily attacked. Behind these "boxes" there were further proposed lines of defense at Wadi Natrun and the Nile Delta. If these could not be held, Eighth Army would split into two, one part retreating north into Palestine, the other going south to Khartoum. If, however, Eighth Army was successful in countering Rommel's thrust, it was then proposed to mount an offensive in late September, and a training area had already been established where divisions could begin to practice mine-field clearance and the like.

Asked what were his personal views on the state of Eighth Army, de Guingand expressed his qualms about the current policy of fighting in mobile brigades and battle groups; the lack of coordination between army and air force; and the worrying tendency of staff and command-ers to "look over their shoulders."

It was undoubtedly the uninhibited accounts given first by Harding and then by de Guingand which set the seal on Monty's intention to "stir things up" at HQ, Eighth Army. "In due course we left the coast road and turned south along a track into the open desert. We were quiet now and I was thinking: chiefly about de Guingand," Monty later related.

De Guingand was well aware his own future now hung in the balance. At 11 A.M. the car drew up at Eighth Army Headquarters, where the acting army commander, Lieutenant General Ramsden, was waiting. It was, in the words of Charles Richardson, an "absurd" head-quarters, far too far forward, so that it was both within German artil-lery range and regularly being attacked by the German air force, as well as being set up at "a not very attractive place: an intersection of camel tracks just behind the Ruweisat Ridge, with a liberal supply of camel dung all around, on which Winston Churchill commented when he came there." More important, it was more than forty miles from Desert Air Force HQ.

"The sight that met me," Monty recalled in his own words, "was enough to lower anyone's morale. It was a desolate scene; a few trucks, no mess tents, work done mostly in trucks or in the open air in the hot sun, flies everywhere. I asked where Auchinleck used to sleep; I was told that he slept on the ground outside his caravan. Tents were for-bidden in the Eighth Army; everyone was to be as uncomfortable as possible, so that they wouldn't be more comfortable than the men. All officers' messes were in the open air where, of course, they attracted the flies of Egypt."

Only the senior officers' dining mess was covered. It was the proud construct of the chief engineer: an aviary-type frame, over which mos-quito netting had been drawn, thus entrapping the very flies it was meant to keep out. Here Churchill had breakfasted; here Monty was expected to take lunch. "What's this?" Monty barked at de Guingand. "A meat-safe? Take it down at once and let the poor flies out."

To some extent Auchinleck's spartan life at Eighth Army Headquar-ters was designed to show officers, men and visitors that Eighth Army's high command was not immune to the ordeal the army had been through in its terrible flight from Gazala; perhaps, unconsciously, it was also Auchinleck's personal atonement for the very failure of command that had led to British defeat.

Auchinleck's biographer, John Connell, later remarked that "Rommel fought and worked under the same conditions," as though this might excuse Auchinleck for imitating him. Yet the fact is that Rommel was in poor health as a result. It was not Rommel's mess conditions that required adoption by Eighth Army, Monty felt, but certain of his techniques, such as the organization of an armored corps. Besides, the staff should stop feeling guilty at their reverses, which no tentless headquarters would mitigate. They should concentrate now on the best way of defeating Rommel and fulfilling the Prime Minister's directive to clear Egypt and Cyrenaica of enemy forces. This would not be effected from a "meat-safe."

Monty's interview with Lieutenant General Ramsden confirmed, moreover, the accounts of de Guingand and Harding—indeed, in response to Monty's blistering interrogation Ramsden revealed an almost incredible scenario, whereby the entire British front-line defense, south of Ruweisat, would be withdrawn on a codeword "Gratuity." Two complete infantry divisions—2nd New Zealand and 5th Indian—would thereupon stream back, the Indian division into "Army Reserve in the area Ruweisat station," the New Zealanders to "ALAM HALFA defended locality," covered by armor. Having reached the Alam Halfa ridge, the New Zealanders would be split up into "mobile battle groups." "The essence of the defensive plan was fluidity and mobility," Auchinleck had laid down, with 1st Armored Division's covering "the withdrawal of the forward infantry to the ALAM HALFA ridge," which was otherwise undefended. Nothing in the order, however, was to be "interpreted as a weakening in our intention to hold the present position or as an indication that our efforts have or are likely to fail."

While the New Zealand and Indian infantry of 13 Corps withdrew, Ramsden's 30 Corps in the north was also to "thin out" the "forward zone" and occupy rear "defensive localities" composed each of "two infantry battalions, one field battery and one anti-tank battery." Between these defended localities "battle groups will counter-attack any enemy who may attempt to attack or outflank our positions." These "Battle Groups will be controlled by brigade and divisional HQs. Arrangements will be made and recces carried out to enable them to operate rapidly in support of neighbouring Divisions or of 13 Corps," their orders ran. The battle groups were to be "organized and trained to act in the above way."

The New Zealand 5th Brigade Commander, Howard Kippenberger, perhaps best summed up the plans: "We did not know whether we would fight where we stood, or in the reserve positions, or run away."

Taking Command

Monty was shocked. "It was clear to me that the situation was quite impossible, and, in fact, dangerous," he summarized in his own diary, "and I decided at once that I must take instant action. I also decided that it was useless to consult GHQ and that I would take responsibility myself."

De Guingand had referred to Ramsden, in his appreciation in the car, as "bloody useless," he later recalled—a verdict shared by most officers at Eighth Army Headquarters at that time. Ramsden had been a mere battalion commander under Monty in Palestine in 1938–39; it was therefore inconceivable that Ramsden should continue as acting army commander for a further three days while Monty "waited in the wings." In the recent view of both Churchill and Field Marshal Brooke, Ramsden was already above his ceiling as a corps commander, let alone an acting army commander.

It is a mark of Monty's authority that, when he now told Ramsden to return to his headquarters at 30 Corps, and that he, Monty, would take command of Eighth Army immediately, Ramsden did not "belly-ache," but accepted Monty's decision without hesitation or even checking it with GHQ in Cairo. "He seemed surprised . . . but he went," Monty recalled. The new army commander thereupon sat down to lunch in the open, beneath the hot sun.

Monty had now declared himself *de facto* Commander of the Eighth Army; he had to inform GHQ in Cairo of this, and to start revitalizing Eighth Army from top to bottom. There was not a moment to lose. "During lunch I did some savage thinking," he later recounted. After lunch was over he issued the first of his historic edicts. The first was a cable to Cairo for a servant:

To Mideast from Main A 8th Army
Army Commander requires best available soldier servant in Middle East
to be sent to Main A Eighth Army at once.

His second cable, to General Auchinleck's chief of staff, explained the
first:

To Mideast from Main Eighth Army
For CGS. Lieut-Gen. MONTGOMERY assumed command of Eighth
Army at 1400 hrs today.

"I learnt later that the arrival of this telegram made Auchinleck very
angry as he had told me not to take over till 15 August," Monty recorded in his diary. "Having sent off this telegram to GHQ, I then set
out to see my Corps Commanders, so as to be away if any protest
came."

His first visit would be to the Acting Commander of 13 Corps—
Lieutenant General Bernard Freyberg of the 2nd New Zealand Division. Before doing so, however, Monty gave two more orders. The first
was a message to every unit, canceling all Eighth Army plans and orders for possible withdrawal. "If ROMMEL attacked we would fight
him on the ground where we now stood; there would be NO WITH-
DRAWAL and NO SURRENDER," Monty noted. The Eighth Army
would remain in its existing positions—dead or alive. His second order
was to summon all staff officers at Eighth Army Headquarters for an
urgent conference.

"When, sir?" asked de Guingand.

"Why, this evening of course," Montgomery replied—and left to see
General Freyberg.

Rommel's Lineup

"The situation when I arrived was really unbelievable; I would never have thought it could have been so bad. Auchinleck should never be employed again in any capacity," Monty angrily confided in a private letter to his former chief of staff "Simbo" Simpson at the War Office some weeks later.

The situation was certainly critical. Benefiting from Ultra—decrypts of top-secret German signals—Eighth Army Headquarters had an extraordinarily accurate picture of the Axis forces massing a few miles away across the scrubby, arid desert. Even on 10 August, the day Auchinleck left Eighth Army Headquarters, it had been estimated that Rommel commanded a German army of some 37,000 highly trained troops, 185 medium tanks, 203 guns, and 295 antitank guns including deadly 88s—by far and away the best tank-busting weapon of World War II. Rommel's Italian army was smaller, numbering 28,700 men and 110 second-class tanks, but with a disturbing 240 guns and 270 antitank guns: a front-line Axis army of 65,700 men, 295 tanks, 443 guns and 565 antitank guns.

Rommel's rate of buildup, however, was even more alarming. Within the next two days, Eighth Army Intelligence currently estimated, Rommel would have at his disposal 200 serviceable Mk III and IV Panzer tanks, 80 guns, and 100 antitank guns in the Afrika Korps alone, which would boast 15,000 men. Moreover, the estimate went on, "90 Light Division should muster 5000 men with possibly 100 anti-tank guns by the same date." The 164th (German) Division would furnish a further 10,000 men, 48 guns, and 50 antitank guns. "Should the enemy then decide to live by 'hunt and peck' supply methods during operations," the report ended, "there can be little else to delay the beginning of his offensive save our own action."

But Monty did not propose to delay Rommel's offensive by any action; he proposed to meet it—decisively.

No Surrender

L ieutenant General Freyberg, Commander of 2nd New Zealand Division and Acting 13 Corps Commander, was still recovering from wounds he had suffered in July. "Egypt is the graveyard of generals," he greeted Monty when the new army commander arrived.

Two years younger than Montgomery, Freyberg shared Montgomery's Christian name and his experience on the Western Front in World War I. Freyberg's disastrous defense of Crete (despite being given decrypts of the enemy's complete order of battle and assault plans) had demonstrated his failings as a higher commander—but as a divisional commander he probably had no equal in the Allied armies. It was said that there was no task which, once given, the 2nd New Zealand Division would not carry out; and, when Monty announced that he was canceling Auchinleck's planned withdrawal from the front line to the rear "defended OP areas," Freyberg was delighted.

There seemed every possibility that Rommel would launch an armored thrust to outflank Eighth Army, Monty acknowledged. Let him—for as long as the British front line, including the New Zealanders, held firm, Rommel would be unable to press on towards Cairo and Alexandria for fear of becoming entirely cut off; he *must* therefore wheel and try to roll up Eighth Army from the rear. Provided that the ridge at Alam Halfa was properly garrisoned, there was nothing to fear. Eighth Army would be meeting Rommel on ground of its own choosing. Given well-sited, cohesively controlled artillery and antitank guns, and judicious husbanding of Eighth Army's own armor, Rommel could achieve nothing.

As part of his new defense plan, Monty instructed, the New Zealanders were to "stay put." There would be no mass evacuation to Alam Halfa, and no fragmentation into battle groups. The front line from the Mediterranean Sea, through the Ruweisat Ridge and down to Alam Nayil would no longer be an FDL: it would be *the* defense line, to be held dead or alive.

When Freyberg asked who would then man the Alam Halfa area, behind this front line, Monty told him not to worry: there were plenty of units wasting in the Delta—they would be brought up. The important thing was to look to the front, not backwards: to see that his defenses were prepared in depth, with proper attention paid to minefields and to artillery so as to enable the chief gunner to bring the combined weight of divisional, even corps, artillery on any one spot. Auchinleck's policy of "mobility and fluidity" was henceforth redundant.

Once Rommel's attack had been halted, however, it would be Eighth Army's turn to take the offensive. 30 Corps would take responsible for the whole front; 13 Corps would be withdrawn to train as a highly mobile, armored break-in corps, in which the New Zealanders themselves would be reequipped as a motorized infantry division, similar to Monty's old 3rd Division, but with its own brigade of support tanks, and would begin preparing for a more aggressive mobile battle role, in conjunction with the new *corps de chasse*—a role equivalent to that of the famous German 90th Light Division.

Leaving Freyberg to draw up orders embodying his instructions, Monty finally left 13 Corps HQ and returned to his own unsatisfactory headquarters on the Ruweisat Ridge, where he had told de Guingand to arrange fighter cover by the Desert Air Force at 6 P.M. The time had come to address his new staff.

An Electric Address

"We thought this 'air umbrella' was a very comic thing," one officer candidly recalled his feeling, "—because we didn't think we were very precious. And, what is more, before Monty actually arrived the 'air umbrella' had disappeared—because he was late! They'd gone before he arrived, which made the 'air umbrella' an even more hilariously enjoyable concept!"

This was twenty-nine-year-old Major "Bill" Williams, G2 Intelligence—who little dreamed that August evening, mocking the arrival of a new commander, that within two years he himself would be the Allied armies' chief of Intelligence for the D-Day landings in Normandy.

Monty did not, after all, have "sand in his shoes," in the parlance of the desert veterans, and probably had no idea of the extent to which Rommel had transformed mobile operations in North Africa, Williams believed. Moreover, when Montgomery did finally appear half an hour late, he looked, in his new desert shirt and slacks, absurdly gaunt and small: a skinny little man with a foxy, pointed face, high cheekbones and long, sharp nose beneath his peaked general's hat.

Although so close to the front line, the headquarters was not a tactical HQ but contained all branches of Eighth Army's staff, from operations to artillery, engineers to administration, Intelligence, plans, signals and staff duties. The sixty officers stood to attention and saluted. Monty returned the salute, stood on the steps of his predecessor's caravan, bade the gathering to sit in the sand and, in a clear and confident voice that rang through the evening stillness of the desert, introduced himself and stated his mission—to end the cycle of British defeat.

"I believe that one of the first duties of a commander," Monty continued, "is to create what I call 'atmosphere,' and in that atmosphere his staff, subordinate commanders, and troops will live and work and fight."

So far, Monty confessed, he was not impressed by Eighth Army:

I do not like the general atmosphere I find here. It is an atmosphere of doubt, of looking back to select the next place to which to withdraw, of loss of confidence in our ability to defeat Rommel, of desperate defence measures by reserves in preparing positions in Cairo and the Delta.

All that must cease.

Let us have a new atmosphere.

The defence of Egypt lies here at Alamein and on the Ruweisat Ridge. What is the use of digging trenches in the Delta? It is quite useless; if we lose this position we lose Egypt; all the fighting troops now in the Delta must come here at once, and will. Here we will stand and fight; there will be no further withdrawal. I have ordered that all plans and instructions dealing with further withdrawal are to be burnt, and at once. We will stand and fight here.

If we can't stay here alive, then let us stay here dead.

The candor and realism of the new army commander came as a shock to those officers who had not met Monty before. Equally, it was clear that the new commander had no intention of being beaten—indeed had every intention of trouncing Rommel in the coming months:

I want to impress on everyone that the bad times are over. Fresh Divisions from the UK are now arriving in Egypt, together with ample reinforcements for our present Divisions. We have 300 to 400 Sherman new tanks coming and these are actually being unloaded at Suez now.* Our mandate from the Prime Minister is to destroy the Axis forces in North Africa; I have seen it, written on half a sheet of notepaper. And it will be done. If anyone here thinks it can't be done, let him go at once; I don't want any doubters in this party. It can be done, and it will be done: beyond any possibility of doubt.

Now I understand that Rommel is expected to attack at any moment. Excellent. Let him attack.

I would sooner it didn't come for a week, just to give me time to sort things out. If we have two weeks to prepare we will be sitting pretty; Rommel can attack as soon as he likes, after that, and I hope he does.

Meanwhile, we ourselves will start to plan a great offensive; it will be the beginning of a campaign which will hit Rommel and his Army for six right out of Africa.

But first we must create a reserve Corps, mobile and strong in armour,

*This was a deliberate exaggeration; the American convoy bringing tanks and supplies was not due to arrive until 2 September 1942.

which we will train out of the line. Rommel has always had such a force in his Africa Corps, which is never used to hold the line but which is always in reserve, available for striking blows. Therein has been his great strength. We will create such a Corps ourselves, a British Panzer Corps; it will consist of two armored Divisions and one motorized Division; I gave orders yesterday for it to begin to form, back in the Delta.

I have no intention of launching our great attack until we are completely ready; there will be pressure from many quarters to attack soon; I will not attack until we are ready, and you can rest assured on that point.

Meanwhile, if Rommel attacks while we are preparing, let him do so with pleasure; we will merely continue with our own preparations and we will attack when we are ready, and not before.

Even the skeptical "Bill" Williams—an Oxford don in civilian life—found his first impression of hilarity over the "air umbrella" altering to one of reluctant admiration as he listened to Monty speak. Williams had been in Intelligence at GHQ Cairo until June, when at de Guingand's prompting he was posted to Eighth Army. In both positions he had been primarily responsible for interpreting and relaying to Auchinleck Ultra decrypts of the enemy's most secret signals—and had become frustrated and testy over the disappointing use to which this unique intelligence had been put.

"I can remember the address," he related almost forty years later. "I think we had this rather arrogant view that we'd had rather a lot of generals through our hands, in our day. And this was a new one—but he was talking sense, although in a very sort of strange way: the manner, the phraseology. You've got to remember that the sort of people I'd talk to would be the intelligentsia, so to speak, and this sort of stuff was straight out of school speech-day. And yet . . . I remember it was, it was a feeling of great exhilaration: a feeling that here was somebody who was really going to use his staff. And I remember relating it purely personally to this sort of feeling: well, God, he's the sort of chap who's going to be able to use Ultra, you see. You had this feeling that we kept producing stuff that was out of this world in terms of the amount of information we were getting about the enemy, and somehow it never seemed to get put to any purpose."

Meanwhile, Monty had not finished:

I want to tell you that I always work on the Chief-of-Staff system. I have nominated Brigadier de Guingand as Chief-of-Staff Eighth Army. I will issue orders through him. Whatever he says will be taken as coming from me and will be acted on at once. I understand there has been a great deal of "belly-aching" out here. By "belly-aching" I mean inventing poor reasons for not doing what one has been told to do.

All this is to stop at once.

I will tolerate no belly-aching.

If anyone objects to doing what he is told, then he can get out of it; and at once. I want that made very clear right down through the Eighth Army.

I have little more to say just at present. And some of you may think it is quite enough and may wonder if I am mad.

I assure you I am quite sane.

I understand there are people who often think I am slightly mad; so often that I now regard it as rather a compliment.

All I have to say to that is that if I am slightly mad, there are a large number of people I could name who are raving lunatics!!

What I have done is to get over to you the "atmosphere" in which we will now work and fight; you must see that atmosphere permeates right down through the Eighth Army to the most junior private soldier. All the soldiers must know what is wanted; when they see it coming to pass there will be a surge of confidence throughout the Army.

I ask you to give me your confidence and to have faith that what I have said will come to pass.

There is much work to be done.

The orders I have given about no further withdrawal will mean a complete change in the layout of our dispositions; also that we must begin to prepare for our great offensive.

The first thing to do is to move our HQ to a decent place where we can live in reasonable comfort and where the Army Staff can all be together and side by side with the HQ of the Desert Air Force. This is a frightful place here, depressing, unhealthy and a rendez-vous for every fly in Africa; we shall do no good work here. Let us get over there by the sea where it is fresh and healthy. If Officers are to do good work they must have decent messes, and be comfortable. So off we go on the new line.

The Chief-of-Staff will be issuing orders on many points very shortly, and I am always available to be consulted by the senior officer of the staff. The great point to remember is that we are going to finish with this chap Rommel once and for all. It will be quite easy. There is no doubt about it.

He is definitely a nuisance. Therefore we will hit him a crack and finish with him.

Monty stepped down. The assembled officers rose and stood to attention. "It was one of his greatest efforts," de Guingand would chronicle some years later. "The effect of the address was electric—it was terrific! And we all went to bed that night with new hope in our hearts, and a great confidence in the future of our Army."

The Formula for Victory

L ooking back many years later, Captain Keating, head of the
Eighth Army Film and Photographic Unit, blessed the energy
and command experience Montgomery brought with him that
first day in the desert, and the "electrifying effect" of his first
"harangue":

> Monty knew all the rules of the conduct of war and the fighting of bat-
> tles. He was like a surgeon, you know: he could take your tummy out
> and put it back. And I was, by this time, the time of his arrival, I had al-
> ready personally experienced endless defeats. I'd been wounded five
> times; and here I was, sure that this was the man who had victory. And
> if you ask me to explain why, I was sure—it was something he exuded,
> it was *professionalism.*

In the days to come Keating would virtually become Monty's PR man.
"I was regarded by the old hands—who were not to be neglected—as
slightly disloyal in throwing my hat in so much with him. Monty of
course was regarded as rather a vulgar chap. . . . But I knew in my
heart of hearts that here was a man who had the formula for victory."

For Colonel Richardson, G1 in charge of plans, Monty's address was
quite simply the turning point of the Second World War. He admired
Auchinleck. "I mean there is no question of the Auk's moral and physical courage. All else had failed," he said, remembering the moment
when he joined Auchinleck on 25 June 1942 after the fall of Tobruk,
and the surrender of 30,000 British troops to the Germans. "Ritchie
[installed by Auchinleck as Eighth Army Commander after the failure
of General Cunningham, its first commander] had failed, everything
else had failed, he [Auchinleck] was being tormented by Churchill and
so forth. He didn't lose his head, but at the end he was a defeated

man. There was no prospect in my mind of him ever—even if he'd been given thousands of new tanks and new divisions and so on—there was no possibility in my mind of that brain ever being able to produce a new élan."

It was Montgomery's historic achievement to produce a new spirit from the moment he arrived: to restore leadership, purpose and morale to an exhausted army. As one of his staff, who joined him before the battle of Alamein, put it: "He made you better than you thought you were"; or another: "Monty absolutely deserved all the credit he could get for the way he changed us. I mean, we were different people. We suddenly had a spring in our step."

The seeds of a new army had indeed been sown. It was as though, in their hearts, the staff of Eighth Army had been waiting for this moment, knowing they were capable of better things. Baffled by the reverses of the summer of 1942, it was leadership *from above* these officers wanted. In his eve-of-Alamein diary entry, Monty penned a scathing indictment not only of the army he had inherited on 13 August, but of the men he held responsible:

> The condition of Eighth Army as described above is not overpainted; it was almost unbelievable. From what I know now it was quite clear that the reverses we had suffered at GAZALA and East of it, which finally forced us back to within 60 miles of ALEXANDRIA, should never have happened.
>
> Gross mis-management, faulty command, and bad staff work, had been the cause of the whole thing.
>
> But the final blame must rest on General AUCHINLECK. . . . Divisions were split up into bits and pieces all over the desert; the armour was not concentrated; the gunners had forgotten the art of employing artillery in a concentrated form.
>
> If changes in the higher command had not been made early in August, we would have lost EGYPT.
>
> Actually, they were made only just in time.
>
> A clean sweep was required in the Middle East, and new Commanders had to be brought in; Commanders who would NOT be influenced by past events, but who would take each situation on its merits and decide on a method suitable to the occasion and to local conditions.

When Churchill came to read a copy of this part of Monty's diary later that year, his heart must have swelled. It had taken courage and ruthlessness to make such changes of command at a critical moment in the war. However, Churchill's pleasure must have been tempered by Monty's succeeding remarks:

GOTT was to have commanded Eighth Army. I am convinced that this appointment was not sound and might have led to disaster. GOTT was one of the old regime and had been in EGYPT all the war; his tactical ideas were influenced by past events; his plan in 13 Corps for fighting ROMMEL if he attacked in August was very bad and if it had been put into effect I consider the Eighth Army would have been defeated.

On the evidence now available to military historians, there is little doubt Monty was right. The chaos produced by the mass exodus of divisions from their forward defense lines, the lingering obsession with mobility, the lack of a proper garrison at Alam Halfa, the dispersion of armor, and the fragmentation of the infantry into battle groups might well have resulted in the greatest British military disaster of the war.

Meanwhile, to defend the crucial Alam Halfa ridge, Monty had promised Freyberg he would bring up all three brigades of 44th Division from the Delta—one of which Auchinleck was still holding east of the Nile, in case of a German breakthrough. "Consider present absence of adequate garrison E and F [Alam Halfa] most dangerous and prejudicial to carrying out fresh policy," Freyberg warned by radio signal at 9:20 P.M. on 13 August—and was relieved to hear the new army commander had already spoken by telephone to General Alexander in Cairo, and got permission for the 44th Division to move up into the line immediately. In the division's War Diary for 1942 there still stands the simple but historic entry:

13 August 1942, 2200 hours: Orders received for 44 Division to move into 8 Army Area.

Whatever the confusion over who was in command in Cairo, and what were the plans of GHQ Middle East, within Eighth Army there was no longer any doubt about who was in charge—nor the "fresh policy" the new army commander had laid down.

That evening Monty had a long talk about the future with de Guingand. Finally he retired to bed in one of Auchinleck's caravans. "By the time I went to bed that night I was tired," Monty recalled. "I'm afraid it was with an insubordinate smile that I fell asleep: I was issuing orders to an Army which someone else reckoned he commanded!"

Preparations for Defensive Battle

"I was woken up soon after dawn the next morning by an officer with the morning situation report," Monty remembered. "I was extremely angry, and told him no one was ever to come near me with situation reports; I did not want to be bothered with details of patrol actions and things of that sort. He apologized profusely and said that Auchinleck was always woken early and given the dawn reports.

"I said I was not Auchinleck and that if anything was wrong the Chief-of-Staff would tell me; if nothing was wrong I didn't want to be told."

The duty officer was not the only one to be surprised. Immediately after breakfast on 14 August 1942, Monty left his headquarters to visit 30 Corps area—where he would acquire his first distinctive desert headgear: an Australian bush hat on which he would, day by day, pin the badges of all the regiments he inspected.

While Monty examined the vital Ruweisat Ridge defenses, comprising the north and center of the British front line, Brigadier de Guingand departed in the opposite direction, to find a new headquarters site by the sea. When Auchinleck's GHQ liaison officer arrived at Eighth Army Headquarters at noon from Cairo, he therefore found the army commander's cupboard bare; moreover Monty's staff now flatly refused to cooperate with Auchinleck's proposed "Deltaforce War Game," for which Eighth Army had been requested to provide two staff officers. "In view of 8th Army's signal U453 timed 0905/14," the officer reported, "it is confirmed that no, repeat no, staff officers will be available." Similarly, Auchinleck's request for a "Plan of Wadi Natrun defenses to be given to staff officer who was organizing it" was treated with utter contempt. Colonel Mainwaring, the senior operations officer, "stated that in view of 8th Army Commander's new order

for 'no looking over your shoulder' and 'fighting on present position'
there is no need for a Wadi Natrun defensive position, therefore there
is no action required."

Monty's edicts and his address to his staff had evidently done the
trick. The staff was behind him. Auchinleck's liaison officer concluded
his report with a note about "Future Moves." Neither army commander nor BGS was seen, "latter being on a recce in the Burg-el-Arab
area, neighbourhood of HQ RAF, Western Desert Force. This recce
was with a view to moving HQ 8th Army to a site in this locality. The
present hope is to move on Sunday 16/8."

As de Guingand reconnoitered the site for the new Eighth Army
Headquarters, Monty carried out a blitz on the front of 30 Corps. By
two o'clock he had reached 5th Indian Division on the Ruweisat
Ridge. Cover was difficult to provide in the rocky, bare ground, but
the ridge was obviously the key position in the north—therefore,
Monty ordered, it would have to be strengthened by further mines,
more dug-in and blasted positions, and the siting of an armored brigade of Valentine tanks behind the front.

South of the Ruweisat Ridge were the New Zealanders, whom
Monty had visited together with Freyberg the previous afternoon.
Monty was satisfied that, reinforced by a brigade of 44th Division, the
New Zealanders would now hold firm. The New Zealanders, equally,
were impressed by the new army commander—as Brigadier Kippen-
berger, Commander of 5th New Zealand Brigade, later recalled:

> The new Army Commander made himself felt at once. . . . He talked
> sharply and curtly, without any soft words, asked some searching ques-
> tions, met the battalion commanders, and left me feeling much stimu-
> lated. For a long time we had heard little from Army except querulous
> grumbles that the men should not go about without their shirts on, that
> staff officers must always wear the appropriate arm-bands, or things of
> that sort. Now we were told that we were going to fight, there was no
> question of retirement to any reserve positions or anywhere else, and to
> get ahead with our preparations. To make the intention clear our troop-
> carrying transport was sent a long way back so that we could not run
> away if we wanted to! There was no more talk of the alternative posi-
> tions in the rear. We were delighted and the morale of the whole Army
> went up incredibly.

The important thing was to make sure the 44th Division got up without delay from the Delta, and Monty ordered that this be given top
priority. Alan Moorehead, then a war correspondent in North Africa,
later reconstructed the scene around Alamein:

Insistently and steadily, hour after hour, the orders went out, and a great commotion spread across the desert. Thousands of men and vehicles on the backward trek were suddenly halted and turned round. Tens of thousands of men, new guns, new tanks and new vehicles began to pour down towards the front from the Nile Delta. Liaison officers in jeeps were dashing about from unit to unit; Cancel the previous orders, here are the new—for immediate action. Headquarters abruptly began to pack their trucks, strike their encampments and set off across the open sand. Huge columns were preparing to move, some going south, some north, some towards the front and others away from it. Isolated convoys carrying landmines and signals, tanks workshops and camouflage gear, hospitals and petrol, barbed wire and food, ammunition and tentage, water and clothing, artillery and spare parts—all the paraphernalia of this strange expedition in the sand—began to chart their courses and drive off through the dust. Everywhere men were digging or on the march.

The transformation of Eighth Army went with alacrity. Moreover there could be no doubt about army command's "grip." A "fed-up," humiliated headquarters now came back to life. Corps commanders were summoned to a conference at Eighth Army Headquarters at 0900 hours on 15 August to "discuss future policy"—and were required to bring "tracings of minefields laid and projected" for inspection.

Monty began the conference by giving an address very similar to his talk to his staff on 13 August. Freyberg was impressed and noted in his diary that he agreed with everything the army commander said. Auchinleck's liaison officer meanwhile reported back to Cairo that evening:

> 8th Army's defence policy is to stand and fight on present positions, and no withdrawal is to be made. The words "Army Reserve Position" are being deleted from printed maps.
>
> Defended localities are being considerably strengthened, in both personnel and e.g. fresh minefields.
>
> The new Army Commander attaches particular importance to the holding of the Ruweisat Ridge.

30 Corps certainly reflected the army commander's new directive in its Operation Order No. 72:

Introduction
1. All orders and instructions which refer to withdrawal from or thinning out of our present positions are hereby canceled.

Intention
2. 30 Corps will defend the present FDLs [front-line positions] at all costs. There will be no withdrawal. . . .

The influence of the new army commander was unmistakable. Later that afternoon the new commander of 13 Corps arrived: Lieutenant General Brian Horrocks. He'd left his division in Northumberland on the evening of 12 August. "I arrived in Egypt," Horrocks related in an account for the Official British Historian in 1945, "three days after General Montgomery. He had wired for me to come out. On arrival I motored up to his Headquarters in the desert, where I spent the first night and where he gave me his appreciation.

"Although he had only been a very short time in Egypt his appreciation was remarkably accurate." Rommel would probably break through Eighth Army's minefields in the south, Monty predicted, then attempt to sweep around the rear of 30 Corps by seizing the Alam Halfa ridge. Horrocks' job, as the new commander of 13 Corps, was to deny Rommel the pleasure by digging in his tanks and guns, and subjecting the Panzer army to a thorough beating, from artillery and aerial bombing, but without allowing his Eighth Army armor to take any unnecessary risks. As Horrocks recalled, Monty was most emphatic about this—for he had no intention of fighting an all-out battle until the new American tanks arrived at Suez early in September. "I will not go into details," Horrocks explained to the Official Historian, "except to emphasize the following points:"

    a) He anticipated that Rommel would make one all-out effort to capture the Delta, and that this attack would be made on the frontage of my Corps, 13 Corps, which was holding the left sector of the Alamein position. He ordered me to defeat the Germans, *but not under any condition to become mauled in the process*, because he was then thinking of his offensive operations. He continually stressed this point afterwards and it is important to consider this when remembering how we fought the battle.

    b) In his appreciation he even showed me on a map the area in which he proposed to launch the main attack during the [subsequent offensive] battle of Alamein. Looking back on this conversation the interesting point is that the plan, as outlined by General Montgomery, was adhered to in almost every detail. . . .

Looking back, in 1960, Horrocks called it "the most remarkable military appreciation I ever heard," for it seemed incredible that the army commander should be more interested in the future Eighth Army offensive than in Rommel's impending thrust.

It was only in his mid-eighties, however, that Horrocks revealed his own diffidence in accepting the role Monty envisaged for him. General Alexander, in Cairo, had been charming but vague, almost out of touch: "All he said was: 'Monty has some great plan for driving the Germans out of Egypt. I don't know what it is, but you are to take part in it, and I'm letting him get on with it'—that's all he said!" Thus when Horrocks first arrived at Monty's Eighth Army Headquarters he still had no idea what command he was to have. Having outlined his plan for 13 Corps' defense at Alam Halfa, Monty then announced that Horrocks would, in the subsequent British offensive battle, command the armored *corps de chasse* to be formed out of 13 Corps, and equipped with the new American Shermans. Horrocks was horrified.

> I said "No, no, Sir, it's no good you know." He said "Why not?" I said, "Well look: I've already commanded an armored division in England— the 9th Armored—and I know they'll resent it." You see, I came from a very humble regiment, the old die-hard Middlesex Regiment, and I knew at once that the reaction of the cavalry to me being put in charge of them would be bad. I said "No! For God's sake don't do that! Put [General] Lumsden in"—because Lumsden was the great hero, he'd won the Grand National, God knows what else, you know what I mean? He was the man. And Monty eventually said "Yes, I think you're right. I will." So he said, "Well, you take command of 13 Corps. . . ."

Monty's decision to give command of his *corps de chasse* to General Lumsden—whom he had never met, but who was highly recommended by Alexander's chief of staff—was one Monty would deeply regret in the weeks ahead. But for the moment he was satisfied Horrocks would obey his orders at Alam Halfa, and ensure the initial defensive battle be fought according to simple, well-rehearsed plan.

For Horrocks, however, it was not to be that simple.

A New Light

I f Horrocks hoped his appointment to command 13 Corps would prove easier than Monty's projected version of the Afrika Korps, he was very mistaken. Even in his eighties Horrocks remembered this bitter and fateful struggle as "about the most difficult time I had in the whole war."

Freyberg, returning to 2nd New Zealand Division Headquarters and resentful at having yet another junior British general promoted above him as 13 Corps Commander, did everything he could to make Horrocks' life hell. "Every order I issued was queried," Horrocks recalled, "and it was a very nasty, difficult time." The commander of the 7th Armoured Division, Major General Renton, was equally recalcitrant. "Renton—that's the man," Horrocks recalled: "he was the man who caused all the trouble." Michael Carver, senior operations officer at 7th Armoured Division Headquarters, later remembered Renton well: "He was an attractive character in lots of ways, but by this time he had seen a great many Riflemen either go 'in the bag,' or gallant attacks which then achieved nothing. . . . He was imbued with a feeling that it was important to preserve his forces 'in being,' rather than to hold any specific bit of ground—such as Alam Halfa. Well, there was a tendency to keep your forces 'in being' in order to take them backwards! That was Horrocks's real criticism of Renton."

Sensing the difficulties Horrocks would have to face, Monty suggested a meeting of senior 13 Corps commanders on the Alam Halfa ridge that day, 16 August. Brigadier "Pip" Roberts, who commanded 22nd Armoured Brigade—the only unit in Eighth Army equipped with Grant tanks capable of meeting German Panzer Mark IIIs and IVs in battle—remembered his first meeting with Monty vividly. Roberts had not seen the new orders for the infantry to stay put. The merit of the new army commander, in Roberts' view, was that, whereas in the past there had been a plethora of plans for the use of British armor, when Montgomery arrived there was one plan:

> Before Monty arrived we had a number of different plans. Plan A was this, Plan B was this, Plan C was that, you see. Now when Monty came, there was only one task; to stay on Alam Halfa. All our job was, was to stay there.
>
> Immediately the air was cleared, as it were. Everybody knew that we were not moving back, we were fighting here! That is that! Certainly a different atmosphere pervaded, at once. [The military historian] Liddell Hart doesn't agree with me quite on this, but he wasn't there, so he doesn't know. I mean, we all had a very high opinion of Auchinleck, we also had a very high opinion of "Strafer" Gott. But Monty gave as it were a new light on the whole thing: a simple, clear, firm light. And there's not the slightest doubt that if it made a difference to me, naturally it made a difference to the people under me. There's not the remotest doubt about the effect his arrival had.

Roberts was delighted to have a role he knew he could fulfill, rather than a series of highly dubious possible tasks, from covering the withdrawal of the New Zealand Division to a flank attack on the combined Afrika Korps:

> You see, the defence is much more powerful than the attack, and to be effective in the attack you have to have a preponderance of 3 to 1 or thereabouts—something like that.

With Rommel enjoying a three-to-one superiority in heavy tanks, Roberts was delighted to abandon Auchinleck's "fluid" schemes. "No, if we were going to stay put like that, fine, we'd stay put. I didn't mind that at all. It was a simple plan. I knew that if we could hold our fire and we stayed put, then we would inflict more casualties than were inflicted on us."

There was, also, the preciousness of 22nd Armoured Brigade's tanks to consider:

> We had all the Grant tanks that were left—all the leftovers from all the other units that had gone back to re-equip. Ours was really the only armored brigade left in the desert—there was another brigade that was left up, called the 23rd Armoured Brigade and they had a few Valentine tanks—these were armed with only a 2-pounder gun so they were not at all effective against the German tanks. So I was in the enviable—you might think rather nervous situation of being in command of virtually the only armored brigade we had in the desert at that time.

Monty's memory of the meeting at Alam Halfa was equally vivid—including a run-in with Roberts' divisional commander, General Renton:

> During the day [16 August] I met on the southern flank the general commanding the 7th Armoured Division, the famous Desert Rats. We discussed the expected attack by Rommel and he said there was only one question to be decided: who would loose the armor against Rommel? He thought he himself should give the word for that to happen. I replied that no one would loose the armor; it would not be loosed and we would let Rommel bump into it for a change. This was a new idea to him and he argued about it a good deal.

As a result of Renton's "belly-aching," 22nd Armoured Brigade was now removed from Renton's division that evening, and put directly under Horrocks at 13 Corps. Renton was furious. As Horrocks confessed to the Official Historian, "this was an untidy picture, as a Brigade should not operate directly under Corps Headquarters, but I did not want there to be any risk of the Grant tanks being launched into battle by 7th Armoured Division without my order." Had Renton been allowed to control the "vital Grant tanks" of 22nd Armoured Brigade, and had he used them as envisaged under the plethora of Auchinleck-Gott plans, Horrocks felt the whole battle would have been in jeopardy: "As we were outnumbered and out-tanked, if this Brigade was launched head-on at the Germans there was every chance that it would be completely written off; in which case we should really have lost the battle."

Brigadier Roberts, meanwhile, set to work with a will. The telltale hunting code words like "Pheasant," "Snipe," "Snippet," "Grouse," "Cheeper," "Gamebirds," "Hamla," "Woodcock," "Lobster" were ordered to be torn up; engineers were brought in to blast and bulldoze a series of hull-down positions for the Grant tanks on the slopes of Alam Halfa, while a screen of antitank gun positions was set up in front of them. On 19 August, Roberts confirmed the orders to his 22nd Armoured Brigade in writing, to the effect that "22 Armoured Brigade is to take up an impenetrable position which it is hoped the enemy will attack," emphasizing that "the position is a strong one and will resist any enemy tank or other attack, the rear of the position being protected by Fortress 'E' [Alam Halfa, garrisoned by 44 Division]." Moreover, he added, "the battle positions for armored regiments are good, give considerable scope for troop commanders' initiative, enable tanks to remain concealed until fire is required and provide good hull-down positions." In particular he wanted antitank guns "so sited that not only do they cover their own front but can cover the front of armored Regiments thereby enabling them to remain concealed until a severe threat develops." In conclusion he repeated: "By taking up these positions it is hoped that for once the enemy may have to attack us in good positions of our own choosing."

The battle of Alam Halfa was beginning to take shape—almost two weeks before Rommel actually launched his assault.

Ultra Intelligence

M eanwhile, asking for Major "Bill" Williams to come to his caravan, the new army commander went over the latest intelligence. "I was summoned pretty early on, 15th or 16th August, 1942, perhaps," Williams remembered. "The new Army Commander had uncomfortably piercing eyes, which also seemed hooded: a disconcerting combination. I can remember his very, very searching questions. You know, at the time one was glad to have good questions because there had been this curious incoherence because—well nobody had been quite certain who was in charge as it were." To Williams, in retrospect, "what was so interesting about the Alam Halfa business was—and I think this is where Ultra played its part—that he believed right away these items of information we supplied him with. It was rather staggering."

Williams at first assumed that Montgomery's receptivity to "the cold hard intelligence estimate" must derive from the army commander's respect for Ultra, the priceless Allied decrypting of top-secret enemy signals. As time went by, however, Williams came to see it went much deeper. Ultra's unique insight into enemy plans, dispositions and forces meant so much to the new army commander because, as Williams came to realize, "he was so very professional. Sometimes [in interpreting the Ultra material], you'd say to him, 'well I think it means this, er, but what would you do, sir, in the [enemy] situation?' And he was very good about that because he was a very good soldier and he could therefore see—because the Germans were also very good soldiers—what a good soldier would do—and so much better than I could do because I wasn't a good soldier!"

Throughout the desert campaigns, Ultra had provided information about the enemy to which Eighth Army could react. What was different now was that there was a commander in charge who wished to use Ultra as a backcloth to his *own* tactical and strategic designs. How would Rommel react to *his*, Monty's, tactics, and what forces did he have to do so?

In his caravan, Monty deliberately hung an artist's drawing of Rommel. From the moment he had begun to think over his task as Commander of Eighth Army on the flight from England, Monty had attempted to "put himself in the enemy's shoes." As Williams came to see, this was not so much a feat of imagination as the logical projection of one supremely professional military mind onto that of another. In the meantime, however, Williams was astonished by the way Montgomery "spent most time that first morning I ever spent with him—I had barely become a major—interrogating me about the enemy *defenses* at Alamein. The new General was already one battle ahead of me."

Moving to Burg-el-Arab, beside the sea, the new Eighth Army Headquarters was soon transfigured, becoming almost overnight perhaps the most professional army staff team of its kind—so much so, in fact, that when Churchill arrived a few days later on his way back from Moscow he could barely credit the change.

Churchill's Visit

Gone, to Churchill's relief, was the "meat-safe" and the "liberal supply of camel-dung." A sea breeze blew in off the shimmering Mediterranean. Colonel Mainwaring, the G1 (Ops), had ensured that the caravans were laid out in such a way as to provide an operations courtyard, with maps both inside the lorries and draped outside. Army and air force officers now worked side by side, sharing intelligence—intelligence which, on the night of 17 August, had, via Ultra, confirmed Monty's judgment that Rommel would strike in the south and had given a target date of 26 August for the battle.

Churchill's visit was paid on 19 August—the same day as the doomed Allied cross-Channel raid on Dieppe. The amphibious landing on the French coast by Canadian infantry, tanks and British commandos proved an utter catastrophe: a disaster brazenly concealed by its architect, Admiral Mountbatten, who, having deliberately and mischievously resurrected the canceled operation, lied to Churchill and reported that losses had been extremely light.

News of Mountbatten's failure duly emerged in the following days, with its painful toll of brave Canadians, mown down in almost cold blood upon the shingled beach of Dieppe, as at Gallipoli. But on the baking sand of the Egyptian desert near Alamein, Churchill's interest was in the state of the Eighth Army under its new commander—and like the headquarters staff on 13 August, Churchill was mesmerized by Monty's authority and confidence. To the Deputy Prime Minister he cabled home the next day to say he was "sure we were heading for disaster under the former regime" and to report the "complete change of atmosphere" he had found. "The highest alacrity and activity prevails. Positions are everywhere being strengthened, and extended forces are being sorted out and regrouped in solid units. The 44th and 10th Armoured Divisions have already arrived in the forward zone. The roads are busy with the forward movement of troops, tanks, and guns."

What astounded Churchill, as it astounded the normally dour British Army Chief of Staff, Sir Alan Brooke, was the speed with which Montgomery, arriving in the desert a mere eight days after the Prime Minister and CIGS, had imposed on Eighth Army his own vision not only of the tactical strategy he intended to adopt, but the kind of professional army he wished Eighth Army to become.

"I knew my Monty pretty well by then," Brooke later wrote, "but I must confess I was dumbfounded by the situation facing him, the rapidity with which he had grasped the essentials, the clarity of his plans, and, above all, his unbounded self-confidence—a self-confidence with which he inspired all those that he came into contact."

There could be no doubt about Churchill's genuine submission to the "Montgomery-magic" that evening. Like an old but obdurate hunting dog, Churchill had finally picked up the scent that had eluded him for two long and wearisome years of war: the smell of victory. It now pervaded everything and everyone Churchill met.

Churchill's response, however, was not only a warming to the prospect of military victory, at last, in Egypt; it was, too, the awareness of an historian, and in Montgomery's visitors' book Churchill searched for a parallel. In the end he found it in his own ancestor, the Duke of Marlborough. "May the anniversary of Blenheim which marks the opening of the new Command bring to the Commander in Chief of the Eighth Army and his troops the fame & fortune they will surely deserve," he wrote the day he left Burg-el-Arab, 20 August 1942.

As Churchill left, Monty showed him the draft of a special message he intended to issue: the first of his famous "Orders of the Day" to the officers and men of Eighth Army:

The enemy is now attempting to break through our positions in order to reach CAIRO, SUEZ and ALEXANDRIA, and to drive us from EGYPT.

The Eighth Army bars the way. It carries a great responsibility and the whole future of the war will depend on how we carry out our task.

We will fight the enemy where we now stand; there will be NO WITHDRAWAL and NO SURRENDER. Every officer and man must continue to do his duty as long as he has breath in his body.

If each one of us does his duty, we cannot fail; the opportunity will then occur to take the offensive ourselves and to destroy once and for all the enemy forces now in EGYPT.

Into battle then, with stout hearts and with the determination to do our duty.

And may God give us the victory.

The Hinge of Fate

W hile Monty's Special Message went out to the troops, Churchill cabled back to Attlee, his deputy at home: "I am satisfied that we have lively, confident, resolute men in command, working together as an admirable team under leaders of the highest military quality"—and added (no doubt reflecting the influence of General Brooke), "It is now my duty to return home as I have no part to play in the battle, which must be left to those in whom we place our trust."

But did Churchill really trust the new army commander, despite his dazzling "grip" of the situation? In truth, Churchill was acquiescing in the very opposite of what he'd intended to happen in the desert. In appointing Alexander to replace Auchinleck as C-in-C Middle East he had hoped to install a fresh, fighting general who would order a British offensive without delay. Equally, in appointing Gott to take command of Eighth Army, Churchill had intended perhaps to highlight what he approved in Auchinleck's plans: namely the accent on offensive mobility and maneuver. Certainly Churchill's original intention, as told to Brooke on the flight back from Moscow, was to stay in Egypt for the coming battle. Moreover, two other of the Prime Minister's statements on 20 August suggest that, though Churchill genuinely applauded the new spirit in Eighth Army, he either misunderstood or disagreed with Montgomery's plans. "Trouble with you generals is that you are defensive minded," he had barked at General Horrocks, on hearing the plans for 13 Corps at Alam Halfa. "Why don't you attack? That's the way to win battles, not by sitting down in defence." Moreover, in his cable to Attlee, Churchill reported that the "strong line of defence" being developed across the Delta from Alexandria to Cairo was "to give the fullest manoeuvring power to the Eighth Army in the event of its being attacked next week."

In reality the Delta defense scheme was being undertaken by the newly arrived 51st Highland Division for the very opposite purpose: namely in order that Eighth Army might remain dug in on Alam Halfa, leaving 51st Division to meet any overambitious German columns that attempted to bypass the Alam Halfa ridge—as the division's War Diary recorded at the time.

The extent to which Churchill misunderstood his new Eighth Army Commander is of the greatest historical interest: for it was a misunderstanding that would be mirrored in an almost identical manner in Eisenhower's headquarters two years later, at the height of the battle for Normandy. In both cases Monty held his superiors in a state of awe by his "grip" and the utter clarity and simplicity of his tactical forecast; yet somehow, the moment Churchill or Eisenhower left him, they became a prey to their own tactical illusions. Indeed it is impossible to resist the impression that Churchill tolerated Montgomery, a soldier so unlike his romantic ideal, only so long as Monty produced victories—and was the first to round on " 'your' Monty," as Brooke recalled, whenever victory took longer to achieve than the impatient Prime Minister was prepared to wait.

"I have had a difficult time out here trying to get things in better shape," Brooke meanwhile wrote from Cairo, "and am leaving with a great feeling of satisfaction at the thought of Alex & you at the helm out here. You have wonderful prospects out here and I have the fullest confidence that you will make the most of them. You can rest assured that if there is anything I can do from my end to help it will be done if it is possible." In the fateful months, even years, ahead, Brooke would be as good as his farewell word.

Obsessed with his own picture of British amateurishness, meanwhile, Rommel paid no attention either to the British announcement of changes in command on 19 August, or to the changes going on within the British lines—indeed his lack of reconnaissance by air or patrol in the southern sector of the British front, though intended to lull the British into a sense of false security there, was also a sign of contempt for his opponents. Trusting to the superior professionalism of his armored forces, Rommel had based his plan on a "decisive battle . . . to be fought out behind the British front in a form in which the greater aptitude of our troops for mobile warfare and the high tactical skill of our commanders could compensate for our lack of material strength."

Rommel's only major concern was the arms race—a race to build up the maximum number of Axis tanks, ammunition and fuel before the British could be reinforced. In this respect Rommel was cautiously optimistic. "The situation is changing daily to my advantage," he wrote to his wife on 10 August. From German agents in Cairo he knew that a large convoy "laden with a cargo of the very latest weapons and war material for the Eighth Army would arrive in Suez at the beginning of September." He therefore delayed his attack to the very final moment in August—unaware that every day's grace was manna to the Eighth Army under its new commander.

Whether Rommel was right in referring to the Axis "lack of material strength" is debatable: it would appear that each side overestimated the other's strength and underestimated its own. To the British, the German Panzer Mark IIIs and IVs were weapons of ominous power, and the knowledge that, already by 15 August, the Germans possessed over 200 of them was a matter of considerable disquiet, dominating all Eighth Army Intelligence reports for the period. The motley array of British Valentine tanks, the single brigade of already ancient Grants—"Egypt's last hope"—and the knowledge that none of the new Sherman tanks would be in line before mid-September was equally worrying.

Fortunately Rommel, in his turn, considerably exaggerated the British forces confronting him. He credited the British 30 Corps with a division still held back in the Delta under Alexander (50th Division), and assumed there were two British armored divisions in reserve behind 7th Armoured Division, south of the New Zealanders—whereas until 27 August there were in the whole of Eighth Army only two armored brigades, one of which was in the north, armed only with Valentines, the other on the Alam Halfa ridge.

In fact Rommel's armored superiority now exceeded the three-to-one ratio deemed necessary for offensive success, and, thanks to Rommel's urgent appeals for more troops and supplies, the Axis buildup far exceeded that of Eighth Army—as the Intelligence staff at Eighth Army were well aware. By 19 August, Major Williams was reporting in his top-secret Eighth Army Intelligence summary, "Enemy strength is still growing," and now included 5,000 elite parachute troops from Crete. By 21 August he reported that there had been a "significant change in the last week." The enemy's "mobile forces have been released from their temporary positional role. He is trying to deny our observation; and he has moved his artillery concentrations further south. His positional infantry, both German and Italian, are now bedded down and anti-tank guns have begun to come up for 164 Div. A definite acceleration of shipping programme is noticeable. There is no reason to believe his supply situation is any longer a strain. The parallel to mid-May begins to be pointed. . . . Further information from German parachutists [a euphemism for information based on Ultra decrypts] makes it evident that the stage is almost set."

In Cairo Churchill sat down with McCreery and Lindsell (Chief of Administration) to "spend a happy couple of hours at the good old pastime of whittling away the enemy's strength on paper," Ian Jacob recorded in his diary. "In the end the Prime Minister was satisfied that he had got a fair comparison of men, vehicles, weapons, etc. and it was generally agreed that taking one thing and another into account, we were about fifty-fifty with the enemy in the desert."

Churchill, however, was counting in numbers, not qualitative comparison. Eighth Army's tank strength was, on paper, 478. Of these, only 71 were Grants; the rest were obsolescent: 117 Valentines, 15 Matildas, 139 Stuarts and 136 Crusaders. Unreliable and boasting only 2-pounder or 37mm guns, they were of little or no account against German Panzers. Indeed, unknown to the British, over 170 of the 234 German tanks now sported long-barreled 50mm guns and extra frontal armor ("Specials"). A further twenty-six German tanks were even more powerful: Panzer Mark IV Specials, armed with 75mm guns. Together with the 281 tanks of the Italian armored divisions Rommel was expected to put into battle over 500 tanks. His Afrika Korps numbered "at least 29,000 men, over 100 guns, 200 anti-tank guns and perhaps fifty 88s," Major Williams recorded in his Eighth Army Intelligence summary on 26 August. Behind his mask of confidence, even Churchill became anxious. "At any moment Rommel might attack with a devastating surge of armour," he recalled in *The Hinge of Fate*, recording with candor how he had hinted to the British Ambassador's wife that she might be safer, with her baby son, in the Lebanon.

Lady Lampson, however, having met Monty on 12 August, refused to go. The days of evacuation were, she was certain, finally over. This time Eighth Army was going to win.

Waiting for Rommel to Attack

Ironically, Eighth Army was now only one-third as strong in medium-gunned tanks as it had been at Gazala—where it had boasted almost 170 Grant tanks alone. At Gazala, Rommel had turned the cumbersome generalship of Eighth Army to magnificent advantage, and was rewarded by Hitler with a field marshal's baton. Now, on the eve of his next great offensive, he showed signs of nervousness—the nervous anxiety of the ambitious performer, captivated by the looming prize of Alexandria and Cairo, and propelled also by the intuitive feeling that, unless either he or the German army in the Caucasus broke through, the greater material output of the Allies would, now that the United States had entered the war, doom Germany to eventual defeat. Should he fail to get through to the Nile, however, he hoped at least to "give the enemy a pretty thorough beating" before the arrival of the September convoy, he boasted to his wife. Indeed, he claimed in his letter to be "feeling quite on top of my form. There are such big things at stake. If our blow succeeds, it might go some way towards deciding the whole course of the war."

Across the minefields his adversary was equally confident, however.

As had become the hallmark of his generalship in England, Monty had insisted that all Eighth Army formations should rehearse their battlefield roles in properly umpired exercises. 30 Corps carried out its first exercise on 22 August; but it was in 13 Corps area that Rommel was expected to make his main thrust, and there that Monty's insistence upon training and rehearsal paid off. The War Diary of 13 Corps records how on 19 August the new corps commander "held conference for senior officers and explained his plans for meeting any enemy offensive"; on 20 August there came "practice moves of 22nd Armoured Brigade ['Egypt's last hope'] to battle positions on Alam Halfa ridge"; on 21 August "BGS held conference of umpires discussing plans for exercise on August 22"; and on 22 August Exercise Gala began at five o'clock in the morning, ending at four in the afternoon, and attended by the army commander himself:

> Tasks: To practice i) Move of 22nd Armoured Brigade into battle positions ii) Control throughout the Corps iii) Actions of commanders in certain situations.

Each eventuality was practiced. If Rommel, having smashed a path through the lightly held southern minefields, wheeled north to roll up the British front line, he would be met by Roberts' 22nd Armoured Brigade, hull-down on higher ground, leavened by medium artillery and antitank guns, and with 23rd Armoured Brigade's Valentines available to back it up if need be. This would be the ideal situation. If, however, Rommel attempted to press on towards El Hamman, 22nd Armoured Brigade would then threaten his rear, with 23rd Armoured Brigade in turn assuming the hull-down positions on the Alam Halfa ridge behind them. "It is a man's job if ever there was one and a great deal will depend on what results we can achieve here," Monty wrote to Brigadier Tomes, his old battalion commander in England, on 25 August. "I am wonderfully fit, as are all the Troops. You could not have a more healthy life," he declared—adding:

> The difficulty is Water: every man has one gallon a day but that is to do for cooking and for the radiator of his vehicle; the net result is that in bad times he has to do on a full water bottle for drinking and washing.
>
> A man soon becomes an expert in performing his complete ablutions in one mess tin of water; it is important to get the right sequence in which to do things, i.e. Shave, Teeth, then Wash.

This concern of the new Eighth Army Commander for the niceties of his troops' toilet, on the day Rommel was expected by British Intelligence to launch his much-vaunted attack, was yet another facet of Monty's strange psychology—though Tomes knew Monty well enough not to be in the least surprised.

Rommel, however, did not attack that night. Nor did he the next; and by 27 August, Eighth Army Intelligence was suggesting from Ultra evidence that the German attack would take place "not tonight but two nights later."

It was in fact this delay by Rommel that removed in the minds of most senior officers of Eighth Army the last vestiges of doubt whether 13 Corps could contain a blitz attack by the Afrika Korps with 234 Panzer Mark IIIs and IVs, as well as the lethal 88s; for on 27 August the 8th Armoured Brigade rejoined 8th Army with a further sixty to seventy refitted Grants. The two Grant-armored brigades were now put under command of Major General A. H. Gatehouse, who set up his 10th Armoured Division Headquarters alongside Horrocks, and, by placing 8th Armoured Brigade squarely on the track leading towards El Hamman, sealed Rommel's only eastern exit from the Alam Halfa trap.

The arrival of the 8th Armoured Brigade, Horrocks later wrote, "was a godsend to me and it altered the whole picture." The next day, 28 August, Horrocks held another training exercise so that Gatehouse could practice not only communication with his two armored Grant brigades, but also the summoning of the third, Valentine-armored brigade from the north in the event that it might be required in the south. By 29 August there was "still no conclusive evidence re timing," and Intelligence put this down as "temporary delay perhaps due to supplies."

In London, Churchill—reading the same Ultra decrypts—began to have doubts whether the Axis offensive would, after all, take place that month. The period of full moon had passed, and the night sky was getting darker. "What do you now think of the probabilities of 'Zip' coming this moon?" Churchill cabled to Alexander on the 28th. "Military Intelligence opinion now does not regard it as imminent." To this Alexander replied: " 'Zip' now equal money every day from now onwards. Odds against increasing till September 2, when it can be considered unlikely."

According to the Official New Zealand History of the war, both Montgomery and Horrocks became convinced, by the morning of 30 August, that "the danger of an immediate attack was passing, if it had not already passed," and therefore the time had come for the New Zealand Division to be withdrawn from the front line in order to start retraining as a motorized division, equivalent to the German 90th Light Division.

Whether Montgomery and Horrocks did, in fact, feel Rommel was "crying off" is difficult to say. According to Eighth Army records, a general "Stand To" was definitely ordered on 30 August in expectation of an attack, and Brigadier Williams could afterwards recall no change in the army commander's policy—a recollection confirmed by publication of the Ultra decrypts, which even on 29 August recorded no change in the enemy's intention to attack as soon as his fuel situation was satisfactory. Y Intelligence (enemy radio messages, monitored by British) indicated, moreover, on 30 August that 15th Panzer Division was moving south—an almost sure sign of impending enemy operations.

Whatever the truth, Monty showed not the least anxiety, and spent 30 August 1942 writing out his general training policy for the future Eighth Army offensive battle at Alamein. Having finished it, in hand, he gave it to his typist, then went to bed in his caravan.

The two New Zealand brigades were just commencing their phased departure from the front line that night, however, when there were reports of an enemy attack against 5th Indian Division on the Ruweisat Ridge. At Burg-el-Arab the Army/Air Headquarters was alerted, and shortly after midnight came the first indications of an enemy advance in the south. Brigadier de Guingand waited until there was enough evidence of a major enemy advance rather than a series of raids, then made his way excitedly to the army commander's caravan.

Monty's response de Guingand would remember to his dying day. The army commander merely murmured, "Excellent, excellent," turned over—and went back to sleep!

Part Two

ALAM HALFA

Monty inspects captured German tank with
Wendell Willkie, FDR's emissary,
5 September 1942.

Rommel's Sixth Sense

P erhaps the most remarkable aspect of the defensive battle which became known as Alam Halfa was its relative importance in the minds of the two opposing army commanders: Field Marshal Erwin Rommel and Lieutenant General Bernard Montgomery.

For Rommel, the battle of Alam Halfa was his last bid for victory in the Middle East. "Today," he announced on 30 August 1942 in a special message to his troops, "our army sets out once more to attack and destroy the enemy, this time for keeps. I expect every soldier in my army to do his utmost in these decisive days!"

By holding his armor behind the center of his line until the last moment, Rommel had hoped to deceive Eighth Army over the axis of his impending thrust. In the event, however, he himself was deceived. Eighth Army had sown much deeper minefields than expected in the south—almost 200,000—and had dug in mortar, artillery and machine-gun posts, which gave the Panzer army a rude shock when it reached the southern sector around midnight on 30 August. Moreover, the moment the first reports of an enemy attack were relayed by 13 Corps to Eighth Army Headquarters, the new Eighth Army partnership with the Desert Air Force came into operation.

The Luftwaffe, with 758 aircraft, considerably outnumbered the 565 Allied planes of the Desert Air Force. It was therefore imperative not to squander Allied bombers and fighter escorts on secondary or diversionary attacks. When, shortly before midnight, the first diversionary raids began in the north, the Desert Air Force was therefore told to wait. The 9th Australian Division easily repulsed the raid in its sector; the 5th Indian Division on the Ruweisat Ridge—which Monty had visited that very afternoon—gave way a little, and had to mount a dawn counterattack.

While Monty slept, de Guingand had sifted the incoming reports, concentrating on those from 13 Corps in the south. Only when the Axis columns were inextricably tied down in the British minefields in the south had he authorized the first bombing attacks to begin. Thereafter, at 2:40 A.M. on 31 August 1942, the area south of the New Zealanders was lit up by parachute flares and soon became an inferno. German casualties began to mount quickly; the Commander of the Afrika Korps, General Nehring, was wounded by a fighter-bomber, while the Commander of the 15th Panzer Division, Major General von Bismarck, was killed by a mortar bomb. It was an ominous beginning for an offensive designed to smash the Eighth Army and capture Cairo and Alexandria.

In his memoirs Rommel recalled:

> Shortly after passing the eastern boundary of our own minefields, our troops came up against an extremely strong and hitherto unsuspected British mine belt, which was stubbornly defended. . . . Before long, relay bombing attacks by the RAF began on the area occupied by our attacking force. With parachute flares turning night into day, large formations of aircraft unloosed sticks of HE bombs among the troops.
>
> The [Panzer] Army staff spent most of the night on the telephone, with reports pouring in in a continual stream. Even so there remained considerable uncertainty about the situation, although it gradually became clear that things could not have gone altogether as planned.

This was an understatement, for Rommel had given orders that his motorized forces were to advance no less than thirty miles east by moonlight, then strike north towards Burg-el-Arab at dawn.

Such optimism, based on poor reconnaissance by air and foot patrols, was a major error for a newly created field marshal (though Monty would commit a comparable error at Arnhem, seventeen days after himself becoming a field marshal), and it is difficult to understand why Nehring, von Bismarck and von Vaerst (Commander of 21st Panzer Division) subscribed to such a bold plan without more accurate information. As Monty had warned in a 1937 "Encounter Battle" article—which at the time Basil Liddell Hart found wholly unconvincing—the clash of two modern armies meeting in battle required a new approach to the layout of formations and their headquarters. Modern warfare allowed less time to recover from mistakes and demanded therefore that battle plans be well thought out, and well rehearsed, using latest Intelligence information. If the plan was poor, he had predicted, it would, in modern conditions, prove difficult if not impossible to rectify one's error.

Rommel's plan for the final conquest of Egypt fell into this category.

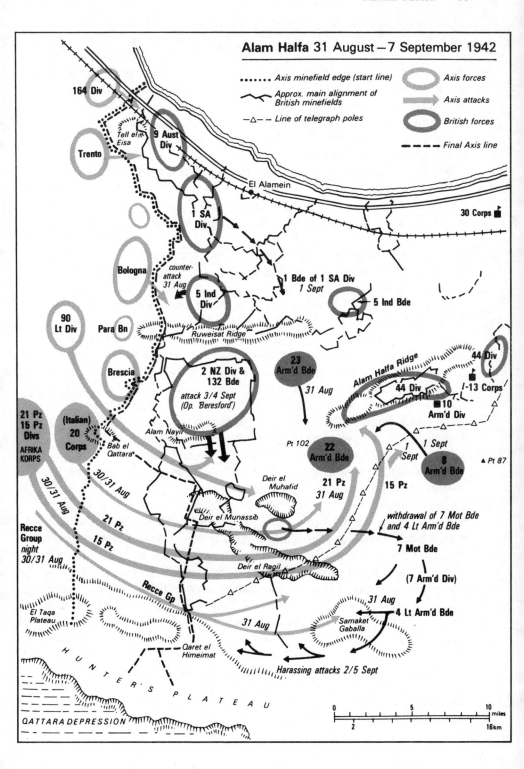

Alam Halfa 31 August – 7 September 1942

- **·····** Axis minefield edge (start line)
- Approx. main alignment of British minefields
- –△– Line of telegraph poles

- Axis forces
- Axis attacks
- British forces
- Final Axis line

164 Div

Tell el Eisa

9 Aust Div

Trento

El Alamein

30 Corps

1 SA Div

Bologna

counter-attack 31 Aug

1 Bde of 1 SA Div 1 Sept

5 Ind Div

5 Ind Bde

90 Lt Div

Para Bn

Brescia

Ruweisat Ridge

2 NZ Div & 132 Bde attack 3/4 Sept (Op. 'Beresford')

23 Arm'd Bde 31 Aug

Alam Halfa Ridge

44 Div

44 Div

I-13 Corps

10 Arm'd Div

21 Pz 15 Pz Divs AFRIKA KORPS

(Italian) 20 Corps

Bab el Qattara

Alam Nayil

Pt 102

22 Arm'd Bde

21 Pz 31 Aug

15 Pz

1 Sept

1 Sept

8 Arm'd Bde

▲ Pt 87

30/31 Aug

30/31 Aug

Deir el Muhafid

21 Pz

Recce Group night 30/31 Aug

15 Pz

Deir el Munassib

withdrawal of 7 Mot Bde and 4 Lt Arm'd Bde

7 Mot Bde

(7 Arm'd Div)

Deir el Ragil

Recce Gp

31 Aug

El Taqa Plateau

31 Aug

Samaket Gaballa

4 Lt Arm'd Bde

Qaret el Himeimat

Harassing attacks 2/5 Sept

H U N T E R ' S   P L A T E A U

QATTARA DEPRESSION

0   5   10 miles
2   16km

The success with which, though vastly outnumbered, he had thrown back Eighth Army at Gazala, snatched Tobruk, and held on to his gains in July 1942 had blinded Rommel to almost all problems save those of supply. He alienated his air force by his derision of its efforts and allowed himself to become almost megalomaniac in his assumptions about the enemy. He had banked on surprise and speed, and when he found his plan had not worked by dawn on 31 August, his heart sank, and his famed *Fingerspitzengefühl*, or military sixth sense, warned him not to go on.

Ironically, such was the legendary effect of Rommel's command that he became now a prisoner of his own reputation. The Afrika Korps chief of staff, Colonel Bayerlein, met Rommel at 8:15 A.M. on the battlefield, having become the Acting Commander of the Afrika Korps when Nehring was wounded. Bayerlein urged they be allowed to continue, since both 15th and 21st Panzer Divisions were at last emerging on the far side of the minefields. But Rommel hesitated, telling the Panzer divisions to halt and wait for new orders.

In his memoirs Rommel claimed that the long delay in the minefields "had given the enemy units in the threatened sectors time to send alarm messages and situation reports back to British Headquarters, and had enabled the British commander to take the necessary countermeasures." Forced to commit suicide for his role in the plot to assassinate Hitler in 1944, Rommel never did learn that "the British commander" had made up his mind how he would fight the battle as early as 13 August 1942, had ensured that Eighth Army rehearse its movements in proper exercises in the intervening weeks, and had simply gone back to sleep when told the battle had begun.

The specially jeweled field marshal's baton being held for Rommel in Berlin was now of no use; he had lost the opening round of the battle and his instinct was to pull back. Bayerlein, however, reflected the legendary courage and ardor of the Deutsche Afrika Korps, which would have felt betrayed if recalled from the far side of the minefields it had so painfully crossed. Not suspecting that the area beyond the minefield was a trap, Rommel now committed his second error. "We no longer had the advantage of the time the British would have needed, in the event of a quick break-through in the south, to reconnoitre the situation, make their decisions and put them into effect," Rommel afterwards summarized. Having lost the advantage of surprise, he now abandoned his overoptimistic objective of reaching Hamman (to the rear of Burg-el-Arab, some fifty miles away), and instead decided to swing north, making straight for Alam Halfa, from which ridge he could then dominate the rear of Eighth Army's front line—much as he had done by capturing the British "Knightsbridge" locality in the Gazala battle. He knew it had recently been fortified and expected a "very severe" battle to take it; but, as at Gazala, he recognized it was "the key to the whole El Alamein position."

That Rommel should so soon have fallen into the Eighth Army trap was a tribute, among other things, to Monty's grasp of the air weapon. Four years before, in August 1938, in the *Army Quarterly*, Monty had defended his "Encounter Battle" theories against Liddell Hart, while reiterating his vision of the proper tactical use of air power in battle. Reflecting on the great German spring offensive of 1918, he remarked that the Allies had done nothing to attack the German concentration of forces from the air. The spring offensive had "very nearly won the war for Germany," he recalled, "whereas, if the entire Allied Air Forces had been used to attack the concentration, it was possible that the offensive might never have taken place at all.

"The lesson seems to be," Monty had written, "that full advantage must be taken of the flexibility of air forces to direct every ounce of power when the decisive moment arrives on to what is then the decisive target. Thus the moment may come for switching off the attacks on the enemy's economic centres and concentrating everything in an overwhelming attack on his assembling armies. The speed at which ground forces can now move suggests that plans for this 'switching over' of air effort must be formulated in advance, so that they can be implemented within a few hours."

The preliminary bombardment of the Axis forming-up positions and depots, then the great Desert Air Force blitz on Rommel's mobile forces as they tried to force their way through the British minefields in the southern sector at Alamein on the night of 30/31 August, was Monty's first opportunity as an army commander to put his theories of air power into effect. While it is true that the sinking of Rommel's petrol-supply ships—by submarines and air attack—sealed the ultimate fate of the Panzer army, there can be no doubt that Rommel's decision to abandon his first plan and to drive up against Alam Halfa was not the immediate product of those sinkings, but the direct result of Monty's two-point plan for the opening phase of the battle: concealed depths of defended minefields and a punitive British air bombardment.

Rommel's hesitation at dawn on 31 August did credit to his military intuition. Both Kesselring, the German C-in-C South, who arrived on the scene at 9:45 A.M., and later Hitler himself failed to understand this pause. Kesselring considered that, since the Axis forces managed to continue in battle for another week, lack of petrol supplies could not be blamed. "The defeat may be attributed to causes of a more psychological nature," he wrote later. "I had at the time the conviction that this battle would have presented no problem to the 'old' Rommel. Had he not been suffering in health from the long strain of uninterrupted campaigning in Africa, he would never have pulled out when he had already completely encircled the enemy—the British 'Last Hope' position, as it was called, had already been outmanoeuvred. I know today that his troops were unable to understand the order to retire."

Kesselring, with his airman's view of strategy, saw the vital importance of taking both Alexandria and then Malta before the British could, with American help, rebuild their tattered strength in the Mediterranean—as Hitler also recognized. Neither appreciated, however, the extent to which the Panzer Army had been outwitted. In fact only Rommel seems to have recognized, in his bones, that his plans had been misconceived: that by relying so heavily on tactical surprise he had failed to do the necessary reconnaissance for such an ambitious thrust, and that to continue his offensive would be to take a massive gamble with his men's lives.

As events were to show, Rommel's intuition was correct—and the assault on Alam Halfa was doomed.

Keeping Faith with the Afrika Korps

Before the launch of his offensive, Rommel had sketched the German and Italian units which would go on to take Alexandria and Cairo, as well as the British airfields at Fayum. Nobody understood better the omens of success or failure, therefore, than the "Desert Fox." If Rommel hesitated on the minefields between Alam Nayil and Himeimat it was not for lack of courage or from exhaustion, but because he recognized that his plan had gone awry. He had failed to achieve surprise; had himself been surprised by the "unsuspected mine barriers" secretly laid by Eighth Army. Moreover, far from being supported by the terrifying Stukas, which had once been the hallmark of German offensives, he was himself being bombed and strafed un-mercifully by the RAF.

In deciding to continue the battle Rommel wished to keep faith with the Afrika Korps he had personally created. It took precious hours to refuel and rearm the Afrika Korps, as well as the Italian Littorio Armored Division. Nevertheless at 1 P.M. on 31 August the Axis army moved forward again. Moreover, as if in answer to a prayer, a desert sandstorm blew up, grounding the RAF. Taking advantage of the weather, the Panzers, armored cars, artillery and motorized infan-try raced on. Eventually, in the late afternoon, the Alam Halfa ridge became visible.

It was now imperative that, to win the battle, the Afrika Korps had to take the ridge, "the key to the whole El Alamein position." Once in possession of Alam Halfa, Rommel could dominate Eighth Army's rear. The British would be forced to contest this move, enticed into battle in such a way that the secret new guns of the Panzer Mark IIIs and IVs could deal with each British attack in turn.

Morale in the Afrika Korps was second to none: soldiers who had fought their way some 1,360 miles along the shores of North Africa, and now at last felt themselves within real striking distance of the cap-ital of Egypt and the port of Alexandria.

To the Eighth Army officers and men waiting on the Alam Halfa ridge, meanwhile, the emergence of the Afrika Korps resembled an ar-mada issuing from a sea mist—hundreds upon hundreds of German tanks, like ships filling the desert.

What then took place was, from Lieutenant General Montgomery's point of view, the vindication in modern battle of his theories of de-fense and of command. But for Rommel it was to mark the end of his belief in the independent power of armor.

In the Middle of a Battle

"On they come, a most impressive array," Brigadier "Pip" Roberts later described the German and Italian assault. "And now they all turn left and face us and begin to advance slowly. . . .

"I warn all units over the air not to fire until the enemy are within 1,000 yards; it can't be long now and then in a few seconds the tanks of CLY [County of London Yeomanry] open fire and the battle is on.

"Once one is in the middle of a battle time is difficult to judge, but it seems only a few minutes before nearly all the tanks of the Grant squadron of the CLY are on fire. The new German 75mm is taking heavy toll. The enemy tanks have halted and they have had their own casualties, but the situation is serious; there is a complete hole in our defence. I hurriedly warn the Greys [the reserve tank regiment] that they must move at all speed from their defensive positions and plug the gap.

"Meanwhile the enemy tanks are edging forward again and they have got close to the Rifle Brigade's anti-tank guns, who have held their fire marvellously to a few hundred yards. When they open up they inflict heavy casualties on the enemy, but through sheer weight of numbers some guns are overrun. The SOS artillery fire is called for; it comes down almost at once right on top of the enemy tanks. This, together with the casualties they have received, checks them. . . ."

Roberts' account wonderfully illustrated the intimate cooperation of hull-down tanks, antitank guns and artillery required to halt a full Panzer advance. But how near the Germans came to luring 22nd Armoured Brigade from their positions emerged from an interview Brigadier Roberts gave almost forty years later, using tableware to describe the positions:

As a matter of fact, although Monty says in his *Memoirs* that the instructions were that the tanks were to stay put in their position on the Alam Halfa position, we did come very near to moving.

You see, the Germans advanced and came up towards Alam Halfa. Now here were we sitting; the Germans came up the [line of] telegraph poles, and when they got there—instead of coming up here, they swung away, like that.

Well my divisional commander was then a man called Alec Gatehouse. And he was sitting further back . . . he could see what was happening too. And here were our forces with all the German Panzers going along like that, *past* our position. And in fact although Monty says he gave instructions that on no account was the 22nd Armoured Brigade to move its position, at that time Alec Gatehouse said to me, over the air:

"I don't want you to think we're peeing in our bags here, but you may have to come out of your position and attack him from the rear."

Now whether he had got Horrocks' permission to make such a statement, whether he'd been told by Horrocks that that might happen, and whether Horrocks had referred it to Monty I've not the slightest idea. However that is what he said to me. So I issued preliminary instructions to people that they'd got to be prepared to move out of their defensive positions—just thinking about it.

However at that moment the German tanks stopped and they all turned towards us—just turned, individual tanks, like that, so the situation never arose. . . . In fact we stayed put, and it was very effective even though they, the Germans, produced for the first time a long-barrelled 75mm gun in their Mark IV tank—which was much more effective than our 75mm gun and it knocked out one squadron of our Grants very efficiently, before we could do anything about it.

As Monty noted in his diary, it was only by meeting the enemy on "ground of its own choosing" that the outgunned Eighth Army had managed to halt Rommel's attack. At 8 P.M. on 30 August he noted: "2000 hours: enemy Panzer Division drew off and went into harbour for the night"—but the RAF had no intention of suspending its bombing operations, nor the British artillery. "2100. Dust now better and the RAF began night bombing," Monty recorded with satisfaction in his diary. "The Albacores found two large concentrations—one of 2000 tanks and MT [motor transport], and one of about 1000. These were bombed all night. One enemy harbour area of about a hundred tanks within range of artillery of 13 Corps was shelled all night."

In his war memoirs Rommel had cause to remember the incessant bombing and shelling:

After nightfall our forces became the target for heavy RAF attacks, mainly on the reconnaissance group, but also—though less severe—on other units. With one aircraft flying circles and dropping a continuous succession of flares, bombs from the other machines—some of which dived low for the attack—crashed down among the flare-lit vehicles of the reconnaissance units. All movement was instantly pinned down by low-flying attacks. Soon many of our vehicles were alight and burning furiously. The reconnaissance group suffered heavy casualties. . . .

While the British artillery and the Desert Air Force pounded the German positions, Monty slept. For Rommel, however, there was little sleep. His famed Afrika Korps was stalled beneath the ridge of Alam Halfa, before the hull-down tanks, antitank guns and supporting artillery of 22nd Armoured Brigade. Alongside 22 Armoured Brigade was a further brigade of more than a hundred Valentines; to the east another armored brigade with Grant tanks; and on the ridge itself the 44th Infantry Division, dug in with minefields, barbed wire and endless artillery. Rommel's hopes of overrunning British petrol dumps had been dashed, and, though the Panzer army was still a composite force with tremendous gun-power, it was like a bull in a ring. There was no way out to the north, for Alam Halfa was impregnable; there was no way out east, for even if the Afrika Korps could smash its way through the seventy-two Grants of the 8th Armoured Brigade, it could not leave its entire lines of communication at the mercy of Montgomery's forces at Alam Halfa, on its northern flank. And to the south there was merely the impenetrable expanse of the Qattara Depression. The Panzer army could only hope to retreat the way it had come.

On the morning of 1 September, Rommel permitted his Panzer divisions a few limited attacks, hoping he might thereby entice the reluctant enemy tanks to leave their hull-down positions. But, as the German 88mm Flak War Diarist recorded, Rommel was disappointed. "The swine isn't attacking," he complained bitterly to Kesselring—knowing that, unless the British came out, the battle was lost.

The British did not come out. Fearing the worst, Rommel signaled to Berlin that the Axis offensive should be played down in the German press and on radio. By denying Rommel the opportunity of a mobile battle, Montgomery had put paid to his last hope of reaching Cairo and Alexandria. "Shortage of petrol" would be the official reason given to the bewildered German troops—though, as Kesselring later commented, with the suggestion of a sneer, there was enough to bring all the units back. "It was this cast-iron determination to follow through that was lacking," Kesselring judged. To Hitler, Kesselring complained: "It was a mystery why he didn't go on with it. We had the British on the run again, we only had to pursue them and knock the daylights out of them."

An American Visitor

A t Eighth Army's headquarters at Burg-el-Arab, shared with the RAF, the realization that Rommel's offensive had failed brought great elation. This was capped, on 4 September, by the arrival of President Roosevelt's personal emissary, Wendell Willkie.

Willkie's world tour on behalf of the American President had put the wind up the Foreign Office in London. Willkie was known to be deeply suspicious of British colonial policies and intentions. Churchill therefore wired anxiously to the British Ambassador in Cairo on 5 September: "I hope you are taking trouble with Wendell Willkie who is a good friend of our country. He should be given every chance to see the front and anything else of interest that he desires. It is most important he should be warmly welcomed. You might mention him to Alexander if the latter is not too busy."

As the war progressed, Monty would often arouse ill feeling by his refusal to allow VIPs to visit his headquarters—indeed, one of his first edicts at Eighth Army Headquarters had been to ban *all* visitors without his own personal permission. However, in this instance he needed no pressure from Churchill to recognize the importance of Willkie's mission, and Churchill's cable arrived in Cairo twenty-four hours *after* Willkie had left for Burg-el-Arab.

Wendell Willkie—the losing, antiwar Republican contender in the 1940 U.S. presidential election—had been worried by State Department and military briefings he'd received en route to North Africa. "On the way to Cairo at the end of August bad news came to meet us," he related in his chronicle of the journey, *One World*. "I recalled the President's warning just before I left Washington that before I reached Cairo it might be in German hands. We heard tales of Nazi parachutists dropped in the Nile Valley to disorganize its last defenses. The British 8th Army was widely believed to be preparing to evacuate

Egypt altogether, retiring to Palestine and southward into the Sudan and Kenya."

Cairo Willkie found "full of rumors and alarms. . . . In a half hour at Shepheard's Hotel you could pick up a dozen different versions of what was taking place in the desert not much more than a hundred miles away. So I accepted eagerly an invitation from General Bernard Montgomery to see the front myself, at El Alamein."

Willkie was bowled over by the new Eighth Army Commander and his approach to modern battle, much as Winston Churchill had been:

General Montgomery met me at his headquarters, hidden among the sand dunes on the Mediterranean. In fact, it was so near the beach that he and General Alexander and I took our next morning's bath in those marvelous blue-green waters. Headquarters consisted of four American automobile trailers spaced a few dozen yards apart against the dunes for concealment purposes. In one of these, the General had his maps and battle plans. He gave me one for sleeping-quarters. In another his aide put up, and in the fourth the General himself lived, when he was not at the front.

This was not often. The wiry, scholarly, intense, almost fanatical personality of General Montgomery made a deep impression on me when I was in Egypt, but no part of his character was more remarkable than his passionate addiction to work. . . .

Almost before we were out of our cars, General Montgomery launched into a detailed description of a battle which was in its last phases, and which for the first time in months had stopped Rommel dead. No real news of this battle had reached Cairo or been given to the press. The General repeated the details for us step by step, telling us exactly what had happened and why he felt it was a major victory even though his forces had not advanced any great distance. It had been a testing of strength on a heavy scale. Had the British lost, Rommel would have been in Cairo in a few days. . . .

At first it was hard for me to understand why the General kept repeating in a quiet way: "Egypt has been saved." The enemy was deep in Egypt and had not retreated. I remembered the skepticism I had found in Cairo, born of earlier British claims. But before I left the trailer in which General Montgomery had rigged up his map-room, I had learned more about desert warfare, and he had convinced me that something more than the ubiquitous self-confidence of the British officer and gentleman lay behind his assurance that the threat to Egypt had been liquidated.

General Montgomery spoke with great enthusiasm of the American-manufactured General Sherman tanks which were just then beginning to arrive in important numbers on the docks at Alexandria and Port Said. . . . Almost his central thesis was his belief that earlier British reverses on the desert front had resulted from inadequate co-ordination of tank forces, artillery forces, and air power. General Montgomery told me that he had his air officer living with him at his headquarters, and that complete coordination of planes, tanks and artillery had been chiefly responsible for the decisive check to Rommel of the past few days.

Monty invited Willkie to dine with him that evening; but, though Willkie accepted gratefully, Burg-el-Arab was soon alight with petty jealousy. The American Army Air Forces had begun to provide both bomber and fighter-escort squadrons in the desert, under the overall command of Major General Lewis S. Brereton: arguably the most incompetent of all senior American generals in World War II. Monty had no idea who Brereton was when introduced together with Willkie, and thus did not think to include him in his invitation to dinner. Brereton took lasting umbrage at this, and only the timely intervention of General Alexander, as C-in-C, Middle East, averted a row. Although dinner was given in Montgomery's mess, Alexander took over as host and invited Brereton to come, and to Brereton's delight General Montgomery was placed "down by the salt."

It was therefore a tribute to Willkie, so naturally skeptical of British war aims, that he became the very first American to see beyond Monty's social failings into the heart of a professional battlefield commander on the very verge of greatness. After dinner, Monty accompanied Willkie to his caravan:

> He made sure my sleeping bunk was in order, and then we sat on the steps of the trailer, from which we could see the whitecaps breaking on the sea under the moon and hear at our backs in the distance the pounding of his artillery against Rommel's retreating forces. He was in a reminiscent and reflective mood and talked of his boyhood days in County Donegal, of his long years in the British Army, with service in many parts of the world, of his continuous struggle since the war began to infuse both public officials and Army officers with the necessity for an affirmative instead of a defensive attitude. "I tell you, Willkie, it's the only way to defeat the Boches"—he always spoke of the Germans as the Boches. "Give them no rest, give them no rest. These Boches are good soldiers. They are professionals."
>
> When I asked him about Rommel he said: "He's a trained, skilled general, but he has one weakness. He repeats his tactics—and that's the way I'm going to get him."

Ironically, the same would one day be said by Germans of Monty. Meanwhile the next morning Monty personally took Willkie round the front, visiting a group of Americans training with a British tank regiment, and inspecting "the dozens of German tanks scattered over the desert. They had been captured by the British and blown up at Montgomery's orders. As we would climb up on these wrecked tanks, he would open the food boxes and hand to me the charred remnants of British provisions and supplies which the Germans had taken when they captured Tobruk. 'You see, Willkie, the devils have been living on us. But they are not going to do it again. At least they are never going to use these tanks against us again.' "

For Wendell Willkie, after Roosevelt's ominous warning and the rumors he had heard all the way from Washington to Cairo, the picture of this small, beaky-nosed army commander, who personalized everything and yet who had such a mastery of military detail, clambering up a wrecked German tank and opening its food boxes was mesmerizing. "Again I was enormously impressed by the depth and thoroughness of General Montgomery's knowledge of his business. Whether it was Corps or Division, brigade, regiment or battalion headquarters he knew more in detail of the deployment of the troops and location of the tanks than did the officer in charge. This may sound extravagant but it was literally true. . . . On the way back to General Montgomery's headquarters he summed up what I had seen and heard. He minced no words at all in describing his situation as excellent, and the battle just concluded as a victory of decisive significance. 'With the superiority in tanks and planes that I have established as a result of this battle, and with Rommel's inability to get reinforcements of matériel across the eastern Mediterranean—for our air forces are destroying 4 out of every 5 of his matériel transports—it is now mathematically certain that I will eventually destroy Rommel. This battle was the critical test.' "

Even the miffed air force general, Lewis Brereton, afterwards noted in his diary that "Rommel's bid for Egypt had failed. It was one of the major turning points of the war."

Monty's diary entry that evening—5 September 1942—recorded more simply: "By 1900 hours enemy was right back in the minefield area, covered only by rearguards."

Monty had won his first battle as an army commander.

Part Three

A TOUGH PROPOSITION

Monty at Alamein with Brigadier "Pip"
Roberts on right, Lieutenant General Brian
Horrocks on left.

A Ruse to Keep Rommel at Alamein

R ommel had withdrawn his battered forces—but should the British trumpet it as a major victory?

"Looking back, I see it was a mistake to remain there," the German C-in-C South, Field Marshal Kesselring, reflected after the war. "All things considered, it would have been better to have retired behind a rearguard to a more easily defended position, for which the Halfaya Pass would have been suitable; or else, under pretence of offering the main resistance from the El Alamein line, to have accepted the decisive battle some twenty miles further west in an area—the so-called Fuka position—which had all the advantages of the El Alamein zone and was better protected on the left wing by the terrain."

This was said with hindsight, however. At the time, Rommel's decision to accept battle with the British at Alamein was one with which Kesselring wholeheartedly concurred—a decision which owed much to Monty who, concerned lest Rommel pull back to more defensible positions further west, decided not to proclaim the battle of Alam Halfa a decisive British victory over the Germans, despite the obvious yearning of both press and public for news of an Allied success.

Monty's prescience in this instance was truly remarkable—and was never acknowledged by later historians. Yet on 5 September, Alexander—after reaching "various decisions" the previous night with Monty—cabled the War Office in London. The text was unmistakably Monty's:

Consider it most desirable to forestall publicity. Please arrange press publicity on following lines:
  Enemy attacked our southern flank with whole Panzer Army. After five days' heavy fighting, at times intense, enemy has been driven back by combined efforts all arms, armoured and unarmoured, magnificently

assisted throughout by RAF. In spite of every effort, enemy failed to penetrate our main defensive system at any point.

Enemy losses in personnel and material have been severe, our own comparatively light.

At Alamein, meanwhile, Monty asked Willkie to help damp down press accounts of the Alam Halfa battle. The Eighth Army Commander had "stopped Rommel," Willkie noted, "but he was anxious for him not to begin to retreat into the desert before some 300 [sic] American General Sherman tanks that had just landed at Port Said could get into action. He estimated that this would take about 3 weeks. He figured that if he made a formal public announcement of the result of the battle, Rommel's withdrawal might be hastened."

Could Willkie address the press, therefore, instead of the victorious Eighth Army Commander? Willkie, as the only civilian witness of the battle, agreed to make, once back in Cairo, a personal statement "which would not be regarded by Rommel as a sign of aggressive action on his [Montgomery's] part."

Monty's refusal to comment on the battle, and the strange use of an American politician instead, "in the language which he [Montgomery] and I had agreed upon in advance," worked wonders. The tidings appeared to be good—Rommel withdrawing—yet the manner of Willkie's announcement was so unaggressive as to cause the war correspondents to remain deeply skeptical. "It was the first good news from the British side that these British newspapermen had had in a long time," Willkie recounted. "They'd been fooled many times and were wary. The battle line, to their eyes, had hardly sagged, Rommel was still only a few miles from the Nile, while the road to Tripoli, from where we were, seemed long and a little fanciful and the road to Cairo painfully short."

Nor were the war correspondents the only ones to be disappointed. Some of Monty's subordinates were downright aghast at the way the army commander allowed Rommel not only to occupy the old British minefield positions in the south, but even the commanding heights of Himeimat, on the southern side of the Axis penetration. "Pip" Roberts, the Commander of 22nd Armoured Brigade, protested at this refusal to contend possession of Himeimat—an opinion he still held almost forty years later:

I do know that the fact that the Germans had Himeimat was a very severe handicap to us when we came to the main battle of Alamein. And I'm thinking of myself because 7th Armoured Division was in the south and had this bloody Himeimat looking right down on us all the time. If we'd taken Himeimat then it would have eased that. From there one saw a very large amount of the battlefield. It was a tremendously useful position—and very difficult to get people off it. . . . I think personally it would have been worthwhile having a try, and if it seemed difficult, then give it up. I don't know how much Monty appreciated that it was a tremendous vantage point, looking up the whole of the Alamein line.

But Monty *did* appreciate its value: a prime piece which, as in a game of chess, he deliberately surrendered in order to keep Rommel at Alamein, at the end of extended lines of communication and in the south, on the edge of the Qattara Depression—thus stretching to the limit Rommel's German-Italian forces, until they became too thin to survive a British armored attack, mounted in overwhelming strength with new American tanks, at one selected point.

As always, it was Monty's opponent who appreciated best the success of Monty's strategy. In his memoirs Rommel summarized the reasons for the 'failure' of the Axis offensive and noted that

British ground forces, as has been shown, had hardly put in an appearance during the [German-Italian] offensive. Montgomery had attempted no large-scale attack to retake the southern part of his line; and would probably have failed if he had. He had relied instead on the effect of his enormously powerful artillery and air force. Added to this, our lines of communication had been subjected to continual harassing attacks by the 7th Armoured Division. There is no doubt that the British commander's handling of this action had been absolutely right and well suited to the occasion, for it had enabled him to inflict very heavy damage on us in relation to his own losses, and to retain the striking power of his own force.

Monty had won round one. Round two, a British offensive battle, would, however, be a much tougher proposition.

Training the Eighth Army

T hough the press remained skeptical, and some of the armored commanders felt frustrated, an air of jubilation had meanwhile permeated the rest of Eighth Army.

"It was a fascinating battle," Robert Priestley, a staff officer in 8th Armoured Brigade, recalled. "For the first time since the Germans came into operations in North Africa we were told to do a job we really felt we could do. . . . The actual battle went, as far as I could tell, absolutely according to plan. I remember on the second day of the battle visibility was superb—and it very rarely was in the desert. You could see 5 miles or more quite easily. And we could see the whole of the German army laid out in front of us. I got on a tank with Derrick Mullins, a regimental CO, and we sat there watching the German army being shelled and bombed. And I remember writing home after that battle saying, 'All right, this battle's changed the war. Now we shall win. No two ways about it. We shall win.' And that confidence never left really."

By contrast, the battle of Alam Halfa broke Rommel's morale and his health. Within twelve days of its end a deputy, General Stumme, would arrive to take temporary charge of Panzerarmee Afrika in order that Rommel could convalesce in Germany; but no rest could restore to Rommel the initiative he had surrendered at Alam Halfa. By the time Montgomery launched his massive October offensive, the African Panzer Army had only just regained the tank strength it had possessed prior to the "Six-Day Race" (as the Germans called the battle for Alam Halfa)—whereas Eighth Army's strength grew and grew. The world at large might not be aware of the change that had been wrought in the Egyptian desert, but the men of Eighth Army were. The first Sherman tanks began to arrive—already by 20 September there were ninety-five ready for action. The lighter Crusader tanks were being fitted with

6-pounder guns, and large numbers of new 6-pounder antitank guns were being issued. A new flail tank had been converted from the old Matildas to clear gaps in minefields.

For Monty, victory at Alam Halfa was especially heartening in that it confirmed almost all the principles on which he had sought to retrain the British army in England since 1940. "I enjoyed every minute of the battle," he confided to the Reynoldses on 21 September, after thanking them for looking after his son, David. "And I fought it in accordance with the doctrine I have been teaching and preaching in England since the Dunkirk days; which makes the victory all the more satisfactory." The desert had rejuvenated him. "I am extremely well in health; better than I have been for years," he boasted. "There is no doubt the desert is a very healthy place. I have not had a bath for 4 weeks; I am convinced we all wash and bath far too much!! . . .

"Tell David that I am very flourishing and enjoyed fighting Rommell [sic]—and that I saw him right off."

It was now that Monty's impact as army commander began to be felt as something more than that of a new general with sound ideas in an old army. Thus far Monty had only made a single change in command or staff: the summoning of General Horrocks to take over 13 Corps. Now, however, heads began to roll. Ramsden, Commander of 30 Corps, was sacked, and one of Monty's former Camberley Staff College students appointed in his place: Lieutenant General Sir Oliver Leese. The commander of the famed Desert Rats, Callum Renton, was also sacked, to be replaced by another of Monty's ex-Camberley students, Major General John Harding from Cairo. Under Douglas Wimberley, yet another former Camberley student of Monty's, the 51st Highland Division also came into the front line.

A host of brigadiers and colonels meanwhile also vanished—such as the CO (commanding officer) of a certain unit who, when asked by Monty who trained the officers, answered that this was done by the second-in-command. "I came across the second-in-command later in the day," Monty recalled in his *Memoirs*. "The poor man denied that he was responsible for training the officers and said that it was done by the CO. I ordered that a new CO be found for the unit at once; it was clear that nobody trained the officers."

What is not generally known is that, for the battle of Alamein, Monty assumed the responsibility of training the Eighth Army himself—he had no officer on his staff to do it, nor probably could have found one. He had already written and issued his own training instructions, "8th Army Training Memorandum No. 1," on the eve of the Alam Halfa battle. Immediately the battle was over he ordered all three corps of Eighth Army to begin to act upon them.

Training instructions in all Eighth Army formations and units—infantry, armor and artillery—now reflected almost word for word those of the army commander: instructions which were almost identical to those which Monty had issued in Home Forces over the past two years. On 10 September, for instance, only three days after the battle of Alam Halfa was over, General Gatehouse's 10th Armoured Division Headquarters issued a new training instruction to the constituent armored brigades as they gathered to become part of 10 Armoured Corps for the battle of Egypt, beginning: "8th Army Training Memorandum No. 1, recently issued by the Army Commander, lays down that training will be directed to ensure that we can fight the battle in accordance with certain fundamental principles which are enumerated below. . . ." The following day General Lumsden, the new Commander of 10 Corps, issued his own Corps Training Instruction. It too laid down that "8th Army Training Memorandum No. 1 be read once a week and carefully studied by all commanders"; that training programs "will be prepared by all commanders down to Commanders of troops, platoons or equivalent sub-units"; and warned that skeleton exercises "down to Division and Brigade HQ will be held by the Army Commander during the month."

Nothing was left to chance. How tough Monty's new grip felt was recalled of one of his staff officers, William Mather, who had been in the desert since 1940, and was wounded in the summer of 1942:

I got wounded in the Gazala battles and I was in the General Hospital at Kantara, recovering. I was there about three months. And one of the things you do in hospital is to try and fix yourself up with a good job when you come out. I got myself fixed up with what I thought was the best job in the army, which was to be Brigade-Major of the 1st Armoured Brigade—which was a very good armoured brigade, and I was only a Territorial [volunteer reserve officer]. I thought it was a tremendous feather in my hat and I was cock-a-hoop. I was just about to be released from hospital when Monty arrived to take command in the desert.

And you know, I was rather surprised because I knew he was quite a good soldier, of course, but it didn't mean very much to me. And I thought, how odd, he wasn't desert-worthy, as we used to say, in any way. One of those . . . sort of 'Ingleezis' coming out to control the desert sweats who really thought we knew the ways of the desert backwards. So I was really rather surprised, even though we'd been pushed back to Alamein. . . .

I was congratulating myself on getting the job when a new posting came out to me just as I was about to leave hospital. I was to go as a Liaison Officer to 8th Army Headquarters!

Well I regarded a Liaison Officer, even a G2 [Grade 2] Liaison Officer as a Major, as a pretty low form of life compared with being Brigade-Major of the 1st Armoured Brigade. So I went to see the Commandant of the hospital and told him—asked him: Can you keep me for another few days until this thing blows over? So he said, Oh yes, fine; and I stayed there for about ten days, thinking that they'd be too impatient, they'd post somebody else to this job.

Not a bit of it! An order came out [after Alam Halfa] for my arrest! And I realized times had changed!! So I shot off post-haste to 8th Army Headquarters, Burg-el-Arab, and I was straightway summoned to Monty. He said:

"Mather, you were malingering!"

I thought, how do you know? And—it was the most extraordinary thing about Monty that he *always* knew what you'd been up to! He was such a rogue himself in many ways that he could see through anybody. *Nobody* could pull a fast one over him, at all. And this was so absolutely apparent that no one bothered after it'd been tried once or twice. Anyway, he said:

"Why?"

So I thought the best thing was to come clean—which people soon realized with Monty. So I said what the position was, that I didn't fancy being a G2 Liaison Officer instead of being Brigade-Major at 1st Armoured Brigade. And he retorted:

"So you think being Brigade-Major at 1st Armoured Brigade is better than a job being one of my Liaison Officers?"

I said, "Frankly, yes, sir."

He said:

"Well may I tell you that *I'm destroying the desert trades union*. And the 1st Armoured Brigade's going to become a Tank *Delivery* Regiment!" Similarly with the Bays, the 10th Hussars and the 9th Lancers—he also broke their brigade up!

Faced with such a prospect, Mather accepted the job of liaison officer. Within days, though, he was made G2 (Plans) under Colonel Mainwaring, whom he considered one of the best operations staff chiefs ever—founder of the system of monitoring radio signals broadcast by Eighth Army's own units ("J"), and the architect of Eighth Army's new operations setup, based on a group of caravans, bringing Intelligence, air, staff duties and plans together.

"It was fascinating because we all used to go down and bathe on the beach before breakfast, all wearing our nothings, and when we were all set the atmosphere was tremendous," Mather recalled, "because Monty had got a complete grip of the Army at once. I mean he was a professional, much more professional—I mean we all thought we were professionals, but by Jove he was in a different class!

"And the two things were: that without any effort he virtually knew everybody by name, down to the rank certainly of second-in-command of regiments and brigade-majors. I mean he knew everybody above major certainly—all senior majors he knew by name—and usually their Christian name and knew all about them. *In the whole of the Army!* It was absolutely fantastic—and without any apparent effort. He would discuss the merits of different people: and he always used to get it right! It was absolutely extraordinary, the way he could sum people up. We called him 'The Oracle.' Because when you had a problem, you asked Monty. And he knew what the answer was—inevitably he got it right. It was absolutely extraordinary! He was always known as 'Master,' but he was also called 'The Oracle.' "

As chief planning officer, Colonel Charles Richardson found the army commander's oracular ability equally amazing:

> At Alamein I was asked, as the Planner, to give a figure for the casualties at Alamein, about a fortnight before the battle. And I had to say to Freddie [de Guingand], "I've got no experience on which to base this estimate and there's nothing in the books." So he said, "All right, I'll ask the Army Commander."
>
> And Freddie came back the next day, and he said, '13,000.' Well now that was precisely, within a matter of hundreds, the figure for killed, wounded and missing at the end of the battle!

Having laid down the principles for training Eighth Army in the coming weeks, meanwhile, Monty had to draw up in writing his plan of battle.

Major Mather remembered the moment vividly. It was 13 September 1942—six days after the end of the battle of Alam Halfa:

> You see, when he wrote the Operation Order for the battle of Alamein it was like a hen giving birth. He walked backwards and forwards on the sands of Burg-el-Arab all day, backwards and forwards, like Napoleon with his head down, his hands behind his back. And we all said: "Master is giving birth."
>
> And he came back into his caravan and in about 4 hours—I remember now it was on 14 sheets of paper—he wrote the whole Operation Order for Alamein. That was it. It wasn't changed, or very few variations were made to it.

The plan was called Lightfoot, and the document Monty wrote out was historic, for it marked the beginning of a series of offensive battles that would take the Western Allies from Alamein to the heart of Germany over the next two and a half years.

Operation Lightfoot

14 September, 1942

LIGHTFOOT
General Plan of Eighth Army

OBJECT

1. To destroy the enemy forces now opposing Eighth Army. The operations will be designed to "trap" the enemy in his present area and to destroy him there. Should small elements escape to the West, they will be pursued and dealt with later.

PLAN IN OUTLINE

2. The enemy will be attacked simultaneously on his North and South flanks.

3. The attack on the North flank will be carried out by 30 Corps with the object of breaking in to the enemy defenses between the sea and inclusive the MITEIRIYA Ridge, and forming a bridgehead which will include all the enemy main defended positions and his main gun areas. The whole of this bridgehead will be thoroughly cleared of all enemy troops and guns. 10 Corps [*corps de chasse*] will be passed through this bridgehead to exploit success and complete the victory.

4. On the South flank, 13 Corps will:
   a) Capture HIMEIMAT.
   b) Conduct operations from HIMEIMAT designed to draw enemy armor away from the main battle in the North.
   c) Launch 4 Lt Armd Bde round the Southern flank to secure DABA and the enemy supply and maintenance organization at that place,

and to deny to the enemy air the use of the air landing grounds in that area. . . .

In extraordinary detail the new Eighth Army Commander proceeded to lay down, in forty-two precise paragraphs, the strategic, tactical, technical, supply, deception, air, training and morale blueprint for one of the decisive battles of human history—five weeks before the battle commenced.

In many respects Monty's plan was the product of a lifetime's military thinking and experience, from the North-West Frontier of India to the trenches of the Western Front, and the grim education of Dunkirk in May 1940. Out of the chaos of modern blitzkrieg warfare a small, beaky-faced misfit had extrapolated the essentials for success in battle. The days of "tip and run" desert tactics, Monty felt, were now over. The free world demanded Allied victory: and to obtain that victory, against a seasoned and professional enemy, protected by minefields, armed with awesome tanks and artillery and covered by a renowned air force, a new Allied weapon must be forged. "All formations and units will at once begin to train for the part they will play in this battle," Monty ordered. "Time is short and we must so direct our training that we shall be successful in this particular battle, neglecting other forms of training. . . . The initial break-in attack by 30 Corps, and the initial operations by 13 Corps, and the move forward of 10 Corps to deployment areas, will all be carried out by night with a full moon.

"Therefore full advantage must be taken of the September full moon period to practice operating on a moonlit night and actually *to rehearse the operations concerned*, using similar bits of ground.

"There will be a great weight of artillery fire available for the break-in battle. During the training period infantry and other arms must be accustomed to advancing under the close protection of artillery fire and mortar fire.

"We must have realism in our training and use live ammunition in our exercises with troops, even if this should result in a few casualties. I will accept full responsibility for any casualties that may occur in this way.

"The accurate fire of mortars will be of the greatest value in the break-in battle. No troops can stand up to sustained heavy and accurate artillery and mortar fire without suffering a certain loss of morale; low category troops will be definitely shaken by such fire, and can then be dealt with easily by our own attacking troops.

"Tanks that are to work in close co-operation with infantry in this battle must actually train with that infantry from now onwards.

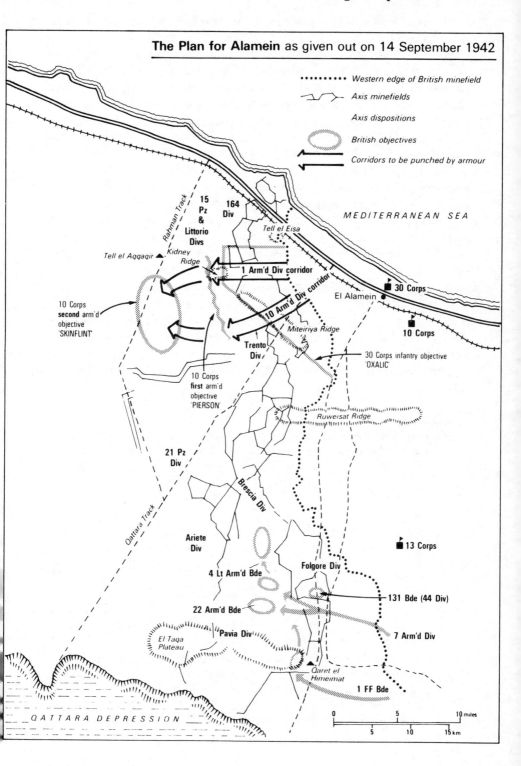

The Plan for Alamein as given out on 14 September 1942

•••••••• Western edge of British minefield

⌐⌐⌐⌐⌐ Axis minefields

Axis dispositions

British objectives

Corridors to be punched by armour

MEDITERRANEAN SEA

15 Pz & Littorio Divs

164 Div

Tell el Eisa

Rahman Track

Tell el Aqqaqir

Kidney Ridge

1 Arm'd Div corridor

30 Corps

El Alamein

10 Corps second arm'd objective 'SKINFLINT'

10 Arm'd Div corridor

10 Corps

Miteiriya Ridge

30 Corps infantry objective 'OXALIC'

Trento Div

10 Corps first arm'd objective 'PIERSON'

Ruweisat Ridge

21 Pz Div

Brescia Div

Ariete Div

13 Corps

4 Lt Arm'd Bde

Folgore Div

131 Bde (44 Div)

22 Arm'd Bde

Pavia Div

7 Arm'd Div

El Taqa Plateau

Qattara Track

Qaret el Himeimat

1 FF Bde

0   5   10 miles

5   10   15 km

QATTARA DEPRESSION

"The individual soldier must be given practice so that he will reach a high degree of skill with the weapons he will use in battle.

"There is plenty of ammunition available for this purpose. Full use will be made of the [sand] model in preparation for this battle. Every formation headquarters and every unit should have a model of the ground over which it is to operate, and on this model all officers will be instructed in the stage-management of the battle.

"Finally all NCOs and men will be shown on the model the part they will play in the battle.

"As far as officers and NCOs are concerned the model will be any ordinary piece of ground; the actual place names must not be shown. As the day of attack approaches more information can be disclosed.

"No information about our offensive intentions will be disclosed to any officer or other rank who has even the slightest chance of being taken prisoner in a raid; this order will not be relaxed until the morning of D1 day.

"I direct the attention of Corps and Divisional Commanders to Eighth Army Training Memorandum No. 1 issued on 31 August 1942. The fundamentals outlined in that memorandum will govern the conduct of our battle operations, and will therefore form the basic background for all our training. . . ."

There was one further theme Monty wished to emphasize, however: morale.

MORALE

38. This battle for which we are preparing will be a real rough house and will involve a very great deal of hard fighting. If we are successful it will mean the end of the war in North Africa, apart from general "clearing-up" operations; it will be the turning point of the whole war. Therefore we can take no chances.

39. Morale is the big thing in war. We must raise the morale of our soldiery to the highest pitch; they must be made enthusiastic, and must enter this battle with their tails high in the air and with the will to win.
There must in fact be no weak links in our mental fitness.

40. But mental fitness will not stand up to the stress and strain of battle unless troops are also physically fit.
This battle may go on for many days and the final issue may well depend on which side can best last out and stand up to the buffeting, and ups and downs, and the continuous strain, of hard battle fighting.
There will be no tip and run tactics in this battle; it will be a killing

match; the German is a good soldier and the only way to beat him is to kill him in battle.

41. I am not convinced that our soldiery are really tough and hard. They are sunburnt and brown, and look very well; but they seldom move anywhere on foot and they have led a static life for many weeks. During the next month, therefore, it is essential to make our officers and men really fit; ordinary fitness is not enough, they must be made tough and hard.

42. This memorandum will not be reproduced or copied. It will form the basis of all our plans and preparations for operation "LIGHTFOOT."

B. L. Montgomery
Lt. Gen.
G.O.C.-in-C.
Eighth Army.

Coming Down to Earth

The next evening, Lieutenant General Sir Oliver Leese arrived from England to replace Ramsden—having, as he candidly admitted in his unpublished memoirs, waited a full day before leaving the Guards Armoured Division in England, then been delayed a further day by engine trouble at Gibraltar. Arriving in Cairo on the morning of 15 September he'd breakfasted with Dick McCreery, Alexander's chief of staff, bought some desert clothes, then finally motored in a leisurely fashion to Burg-el-Arab. "I soon came down to earth as the Army Commander greeted me warmly and then quickly asked me why on earth I had taken so long to get to him!" Leese recalled.

Asking Leese to stay overnight in one of his caravans, Monty gave him the exact date of the Eighth Army's forthcoming offensive—23 October—and his task: to smash through the enemy's northern defenses with four infantry divisions, so that the new Eighth Army armored corps could pass through onto the Miteiriya Ridge and destroy the Afrika Korps. The next day, at a gathering of all Eighth Army corps and divisional commanders, Monty personally went over his Lightfoot plan. No one dissented.

All three corps commanders—Leese, Lumsden and Horrocks—were, however, "new," having all been divisional commanders only four weeks previously. Moreover they were all English, which distinctly irritated the Commonwealth divisional commanders—Pienaar, the South African, Morshead, the Australian, and Freyberg, the New Zealander—who saw themselves as being passed over for promotion. Nevertheless, all were impressed by the Eighth Army Commander's authority, determination and zeal. As before the Alam Halfa battle, the objectives were crystal clear, presented by a general who had now proved himself in battle against the "bogeyman" Rommel.

It was only after the senior commanders returned to their formations that the true enormity of the undertaking began to sink in—and the problems began.

Churchill Objects

The first objection came from Churchill. Never a patient man, the Prime Minister had already cajoled and harried two Middle East Commanders-in-Chief—Generals Wavell and Auchinleck—to their professional doom. In recently installing Alexander as his third appointee, Churchill had intended to install an obedient soldier who would do what he was told. On 17 September, therefore, having heard nothing from the desert since Montgomery's victory at Alam Halfa, Churchill impatiently cabled Alexander that he was "anxiously awaiting some account of your intentions. My understanding with you was the fourth week in September." Perturbed, Alexander went straight to Burg-el-Arab, where he showed Monty the Prime Minister's telegram.

Monty, however, had no intention of attacking Rommel in September. In his diary, written up on the eve of the battle of Alamein, Monty noted laconically: "About the middle of September the C-in-C was pressed by the Prime Minister to start the Eighth Army offensive at an early date. A reply was sent that this was not possible."

De Guingand, however, later recalled the incident in more detail. "Monty called me in," de Guingand remembered. "I was the only other person there. He said: 'Now, Alex, I won't do it in September. But if I do it in October it'll be a victory.' And Alex said: 'Well what shall I say to him?'

"Monty said: 'Freddie, give me the pad'—I always carried a note pad—and he wrote out the message himself for Alex to send. I quote it in my book [*Operation Victory*]. And Alex said: 'Thank you very much, Monty, I'll do that'—and he sent off the signal which was not his but Monty's!"

Since the signal bore Alexander's name, however, it was against Alexander that Churchill ranted and railed when he received it—as well as against the hapless CIGS, Sir Alan Brooke, who had gone grouse shooting on the Durham moors near Catterick. A furious interchange took place on the "scrambler," Churchill accusing Brooke of being "out of touch with the strategic situation," and Brooke replying that he had "not yet solved how I am to remain in touch with the strategic situation whilst in a grouse-butt."

Monty's cable was duly sent by Churchill to the shooting-butt at Catterick by messenger. Brooke, reading the cable, thought "Alexander's reasons . . . were excellent. I told him [Churchill] so on telephone and thought he said that he agreed with me."

In this, however, Brooke was mistaken. Whilst Brooke continued his brief vacation, Churchill bombarded Alexander with signals, stressing the need to draw German forces and attention away from Torch, which was currently scheduled to begin on 4 November. To each signal Monty had to formulate a reply, and in his diary he recorded: "After some protesting and 'belly-aching,' the Prime Minister accepted the inevitable, and agreed; when the true facts were put to him clearly he saw the point at once."

Like Brooke, however, Monty was also mistaken—for the truth was, Churchill was under enormous strain. As the Prime Minister confessed later to his doctor, the months of September and October 1942 were, for him, the most anxious months of the entire Second World War. He had promised Stalin Torch; but only after tremendous and sustained pressure had he got the Americans to back the operation wholeheartedly, on 5 September. Then Stafford Cripps, Leader of the House of Commons, announced on 21 September that he wished to resign—in protest at the way Churchill was running the war! Cripps gave voice to a "widespread sense of frustration and discontent" in Britain—a feeling that, despite the great exertions of the people, the conduct of the war left much to be desired.

What was wanted, Churchill knew, was a victory: a tangible sign of battlefield success. Alam Halfa, owing to Monty's strategic intentions, was not popularly regarded as a victory. By begging Cripps to delay his resignation until the outcome of Eighth Army's desert offensive, Churchill managed to buy himself a breathing space, but he was well aware, as he recalled in his history of the war, that Cripps' resignation would precipitate a "political crisis" that might well bring the government down. Churchill had survived one recent vote of confidence in the Commons; whether he would survive another was less certain. As Brendan Bracken, Minister of Information, said to Churchill's physician at this time: "There may be trouble ahead. The Prime Minister must win his battle in the desert or get out."

Nor was Churchill's anxiety merely political. Lord Trenchard, legendary father of the RAF, was adamant that direct confrontation with the German army, either on the continent or elsewhere, would inevitably result in defeat or, at best, a return to the stalemate trench warfare of the First World War. The crippling casualties involved in land warfare against the Nazis, Trenchard believed, could only be avoided by air offensive—a "bomber 'blitz,' " as he put it in a widely read paper at the end of August 1942.

Little wonder, then, that Churchill "belly-ached." Although he gave in on 23 September—at Brooke's behest—and promised Alexander that "we shall back you up and see you through," he was in fact far from satisfied—and forced Alexander to divulge Monty's Lightfoot battle plan.

This was meddling of a typically Churchillian kind. Through Ultra decrypts of German top-secret signals (which he liked to read "naked," i.e., without the benefit of an experienced operational Intelligence analyst) Churchill was receiving in London his own accurate picture of Axis dispositions and measures for meeting Eighth Army's offensive in the desert—and therefore knew of the ever-deepening belt of German minefields at Alamein. In conversation with his military advisers Churchill began seriously to doubt whether, having postponed his offensive from September to October, Montgomery could possibly "blow a hole in the enemy's front," as Churchill signaled to Alexander:

There is a point about the fortifications which the enemy will make in the interval which I should like to put to you. Instead of a crust through which a way can be cleared in a night, may you not find twenty-five miles of fortifications, with blasted rock, gunpits, and machine-gun posts? The tank was originally invented to clear a way for the infantry in the teeth of machine-gun fire. Now it is the infantry who will have to clear a way for the tanks, and it seems to me their task will be a very hard one now that fire-power is so great. No doubt you are thinking about all this and how so to broaden your front of attack as to make your superior numbers felt.

Once again, all Alexander could do was show Monty the signal.

A Tough Proposition

Churchill's "belly-aching" Monty simply ignored. The Prime Minister—an enthusiastic promoter of the use of the first tanks on the Western Front in 1917—was obviously haunted by past memories, Monty felt. Moreover his idea of broadening the front of the attack flew against the cardinal principle of concentration that characterized modern military thought.

Yet, in his maddening, illogical and intuitive way, Churchill had put his finger on the nub of the problem—for the task of breaking into Rommel's prepared defenses looked increasingly formidable, at least to Oliver Leese. In his unpublished memoirs, Leese later reflected that, of his five infantry divisions, one (4th Indian) was incapable of offensive action; another (51st Highland, reconstituted after the surrender of the original division at Saint-Valéry in 1940) had never been in battle before; two (2nd New Zealand and 1st South African) were a brigade short and therefore only "good" for a single attack in the battle; indeed only one, the 9th Australian, was up to strength and capable of sustained operations:

After the Conference [15 September] my first decision was to see for myself the ground over which I was to do the attack....

We were obviously up against a tough proposition. The whole area was quite flat, except for the Miteiriya Ridge which was some 300 ft high and which was mostly in German hands. And it stuck out a mile that it was going to be very difficult to conceal our guns, ammunition, tanks and infantry during the concentration prior to the battle....

I spent three days in reconnaissance and then I had to decide on the actual point of attack. I had too few Divisions and also too few guns to attack all along my front. I found a certain defilade to cover my right flank about Tel-el-Eisa and I rested my left as best I could on the Miteiriya Ridge. It gave me an initial frontage of 12,000 yards on the first objective, unfortunately extending to 16,000 yards on the second. I have often thought that if I had to do the attack again, I would somehow have shortened it still more.

Contrary to popular legend, Leese was acutely aware that, for a ten-mile-wide break-in, he was short of artillery—"In point of fact I only had 452 field guns and what was more worrying only 48 medium guns to cover the 30 Corps break-in attack."

If Leese worried whether he had sufficient infantry and artillery to achieve the "break-in," however, he was even more alarmed when he found that his infantry divisional commanders doubted whether the armor would push through the minefield gaps the infantry made.

Faith and Doubt

"When I held my first Corps conference my divisional Commanders listened politely to what I had to say, and then said quite quietly that the Armor would not pass through their gaps in the minefields. I replied that they would of course do so as the Army Commander had issued the order to that effect. The divisional Commanders just repeated again quite quietly their previous opinion that the Armor would not do so."

Freyberg never subsequently attempted to conceal his misgivings about the British armor. Indeed, when shown a draft of the British Official History relating to these "doubts," Freyberg commented tartly in his large, childlike hand: "It was not that we doubted. We did not feel it was possible. And it wasn't."

Whether at this stage Monty realized that he had so many doubters is unknown; he made no mention of the problem either in his diary or his *Memoirs*, mentioning only that GHQ Cairo disliked the idea of a northern thrust and would have preferred to see the conventional inland hook around the south. Yet it seems unlikely that Monty—who as Major Mather quickly discovered "knew everything"—was unaware of such dissension. Treating it as "belly-aching," however, he ignored it as he had Churchill's objections, and stuck strictly to his "masterplan."

Preparations went ahead inexorably. With each day the morale of the troops rose steadily higher. The deception plan in the south, under Colonel Richardson, was destined to become a classic of its kind, guaranteeing—as it would at D-Day in Normandy—complete tactical surprise. The artillery plan, meanwhile, was to Monty even more important. The artillery must pave the way for the infantry, then protect it once it had reached its objectives. It must also cover the complicated leapfrog of the armored corps through and beyond the conquered minefield sector. In order that the full, concentrated weight of Eighth Army artillery could be brought to bear on the two break-in points, Monty now entrusted the artillery plan to his erstwhile chief gunner at South-Eastern Command, Brigadier Sidney Kirkman, whom he had summoned with Horrocks, but who had had to come out the long way from England.

Like Leese, Kirkman stayed his first night in the desert in Monty's guest caravan. After dinner Monty took him to his map lorry, explained his plan of battle and instructed Kirkman to see that "the gunner plan is absolutely as good as it can be—'it's one of the most important factors,' " Kirkman recalled Monty's words many years later. "And I said, 'Yes, sir, I understand.' "

Recalling the incident almost four decades later, Kirkman felt this to be remarkable:

> I mean if one looks back, almost any other Commander in history, having attached importance to an event of that sort would probably have said "Is everything going all right—are you happy?" Not a bit of it. He never mentioned it again. I mean I had plenty of interviews with him, mostly at my request. But between that moment and the Alamein offen-

sive he never again referred to the gunnery plan. He was satisfied that since I was there it would be as good as it could be. There are very few people who have that faith!

Monty's faith was not misplaced. Indeed he was quite satisfied that the infantry, by the last week in October, would be trained and ready for their role, as would the artillery. The problem, in his view, was the armor. Would it really penetrate beyond the Axis minefields in the north by the first morning of the battle; and if it did, was it to be trusted to remain concentrated and destroy Rommel's armor on ground of its own choosing? Could one realistically hope to create and train a cohesive British armored corps, akin to the celebrated Afrika Korps, with new tanks about which the crews and maintenance teams knew nothing, in a bare five weeks? Moreover, Churchill's fear of a twenty-five-mile-deep system of fortifications, although exaggerated, was in essence well founded. On 27 September, Eighth Army Intelligence reported that the Italian Trento Division had been "sandwiched between German units" and that elite German parachutists were forming "iron lungs for Italian infantrymen" by being peppered in battalion strengths within the Italian defensive layout.

To test the strength of Rommel's defenses, two brigades of the 44th Division carried out an attack on the last day of September. The results were depressing: the troops ran into both Ramcke and Folgore Brigade paratroopers, sustaining heavy casualties, and failed to achieve their object.

It was clear that, as fast as Monty trained his revived Eighth Army for a decisive *offensive* battle, the African Panzer Army was preparing itself for a decisive *defensive* battle. On 5 October, Eighth Army Intelligence drew up its latest and most accurate analysis of Rommel's defensive layout, instituted before Rommel left for his cure on 21 September. Using half a million mines, Rommel had ordered the sowing not only of conventional mine belts, but also a system of "dividing walls connecting the two main north to south belts at intervals of 4 to 5 kilometres," thus forming a series of "hollow areas." These "hollow areas" were intended as "traps for penetrating troops" who breached the first minefield belt, since they would be forced to move either right or left of the "dividing wall," thus "dissipating the force of the attack."

This was ominous—though not as much as news that the British armored commanders were now on the point of open mutiny.

Mutiny in the Desert

D
e Guingand later recalled the circumstances clearly. "Monty had been called away to give a lecture at the Staff College, Haifa. Lumsden was commander of 10 Corps, and I thought I'd better go over and listen to what he'd got to say [at a conference of his divisional and brigade commanders]."

To de Guingand's horror, Lumsden applauded Monty's plan—then declared he would not follow it: " 'Monty's plan—there's one point I don't agree with: that tanks should be used to force their way out of the minefields. Tanks must be used as cavalry: they must exploit the situation and not be kept as supporters of infantry. So I don't propose to do that.' After the conference I went up to Herbert and I said: 'Look here, my dear boy, you can't do this. You know Monty. You must know him well enough—he won't permit disobedience to his orders.' " Lumsden, however, was unruffled, telling de Guingand to "leave that to me."

Such refusal to obey orders had come to characterize the disparate Commonwealth units of Eighth Army over the past year, and illustrated how little the so-called superiority in arms and men enjoyed by Eighth Army really meant to the generals at the time. By late October, Rommel's German-Italian African Panzer Army mustered approximately 100,000 troops, while Eighth Army's strength had risen to almost twice that number. Historians, noting this growing imbalance, often assumed the numerical ascendancy of Eighth Army somehow guaranteed Montgomery success. Yet the truth is, Eighth Army had enjoyed relatively greater superiority over Rommel in the Crusader operations of November 1941, and again at Gazala in May 1942—and had been defeated. Herbert Lumsden, supposedly the most experienced armored commander in the desert, had now been given the first truly armored reserve corps in Allied battle history, with first-class American tanks—yet his diffidence over the chances of breaking out through the Axis minefields became known to all the senior commanders of Eighth Army and their staff.

"Monty came back the next day and I repeated to him this conference," de Guingand recalled.

What was to be done? Only two and a half weeks now remained before D-Day. The situation was critical. There could be no question of postponing the most important Allied offensive of the war, upon whose success the outcome of the Torch landings depended—indeed upon which was predicated the entire American commitment to the war in the Mediterranean. Failure at Alamein would, it was generally believed, lead the Vichy French to challenge the Torch landings on their shores in Morocco and Algeria, as well as giving Hitler ample reason to reinforce his German armies in North Africa, concentrating then upon the final capture of Malta—which was only expected to hold out if resupplied by 16 November, when a British convoy was due to sail: ships which could only enjoy air protection if Eighth Army recaptured the Martuba airfields, west of Alamein, by that date.

Instinctively, Churchill had recognized the magnitude of Monty's problem. Because the Prime Minister's suggested solution—broadening the attack—was impossible, as well as tactically unsound, Monty had simply ignored it. Now, however, he had to face the fact that Churchill was right: Eighth Army was faced with an almost impenetrable line of fortifications. Though he "whistled in" General Lumsden and reiterated Lumsden's task as Eighth Army's armored corps commander, Monty knew his words alone would not suffice. It was too late, however, for a wholesale change of armored commanders; too late to start again and completely retrain the British armor for its new role. The Allied Torch landings and the very survival of Malta were at stake. Reluctantly, therefore, Monty took the only course open to him: he altered his plan.

A Killing Match

T he more Monty thought about the problem, the more he realized that despite the arrival of so many new antitank guns and
the imposition of corps artillery programs under Kirkman, the
infantry themselves were at heart frightened of making such a deep
penetration into the Axis lines without tank support. Conversely, the
armor was still terrified of being caught in a "trap," unable to maneuver
in the German minefields and picked off like stranded ducks by the
dreaded German 88mm guns. Lumsden's personal bravery was un-
questioned, but his experience at Gazala had made him reluctant once
again to risk crippling casualties: and this was reflected in his subordinate commanders.

One answer was to close down the *corps de chasse* altogether and allot its armored divisions to Leese's 30 Corps. However, such infusion
would make the formation too large for Leese, an as yet completely inexperienced corps commander, to handle. The only possible way out,
Monty felt, was to alter his Lightfoot plan so that 10 Corps fought
with 30 Corps, giving the infantry the security they so lacked, while
the armor would receive the full benefit of a corps of infantry, replete
with artillery and antitank guns. In such a scenario there need be no
interruption or alteration in the planning: the attacks would go in as
arranged. Only, instead of breaking into the open to engage the Afrika
Korps, well beyond the German minefields and the Eighth Army's infantry, the British armor would simply settle itself on good ground of
its own choosing and "shield" the infantry whilst *it* now undertook the
major battle-role: that of methodically eating away or "crumbling" the
defending Axis troops. The German armor could not possibly watch
its defending infantry being so destroyed; would be forced therefore to
attack the armored shield of 10 Corps on ground of the latter's own
choosing—with the same result as at Alam Halfa.

How this idea came to Monty at this critical moment is a mystery which none of his staff could ever explain. It transformed an imaginative but overambitious "masterplan" into a much more basic proposition, a battle of attrition—and for this, romantic military historians would never forgive him. By contrast, veterans of the desert campaign could only marvel at the way Monty turned an ominous situation to advantage: an intriguing example of Monty's underlying realism, yet—because it implied that his original concept of a *corps de chasse* was wrong—something for which Monty, who hated *ever* to admit to having made a mistake, never took the credit he deserved.

In his diary, after the battle, Monty recorded the change of plan, but made no mention of the "mutiny" by his armored commanders:

By the first week in October I was satisfied with the leadership.

The equipment situation was also good; we had a good heavy tank and it contained a good gun; we had a great weight of artillery and plenty of ammunition; I could concentrate some 400 guns for the operation of blowing the hole in the enemy positions in the North.

But the training was not good and it was beginning to become clear to me that I would have to be very careful, and that I must ensure that formations and units were not given tasks which were likely to end in failure because of their low standard of training.

The army had suffered 80,000 casualties, and the re-born Eighth Army was full of untrained units.

The troops had fought a successful defensive battle on 31 August and following days. But this next battle was to be an offensive battle, which is a very different proposition. I was determined to have no more failures. The troops in the Middle East had a hard life and few pleasures; they put up with it willingly. All they asked for was success—and I was determined to see that they got it. It was clear that I must so stage-manage the battle that my troops would be able to do what was demanded of them, and I must not be too ambitious in my demands.

And so, on 6 October, I issued a Memorandum of how I intended to fight the battle.

The memorandum was five typescript pages long. Although the original plan of Lightfoot envisaged very tough fighting, the accent had been—just like Rommel's at Alam Halfa—on speed, armor and surprise. Now, seventeen days from D-Day, the Eighth Army Commander's new plan anticipated a battle of armored and infantry attrition. "This battle will involve hard and prolonged fighting," Monty's memorandum ran.

Our troops must not think that, because we have a good tank and very powerful artillery support, the enemy will all surrender. The enemy will not surrender, and there will be bitter fighting.

The infantry must be prepared to fight and to kill, and to continue doing so over a prolonged period.

It is essential to impress on all officers that determined leadership will be very vital in this battle, as in any battle. There have been far too many unwounded prisoners taken in this war. We must impress on our officers, NCOs and men that when they are cut off or surrounded, and there appears no hope of survival, they must organize themselves into a defensive locality and hold out where they are. By so doing they will add enormously to the enemy's difficulties; they will greatly assist the development of our own operations; and they will save themselves from spending the rest of the war in a prison camp.

Nothing is ever hopeless so long as troops have stout hearts, and have weapons and ammunition.

This new policy, however, meant training and bringing Eighth Army's infantry and armor to such a pitch of determination and enthusiasm that it would be able to sustain its offensive for perhaps ten days or more.

Taking His Gospel to the Troops

That Monty managed to inspire Eighth Army with the will and determination to undertake such a decisive "killing-match" was, in the end, what raised him head and shoulders above any other Allied general in the war so far—indeed, Field Marshal Templer would later remark that it was this quality, far more than any tactical ability, which was Monty's true genius, and the reason why he would go down as one of the great captains of history, just as Churchill would for his moral leadership of a beleaguered nation in 1940 and 1941.

Churchill had inspired the free world by a rhetoric that did justice to the cause of humanity and civilization. Even on his brief visit to selected units of 13 Corps on 20 August, Churchill had evoked images that would remain forever in the minds of the men of his old regiment—the 4th Hussars—on the eve of the battle of Alam Halfa:

> Gentlemen, you will strike—ah—an unforgettable blow—ah—against the enemy. The corn will be ripe—ah—for the sickle—ah—and you will be the reapers.
> May God bless you all.

The Prime Minister's courage was born of an indomitable spirit, of a lifetime's political struggle, and a deep awareness of the epic nature of history. His confidence, however, was subject to moods of profound depression—his "dark fears" as his doctor called them—and his night's rest only guaranteed by a "red tablet."

By contrast, perhaps the most extraordinary facet of Monty's whole character was his infectious, unshakable self-confidence. If he was mad, as some claimed, then it was a strange madness that eliminated doubt, exuded confidence and guaranteed his sleep.

This gift of self-confidence Monty now brought to bear in a tireless bid to enthuse and prepare his army for the coming battle. He made it his business to visit virtually every unit of Eighth Army, formally and informally. Like his missionary father before him in Tasmania he took his gospel out to the troops. "It was a great achievement," Sir Oliver Leese recorded in his unpublished memoirs, "as day by day his own personality was spreading through the Army, and in the end the battle plan became the personal affair and interest of each man."

Monty's orders had always borne the unmistakable imprint of his mind—that talent for clarifying complex problems until they appeared to be quite straightforward. Yet, as if to mirror the contradictions of his character, an impish vanity revealed itself in tandem with his awesome professionalism, striking a bond with ordinary soldiers that would be unique in the history of his country. Churchill was admired, but as his wife, Clemmie, once said: "He knows nothing of the life of ordinary people. He's never been in a bus, and only once on the Underground"; whereas Monty's mischievous, schoolboy humor and his evident, almost messianic concern for the welfare of his men began to turn soldierly respect into loyalty of a new kind. His phrases and sayings swept through an army that had no other diversions or distractions than preparing for the impending battle. As General Horrocks later emphasized, the bare, scrubby desert imparted a classical military quality to the confrontation between the two armies, quite unlike that of any other theater of war.

"I have been very busy since I last wrote," Monty apologized in a letter to the Reynoldses on 6 October—the day he issued his revised plan for Alamein. "In fact one has no spare time at all; this is probably just as well as there is not a great deal to do in the desert. . . . It will be very interesting when I begin to get the *Times*. I take it by the year but the copies all come by sea and I suppose I shall get about 80 back copies on one day!!" he remarked—adding, with characteristic, almost unconscious egoism: "I shall be able to read what the Press said about my appointment." He was meantime instructing his bank in London to transfer some £500 to the Reynoldses, "and to keep you always on that mark or thereabouts. Then if anything should happen to me David would be all right for about a year or so; this would tide over the time they always take to wind up one's affairs. Actually," he assured the Reynoldses, "I haven't the least intention of letting anything happen to me, and I know it will NOT. But I would like you to have the money and then I needn't bother."

Meanwhile Monty had on 29 September laid down the system and timing by which Eighth Army would be informed of the plan of battle. Except for those units furnishing patrols, every man in Eighth Army would eventually be told, at least in outline, what the plan was: brigadiers and CREs (engineer commanders) immediately, battalion and regimental commanders on 10 October, company and battery commanders on 17 October, and all remaining officers on 21 October—officers whose duty was to see that "all troops" were then properly informed: "Wed 21 October and Thurs 22 October will be devoted to the most intensive propaganda as regards educating the attacking troops about the battle, and to getting them enthusiastic," he ordered.

> We have great superiority over the Germans in artillery and tanks, and the Germans have no conception of what is coming to them in this respect. . . .
>
> If every tank crew, and every 6-pdr A[nti].T[an]k. gun team, will hit and disable one enemy tank, then we must win.
>
> If every disabled enemy tank is destroyed at once by the RE [Royal Engineers] before it can be towed away, our win becomes all the easier.
>
> These, and other, facts must be got across to the troops in no uncertain voice. They must be worked up to that state which will make them want to go into battle and kill Germans.

Having altered his tactical policy for the battle, Monty himself seems to have had no doubt about the outcome. He summarized in his diary relating to the eve of the battle:

As the days passed, it became clear to me that if 30 Corps was successful in blowing the hole, and if 10 Corps could get its leading armoured Brigades out through the gaps unopposed before daylight on D plus 1, then we would have no difficulty in winning the battle. It would merely be a question of time.

There would be much hard fighting, and I was prepared for a real dog-fight to go on for at least a week; but our resources were such that we must win.

I could see that great determination and willpower would be necessary; the enemy would fight hard and there might be many awkward periods; if we wavered at these times we might lose the battle.

The critical essentials would be:

To keep the initiative

To maintain the pressure and proceed relentlessly with the Army plan.

To preserve balanced dispositions so that we need never re-act to enemy thrusts. . . .

An essential feature of my plan was that every Commander in the Army, right down to the Lt-Col level, should know my whole plan, how I meant to fight the battle, what issues depended on it, and the chief difficulties the enemy was up against.

I was also determined that the soldiers should go into battle having been worked up to a great state of enthusiasm.

This was essentially an Army battle, fought on an Army plan, and controlled carefully from Army HQ. Therefore, everyone must know how his part fitted in to the whole plan; only in this way could perfect co-operation be assured.

For this reason, apart from daily visits and inspections of units, Monty relied on the technique he'd developed in Home Forces in England, addressing his officers down to lieutenant-colonel level at specially convened gatherings. In England he had done this at postmortem conferences following an exercise; now he began doing it *before* the battle. As one of his staff officers, Major Oswald, later acknowledged, it was this willingness of the army commander to announce openly to his men what he intended to do in the coming battle that astonished even those who admired the way Alam Halfa had been won. "After Alam Halfa people paid more and more attention," Oswald related.

But when he really stuck his neck out before Alamein and said "This is how it's going to go, and what is more, see that every single soldier knows this"—now that's taking a hell of a chance. Because if you're wrong, there's nothing for you to do but remove yourself from the scene. . . .

You could see from the faces of the people who were there, some of whom had long experience of the desert: they said, "By golly, he must be pretty sure—he fairly stuck his neck out. We've never heard anybody say in such detail exactly what's going to happen in the ensuing battle. We've heard generals explaining why we didn't quite manage to win the last one. But here he stuck his head out and he must be jolly certain of himself."

Now that made a very profound impression.

Major "Bill" Mather was given the task of organizing one of these officer briefings at Amiriya. "It was absolutely amazing. We were there for two hours. . . . He went through it, day by day, and told us how we'd be feeling; how we'd come to a point where we might start to lose hope—and saying but we would carry on."

The battle, Monty predicted, would have three phases: the "break-in," the "dogfight," and the "final 'break' of the enemy." He warned officers not to "expect spectacular results too soon"; it would be a steady, methodical battle which the enemy could not withstand, but which Eighth Army could. He predicted it would last twelve days. Provided they operated "from firm bases," reorganized quickly on gaining their objectives, kept balanced, and kept up pressure, then there was no way in which the Panzer army could succeed in holding Eighth Army. "If we do all this, victory is assured."

As de Guingand later recalled, Monty drummed in the need to retain the initiative, "and how everyone everyone must be imbued with the burning desire to 'kill Germans. Even the padres—one per weekday and two on Sundays!' This produced a roar."

Finally, on 21 and 22 October, the men of the Eighth Army were "let into the secret. . . . And, as a result of everything, a tremendous state of enthusiasm was produced. I have never felt anything like it," de Guingand recorded. "Those soldiers just knew they were going to succeed."

Damned Rude to Alex

Meanwhile the way Monty treated his Commander-in-Chief, General Sir Harold Alexander, had become ominously arrogant; to Alexander's staff, indeed, a matter of great indignation. "Bill" Williams, briefing Monty, and sometimes Alexander, on Ultra intelligence, remembered being surprised by Monty's far from subordinate attitude towards his nominal superior:

> Monty was really rather rude to him. I was only a very junior officer, but in front of me he almost said, you know . . . not exactly "shut up" [to Alexander], but that sort of feeling. He wasn't—you got the impression in a way—Monty had taught Alex at the Staff College, that was it; there was this sort of atmosphere that, you know: "I'm telling you"—and I think it rubbed off on oneself in a sense that you talked to Monty on—you didn't spell it all out because he knew it, you didn't have to make it in rounded sentences, you could do it sort of quickly and then in a sense you had to turn to Alex and elaborate somehow, because he didn't have the context quite so much at his fingertips.
>
> Alexander's deputy Chief-of-Staff was James Steele, who was a great friend of mine, and since the war we've often discussed those days and there's no doubt, according to what Jas Steele said to me, that Monty was incredibly off-hand with Alex—in fact damned rude! Alex came to see him one time and Monty said: "I'm sorry Alex, I can't stop now, I'm going off to . . ."
>
> Monty was, after all, the most difficult subordinate to anyone.
>
> The great thing about Alex was: he was a very sensible man, very charming . . . and he saw that Monty was likely to win this battle. He saw that he was saddled with Monty, so he—well, you'll put up with any insubordination in war from a subordinate if he'll win battles—and Alex was sufficiently astute to see that Monty would win the battle.
>
> There was no object in having a row, so there it was. . . . But there's

no doubt that Monty was damned insubordinate to Alex. To the end they remained amiable, and laughing together. But in point of fact Monty had no great respect for Alex, and Alex disliked Monty.

Such open contempt for subordinates and superiors who did not measure up to Monty's professional military expectations had characterized Monty's entire professional life, bringing him many times to the brink of dismissal, and often leading to his being passed over for promotion.

Fortunately, however, Monty was "out of the way" in the Egyptian desert, with less "opportunity for clashes" with his superiors, as Sir Sidney Kirkman later reflected. The desert, in short, suited the simple, ascetic, somewhat messianic Monty, as it had so many of his biblical predecessors; was one area of the modern world where Monty could introduce his vision of how a modern army should be created without the constraints of civilians, without political considerations; and, above all—thanks to Alexander's wise forbearance—without a difficult Commander-in-Chief over him.

This latter advantage could not, and would not, last. But for the moment, however, Monty was the monarch absolute—and how he relished the role! On the morning of 23 October 1942, for instance, Monty addressed the war correspondents at a specially convened press conference. "Many of the war correspondents were rather shaken by the confidence—this bombastic confidence he displayed," de Guingand remembered. "They felt there must be a catch in it—how can he be so sure?"

Wiping the Floor with the British

I f Monty was confident, so too was his opponent, Field Marshal Rommel, recuperating near Wiener-Neustadt, where he had,
in 1938, been commandant of the Kriegsschule.

To an old colleague Rommel boasted that with three shiploads of
fuel for his tanks he could be in Cairo within forty-eight hours: a
strange boast for a man who had lost his great chance of breaking
through the British defenses when they were at their weakest, and
now faced, at Alamein, a burgeoning Eighth Army, armed with hundreds of powerful new American tanks.

To British observers, it scarcely seemed possible that an army of
such magnitude could be assembled and launched into battle with
complete tactical surprise. Yet such proved, in fact, to be the case—
helped by the fact that Rommel remained in Austria. Yet at Alamein,
Rommel's Panzer army subordinates remained equally confident they
could hold the line, even if they had given up hope of breaking
through to Cairo after their defeat at Alam Halfa. The Acting African
Panzer Army Commander, General Stumme, the C-in-C South, Field
Marshal Kesselring, and the chief of operations at Panzer Army HQ,
Colonel Westphal, all predicted defeat for the Eighth Army if and
when it attacked—Stumme having even written to Rommel that the
British "are none too happy about it [the impending offensive]. We're
going to wipe the floor with the British."

The complacency of these senior German commanders was mirrored in the visit of Colonel Liss—Chief of Western Intelligence in
Berlin—to the Alamein line on 23 October, and Liss' confident prediction to Berlin, early that evening, that no attack was expected before
November.

While Liss reported all was quiet on the Egyptian front, Monty had, that same day, issued his historic "Personal Message from the Army Commander" to be read out to every soldier in the Eighth Army:

1—When I assumed command of the Eighth Army I said that the mandate was to destroy ROMMEL and his Army, and that it would be done as soon as we were ready.

2—We are ready NOW.

The battle which is now about to begin will be one of the decisive battles of history. It will be the turning point of the war. The eyes of the whole world will be on us, watching anxiously which way the battle will swing.

We can give them their answer at once, "It will swing our way."

3—We have first-class equipment; good tanks; good anti-tank guns; plenty of artillery and plenty of ammunition; and we are backed up by the finest air striking force in the world.

All that is necessary is that each one of us, every officer and man, should enter this battle with the determination to see it through—to fight and to kill—and finally to win.

If we all do this there can be only one result—together we will hit the enemy for "six," right out of North Africa.

4—The sooner we win this battle, which will be the turning point of this war, the sooner we shall all get back home to our families.

5—Therefore, let every officer and man enter the battle with a stout heart and with the determination to do his duty so long as he has breath in his body.

AND LET NO MAN SURRENDER SO LONG AS HE IS UN-WOUNDED AND CAN FIGHT.

Let us all pray that "the Lord mighty in battle" will give us the victory

B. L. Montgomery,
Lieutenant-General, G.O.C.-in-C., Eighth Army.
MIDDLE EAST FORCES
23-10-42

Everything Is Set

General Leese later remembered the final hours leading up to the battle. "I motored slowly round the battlefield talking to as many platoons, gun and tank teams, sapper parties as I could. One went very slowly to keep down the telltale dust and as usual one had no windscreen to catch the rays of the sun. The men were quiet and thoughtful—many were writing letters and you often found the Padres giving a last service to their men. Everywhere there was a feeling of expectancy and of high confidence, but a realization of the magnitude of the task that lay ahead. Everyone knew what they had to do and I think that somehow we all realised the terrific issues at stake. The morale of the army was tremendously high and the will to succeed and confidence in their preparedness was evident everywhere. . . .

"I dined with the Army Commander on the eve of the battle. After dinner he asked me what I was going to do. I said I was going to look at the [artillery] barrage. He asked what I'd see and what good I'd do; and he then went on to say that there was now nothing further that I could do to influence the battle. My job, he said, was to go to bed early so as to appear fresh in the morning and be able by my appearance to give confidence to the troops. I had then to be on top of my form so as to accept the inevitable shocks of battle; and be able to plan quickly and soundly the next night's attacks."

Retiring to his caravan, Monty wrote up his diary. Major Williams had reported that, according to German signals, the enemy seemed to have no suspicion that the battle was about to begin that night—but that his tank strength was now up to 600, and his army more than 100,000 strong.

Eighth Army, numbering almost 195,000 men now that the 51st

Highland Division and copious reinforcements had been sent up to the front line, still lacked the three-to-one ratio which most military theorists felt essential to ensure offensive victory, particularly in the flat, scrubby terrain that offered no cover whatsoever.

"And so we come to D day," Monty wrote, "and everything is set for a great struggle."

> The enemy knows we intend to attack, and has been strengthening his defenses. On our side we have the initiative and a great superiority in men, tanks, artillery and other material.
>
> We also have an Army in which the morale is right up on the top line; and every officer and every man knows the issues at stake, knows what is wanted, and knows how the battle will be fought and won.
>
> The leadership is all right, and the equipment is all right.
>
> The training is NOT all right and that is why we have got to be very careful. Having made a successful "break-in," we must not rush madly into the mobile battle with wide encircling movements and so on; the troops would all get lost.
>
> We must finish up the "break-in" battle so positioned that we have the tactical advantage, and will be well positioned to begin the "crumbling" operations which are designed to destroy all his holding troops.
>
> His armor cannot stand back and look on; it will have to counterattack, and then we can destroy that too.
>
> The "break-in" battle has been planned accordingly.

There would be much blood shed, he knew, but it could not be avoided—indeed, in the long run it would, if the battle proved decisive, save lives. He ended gravely:

> The battle will be expensive as it will really become a killing match. I consider that the dog fight of the "crumbling" operations may last for a week, during which time we shall never let go our stranglehold. I have estimated for 10,000 casualties in this week's fighting.
>
> All we need now is average luck and good weather.

Sometime after nine o'clock, having written further reflections on the future of the army after the battle was won ("What will the situation be when I have had 10,000 or 20,000 casualties in the forthcoming operations, and have also lost a lot of tanks? When we have cleared the Germans from North Africa we shall have to re-organize our forces. The plan for it should be considered now"), and having read a few pages of a novel, Monty went to sleep.

At 9:40 P.M. the artillery barrage opened—the biggest of its kind in the war so far. The ground shook, the cloudless black of the night was lit by the flashing of over 800 guns, and twenty minutes later the first infantry crossed the starting line. The battle of El Alamein, the turning point of the Second World War, had begun.

Part Four

THE BATTLE OF ALAMEIN

Lieutenant General von Thoma surrenders
to Monty at the climax of the battle of
Alamein, 4 November 1942.

The "Break-in"

The chaos of the first night—the mines, mortar, dust, breakdown in communications, casualties—had cleared miraculously by the time the Eighth Army Commander awoke at dawn on 24 October 1942.

The attack had achieved complete surprise. For at least an hour there had been virtually no response by the German or Italian artillery. Moreover the series of simultaneous Eighth Army raids, from the Mediterranean Sea to the Qattara Depression, meant that Stumme—who believed the eventual Eighth Army attack would be delivered just south of the center of his line—had no means of knowing which thrust he should concentrate upon. Indeed for the Panzer army it was a disastrous opening to the battle. It was by no means lost, but Rommel's fire-fighting doctrine, by which he had hoped to smother any attack before it could break out of the minefields, had invited disaster, and by failing to garrison adequately the Miteiriya Ridge Rommel had given Montgomery a lever by which Eighth Army could prize open his whole defensive layout.

Stumme's complacency was to be, literally, fatal. However, in blaming him for the eventual African Panzer Army defeat at Alamein, historians did his memory much wrong. Stumme was an experienced armored commander, well liked, and had seen much action on the Russian front. Despite this, Rommel refused to entrust the battle to him, except on a temporary basis, as Rommel confessed quite blandly in his memoirs: "General Stumme was to deputize for me as Army Commander during my absence. . . . He was rather put out when he heard that I proposed to cut short my cure and return to North Africa if the British opened a major offensive. He supposed that I had no confidence in him."

Stumme was right. It was Rommel's choice of battlefield, Rommel's detailed plan of defense, and Rommel's iron conviction about the way the battle should be fought that doomed the Axis forces to defeat, not Stumme's temporary command of the Panzerarmee Afrika. However, it was Stumme, not Rommel, who paid for this mistake with his life.

The Death of Stumme

T hat Eighth Army, in a single night, could breach the most thickly held part of the German defenses and position itself on the key terrain of the Miteiriya Ridge with infantry, armor, artillery and antitank guns was simply inconceivable to Rommel—who believed he would have at least two days' warning of the move of enemy armor and main bodies of supporting infantry.

Adding to the German and Italian surprise and confusion, moreover, was the fact that Eighth Army's artillery barrage and Desert Air Force bombing had knocked out most normal Axis communications, with Allied aircraft also jamming German radio frequencies. All night, from all parts of the Axis line, news of British attacks kept coming in to Stumme's headquarters by messenger. Desperate to assess, as soon as possible, the main sector of the British offensive, Stumme therefore did what Rommel would also have done—he set out to see for himself. The depth of the Australian penetration north of the Miteiriya Ridge must have been completely unknown to him, for it was there, on Minefield "J," that his staff car was shelled and he died of a heart attack. As Kesselring later wrote: "Anyone who knows how decisive are the first orders in a defensive engagement will have no difficulty in understanding what the loss of General Stumme meant for the whole battle."

Command of the Panzer army passed temporarily to General von Thoma, Commander of the Afrika Korps, at midday; but since there were no signs of enemy armor breaking out of the "Devil's Gardens" (the British nickname for Rommel's minefield areas), von Thoma stayed his hand.

Would Rommel have reacted differently? In his memoirs Rommel wrote: "I was convinced that even the most skilful Panzer General would be unable to take the right decisions in an emergency on the Alamein front unless he were familiar with the British. Words alone cannot impart one's experience to a deputy. . . ."

This, however, was written with hindsight. Moreover, almost two years after Alamein, Rommel would face the same British general on the beaches of Normandy and make the same mistake: not only being absent from his post at the start of the battle, but employing the same "fire-fighting" technique as he had laid down for Alamein.

Had the British 30 Corps attack been immediately counterattacked in force and driven back it is very doubtful whether Eighth Army would have mounted a second "break-in" operation—indeed, in all previous cases where an attack had failed to start off on the right foot, the new Eighth Army Commander had authorized withdrawal rather than futile further expenditure of life.

The situation at dawn on 24 October was therefore very largely of Rommel's own making—though he would not be recalled until 3 P.M. that afternoon, and would not arrive until the evening of the following day. He had made no plans for an imaginative defense, as the British had done at Alam Halfa, allowing the enemy armor to penetrate the minefields and luring it onto concealed garrisons. After the death of General Stumme all that von Thoma could do, however, was to carry out the fire-fighting policy which Rommel had laid down before leaving—and hope that the enemy's nerve would fail in the bitter fighting that must still come. After all, Auchinleck had failed to press his advantage in July, and the Axis positions and strength were inestimably greater now. Thus the African Panzer Army accepted battle on Montgomery's terms: and the "dogfight" began.

A Lost Opportunity

If the German reaction to the British break-in was confused, the British reaction was even more so. First reports were so optimistic about the progress on the right of 30 Corps that, at Eighth Army's main headquarters at Burg-el-Arab, de Guingand warned Colonel Mainwaring, the chief operations officer, that "if Aust Div had only slight casualties the Army Commander may decide to attack on coastal sector to clear up that while the going is good. Heavy bomber support will be required. . . ." This was at 5:50 on the morning of 24 October.

At 9:15 A.M., however, the picture had reversed. *No* British armor was through the minefields on the right, and on the left, the armor that had got through was said to be retreating!

Leese, desperate that the armor exploit the clear passage through the minefields on the New Zealand side of the break-in, had suggested as early as 8 A.M. that Lumsden use the left "funnel" to get not only his left but also his right division (1st Armoured) through the minefields, thus bypassing the holdup. Lumsden, however, was out of touch, and his BGS would take no decision without referring it to him.

By ten o'clock it was obvious that all value of surprise had gone. To Sir Oliver Leese, this was the lost opportunity of Alamein. "The armour now had a great opportunity," he wrote in his unpublished account of the battle. "Rommel had not yet returned from Italy [sic]. There was no controlling head and for once the Panzer Corps was fighting piecemeal. General von Stumme had been killed by shell fire . . . and if we could only have broken out during the early morning of the first day, we would have had a good chance to destroy the German armour piecemeal. But by midday on that day it was obvious that the armour had not broken through and to me it was very doubtful whether they could now do so."

Monty felt the same. "I began to form the impression at about 1100 hours," he noted in his diary, "that there was a lack of 'drive' and pep in the action of 10 Corps. I saw Herbert LUMSDEN and impressed on him the urgent need to get his armoured divisions out into the open where they could manoeuvre, and that *they must get clear of the mine-field area*. He left me about 1130 hours to visit his Divisions. So far he has not impressed me by his showing in battle; perhaps he has been out here too long; he has been wounded twice. I can see that he will have to be bolstered up and handled firmly.

"Possibly he will be better when the battle gets more mobile. This 'sticky' fighting seems beyond him."

In the Devil's Gardens

Lumsden's divisional commanders, however, were even stickier. Leese, who visited the New Zealand Headquarters behind the Miteiriya Ridge, finally found Gatehouse, commander of the 10th Armoured Division, and was infuriated by Gatehouse's unwillingness to exploit the success of the infantry, as he reported by telephone to Monty. Freyberg was personally offering to take his own armored support brigade (9th Armoured Brigade) "over the top" provided Gatehouse gave him some support from 10th Armoured Division. This Gatehouse refused to do, as Leese explained:

Gatehouse says . . . anything that puts its nose over the ridge gets shot up. G[atehouse]'s main preoccupation at moment is to get 10 Armoured Div into position to receive attack from someone else. . . . He keeps saying he is trained for a static role. I think that is getting above him. I have told Bernard [Freyberg] to hold a meeting with Gatehouse and Brigadiers. I am placing whole Corps artillery at his disposal and am suggesting that under smoke they try and do something later in day. . . . Now there is hardly anything happening.

"I gained the impression during the morning that the Armoured Divisions were pursuing a policy of inactivity." Monty noted in his diary at midday; "they required galvanising into action, and wanted determined leadership. There was not that eagerness to break out into the open on the part of Commanders; there was a fear of casualties; every gun was reported as an 88mm." At 12:25 Monty, worried by the way the Germans were laying new minefields around the salient, signaled urgently to Lumsden:

> From Army Commander: It is necessary to get the two armoured divisions out through the 30 Corps final objective before the enemy can ring them in still further. Steps are already being taken to get 1st Armoured Div forward with 51 Div. Gen. Lumsden should meet Gen. Leese at NZ Div HQ and arrange support of 30 Corps artillery to get 10 Armoured Div out through the NZ Div front. The plan must be really properly teed-up with adequate artillery support, hence the necessity of starting early, if the operation is to be brought off this afternoon.

Speed and artillery, Monty felt, were of the essence. The two corps commanders, Leese and Lumsden, duly conferred. When Monty heard of Lumsden's proposal—a night attack rather than an afternoon assault—he telephoned Lumsden's BGS directly at 1:05 P.M. and told him to "inform Corps Commander that Army Commander considers it essential to get 10 Armoured Div out *this afternoon*." An hour later he called again to emphasize that "one more effort to get through bridgehead must be made. He is prepared to accept casualties provided armoured divisions get out into open so he can continue NZ [crumbling] operation. Corps Commander to be informed of this."

Meanwhile, if there was a danger of the British armor getting bogged down in the left-hand funnel through the minefields, the situation in the right-hand funnel was even worse, for *no* armor had yet reached the infantry front line, let alone got "out." At 1:50 P.M. the chief engineer, Brigadier Kisch, had signaled to Monty that the forward brigade of 1st Armoured Division "appears to be making no progress." If Lumsden had only diverted the rest of the division via the New Zealand bridgehead early that morning, as Leese had suggested, there would have been no problem; as it was Monty now had to intervene directly.

"I was beginning to be disappointed somewhat in LUMSDEN, BRIGGS (1 Armd Div) and FISHER (2 Armd Bde), and also in GATEHOUSE," Monty noted in his diary—having warned Lumsden "he must 'drive' his Divisional Commanders, and that if BRIGGS and FISHER hung back any more I would at once remove them from command and replace them by better men. This produced good results and plans were made in conjunction with 30 Corps for Armoured Divisions to break out."

An infantry attack by 51st Division was launched at 3 P.M. to clear a passage for 1st Armoured Division, and at 3:45 P.M. it was reported that "in the North 1st Armoured Division is being pressed to push on by Army Commander." Within half an hour news came that the forward armored brigade had at last "found a gap and will go through when they have finished mopping up." By early evening 1st Armoured Division seemed finally "out" beyond the forward infantry. "My application of 'ginger' had worked," Monty noted with relief in his diary, for by 5:20 P.M. one brigade of 1st Armoured Division reported itself to be on "Pierson," the original Lightfoot objective of the armored corps, bounded on the northern extremity by a mild, kidney-shaped elevation known as Kidney Ridge.

But Monty was wrong. 1st Armoured Division, though beyond the minefield on the right of the salient, was still far from its objective, Pierson; the New Zealanders' 9th Armoured Brigade, on the left of the salient, had barely moved out a mile from the Miteiriya Ridge; and 7th Armoured Division in Horrocks' 13 Corps at Himeimat was nowhere near passing through into the open—having failed utterly to breach the second "February" minefield confronting it. Rommel's "Devil's Gardens" were proving extraordinarily effective.

A Frustrating First Day

U naware of the true situation, Monty felt only the failure of Gatehouse's 10th Armoured Division was now hindering its Lightfoot plan from proceeding:

Gatehouse's 8th Armoured Brigade had begun a reconnaissance attack across the Miteiriya Ridge at four o'clock that afternoon but, despite Monty's special signal, it was very halfhearted, and at 6:45 P.M.

Lumsden's chief of staff reported to the army commander that the brigade was "held up by minefields South of Miteiriya Ridge on the 289 grid. This minefield was laid today. The minefield is covered by guns and MG's [machine guns] and a force of tanks—probably 21 Panzer. Littorio Group has been operating South of this minefield and has been engaged with 8 and 9 Armoured Brigades. Up to 17 tanks have been claimed, with small loss to ourselves. An operation is being staged tonight to get [Gatehouse's] 10 Armoured Division into the open. Location of 24 Armoured Brigade not known."

Relieved that 1st Armoured Division was at least on Pierson—which was confirmed by 10 Corps at 9 P.M. ("General Lumsden is satisfied that 2nd Armoured Brigade is on kidney-shaped feature")—Monty meanwhile retired to bed. It had been a frustrating first day of battle. The surprise and violence of the initial infantry night assault had, however, served to outweigh the subsequent failure of the British armor. Armored operations were now running almost twenty-four hours behind schedule, but once Gatehouse's 10th Armoured Division fought its way out alongside Briggs' 1st Armoured Division during the coming night, Monty could begin "crumbling," and relentlessly annihilate the enemy. He still held the initiative, he felt, and he was determined not to surrender it.

The Crisis

When the Eighth Army Commander awoke in the early hours of Sunday, 25 October, it was to see the pale and anxious face of his chief of staff, Brigadier de Guingand. Looking at his watch, Monty saw it was 2 A.M.

De Guingand apologized for waking the army commander, but explained that there was something of a crisis brewing. He had spent the hours since 10 P.M. in the Armoured Command Vehicle at Main Headquarters, Burg-el-Arab, monitoring reports of Gatehouse's armored attack, and had grown alarmed when, after three hours of moonlight, 10th Armoured Division had not even set forth. He had gone then to see General Leese—who had a sad story to tell.

To the British Official Historian Leese later confided the events of that night:

> Soon after nightfall General Freyberg spoke to me on the telephone and said that he was not at all confident that 10th Armoured Division were properly set up for the attack.
> General Lumsden's HQ was fairly close to mine and he came round to see me. He told me in as many words that he did not feel confident in the decision to break out with the armor during the night, and though I told him that if he really felt this he should go at once to see General Montgomery, he left me.

Lumsden had no intention of going to Montgomery, for he resented the new Eighth Army Commander and disliked him intensely. Major Williams later sought to explain Lumsden's attitude:

> I can remember in the days when he was coming back at odd times to Army Headquarters for consultations with Monty about training for the plan. I had a sort of feeling that whereas Horrocks and Leese were clearly subordinate—they just were, Horrocks almost going out of his way to be subordinate, sort of saying "isn't he wonderful?," this sort of stuff—and Lumsden not having that sort of business at all. Arriving rather elegant—you know, his scarf was always silk, bush shirt—always bandboxy as it were, and having an insouciance about it. All this stuff—Monty's comic hats—he obviously didn't go for that sort of stuff at all.
> It was almost a social difference between them. It was this old-fashioned sort of cavalry approach to this funny little man who was arsing about in these comic hats. I'm making it up, I'm only giving you the impression it left on *me*. But this was his poise and attitude. . . .
> I think Lumsden had a jealousy of Monty, plus a sort of contempt: it was partly Monty's manner of walking, the way he carried his head—"arrogant bastard"—that sort of thing.

Lumsden was sacked after Alamein, and killed in combat in 1945, but Freyberg later felt that Lumsden had been right to question an armored assault on positions "held in depth with 88mm guns," without infantry support. "I felt it could not be done until a hole was made," Freyberg wrote to Kippenberger in 1949. "I do not think General Lumsden was wrong in his appreciation, either before or during the battle. It must be conceded to him that he was the most experienced tank Commander in the Western Desert at the time, and he had seen what had happened to our tanks at Knightsbridge [during the battle of Gazala] in a few minutes. He, I know, did not believe in the plan for armour to break out unless there was a hole in the defenses. In my opinion General Lumsden was right; but he was quite wrong not to have made his case clear to the Army Commander."

This, however, was written in hindsight. At the time Freyberg was incensed at the sheer cowardice of the British armored formations: for his own New Zealand Cavalry had led the way across the Miteiriya Ridge at 10 P.M. on 24 October, and were followed by his supporting 9th Armoured Brigade—but then let down by the heavy armor of 10th Armoured Division which, having sustained minor casualties, held back.

Puzzled by the failure of the British to press their advantage either that morning or that afternoon, the Germans had ringed the salient with more guns, had laid more mines, and had correctly predicted a night attack—but with infantry. A Stuka, or dive-bomber, attack had therefore been arranged. This had set light to a column of New Zealand supply vehicles, which rapidly became a beacon for German shelling. Instead of urging his armor past the burning vehicles, the commander of 8th Armoured Brigade had appealed to General Gatehouse as divisional commander to cancel the attack, and meanwhile allowed his regiments to disperse. Freyberg's units had thus sat alone beyond the Miteiriya Ridge, waiting for support from the heavy armor that did not come. At 1:40 A.M. on 25 October, Gatehouse referred the decision to Lumsden—who prevaricated.

It was at this moment in the battle that de Guingand had decided, notwithstanding Monty's edict about not being disturbed, to wake him. Here was a crisis, de Guingand felt, which only the army commander could resolve.

Galvanizing the Whole Show

"I told him the situation," de Guingand recalled many years later. " 'They're coming along at 3:30?' " the Army Commander responded. " 'I agree with you—quite right. I'll be there.'

"Shortly before the appointed time I went to his map lorry and there he was, sitting on a stool facing his maps, pencil chalks, you know. . . ."

Whether it was de Guingand's briefing that misled Monty is difficult to say. According to Monty's own diary he began the conference believing that all was going well save on Gatehouse's sector of the Miteiriya Ridge. At 2:30 A.M., he recorded, 1st Armoured Division was "out in the open" on the right of the salient; that on the left of the salient "9 Armd Bde of NZ Div was through the minefield and was planning to move SW in accordance with the [crumbling] plan"; while Horrocks's 13 Corps in the far south, near Himeimat, had reported that "7 Armd Div had cleared gaps in the minefield and that the leading Armd Bde was moving West to pass through into the open."

In contrast to this optimistic picture, Monty noted in his diary, "10 Corps reported that the break-out of 10 Armd Div was not proceeding well and that minefields and other difficulties were delaying progress. GATEHOUSE had said he did not care about the operation and that if he did get out he would be in a very unpleasant position on the forward slopes of the MITERIYA [sic] Ridge; his Division was untrained and not fit for such difficult operations; he wanted to stay where he was. LUMSDEN was inclined to agree with GATEHOUSE."

By 3 A.M., Monty's diary entry read, "It was clear to me that my orders about the armor getting out into the open were in danger of being compromised by the disinclination of GATEHOUSE to leave his hull-down positions on the MITERIYA Ridge. LUMSDEN was agreeing with GATEHOUSE and some quick and firm action was necessary."

How was Monty to get the Germans to counterattack the British, on ground of British choosing, if the British armor posed no threat to the German defenses? This was the root of the problem. As the New Zealand Official Historian remarked: "The armour was perpetuating the tradition, established by General Gott (under whom both Lumsden and Gatehouse had served), of giving lip service to the plans but holding to a determination to run the armoured battle its own way." Lumsden had warned Freyberg, when setting up the attack, that playing with armor was "like playing with fire. . . . It is like a duel. If you don't take your time you will get run through the guts. It is not for tanks to take on guns."

In Monty's map lorry, Lumsden now begged the army commander to speak personally to Gatehouse on the telephone—an admission of Lumsden's own weakness of authority which Monty noted in his battle diary: "GATEHOUSE wanted to withdraw both . . . Armd Bdes back behind the minefields and to give up all the advantages he had gained; his reason was that his situation out in the open would be very unpleasant and he might suffer heavy casualties. LUMSDEN agreed with GATEHOUSE. The real trouble is that LUMSDEN is frightened of GATEHOUSE and won't give him firm orders."

Neither Lumsden nor Gatehouse seemed able to understand that unless the armor got out beyond the minefields, not only could the infantry's "crumbling" operations not begin, but the enemy might not be obliged to counterattack at all. The battle would then come to a halt.

Whatever the casualties, therefore, Monty knew he must keep the initiative, and therefore must step up the pressure. Having berated Gatehouse and insisted he "fight his way out," Monty

spoke very plainly to LUMSDEN and said I would have no departure of any sort from my original plan and orders; I was determined that the armor would get out from the minefield area and out into the open where it could manoeuvre; any wavering or lack of firmness now might be fatal; if GATEHOUSE, or any other Commander, was not "for it" and began to weaken, then I would replace him in command at once.

I then issued definite orders to 10 Corps and to 30 Corps.

The result, Monty felt certain, was decisive. Four hours later, at 8 A.M. on 25 October, he noted with satisfaction in his diary that Gatehouse's other armored brigade, 24th Armoured Brigade, "had broken through into the open," indeed was alongside the left regiment of 2nd Armoured Brigade on Pierson. Moreover, the whole of the 9th Armoured

Brigade were "through the minefield" and ready to support Freyberg's crumbling operations, with one regiment of Gatehouse's 8th Armoured Brigade "out" in the middle. "And so all was now working out well, and we were in the positions we had hoped to have been in at 0800 hours on 24 October," Monty added. "It is a good thing I was firm with LUMSDEN and GATEHOUSE last night.

"It is amazing how many weak Commanders we have," he went on. "At one stage in the battle yesterday the whole of 10 Corps was inactive and doing nothing, waiting for other people to do things. There was no 'drive' to get things done, and to get a move on; the whole show had to be galvanized into action, and I had to do this myself. However, all is now well-placed for us to crack along and to keep the initiative; there was a danger yesterday that we might lose the initiative."

De Guingand, both in his postwar account *Operation Victory* and to the end of his life, maintained that without this display of resolution by the Eighth Army Commander, the whole British offensive at Alamein might have foundered: "Unless it had been made I am firmly convinced that the attack might well have fizzled out, and the full measure of success we achieved might never have been possible. The meeting broke up," de Guingand declared, "with no one in any doubt as to what was in the Commander's mind." Sir Oliver Leese felt exactly the same: "There is no doubt in my mind that this Conference cleared any shadow of doubt from anyone's mind as to the Army Commander's intention."

But in truth, they were wrong. However crucial Monty's "removal of doubt" from a psychological point of view, the fact was, Eighth Army's armored offensive had already foundered.

Failure of the Masterplan

A t 7:15 A.M. on 25 October, under the illusion that Gatehouse had cleared the minefields so that he could pass through the remaining regiments of 8th Armoured Brigade, Monty confirmed his orders to Lumsden: namely to "locate and destroy enemy armoured Battle Groups" and to "ensure that [crumbling] operations of 2 New Zealand Division South-West from Miteiriya Ridge are not interfered with by enemy armoured forces in the West."

Even at 10 A.M. that day, Monty firmly believed he could carry out Operation Lightfoot as planned. Monty's confidence in this assessment was, however, greatly upset half an hour later when 10 Corps finally informed him that 1st Armoured Division was not on its objective, Pierson—indeed, 10 Corps now admitted that 2nd Armoured Brigade held "only Eastern end of kidney-shaped feature," the majority of which was occupied by dreaded German 88mm guns.

Nor was this the only bad news. Down in the south, at Himeimat, 13 Corps also confessed that they were not, after all, "in the open"; in fact it was revealed that the corps commander, General Horrocks, had ordered 7th Armoured Division to *give up* its assault on the "February" minefield. Horrocks had completely misjudged the enormity of the task of penetrating the Axis minefields, as "Pip" Roberts later recalled:

There were two minefields to be got through—"January" and "February"—and clearly one needed infantry to co-operate to get through. We had infantry from the 44th Brigade and we had our own infantry; but instead there was a little plan—I think it was hatched up by Horrocks—in which we tried for the first time to use what were called "Scorpions"—they were flails being used on what were old Matilda tanks, and they were very unreliable. They were going to clear a gap through the minefield.

Well, to follow them Horrocks collected together an enormous number, almost a battalion of carriers, which were then going to rush through the gaps and bug the area with carriers, you see, taking everybody off the ground. It was nothing to do with me. I honestly didn't have much faith in what the carriers could do, because it was very vulnerable, a carrier. I mean it's got very thin armor and so forth, and I never put much faith in what their armor could do. The carriers were to precede us—22nd Armoured Brigade.

Oh yes, they would have been under fire from artillery, et cetera. I never thought they had a hope in hell myself. But they weren't under me, they were directly under the [7th Armoured] Divisional Commander, so O.K., let them have a shot.

But then, as our main effort to make gaps in the minefields was to be done by these Scorpions, and the Scorpions broke down and got in the way and then the Sappers had to come up and do it by hand—there was a great deal of delay. And after the first night all we'd got through was the first minefield. And then we sat between the minefields—and the two minefields were here, like that, and Himeimat was there—I mean within 2,000 yards—absolutely looking down on us. It was the most uncomfortable situation.

And then we tried again the next night. And then we didn't have Scorpions working, we only had Sappers and the Queen's Regiment, and somehow or other—I couldn't quite tell you how, the Queen's Regiment—who were going to form the bridgehead in front of the gap that had been made by the Sappers—they went one way and some people went another and we went where the gap was, and there were no other infantry there. And then we got every tank knocked out, either by mines or by anti-tank fire. We struggled all night and made no progress. We came back.

And so we called it off. . . .

I know that Horrocks was disappointed that we didn't get through. I think he felt we ought to have exerted more push, but that was it: tanks going through this one gap which was made, knocked out, one after the other. John Harding [Commander of 7th Armoured Division] came up and saw the situation too; but I'm sure Horrocks felt we ought to have dashed through. But it was a very, very narrow funnel, with anti-tank guns covering it. . . .

In the light of this failure, Roberts afterwards had great sympathy for Lumsden and Gatehouse in the north: "Oh, I do think he [Monty] expected much more than they could possibly achieve—much more. I mean whenever you attack with tanks—and this was on a really detailed, pre-conceived plan—you get heavy casualties—very heavy casualties. When you give the enemy heavy casualties is when he attacks you."

This, in reality, was the *real* crisis of the battle. Shaken, but not revealing any signs of anxiety, Monty left at 11:30 A.M. for Freyberg's headquarters in order to ensure that at least the New Zealand Division's "crumbling" operation was properly set up. There the bitter truth was at last revealed to him. Gatehouse's "Sitreps" from 10th Armoured Division had been utterly misleading. In fact, *no armor whatsoever* was out on the forward slopes of the Miteiriya Ridge.

Monty's left-hand armored "hinge" did not exist.

There would be no armored shield to protect the New Zealanders' "crumbling" operation.

Far from having "galvanized the whole show into action," Monty's night-time conference and his obsession with keeping to his battle-script had only served to obfuscate the truth, frightening Lumsden into resentful silence, Gatehouse into a suppression of the true facts, and Briggs into wildly overoptimistic reports of progress on 1st Armoured Division's front on the right.

Further south, Horrocks' 13 Corps had stalled too.

Monty's "masterplan" had failed, utterly.

Second Thoughts

"The scene of chaos was absolutely unbelievable," Monty's chief planner, Colonel Richardson, recalled. "Monty had planned for 30 Corps to clear the minefields for the armor. Well this never happened at all. They became inextricably mixed. It was a fundamental difference between the plan and the actual battle that the armor was stopped in the dog-fight area." The battle "*didn't* go according to plan—and we at his Tactical Headquarters, we thought the battle was going bloody badly for a time!'

At the New Zealand Division Headquarters shortly before midday on 25 October, Monty assessed the local situation with Freyberg and then spoke to Leese and Lumsden, who had once again been summoned for a conference. Freyberg, angered by the excessive caution of Gatehouse's armored brigades, considered it impossible to go ahead now with the intended "crumbling" operations. In fact he had no faith that Gatehouse would *ever* break out beyond the Miteiriya Ridge; he therefore advised the army commander to postpone further operations until the evening, and then allow the New Zealand infantry to mount an artillery-supported attack to gain the Pierson line for Gatehouse's armor, about 4,000 yards beyond the ridge. The armor could then follow up and occupy the captured positions. Lumsden agreed.

Monty did not.

In his diary Monty recorded the conference in the very briefest essentials, and made no mention of the Freyberg-Lumsden proposal—not only because he disliked admitting to failure, but because his rejection of Freyberg and Lumsden's suggestion was intuitive, and came from the heart as well as the head. Though Monty liked to refer to his military approach as "scientific"—reducible to principles and systematic knowledge—his own talent for command had a deeper, more personal, more *competitive* core. From the moment of his arrival in the desert he had personified the German-Italian Panzer army as "Rommel." His plan for the battle of Alamein had rested on surprising the enemy—and in this respect it had worked, not only catching the Panzer army without its commander, but within hours smashing a savage wedge into Rommel's defensive line where least expected.

Thereafter, however, the British armor had failed to exploit Eighth Army's advantage. Some thirty-eight hours of battle had now passed, and von Thoma—to judge by counterattacks, with tanks, that had begun to build up that morning—was now well aware that the thrust from the Miteiriya Ridge was the principal effort by Eighth Army. Even a night attack with infantry would be likely to sustain heavy casualties—casualties which would blunt the very infantry weapon Monty wished to preserve for the real dogfight, or "crumbling" operations, of the coming week.

The infantry weapon, Monty was well aware, must be used sparingly, for it was already fragile following its magnificent performance on the first night of the battle. The South African Division, as Leese later recalled, had already been "fought to a standstill and its two brigades were now too weak for further offensive operations." The New Zealanders also possessed only two brigades and had had heavy casualties—as had 51st Highland Division in this, its first battle since reconstitution. Only the Australians were up to full strength, their losses made good by reserves.

Although he wished to keep to his overall strategy, Monty nonetheless felt in his bones that he must continue to *surprise* the enemy.

Somehow he must reinforce not weakness but strength. If the New Zealanders failed in their infantry assault beyond the Miteiriya Ridge, or if Lumsden's armored commanders found further pretexts for refusing to obey, the battle would, to all intents and purposes, be lost or reduced to stalemate.

"The Army Commander sized up the situation very quickly," Leese wrote later, "and made one of his characteristic quick tactical decisions which he so often did in the midst of the heat of a battle and which enabled him to pull an awkward situation out of the fire, without appearing in any way to alter the shape of his original battle plan." Gatehouse's armor, in the left "funnel," was to be withdrawn from the battle, Monty now ordered. Freyberg's infantry would undertake no night attack; they would rest.

Instead, everything would now be thrown into the right-hand sector of Eighth Army's break-in, pushing out the 1st Armoured Division shield and starting crumbling operations northwards, to the sea, by the infantry of the 9th Australian Division. "This really meant a new thrust line or axis of operations, from South to North, a switch of 180 degrees. I hoped that this completely new direction of attack might catch the enemy unawares," Monty noted in his diary—the decision, duly recorded, dated and signed by the army commander, being attached to the Tactical Eighth Army HQ Diary:

1: Direction of "crumbling" operations being undertaken by 30 Corps to be changed. 30 Corps to hold Miteiriya Ridge strongly and *not* operate SW from it.

2: Instead 30 corps to undertake crumbling operations Northwards towards the coast using 9 Aust Div. . . .

The conference at the New Zealand Division HQ at twelve noon on 25 October 1942 thus marked the first major turning point in the battle. Although Monty's insistence, in the early hours of the morning, on the armor getting out beyond the Miteiriya Ridge would go down in military annals as the mark of his superlative generalship, *pace* de Guingand, it was not. His "ginger" had *not* worked; the armor had *not* got out on the left, beyond the Miteiriya Ridge, and it was futile to expend further brave New Zealand lives getting it out.

Instead, the New Zealand artillery would, Monty decreed, defend the New Zealanders *in situ* on the Miteiriya Ridge, while the Australian infantry took upon themselves the major offensive role in the battle.

A Fateful Day

At midnight on 25 October 1942 the Australians successfully carried out the first "crumbling" attack ordered by the army commander, advancing 3,000 yards, taking the vital "Point 29," and overrunning a German battalion whose orders showed that no large-scale German counterattack by the Afrika Korps was envisaged.

Monty's switch of "crumbling" axis thus proved a complete surprise to the enemy, and the courage of the Australian infantry was salutary. However, there was a price to be paid. The casualty figures spoke for themselves. By the morning of 26 October, Leese's 30 Corps had sustained 4,643 casualties, whereas Lumsden's 10 Armoured Corps had suffered a mere 455.

Despite the urging of the Australians, however, 1st Armoured Division failed to push the armored "shield" onto the kidney feature in order to help screen the Australian "crumbling" attacks and entice the Axis armor to counterattack. In his diary Monty recorded the situation as it was reported to him on the morning of 26 October:

> 0600 The attack Northwards by 9 Aust Div was completely successful. . . .

> 0800 1 Armd Div had failed to progress Westwards and North-Westwards.

The British armor was proving a broken reed. Their navigation was so poor 1st Armoured Division refused at first to admit they had failed to take the kidney feature, and would not cooperate with the Royal Engineers in surveying-in their exact geographical positions as the infantry did. Worse still, they had insufficient grasp of corps artillery cooperation.

What worried Eighth Army's Intelligence, however, was the enemy. In his daily Intelligence summary for 26 October, Major Williams commented that, following the British break-in, "the enemy response has been to wear down our attack piecemeal without committing his main mobile forces for a decisive blow."

Where would the enemy's "decisive blow" be delivered? And could the Eighth Army salient withstand it, if it came in the north?

Monday, 26 October 1942, was to be the fateful day for both armies. At 11:00 the previous evening, Field Marshal Rommel had finally reassumed command of the German-Italian African Panzer Army. Early on 26 October, Rommel made his own personal reconnaissance of the northern salient, particularly the new bridgehead—Point 29—taken by the Australians during the night. There were a number of courses open to him, including the "decisive blow" which Eighth Army Intelligence feared. But to the relief of the Eighth Army, Rommel decided against this. He later wrote: "What we should really have done now was to assemble all our motorized units in the north in order to fling the British back to the main defence line in a concentrated and planned counter-attack."

Why did Rommel pass up such a retrospectively glittering opportunity?

The truth was, as at Alam Halfa, Rommel was hobbled by his own initial error of judgment. Before leaving for his rest in Austria he had ordered the splitting of the Afrika Korps into two, so that half its units were tied down in the southern sector. With only half his Panzers in the north, he could not have "flung the British back," for by now the British had moved so many guns into their salient it was doubtful whether the assembling of "all our motorized units' armor" could have been achieved without unacceptable losses "from air and artillery bombardment," as Rommel himself later acknowledged.

If Rommel felt dubious of successfully mounting a grand German counterattack against the British on ground of their choosing, ought he to have, instead, lured the British armor away from that ground? With considerable honesty, Rommel posed this question in retrospect, wondering whether he "could have made the action more fluid by withdrawing a few miles to the west and could then have attacked the British in an all-out charge and defeated them in open country. The British artillery and air force could not easily have intervened with their usual weight in a tank battle of this kind," he reflected, "for their own forces would have been endangered."

Once again, however, such retrospective alternatives were academic. At the time, to take the risk of giving ground and encouraging mobile battle in the north would have entailed withdrawing his German-

Italian armor from the south—where the British 13 Corps was already through the first minefield belt and threatening, according to current reports, to burst through the second at any moment. Rommel thus had no option but to continue the fireman's policy he had laid down before he left Africa a month earlier. Moreover he was doomed to react in the way Montgomery had intended, for despite the relative failure of the British armor he could not stand and watch the Australian forces "crumbling" his infantry and artillery defenses. As at Alam Halfa he was thus now forced to fight the battle in the way which Montgomery dictated by launching attack after attack to stop or drive back the Australians. As a result, "rivers of blood were poured out over miserable strips of land which, in normal times, not even the poorest Arab would have bothered his head about," he acknowledged sadly. He had failed to train his infantry for night attacks with coordinated air, artillery and tank support, and—provided the determination of Eighth Army did not weaken—the situation was critical.

For Monty, by contrast, the position was both encouraging and disappointing. He had estimated for a minimum of 10,000 casualties in the first seven days of the battle. Already, after three nights' fighting, he had reached two-thirds of that figure. It was important now, Monty felt, not to squander the magnificent achievements of the infantry, nor to overtax them with casualties. The British salient was secure, and the Australians had, on the night of 25/26 October, driven a deep further wedge into Rommel's northernmost defenses. The infantry, Monty decided, must now be given a chance to rest before undertaking further "crumbling" operations. It was time at last for the British armor, which had sustained only nominal casualties so far, to begin to *fight*.

At 9 A.M., 26 October 1942, Monty therefore issued a new battle directive, which he then gave out personally at a conference of corps commanders held at the headquarters of Morshead's 9th Australian Division at 11:30 A.M. "After thinking the problem over, I came to the conclusion that 30 Corps needed a short period with no major operations," Monty noted in his diary. "Divisions had been fighting hard since 2200 hours 23 October, and were somewhat disorganized; a period was wanted in which Div areas could be tidied up, and things sorted out." General Leese was told that, although 30 Corps was to be responsible for defending the bridgehead, it would carry out no major offensive operations for the moment—"Divisions of that Corps are to be so re-organized and rested that they can conduct major operations in the near future." In the south, in Horrocks' 13 Corps, the armor of 7th Armoured Division was also to be relieved of offensive tasks. The only offensive action would now be conducted by Lumsden's 10 Corps—whose job was "to make progress to the West and NorthWest from the Kidney Hill area." General Lumsden was to concentrate on this "one hundred per cent," and to stop worrying about the "security of the bridgehead."

Lumsden duly returned from this conference to his headquarters to prepare a 10 Corps plan for a night attack, the object of which was to push out westwards from the British toehold on Kidney Ridge.

While he did so, however, Monty examined the tank casualty figures—which at noon that day showed a combined loss of 239 tanks of all types, mostly on minefields and easily repairable. Together with the very light casualties in officers and men in 10 Corps it was difficult for Monty to understand the ineffectiveness of the armored performance. The success of the infantry's "crumbling" concept had already been reflected in the number of piecemeal counterattacks put in by Rommel's armor; but it was the *infantry* of Eighth Army that was still having to take the brunt of the casualties. On the right of the break-in salient, a single Australian sergeant had knocked out no fewer than five enemy tanks with his 2-pounder antitank gun, but there was a limit to the number of further "crumbling" operations the infantry could be expected to mount in the battle. Half the Afrika Korps had still not been engaged; yet it seemed impossible to make Lumsden understand that the British armor *must* play its part in the battle and not simply sit back doing a job that could be done by 30 Corps' own antitank guns. Skeptical of Lumsden's zeal for the battle, Monty had therefore told him he wanted to see a copy of his plan of attack, to make sure it was properly tied in with full corps artillery support.

It was at this point, waiting to see Lumsden's plan at his small new Tactical Headquarters, that Monty decided to check out with his chief gunner the artillery situation.

Not a High-Class Soldier

Brigadier Kirkman clearly recalled the meeting. "I said to him, 'As far as I can find out we can go on with this battle for ten days at the present rate—but we can't go on indefinitely.' "

"And Monty replied: 'Oh, it's quite all right, absolutely all right, don't worry about ammunition. This battle will be over in a week's time. There'll be no problem.' "

Monty was not worried about the *eventual* outcome of the battle. "If we fire 150 rounds [in the north] a gun per day, we can continue the battle [in the north] for three weeks," he noted confidently in his diary. What worried him much more was the amateurishness of his armored commanders—especially when Kirkman reported that Lumsden was failing to keep in touch with his chief gunner. As Kirkman remembered, "I said, 'The next time you see Herbert Lumsden, I wish you would point out to him that he must keep his corps artillery chief in the picture. He wanders about the country by himself and the corps artillery chief doesn't know what's going on.' "

To Monty this was exasperating. In his diary he noted at 5 P.M. that day:

> I have just discovered that LUMSDEN has been fighting his battle without having his CCRA [corps artillery chief] with him. I have ordered him up at once.
>
> There is no doubt these RAC [Royal Armoured Corps] Generals do not understand the co-operation of all arms in battle. I have had many examples of this since the battle started.
>
> LUMSDEN is not a really high-class soldier.

It was in fact his final revelation that Lumsden was not even fighting with his chief of artillery alongside him that caused Monty now to abandon his latest plan. The British armor had proved utterly "useless" in close combat with the enemy. In such circumstances, what was the point of risking further failure by insisting they play a constructive role in the dogfight phase of the battle?

It was imperative, Monty felt, not to allow the offensive to peter out into stalemate. Rommel had failed to deliver a "decisive blow." Perhaps it was time to consider an Eighth Army "decisive blow," rather than pitching Lumsden's armor into the same sort of piecemeal assaults that Rommel was conducting.

At 6 P.M. on 26 October, therefore, Monty summoned Leese, and gave the orders which, six days later, were to lead not only to the victory of Alamein, but to the almost complete annihilation of the German-Italian African Panzer Army.

Creating Fresh Reserves

I n his diary on the evening of 26 October 1942, Monty recorded his new decision: "After careful thought, I decided to regroup, and reposition, with a view to creating fresh reserves for further offensive action."

"In order to produce a reserve the following moves would take place," the minutes of the subsequent 7 P.M. conference began, recording in detail the wider frontage and sidestepping required to bring the New Zealanders and possibly 10th Armoured Division into reserve, while enabling the Australians to renew their "crumbling" operations northwards from the salient towards the sea "so as to write off all the enemy in his original positions in the coastal sector by getting in behind them," as Monty described his intention in his diary. An hour later General Lumsden's corps headquarters were ordered to drop all orders for attack and instead produce plans for an armored reserve corps, consisting of "the New Zealand Division and 9th Armoured Brigade, 10 Armoured Division and possibly 7 Armoured Division." Re-grouping, Lumsden's 10 Corps would, at last, become the British equivalent of the Afrika Korps, ready to deliver the "decisive blow" of the battle.

General Leese was enormously impressed by the army commander's refusal to be put out by the failure of the armor in the battle of Alamein thus far. Instead of being allowed to feel that the offensive was "fizzling out," Leese was given a new and crystal-clear challenge: to lock the enemy in close combat, while the British armor withdrew from the line, in preparation for a knockout blow.

"The Australians on the right were already in the midst of desperate fighting with the Panzer Divisions," Leese recalled in his unpublished memoirs:

> Their job was by offensive action to contain the Panzer Corps on their front. He [Montgomery] told me to reorganise the remainder of the line—to pull out the New Zealand Division and to form a new striking force under General Freyberg. . . . He was making use of the magnetic leadership and personality of General Freyberg, with his most efficient Headquarters, to drive the final wedge into the enemy front. The line was to be held very thinly by the South African and Highland and Indian Divisions. There appeared little chance, if any of [successful] enemy counter-attacks. The Australian Division was to continue its attacks with the object of drawing the Africa Corps on to its front. . . . The Armour was to be re-fitted and with the exception of the 9th and 23rd Armoured Brigades was to be held in reserve ready for the break through. . . .

Leese was revitalized by his new assignment:

> Directly I received my orders verbally from the Army Commander I held a conference in a tiny corrugated dug-out by the sea to arrange the take-over and reliefs in the line. I have never had such willing co-operation and help. Everyone realised the urgency and the importance of the situation; and very soon Divisional Commanders were vying with each other to find ways and means by which they could help each other to speed up the necessary moves. It was a wonderful tonic to me. Speed was the essence of the plan and when the Army Commander gave me my orders, I fully realised that it could never be done without a super-human effort by all Divisional Commanders. That they did it so willingly is a great tribute to the spirit and efficiency of their Divisions and of themselves. Moreover, it was a particularly fine effort on the part of a Division like the South African Division who had been over-run more than once in the past, and who now willingly took over a very long front with complete faith in our future.

Leese's confidence that there would be no concentrated armored counterattack by the enemy was partly based on his experience of the battle so far, and partly on an appreciation given by the head of Eighth Army Intelligence, Colonel "Spud" Murphy. Shortly after the army commander's evening conference on 26 October, Murphy reported the capture and translation of the "Defensive Policy Plans" of the Italian Trieste Division—which were to "wear down" the attack with all means in their power *without* using concentrated armoured division counter-attacks." Murphy thus gave the army commander his considered opinion:

> It looks as if this is in fact happening and I do not expect concentrated counterattacks from DAK [Deutsche Afrika Korps] until either our armor has completely broken through or until the infantry have been so weakened that they cannot continue to resist in the Northern sector.

In fact Murphy was spectacularly mistaken, as the next day's fighting would reveal. Already during the afternoon of 26 October Rommel grew more and more anxious about the Australian salient; he brought in 90th Light Division from his northern reserve to try to retake "Hill 28" (Point 29) from the Australians, and when this failed, he finally made the irrevocable decision to risk a further British armored offensive in the far south by bringing up 21st Panzer Division to the north.

It was too late, however. Monty's insistence that Lumsden at least push out his remaining armor a little beyond the kidney feature, in order to shield the Australian "crumbling" operations, had finally borne fruit: for on the night of 26 October, 1st Armoured Division, at its second attempt, finally got its motor brigade forward almost onto its objectives, "Woodcock" and "Snipe," thus forming an armored shield for the advancing Australians—and forcing Rommel to react, which he did the next day. In his memoirs, Rommel remarked on the brilliance of Eighth Army's "crumbling" attacks by infantry at night—"particular skill," he acknowledged, "was shown in carrying out this manoeuvre at night and a great deal of hard training must have been done before the offensive."

The sight of British armor accompanying the relentless progress of the Australian infantry was too much for Rommel. Mistakenly assuming that Eighth Army was seeking to break out of its salient, he now hurled the entire Afrika Korps into battle. The northern front on 27 October thus became an inferno of shelling, bombing, dive-bombing, and infantry and tank engagements. "No one can conceive the burden that lies on me," Rommel wrote in his daily letter to his wife. "Everything is at stake and we're fighting under the greatest possible handicap. However, I hope we'll pull through. You know I'll put all I've got into it."

He did. Time and again the Germans and Italians attacked to try to prevent the presumed British breakout: "Every artillery and anti-aircraft gun which we had in the northern sector concentrated a violent fire on the point of the intended attack. Then the armour moved forward," Rommel recalled in his memoirs. "A murderous British fire struck into our ranks and our attack was soon brought to a halt by an immensely powerful anti-tank defence, mainly from dug-in anti-tank guns and a large number of tanks. We suffered considerable losses and were obliged to withdraw. There is, in general, little chance of success in a tank attack over country where the enemy has been able to take up defensive positions; but there was nothing else we could do."

Even at 12:30 P.M. on 27 October, Colonel Murphy refused to believe that the whole Afrika Korps had been committed to battle, reporting to Monty that "evidence is against 21 Pz being in the North." Later in the afternoon, however, the headquarters of 21st Panzer Division was pinpointed, and the violence of the assault on the northern salient thereby explained.

Monty had begun the day disgruntled by the seemingly desultory results of Lumsden's latest attack, since this put yet more burden on the infantry divisions, whose casualties were mounting. The 9th Australian Division had lost over 1,000 officers and men, he noted; the 51st Highland Division some 2,000. Compared with this, the losses sustained by the British armor appeared minimal, and Monty's frustration, in his diary entry at 8 A.M., had been marked:

> My own armor is at present breaking out through the Northern "funnel"; it is actually out, but its progress Westwards and North-Westwards is very slow.
>
> It is a "sticky" fight and artillery plays a great part in it.
>
> But the Armoured Div Commanders do not know anything about artillery; they are used to having it decentralised by batteries; there is no CRA [chief gunner] of an Armoured Division who understands how to handle a Div artillery; they have never been trained by their Div Commanders or by the CCRAs of Corps.

The bravery of the tank and antitank gun crews during the day, however, heartened the army commander. "All day the enemy has been attacking the 1st Armd Div which is in the open to the West of the 'funnel'; all attacks have been beaten off and there seems no doubt that we have destroyed about 40 tanks," he recorded in his diary late in the afternoon of 27 October. In the evening he added: "The one thing we want is that the enemy should attack us. 1st Armd Div have today destroyed 50 enemy tanks (all burning) without loss to themselves."

It was the stalwart defense of Kidney Ridge by 1st Armoured Division on 27 October which to some extent restored Monty's faith in the guts of his British armored formations. However, his hopes of using the "infantry-cum-tank assault" force he was amassing in reserve to exploit this success were dampened the following morning when he heard that the 2nd Battalion of the Rifle Brigade had been overrun after the most valiant effort by their antitank gunners, unsupported by either 2nd or 24th Armoured Brigade; moreover 24th Armoured Brigade had inadvertently run into a minefield, causing heavy losses to their tanks—"24 Armed Bde had suffered considerable casualties owing to mishandling by KENCHINGTON," Monty noted testily at 7 A.M. on 28 October.

Reflecting on the fury of Rommel's counterattacks in the Kidney Ridge area, however, Monty recognized that his armored reserve would never be able to break out via the Kidney Ridge, any more than it had beyond the Miteiriya Ridge. Yet again, he would have to alter his plan. Having locked the Afrika Korps in combat in the Australian sector, he must deliver his blow elsewhere. But it would not be an armored assault—for the lesson of Alamein was that the British armor was completely useless in close combat, save when in hull-down defensive positions. Thus, he decided, he would secretly withdraw 1st Armoured Division and 24 Armoured Brigade, and add them to his own Afrika Korps, ready for the *coup de grâce*—when the battle of Alamein was over.

A New Plan

The Battle of Alamein was now entering its fifth day. At 8 A.M. on 28 October 1942, Monty recorded the results of his conference with Lumsden and Leese—at which he ordered the complete withdrawal of Lumsden's armored corps headquarters, troops and tanks from the current battle, and the handing over to General Leese of all offensive operations. "We now have the whole of Panzer Army opposite the Northern funnel," Monty explained. While keeping Rommel's Panzers committed in the Australian sector, Leese was now to switch the thrust of his attack to Rommel's main supply route to the west of Alamein station—indeed, the New Zealanders were to be put back into the line, rather than be withdrawn into the armored reserve corps:

> I explained that after 9 Aust Div operation tonight, the next operation would be a "drive" NW by 30 Corps to get SIDI RAHMAN; I then wanted to launch armoured cars South-West from that place, to get across the enemy supply routes and to prevent rations, petrol, water, etc. from reaching the forward troops.
>
> The NZ Div would be used for this operation, but it was now very weak.

Freyberg's New Zealanders would have to be "beefed up." Summoning Horrocks from 13 Corps at 11 A.M., Monty explained his intention, and together they agreed on infantry formations which could be spared in the south if 13 Corps sector now became a defensive front. About his divisional commanders, Monty was, in his diary, quite emphatic:

Easily my best fighting Divisional Commander is FREYBERG, and then MORSHEAD.

I am therefore going to fight the battle for the present with 30 Corps, and have placed one armoured div under command of 30 Corps.

The NZ Div will be used to "drive" along the coast towards SIDI RAHMAN and beyond. To keep the NZ Div up to strength and to enable it to operate offensively, British Inf Bdes in turn will be put into it:

First: 151 Bde (DLI)

Second: 131 Bde (Queens)

Third: Greek Bde

This will enable 2 NZ Div to keep going. As each Inf Bde in turn becomes exhausted, so it will rejoin its own Division in 13 Corps and the next Bde will come up.

If Leese could do this, the battle of Alamein would be won—by the infantry. The enemy's unmotorized infantry could not get away, while Eighth Army's armored cars could harry Rommel's supply route. This would still leave Monty the three armored divisions of his *corps de chasse*—1st, 10th and 7th—which could then be launched to finish off any pockets of enemy resistance, a task he hoped would not, this time, be beyond them. Such was the confident new plan Monty gave out at midday on 28 October.

Monty had not, however, reckoned on the political repercussions thousands of miles away in England.

Anxieties in London

News of the withdrawal of Eighth Army's armor caused consternation in Cairo and London, for there had been no mention of such an eventuality in the Lightfoot plan which had been sent to London. Churchill, combining the offices of Prime Minister and Minister of Defence, had assumed that the armor would remain "out" until it had destroyed the Axis armor. Now, according to latest reports, Monty was withdrawing the whole of 10 Armoured Corps.

Quite who began to spread the rumor that this withdrawal implied grievous losses, even retreat, was for years unknown. Eventually, from the unpublished portion of Field Marshal Brooke's diary, it became clear the culprit was none other than Foreign Secretary Anthony Eden—in London! On the night of 28 October 1942, Eden went round to 10 Downing Street "to have a drink with him [Churchill] and had shaken his confidence in Montgomery and Alexander and had given him the impression that the Middle East offensive was petering out!!" Brooke noted in exasperation the following day. "Before I got up this morning I was presented with a telegram which PM wanted to send Alexander. Not a pleasant one!"

Brooke managed to scotch the unpleasant telegram, but at Eden's insistence the British Minister of State in Cairo, Richard Casey, was ordered by cable to go straight up to the Alamein front and re-port back—a sad reflection of Eden's conspiratorial and meddling faithlessness.

When Brooke heard about this a little later he was beside himself with rage. "During COS [Chiefs of Staff meeting] while we were hav-ing final interviews with Eisenhower [prior to Torch] I was sent for by PM and had to tell him fairly plainly what I thought of Anthony Eden and [his] ability to judge a tactical situation at this distance," Brooke recorded in his diary. In his subsequent "Notes on My Life," Brooke later elaborated:

> What, he [Churchill] asked, was MY Monty doing now, allowing the bat-tle to peter out? . . . He had done nothing now for the last three days, and now he was withdrawing troops from the front. Why had he told us he would be through in seven days if all he intended to do was to fight a half-hearted battle? Had we not got a single general who could even win a single battle etc. etc. When he stopped to regain his breath I asked him what had suddenly influenced him to arrive at these conclusions.

On hearing that the offender was none other than Anthony Eden— architect of the British catastrophe in Greece the previous year and thus the whole train of disasters in North Africa—Brooke lost his tem-per. "The strain of battle had had its effect on me," Brooke acknowl-edged in retrospect, "the anxiety was growing more intense every day and my temper was on edge. Churchill retorted that he was entitled to consult whomsoever he pleased. He continued by stating that he was dissatisfied with the course of the battle and would hold a Chiefs-of-Staff meeting under his chairmanship at 12:30 to be attended by some of his colleagues." Then, in front of Field Marshal Smuts and the Chiefs of Staff of the three services, Churchill produced his draft telegram once again, criticizing Alexander and Montgomery.

All Churchill's earlier fears about the depth of the Axis minefields at Alamein and the peril of delaying the British offensive beyond September seemed to him to have been borne out. Once again the Prime Minister's own political position was at stake, not only in terms of possible parliamentary rejection of his premiership, but in terms of his relationship with the Prime Ministers of the Commonwealth, whose troops were so deeply committed in the Alamein battle. On top of the wartime losses suffered by New Zealand, Australian, South African, Indian and Canadian forces in Greece, North Africa, the Far East, and recently at Dieppe, the heavy casualties already sustained at Alamein promised—unless Montgomery failed to achieve decisive victory—to cost Churchill his head.

Field Marshal Brooke, however, was in the same critical situation. Indeed his nightly diary records quite unequivocally how much he felt his position as head of the British army now hung on the successful outcome of the battle of Alamein—"if we had failed again," he confessed at the end of the battle, "I should have had little else to suggest, beyond my relief by someone with fresh and new ideas!"

Yet it was precisely the critical importance of the battle to Allied military strategy and to his own personal position that now made Brooke stand up to Churchill in a way that he had failed to do in August, when Churchill appointed Lieutenant General Gott to command Eighth Army, in preference to Monty. Brooke had heard nothing from Montgomery directly, during the Alamein battle, but he felt certain Monty was withdrawing formations in order to create new striking reserves. "I then went on to say that I was satisfied with the course of the battle up to the present and that everything I saw convinced me that Monty was preparing for his next blow."

Churchill, humbled, thereupon climbed down and lied to Smuts, pretending he had not previously discussed the matter with Brooke, and that he agreed with the CIGS entirely. The telegram was scrapped.

Brooke, however, was far from convinced by his own military logic. "On returning to my office," he later recalled, "I paced up and down, suffering from a desperate feeling of loneliness. I had during the morning's discussion tried to maintain an exterior of complete confidence. It had worked; confidence had been restored. I had told them what I thought Monty must be doing, and I knew him well, but there was just that possibility that I was wrong, and that Monty was beat. The loneliness of those moments of anxiety, when there is no one one can turn to, have to be lived through to realize their intense bitterness."

Radiating Confidence

To his staff and his commanders Monty meanwhile showed nothing but confidence—retired to bed at the same time each night and exuded optimism by day. Thus, while Rommel made himself ill with anxiety, Monty appeared quite unruffled each morning at breakfast. He was not relaxed—as General Sir Charles Richardson later made clear:

> I don't think relaxed is the right word because his style in fact was very taut. Of course there was never any hurry, no flap and that sort of thing, and this was really due to his iron self-discipline—his professional approach to the art of command—rather than to a relaxed style.
>
> His philosophy really went like this: that a Commander must radiate confidence at all times—that was his great expression: "radiate confidence." And if he couldn't control his emotions and conceal his fears, then he shouldn't be a Commander at all. So in order to preserve the nervous energy to carry out that bit of self-discipline, he would have a very orderly regime of sleep and rest and diet and so on.
>
> Now secondly, a Commander must personally control the battle throughout; and in order to be able to do that he must plan it so that he remains in balance—what he called "poise" ("always retain poise"), and he would personally encourage his subordinates—visit them, and control the battle by word of mouth personally.

Behind the facade of confidence, however, Monty was far from satisfied with the way the battle had gone since the break-in on the first night. Moreover, in withdrawing the armor of 10 Corps he was in fact bowing to the inevitable. From the very beginning of the battle,

Lumsden and the armored commanders had been unwilling to fight offensively "up front." The years of failure and defeat, of being outgunned and outmaneuvered, had bred a fatal lack of confidence, and one which could not be dispelled overnight. Moreover there was as yet no Patton-like corps or even divisional commander capable of instilling the necessary resolution within the armored formations, nor the cooperation with other arms—air, artillery, and infantry—which Monty expected of professional battlefield commanders.

In withdrawing his armor, Monty was in effect abandoning the policy he had laid down for the battle—that of an armored shield to protect the infantry's crumbling attacks and draw upon itself the German armored counterattacks—and instead reverting to an infantry-style battle that would entail even heavier casualties than he had anticipated, while keeping his armor in reserve.

Thus, on the night of 28 October, the Australians delivered yet another "crumbling" attack northwards from the bridgehead towards the Alamein railway and the sea. Switching axis, in the next stage of the battle, Monty hoped then to launch the infantry reserve he was assembling under Freyberg westwards, after which the *corps de chasse* could be passed out.

It was not, however, to be so simple.

A Battle for Life or Death

Without armored support it was becoming increasingly difficult for the intrepid Australians to make headway in such a narrow area, with the larger part of Rommel's famed Afrika Korps contesting every yard. For Rommel the battle had already become, quite literally, a matter of life or death.

On the morning of 28 October, at the same time that Churchill was ranting against his generals in the field, Rommel had written to his wife: "Whether I would survive a defeat lies in God's hands. The lot of the vanquished is heavy. . . . My last thought is of you. After I am gone, you must bear the mourning proudly." The capture of a British map showing Montgomery's intended drive northwest from the Australian salient confirmed Rommel's feeling that the critical moment of the battle had arrived—though he mistakenly thought Montgomery was about to launch an armored attack. Accordingly "the whole of the Afrika Korps had to be put into the line," he recorded in his memoirs, and he "again informed all commanders that this was a battle for life or death and that every officer and man had to give of his best."

Meanwhile, Rommel's situation report to OKW (the German high command) for 28 October was quickly decrypted at Bletchley Park in England, the decoding center for Ultra signals, and forwarded both to Churchill in London and to Montgomery at Alamein. The report described the situation as "grave in the extreme." Excited, Churchill summoned Brooke at 11:30 that night and showed him Rommel's message. "He had a specially good intercept he wanted me to see and was specially nice," Brooke recorded in his diary. Referring to the Middle East, Churchill now asked: "Would you not like to have accepted the offer of Command I made to you and be out there now?"

After Churchill's tirade that morning, this volte-face astonished Brooke, especially when Churchill went on to say how grateful he was that Brooke had elected to stay and serve the Prime Minister in London. The angry telegram to Alexander and Monty was forgotten, and as the Australian infantry smashed their way northwards—often in hand-to-hand combat—Brooke and Churchill retired to bed, much relieved.

Pressure from London

The courageous resistance put up by the Germans in the north succeeded in blunting the Australian attack, however, which reached the coastal railway line, but not the sea. For Rommel, though, it seemed but the tip of the iceberg. "No one," he wrote afterwards, "can conceive the extent of our anxiety during this period.

"That night I hardly slept and by 03.00 hours was pacing up and down turning over in my mind the likely course of the battle, and the decisions I might have to take. It seemed doubtful whether we would be able to stand up much longer to attacks of the weight which the British were now making, and which they were in any case still able to increase. It was obvious to me that I dared not await the decisive break-through but would have to pull out to the West before it came. Such a decision, however, could not fail to lead to the loss of a large proportion of my non-motorized infantry, partly because of the low fighting power of my motorized formations and partly because the infantry units themselves were too closely involved in the fighting. We were, therefore, going to make one more attempt, by the tenacity and stubbornness of our defence, to persuade the enemy to call off his attack. It was a slim hope, but the petrol situation alone made a retreat, which would inevitably lead to mobile warfare, out of the question."

Throughout the battle the Allied air forces and the Royal Navy had kept up their pressure on Rommel's petrol supply—as during Alam Halfa—and by the morning of 29 October Rommel was clear he must prepare for withdrawal to Fuka "before the battle reached its climax." At 2:45 P.M. that day his aide noted in his diary: "C-in-C enlarges over lunch on his plan to prepare a line for the army to fall back on at Fuka when the time comes, now that the northern part of the Alamein line is no longer in our hands." To his wife Rommel confessed in his daily letter: "I haven't much hope left. At night I lie with my eyes open, unable to sleep for the load that lies on my shoulders."

For Bernard Montgomery there was no such problem over sleep. Nevertheless the responsibility for ensuring victory weighed equally heavy. The battle had now raged for eight nights and seven days. From the tally kept of enemy tanks and guns destroyed, as well as mounting numbers of prisoners and his Ultra decrypts, Monty knew how desperate the situation must look to Rommel. At 11:15 the previous night, 28 October, his Intelligence staff had identified 90th Light Division fighting in the extreme north, to the west of the Australians—an indication that Rommel was throwing everything he had into that sector in order to prevent Eighth Army breaking out. However, the heavy casualties sustained by the Australians and the damage done to their support tanks on minefields forced Monty now to postpone their follow-up attack. In his diary for Thursday, 29 October, he noted that the "attack of 9 Aust Div made good progress and some 200 prisoners were taken." However, the Australians "got hampered by minefields and did not reach the railway as I had hoped."

Disappointed but more than ever convinced of Eighth Army's impending victory, Monty was concerned not to expend further human life until the Australians had had time to sort out their positions and reorganize their artillery and tank support: "The new front is being reorganized and the attack will be resumed tomorrow night, i.e. Friday, 30 October, when I hope the Australians will reach the sea and clean up the whole area."

It was at this juncture, while preparing for a renewed infantry coastal offensive, that Monty was for the first time in the battle made aware of the political pressure being brought to bear from London. At 11:50 A.M. on 29 October he was informed that Churchill's son-in-law, Duncan Sandys, would visit his headquarters the next day; meanwhile, Alexander himself suddenly appeared with the Minister of State in Egypt, Richard Casey, bearing Churchill's revised telegram. In this, the Prime Minister pointed to the imminent Allied landings in northwest Africa (Torch), and painted a rosy (though illusory) picture of their prospects—namely that the French would assist the Allies in Tunisia and perhaps even rise up in Vichy France. "Events may therefore move more quickly, perhaps considerably more quickly, than had been planned," Churchill signaled, urging that everything now be done to expedite a victory by Eighth Army.

De Guingand recalled the deputation in his book *Operation Victory:* To Casey "the Army Commander described the situation and his plans, and radiated confidence. There had been a signal or two which suggested that some people were a bit worried that things had not gone faster," de Guingand admitted, but "Montgomery's reply to such suggestions was that he had always predicted a ten-day 'dog-fight' and he was perfectly confident that he would win the battle. I was taken aside by Casey, who asked me whether I was quite happy about the way things were going."

So alarmed was Casey, in fact, by the apparent stalemate and the withdrawal of the entire *corps de chasse* that he showed de Guingand a draft signal to London preparing Churchill for a possible reverse. Brigadier Williams remembered the moment quite clearly. "I had a curious sort of truck which had a shelf-cum-bench in it, and Freddie brought Casey into it and we sat on this bench. I talked to Casey and told him the enemy point of view—and then suddenly there was this business of Casey mumbling away that he ought to go and prepare a signal to warn Winston that things weren't going well, and Freddie having this incredible burst of temper, saying: 'For God's sake don't! If you do, I'll see *you're drummed out of political life!'* "—a threat which greatly amused young Major Williams, since de Guingand evidently had "no appreciation that he [Casey] wasn't in political life anyway!"

In his *Memoirs* Monty claimed to have been too busy to bother about what signal Casey eventually sent. However, the evidence of his diary confirms that, on the contrary, he took the pressure from Casey and Churchill very much to heart. " 'Torch' is on 8 November," Monty noted. "It is becoming essential to break through somewhere, and to bring the enemy armor to battle, and to get armoured cars astride the enemy supply routes. We must make a great effort to defeat the enemy, and break up his Army, so as to help 'Torch.' I have therefore decided to modify my plan," he concluded—and set down his new intention.

Rather than driving the New Zealanders in a self-replenishing infantry offensive westwards through the Australian "thumb" (as it was nicknamed at Eighth Army Headquarters) and along the coast road to Sidi Rahman, he would allow the Australians to continue their assault towards the sea in the far north; however, instead of exploiting it, he would put all his reserve forces into a blitz infantry-cum-armored attack westwards from the Kidney Ridge area. This "hole" would be "blown" by Freyberg, and would be some three miles deep; through it Monty would then pass his entire armored corps and two armored car regiments:

> The Armd Car Regts will be launched right into open country to operate for four days against the enemy supply routes.
> The two Armoured Divisions will engage and destroy the DAK.
> This, in effect, is a hard blow with my right, followed the next night with a knock-out blow with my left. The blow on night 31 Oct/1 Nov will be supported by some 350 guns firing about 400 rounds a gun.
> I have given the name "SUPERCHARGE" to the operation.

Thus, instead of being held back in reserve until Leese's 30 Corps had smashed an infantry path all the way through the Axis forces along the coast, Lumsden's armored corps was once again being asked to take part in an assault capacity—"a knock-out blow."

Whether the armor would perform any better than it had in the battle so far, however, remained to be seen.

A Change of Direction

Before breakfast on 29 October, according to Charles Richardson, de Guingand went to brief Montgomery and presented new Intelligence reports indicating that 90th Light Division was definitely committed in the coastal sector. De Guingand, Mainwaring, Richardson and Williams all felt that, with so many Germans committed by the sea, abandoning their erstwhile policy of corseting the Italian units all the way down the line, it might be wiser to strike not from the Kidney Ridge area, north of the Miteiriya Ridge, but further inland, against weaker, largely Italian opposition.

"It wasn't a specially brilliant idea," Williams recalled, "because I mean it was a fairly obvious thing to do, and I can remember it was mainly a matter of one's chinagraph [crayon]—there was this great map hanging on the side of the operations truck; I can remember my own sort of feeling that you'd leave the Panzers the wrong side of the track so to speak if you did it down there rather than across here. We had the chance to leave the Germans the wrong side of it, stranded as it were, while they were virtually cut from below and by-passed."

At first, Monty would not hear of the idea, as Richardson recalled:

The sequence of events really was the Ultra—showing 90th Light having been moved north—Bill Williams appreciating the significance of the Ultra, discussing it with Freddie and Freddie deciding, coming to the conclusion that instead of going, absolutely charging straight at 90th Light, wouldn't it be better to move further south and to attack on the German-Italian boundary and then get around behind? Now that, I'm quite certain, was Freddie's idea, perhaps prompted by Bill Williams. But it took some persuasion, because he went to discuss it with Monty and came back saying, "No, he won't have it."

De Guingand discussed the matter with McCreery when he came up with Alexander and Casey that morning. "McCreery also felt that 'Supercharge' might work better further south," de Guingand recalled in *Operation Victory*, but Williams remembered quite clearly de Guingand's injunction against McCreery mentioning it to the army commander. "I can remember Freddie tried to say to Dick McCreery: 'Look I will go and talk to Monty about it again—don't you, for goodness sake, because if you do, he won't do it. But if one can persuade him it's his own idea, so to speak, then I'm sure it's the right thing to do.' I can remember the atmosphere: 'for God's sake don't go and muck about now' because it'll only cloud the issue."

Richardson remembered de Guingand's success on his second attempt, after Alexander's visit was over—"He [de Guingand] went back and had another go; and the second, final time Monty did accept it." A sigh of relief went through the headquarters staff.

Whether Monty's staff were right will be debated as long as military history is studied. Monty's soldierly instinct was to smash his way with infantry and tanks onto the coast road, however long and however many casualties this would entail. Certainly this was what Rommel feared. In his memoirs Rommel recalled that his army "had been so badly battered by the British air force and artillery that we could not now hope to stand up for long to the British break-through attempt, which was daily or even hourly expected."

However, the success of the Allied landings in Morocco depended upon an accelerated victory at Alamein—and in the end it was this necessity to help Torch that caused Monty to alter his plan for Supercharge. Ultra decrypts indicated Rommel was becoming critically short of petrol—in which case a British mobile thrust inland, through the desert, might be able to encircle the German armored units better than a coastal assault. For good or ill, Monty therefore noted in his diary that "at 1100 hours on 29 October I changed my plan and decided to attack further to the south, because I had learnt that 90 Light Div was in that [northern] area, also that the enemy is very short of petrol."

Historians would hail this as the decisive moment of the battle of Alamein. But if truth be told, Churchill's signal and the necessity of speeding up the conclusion of the battle in the interests of Torch were to produce a tantalizingly disappointing armored finale to one of the decisive battles of human history—indeed threatened, at one moment in the following days, to squander it.

The Heroism of the Australians

The situation on the desert battlefield was meanwhile fantastically confused—so confused in fact that the chief of staff of the New Zealand Division and the G1 (Plans), Eighth Army, were told to go and identify all units on the ground and, by authority of the army commander, order those not involved in Supercharge to withdraw to the rear immediately!

Meantime, at 6 A.M. on 31 October, Monty recorded in his diary that the Australian assault in the north had been "a great success. By dawn over 400 prisoners had been taken, all Germans, and the attack had reached the coast. The rest of 164th German Division were trapped and will not be able to escape."

If Monty began to wish he had held to his intention to break out from the base of the Australian sector, given the apparent success of the Australian night attack, such thoughts must have been quickly erased by the fierceness of the German counterattacks at dawn. Far from reaching the coast, the Australians were able only to take the coast road and railway—to which they clung tenaciously despite everything Rommel did to dislodge them. Some of the most savage fighting of the battle now occurred, as ground was taken, lost, and retaken on both sides. Leese recalled the heroism of the Australians with enduring admiration:

> The Australians . . . established a very difficult salient beyond Point 29 which they held against continuous Panzer counterattack. If the front of that Division had been penetrated during their four-days' ordeal, the whole success of the 8th Army plan could have been prejudiced. As it was, they suffered over 5,000 casualties, but they beat off all enemy attacks, withstood intense hostile shelling and maintained a firm base for subsequent operations by 8th Army. They drew on their front most of

the Panzer Corps of which they destroyed a great part with their antitank guns. It was a magnificent piece of fighting by a great Division, led
by an indomitable character, Leslie Morshead.

Rommel personally directed the Panzer and infantry counterattacks
against the Australians, summoning the Afrika Korps Commander to
his side. The next day, 1 November, he wrote to his wife: "It's a week
since I left home—a week of very, very hard fighting. It was often
doubtful whether we'd be able to hold out. Yet we managed it each
time, though with sad losses. I'm on the move a lot in order to step in
wherever we're in trouble. Things were very bad in the north yesterday morning," he confided, "although it was all more or less cleared up
by the evening"—causing him to wonder why Montgomery did not
now commit his British armor.

In his *Memoirs* Rommel still pondered the question. Why had the
British not thrown in "the 900 or so tanks, which they could safely
have committed on the northern front, in order to gain a quick decision with the minimum of effort and casualties"? he queried. "In fact,
only half that number of tanks, acting under cover of their artillery and
air force, would have sufficed to destroy my forces, which frequently
stood immobile on the battlefield."

Thus, to the end of his life, Rommel failed to appreciate the reasons
why Monty did not commit his armor in the battle, after the break-
in—in fact, had withdrawn 10 Corps from the fighting entirely, and
only allocated it, behind Freyberg, well away from the primary
battle—lest it fail again in close combat.

Even Operation Supercharge had had to be postponed, after
Freyberg informed Leese he needed more time to set up his attack. 10
Corps had refused to move out of their rear positions in order to allow
the New Zealanders to assemble their forces, until de Guingand overruled Lumsden; more important, Freyberg found many of the infantry
tired and the artillery bewildered by the need first to support the Australians in the north, then the New Zealander attack further south and
towards the west. Since the success of Supercharge hinged on
Freyberg's front-line leadership and willingness to accept casualties,
Monty had not been able to refuse, and the assault was therefore postponed to the night of 1 November.

The Approaching Climax

That evening, as the minutes ticked away, Monty wrote to his boss and mentor, Sir Alan Brooke, describing the battle and its approaching climax:

I have managed to keep the initiative throughout and so far Rommel has had to dance entirely to my tune; his counter-attack and thrusts have been handled without difficulty up to date. I think he is now ripe for a real hard blow which may topple him off his perch. It is going in tonight and I am putting everything I can into it; I think we have bluffed him into where it is coming. I hope to loose two regiments of Armd Cars into open country where they can manoeuvre. If everything goes really well there is quite a good chance we may put 90 Light Div and 21 Panzer Div both in the bag. But battles do not go as one plans, and it may be that we shall not do this. We have got all the Germans up in the north in the Sidi Rahman area, and I am attacking well south of that place. There will be hard and bitter fighting as the enemy is resisting desperately and has no intention of retiring.

I am enjoying the battle, and I have kept very fit and well. It is getting chilly now, especially at night, and I have taken to 4 blankets at nights. Tonight's battle I have called "Supercharge" and I enclose a copy of my orders for it. If we succeed it will be the end of Rommel's army.

Oliver Leese has been quite first class; so has Horrocks, but he is away in the south and has little to do.

Lumsden has been very disappointing; he may be better when we get out into the open. But my own view is that he is not suited for high command, but is a good fighting Div Commander. He is excitable, highly strung, and is easily depressed. He is considerably at sea in charge of a Corps and I have to watch over him very carefully. The best of the lot is Oliver Leese, who is quite first class. Freyberg is superb, and is the best fighting Div Comd I have ever known. He has no great brain power and could never command a Corps. But he leads his Division into battle, go-

ing himself in front of a Honey tank with two other Honies in attendance. The only way to find him during a battle is to look for a group of
3 Honey tanks in the NZ area; that will be Freyberg!!

My great task is to keep morale high and spirits up.

I believe that the attack we launch tonight may just do the trick. I am
placing great reliance on the Armd Cars, and if I can launch them into
enemy rear areas the morale and material damage they will do will be
immense.

I hope you are keeping fit.

Yours ever
Monty

With this, Monty retired to bed in his caravan. Just after 1 A.M. on 2
November 1942 the combined artillery of two British corps thun-
dered: a shattering and ominous herald of the major British attack
most Axis troops in the north of Alamein had feared must, eventually,
come.

Victory or Death

0100 ATTACK went in under a creeping barrage on a front of 4000 yds
fired by over 300 25-pdrs. It was probably the first creeping barrage ever used in EGYPT. The attack was a complete success.

Thus ran Monty's initial diary entry for 2 November 1942. Once
again, however, as on the first night of the battle, the performance of the British armor failed to exploit the magnificent feat
of the infantry in reaching their objectives. Indeed in many respects it
was a carbon copy of the opening phase of Lightfoot, with Rommel
quite certain that the thrust was coming on the front further north,
through the Australian "thumb." So certain was Rommel that this was
so, he did not order the Afrika Korps to concentrate on the actual
breakthrough towards Tell el Aqqaqir until well after dawn on 2 No-

vember—by which time Monty hoped to have many hundreds of tanks and armored cars debouching beyond the Rahman track, thrusting northeast to put 21st Panzer and 90th Light Divisions "in the bag."

It was not to be.

In his unpublished memoirs, Sir Oliver Leese was caustic. "The attack [by 30 Corps] exceeded all expectations," he wrote. "The effect of the tanks of the 9th Armoured Brigade [the NZ support brigade] moving along the lanes in rear of the infantry was devastating to the enemy morale; and neither infantry brigade had even to mop-up. By dawn all objectives were captured and the 9th Armoured Brigade were on the Tell el Aqqaqir feature.

"Once again there seemed to be a chance for the Armor to break out. Two Armoured Car Squadrons of the Royals had got out but the armour was again unable to get beyond our FDLs [front line]. The 9th Armoured Brigade themselves had had a great success but they had had many casualties and were forced to withdraw.

"Once again it was up to the infantry soldier. I almost said: 'as usual.'"

The records of the individual units bear out Leese's contention, for the only Axis antitank guns facing 9th Armoured Brigade at that time were 47mm and 50mm caliber, which could halt Shermans or Grants only at short range. Had 1st Armoured Division pressed on the heels of the self-sacrificing Brigadier Currie's 9th Armoured Brigade, the battle might then have been won. Again and again Freyberg signaled to Leese to urge on 1st Armoured Division, but without avail. As Monty had warned Brooke, "battles do not go as one plans." By 7 A.M., wireless intercepts made it clear that the chance had already been missed, since Rommel was now ordering the whole of the Afrika Korps to counterattack. The opportunity to get behind Rommel and cut off his armor had been lost, but, provided Leese and Lumsden brought up plenty of antitank guns and concentrated their artillery fire, there was at least the likelihood of destroying the bulk of Rommel's remaining armor—which to the credit of the British armor, artillery and antitank gunners they now did. By the evening of 2 November 1942, in fact, the Afrika Korps' tally of fit tanks had been halved, with only thirty-five German tanks and twenty Italian still in battle order.

Freyberg was understandably distressed by the failure of the intended breakout, but Monty, as army commander, was more sanguine. He had a further two armored divisions—10th and 7th—in hand, and all day he and Leese had been assembling infantry reserves. If 1st Armoured Division could hold the Afrika Korps to the north and west, Monty felt certain he could follow up the success of his armored cars in breaking out to the southwest of the salient, thus completely bypassing the remaining Afrika Korps. Planned originally for 4 P.M. on 2 November, the first stage of this operation—an infantry attack supported by tanks—took place at 6:15 P.M., and was completely successful.

Rommel, meanwhile, had already admitted defeat to his staff. At 4:30 P.M. on 2 November he had announced to them that the cordon around the enemy salient was only to be a rearguard: the retreat of the Panzer Army to Fuka was to begin. He delayed a final decision on this until he had spoken to the Commander of the Afrika Korps, General von Thoma, but von Thoma confirmed it was now impossible to hold back the British, he had lost so many tanks during the day.

German and Italian infantry not locked in combat began retreating that very night. To his wife Rommel wrote of "the end" and to OKW he radioed at 7:50 P.M. on 2 November his famous admission of defeat:

> After ten days of extremely hard fighting against overwhelming British superiority on the ground and in the air the strength of the Army is exhausted in spite of today's successful defence. It will, therefore, no longer be in a position to prevent a new attempt to break through with strong enemy armoured formations which is expected to take place tonight or tomorrow. An orderly withdrawal of the six Italian and two German non-motorized divisions and brigades is impossible for lack of MT [motor transport]. A large part of these formations will probably fall into the hands of the enemy who is fully motorized. Even the mobile troops are so closely involved in the battle that only elements will be able to disengage from the enemy. . . . The shortage of fuel will not allow of a withdrawal to any great distance. There is only one road available and the Army, as it passes along it, will almost certainly be attacked day and night by the enemy air force.
>
> In these circumstances we must therefore expect the gradual destruction of the Army in spite of the heroic resistance and exceptionally high morale of the troops.

Did the message mean Rommel was withdrawing; was seeking permission to withdraw; or standing fast and expecting to be annihilated? Not until the early hours of the next day, 3 November, did Rommel's follow-up report reach OKW, in which he retrospectively announced his orders for the retreat of the Axis infantry, to begin at 10:00 on the night of 2 November.

These two messages were decoded at Bletchley Park in England, and were in Brooke's hands by midday on 3 November, as Brooke ecstatically recorded in his diary:

Whilst at lunch I was called up by DMI [Director of Military Intelligence] and informed of the two recent intercepts of Rommel's messages to GHQ and Hitler in which he practically stated that his army was faced with a desperate defeat from which he could only extricate remnants!

In his "Notes on My Life" Brooke wrote: "It can be imagined what the receipt of this message . . . meant to me. I dared not yet allow myself to attach too much importance to it, but even so felt as if I were treading on air the rest of that day."

Even Monty's own staff, given the failure of the British armor to break out in Supercharge, were surprised by the defeatism of Rommel's signals. "This Ultra message reached us extremely quickly," Charles Richardson recalled. "Being somewhat skeptical of the Army Commander's optimistic view of events, I shall never forget the elation of myself and of Bill Williams."

Hitler, however, was flabbergasted. The second report, announcing Rommel's order to retreat, only reached him at 9 A.M. on 3 November, and immediately Hitler countermanded it: "In your present situation nothing else can be thought of but to hold on, not to yield a step, and to throw every weapon and every fighting man who can still be freed into the battle. . . . You can show your troops no other road than to victory or death."

In his memoirs, Rommel claimed that without Hitler's countermand, he might still have rescued his army:

Looking back, I am conscious of only one mistake—that I did not circumvent the "Victory or Death" order twenty-four hours earlier. Then the army would in all probability have been saved, with all its infantry, in at least a semi-battleworthy condition.

This, however, was wishful thinking, for Hitler's countermand was only decoded at Rommel's African Panzer Army Headquarters at 1:30 P.M. on 3 November—by which time the retreating Axis infantry had been on the march for more than fifteen hours, and could not be stopped, let alone be put back into line. Moreover, Leese's second infantry attack southwestwards had paved the way for an armored night assault by Lumsden's 10 Corps, which, although poorly executed, so threatened the Italian-German line in the north that Rommel was forced to throw in his entire motorized and armored reserves in order to prevent a rout.

How, in these circumstances, Rommel could have hoped to save a "semi-battleworthy" army is hard to understand. Already a whole regiment of British armored cars were causing havoc as far west as Daba,

British and American aircraft of the Desert Air Force were mercilessly bombing the retreating infantry columns, and to speed up Lumsden's still-stalled breakout Monty asked Leese at 9 A.M. on 3 November to undertake yet another infantry attack "in order finally to push out the armor," as Leese recalled.

Leese decided to make three separate infantry assaults, beginning late that afternoon, the first of which was to be carried out by the 1st Gordons supported by a battalion of tanks, in the evening, west of Tell el Aqqaqir.

Once again, however, Lumsden's 10 Corps headquarters fouled up the operation—leading to heartbreaking and wholly unnecessary Scottish casualties.

The Battle Is Won

"Three or four hours before the attack was due to go in, 10 Corps informed us that their armor was 2,000 yards beyond the Sidi Rahman track and were therefore in possession of our objective," General Leese chronicled in his unpublished memoirs. To avoid shelling Lumsden's tanks, Leese therefore canceled the corps artillery barrage ahead of his attack, making do with smoke. "Just before zero hour the armour informed us that in actual fact they were still 2,000 yards short of the Sidi Rahman track," Leese recalled. "It was too late to do anything; the attack went in unsupported and failed."

The commander of the 51st Highland Infantry Division, Major General Douglas Wimberley, had pleaded with Leese to clear Lumsden's tanks, "if there were any there," and to "let my attack go in properly under a Barrage. The position was, as we had reported, strongly held, not a sign of our tanks was to be seen, but plenty of enemy ones," Wimberly recounted later. "The Gordons made little progress, and lost a lot of men; I felt it had been sheer waste of life and was sick at heart.

Worst of all, thinking that it was an advance rather an attack, the Gordons put a number of their Jocks on the top of the tanks, to be carried on them forward to the objective. I saw the tanks, later, coming out of action, and they were covered with the dead bodies of our Highlanders. It was an unpleasant sight and bad for morale."

Leese was mortified by this waste of human life—and furious with Lumsden's staff. "I had learnt a lesson never again to cancel an artillery programme. Armour can always be moved quickly off any area at will by R/T [radio]. An artillery programme once decided on," he later reflected, "must be allowed to run."

Monty too drew the lesson; and though historians scoffed at later artillery programs which proved unnecessary—as during the first Allied landings on the mainland of Europe at Reggio the following year—Monty himself remained unrepentant. An infantryman's courage depended on his loyalty to his commander: and no good commander should abuse that loyalty simply to save shells.

Wimberley, meanwhile, was so distraught that when Leese explained the armor reported it was *still* unable to gain the Tell el Aqqaqir feature, and that a *further* Highland infantry attack would be necessary to take it, Wimberley broke down. "I was so sick at heart at being overruled regarding not firing my barrage for the Gordon attack that I must have shown it over the phone, unmistakably," he recalled. "I remember Oliver [Leese] said over the phone, 'Surely now you, Douglas, of all people are not going to lose heart.'"

Wimberley did not. Argyll and Sutherland Highlanders and an infantry brigade from 4th Indian Division, under command, were ordered to pave the final path for Lumsden's armor. At last, at 2:30 A.M. on Wednesday, 4 November 1942, by the light of the waning moon, Brigadier "Pasha" Russell's 5th Indian Brigade advanced behind a creeping barrage, with medium artillery pounding known centers of resistance, and clearing a path for 10 Corps, some five *miles* deep. At 6:15 A.M. a battalion of Argyll and Sutherland Highlanders, in a separate attack, began racing for its objective: Point 44, at the heart of the Tell el Aqqaqir feature.

By dawn on 4 November, therefore, Bernard Montgomery knew he had finally and irrevocably won the battle of Alamein. At 6:30 A.M. he recorded in his diary:

The armour went through as the dawn was breaking; it got clear away and out into the open, 1 and 7 Armd Divs leading. We had at last passed our armoured formations into the enemy rear areas, and into country clear of minefields, and into country where they could manoeuvre.

The armoured cars raced away to the West, and were directed on FUKA and BUQQUSH.

I ordered the 2 NZ Div, with 4 Light Armd Bde under command, to move out SW, get on to the FUKA track and move with all speed to secure the FUKA bottleneck.

A wave of exhilaration went through the whole of Eighth Army. After thirteen nights and twelve days of battle, Rommel's army was beaten. It was the first major offensive battle won by the Allies against a German-led army in the war, and the fact that it had been won by perseverance and dogged determination made it all the more moving a victory. De Guingand wrote shortly before his death in 1980:

El Alamein was the proving ground of British military renascence in the Second World War. Without it one frankly cannot imagine the feats which were subsequently achieved. Behind us stretched a pathetic catalogue of bungled efforts and ultimate failures: the defence of Belgium, Dunkirk, Norway, Greece, Crete, Dieppe, and the loss of North Africa to the very gates of Cairo. Democracy had shown itself a poor opponent on the field of battle, when one must be willing to lay down one's life.

In his retirement, Monty visited the battlefield; but when asked if he wished to see the German and Italian cemeteries he shook his head. "I think," he said, having seen the serried rows of British headstones, white and rigid beneath the Egyptian sun, "I've been responsible for enough deaths without seeing those too." Moreover the passage of the years made him feel less negative about the performance of the British armor in the battle. The self-sacrificing courage of Brigadier Currie's 9th Armoured Brigade at Tell el Aqqaqir "paid in blood any debt they owed the infantry."

Meanwhile, on 4 November 1942, Churchill wept when he received General Alexander's telegram announcing British victory. He had already seen, at breakfast, the Ultra decrypt of Hitler's telegram to Rommel, ordering his soldiers to choose death or victory.

While Hitler was now urged to relent over his victory-or-death order, Winston Churchill was free to dictate the messages he had dreamed of. "I send you my heart-felt congratulations on the splendid feat of arms achieved by the Eighth Army under the command of your brilliant lieutenant, Montgomery, in the Battle of Egypt . . ." he began by cabling Alexander, moving then to the Prime Ministers of the Commonwealth.

Shortly after midday, 4 November, the Commander of the Afrika Korps was captured, carrying out Hitler's order to the letter, and standing unbowed amidst a raging tank battle, while his chief of staff, Colonel Bayerlein, ran away on foot as fast as his legs would carry him. David Irving, in his biography of Rommel, branded von Thoma a traitor to the Nazi cause for surrendering, but Major Oswald, in charge of Montgomery's Tactical Headquarters, later well remembered the circumstances of von Thoma's capture, and his soldierly bearing when brought before the Eighth Army Commander that afternoon:

A traitor? Nonsense, of course he wasn't. I've heard it said that he was pretty suicidal. But he was a very experienced officer. He'd commanded the Africa Korps throughout the battle, had commanded the Condor Legion in the Spanish Civil War and was probably one of Germany's leading experts on the use of armor. He was rather a fine-looking chap. I thought he preserved a very soldier-like demeanour—after all his truck had been shot from under him in the heart of the battle, he'd had a pretty good dusting, and had been brought straight before the Army Commander.

Monty, bare-headed and wearing a light-colored pullover without insignia of rank over his desert shirt and trousers, greeted his adversary's salute by staring intently into his gaunt, haggard eyes. Studying von Thoma's face he saw the bearing not of a politically motivated individual, nor of a traitor, but that of a fellow soldier, a fellow professional. Disregarding the possible publicity or even political consequences, Monty told the Commander of the Afrika Korps he wished him to dine in his headquarters mess that evening, before going into captivity. In his diary Monty noted:

General VON THOMA, the Commander Africa Corps, was a prisoner at my HQ and he dined with me in my mess. He is a very nice chap and was quite willing to talk about past events. We discussed the battle in Sept. when ROMMEL attacked me, and we discussed this present battle.
    I doubt if many Generals have had the luck to be able to discuss with their opponent the battle that has just been fought.

More than any other episode during the battle, this image of the Eighth Army Commander on the evening of possibly the most historic British victory of World War II is perhaps the most revealing. While Churchill sought Brooke's approval to ring the church bells of Britain and frantically dispatched telegram after telegram to the heads of state of the Allied nations—to Roosevelt, Stalin, Fraser, Curtin and others—Lieutenant General Bernard Montgomery sat beneath the camouflaged canvas of his mess tent and, as soon as the meal was over, had the table cleared and a map of the Egyptian desert produced.

"Now, tonight my forces are approaching Fuka—what do you think about that? Come on, what would you do, von Thoma?" Monty harangued his "luckless opponent," as General Oswald later recalled. But von Thoma would give nothing away:

> He said: *"Sehr kritisch, wirklich sehr kritisch—"*
> Monty was leading him on a bit, I'm afraid, for we weren't half as far forward as that, we hadn't even got to Galal, but anyway . . .

Four days later, when informed that three Italian generals would be joining him in captivity, von Thoma—who felt the Germans had had to bear the brunt of the fighting in the battle of Alamein—"asked that they [the Italian generals] should not be put in his compound, and if they were, a barbed wire fence to be put between them," Alexander cabled with amusement to Churchill.

But if von Thoma felt resentful towards his Italian allies, for the Eighth Army Commander who had dined him on the night of 4 November 1942 he maintained a lasting admiration. "I thought he was very cautious considering his immensely superior strength," he declared after the war was over, "but he is the only field marshal in this war who won all his battles. In modern mobile warfare, the tactics are not the main thing. The decisive factor is the organisation of one's resources—to maintain momentum." And Bernard Montgomery, despite all the vicissitudes of battle, had done just that: given the peoples of the Allied world the victory they had longed for.

Part Five

MEDITERRANEAN INTERLUDE

Ike's first visit to Monty in the field,
29 March 1943.

General Sir Bernard Montgomery

One week after his victory at Alamein, Lieutenant General B. L. Montgomery was promoted to the rank of full general and knighted, becoming Sir Bernard Montgomery "for distinguished service in the field."

He had stepped into history.

The Panzerarmee Afrika had been destroyed, suffering an estimated 50,000 casualties. In America, Wendell Willkie, Franklin Roosevelt's emissary, told newsmen: "It is a thrilling and far-reaching accomplishment. When I visited General Montgomery some two months ago, I was convinced the present results would follow in a short time. Montgomery told me he would eliminate Rommel. He is apparently well on the way."

Rommel had now to learn the pain of retreat, not attack. "We have to be grateful for every day the enemy does not close in on us," Rommel confided to his wife as he retreated to the Libyan border with the remnants of his Panzer army, adding: "I wish I were just a newspaper vendor in Berlin."

At last an Allied general had proved the spell of German predominance could be broken. The journalist C. V. R. Thompson reported to London's *Daily Express* from New York: "Americans have forgotten their criticisms of Britain, and full credit to the British is given in the American Press and by the American people for the desert victory. . . . The International News Service, which goes to 700 American newspapers, had this to say: 'The question, can the British soldiers really fight? need never again be asked. The Germans themselves are the best judges of their fighting spirit.' . . . Montgomery has driven the [midterm] election off America's front page."

Perhaps no general ever has so assiduously prepared himself for high command, or so dramatically imprinted his concepts upon an ailing army in the field. However, Monty's hour of glory was short-lived. Once British and American forces landed in northwest Africa on 8 November 1942, Monty became a member of an Allied team. Thanks to him, the tide of war had turned; but the great victory at Alamein soon paled amidst the preoccupations and setbacks of Allied strategy in the Mediterranean. After a brilliant start, the Torch landings in Morocco and Algeria led to stalemate in Tunisia, as Hitler occupied the rest of Vichy France, reinforced his North African forces, and put paid to any possibility that Eisenhower, with inexperienced generals and unblooded troops, could force a victory without Monty's help.

As a result, Eighth Army had to press Rommel's remnant Panzer army thousands of miles through Cyrenaica, Libya and eastern Tunisia in order to join up with Eisenhower's forces. While Monty halted to replenish his army at Tripoli in February 1943, Rommel launched an armored offensive at Eisenhower's eastern flank that vividly demonstrated the naïveté of those who had favored a Second Front on the mainland of Europe in 1942. Some 4,000 American troops were captured at Kasserine, and 6,000 casualties sustained by 2 U.S. Corps—almost half the 13,000 casualties Eighth Army had sustained at Alamein. Turning his attention back to Eighth Army, Rommel thereupon attempted to repeat his Kasserine success. At Medenine, Rommel ran up against the same professional tactics, however, that had doomed his offensive at Alam Halfa: dug-in tanks, courageous antitank gunners, and devastating artillery.

Monty's defensive victory, on 6 March 1943, marked the end of Rommel's military career in North Africa. The legendary "Desert Fox" had met his match and was withdrawn from the theater, after disagreements with his superiors and fellow generals. He would never launch an offensive again.

Monty as Napoleon

M onty's fate was to be markedly different—indeed, save for the battle of the Ardennes, Monty would spend the rest of the war mounting offensive battles. However, there can be no doubt that his personal ego, after a lifetime of frustration and conflict with his superiors, became inflamed by victory, and he found it hard to forgive what he saw as criminal mistakes by his allies and fellow generals—criminal in that they resulted in wholly unnecessary loss of life after the lessons of 1940–43.

Nowhere would this self-righteousness be more ominously displayed than in the planning—or misplanning—of Operation Husky, the Allied invasion of Sicily, and the subsequent campaign to "knock Italy out of the war."

Monty had, by seizing the Tunisian city of Sfax by 10 April 1943, won a bet with Eisenhower and demanded as payment a Flying Fortress from Allied Headquarters in Algiers, complete with an American crew, on the American payroll, for his exclusive use for the rest of the war. This outrageous demand (met by giving Monty a Fortress earmarked for the U.S. Army Air Forces Commander, General "Tooey" Spaatz) was only the first of Monty's many imperious demands, disagreements and dire warnings if he did not get his way. He simultaneously declared all Allied planning for the invasion of Sicily to be incompetent, and threatened, if his own plan of assault was not adopted, to resign. Worn down by Monty's insistence, General Eisenhower, who favored multiple landings around the island, and General Alexander, who had become Allied field armies commander in Tunisia under Eisenhower's overall aegis in Algiers, finally gave in—only for Monty to demand he take Patton's 2 U.S. Corps under command for the invasion.

Clearly, Monty was inciting resentments that would last throughout the war—and beyond. "Monty thinks himself as Napoleon," Air Marshal Tedder complained to Patton. Tactless, vain, indiscreet, Monty behaved with an arrogance almost calculated to offend—the once-colonial boy, swaggering around in a tank commander's beret with two badges, conscious of the fact that he had become the greatest battle-winning general on the Allied side: the victor over Rommel.

"Montgomery is of different caliber from some of the outstanding British leaders you have met," Eisenhower had described Monty to his boss in Washington, General Marshall, after staying several days at Monty's tactical headquarters at Mareth, and viewing the scarred battlefield. "He is unquestionably able, but very conceited. For your most secret and confidential information, I will give you my opinion which is that he is so proud of his successes to date that he will never willingly make a single move until he is absolutely certain of success—in other words, until he had concentrated enough resources so that anybody could practically guarantee the outcome. This may be somewhat unfair to him, but it is the definite impression I received."

The Battle of Sicily

Monty's view of Eisenhower was no less patronizing. To Alexander, Monty confided that he "liked Eisenhower." However, he added, "I could not stand him about the place for long: his high-pitched accent, and loud talking, would drive me mad. I should say he was good probably on the political line; but he obviously knows nothing whatever about fighting."

The stage seemed set for conflict and misunderstanding. Eisenhower was by temperament and intelligence supremely able at maintaining Allied solidarity in his command—but always at the cost of haphazard operational planning, which he delegated to others.

At loggerheads with his British and American colleagues over the future conduct of the land war in the Mediterranean, Monty now found that the very virtues which gave his leadership its inspiring quality—absolute conviction, insistence on proper planning, ruthless professionalism—made him an infuriating and stubborn ally. Walter Bedell Smith's famous remark—"You may be great to serve under, difficult to serve alongside, but you sure are hell to serve over!"—was to become uniquely apt.

In American eyes, Monty's belief in careful planning and adequate logistical backup seemed pedantic at best, slow at worst. What American newcomers to the Mediterranean could not always appreciate was that Monty's philosophy of military tidiness had crystallized in the years of British defeat, from Dunkirk to Tobruk. Dispersion of effort, failure to plan properly, lack of adequate weaponry, absence of rehearsal, feeble cooperation between different arms and services, and a pervasive distrust of the high command among the soldiery had had a disastrous effect—something he saw being repeated almost before his eyes in the early American failures in Tunisia. "The real trouble with the Americans," he wrote to "Simbo" Simpson at the War Office in London, "is that the soldiers won't fight; they haven't got the light of battle in their eyes.

"The reason they won't fight," he went on, "is that they have no confidence in their Generals. If they had confidence that their Generals would put them into battle properly, then they would fight."

Morale, Monty felt, was not a matter of simple exhortation. It was a matter of battlefield commanders winning the confidence of their troops: of professionalism *from the generals down*. "I showed him soldiers," Monty boasted after Churchill's visit to North Africa in the spring of 1943, "that I do not believe you would see in any other Army in the world; magnificent fighting men from all over the world; the parade and march past in the main square of Tripoli was a wonderful sight; the P[rime] M[inister] was deeply moved and could hardly trust himself to speak. I do not think you would see such a display of fighting men in any Army in the world except in the Eighth Army. The morale is right up on the top line and the sick rate is 1 man per 1,000 per day; you cannot want anything better than this."

As the Mediterranean campaign progressed, however, Monty's respect for Churchill and for Eisenhower even at the political level diminished. Not understanding the difficulties of dealing with de Gaulle and his competing French generals, or of negotiating with Italian emissaries for a secret peace treaty, Monty saw only a tragic military quagmire into which, on behalf of his proud soldiery, he refused to get sucked. The original plan for isolated, mutually unsupporting landings on different coasts of Sicily he felt was harebrained. Wherever the Allies fought with overwhelming concentration of force, he argued, they prospered; wherever the Allies dispersed their efforts, they were defeated in detail by such veteran combatants as the Germans.

Monty's revised plan for the invasion of Sicily, for all the resentment it caused, guaranteed the Allies success ("I begin to think that the new operation is better in many ways than the old," Patton acknowledged in his diary on 7 May 1943)—and success, four weeks later, on 10 July 1943, duly began, despite disaster in the parachute operations. By landing side by side in a cohesive assault upon the south coast of Sicily, the Allied assault proved triumphant.

If Monty had cause to feel militarily vindicated, his pride was soon rocked by the fierceness of fighting in the Catania plain. The Germans, with vast reserves of men and ammunition in Italy, flew in elite parachute units to fight as infantry. Patton's 2 U.S. Corps had been pumped up to become Seventh U.S. Army, with General Patton its army commander. Impatient with what he saw as his subordinate American role in the campaign, Patton was determined to blaze a trail in Sicily that would avenge the American disaster at Kasserine. Flying to Alexander's headquarters in Bizerta, North Africa, he wrested permission to advance westwards to Palermo, instead of fighting with Eighth Army. "We took the northwest corner of Sicily. It was a pleasure march. . . . Nicest war I've ever been in!" General Maxwell Taylor, artillery chief of 82nd U.S. Airborne Division, later recalled. "Monty—he had a different problem—he was up against Germans."

Too late, Monty called upon Patton for help, begging Alexander on 19 July 1943 to get the Americans to "develop a strong thrust eastwards towards MESSINA . . . and possibly repeat the BIZERTA manoeuvre [when 250,000 Axis troops were outflanked, and surrendered, at the climax of the Tunisian campaign]." Alexander duly sent Patton a signal to this effect, but Patton's chief of staff deliberately withheld transmission of the order, and Patton raced on to Palermo—causing his 3rd U.S. Division commander to later confide: "It is my belief that the glamour of the big city was the chief thing that attracted Gen. Patton."

Not until a week later, at Syracuse airfield on 25 July 1943, was Monty able to lure Patton from his palace in Palermo and concert an Allied strategy to end the campaign—a campaign that could have been far better run by a single army commander, on the spot, instead of two separate army commanders, hundreds of miles from each other, reporting to an army group commander—Alexander—still in North Africa.

Despite his reservations about Monty, Patton threw everything into his northern thrust to Messina, which he entered triumphally three weeks later, on 17 August 1943. Yet it had proved impossible to get the Allied air forces to agree on a plan to stop the German evacuation—just as the Luftwaffe had failed to coordinate a plan for halting the British evacuation at Dunkirk in 1940—and the entire German army defending Sicily had got away by ferry to the mainland.

"The trouble is there is no high up grip on this campaign," Monty had complained already on 7 August. "It beats me how anyone thinks he can run a campaign in this way, with the three Commanders of the three Services [army, navy and air force] about 600 miles from each other. The enemy should never be allowed to get all his equipment out of Sicily, and we should round up the bulk of his fighting troops . . . but such a plan does not exist."

Patton's specially photographed and filmed triumphal entrance into Messina masked an incredibly mismanaged campaign, in Monty's eyes. General Bradley felt the same. Indeed, so incensed was Bradley by Patton's megalomania (particularly his bragging at having slapped and threatened a number of hospitalized American soldiers on 3 and 10 August) that Bradley refused even to appear at Patton's parade in Messina.

The Allies, in both Bradley's and Monty's view, were in grave danger of allowing public relations to masquerade for military professionalism—and brave soldiers' lives would be squandered as a result, Monty warned. The latest wild Allied planning for the invasion of the Italian mainland—due to take place early in September 1943—was a "recipe for disaster," Monty predicted—and at Salerno it very nearly would be.

However, the prize for military mismanagement of the Allied effort, in Monty's opinion, undoubtedly went to those responsible for the failure to plan and rehearse the major Allied assault of the war: the forthcoming invasion of France, or "Second Front."

The Need for a
Cross-Channel Commander

Monty's two-week trip to London in May 1943 had convinced him the Allies would never succeed in an invasion of France unless they finally appointed a commander.

"A cross-Channel operation is being envisaged," he complained to the Director of Military Operations at the War Office; "various planning staffs are at work; no outline has been produced by the Commander who is to take charge of the operation, because no Commander has been appointed. The staff of the Commander have been appointed and they are busily engaged in planning; but none of them have fought in this war and they know nothing about the battle end of the problem," he protested. "A further point is that the Commander, when appointed, has got to create his fighting machine and train his forces for the battle. This takes time, and it is not being done.

"There seems to be no one person in England who knows what is wanted, who says so quite clearly, and who has such prestige and fighting experience that everyone will accept his opinion and get on with it. Until such a person is appointed to "take hold" of the Army in England, we will do no good.

"At present there are too many people in England who think they know what is wanted; but they all disagree with each other; and they have got the basic set-up wrong; and they bellyache about nonessentials; they do not really know what are the essentials"—at which Monty listed the essentials of modern war as he saw them: namely the need to win air superiority; the necessity for good and simple army planning; the seizing and retaining of the tactical initiative once ashore; targeting the vital hinges in the enemy's defensive layout; regrouping, if necessary, to capture or outflank those hinges; and appointing only commanders with terrific "drive" and energy. To Admiral Mountbatten, the Chief of Combined [amphibious assault] Operations in Britain, Monty also appealed for help in getting a commander appointed. "There are so many people at the top who do not really understand the matter; and there are so many vested interests. In order to win battles, and so carry out the policy of the Government, certain basic things are essential; if you don't have them, then you don't win the battle. Someone has to fight for these things, and whoever takes on this job is bound to make enemies and get a lot of mud slung at him. Ever since I went to Africa in August 1942 I have fought for these things—for first principles—to get the big thing right. And as a result I have won my battles. I do not in the least mind the mud that is slung about; I shall go on fighting for the things that matter. All I want to do is win the war. With your very great enthusiasm and sound practical common sense, and knowledge of what is wanted, you are exactly the man we want to help us."

Monty felt certain that only by transferring Alexander and himself to London could the cross-Channel assault be put on a sure footing. "But I also feel that Alex and myself cannot both leave here if it is the intention to carry on against Italy and knock her out of the war. Someone will be required to command the field armies for Eisenhower i.e. 15 Army Group; we shall probably have three Armies, two American and one British. It would be a biggish undertaking and the Army Group Commander would have to know his stuff 100%. If Alex and I both go home there is no one out here who could command the three armies and knock Italy out. So if Alex goes home, as I think he must, then I must stay here and take on his job—and knock Italy out. I could come home early next year, in the spring, to help Alex. That is how I see the matter."

Others, however, saw it differently. Only General Marshall in Washington had the necessary vision and commitment to the cross-Channel attack to bring back to England an experienced field commander at the end of the Sicilian campaign—Omar Bradley. Field Marshal Brooke, by contrast, ignored Monty's suggestion, and left *both* Alex and Monty in the Mediterranean. "I think as things go at present it is probably right to leave the 1st XI [i.e., team] out here," Monty wrote with resignation to Mountbatten on 3 August 1943. "But they must remember the need in England; and if anything is contemplated then someone must 'catch hold' at home. To delay after November would be very dangerous."

What Monty feared was a repetition of Sicily, as he pointed out in a further letter to Mountbatten a week later, after reading a report on the Sicilian landings: "What is past is past. But do not let us make the same mistake again. Let us learn from our mistakes. Unfortunately I see no signs that we are doing so."

Everything Monty heard from England gave him cause for anxiety.

A Savage Indictment

However logical Monty's approach to military undertakings and the need for battle-hardened commanders, the flaw in his argument was the plain fact that the Allies possessed very few such commanders. Monty had himself suggested that Alexander should return to England to "take hold" of the cross-Channel attack. But did Monty really think Alexander capable of such a feat? As the Sicilian campaign lurched to its disappointing conclusion, Monty remarked caustically in his diary: "I am afraid it has to be admitted that throughout the preliminary planning stage, and during the actual operations in SICILY, 15 Army Group has been completely and utterly ineffective." Both Alexander's chief of staff and his chief of administration were "out of their depth"; moreover Alexander's vast staff of 480 officers—excluding other ranks—was "definitely a great waste, and in fact a scandal.

"A further trouble is that Alexander cannot make a decision when faced with a difficult and complex problem. Therefore his staff have a very difficult time.

"He is so used to reaching agreement by compromise, and to finding a formula that will suit all parties, that he has lost the gift of quick decision—if he ever had it.

"He will take action at once when the form is given him by me, or by someone else whose opinion he trusts," Monty went on. "If his staff would give him the proper line, he would be all right. But his staff is a very poor one. . . . The whole set-up at 15 Army Group has been bad; the planning for operations, the grip on the battle and the conduct of the war generally, has been a complete failure."

This was a savage and insubordinate indictment. In the light of what Monty would have to say about the subsequent campaign in Italy, it was, however, positively charitable.

No Grip or Control

Monty's frustration in the fall of 1943—though it never reached the point at which, like Patton, he lost his self-control and abused sick men—grew worse and worse. Monty did not blame his troops; he blamed the commanders—including, increasingly, the Commander-in-Chief, General Eisenhower. By concentrating on the political aspect of the Italian campaign, Eisenhower had failed to foresee the military problems inherent not only in landing on the Italian mainland, but in facing some twenty German divisions established in Italy, and confronting them in terrain and weather that were ideal for defense. Moreover, despite Eisenhower's great coup in getting Badoglio to agree to an armistice of anti-Mussolini Italians, Monty put no faith in Badoglio's promise to switch sides and fight against his former allies.

Having been given a completely subsidiary task in Italy—landing Eighth Army at Reggio, across the Strait of Messina on 3 September 1943—Monty thus warned Alexander on 8 September of his deep misgivings. Eisenhower's plan to drop an American airborne division on Rome he thought the most ridiculous scheme in modern military history, and even the projected Allied landing at Salerno, "Avalanche"—set for 9 September—looked ill-conceived and likely to be quickly fenced in by German forces in the area, as he noted in his diary:

ALEXANDER was very optimistic and was obviously prepared to think that the Italians would do all they said. I took him aside for a talk. I told him my opinion was that when the Germans found out what was going on, they would stamp on the Italians.

The Italian soldiers were quite useless and would never face up to the Germans.

I said that he should impress on all senior commanders that we must make our plans so that it would make no difference if the Italians failed us. I said the Italians might possibly do useful guerilla work, sabotage, and generally insure complete non-co-operation on the part of the entire population; but I did not see them fighting the Germans.

They were carrying out a colossal double-cross, and we must not trust them too much, or tell them our plans just at present.

The Germans were in great strength in ITALY and we were very weak. We must watch our step very carefully, do nothing foolish, and on no account must we risk a disaster. If we knock Italy out of the war, and contain 20 German divisions in Italy, and get the Italian fleet, we would have done very well.

I begged him to be careful; not to open up too many fronts and so dissipate our resources; and to be quite certain before we landed anywhere that we could build up good strength in that place, sufficient to be quite safe in that area. I said that we knew the Germans were strong about ROME and NAPLES, and could concentrate against AVALANCHE [Salerno] quicker than we could build up; if there was any danger of a disaster to AVALANCHE we should cancel it, and put that effort in to TARANTO and so get a firm grip on Southern Italy.

In the end, the airdrop on Rome was canceled, after General Maxwell Taylor—dispatched on a clandestine trip to Rome—reported by radio there was no chance whatsoever that the Italians there would fight the Germans. Meanwhile, however, Avalanche went ahead—and almost met disaster.

From Intelligence sources Monty was aware that Rommel was once again in charge of German troops in the theater. "It was known from agents, and from the Italians that the Germans had twenty divisions in Italy, and that Rommel was in command in the north. I look forward to taking on my old opponent again," Monty had recorded on 5 September. He himself felt secure, in the toe of Italy; but about Fifth Army's Anglo-American Salerno invasion under General Mark Clark he was much less sanguine.

Ironically, Monty's caution was mirrored by that of Rommel in the north of Italy, for despite their vastly superior strength the Germans were too concerned with the possibility of Allied landings there to risk sending forces south, and being outflanked. Thus, while Rommel and Montgomery watched each other warily from north and south, the battle for Italy took place in the gap between them. In spite of the Italian surrender to the Allies, Rome and Naples were instantly secured by the Germans. Meanwhile, from 9 September 1943, the Allies fought a life-and-death struggle for a fragile beachhead in the Bay of Salerno. Eighth Army was once again summoned to assist—Alexander sending frantic messages to urge Monty to drive hundreds of miles north from Reggio, while Hitler vainly urged Rommel to drive hundreds of miles south. "As my mother and I well remember," Rommel's son later recalled, "Hitler discussed with my father the possibility of launching a counter-offensive to retake southern Italy and possibly Sicily. My father saw not the smallest chance of this." In fact Rommel specifically refused to release the two Panzer divisions which Kesselring begged for.

To his great credit, General Mark Clark managed to stave off defeat at Salerno, but plans for an American evacuation were at one point drawn up, and until 16 September the situation remained critical in the extreme. Thereafter the Allied campaign in Italy deteriorated into a series of ill-coordinated offensives, resulting in terrible casualties for strategically nominal gains.

Disappointed, even the normally dispassionate General Marshall blamed Monty rather than his own protégé, General Eisenhower. As Marshall later confided to the American Official Historian, Dr. H. M. Smyth, he had been " 'strongly in favor of the Salerno operation' but had been irritated by the slowness with which this operation was mounted. The Logistical people were too cautious about what could be done, and the speed with which it could be done." In Marshall's postwar view "the British in the Middle East (8th Army) had committed about every mistake in the book." Far from applauding Montgomery's march across North Africa from Alamein to Tunis, Marshall considered it was "no model campaign. The pursuit of Rommel across the Desert was slow. . . . Here Marshall formed an opinion: that Montgomery left something to be desired as a field commander."

It seemed, the further away the bystander, the less he understood the military realities of fighting against German forces—and the more he misunderstood Monty's battlefield professionalism.

Understanding the Business

More and more, after Sicily, Monty began to feel the rift between his own concept of the professional conduct of war and the daydreams of his superiors. General Marshall might well scoff at El Alamein as being a battle "blown up out of proportion to its importance," but Monty himself knew how much the encounter still meant in the hearts and minds of his soldiers. On the first anniversary of the battle he had received messages from all over the world, but it was those of his headquarters staff, commanders and men he most valued. The battle had not only begun an historic march of victories unknown in the British army since the days of Wellington, it had demonstrated in its agonizing course the bravery and professionalism of the German soldier: a lesson repeated again and again in the long crusade across North Africa, as it was in the plains and olive groves of Sicily. The German soldier was not to be underestimated.

Though he did his best to do his duty as Eighth Army Commander, Monty was scathing in private. "You remember I told you I could write a book about the whole HUSKY [Sicily] affair," he wrote on 29 September 1943 to Mountbatten—who had been made Supreme Commander of the Southeast Asian Theater—"but it would be quite impossible to publish it!! It is nothing to what I could write about what I was asked to do when we invaded the mainland of Europe. The trouble we had to get the thing on a good wicket is almost unbelievable. . . .

"But my advice to you as a Supreme Commander is to get a good sound plan drawn up before you begin detailed planning; get an experienced fighting commander 'in' on it and make certain that what you want to do is possible and that you have the necessary resources to do it.

"And do one or two things really properly; and don't try to do five or six things all of which are starved for lack of resources—and which will probably all produce no results."

A month later, Monty was even more disheartened. Rommel had been transferred to take command of all German forces defending Northwest Europe—"Fortress Europe"—but Allied progress in Italy was held up by administrative chaos and an almost total lack of clear priorities and firm leadership at the top. "What we want in ITALY is a proper and firm plan for waging the campaign. At present it is haphazard and go-as-you-please," Monty complained in his diary.

> I fight my way forward as I like; I stop and pause when I like; I choose my own objectives.
>
> CLARK (Fifth Army) does the same; I have very close touch with him and we see that our actions are so coordinated that all is well.
>
> But we each do what we like, when we like; the total military power in the two Armies is not applied on one big plan. In other words, there is no grip or control by 15 Army Group.
>
> As far as I know no high authority has ever said what is wanted. Do we want ROME and its airfields? Do we want the Po valley?
>
> What do we want, and when?
>
> Until some very clear directive is issued we shall continue to muddle on.

To Monty, this was scandalous—especially since the Germans now had twenty-four divisions in Italy, almost twice as many as the Allies, and easily supplied from Germany.

> The Allies have not got the resources in craft and shipping to fight two major campaigns at the same time. If ITALY is to be the main theater, then turn the tap on there and leave it on till you have got what you want.
>
> We turned the tap off before we got what we wanted.
>
> If Western EUROPE is to be the main theater, then turn the tap on there; in this case you must not expect spectacular results in ITALY.
>
> I put all the above very plainly to ALEXANDER when he came to see me today. I said it was my opinion that we should have as our objective the ROME line; we should then halt for at least three months in order to bring up reserves in our depots and prepare for the spring campaign; in the spring we should launch an offensive into the PO valley.
>
> If some simple plan as above was laid down, we could all plan ahead.
>
> But nothing is laid down.
>
> ALEXANDER agreed, and said he would order the above plan. There is no doubt we conduct our wars in a most curious way; ALEXANDER is the nicest chap I have ever known, but he does not understand the conduct of war; the indecision and lack of grip at 15 Army Group is

bad—it is more than that, it is a scandal. I very much doubt if we shall now get the ROME line without great difficulty—and not before the middle of December.

This was prophetic, as Monty himself discovered a few days later, when rain, mud and slush brought the right flank of Eighth Army's advance to a complete standstill. Rome was out of the question, now. The reason, he confided in his diary, "is that we are now paying for the lack of fixed policy, lack of planning, and lack of 'grip,' that has been noted in this diary all through the Italian campaign." He had warned Alexander again and again in his signals, and in person on 7 October 1943. "I also put the whole thing very clearly to EISENHOWER when he visited me on 11 October. But nothing was done.

"An enormous Air Force is pouring in," he noted. "But the land armies remain unchanged, I have many units still in AFRICA. I have four infantry divisions. I cannot get to the ROME line with these. . . .

"Now another complication has arisen," Monty went on, for Alexander, shamed by the slow progress of the campaign, had dreamed up another fantasy, on a par with Eisenhower's plan for the American airborne assault on Rome, Giant II—this time an amphibious landing at Anzio, behind the German lines, but ringed by easily defensible mountain ranges.

"ALEXANDER has now told the CIGS that he must be allowed to keep craft and shipping for one division, so that he can land this division up near ROME in an assault operation; he has said that if he cannot have the craft he cannot get to ROME.

"In my opinion this is complete nonsense; the weather is too uncertain now for assault landings; one division landed near ROME would find itself taken on by several enemy armoured Divisions, as the Germans are withdrawing their armoured Divisions to rest in the ROME area; there are very few beaches where such a landing could be made," he warned, "and they will all be closely watched.

"To keep a division locked up in craft, waiting for an assault landing that may never come off because of adverse weather or of enemy concentrations, is monstrous," he felt. "ALEXANDER is trying hard to find a way out of the mess. But he won't do it by landing a Division at ROME; he will merely make it worse and the Division may well be written off by the Germans.

"The answer," Monty contended, "is quite simple. If you want to wage successful war, you have got to have a commander who understands the business.

"ALEXANDER is my great friend. But he does not understand the business."

A Hell of a Battle

D espite his frustration, Monty loyally fought his way up the Adriatic coast with four divisions; indeed, for a moment in November 1943, with Mark Clark's Fifth Army stalled just beyond Naples, Monty believed there was a sudden chance for Eighth Army to outflank the German winter line and take Rome from the east. He had planned a Blitzkrieg infantry-and-tank attack across the river Sangro, in the manner of his desert offensives; but without fine weather, as he himself acknowledged in his diary, "I am done."

Monty's worst fears were soon realized. The heavens opened, the armor became immobilized, and the air support squadrons were grounded. Vainly Monty tried to modify his plan, dispense with surprise and try to sneak enough light forces, under heavy artillery cover, to secure the high ground dominating the far side of the Sangro. This was already done on the night of 19 November, but despite Monty's insistence that his 5 Corps Commander, General Allfrey, "stiffen up the forward companies across the river," they were thrown back on the left flank the next day. "I discovered that no gunner F[orward] O[bservation] O[fficer] was with his company, or with any of the other companies over the river. I spoke very severely to the Corps Commander on that subject; I am informed that this is now in hand and that gunner FOOs are across the river," he recorded in his diary. But on 21 November, with heavy rain still suspending all activity from the Desert Air Force's airfields, the right-flank company of General Evelegh's 78th Division was thrown back across the Sangro. "On enquiring I ascertained that there was no gunner FOO with this company. This made me very angry. . . . I sent for ALLFREY, GOC 5 Corps, and told him that his Corps was completely amateur according to Eighth Army standards; there was a lack of 'grip' and 'bite,' and things must change at once." Five battalions were to be put across the river that night, and three Bailey bridges to be constructed. Antitank guns were to be got over, as well as tanks, one by one, even in daylight. This was duly done, and by dawn on 22 November one Bailey bridge was ready, and the two others almost completed. "A fine day," Monty recorded hopefully. "I believe we are at last in for a fine spell."

But Monty was wrong. The next day he noted in his diary: "Heavy rain all day. The SANGRO valley is completely waterlogged, and for the moment offensive operations are at a standstill."

Already he had begun to revise his expectations. Instead of the New Zealanders racing up to the Pescara line, the high ground overlooking the Sangro would have to be secured and held while Eighth Army bridged the river properly and ensured that the forward units could be adequately maintained. "A breakthrough attack by a complete Division, supported by 200 tanks, was clearly not possible unless we got dry weather; we do not seem to be able to get dry weather; therefore we must employ methods which can be used in wet conditions and which are independent of tanks." Yard by yard the Eighth Army bridgehead across the Sangro was extended until it was a mile and a half deep and seven miles wide. Then on 27 November the New Zealand Division crossed, and the dogfight for possession of the high ground began in earnest. "Tomorrow (28 Nov) I am attacking from the bridgehead with 78 DIV, 8 Ind DIV, centre (5 Corps), 2 NZ DIV, left (under Army HQ)."

The fight to gain the bridgehead had been arduous, he acknowledged in a letter to Brooke's deputy in London, General "Archie" Nye:

> In spite of continuous rain and acres of mud I managed to get a good bridgehead over the SANGRO; the trouble was to get any tanks and supporting weapons over, as the river was in flood and low level bridges merely disappeared. I took a good few risks.
>
> Twice I was pushed back to the river—once on my right, and once on my left. But we came again and refused to admit it couldn't be done.
>
> The troops were quite magnificent, and in the most foul conditions you can ever imagine; the SANGRO, normally, is about 80 feet wide, and it became swollen to 300 feet and rose several feet; the water was icy cold as heavy snow fell in the mountains where the river rises. Many were drowned.
>
> Eventually we succeeded.

Further success, however, was to be measured in yards. Within days Monty was acknowledging:

I am fighting a hell of a battle here. The right wing of my Army on the Adriatic side consists of three divisions. I am opposed there by 3½ divisions; this, combined with the mud, makes it not too easy.

I am now going to move troops over to my right, from my left—i.e. I am sending 5 DIV over.

I don't think we can get any spectacular results so long as it goes on raining; the whole country becomes a sea of mud and nothing on wheels or tracks can move off the roads. Given fine dry weather we could really get a move on.

My total casualties in the SANGRO battle were 113 officers, 1,650 Other Ranks—which was quite light considering what was achieved.

By dawn on 1 December 1943, Eighth Army had captured 1,000 German prisoners, and in a desperate attempt to stop the British breaking out, the Germans began to throw in units of 90th Light Division, reconstituted after its surrender to the New Zealand Division in May that year. "We now had to smash our way forward to the PESCARA before the enemy could recover," Monty noted in his diary, elated that he had apparently broken open the so-called Gustav Line.

Monty's satisfaction was short-lived, however. Not only did the Germans fiercely contest further movement forward by 5 Corps, but on 4 December the heavy rain caused the Sangro to rise another eight feet, and by the morning of 5 December "all bridges over the river were under water and most washed away. All communications across the SANGRO were cut. There was nothing to be done except to put all the RE on to the job, and to stop all movement. It rained in the mountains for 18 hours without a break." Offensive operations came to a standstill, and when on 7 December the New Zealanders tried to take Orsogna, insufficient supporting weapons could be brought up—"finally our troops were withdrawn clear of the village to save casualties."

Reinforcing 5 Corps with a division from his mountain flank, Monty attempted to rekindle his breakthrough to the Pescara River. But on 10 December the rain yet again brought operations to a standstill, and Eighth Army was fortunate to reach both Orsogna and Ortona, across the river Moro. Three further German divisions had been put into the line, one from Clark's front, one from Genoa and one from Venice, and it was unlikely that a British breakthrough was now attainable. Nor was one likely on Clark's Fifth Army front, as Monty quickly perceived when he flew over to see Clark on 8 December. Indeed both army commanders discounted each other's chances of offensive success, Clark because he found his own British 10 Corps so unwilling to take further heavy casualties and assumed Eighth Army was all the same, and Monty because he felt Clark's piecemeal fighting "gave the Germans ample time to regroup between the Fifth Army attacks."

What was clear was that time had run out, and the Allies had failed in their bid to reach Rome that year. Already on 18 November 1943 Monty had written to "Simbo" Simpson, Director of Military Operations:

> I have been thinking a great deal about the whole Italian campaign. I consider that we (the Allies) made a great many mistakes and have made a sad mess of it; if our strategy, and the conduct of the campaign, had been kept on a good wicket we would have had ROME by now easily. . . . If you make mistakes in war it is not easy to recover.

To Mountbatten, on 14 November, he had written the same, ending: "I understand Caesar used to go into winter quarters about this time, when he commanded an Army in these parts!! And very wise too!!"

By 23 November, Monty had begun to doubt his chances of reaching Rome in December, and begged Simpson to give him some idea of current War Office strategic thinking. "The great point that seems to want a firm decision is: where will we make our major effort from now on?" Italy or France, Monty counseled—but not both.

As Monty explained to Simpson a few days later, Italy ought to be held as a dormant front for the rest of the winter, with a drive to secure the Po valley in the spring of 1944, thus drawing away German strength from France, and providing an alternative front to reinforce in the case that Overlord—the name that had been given to the Allied invasion of France—proved less than one hundred per cent successful. But the state of the army in England worried him still, as it had all summer:

> We must get the Army in England in good shape, and tee-up the cross-Channel venture so that it could be launched when the moment is opportune.
>
> I am not certain from what I hear that the Army in England is in good shape. Some fresh air seems to be needed. And a good deal of dead wood needs to be cut out, and the whole show made younger, and more virile. . . .
>
> I have no doubt you will decide all these things in due course!!

In similar vein Monty wrote the next day to Sir Oliver Leese, one of the few corps commanders to have been brought home to England. "It would be interesting to hear your private views of 21 Army Group, Second Army, and the set-up in England generally. Eventually we must go across the channel, and the 'weapon' in England wants to be prepared. Can the present chaps do this?"

"Who Will Command Overlord?"

A lready in October 1943, General Eisenhower had heard from the American Secretary of the Navy that George C. Marshall "had been named supreme commander" for the invasion of Western Europe, and it was "probable" Ike would be recalled to Washington to take Marshall's seat as Chief of Staff of the U.S. Army.

Pressure to announce the appointment of a commander for the invasion of France had then waned. Only with the likelihood of stalemate in Italy and looming inter-Allied conferences in Cairo and Tehran, however, did the controversy once again rekindle. President Roosevelt pressed for a dual Supreme Commander, responsible for both the cross-Channel invasion and the Mediterranean, but Churchill torpedoed this—having told Bedell Smith at Algiers that Marshall was still "certain" to be Supreme Commander for the invasion of France—*if* the Americans still insisted upon a cross-Channel attack! As Bedell Smith reported, "the P[rime] M[inister] and the British are still unconvinced as to the wisdom of OVERLORD—the cross-Channel operations—and are persistent in their desire to pursue our advantages in the Mediterranean, especially through the Balkans."

This was a matter of great concern to the Soviet dictator, Joseph Stalin, since the Soviet armies were currently taking catastrophic casualties on the Eastern Front. On 29 November, at the Allied summit in Tehran, Stalin therefore looked both Churchill and Roosevelt in the eyes and posed his devastating question: "Who will command Overlord?"

Churchill, stunned by Stalin's directness, faltered. Roosevelt was forced to admit no commander had been chosen.

Visibly shamed—since the absence of a commander implied an absence of serious intent to mount a Second Front—Churchill offered to hold a meeting of the three heads of governments (i.e., Soviets, Americans and British) to choose a commander: an idiocy Stalin crushed by saying the Russians merely wished to know who the commander would be. Abashed—and concerned always lest the Russians make a separate pact with the Germans as they had in 1939, shortly before the invasion of Poland—Churchill promised a commander for the invasion would be appointed within a fortnight.

News of Churchill's promise now spread through American, British and Allied military headquarters in the Mediterranean. Tension—and bets—mounted as to who the Overlord commander would be. When Eisenhower returned from Cairo on 1 December 1943, it still looked as though General Marshall would be the Supreme Commander, with Sir Alan Brooke as the commander of Allied field armies under him and Eisenhower slated to go to Washington. On 5 December 1943, Eisenhower's naval ADC recorded, Eisenhower was "practically resigned to his prospective assignment."

Eisenhower disliked the idea of returning to Washington for a variety of reasons—personal as well as military. Though he had so far only visited his Eighth Army Commander on a single occasion during the entire Italian campaign (and not once during the Sicilian campaign), he still liked to think of himself as a battlefield commander. He was thus astonished and delighted when a cable from Marshall arrived at Allied Headquarters in Algiers on 10 December 1943, announcing, as Eisenhower's naval aide noted, that "Ike is to be Supreme Commander of the Allied Expeditionary Force in England after all." According to Roosevelt, who passed through Tunis later that day, Eisenhower's "demonstration of his grasp of the military situation," as well as "Ike's battlefront knowledge" were the main reasons for the appointment.

Monty, commanding Eighth Army in the mud and rain in the mountains above the river Moro, did not agree with Roosevelt's assessment of Eisenhower's "battlefront knowledge." Nor did Monty, in all honesty, share Churchill's high opinion of Alexander. There was nothing, however, he could do but wait—and hope against hope he would be summoned to England to command the invasion armies in Overlord, in preference to Alexander.

"We had this sort of Tactical Headquarters overlooking the Sangro and it was a very simple Tac headquarters—just tents and the two caravans and the ACV [Armoured Command Vehicle]," Major "Bill" Mather later recalled. "And one day an Australian fighter pilot was shot down quite near us. Monty saw a parachute going down, so he said 'Send somebody out, bring him back to lunch.' "

This done, Monty had the pilot seated beside him at lunch in the mess tent. "Now Monty had decided to rewrite the Principles of War," Mather explained, "at least to introduce his new principle of war, the first and greatest principle of war, which was: 'Win the air battle first.' And he was very proud of this and kept telling everybody, 'You know the first principle of war? Win the air battle first!'

"About halfway through lunch he turned to this Australian and said, 'Now, do you know what the first and greatest Principle of War is?'

" 'Well, I don't know much about principles of war, but I should say it's *stop frigging about!*'

"Monty was absolutely speechless," Mather recalled.

In his artless way, the Australian had summed up Monty's feelings exactly.

Daffodil

The truth was, the strain of almost eighteen months of continuous battle command had begun to tell. Sir Alan Brooke, when he finally visited Monty on the way back from Cairo on 14 December 1943, found Monty was "looking tired and definitely wants a rest and a change."

Was Monty to get it, though? As Roosevelt had been unwilling to release his Army Chief of Staff, General Marshall, so Churchill proved unwilling to release *his* Army Chief of Staff, Sir Alan Brooke—but remained undecided whom to choose as invasion armies commander for Overlord, telegraphing Clement Attlee, the Deputy Prime Minister, on 14 December that he had "not made up my mind whether it will be Alexander or Montgomery but the CIGS is staying with Alexander now and when he rejoins me in a few days I shall be able to make a decision."

Brooke was now also in two minds. Time after time he had chronicled in his diary his misgivings about Alexander. "Alexander, charming as he is, fills me with gloom," he had noted on 18 November 1943.

"He cannot see big . . . he will never have either the personality or the vision to command three services." Nevertheless Brooke did not rule out Alexander as the appropriate armies commander for Overlord, for he continued to have grave misgivings about Monty's ability to get on with his American counterparts. "He [Monty] requires a lot of educating to make him see the whole situation and the War as a whole outside the Eighth Army orbit," Brooke had written in June 1943. "A difficult mixture to handle, brilliant commander in action and trainer of men, but liable to commit untold errors, due to lack of tact, lack of appreciation of other people's outlook. It is most distressing that the Americans do not like him, and it will always be a difficult matter to have him fighting in close proximity to them."

Still undecided after visiting Monty and Alexander in Italy, Brooke then returned to Tunis, where Churchill had taken to his bed with suspected pneumonia, and for some considerable time they discussed the new appointments, exchanging views by telegram with the Deputy Prime Minister and the War Cabinet in London—but without asking the newly designated Supreme Commander, General Eisenhower!

Eisenhower, by contrast, knew exactly whom he wanted to command the Allied armies under him, writing on 17 December to Marshall to say that he would like a "single ground force commander" for Overlord. However, he did not want Monty. "If the British could give him to me, I would like to have Alexander. My conception of his job would be that his eventual assignment would be in command of the British Army Group but that until the time for employment of two complete army groups arrived, he would be my single ground commander. Under him a British Army and an American Army will carry out the direct assaults and will expand as rapidly as possible." With this, Eisenhower left to see Alexander, and to pay only his second visit to Monty's Italian front in four long months.

Monty hoped Eisenhower would put him out of his misery. "We all thought we would hear the answer—but we didn't," de Guingand later recalled. Indeed, so anxious did Monty become, after Eisenhower's departure, that he even arranged a set of codes with "Simbo" Simpson at the War Office—names of garden flowers each denoting a possible combination of appointments.

Almost a year and a half had now passed since the last round of musical chairs, when Churchill and Brooke traveled to Egypt and sacked General Auchinleck—but chose an inappropriate commander to take over Eighth Army: Lieutenant General Richard Gott. "The 'great ones,' having decided how they will win the war, will now presumably re-group the generals to get on with it," Monty had written of Churchill's summit with Roosevelt and Stalin. "I suppose they know the real and true form; I often wonder if they really do; if they make mistakes, and get the generals in the wrong places, we will have endless trouble."

On tenterhooks—for Eisenhower left Italy knowing as little as Monty whom the British government would appoint as his Overlord ground commander—Monty concentrated on the task at hand, mopping up at Orsogna and Ortona after the bitter Sangro battle. "Our casualties since the SANGRO battle began on 27/28 Nov have been as follows," he noted in his diary, and entered the figures: almost 5,000 men. The 8th Indian Division, in particular, had already lost so many troops and had so few reinforcements that it would have to be taken right out of line. There was no chance on earth of continuing to Rome before March 1944 at the earliest, he had told Brooke, but having gained the Sangro, Eighth Army must secure a strong defensive line through Orsogna and Ortona, he insisted. If this could be done, operations could be closed down on Christmas Day, and thereafter for a full week. Eighth Army would then push on towards its next objective: Pescara.

But would Monty still be in command of Eighth Army? "Poppy" was the code word for Alexander's departure to become Allied Army C-in-C Western Europe; "Daffodil" if Monty was chosen.

Before Simpson could send the agreed code word, however, a signal arrived direct from the CIGS, Sir Alan Brooke. The Secretary of State for War, Sir James Grigg, had replied to Churchill's cable that the War Cabinet, alarmed by the choice of the easygoing Eisenhower instead of the tough, no-nonsense Marshall, were "disposed to think Montgomery would be a better choice than Alexander for 'Overlord.'" Churchill's pneumonia made him less willful than normal, and Brooke had had little difficulty in finally proposing Monty for Overlord.

It has been decided you are to come back to U.K. to . . . command 21 Army Group the date to be decided according military exigencies. This decision is subject however to governmental approval but there is NO reason to suppose this will NOT repeat NOT be forthcoming. This is for your personal information and is NOT repeat NOT to be disclosed to anyone else.

The date was 23 December 1943. The next day, Christmas Eve, confirmation was received. There was low cloud and heavy rain, making flying impossible. But Monty was over the moon.

Farewell to Eighth Army

"This is a very fine job," Monty remarked of the new Overlord appointment in his diary, "and it will be about the biggest thing I have ever had to handle." Indeed he was quite certain that Overlord would be the deciding battle of the war.

On 27 December, Monty arrived in North Africa. "I am in Algiers discussing the problem with Eisenhower and Bedell Smith," Monty wrote to Sir Alan Brooke. "Eisenhower has told me that he wants me to be his head soldier and to take complete charge of the land battle."

From Algiers Monty returned to his tactical headquarters in Italy on 28 December 1943. He had already drawn up a list of officers he wished to take home with him, and had cabled it to the Military Secretary in London. On 30 December he convened all officers and men of his Main Eighth Army Headquarters in Vasto, together with corps and divisional commanders, to say goodbye.

It was a moving occasion, and the tension was high. In August 1942 Monty had assembled, in the desert at Alamein, the headquarters staff of a beaten army—an army which had been run back 700 miles across North Africa and had suffered over 100,000 casualties. Now, eighteen months later, he was leaving an army that had victoriously fought its way across North Africa, had conquered Sicily, and had successfully secured southern Italy for the Allies; an army unbeaten in battle; an army whose reputation stood perhaps higher than that of any other British army in the twentieth century; and, most remarkable of all, an army which by December 1943 contained only a single division that had served in the desert campaign.

In his final Farewell Message to the troops of Eighth Army, Monty had written, "It is difficult to express to you adequately what this parting means to me."

I am leaving officers and men who have been my comrades during months of hard and victorious fighting and whose courage and devotion to duty always filled me with admiration. I feel I have many friends among the soldiery of this great Army. I do not know if you will miss me; but I will miss you more than I can say, and especially will I miss the personal contacts, and the cheerful greetings we exchanged together when we passed each other on the road. . . . What can I say to you as I go away?

When the heart is full it is not easy to speak. But I would say this to you:

You have made this Army what it is. You have made its name a household word all over the world. Therefore you must uphold its good name and its traditions.

Monty's address to the senior officers of Eighth Army in Vasto, though unscripted, would never be forgotten. Even the sometimes sardonic BBC correspondent Denis Johnston was moved, recalling Monty "talking away on the stage, having the time of his life. He was sorry to go, he said, and to take with him so many experienced officers. But duty called, and he was leaving the Army in the charge of a good soldier—a fighting soldier, who would maintain the traditions of the past. But before he went, he would give them a few pointers—he would tell them how to win wars, so that they could continue to do their best, even without him.

"He did not put it quite like that, but it is what he meant; and as I listened to him, I thought to myself, what a headache, what a bore, what a bounder he must be to those on roughly the same level in the service. And at the same time what a great man he is as a leader of troops, and how right he is to wear funny hats so that the soldiers along the roads will know their general and answer his friendly wave. Maybe he is not as great as he thinks he is, but by God there's no getting away from the fact that he out-foxed Rommel, and turned the men of the Desert Army from the shoulder-shrugging cynics they used to be into the confident, self-advertising crowd they are now."

Part Six

OVERLORD

Monty leads the D-Day armies, Birmingham,
England, 1944.

A Visit to Marrakesh

S wallowing his personal vexation over Monty's, rather than Alexander's, appointment to command the Allied field armies in the cross-Channel invasion, Eisenhower nobly asked Monty to accept the offer of a bigger private airplane than his current C-47 (his Flying Fortress had crashed in Sicily) to take him back to England. "I do not look with favor on risking your neck on a two engine transport," Eisenhower signaled. "I can arrange the very highest priority for you and whatever small staff may be accompanying you personally and I strongly urge that you allow me to do this."

Monty thus flew to Britain in a giant C-54, taking with him an unknown young French resistance leader, François Mitterrand. On the way, however, he was invited to stay the night with Winston Churchill at his villa in Marrakesh, and it was there, at 6 P.M. on 31 December 1943, that Monty found Churchill "in bed reading a copy of OVERLORD"—the current Allied plan for the invasion of France, prepared by General Frederick Morgan, chief of staff to the Supreme Commander Designate of the Second Front and known to all by his Russian-sounding acronym, COSSAC.

Churchill was "recovering from his recent illness and did not look very fit," Monty confided in his diary. "He said I was to read OVERLORD and give him my opinion about it. I replied that I was not his military adviser. He then said he was very anxious to have my first impressions of OVERLORD, which I had never yet seen. So I said I would read it through and would give him my 'first impressions' in the morning."

The COSSAC Plan

T
he next day, sitting beside Churchill in his car on a two-hour drive to the Atlas Mountains, Monty went over the invasion plan with the Prime Minister.

Targeted at Normandy rather than the Pas de Calais, Morgan's COSSAC plan envisaged a landing by three divisions across sandy beaches at Arromanches, near Caen, the major road center controlling access to Normandy from north and northwest France. In charge of this three-divisional landing would be the Commander of the First U.S. Army, General Bradley, with a Canadian, a British and an American corps built up under his aegis over the succeeding week of fighting. Only then would the British Commander of 21 Army Group assume battlefield command of the bridgehead. Under him, General Bradley's First U.S. Army would absorb all American troops, while the British and Canadian soldiers would come under command of a newly created First Canadian Army.

As if this command plan were not complicated enough, General Morgan envisaged a campaign in Normandy whereby the Allies established a narrow corridor to Caen, then swung west more than a hundred miles to take Cherbourg, then—while sending an American subsidiary column down the west Cotentin Peninsula to Brittany— struck back due east from Caen to the Seine and to Paris.

In Monty's view the plan—though he liked the notion of attacking in Normandy, at the furthest extremity of the German defenses in France—had not the remotest chance of succeeding. Not only was the size of the initial Overlord invasion force far too small, Monty explained to Churchill, but it committed the assaulting army to the same error that had doomed the Allies at Salerno: namely the confinement of the Allied invasion to one easily contained beachhead.

Worse still, in terms of subsequent buildup, was the attempt to land too many formations, both on D-Day and during the succeeding days, across the same few beaches—beaches that would become fatally congested. "By D + 12 a total of 16 divisions have been landed on the same beaches as were used in the initial landings. This would lead," Monty pointed out to the Prime Minister, "to the most appalling confusion on the beaches, and the smooth development of the land battle would be made extremely difficult—if not impossible."

The answer, by contrast, was simple: an attack, as at Alamein and in Sicily, in such strength and magnitude *on the first day* that the enemy could not possibly repel it. "The initial landings must be made on the widest possible front," Monty emphasized to Churchill. Simplicity of reinforcement was crucial. "British and American areas of landing must be kept separate," he warned. "Corps must be able to develop their operations from their own beaches, and other Corps must NOT land through those beaches." Once ashore, moreover, "operations must be developed in such a way that a good port is secured quickly for the British and for American forces. Each should have its own port or group of ports." Air supremacy was vital, too: "The air battle must be won before the operation is launched. We must then aim at success in the land battle by the speed and violence of our operations."

Churchill, as in the Egyptian desert in August 1942, was won over by the clarity and authority of a commander he had only reluctantly appointed. Though unimpressed by Morgan's plan, Monty was obviously "a firm believer in the operation," Churchill recorded, "and I was very pleased at this."

When Churchill then suggested they drive up to his favorite panoramic viewpoint, Monty asked Churchill to stop the car, "got out and walked straight up the hill 'to keep himself in training,' as he put it. I warned him not to waste his vigour, considering what was coming." Churchill later recalled with wry amusement, "that athletics are one thing and strategy another. These admonitions were in vain. The General was in the highest spirits; he leaped about the rocks like an antelope, and I felt a strong reassurance that all would be well."

Monty's Harangue

In truth, Monty was deeply worried by the outlook. He had been pressing for Overlord ever since his victory at Alamein, the year before. On 27 November 1942, indeed, he had begged Brooke to consider the idea of mounting Overlord in 1943. "Given a large number of Americans," he had written, "I believe the invasion of Western Europe could be brought off successfully next summer about June when the weather is good. But the Army in England would have to be tuned up, and made battle worthy in no uncertain manner."

Now, thirteen months later, the Second Front was still more a fiction than a reality, reducing Monty almost to despair by the way—as in Sicily and as in Italy—critical Allied military operations were planned by inexperienced staffs on paper and only handed over to their commanders when it was too late for them to make the alterations that would ensure their battlefield success. As he recorded in his diary, "I impressed on him [Churchill] the need to get experienced fighting commanders 'in' on any future operational plans early. . . . In every operation in which I have been brought into in this war, changes in plan have been necessary and there has been all too little time, e.g., HUSKY [Sicily] in May, 1943, and now OVERLORD did not look too good."

Leaving Churchill to recuperate in Morocco, Monty flew to England, while Eisenhower flew to Washington for consultations with General Marshall and the War Department.

Monty's new 21 Army Group Headquarters in West London, controlling the million British and Canadian soldiers training for D-Day, had been set up in his old school, St. Paul's, and it was there at 9 A.M. on 3 January 1944, the morning after his arrival, that Monty held his first, historic Overlord conference—attended not only by his new 21 Army Group staff but also by Eisenhower's chief of staff, General Bedell Smith, and members of Eisenhower's new Supreme Command staff, who were to occupy Norfolk House in Piccadilly, taking over General Morgan's COSSAC organization.

To begin the conference, Monty asked for a brief presentation of the latest Overlord plan by the senior officers of COSSAC's planning section, General West and Brigadier McLean. "21 Army Group churned OVERLORD around half-heartedly before Monty got there," McLean later confided to the American Official Historian. "Things dragged along. Monty arrived in January 1944—couple of weeks before Ike. Then I had to explain OVERLORD to Monty and [Bedell] Smith. Went into great detail."

When McLean was done, Monty stood up. There would be a pause of twenty minutes, he declared.

Thereafter it was Monty's turn to speak. "Monty gave his harangue," McLean recalled. "Was not convinced of my arguments. Thought that we could land more troops in the first assault from the craft we had." Moreover, in Monty's view it was no good attempting to drive inland towards Caen with only a narrow corridor for reinforcements, entailing congestion, muddle and confusion. Caen was an important road center, Monty conceded—but the vital need was for a port, not a town, and Morgan's plan did not give him much confidence that Cherbourg could be swiftly captured from a tiny, three-divisional landing north of Caen, more than a hundred miles away. Why, he asked, could the Allies not land further west *also*—even on the west coast of the Cotentin or Cherbourg Peninsula?

Morgan's American deputy, Major General Ray Barker, vividly recalled the challenge. "Monty took the floor," he remembered. "In grandiose style he said the plan was too restricted. Wanted to attack north side of Brittany Peninsula or at least as far south as Granville and St Malo. Wanted to broaden left flank, but realize[d] could [not] go too far because of shore batteries. Said he wanted the planners to study the situation and give him an answer the next day. It was quite clear that Monty was the ground commander. Entirely within his rights."

Monty had confronted the planners, who had labored for a year and a half on a Supreme Command plan without a Supreme Commander. The meeting broke up in some consternation.

"Next day Monty challenged all our figures. Quoted Sicily to us," McLean recalled. Though Monty moderated his objection after Admiral Ramsay explained why he could not "guarantee landings on the west side of the Cotentin," there seemed no good reason why the Allies could not land nearer to Cherbourg, around Carentan. "On the second day's meeting," General Barker recalled, "Monty said if we can't go any further west, we must at least go to Utah Beach [near Carentan]. This was fully accepted that day. It was decided that we would prepare an outline and develop a statement of requirements in craft."

History, military history, was being made—in hours now, not months or years. On the third day, McLean summarized, "we reduced his demands to extending to 'Sword' beach [north of Caen] . . . and to the Cotentin": a sixty-mile front. In order to ensure success on his west flank, moreover, Monty declared he was willing to switch the airborne forces allotted for the capture of Caen, in the east: "He decided not to use airborne for Caen, but to land on the Vire and the neck of the Cotentin . . . stressed Cherbourg heavily, which we didn't. This is partially why he wanted the Cotentin. On the third day Monty took the line we must have more craft. He said it must be a five division front or no show. *Give me this or get someone else.*"

The new invasion commander obviously meant business—and was prepared to resign rather than carry out an impractical plan, involving millions of Allied lives. "A wave of relief came over us," Brigadier McLean admitted to the American Official Historian—though his boss, General West, remained "extremely insistent on the three division assault. He and [General] Bull [Eisenhower's chief of operations] made a last despairing visit to Monty at night. He chased them away. . . . Monty's action was like a breath of fresh air."

Ralph Ingersoll, an Intelligence officer who was later to be Montgomery's most vitriolic critic in the United States, recorded the feelings of American planners involved in the COSSAC plan: "Now that the great Montgomery was in command, I think we all experienced a kind of relief; at least we no longer carried our dreadful burden of responsibility."

Honor Is Satisfied

S o impressed was General Omar Bradley, the First U.S. Army Commander, when he attended Monty's first gathering of the Overlord army commanders on 7 January 1944, that he not only accepted Monty's new plan as a *fait accompli*, but even surrendered his right—enshrined in Morgan's COSSAC plan—to command the "assault phase" of the landings themselves.

Monty's new plan envisaged not one but two Allied armies landing abreast, as in Sicily. On the west flank, the conference minutes recorded, "the task of the American army will be the capture of Cherbourg and the clearing of the Cherbourg Peninsula. They will subsequently develop operations to the south and west." On the east flank of the beachhead would be not a Canadian army—as Morgan had planned—but a British army, whose task would be "to operate to the south to prevent any interference with the American army from the East."

Such complete clarity of conception was much to Bradley's liking, after four and a half months commanding First U.S. Army in England without any real faith in either Morgan or Paget, Monty's predecessor at 21 Army Group. Thus when Monty said he wanted to create a truly Allied headquarters at 21 Army Group for the Overlord invasion and battle, Bradley offered Monty a number of his own senior American staff.

There were, however, limits to Bradley's coalition loyalty. Given the importance of the British-Canadian shield to protect the American First Army against counterattack from the powerful German Panzer army being held in the Pas de Calais that Monty had declared his intention of landing five brigade groups in the British sector, leaving only three to be put ashore in the American sector. "Commander FUSA [First United States Army] stressed it would be difficult to explain to the American public the small U.S. part," Monty's military assistant recorded.

It was Monty's first taste in Overlord of the ramifications of his new broom on public relations in America. "To be discussed on the 12th," his assistant added.

As a result of Bradley's objection, Admiral Ramsay agreed to furnish enough transport vessels and naval forces for five American brigades to land on D-Day.

Honor was satisfied. The British and Americans would land in parity with one another.

Starting Another War

Immediately the plan had been altered to his satisfaction, Monty left to meet the men who would have to fight the battle. On 13 January 1944 he addressed all the generals of the Overlord field armies, British and American, together with their principal staff officers, then packed his bags and left London on a five-day tour of Bradley's First U.S. Army. "I was anxious to visit the American troops at once, and to talk to them, and so gain an impression of the quality of the American Divisions. It was also essential that they should see me, and that personal touch should be established between us," he recorded in his diary. "I arranged that there would be about three parades of about 3,000 to 4,000 each in each Div area, and I would address the officers and men using a loud speaker. I would see them and talk to them; they would see me; in this way I hoped that mutual confidence would be established."

The tour, organized by Bradley's staff, was certainly a novelty, for no British field commander, whether in North Africa or Italy, had ever gone out of his way to assemble and address large numbers of American troops on the eve of battle. "Before D-Day in England he went round, as he called it, to 'binge up' the people," recalled Lieutenant Colonel Trumbull Warren, Monty's Canadian personal assistant, who traveled with him—"sales talk, you know! He would commandeer a big common and he would have a jeep in the center and he would get up on the hood—what you call the bonnet: 'Now get gathered round here fellows—this is how we're going to knock the Germans all to hell,' and so on.

"The first one he did with the Americans, he was very nervous. He didn't really know the Americans. And he got up there and he called them around and said: 'Now I don't know you people, but I know General Eisenhower—Ike and I are good friends and we're going to do this business together. Now,' he said, 'I've never been to the States, but Ike has asked me to come over after the war and visit your country. And I hear so much about it, and I don't know whether to start in the North or the South.'

"And some black soldier at the back shouted: 'What the hell are you trying to do? Start another war?' "

Monty had learned his first American lesson—the subject of North and South being dropped from all subsequent addresses. However, his abiding message touched the men's hearts in an extraordinary manner, for with a growing grasp of the psychology of citizen soldiers, Monty recognized their desire to see the end of the war and to return to their homes. Around this perception he cast his simple spell: the heavy responsibility carried by Allied troops about to launch the Second Front; the need to rehearse their roles in order to carry out their forthcoming task professionally; thence to go home to wives and families proud men.

Some troops sniggered; some found Monty's clipped English accent and his swagger irritating. However, the vast majority of American troops were amazed that the new Commander-in-Chief of armies totaling almost two million men should come to speak and be known to them, personally, before the battle. One divisional commander, General Leroy Watson, was unhappy that "every man of the [3rd Armored] division did not get to hear and see our new Allied ground commander. I am sure that all those who did see and hear him were instilled with a feeling of great confidence in our leader," he stated in a General Order to read to every man in the division on 18 January 1944. "To know him is to understand his sincerity of purpose, complete confidence in himself and in his plans."

Unfortunately, once Eisenhower arrived from Washington, not everyone accepted Monty *was* the Allied ground commander, let alone his new plans.

In Sole Charge of the Land Battle

E isenhower had given Monty authority to act as his deputy until he reached London—but had no idea that Monty would so radically alter the COSSAC plan, nor that he would start taking his gospel to the troops so quickly.

At a press conference on 17 January 1944, therefore, when asked point-blank if Monty was to be the Land Forces Commander in Chief for the invasion, Eisenhower failed to answer, cautioning reporters not to "go off on the end of a limb"—indeed, when reports came in of Monty's address to the U.S. 29th Division, quoting Monty directly ("I came home the other day from Italy to take command of the British Army and the American Army of which General Eisenhower is the Supreme Commander and he has put one Army, the First American Army, under me for the battle"), the report was actually censored.

Concern about public perception in America was the problem, Eisenhower's chief of staff pointed out the next day. "Ike again will be the target for those critics who say the British have cleverly accepted an American as Supreme Commander but have infiltrated British commanders for land, sea and air, even though a majority of the troops are American and the ratio of British to American planes in the U.K. is 4 to 7. This is something," Eisenhower's naval aide noted in his office diary, "on which we shall be on the defensive, and therefore Beetle [Bedell Smith] was anxious for Ike ultimately to take over the ground operations, particularly after we have two army groups and he can get his advanced command post in France."

To clarify the situation, therefore, Eisenhower convened his first Supreme Commander's Conference on Friday, 21 January 1944. Eisenhower's Deputy Supreme Commander for Overlord, Air Marshal Arthur Tedder; the Navel C-in-C, Admiral Sir Bertram Ramsay; the Air Forces C-in-C, Sir Trafford Leigh-Mallory; the Supreme Commander's chief of staff, General Bedell Smith; the COSSAC chief of staff, General "Freddie" Morgan; the Commander of First U.S. Army, General Bradley; the Commander of Second British Army, General Anderson; the Commander of the American Air Forces, General Spaatz; the new chief of staff, 21 Army Group, Major General de Guingand—all the senior commanders and staff officers of Supreme Headquarters and the field armies gathered at Norfolk House as Brigadier McLean once more outlined the original COSSAC plan.

Monty then stood up—and again demolished it.

For General Morgan the occasion was excruciating. Though the minutes of the meeting, kept among Eisenhower's papers, were denied to historians for almost forty years, they clearly bore out Monty's notion of a British shield at Caen: the American army seizing Cherbourg, then driving towards the Loire, while in the meantime "the BRITISH-CANADIAN forces would deal with the enemy main body approaching from the EAST and South-East." Surviving witnesses, moreover, clearly recalled Monty's address after the war. In particular General Charles West, the chief of the operations staff at COSSAC, in 1947 explained to Dr. Pogue, the American Official Historian of the Supreme Command, that it was "true that at first Norfolk House conference with Monty he [Monty] stressed the firm left flank, which would make Caen a hinge," something which West felt to be entirely logical, since even "in our original plan we supposed the Germans would counter-attack at Caen. Germans couldn't afford to give way there. *That had to be the hinge.*"

To achieve this British-Canadian shield or hinge, Monty was determined, as at Alamein, to break into the vital sector of the German defenses, push out his British armor, and *force the Germans to counterattack on ground of British choosing*, while behind them the Americans "crumbled" Rommel's Cherbourg and Brittany formations. "In the initial stages, we should concentrate on gaining control quickly of the main centres of road communications," Monty declared. "We should then deeply push our armoured formations between and beyond these centres and deploy them on suitable ground. In this way it would be difficult for the enemy to bring up his reserves and get them past these armoured formations."

"As at present planned," the minutes of the first Overlord conference at Norfolk House solemnly recorded, "he [Monty] did not consider that 'OVERLORD' was a sound Operation of War. He had throughout been considering how he wanted to fight the land battle; and it remained to be seen whether the Navy and the Air would be able to meet his requirements. . . . As for the timing of the Operation, in order that we should be in a position to achieve our 'quick success' it was desirable that we should leave ourselves the maximum number of months of good campaigning weather. From the point of view of the army, therefore, the Operation should if possible begin early in May."

Until now, Eisenhower had remained undecided—particularly as he had "inherited" the COSSAC organization in its entirety, and had not the heart to sack Morgan or any of his colleagues. Monty's presentation, however, proved decisive. To Morgan's embarrassment—and lasting resentment—the COSSAC plan was now officially thrown out, and Monty's plan, treating Cherbourg as the Allies' first and major priority, was formally accepted by Eisenhower. "The Supreme Commander agreed with General MONTGOMERY that it was desirable that the assault should be strengthened and that CHERBOURG should rapidly be captured," the minutes of the conference recorded. Moreover, to confirm his faith in Monty, Eisenhower "proposed that General MONTGOMERY should be left in sole charge of the ground battle."

Monty's new plan had been affirmed—and his command of the Anglo-American armies too.

Anvil

"After detailed examination of the tactical plan I clearly understand Montgomery's original objection to the narrowness of the assault. Beaches are too few and too restricted to depend upon them as avenues through which all our original build-up would have to flow," Eisenhower reported to his boss in Washington, General Marshall. "We must broaden out to gain quick initial success, secure more beaches for build-up and particularly to get a force at once into the Cherbourg Peninsula behind the natural defensive barrier separating that feature from the mainland. In this way there would be a reasonable hope of gaining the port in short order. We must have this."

"We had a meeting of Cs-in-C (Self, Ramsey, Leigh-Mallory) under the chairmanship of Ike, and my revised plan has now been accepted in all its details," Monty simultaneously informed his successor at Eighth Army, General Leese. However, he added wearily, "this will have repercussions in other theatres of war, and so we have now got to get the Allied Chiefs of Staff to agree. It is all very exhausting work. And it is curious how history repeats itself and we never seem to learn from our mistakes; it is 'Husky' all over again with all the frightful troubles in the planning stage. But this time it is very serious as if Overlord were to fail, or to be only a partial success, it would put the war back months and months."

The "repercussions" largely related to the desire of the American chiefs of staff to start up a third front, on the Mediterranean coast of southern France near Marseilles—a suggestion put to Stalin at the Tehran summit by President Roosevelt, without prior consultation with Churchill, and code-named "Anvil." Anxious lest the Allies develop the Italian campaign into a thrust towards central Europe and Russia through the Balkans, Stalin had applauded the Marseilles scheme, and Marshall had subsequently ordered Eisenhower to include it in his strategic planning.

From the moment he heard of Operation Anvil, Monty was against it. Once again Eisenhower was, in Monty's view, failing to focus on his primary task: Overlord. If Anvil was canceled, and merely mounted as a threat (in the same way as Fortitude, the operation which was currently being organized under Colonel Johnny Bevan to deceive the Germans into thinking the Allies would land in the Pas de Calais area), then all the Anvil landing craft, naval and air support, troops and maintenance could be concentrated instead upon Overlord, thus guaranteeing it could be mounted in May.

Eisenhower, however, aware that his mentor General Marshall favored Anvil, turned down Monty's plea, asking him to remember "that the Russians had been led to expect that that Operation [Anvil] would take place. . . . We had to make recommendations to the Combined Chiefs of Staff not later than 1st February as to the future of 'ANVIL'. . . . We must consider whether we could not manage a successful 'OVERLORD' without damaging 'ANVIL.' "

Thus, though Monty got his way over the Normandy landings, he failed to eliminate Eisenhower's penchant for Anvil—with potentially fatal repercussions on Overlord once Rommel began to infuse his legendary charisma into the German defenders in France.

Shingle

_____

S ince 15 January 1944, Rommel had been given tactical command of all Axis troops in Europe facing invasion from Britain.
For Monty this was of special interest, since he was the only Allied commander to have defeated Rommel in battle. He had greatly
looked forward to a renewed military confrontation with Rommel in
Italy—a duel Hitler had thwarted by removing Rommel from command in Italy in October 1943.

Now the contest was to be revived, on the beaches of northwest Europe. Tirelessly Rommel toured the German defenses, and though he
misjudged the real site of invasion (he felt it was bound to come in the
Pas de Calais area, or at least north of the Somme), his energy and in-
genuity were such that even the less-well-defended Normandy and
Brittany coasts received the full blast of his endeavors. He too became
headline news in the German press—a popularity he encouraged because it undoubtedly raised the morale of the soldiers defending the
coast.

That he could defeat Rommel, Monty had no doubt. At Alamein
Rommel had laid hundreds of thousands of mines and had inspected
every inch of the front, but although it had led to a much "rougher
house" than many had expected, it was always clear to Monty that, if
the British could successfully smash a way into Rommel's defenses,
then by sheer guts and dogged determination they must eventually
prize open Rommel's overextended line. For Monty, Overlord presented itself in an almost identical way. The Allies could not conceal
their intention of mounting an offensive; but where that blow would
fall, and when, were matters the Allies _could_ disguise, as at Alamein:
forcing Rommel to spread his forces and subjecting the defenders to a
war of nerves.

About his own Allied colleagues, and particularly his superiors,

Monty was less sure. Churchill, he felt, was in his pocket; Brooke too was solidly behind him; but Eisenhower's desire to have his cake and eat it, by mounting both Anvil and Overlord, as well as continuing the offensive campaign in Italy, reminded him uncomfortably of Eisenhower throughout 1943: particularly Eisenhower's final fantasy in Algiers, Operation Shingle.

Designed to bypass German opposition by landing behind the German lines at Anzio, further up Italy's Mediterranean coast, Eisenhower's plan was carried out on 21 January 1944. "Shingle has started well," Eisenhower's naval ADC stated, recording the excitement in Eisenhower's headquarters two days later. It was, he claimed, a "brilliant maneuver" of which Eisenhower was the true progenitor, whatever the British press might say: "Under Ike's direction SHINGLE was already well advanced. . . . Thus another [i.e., Alexander] gets credit for a long-laid plan which developed under Ike. But the truth eventually 'will out.' "

The truth, however, never did out. Within a week Anzio was acknowledged to be a failure, "a stranded whale" in Churchill's vivid phrase—and without hope this time of miraculous Eighth Army rescue. (Butcher deliberately excised this passage from the published version of his office diary, *Three Years with Eisenhower*, and the passage was only declassified by the American government in the 1970s, after Eisenhower had ceased to be President and had died.)

Eisenhower, meanwhile, found it hard to credit the flop of the Anzio landing—indeed, he attempted to excuse it in a long cable to Marshall a few days later, wagering that "bad weather in the early days of the landing made it impossible to give the necessary mobility to strong armored detachments that could have safely pushed forward across the Appian Way and secured the high ground to the east thereof." In his diary he nevertheless recognized that, "with SHINGLE stalemated," the resources for a landing at Marseilles would have to go into Italy to rescue the troops surrounded at Anzio. "It looks as if ANVIL is doomed," Eisenhower concluded. "I hate this—in spite of my recognition of the fact that Italian fighting will be some compensation for a strong ANVIL."

What irked Eisenhower was to be thought timid. "Generally speaking the British columnists," he complained in his diary, "try to show that my contributions in the Mediterranean were administrative accomplishments and 'friendliness in welding an Allied team.' They dislike to believe that I had anything particular to do with campaigns. They don't use the words 'initiative' and 'boldness' in talking of me—but often do in speaking of Alex and Monty."

It was this understandable desire to be seen as a bold commander which now led Eisenhower to resurrect Anvil—for when, on 11 February, the American chiefs of staff decided to "pass the buck" and leave the Anvil decision up to Eisenhower as Supreme Commander in the field, Eisenhower refused to cancel the operation, even though it would cut down the strength of the Overlord landings and delay them till June.

Such procrastination drove Monty, as a no-nonsense combat soldier, almost crazy. "On return to London," he noted in his own diary on 10 February, "I found that telegrams were still going on between London and Washington as to the whole question of 'ANVIL,' and the five-div lift for OVERLORD. The Combined [i.e., Allied] Chiefs of Staff had been invited to come to London to discuss the matter but had declined to come; instead they had given EISENHOWER full power to act for them. But EISENHOWER seemed to be trying to please both parties and did not come down hard on the side of OVERLORD; he still wanted an 'ANVIL.' "

That evening Monty went again to see Churchill. "I told him that we were fighting hard in ITALY, and would have to fight hard in OVERLORD; to open up a third front in Southern FRANCE was quite absurd. I also said that a successful OVERLORD required a five-divisional assault with a good build-up behind it, and to cut this down in any way would be to risk failure. The Prime Minister agreed."

Eisenhower, torn between his loyalty to Marshall, Monty's plea that every Allied resource be thrown into Overlord, and the desire to "keep his options open," did not agree. "Ike and Beetle had been in a sweat because of questions relating to OVERLORD," Eisenhower's aide noted in his office diary—questions that were "boiling and Beetle had advised Ike against leaving London at this time."

It was in this frustrating atmosphere, with Eisenhower postponing Overlord by a full month in order to be able to mount both Overlord and Anvil, that Monty convened his second conference of Allied army commanders on 11 February at his headquarters at St. Paul's.

The Miracle of the War

A clear Allied approach to amphibious invasion was vital, Monty felt, so that the Allied commanders could move straight on to the next problem: the development of the Normandy battle on land. "I emphasized the need for simplicity," he noted in his diary. "Complicated fire-support methods" were to be canceled. Given the propensity for things to go wrong in war it was essential, he declared, to get all five divisions ashore on the first tide—with their own supporting weapons and with tanks. In contrast to the original COSSAC plan for a "silent" assault, he wanted "heavy air bombing before, and at, H hour" (between daybreak and sunrise). The maximum number of special tanks were to be put ashore *with* the first troops—DD-tanks, Arks, Flails, Ploughs and Snakes—"so as to develop the land battle quickly."

General Anderson, the Commander of the British Second Army, had quickly been replaced by Lieutenant General Miles Dempsey, whom Monty had "brought on" as a young corps commander in Sicily. Meanwhile it had also been decided, with Monty's approval, that General Patton should command the Third U.S. Army—against Bradley's wishes.

Bradley, who had served under Patton as a corps commander in Sicily, was wholly against Patton's reemployment in the cross-Channel invasion. "Had it been left up to me," the First U.S. Army Commander later confessed, "frankly I would not have chosen Patton. I had so many misgivings about George. I had seen so many things he had done in Sicily . . . that I disapproved heartily of him. I was soured on him. I didn't think he was too good an Army Commander."

By contrast, Bradley considered Monty an excellent commander for the invasion. "Psychologically," he reflected later, "the choice of Montgomery as British commander for the OVERLORD assaults came as a stimulant to us all." Even Patton waxed complimentary about Monty in his diary: "an actor but not a fool," he noted after the conference.

Victory would certainly not be won by being nice, Monty felt. "A very large number of major generals and other senior officers who were in this party have gone to their homes, to await other jobs," he reported with satisfaction to Oliver Leese; "they were mostly quite useless."

Brigadier Otway Herbert, one of the few survivors of Monty's Augean clear-out at 21 Army Group, later agreed—indeed was astonished that his own services were retained. "Everybody else was sacked, of any consequence," he recalled. "Some senior officers departed even without being sacked! For example, Willoughby Norrie, who had been a Corps Commander in the desert—he and Monty didn't hit it off, so I remember him coming in to me, to my office: 'Well I'm off, anyhow—that's absolutely certain,' the moment he heard Monty was coming! And off he went!

"I don't think anybody expected to be kept on. 'Monkey' Morgan—he was already a lieutenant-general, [Paget's] Chief of Staff—I think he was a bit upset about being outed. But he expected it.

"The BGS Intelligence was no good at all—he should have been out before—so that he was a certainty to go. . . .

"The major-general Administration—he was a bit of a dud too. . . .

"And the BGS Operations—that was a shambles! He was hopeless— honestly, that was a frightful disaster. . . . He was, I consider, a pretty poor number altogether. I'd known him for years—a perfect misery, didn't grasp the thing at all."

Monty's cruel ax was wielded, in Herbert's view only just in time— for a dangerous air of defeatism had pervaded the headquarters. De Guingand took over as chief of staff, Brigadier Richards took over as head of armor, Williams as head of Intelligence, Graham as head of administration, Belchem was summoned from Eighth Army to become BGS Operations, and Charles Richardson, still on loan as deputy chief of staff to Mark Clark, was even brought back from Fifth Army to be head of plans. As a consequence, by early February 1944, barely four weeks after Monty's "takeover," the new staff at 21st Army Group had drawn up Monty's complete, detailed new plan for Overlord—the "miracle of the war," as General Paget himself later called it.

The Human Factor

A Messianic fervor now gripped Monty. Certain that Overlord was to be the supreme test of his life, he was resolved, especially after the Allied failure at Anzio, that there should be no weak links in the Allied chain of preparations. Everything must be right, with the odds stacked in favor of the Allies, from planning to training, from air support to intelligence. Not since the eleventh century had there been a successful cross-Channel invasion. Napoleon had prepared for one, then balked at the prospects. Likewise Hitler in 1940, after Dunkirk.

To mount the greatest amphibious assault in human history and to triumph over the sixty enemy divisions guarding "Fortress Europe," however, would need men determined to win—and to this end Monty made it his aim to visit every unit participating in the invasion. "Nowhere did the slight erect figure of Montgomery in his baggy and unpressed corduroys excite greater assurance than among the British soldiers themselves," Bradley remembered. "Even Eisenhower with all his engaging ease could never stir American troops to the rapture with which Monty was welcomed by his. Among those men the legend of Montgomery had become an imperishable fact."

Encouraged by the growing confidence of his men, Monty was concerned, however, by the downcast spirit of ordinary civilians and workers he met. For them the war was now in its fourth year. "I would say that the great mass of the people are getting war weary," Monty observed in his diary. "The miners, the factory workers, the dockers, the railwaymen, the housewives—all have been working at high pressure and the tempo has been great. They cannot get away for holidays; so holidays have to be spent at home. The blackout lends a dismal tone. I consider it is very important to try and win the war in EUROPE early next year. I consider also that it could be done—providing we make no mistakes. But to do so requires a great effort on the part of everyone, and the nation must be roused to make the effort. And above all, there must be great enthusiasm."

Few commanders in history have recognized the part played by the wives, children, relatives, neighbors and friends of soldiers fighting in battle. In the first of his evangelical attempts to raise the morale of the English nation Monty now addressed, by arrangement with the Ministry of Transport, some 500 leaders of the railway trade unions at Euston Station in London.

The key to success in battle, Monty maintained, was essentially democratic: the need to understand that, in contrast to the armies of the dictatorships, the human factor was paramount. As he sketched in his notes for the address, he wanted "to tell you something of the Army, and my methods. I want to interest you in what we are doing, and I will tell you how I fight my battles and what influences everything I do. . . ."

4. *The human factor*
The big thing in war. It is the man that matters and not the machine; the men in the tank and not the tank itself.

It is the same in every profession, and in every concern.

Study the human factor. The team—tank and crew.

5. *The German General*
Apply this to the German commander. He is good so long as he is allowed to dictate the battle. Therefore he must be made to dance to your tune. How is this done? Decide how you will fight the battle before you start it, and force it to swing your way. *Examples:* Alamein, Mareth.

6. *No failures*
How is this done? Limit the scope to that which can be done successfully. Tell the soldiers what you are going to do. Then do it. Every man knows that when the army gets on the move it is going to win. Having won, he then has great confidence. And *that* is a pearl of very great price. The British soldier IS a wonderful person—and never fails you.

7. *The sick and wounded*
Sick always about 6 times the wounded. Obvious importance of a healthy army. The 4 things that save many lives: Surgical teams. Blood transfusion. Air Evacuation. Nursing sisters well forward.

8. *The German soldier*
His three main characteristics. Technical ability. Eye for country. Obedience. Very good soldier. But well trained British soldier is better. . . .

Item by item, Monty laid out the lessons of a lifetime spent in studying the art of command—and the railway leaders who listened were enthralled. "The war has gone on long enough," Monty eventually concluded. "The women bear the real burden. Let us all rally to the task and finish off this war; it can be done; and together, you and I, we will see this thing through—to the end."

Much Jealousy

Inevitably, with so little time left to go, Monty's increasingly megalomaniacal view of his role in Overlord aroused resentment among the men he'd sacked, among politicians dubious about his burgeoning popularity—and among the staff of Supreme Headquarters.

Monty was well aware of this. "The public, and the Army, are firmly behind me and would support me to the end," he noted in his diary. "But not so the Generals; my own Generals in the field armies are my firm supporters, but outside the field armies is much jealousy."

Monty's answer was to fight even harder for the things he knew were important, since he was, he acknowledged, "bound to make enemies whatever I do. I shall go on doing my duty, come what may." Yet there can be little doubt that, as in the desert when Eighth Army captured Tripoli and commenced its final triumphant drive into Tunisia to "rescue" First Army after the débâcle at Kasserine, the pressure upon him began to tell, in small but biographically significant ways: ways that may be seen to prefigure the somewhat isolated, bitter army group commander who would later refuse to attend the liberation of Paris ceremonies, or confer personally with his Supreme Commander; ways that in time, by his self-righteous intransigence, would threaten to bring the warring Allied alliance in the West to the very brink of collapse.

As in the desert, the symptoms were first to be seen in Monty's relations with his kith and kin, for he now began to "freeze" members of his family in a way which even his own personal staff officers sometimes found difficult to credit.

"We were on one of these tours [of troops]," Monty's Canadian assistant, Lieutenant Colonel Warren, later recalled, "and when we were standing there a policeman came up—a civilian policeman—and said, 'General, your sister is up on the hill, by the car, about a quarter of a mile away.'

"Monty said, 'Thank you very much.'

"As we were walking up to the car I said, 'Sir, your sister's there.'

"He said, 'Thank you very much.'

"We got up to the car—it took a bit of time because he stopped and spoke to several people on the way. Then he got into the car. I thought he had forgotten about her. So I put my head in through the window and said, 'Sir, your sister—'

"He said, 'I heard you the first time! Get in and drive off!' Just as cold-blooded as that!"

An almost identical occasion was witnessed by Monty's stepson, Dick Carver, when accompanying Monty on a tour of troops near Guildford, home of another of Monty's sisters, Una. He even refused to meet his own elderly mother when she came over from Northern Ireland in hopes of seeing him. Old friends, too, were cold-shouldered if they posed a threat to Monty's increasingly Napoleonic self-image—men such as Basil Liddell Hart, the military theorist and writer, towards whom Monty had shown an almost exaggerated respect throughout the interwar years. "I fear I am too busy at present to meet you for a talk," Monty responded to Liddell Hart's polite inquiry—and even two years later, after the war was over, remained "too busy," he claimed—adding, on that occasion: "I have come to realise in the last few years that the way to fame is a hard one. You must suffer, and be the butt of jealousy and ill-informed criticism; it is a lonely matter. One just has to go on doing what you think is right, and doing your duty: whatever others may say or think; and that is what I try to do." (Liddell Hart was deeply offended; in a scribbled memorandum he remarked: "what a pathetic self-defensive note is sounded in the long postscript. Very small-boyish—rather touching, yet hardly worthy of a man who has reached such eminence. . . . A curious psychological case!")

Monty was. Neither then nor later did he rise to the heights of statesmanlike maturity and magnanimity which so marked Eisenhower's performance as soldier and statesman. But then, it was Eisenhower who so continually foisted onto his subordinate field commanders the responsibility for his *own* military failings—above all, his inability to decide upon a strategy and to stick to it through thick and thin. Eisenhower had never intended, as a youth, to become a soldier, had remained in the United States during World War I, and was neither by nature nor by circumstance a battlefield commander, however much he longed to become one. "Ike stepped in only to sort out disagreements," General West later confided to the Official Historian of the Supreme Command. Colonel Bonesteel, a senior American planner, was more caustic: "Ike never really commanded. He was an arbiter or tribunal between services."

For the moment, save for the problem of Anvil, this did not become a serious obstacle, since Monty proved more than willing to supply the battlefield vision that Eisenhower lacked, while the trouble-free cooperation of services and nations was guaranteed by a Supreme Commander in a genial and selfless manner that Monty entirely lacked.

However historic in the spring of 1944, it was a partnership, however, that could not, and would not, last.

Exercise Thunderclap

Meanwhile preparations for D-Day were proceeding inexorably towards combat. "By the end of March everything was 'set' for OVERLORD and the Armies were mostly on the move to concentration areas," Monty noted in his diary. "These moves were to take some time and had to begin early; they would seriously test the transportation and railway services." Moreover "the whole of April was to be taken up with exercises, culminating in a very large 'grand rehearsal' by all assault forces between 3rd and 5th May."

Rehearsal was at the heart of Monty's undertaking—not only rehearsal by the troops, but by the commanders. Thus, while the soldiers began to move nearer their embarkation points, Monty summoned all combat generals of the invasion armies to his headquarters on 7 April 1944—his object being to put them at last "completely into the whole

OVERLORD picture—as affecting the general plan, the naval problem, and the air action."

Staged entirely by his own 21st Army Group Headquarters at St. Paul's School, and based upon the exercises and tactical conferences Monty had been refining since World War I, Exercise Thunderclap was a *tour de force*: a stunning demonstration of how Monty transformed a contentious though deeply researched proposal, in which few commanders had had any faith, into a clear, simple plan of invasion.

Field Marshal Brooke, Air Marshal Portal, Admiral Cunningham, the Secretary of State for War, P. J. Grigg, and their senior staffs were there to hear the presentation. "Monty led off with a talk of an hour and a half, broken by a ten-minute interval in the middle," Major General Kennedy, the Assistant GIGS (Operations), noted; "he went over the Army plan with great lucidity."

In the unheated lecture room, in front of two huge maps of Normandy, Monty set out in detail for the first time his intended campaign strategy. As before Alamein, he predicted almost exactly the length of the battle: not ten to twelve days, as at Alamein, but this time three punishing months. "The most striking feature of his conception is the deliberate nature of his proposed operations," General Kennedy added. "He means to expand the bridgehead gradually, get ports, and eventually arrive, in about three months, on the line of the Seine–Paris–Brittany ports. Of course, if an opportunity offered for a quick advance towards Germany, he would take it. But the main idea is to get established in great strength."

The calm authority with which Monty outlined his battle plan, the likely enemy response, and the phases through which the battle would go were almost incredible to those present—at least those who did not already know Montgomery. By personalizing the enemy as "Rommel," he was able to streamline the scenario—alerting all to the sense of contest between opposing wills:

Since ROMMEL toured the "Atlantic Wall" the enemy has been stiffening up his coastal crust, generally strengthening his defences, and redistributing his armoured reserve.

The present general trend of movement of his mobile reserves is SOUTH—i.e. away from the NEPTUNE [invasion beaches] area; this shows that our target is not yet known to the enemy.

ROMMEL is likely to hold his mobile Divisions back from the coast until he is certain where our main effort is being made. He will then concentrate them quickly and strike a hard blow; his static Divisions will endeavour to hold on defensively to important ground and act as pivots to the counter-attacks.

By dusk on D-1 day the enemy will be certain that the NEPTUNE area is to be assaulted in strength. By the evening of D day he will know the width of our frontage and the approximate number of our assaulting Divisions; it will be quite evident that ours is a major assault. The enemy is likely that night to summon his two nearest Panzer Divisions to assist.

By D+5 the enemy can have brought in 6 Panzer Type Divisions. If he has decided to go the whole NEPTUNE hog, he will continue his efforts to push us into the sea.

As at Alamein, Monty did not think Rommel would succeed:

We ourselves will have 15 divisions on shore by then. After about D+8 I think the enemy will have to begin to consider a "roping-off" policy i.e., trying to stop our expansion from the lodgement area.

Nevertheless Monty acknowledged Rommel was a tough foe. "Some of us here know ROMMEL well. He is a determined commander and likes to hurl his armour into the battle," he remarked, remembering the fierce armored engagements during Alamein. "But according to what we know of the chain of command the armoured divisions are being kept directly under RUNDSTEDT, and delay may be caused before they are released to ROMMEL. This fact may help us, and quarrels may arise between the two of them."

Command disagreements, and the hoped-for punitive effect of Allied air superiority on German road and rail movement, might give the Allies a period of perhaps four days' grace in which to face their crucial test. "Obviously therefore we must put all our energies into the fight," Monty exhorted, "and get such a good situation in the first few days that the enemy can do nothing against us."

Once it had established a secure beachhead, the British Second Army was "to assault to the west of the R. ORNE and to develop operations to the south and south-east, in order to secure airfield sites and to protect the eastern flank of First U.S. Army while the latter is capturing CHERBOURG. In its subsequent operations the ARMY will pivot on its left [CAEN] and offer a strong front against enemy movement towards the lodgement area from the east." Behind this protective shield General Bradley's First U.S. Army would, after seizing Cherbourg, cut off the Cotentin Peninsula and break out southwards towards the Loire. Patton's Third U.S. Army was to push through First U.S. Army's front, "clearing the BRITTANY peninsula and capturing the BRITTANY ports"; then, having seized Saint-Nazaire and Nantes on the Loire, it was to cover "the south flank of the lodgement area

while the First US Army is directed N.E. with a view to operations towards PARIS."

In comparison with the American "breakout" scenario, the task of
Dempsey's Second British Army—holding off the enemy's "main forces
from the east"—promised to be long and bloody, but it was, Monty reiterated, vital to the success of his tactical strategy in Normandy, for it
was upon this firm left flank that the whole Normandy battle would
depend. Dempsey would be reinforced, when sufficient formations had
been landed, by the headquarters of First Canadian Army, which
would take over Dempsey's left, or northern, corps in the Caen area
and have as its ultimate task the capture of the port of Le Havre.

To illustrate his plan, Monty pointed to a large-scale map of northern France. There would, he anticipated, be three phases. Phase One
would last perhaps three weeks, while the Allies expanded their
beachheads in Normandy into a cohesive bridgehead of impregnable
size and power. "This gives us a good base for subsequent operations.
I estimate we may have this area by D+20, and we will fight continuously till we get it. There may then have to be a pause to see how we
stand administratively; if not, so much the better."

Phase Two would then see the British Second Army pushing mar-
ginally forward on its left flank to the line of the river Touques, maintaining its shielding position in the center, but swinging out its right
flank, hitherto anchored on Falaise, to Argentan, near the rise of the
Orne. Behind Second Army's shield, First U.S. Army would break out
"southwards toward the LOIRE and QUIBERON BAY. . . . I estimate
that, if all goes well, we may have the area up to the Yellow [Phase
Two] line by D+35 to D+40"—though the actual clearing up of the
Brittany peninsula, by the newly introduced Third Army under Patton,
was "not possible to estimate with any likelihood of accuracy; it may
be up to D+60."

Phase Three, the final phase of the battle, would take the Allies to
the Seine, with the Canadians responsible for the front from Rouen
northwards to Le Havre and the Channel; British Second Army the
front between Rouen and Paris; and First U.S. Army "directed on
PARIS, and the SEINE above [i.e., east of] the city. It will be prepared
to cross the river and operate to the N.E.," he laid down, with Patton's
Third Army given a role "to protect its right or southern flank" in the
subsequent drive towards the Ruhr and Berlin—currently identified by
Eisenhower's long-term planners as the strategic Allied objective. "We
might reach the black [Phase Three] line by D+90," Monty suggested.

In subsequent bickering in rear headquarters, the failure of Monty's
armies to conform precisely to the phases and contours of this outline
plan would cause endless arguments—the more so since Monty would

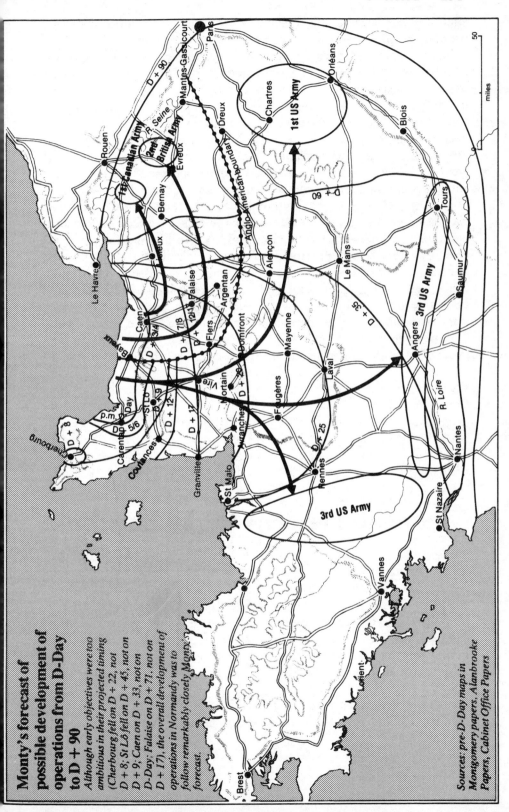

Monty's forecast of possible development of operations from D-Day to D + 90

Although early objectives were too ambitious in their projected timing (Cherbourg fell on D + 22, not D + 8; St Lô fell on D + 45, not on D + 9; Caen on D + 33, not on D-Day; Falaise on D + 71, not on D + 17), the overall development of operations in Normandy was to follow remarkably closely Monty's forecast.

Sources: pre-D-Day maps in Montgomery papers, Alanbrooke Papers, Cabinet Office Papers not afterwards admit that the battle of Normandy had not gone "according to plan." Ought he therefore to have kept quiet, in the days before D-Day, about his intended strategy? Was he not offering a hostage to fortune by being so explicit in his long-term intentions, and the timing of his phases?

The task of a true general, however, is not to please historians or Monday-morning quarterbacks. It is to mount and conduct his operations so that they have the best possible chance of success. By presenting such a clearly defined strategy in advance there can be no doubt Monty brought to the Allied ground, sea and air forces in the spring of 1944 a unity of purpose and conception that was remarkable—and often confused later with Eisenhower's role as Supreme Commander. Against a background of uncertainty over Allied strategic and tactical bombing policy, of continued naval concern over the possible resurrection of Anvil, Monty presented an army plan that gave all those present at the conference a surge of confidence. Moreover, though Eisenhower never said so publicly, both he and Bedell Smith remained to the end of their lives clear how much the free world owed to Monty in the mounting of Overlord. "No one else could have got us there," Eisenhower confided to Drew Middleton years later. "It was his kind of battle. Whatever they say about him, he got us there."

Churchill Hardens to the Enterprise

"As he [Monty] dismissed us for a ten-minute break late that afternoon," Omar Bradley remembered, "he sniffed the air of the room and grinned. 'When we reassemble, gentlemen,' he said, 'you may smoke if you wish.' There was a ripple of laughter in the audience, for both the Prime Minister and Eisenhower were to join us."

Churchill duly entered the school hall. "He looked puffy and dejected and his eyes were red," Major General Kennedy recorded.

"When he had taken his seat, Montgomery spoke again for ten minutes, as he said, to emphasize three main points. The first was that he himself had the most complete confidence in the plan. This confidence must be imparted all the way down the chain of command—he had no room for any doubters. He said that, in effect, the assault was by two armies against two German battalions, which was all they had on the coastal sector at that moment."

Monty's second point, however, made Churchill prick up his ears—namely, "to emphasize the need for boldness and enterprise in pushing forward mobile forces," Kennedy recorded; "even a few armoured cars 20 miles inside the German lines would create confusion and delay."

At this, Churchill became inspired—indeed his Fourth Hussars blood tingled at such cavalry notions. Ignoring Monty's third point—the need to take airfields—Churchill mounted the platform to give what he intended to be one of his finer military orations.

"He was in a short black jacket and had a big cigar as usual. He said he had not been convinced in 1942, or in 1943, that this operation was feasible. He was not expressing an opinion on its feasibility now. But, if he were qualified to do so, and if he were one of us, he would have the greatest confidence from all he had heard of the plans." As Eisenhower later recalled the scene: "Gripping his lapels firmly in his hands, he said, 'Gentlemen, I am *now* hardening to this enterprise.' "

This was a phrase Churchill had first used the month before in a signal to General Marshall, but it appalled Eisenhower. "I then realized for the first time that Mr. Churchill hadn't believed in it [Overlord] all along and had had no faith that it would succeed," Eisenhower later confessed. "It was quite a shocking discovery."

Churchill, struggling to hold the attention of his audience at the end of a long day, declared, as Kennedy recorded, "that the time was now *ripe*" for Overlord. "We had experienced commanders, a great Allied army, a great air force. Our equipment had improved. All the preparations, strategical and tactical, had been made with the greatest skill and care. We were now going to write a glorious page in the history, not of one country or of two, but of the world."

From glory Churchill passed to tactics. "He felt very strongly that this should not be an operation designed to dig in on a bridgehead. At Anzio we had lost a great opportunity—*there* was a lesson for all to study."

"The object," Kennedy concluded by paraphrase of the Prime Minister's remarks, "must be to fight a battle. We needed a battle to break the will of the Germans to fight. Therefore he was glad to hear what had been said about pushing forward armoured spearheads, and *unar-

moured spearheads. He ended by wishing good luck to all those engaged in the operation."

Monty was disappointed. "He looks tired and worn out," he confided to his own diary that night, "and I fear did not create the inspiring influence I had wanted." Brooke was equally disenchanted. Churchill was "looking old and lacking a great deal of his usual vitality," he noted—as did General Kennedy: "He spoke without vigour. He did not look up much while he spoke. There was the usual wonderful flow of fine phrases, but no fire in the delivery. . . . But I heard afterwards that members of the audience who saw him on that day for the first time were tremendously impressed and inspired."

Patton certainly was. "The Prime Minister made the last talk and the best," he noted. " 'Remember that this is an invasion,' " the Pasadena cavalryman quoted the Fourth Hussar, " 'not a creation of a fortified beachhead.' " Of Monty's careful exposition, involving a three-month-long battle, Patton recorded nothing, save that he, Patton, "was the only one . . . to be mentioned by name. The other three he mentioned by number [of the Army]."

Patton—brilliant, self-centered, mercurial—was all for bravado. Monty's deliberate, unfolding strategy for Overlord he felt to be cautious and pedantic. The fact that he, Patton, would not be called to fight for several months until the breakout towards the Loire and Brittany taxed his notoriously combustible patience to the limit (he had not been in battle since disciplined and removed from combat command in Sicily the year before). Within weeks he would be compromising his appointment to command Third U.S. Army in Overlord by giving an outspoken speech at his first public engagement in England: the "Knutsford Incident." General Marshall recommended he be cashiered, with the lackluster but obedient General Hodges promoted to replace him.

However undiplomatic his language, however, Patton was a thruster: and in the difficult days that lay ahead there might well be need of thrusters. Patton—blinkered, megalomaniacal, but living and breathing breakout—was retained.

Gulliver's Travels

The day after Monty's presentation of plans at St. Paul's, meanwhile, the Overlord plans were "second-guessed." A huge scale model of Normandy had been made—in the same manner as the amphibious invasion exercise which Monty had mounted as a junior brigadier in Studland Bay in 1937—and, resting on the floor, was tilted to give a better view from the tiered auditorium: "a relief map of Normandy the width of a city street." Across this, Monty strode "like a giant through Lilliputian France," Bradley later recalled, while firing hypothetical questions at the commanders of each corps, division and brigade participating in the assault. When the turn came of General Joe Collins, commanding 7 U.S. Corps, Collins had no hesitation in responding.

"Sir, if my ship sinks," answered the veteran of Guadalcanal, "you'll find me swimming like hell for the shore!"

Monty collapsed in laughter.

Two days later Monty was once again on tour. He attended 3rd Canadian Division's exercise at Slapton, inspected establishments and ships of the Royal Navy's Plymouth Command, visited 4th U.S. Division in the Exeter area, followed by 30th U.S. Division near Oxford. Breaking the tour in London for a single day on 16 April, he set off to attend a 50th Division exercise assault at Studland, followed by a journey to Scotland to help speed up production in factories in Glasgow and inspect airborne troops of the SAS (Special Air Service) Brigade. After three days at his headquarters in London he left again on 26 April to attend an air bombing exercise at Studland, followed by an assault landing exercise by 4th U.S. Division at Slapton.

It was at this latter rehearsal that a group of German patrol boats penetrated the meager British naval screen (several British destroyers had not turned up for the rehearsal) and sank two large American landing ships (LSTs). More than 600 men lost their lives in the incident—more fatalities, as General Bradley later lamented, than would be suffered by the whole 7th U.S. Corps on D-Day itself.

Monty was chastened, but unbowed. Almost single-handedly he had re-created the morale of the British army in England after Dunkirk, then in the field of battle after Alamein. His parish now extended to some two million invasion troops: American, British, Canadian, Free French, Polish and Belgian. Employing the techniques of a lifetime's study in training men for combat, he was convinced he had found the passkey to professionalism among the armies of the democracies: the art of imaginative preparation and rehearsal. The Slapton Sands disaster was unfortunate, but it did not in any way lessen the need for Allied invasion troops to enact their roles in realistic settings prior to D-Day—for without such rehearsal, the Allied assault landings might well fail.

General Patton might chafe, but General Bradley was awed by Monty's drive, energy and perfectionism. "Monty's incomparable talent for the 'set-piece' battle—the meticulously planned offensive—made him invaluable in the OVERLORD assault," he later acknowledged. "Nothing was left to chance or improvisation in command."

Nor was Bradley exaggerating. Monty was determined, this time, to show that the Allies could be more professional even than the Germans. Thus, on 15 May at his St. Paul's headquarters, Monty mounted one final presentation of the Overlord plan: a last chance to make sure every commander understood his strategy.

A Cold Max

The King, Churchill, Field Marshall Smuts and the British Chiefs of Staff sat in chairs placed as a front row. Behind them sat the generals and their senior staffs on wooden benches.

The Supreme Commander opened the meeting with an almost

priestlike exhortation to be honest: "I consider it to be the duty of anyone who sees a flaw in the plan not to hesitate to say so." Then, to
present the ground-force plans, Eisenhower asked Monty, as Allied
Land Forces Commander, to come forward.

For once Monty was "wearing a very well cut battle-dress with a
knifelike edge to the trouser creases." He also spoke, Leigh-Mallory recalled, "in a tone of quiet emphasis, making use of what is evidently a
verbal trick of his, to repeat the most important word or phrase in a
sentence more than once."

"General Eisenhower," Monty began his presentation, "has charged
me with the preparation and conduct of the land battle.

"There are four armies under my command:

"First American, Second British: Assault armies.

"Third American, First Canadian: Follow up."

As in his address the month before, Monty opted to personalize the
impending contest:

The Enemy
Last Feb. Rommel took command from Holland to the Loire. It is now
clear that his intention is to deny any penetration; Overlord is to be defeated on the beaches.
To this end Rommel has:
(a) Thickened up the coastal crust.
(b) Increased the number of infantry DIVS not committed to beach defence, and allotted them in a layback role to seal off any break in the
coastal crust.
(c) Redistributed his armoured reserve.

Nor was this all. "Fortress Europe," Monty acknowledged, had in the
meantime become more and more formidable, with sixty German divisions stationed in France, ten of which were elite Panzer divisions,
and twelve more were mobile divisions. No less than four of the Panzer divisions were actually quartered in the Normandy area—21st Panzer Division at Caen, 12th SS Division at Lisieux, 17th at Rennes and
Panzer Lehr at Tours. Given such enemy armor, what reception could
the Allies expect on D-Day?

Using his pointer, Monty turned to the wall map. Facing each assaulting army was only a single, static German coastal division. Echeloned behind these was a German field infantry division at Saint-Lô, a
field infantry division at Coutances, and 21st Panzer Division at Caen:
a total of five divisions. By midday, perhaps, a further enemy division
could be expected, 12th SS Division, from Lisieux: "Total six." By the

evening of D-Day there could be yet another enemy Panzer division on the scene: 17th SS Division from Rennes. "Total seven." The Allies, by contrast, would have ashore only six divisions—if all went well.

In order to clarify the likely progression of the battle, Monty now began to chart the opposing tallies of forces: the Allies on the left of a special blackboard, the Germans on the right.

By the evening of the second day (D+1), the Allies would have improved their strength to a slight numerical superiority: ten and one-third Allied divisions facing a total of nine German divisions—of which, however, five were Panzer divisions.

By the third day even this slight Allied superiority would have been lost: twelve Allied divisions fighting twelve German divisions.

At this stage Monty foresaw danger, for "by now Overlord will have become an overriding menace requiring the concentration of all available [German] formations that can be spared." Some thirteen enemy divisions "may begin moving to the Neptune [invasion] area," he surmised, including five Panzer divisions from Amiens, Toulouse, Bordeaux, Sedan and Belgium, and eight infantry divisions from West Brittany and the Pas de Calais.

Within five days of the invasion, therefore, a frightening enemy army could be assembling, and although not all the German divisions might have arrived—especially if the RAF and United States air forces managed to interdict road and rail access to the battlefield—the enemy would nevertheless be starting "to have the necessary ingredients for a full scale counter-attack after proper recce and deployment," with infantry holding essential ground and some ten Panzer divisions "available for the blow."

"The full blooded counter-attack is likely at any time after D+6," Monty emphasized, his voice betraying no emotion as he relentlessly painted the picture to the assembled audience—a picture in which the Allies were now outnumbered: for by the eighth day of the invasion the Allies could hope to have landed, weather permitting, a maximum of eighteen divisions, against which the total number of enemy divisions would "now be up to 24—of which 10 are Pz [Panzer]. The majority will be securing the vital ground forward of the lateral which links his front and which controls the essential routes and nodal centres.

"The Pz divisions will have the mobile role to push us back into the sea," Monty posited. But he did not think Rommel would succeed—indeed, after prolonged discussions with Brigadier Williams, his chief of Intelligence, Monty was convinced, particularly in view of the alarming number of new obstacles appearing on the Normandy beaches, that Rommel would not, in fact, wait until D+8 before launching a counterattack—*and it was vital that all Allied assault commanders should understand this:*

> Rommel is an energetic and determined commander; he has made a world of difference since he took over. He is best at the spoiling attack; his forte is disruption; he is too impulsive for the set-piece battle.
>
> He will do his level best to "Dunkirk" us—not to fight the armoured battle on ground of his own choosing, but to avoid it altogether by preventing our tanks landing by using his own tanks well forward. On D day he will try to:
>
> (a) Force us from the beaches.
> (b) Secure:
> > Caen
> > Bayeux
> > Carentan

"His obsession is likely to be Bayeux," Monty emphasized, for "this important nodal point splits our frontal landings in half. If he can hold firm in the above three nodal points, we would be awkwardly placed."

Alive to this, the Allies *must* seize and hold fast these three key nodal points—in which case, Williams had predicted, Rommel would revert to his Alamein tactics. "Thereafter he will continue his counterattacks. But as time goes on he will combine them with a roping-off policy, and he must then hold firm on the important ground which dominates and controls the road axes in the 'bocage' country. The areas in question are: (a) the high ground east of the R. DIVES; (b) the high ground between FALAISE and St LO, between the rivers ORNE and VIRE; (c) the high ground west of the R. VIRE."

Several hundred generals and their senior staff officers craned forwards as Monty's chief of operations, Brigadier Belchem, tapped the high ground on the huge model in front of them. No one could but be aware of the magnitude of the Allied undertaking. Anticipating this, Monty addressed the issue head-on:

The Problem
The enemy is in position, with reserves available.

There are obstacles and minefields on the beaches; we cannot gain contact with the obstacles and recce them.

There are many unknown hazards.

After a sea voyage, and a landing on a strange coast, there is always some loss of cohesion.

We must time our assault so as to make things as easy as possible for the leading troops. Therefore we shall touch-down so that all obstacles

are dry, and so that we have 30 minutes in which to deal with them before the incoming tide reaches them.

Regarding the wider problem—winning the subsequent Overlord
battle—Monty now gave his own answer:

The Solution
We have the initiative. We must then rely on:

(a) the violence of our assault.
(b) our great weight of supporting fire, from the sea and air.
(c) simplicity.
(d) robust mentality.

   We must blast our way on shore and get a good lodgement before the
enemy can bring sufficient reserves up to turn us out.

   Armoured columns must penetrate deep inland, and quickly, on D
day; this will upset the enemy plans and tend to hold him off while we
build up strength.

   We must gain space rapidly, and peg out claims well inland.

   And while we are engaged in doing this the air must hold the ring,
and must hinder and make very difficult the movement of enemy reserves by train or road towards the lodgement area. The land battle will
be a terrific party and we will require the full support of the air all the
time, and laid on quickly.

   Once we can get control of the main enemy lateral Grandville–Vire–
Argentan–Falaise–Caen, and the area enclosed in it is firmly in our possession, then we will have the lodgement area we want and can begin to
expand.

As in April, Monty ran through the tasks of the four armies, as well as
those of the commandos and airborne troops. Turning to the wall
maps, he gave his strategic intentions for "the development of Operations up to D+90," outlining again the manner in which the British
and Canadians would in those three months "contain the maximum
enemy forces facing the eastern flank of the bridgehead" while the
American forces, "once through the difficult bocage country," were to
"thrust rapidly towards Rennes," seal off the Brittany peninsula, and
wheel round towards Paris and the Seine, pivoting on the right flank of
the British shield. As Bradley recalled, "the British and Canadian armies were to decoy the enemy reserves and draw them to their front
on the extreme eastern edge of the Allied beachhead. Thus while
Monty taunted the enemy at Caen, we were to make our break on the
long roundabout road toward Paris. When reckoned in terms of national pride, this British decoy mission became a sacrificial one, for

while we tramped around the outside flank, the British were to sit in place and pin down Germans. Yet strategically it fitted into a logical division of labors, for it was toward Caen that the enemy reserves would race once the alarm was sounded."

This strategic vision of the Normandy campaign now filled the assembled audience with a sense of pride and anticipation, as it had Monty's own chief of Intelligence when Monty first laid down his Normandy strategy soon after changing the COSSAC plan.

Looked at on the larger map of France, there was indeed something majestic in Monty's strategy: as though a giant boxer were holding off his opponent with his left hand, only to swing with his right and deliver a punch to the enemy's solar plexus that would send him reeling against the ropes—the river Seine.

"*Morale*. We shall have to send the soldiers in to this party 'seeing red,' " Monty concluded his address:

> We must get them completely on their toes; having absolute faith in the plan; and embued with infectious optimism and offensive eagerness.
>
> Nothing must stop them.
>
> If we send them in to battle in this way—then we shall succeed.

Monty stepped down. One American general, John Lee, afterwards wrote to congratulate him: "Your clear and convincing estimate of the situation at St. Paul's yesterday would merit in West Point language 'a cold max.' "

"It went off superbly, I thought, on that occasion," Monty's military assistant, Lieutenant Colonel Dawnay, recalled. "Monty was at his best. He was a supremely confident man—it was astonishing how confident he was."

The invasion was now three weeks away.

A Question of Clerks

Monty's air of confidence was not a mask. His genius had been to take an "unsound operation of war" and to recast it into a simple, clear-cut plan in which all the participants would have, at last, complete faith.

Monty's naval and air colleagues, by contrast, were uninspiring. Ramsay, exhausted by the detail of the naval operation, seemed "indifferent and overwhelmed by all his own difficulties," Field Marshal Brooke recorded. Air Marshal "Bomber" Harris then "told us how he might have won the war if it had not been for the handicap imposed by the existence of the two other Services," Brooke noted with sarcasm. Spaatz did not trust himself to speak from notes but "read every word" of his address. Leigh-Mallory was clear but tedious.

By contrast, "throughout the day EISENHOWER was quite excellent," Monty noted in his diary; "he spoke very little, but what he said was good and on a high level." King George VI, roused by Monty's presentation, even sprang up to give a surprise speech: "absolutely first-class, quite short, and exactly right," Monty noted in his diary. Field Marshal Smuts, on the other hand, dwelled gloomily in his address on the German strength in France in 1940—armies which had overrun the country in 1940 with a ruthlessness the Allies could now reasonably expect to meet again in Normandy.

Churchill, fortunately, was a tonic. "Today he was quite a different person and was full of life," Monty recorded after Churchill had given a stirring speech to end the presentation of plans.

Two days later, however, having moved to his final headquarters in Broomfield House, Portsmouth, overlooking the English Channel, Monty received a disturbing message from 10 Downing Street. "The Prime Minister has asked me to tell you that he was much concerned by some of the statements made at last Monday's Conference on the subject of administrative arrangements for OVERLORD," Churchill's military assistant, General Ismay, wrote. "He was told, for example, that 2,000 officers and clerks were to be taken over to keep records, and he was given a statement (copy attached) which shows that at D plus 20 there will be one vehicle to every 4.84 men.

"The Prime Minister would like to have a discussion with you and your staff on the whole question of the British [administrative] tail, and he wonders whether it would be convenient to you to have this before dinner at your Headquarters next Friday, 19th May."

There was nothing Monty could do but acquiesce.

Churchill Weeps

Monty had no intention, however, of allowing Churchill to interfere with the business of his, Monty's, staff. Steering Churchill instead into his own office that Friday, Monty asked the Prime Minister to be seated. Before Churchill had time to speak, Monty preempted him. "I understand, sir, that you want to discuss with my staff the proportion of soldiers to vehicles landing on the beaches in the first flights," he began.

"I cannot allow you to do so. My staff advise me and I give the final decision; they then do what I tell them." The staff had done a "terrific job preparing the invasion; that work is now almost completed, and all over England the troops are beginning to move towards the assembly areas, prior to embarkation." To make a change now would cause tremendous disruption, Monty asserted, and shake their confidence in their Commander-in-Chief, who took ultimate responsibility for all decisions.

One by one Monty ran through the battles he had won in the past two years: Alamein, Tripoli, Medenine, Mareth, Wadi Akarit, the amphibious assault upon Sicily, the invasion of the Italian mainland, the conquest of southern Italy—all under the overall leadership of the

Prime Minister. The invasion of Normandy was now all set, the men confident they could and would succeed. Did the Prime Minister wish to shake that confidence—to come between a battlefield general and his men, his own staff in fact?

"I could never allow it—*never*," Monty emphasized. "If you think that is wrong, that can only mean you have lost confidence in me."

The two men sat alone, closeted together. Monty's steel-blue eyes stared into those of the Prime Minister, and there was silence.

What could Churchill possibly say? Behind the immaculately tidy desk sat a general who, for all his eccentricity of dress, of behavior and of mind, had become associated, if not positively identified, with the renascence of British military performance in battle. In the coming campaign Monty would be commanding not only the premier British army in the field, but a Canadian one, as well as two American armies.

That Churchill was moved there can be no doubt—indeed he threatened to sue Monty's first biographer, Alan Moorehead, in 1946 if he dared print his account of the episode. Moorehead was aggrieved. "He didn't tell in the book about Churchill breaking down and weeping, which was true," Dr. Pogue, the American Official Historian, confidentially noted after an interview with Moorehead.

To Monty, however, Churchill's weeping was not a sign of weakness; nor did he ever cause it to appear so when recalling the incident. Indeed, the sight of Churchill giving way to tears in his office remained one of the most striking memories Monty retained of the war. Two tireless and egotistical tyrants had confronted one another—and Monty had won. Yet in losing, Churchill had touched the heart of a man who revered him, just as Monty genuinely revered Sir Alan Brooke. Not in triumph therefore but in humility, Monty offered Churchill his handkerchief. Then, when the Prime Minister had dried his tears, Monty quietly suggested they go next door, where he would like to present his staff. "Everyone there sensed there had been a crisis. Most of them guessed what had taken place in the study," Moorehead narrated.

"I'm not allowed to talk to you, gentlemen," Churchill announced, clearing his throat. Then they all went in to dinner: "one of those unforgettable occasions," de Guingand later said. The Prime Minister was "in great form, and prepared to talk—we let him. The Commander-in-Chief's betting book was brought out, and several wagers were laid on diverse subjects. The date by which the war in the West or in the East would end. The type of Government we would elect after the war. . . . Monty never laid a bet himself, but he was always prepared to accept one."

Before leaving, Churchill added a new "chapter" to the autograph book which Monty kept: "Chapter V"—searching for a way in which he could compliment Monty, yet still record his anxiety about the administrative "tail" of 21st Army Group. Eventually, in his small, curling hand, he wrote:

Chapter V
On the verge of the greatest Adventure with which these pages have dealt I record my confidence that all will be well & that the organizations and equipment of the army will be worthy of the valour of the soldier & the genius of their chief

Winston S. Churchill 19.v.44

A Triumph of Leadership

O utside Broomfield House, camouflaged beneath the great beech trees, stood the caravans and tents of Monty's mobile or battle headquarters. Paul Odgers, a young officer who had been brought back from Eighth Army Headquarters in Italy, vividly recalled the creation of Monty's "Tac HQ" for Normandy. "I remembered I'd first seen Monty in Malta, and it was the most awe-inspiring sight, I remember at the time almost shaking in my shoes. Only two people have ever made me shake in my shoes—Monty, and a very great headmaster at Rugby where I was at school." The new Tactical Headquarters was to be composed of tents, grouped around Monty's famous desert trailers or caravans, and with a "marquee for Monty's dining room."

De Guingand, however, as Monty's chief of staff, looked upon the creation of this new mobile headquarters with considerable misgiving. It would enable Monty, as in North Africa, Sicily and Italy, to impose a "grip" on the land battle well forward. The danger, however, was that Monty's two headquarters—Tac and Main—might become divorced from one another, with Main Headquarters remaining in England during the early stages of the battle to coordinate air support, administrative supplies and reinforcements. De Guingand therefore asked Monty to accept as Tac HQ Commander one of his senior colonels from 21st Army Group Operations staff: Leo Russell.

Without question this was to prove a grave mistake, not only because of Russell's incompatibility with the Land Forces Commander, but because the Land Forces Commander was already becoming, in many ways, a law unto himself.

Meantime, three nights after Churchill's tearful visit, it was the turn of King George VI to come to dinner. He too was given a copy of Monty's intended final sermon or address to senior officers, as well as the latest printed edition of Monty's "Notes on High Command in War." These "Notes" Monty had sent to leaders and commanders all over the world—to Wavell, Auchinleck, Marshall, Mountbatten, Smuts, Fraser, Mackenzie-King—often with a photograph of himself, and a request for a return photograph of the recipient.

Though they all thanked Monty kindly and reciprocated, many found this form of self-advertisement embarrassing, if not distasteful. The Reynoldses' house at Amesbury, in fact, would now fill to overflowing with paintings, trophies and signed photographs of Montgomery and his fellow leaders in the free world—so much so that the Reynoldses' own son Tom would find himself treated almost as an outcast when he returned home from combat in Italy.

Such burgeoning vanity was certainly pretentious. Yet, as at Alamein, it rested in part upon Monty's understanding of the significance of D-Day in what would become the history of the Second World War. The Allies, as Monty had admitted in his final address to senior officers, had "worked themselves into a position where they cannot lose." No longer were Britain and the Commonwealth under threat—it was Germany now that was fighting for her life. But the Allies had by no means won the war, and in his address Monty had been careful not to minimize the difficulties in mounting a successful Second Front. The Germans were in prepared positions, with powerful reserves, and only "offensive eagerness" would ensure the Allies were successful:

> Once on land we must be offensive, and more offensive, and ever more offensive as the hours go by. We must call on the soldiers for an all out effort.
>
> Every officer and man must have only one idea, and that is to peg out claims inland, and to penetrate quickly and deeply into enemy territory. After a long sea voyage and a landing followed by fighting, a reaction sets in and officers and men are often inclined to let up and relax. This is fa-

tal; senior officers must prevent it at all costs on D-Day and on the following days. The first few days will be the vital ones; it is in those days that the battle will be won, and in those days that it could well be lost.

Great energy and "drive" will be required from all senior officers and commanders.

I consider that once the beaches are in our possession, success will depend largely on our ability to be able to concentrate our armour and push fairly strongly armoured columns rapidly inland to secure important ground or communications centres. Such columns will form firm bases in enemy territory from which to develop offensive action in all directions. Such action will tend to throw the enemy off his balance, and will enable our build-up through the beaches to proceed undisturbed; it will cut the ground from under the armoured counter-attack. . . .

Inaction, and a defensive mentality, are criminal in any officer—however senior.

For a further week Monty toured his assault armies, visiting every corps and divisional area and addressing in person, as before Alamein, all senior and even junior officers. The response was, even among American forces, tumultuous. "Confidence in the high command is absolutely without parallel," one American officer later reported to Eisenhower's chief of staff—"and unanimously what appealed to them [the assault troops] was the story . . . that the General visited every one of us outfits before going over."

Perhaps no general in history had done as much as Monty to ensure *at every level*, from the generals to the clerks, the success of the battle that lay ahead. It was, as Bedell Smith wrote to Monty after D-Day, a "triumph of leadership"—yet one which, in the bitter Anglo-American wrangles thereafter, would often be forgotten.

The Last Supper

On 1 June 1944, Monty summoned his four army commanders, General Bradley, General Patton, General Dempsey and General Crerar, to a "final conference," and to stay for a last supper together in Broomfield House, before the historic invasion.

A year before, during the Sicily campaign, Patton had been Bradley's boss. Now they were fellow army commanders—with Bradley scheduled to become Patton's boss as 12 U.S. Army Group Commander once Third Army became operational in Normandy.

"General Patton, of course, is extremely unpopular in this Headquarters," Bradley's aide, Major Chester Hansen, wrote in his diary, disclosing the hostile feeling at First U.S. Army. "Most of our officers have carried with them the punctured legend from Sicily. When I told the Captain of the MPs to provide a motorcycle escort for Patton's arrival, he grinned and asked, 'Shall we have them wear boxing gloves?' He was referring, of course, to the slapping incident."

In his own diary Patton recorded: "Bradley and I left at 1530 and flew to Portsmouth to see General Montgomery who lives at Southwick. Montgomery, Bradley, and I had tea, and then we went to his office, and without the aid of any staff officers, went over the plans."

Bradley, shy, diffident—a soldier's soldier—abhorred the braggardly bearing of his erstwhile Seventh U.S. Army Commander, and hoped, understandably, that his own First Army's progress in Normandy would render Patton's Third Army Headquarters almost unnecessary, save as an adjunct. "If everything moves as planned there will be nothing left for me to do," Patton noted with disappointment.

Monty, however, reassured Patton there would be a great deal for Third U.S. Army to do. Patton had rehearsed the hopeful breakout role of Third Army with his staff on 29 May in the presence of the Ninth

U.S. Army Commander, General Simpson, "so I was very fluent," Patton afterwards claimed—prompting Monty, after listening to him, to say twice to Bradley that "Patton should take over for the Brittany, and possibly the Rennes operation."

Bradley quietly demurred. Meanwhile Patton, attempting to keep his injured pride in check, shook hands with Miles Dempsey and Harry Crerar when they arrived. Neither the British commander nor the Canadian made much impact on him, "I take him to be a yes-man," Patton noted of Dempsey—the former corps commander who "failed to take Catania" in the early days of the Sicilian campaign. "The Canadian is better—but not impressive," Patton commented on Crerar.

The dinner, however, was convivial. Monty toasted his four army commanders, and Patton, "as the oldest Army commander present," replied by toasting "the health of General Montgomery" and declaring "our satisfaction in serving under him." The "lightning did not strike me," Patton noted candidly in his diary—for his pleasure at serving under a Briton was a complete invention. Nevertheless he acknowledged, "I have a better impression of Monty than I had."

"They all stayed to dinner and we had a very cheery evening," Monty meanwhile noted in his own diary, indifferent to the undercurrents of envy, pride and personal ambition. Besides, Monty had his own opinions on those present. Patton he regarded as a saber-rattler: ignorant of battle in its larger dimensions, as well as of army/air cooperation, but still the most aggressive "thruster" in the Allied camp. Bradley he considered conscientious, dependable and loyal (Bradley would continue to call Monty "sir" until September 1944). Dempsey, though he lacked the Guardsman's ruthlessness and the drive of Oliver Leese, was cleverer, and possessed a legendary eye for terrain, ran a high-caliber headquarters, and was, behind his quiet manner, completely imperturbable.

Only Crerar really worried Monty. He had known the Canadian ever since Crerar accepted demotion in order to command a division and subsequently the Canadian Corps in Monty's South-Eastern Army Command in 1942, prior to Alamein. Though Crerar was undoubtedly an efficient headquarters manager, Monty felt grave doubts about Crerar as a battlefield leader—doubts which, in Monty's eyes, were to be unhappily confirmed in the months ahead.

It was not, therefore, the most spectacular team of army commanders to be leading the largest invasion in human history. Indeed, of the four army commanders serving under Monty, only Patton had actually commanded an army in battle before—a campaign which had ended in Patton's dishonor and near dismissal. Yet Monty allowed no doubts about the victorious outcome of the impending operations. He had, after all, commanded far less satisfactory generals at Alamein, and had triumphed. He, Monty, would be in sole command of the Allied armies in Normandy. As at Alamein, he wanted only sufficient luck to help achieve his break-in: the landings themselves. Once ashore, luck would be unnecessary, only nerves. Rommel would fight like a tiger, Monty knew, but so long as he, Monty, kept his head, he was certain he had the measure of his opponent, and could best him in a long-drawn-out battle.

What Monty was less sure about was his superiors: the "desk soldiers" and politicians. Like children, all were now clamoring for a ringside seat to witness the historic occasion—Grigg, Churchill, Ismay, Smuts, King George VI. . . . As Patton recorded in his diary, during the meal a phone call came from General Ismay, announcing that Churchill wished to visit the Portsmouth area over the weekend. Monty's reaction was memorable. "If Winnie comes, he'll not only be a great bore, but also may well attract undue attention here," Monty barked back. *"Why in hell doesn't he go and smoke his cigar at Dover Castle and be seen with the Lord Mayor? It would fix the Germans' attention to Calais."*

In vain Monty appealed to Eisenhower and even Brooke to stop Churchill's visit. "He also wants to go to sea in a cruiser and see the assault and the bombardment on D day," Monty lamented in his own diary; "wherever he is he must be an embarrassment and a liability, and might compromise success in that area; I hope the Cabinet will not allow him to go.

"Quite apart from everything else, he is too valuable and should not take such risks; if anything were to happen to him we should be in a bad position. His own good sense and judgement may prevail over his great fighting spirit, but I doubt it!!"

Monty's doubts were soon confirmed. In the meantime, only Eisenhower seemed to him to have grown greatly in stature in this testing period—and that because Eisenhower had had the sense (in Monty's view) to give his Land Forces Commander—as Alexander had, at Alamein—free rein to plan, prepare and rehearse the invasion without hindrance.

Save for the distraction over Anvil, Eisenhower had indeed supported his Land Forces Commander with a firmness that surprised even Monty. On 2 June 1944 the two men dined together at Monty's Tactical Headquarters. "I do like him tremendously," Monty jotted in his diary; "he is so very genuine and sincere."

Together, after dinner, the two men then "went up to Southwick House and had a conference with the Met experts on the weather" at 9:30 P.M. The sea forecast was good, but the air forecast poor—

"making the airborne operations difficult, and especially the landing of gliders."

Monday, 5 June 1944, was still the target date for D-Day. "It was decided to lay on the whole operation," Monty recorded—with the proviso they meet the next evening, 3 June, at the same time to review the weather forecast.

Eisenhower's Dilemma

T he weather worsened by the hour.

By Saturday, 3 June, Monty was aware that a crisis was brewing, in which cast-iron nerves would be required. Some would probably caution cancellation until the next appropriate tides, a fortnight later. His own view was unshakable:

> The weather forecast is not so good. The depression over ICELAND is spreading to the south and the high pressure system which was coming up this way from the AZORES is now being pushed back. So the chance of a good belt of high pressure over the Channel area is now receding.
> All this is awkward, and some very big decisions may be necessary. My own view is that if the sea is calm enough for the Navy to take us there, then we must go; the air has had very good weather for all its preparatory operations, and we must accept that it may not be able to do so well on D day.

Monty had laid down the plan, prepared the armies. It was now up to Eisenhower, as Supreme Commander, to say whether those armies should go. The decision whether to cancel the landings had to be made, at the latest, twenty-four hours before the invasion, i.e., on Sunday, 4 June, since a large proportion of the 4,000 invasion vessels would already be assembling at sea, prior to their passage across the Channel.

Eisenhower's meteorologist became more and more pessimistic. At Southwick House on Saturday evening, Group Captain Stagg presented a gloomy picture: "From tomorrow winds will be . . . force 4 to 5, maybe 6 at times, on the English side of the Channel. . . . They will continue fresh, even strong at times, till Wednesday (June 7)."

Stagg left the room, and an argument amongst the commanders broke out. It was an hour or more before Stagg was recalled, to be told that no irrevocable decision had been made.

"We are now on the eve of the Second Front. The weather forecast does not look too good, and tomorrow, 4 June, will be an interesting day; at 0800 hours tomorrow the final decision must be taken," Monty noted in his diary, "and once taken must be stuck to; everything will be at sea, and if it is to be turned back, it must be turned back then. Strong and resolute characters will be very necessary."

Meanwhile the very Winston Churchill who had once depicted his fears of the English Channel "running red with the blood" of brave Allied troops was now in a state of high excitement. Though denied access to Monty's headquarters, he was using his prime ministerial status to watch the grand embarkation of troops. "They are on a special train parked at Southampton from which they set out to see troops loading on Friday, but had bad luck hitting the right loading places at the wrong time, and vice versa, so the P.M. didn't do so well," Eisenhower's naval aide recorded. Just as Eisenhower and his staff "returned to camp last night, the P.M.'s caravan of cars and dashing cyclists swirled in behind unexpectedly. Filled their gas tanks and diminished our small supply of Scotch like the devil, there being some ten or more parched mouths to moisten."

While the inebriate Prime Minister slept aboard his special train in the early hours of Sunday, 4 June, Monty meanwhile rose and made his way across to Southwick House to hear Group Captain Stagg's latest weather forecast. The outlook was no better than the night before, but this time there was open dissension among the forecasters, with Spaatz's American team at Widewing predicting a favorable upturn—a fact which had become known to the assembled commanders via Ramsay's naval meteorologist, next door to Monty.

"The tension in the room was palpable," Stagg later recalled. Admiral Ramsay branded Stagg a defeatist. "The sky outside at the moment is practically clear and there is no wind: when do you expect the cloud and wind of your forecast to appear here?" Ramsay asked. Stagg answered, "In another four or five hours from now, sir."

Ramsay counseled the Supreme Commander that the invasion should go ahead. Eisenhower turned to Leigh-Mallory. Leigh-Mallory was against, saying the air forces would not be able to carry out their program.

Eisenhower then turned to Monty as Commander-in-Chief of the invasion armies.

Monty was emphatic. Some of Leigh-Mallory's program would probably have to be canceled, he allowed, but the majority of it could go ahead. It was a moment for resolution, for the sort of courage Monty had quoted in his message to be read out to the troops as they set sail: "O God of battles, steel my soldiers' hearts. . . ." "We must go," Monty recommended. Every hour's delay diminished the ability of the troops to face their ordeal and complicated the entire mounting procedures.

It was now the turn of Eisenhower's deputy, Air Marshal Tedder. Tedder disagreed with Monty—in fact he later referred to Monty's "amazingly asserted willingness" to undertake the operation with reduced air support.

There was a pause.

Eisenhower then stood up. "In that case, gentlemen, it looks to me as if we must confirm the provisional decision we took at the last meeting"—i.e., to postpone the invasion pending better weather. "Compared with the enemy's forces ours are not overwhelmingly strong: we need every help our air superiority can give us. If the air cannot operate we must postpone. Are there any dissentient voices?"

Monty was chagrined. The early morning sky was clear outside, yet the entire Overlord operation was being postponed because of a weather forecast which was itself the subject of dissenting meteorological opinions! The recall of so many vessels would be a tremendous operation—increasing the chance of German air or naval craft spotting the armada. On the other hand, Monty had himself decreed, as his number one maxim on the prosecution of modern battle, the cardinal importance of air supremacy. Moreover, it was vital there should be unity of purpose and decision making under the Supreme Commander.

For once, therefore, Monty remained silent.

D-Day, 5 June 1944, was off.

"I Would Say—Go"

Ironically, a "beautiful dawn glow" was lighting the northeastern horizon as the Allied commanders filed out of Southwick House to their cars, and instead of the low cloud that had made Tedder and Leigh-Mallory oppose launching the invasion, the skies remained clear all day.

By one o'clock on the afternoon of Sunday, 4 June, however, a stiff breeze began to blow: evidence of the expected cold front. Yet even now the prognosis was reversing itself: the skies would be clear enough for the air forces to operate—but the sea would be too rough to guarantee naval success!

In the midst of this meteorological nightmare, a new hope suddenly began to appear. The depression in the mid-Atlantic had intensified to the point where it must slow down, giving a breathing space of possibly a full day on Tuesday, 6 June: "a heaven sent break," as Stagg recalled. Excitedly Stagg attended a conference of forecasters at 4:30 P.M.—but instead of being a "short and happy" discussion of the possible break in the weather, the session turned into "the most heatedly argumentative and most prolonged of the whole series," Stagg recorded; "it lasted well over two hours."

If the forecasters could not agree, how could the commanders responsible for the invasion? When, at 9:30 that evening, Eisenhower asked what the weather would be like after 6 June in the Channel and over the French coast, Stagg "hesitated . . . for two dramatic minutes and finally said, conscientiously and soberly, 'To answer that question would make me a guesser, not a meteorologist.' "

Stagg's forecast for 6 June itself, nevertheless, remained good: little cloud, and quieter seas than at present or on Monday, 5 June. Rear Admiral Creasy, Air Marshal Leigh-Mallory and Major General de Guingand cross-examined Stagg. Ramsay seemed moderately content,

Leigh-Mallory still worried about the effectiveness of his heavy bombers in such conditions. Tedder supported Leigh-Mallory. Finally Eisenhower turned to Monty.

'Do you see any reason why we should not go on Tuesday?"

"No. I would say—*Go.*"

After further discussion of the air ramifications of a decision to go, Eisenhower sided with Monty. The convoys that had been ordered to return were now ordered to put to sea again. A final, irrevocable decision would be made at 4:30 the next morning, Monday, 5 June.

The depression Stagg had forecast the night before had meantime arrived, bringing driving rain and high winds. Yet most of the forecasters agreed that Tuesday, 6 June, would see fair weather. Only the forecast thereafter was in doubt.

Once again, in the early hours of Monday, 5 June, the senior commanders of Overlord met again at Southwick House. "All were in battle-dress uniform except General Montgomery," Stagg recalled. "Conspicuous in his customary front seat he was dressed in a high-necked fawn coloured pullover and light corduroy trousers." Chairing the conference, "General Eisenhower seemed as spruce and immaculate as ever. At the earlier meetings the Cs-in-C and their staff chiefs exchanged pleasantries among themselves as they settled into their easy chairs and sofas: but at this meeting, as at the last, the atmosphere was sombre. Faces were grave and the room was quiet."

Stagg's latest weather forecast was hopeful. "Immediately after I had finished tension seemed to evaporate and the Supreme Commander and his colleagues became as new men. Winds along the assault coasts would not exceed force 3 generally, cloud would be high enough to permit both bombing and naval spotting. The further outlook was variable but with sunny intervals."

As a result, Eisenhower confirmed his decision of the previous night. D-Day, 6 June 1944, was on.

In a matter of hours the Allied armies would be in combat. Some 500 warships of all kinds and 3,000 landing craft were already at sea. Aircraft fitters throughout Britain were checking the planes that would participate in an aerial armada greater even than that sailing across the Channel. Meanwhile, as the invasion craft dipped and swayed in the sea that had once kept Hitler from overrunning Britain, the secret of the past five months was at last revealed to the 130,000 men of the two armies whose task it was to breach the Atlantic Wall, and to storm the beaches of Saint-Laurent, Varreville, Ouistreham, Courseulles and Asnelles.

The "Great Adventure" was beginning.

Part Seven

D-DAY

D-Day rehearsals on 5 May made the Allied
landings 6 June 1944 a triumph.

D-Day

———

Certain no invasion could take place in such rough conditions, Field Marshal Erwin Rommel decided on 4 June to drive to his home in Germany for a brief vacation. Thus, as at the opening of the battle of Alamein, he was absent from his post when, early on the morning of 6 June 1944, Monty's blow fell.

As at Alamein, however, the D-Day landings on Gold, Juno, Sword, Omaha and Utah beaches masked a number of crises. "The first vital moment in the battle was, I think, on the afternoon and evening of D day when the left American Corps had a beachhead of only 100 yds after fighting all day," Monty later wrote to Field Marshal Brooke. "Other parts of the lodgement area were not linked up, and we were liable to defeat in detail." 21st Panzer Division sent an armored column right through the center of the British eastern flank, reaching the sea—showing how straightforward such defeat could be. "The answer to invasion from across the sea is a strong counterattack on the afternoon of D day, when the invading force has no proper communications and has lost certain cohesion. That was Rommel's chance. It was not taken, and we were given time to recover—thank goodness. If you saw OMAHA beach," Monty remarked in admiration, "you would wonder how the Americans ever got ashore." This was very much in line with Bradley's "someday I'll tell Gen. Eisenhower just how close it was," as he confided to his ADC.

The position on Bradley's Omaha Beach became so precarious, in fact, that Dempsey was asked if he could take the next wave of American troops onto one of the British beaches—a signal so alarming it was afterwards hushed up. ("It is not usually known that Monty wired me on the night of D-Day asking, 'Can you take V Corps?'" Dempsey confided to the American Official Historian. "I said, 'No, unless you want to leave our people out, because it is too crowded to go in together.' ")

Nevertheless, by the evening of D-Day more than 156,000 British, Canadian and American troops were ashore. No single German patrol boat had put to sea, and the German Seventh Army in Normandy had not even been on alert. Only at 10 P.M. on the night of 6 June did Rommel finally get back to his headquarters—by which time it was too late.

Monty had won round one.

Altering the Initial Plan

Monty's concern, as Allied Land Forces Commander, was the urgent need to link the two Allied armies before the Germans began to react with their Panzer divisions. On the evening of D-Day he thus decided to leave his Broomfield House headquarters and to go straight over to France on board the British destroyer HMS *Faulknor*. "If things were not going well," General Kennedy logged Monty's brief phone call to the War Office, shortly before his embarkation at 9:30 P.M., "he would put them right; if they were going well, he would make them go better."

The next morning at 5:30, Monty's ADC recalled, "I went up on the bridge and said, 'Well, where are we?' "

"I wish to hell I knew!" the ship's captain confessed. "We lost the swept channel two hours ago and we've heaved to—we're waiting for daylight to see if we can see where we are."

Daylight brought confirmation that they were utterly and literally at sea.

Monty was more amused than upset. "Angry? No, not at all. Got dressed, came up on the bridge, and said, 'Ah, I hear we're lost!' "

The captain was soon put out of his misery. "As it started to get lighter, you know, there was suddenly a cry from wherever, that a battleship was in sight. Immediately there was 'Action Stations!,' everyone at their guns. It transpired it was an American battleship; we had floated down right off Cherbourg peninsula!" Henderson remembered. "And jolly lucky with the minefields!"

Within a short time, however, Captain Churchill was able to locate Bradley's command ship, the *Aurora*, and Bradley came aboard the *Faulknor*. "Bradley was concerned about the operational situation on Omaha, his eastern beach. We discussed his problem," Monty later noted simply, "and agreed on how it could be solved."

Monty felt there was only one answer: to delay the American dash for Cherbourg. Collins' 7 U.S. Corps must fight eastwards from Utah Beach in order to help Gerow, instead of immediately westwards, to take Cherbourg.

"Monty told us we gotta join up—before pushing west or north [to Cherbourg]," Hansen recorded Bradley's message to Collins' 7 U.S. Corps Headquarters. "Brit may have to pull us out on Omaha. When they take Bayeux and get farther inland that should relieve the pressure on us." Later in the morning Eisenhower's British minelayer, HMS *Apollo*, arrived off the British beaches, and Monty informed the Supreme Commander of his decision. "On the whole U.S. Army front the immediate tactical plan has been altered," Eisenhower signaled to the Combined Chiefs of Staff in Washington the following day, "after which the original conceptions will be pursued."

No Effective Bombing

The British Second Army landings, meanwhile, had gone excellently. 50th Division had already begun attacking Bayeux "yesterday and 3rd Division was in possession of Ouistreham and Bieville and advancing on Caen today," Monty signaled to his chief of staff in England. The 6th British Airborne Division was across the Orne, to the northeast of Caen. Since it appeared "likely 21 Pz Div intends to hold Caen," Monty had agreed with Dempsey, it would be better to capture the city by envelopment than by a frontal attack: "Dempsey to proceed relentlessly with the original plan. He will hold a flank on the River Dives and capture Caen and Bayeux. He will then pivot on Caen and swing his right forward."

The lucky break in the weather which had made the D-Day landings possible was, however, already over. In his diary Dempsey noted that "unless the wind drops and the sea moderates, the build-up is going to be very difficult." Though pleased with the progress of his two corps, Dempsey was growing anxious about Caen. "The situation of 3 Div North of Caen and 6 Airborne East of the two rivers is still rather obscure," he noted ominously at 6 P.M. on 7 June.

The Allied air picture was equally disturbing. At the headquarters of the Allied Expeditionary Air Force at Stanmore, Air Marshal Leigh-Mallory was puzzled by the lack of German air response to the invasion. He saw his historical task not only in the winning of air superiority in the sky, but as the provider of air support to the Allied ground forces—support he had been unable to provide.

The "six-tenths cloud over Normandy at 2,000 feet" had made "effective bombing by the American heavies impossible" on D-Day, Leigh-Mallory complained to his diarist—the result being that all the carefully laid plans for the delay of German movements by creating "choke-points in towns on the roads could not be executed." Low cloud throughout 7 June was even worse, however—"in many places 10/10th at 1500–3000 ft." This had permitted the Germans "by the end of the day to have moved their nearer reserves into the battle area," he acknowledged. "The German army is being reinforced and I cannot bomb the reinforcements in daylight. . . . I have a feeling we are losing precious time at a moment when the main movements of the enemy are beginning. . . . Generally speaking, Allied Air Forces are not doing as well against the German army as I had hoped. No effective day bombing has yet taken place, and this is most unfortunate." Nor did he believe that the inactivity of the Luftwaffe denoted Allied air superiority had been won—"it may be," he warned, "that the Hun is trying to lull us into a false sense of security. We shall soon know."

Monty, however, was "well satisfied with results of today's fighting," as he signaled to Eisenhower at 8 P.M. "7 U.S. Corps has a lodgement area nearly 8 miles deep. . . . 5 Corps has made a grand recovery from a difficult situation and I have asked Bradley to congratulate the Corps from me. Have ordered Bradley to join up his two lodgement areas and to thrust towards La Haye du Puits [to cut off the Cherbourg Peninsula]. Dempsey has captured Port en Bessin and Bayeux and is on the general line of the railway between Bayeux and Caen." Caen itself, however, was "still held by enemy. Will pursue vigorously plans out-lined to you today."

Eisenhower, when he had to address war correspondents at Southwick, was less satisfied. He "seemed tired and almost listless," his naval aide, Lieutenant Commander Butcher, recorded in the Supreme Commander's desk diary. "He said the operation was still 'hazard-ous.' . . . He wanted them to report faithfully but not paint a false pic-ture of optimism; indeed the situation is somewhat critical and we are now in the inevitable race for build-up."

The Fist Is Unclenched

Immediately after breakfast, at 6:30 A.M. on 8 June 1944, HMS *Faulknor* "began to move in towards the beach on which I had asked to be landed," Monty recounted. "It was low water and, as I had asked we should get in as close as possible, the captain began sounding with hand leads and started the echo sounder. All beachmarks were obliterated by smoke-screens. The next thing that happened was that a slight shudder went through the ship; we were aground aft on some outlying sandbank or boulders. I was on the quar-ter deck with an ADC, and I sent him up to the bridge to ask if we were going to get any closer to the shore. This was not well received by the captain."

Ashore, Monty was shocked by the field headquarters which his staff, under Colonel Russell, had set up. It was, as the senior operations officer chronicled, an "exceedingly moderate location: a series of fields interspersed with German trenches," selected off the map, and under enemy artillery fire.

As on his arrival at Alamein two years before, Monty took one look and ordered the headquarters to be moved. His Canadian assistant, Lieutenant Colonel Warren, had fortunately stumbled on a better lo-cation at Creully, a village two miles further inland. There, in the grounds of the local château, Monty would set up his field headquarters for the next fortnight—missing, as he later recalled, only a chamber pot in his caravan, which had somehow been left behind in England. There followed a ritualistic English circumlocution, as Monty's staff sought, in the heat of battle, a replacement for the Allied Land Forces Commander. Only after she had vainly paraded the château's entire collection of "vases" did it dawn on Madame de Druval what General Montgomery might really require.

Meanwhile, that same morning, the anticipated counterattack by Rommel's 1 SS Panzer Corps began—but it made little headway and lacked cohesion. By evening over half of 21st Panzer Division's tanks had been lost, and Rommel made perhaps his greatest error since leaving his post shortly before D-Day. Sensing that the British were already too strong for a successful German counterattack north of Caen, he split off half of 21st Panzer and 12th SS Panzer Divisions and sent them twelve miles westwards in an attempt to recapture Bayeux. "Thus the fist was unclenched just as it was ready to strike," the Commander of Panzer Group West, General Geyr von Schweppenburg, later wistfully remarked.

Monty, by contrast, was delighted. Though the invasion was proving problematic in terms of linking up the Anglo-American bridgeheads, it was obvious that the very size and breadth of the Allied "break-in" had, as at Alamein, confused Rommel, catching him between three stools: defending Caen in the east, recapturing Bayeux in the center, and retaining Carentan, at the base of the Cherbourg Peninsula.

At 2:30 P.M., Monty visited Dempsey at the latter's headquarters. Dempsey felt that the Canadian and British 3rd Divisions north of Caen were "a bit messy" and needed to get their armor and artillery under better control; once this was done he wanted General Crocker, the corps commander, "to be prepared to operate offensively" from the 6th Airborne Division's bridgehead "with a view to capturing CAEN from the EAST in two or three days' time."

Monty did not agree. As he explained in a letter that evening to Major General Simpson at the War Office, Caen was only a name; he did not want to waste British and Canadian lives unnecessarily:

> The Germans are doing everything they can to hold on to CAEN. I have decided not to have a lot of casualties by butting up against the place; so I have ordered Second Army to keep up a good pressure at CAEN, and to make its main effort towards VILLERS BOCAGE and EVRECY and thence S.E. towards FALAISE.

This switch of axis was in accordance with Monty's promise to Leigh-Mallory that he would take the airfields southeast of Caen. Once established in that area, the British Second Army would present an offensive shield, behind which the Americans could build up their lodgement area, cut off the Cherbourg Peninsula, and gradually swing south, pivoting on the Falaise-Argentan ridge before taking Brittany, ultimately striking east to Paris.

All day Monty toured the British sector—still peppered with German snipers left behind by the speed of the assault. "Our initial landings were on a wide front," Monty explained to General Simpson at the War Office, "and there were gaps between landings. The impetus of the assault carried us some way inland and many defended localities were bypassed; these proved very troublesome later. In one case a complete German B[attalio]n, with artillery, was found inside 50 Div area; it gave some trouble but was eventually collected in (about 500 men). There is still one holding out—the radar station west of DOUVRES; it is very strong and is held by stout-hearted Germans." The Germans, he felt, were "fighting well," though "the Russians, Poles, Japanese, and Turks, run away, and, if unable to do so, surrender." Sniping, however, continued to be a problem. Two British infantry brigade commanders had been wounded, and a "good many C.O.'s killed," including Lieutenant Colonel Herdon, commanding the 2nd Battalion of his old regiment, the Royal Warwicks. Nor was the situation any better in the American sector, as Bradley's ADC noted in his diary: "Talk of sniping and Brad says he will not take action against anyone that decides to treat snipers a little more roughly than they are being treated at present. Sniper cannot sit around and shoot and then [ask to be] capture[d] when you close in on him. That's not the way to play the game."

The most perplexing problem, however, remained that of resupply. The Americans were "two tides behind now," Bradley acknowledged. Though the British had so far held all German Panzer attacks, the move of some of Rommel's armor westwards would expose the gaps in the Allied front. To Monty's intense relief, however, Dempsey sent word at 4:30 P.M. that Port-en-Bessin had been captured and that the Anglo-American armies had joined hands there. "The two armies," Monty proudly informed the War Office, "have now joined hands west of BAYEUX," and to Eisenhower at 8 P.M. he signaled that, while the Americans concentrated on linking their Utah and Omaha bridgeheads, Dempsey would strike south of Caen with his British armor, thus checking, as well as magnetizing, German interference: "Am organizing strong thrust south towards VILLERS BOCAGE and EVRECY. Am very satisfied with the situation."

Leigh-Mallory, however, became so worried by the failure of the Americans to join up their two bridgeheads at the base of the Cotentin Peninsula that, though he had once bitterly opposed the American airborne division drop north of Carentan, he now even offered to drop 1st British Airborne Division into the sector.

Far from sanguine, Leigh-Mallory felt dejected by his very impotence to help Monty by employing his heavy bombers. "It is a terrible thing to me," he recorded to his diarist for the third day running, "to feel all these [German] troop movements going on while I am not able to stop them because of bad weather and low cloud."

But would the Allied bombers blitz German troop movements *even if the clouds lifted?* At the 11 A.M. Allied air commanders' conference that day, it was secretly recorded "there was a resurgence of the old controversy between the Air C-in-C [Leigh-Mallory] and the U.S. Strategic Air Force Commanders over the use of strategic bombers for attacking rail communications in support of the Army, instead of for direct offensive against the German Air Force." Leigh-Mallory admitted the Luftwaffe was not beaten, merely absent thus far from the battle. The time might come when it "would constitute a major threat, but it had not come yet," he argued, "whereas the threat to our Armies from the quick build-up of German reserves was a very real threat."

Either way, without clear skies, the heavy bombers were grounded. That night, 8 June 1944, with the sky completely overcast, Leigh-Mallory fell into a somber mood. "The weather is still lousy. . . . it depresses me, though the met[eorological] people say it will clear tomorrow. I doubt this myself. There is another depression in the Atlantic, they tell me, eight hours away."

The outlook, from the Allied air standpoint, looked bleak.

A Chance to Checkmate the Enemy

Monty, retiring to bed in his sleeping truck for the first time since he left Eighth Army, did not share Leigh-Mallory's gloom. "There is no doubt that the Germans were surprised, and we got on shore before they had recovered. The speed, power, and violence of the assault carried all before it," he reported with satisfaction to Major General Simpson at the War Office.

The slowness of the American buildup ("First US Army had a very sticky party at OMAHA, and its progress at UTAH has not been rapid") still bothered him, but with regard to the British sector he was, as in Sicily, so excited by the way things seemed to be going that he began to imagine he was on the threshold, already, of a major coup. For if the Germans continued to fight around Caen with their Panzer corps, then there was a chance that, by vigorous offensive tactics, he could actually entrap it there.

On 9 June, therefore, as 30 Corps began to drive south from its salient, Monty bristled with confidence. At 10 A.M., General Dempsey arrived, and for an hour and a half the two men went over Second Army's plans for the thrust south to Falaise and Argentan. It was now that the first mention was made of a British airborne operation to assist in the encirclement of the German Panzer corps—Dempsey stressing he would want the American 5 Corps to join with him in the thrust by driving south to Caumont. Meanwhile, "if the attacks of 7 Armd Div and 51 Div went well," Dempsey noted in his diary, "the landing of 1 Airborne Div to the SOUTH of CAEN might well be decisive."

From Creully, Monty drove now westwards to see Bradley. General Collins, commanding 7 U.S. Corps, was "exuding great gusts of optimism over the situation. He is anxious to drive through to Cherbourg," Bradley's aide noted, and was disappointed when Bradley gave him Monty's "verbal order . . . suggesting that main effort be fixed first in joining the corps and thereafter in cutting over the peninsula to cut off the German."

Collins, made in the same mold as the swashbuckling Patton, protested, and asked Bradley for greater latitude. "Collins is independent, vigorous, heady, capable and full of vinegar. Needs a check rein if anything," Hansen recorded. Bradley, however, was adamant that Monty's orders be obeyed. There was no prospect of the Germans being able to reinforce the Cherbourg Peninsula quickly; Cherbourg would therefore fall in good time. What was important now was to ensure that the last gap in the Allied bridgehead be sealed. "Want the corps connected up as quickly as possible," Bradley instructed. "Use the air. Dump 500 or 1,000 tons of air [i.e., bombs] on it [Carentan] and take it apart. Then rush it fast and take it. We've got the Navy here and they can help you with fire."

Monty was confident Bradley would close the Carentan gap "by tomorrow," as he wrote to de Guingand during the afternoon of 9 June. Rommel, in Monty's view, had now clearly divided his counterattack into two main efforts—21st Panzer and two infantry divisions (711 and 346) east of Caen, and two Panzer divisions (12th and Lehr) west of Caen around Bretteville. In both sectors Monty was quite certain of holding the attacks, while hatching his own masterstroke. The American 5 Corps would attack southwards towards Caumont; alongside it Dempsey would unleash 7th Armoured Division, the famous Desert Rats, through 8th Armoured Brigade's bridgehead at Tilly on the Seulles River. The Desert Rats were to be "launched tomorrow southwards through BAYEUX to secure VILLERS BOCAGE and NOYERS and then EVRECY; then to exploit to the S.E." Meanwhile, east of Caen, through the Orne bridgehead, he would "pass 51 Div across R. ORNE, through 6 Airborne DIV, to attack southwards east of CAEN towards CAGNY." To complete the encirclement of the German armored forces he would drop 1st Airborne Division in the gap created by these pincers—"to put down 1 Airborne Div somewhere south of CAEN as a big air hook, and to link up with it from EVRECY and CAGNY. This is being worked out now; would want the whole Division, which should get ready to load now."

Thus Monty *welcomed* the very German counterattacks which so worried Leigh-Mallory. "If the Germans wish to be offensive and drive in our lodgement area between CAEN and BAYEUX, the best way to defeat them is to be offensive ourselves," Monty remarked confidently to his chief of staff, "and the plan given [above] will checkmate the enemy completely if we can pull it off."

But could he?

Eisenhower in a Snit

As instructed, de Guingand went straight to the Supreme Commander's headquarters to show Monty's letter. But Monty's own signal, direct to Eisenhower, though it reached Eisenhower's British ADC, Lieutenant Colonel Gault, that night, never got through—Gault "having deferred handling it until he got up at eight" on 10 June. The signal was then found to be—naturally enough—in Most Secret cipher, and by the time a signals officer decoded it, Eisenhower had left his headquarters in a rage. "He had awakened in a snit . . . no information from Monty, who had agreed to cable every night his latest impression of the way of the battle."

Eisenhower, itching to become at long last a field commander and feeling lonely and isolated now that the Allied assault armies had departed from England, was a frustrated man. "I could see from his questions," his naval aide noted, when Eisenhower went to the war room to hear the latest information from the front, "he wished he were running the 21st Army Group."

Legends would grow after the war that Monty had not kept Eisenhower, the Supreme Commander, fully in touch with his plans and strategy in Normandy, and that because of this, Eisenhower had failed to understand the logic of his Land Forces Commander's operations. This view, however, was completely without foundation, as de Guingand angrily attested when the point was raised. De Guingand—also kept back in England with 21st Army Group's main headquarters at Portsmouth—saw or spoke on the telephone to Eisenhower every day of the campaign, as he had done in the buildup to Overlord.

The truth was, General Eisenhower—who was nothing if not intelligent—understood *exactly* what Monty was attempting to achieve. Like Churchill, however, he was moody and a prey to depression, followed by periods of ebullient optimism when his quick mind would seize upon the hopeful, and became impatient at having to wait for battlefield progress or the fulfillment of battle plans. The unexpected chance that Monty might surround the whole of Rommel's immediate Panzer force in Normandy fueled him with nervous anticipation. When his idle British ADC finally brought him Monty's decoded signal, Butcher noted, "its contents buoyed Ike." Leigh-Mallory's gloom and the failure of the Allied air forces to halt German Panzer division movements were forgotten as, all day on 10 June, the Supreme Commander nervously waited for further news.

A Thurber Cartoon

In Normandy, meanwhile, Monty summoned Bradley and Dempsey to meet him at Port-en-Bessin, the junction between the Allied armies. The conference took place at 11 A.M. in a field "next to an ordinary Fr[ench] stucco house, fixed with many gables and a curious Fr. maid that peered through the open window with several moppets in her arms," Bradley's aide recounted with amusement.

Monty himself "was in an old loose-fitting grey gabardine hunting jacket with bellows pockets that seemed to accentuate its flappiness, a grey sweater, corduroy trousers and the well known beret with its double insignia—one of them nicely fixed in gold embroidery. Map case spread on hood of his open tonneau and he lounged easily behind his sharp beaklike nose, the small grey eyes that dart about quickly like rabbits in a Thurber cartoon.

"Gen Dempsey next to him in a camouflage coat of paratroop length, flat hat and regulation insignia. Monty wore none although his car carried the Brit flag and carried the four stars of an Amerk commander with the 21 Group flash. Brad shook hands (dressed in OD's with combat jacket, helmet—GI) broad grin. "Glad to see you here, sir.' . . . Proceeded to go over their plans."

"Dempsey had plotted an attack south of the unspoiled town of Bayeux, partly to extend his bridgehead and partly to envelop Caen from the west," Bradley later recalled. "Two Panzer divisions were dug in before Caen and Dempsey and his staff sought to outflank them in his attack from Bayeux. We were to parallel this British attack and drive south in the direction of Caumont. There Gerow was to establish a strong defensive outpost for V Corps. An attack on this end of the lodgement, we estimated, might also help divert enemy reinforcements from Collins' attack towards Cherbourg."

With American buildup twenty-four hours behind schedule, and

with the pressing need still to link up his two American corps beachheads, Bradley could not promise Dempsey any immediate assistance.
The Omaha beachhead was still only two miles deep—so shallow, in
fact, that Bradley, four days after D-Day, was still commanding First
U.S. Army from the USS *Augusta*. Regretfully, therefore, he felt he
would be unable to help Dempsey before 12 or 13 June, when he
hoped to send one division through to Caumont, about six miles west
of Villers-Bocage. The Desert Rats, who were already advancing
through the 8th Armoured Brigade's shield on the high ground east of
Tilly, would thus have to go it alone.

Monty was disappointed. "The bad weather is a great nuisance as
what we want is to take quick advantage of our good position by striking deep before the enemy can build up strength against us," he had lamented in a second letter to de Guingand the night before. "However
we are not doing too badly." Sympathetic to Bradley's precarious
beachhead, he accepted the American commander's delayed undertaking. If Dempsey could not get immediate American support, he made
up his mind, he would do his best to get Allied air and airborne help
instead.

This was not, however, to be so easy.

Joining Hands

"It is depressing to think that I have, as the P.M. said, more than
11,000 aircraft and cannot make full use of them, and I confess to
experiencing a certain sense of frustration," Air Marshal Leigh-
Mallory had chronicled in his diary the night before. "I repeat that it
is very annoying, when we have reached a stage on land where the
army has got enough elbow room to do a proper build-up, not to be
able to mount a decent air attack on the enemy's ground forces. I believe that if I had been able to carry out intensive air operations today
I could have delayed them at least twenty-four hours and thus in-

creased our own chance of making a successful attack on land. Today seems to me a very crucial day and very little has been done in the air. This is, indeed, the first critical moment."

Though disappointed by the lack of air support, Monty was again "very pleased with today's operations," he signaled to Eisenhower on the evening of 10 June, for during the day he had heard that the American 5 and 7 Corps had at last joined hands, and he had therefore given Bradley the green light for Collins to cut the peninsula and race for Cherbourg.

Although he remained keen to envelop Caen and, if possible, trap the Panzer divisions there, Monty was, however, concerned at the growing enemy resistance in the Second Army sector and the rising British casualties, which currently exceeded American casualties by four to three. He had thought for a while that he could, by seizing the enemy's Queen—his armor—checkmate him; but as the hours went by he became realistic. The troops were tiring, and the ideal defensive country, though it gave security to the Allied bridgehead now that it was homogeneously established, also favored the German defenders. Against fourteen enemy divisions *in situ* the Allies had put ashore sixteen divisions, but casualties already exceeded those of Alamein, at around 15,000, and had blunted the initial impetus of the landings. Heavier casualties, moreover, were expected, once the Germans brought in more troops and weapons. The drive to encircle Caen might or might not succeed, he felt, but it was not the real business—which was to shield the American right wing as it raced for Cherbourg. As he reminded Brooke at 9:00 the next morning, 11 June, his "general policy is to pull the enemy on to Second Army so as to make it easier for First Army to expand and extend the quicker." To de Guingand and Eisenhower he signaled the same: "My general object is to pull the Germans on to Second Army so that First Army can extend and expand"—and later that day Eisenhower replied: "Thanks for your messages. They are very helpful. Please pass my congratulations on to your commanders."

The situation was, all in all, heartening. Despite weather that precluded heavy air support, and with naval resupply running more than twenty-four hours behind schedule, the Allies had nevertheless achieved what had not been done for almost a thousand years, since the time of William the Conqueror: they had crossed the English Channel and had established themselves ashore in a single, cohesive bridgehead almost a hundred miles wide, in five days.

The Turning Point of the Battle

Montgomery had two options or intentions, Rommel meanwhile felt: to build up a bridgehead in the east around Caen "for a powerful attack later into the interior of France, probably towards Paris," or secondly, to "cut off the Cotentin peninsula and gain possession of Cherbourg," which would give the Allies a major port. Anxious to cripple the threat to Cherbourg, Rommel now declared he would switch his Panzer strength to the American sector (as he had so successfully done at Kasserine), returning thereafter to stifle the British threat to Paris. His army group, he explained to Hitler, would "shift the gravity of its operations into the Carentan–Montebourg area during the next few days, in order to destroy the enemy in that sector and divert the danger from Cherbourg. Not until then can any attack be made against the enemy between the Orne and the Vire."

As Dempsey's armor pushed out towards Villers-Bocage on 10 June, however, Hitler became alarmed—and decided to overrule Rommel. Rommel was *not* to switch his counteroffensive to the American front, he ordered; he was to put everything he possessed into stopping the British breakout. "Hitler vetoed Rommel's plan to move against the American bridgehead in the Caen–Montebourg area," General Bayerlein later lamented, "and gave orders instead for Army Group B to mount an attack against the British bridgehead from the Caen area, using the reinforcements with which it had been supplied."

For General Collins, on the right flank of the American bridgehead, this was a crucial reprieve. But for Dempsey, planning the envelopment of Caen and the German Panzer divisions, it was a decision which effectively ruled out the possibility of spectacular success. By 11 A.M. on 11 June, Dempsey was noting that "it appeared from various indications during the morning that the enemy was preparing an attack North-West from CAEN." Could he then risk removing his tanks from that sector and sending them in support of 51st Highland Division's thrust through the Orne bridgehead? An hour and a half later he met Crocker at 1 Corps Headquarters and canceled the plan for 4th Armoured Brigade to participate in the encircling attack—"told him to retain 4 Armd Bde in the COLOMBY area today." The Desert Rats, meanwhile, were "still meeting considerable resistance" in the other pincer of the intended attack towards Villers-Bocage, and by the following day, 12 June, both Dempsey and Monty became seriously alarmed. Intelligence indicated that *more* Panzer divisions were on their way to Normandy; there was thus little time to lose if Second Army was to seize Caen before these extra Panzer divisions arrived. An Ultra decrypt on 12 June, for instance, showed that 2nd Panzer Division was on the move to reinforce Panzer Lehr in the Villers-Bocage area; it was imperative, then, that 7th Armoured Division move faster.

All morning on 12 June, Dempsey conferred with General Erskine, the commander of the Desert Rats, at the latter's headquarters. "Their advance is going very slowly against stiffening opposition, and the country is very close and difficult," Dempsey lamented. However, at 11:45 A.M., Dempsey met Bucknall, the 30 Corps Commander, at Bayeux railway station. Bucknall told him that the 11th Hussars, on the extreme western flank of Second Army, were "in contact with American 5 Corps" and "were making good progress SOUTH of the road from BAYEUX to CAUMONT." By sidestepping 7th Armoured Division onto this easier axis, Dempsey hoped he could increase the tempo of his thrust—"I told him to switch 7 Armd DIV from their front immediately, to push them through behind 11 H[ussars] and endeavour to get VILLERS BOCAGE that way. Provided this is carried out with real drive and speed, there is a chance that we will get through before the front congeals."

Rushing to Monty's headquarters, Dempsey outlined his latest outflanking plan, which looked increasingly promising as units of both First U.S. Army and Second British Army reached Caumont that evening. As Monty would claim to Brooke, this was now "the turning point of the battle." Hitler had overruled his army Commander-in-Chief in the field. Cherbourg was assured. And, if all went well, Rommel's armor, thanks to Hitler, might be caught in Dempsey's noose.

Distinguished Visitors

I n the midst of these developments, the Prime Minister and his entourage descended on Normandy, as did the American Chiefs of Staff: General Marshall, Admiral King, and General Arnold, the American air chief. Thus the conference Monty had arranged with Bradley at 10 A.M. on 12 June had to be canceled, while the two senior American and British field commanders spent most of the day receiving their distinguished guests.

Bradley's headquarters had only been established ashore a day, and the American Chiefs of Staff had thus to lunch on "C rations and hard tack biscuits," Major Hansen recorded.

Monty's welcome, at his tented compound in the grounds of the Château de Creully, was more lavish, but the visit was equally distracting. Indifferent to the nuisance he was causing, Churchill was excited and, as on his first visit to Monty's headquarters at Alamein, relished the historic moment. "We lunched in a tent looking towards the enemy," he later chronicled. "The General was in the highest spirits. I asked him how far away was the actual front. He said about three miles. I asked him if he had a continuous line. He said, 'No.' 'What is there then to prevent an incursion of German armour breaking up our luncheon?' He said he did not think they would come."

The Prime Minister's presence was an honor, but his indefatigable curiosity was a trial to Monty, who had prefaced luncheon with an "explanation on the map of his dispositions and plans. All, as usual, wonderfully clear and concise," Brooke noted in his diary, reflecting on the wondrous change in fortunes since the same day in June 1940. "I knew then that it would not be long before I was kicked out of France. . . . But if anybody had told me then that in four years I should return with Winston and Smuts to lunch with Monty commanding a new invasion force, I should have found it hard to believe."

On the great wall map of Normandy in his newly built operations trailer, Monty outlined his strategy: the drawing of main German forces onto the British east flank so that the Americans could "expand" behind; indeed now that the beachheads were all conjoined, he had given Bradley the green light to cut off the Cotentin Peninsula and go for Cherbourg. Within this overall strategy, Monty pointed out, the Allies would seize every opportunity to exploit German mistakes. The Germans had, for instance, concentrated their Panzer strength in a bid to hold Caen and to smash what they considered to be an Allied thrust towards Paris. Second Army currently had an excellent chance of encircling the Panzer Corps, and on the colored wall map he pointed to the two pincers Dempsey was trying to create. As Churchill excitedly informed Stalin on his return, "we hope to encircle Caen, and perhaps to make a capture there of prisoners."

At no point in this military lecture, however, did Monty ever suggest that Dempsey was to do more than bring the German forces to battle around Caen and "capture prisoners"—and when, after the war, Eisenhower wrote in his official record of the campaign (*Eisenhower's Own Story of the War*, published in 1946) that "in the east we had been unable to break out towards the Seine," Monty was understandably furious, for this was a complete travesty of the facts. Both to Eisenhower and to Churchill, Monty made it quite clear that there was no question of wild breakouts towards the Seine. How could there be when the Allies had only sixteen divisions ashore, many of which, particularly the parachute and first assault divisions, were inevitably running out of steam? As Churchill explained to Stalin, the battle for Normandy would be a slow and deliberate one: "I should think it quite likely that we should work up to a battle of about a million a side, lasting through June and July. We plan to have about two million there by mid-August."

Eisenhower's unfortunate obfuscation would, however, color military accounts ever afterwards, polarizing chroniclers into nationalistic camps. This was, Monty felt, a tragedy, for the battle for Normandy was, at all stages, an Allied battle: a battle in which Allied soldiers risked and gave their lives conforming to an Allied plan to defeat the German armies in the West—not to "break out towards the Seine."

Eisenhower's account was the product, however, of an idle Supreme Headquarters at the end of the war. At the time in question Eisenhower was fully "in the picture," as were Marshall and the American Chiefs of Staff after their visit. Some days later Eisenhower cabled to Washington: "The plan of battle of that [British] flank remains almost identical with that explained to you when you were here. I am very hopeful it will actually *break up the German formations on that front.*"

Meanwhile, having packed off his distinguished visitors after a tour of the bridgehead, Monty was able to redirect his attention to the battle. The weather was fine and sunny, and the air forces could at last support the land armies.

Monty had exuded optimism to his superiors. But behind his facade of high spirits he was boiling with anger—for, as Allied Air Chief, Leigh-Mallory was refusing to drop the 1st British Airborne Division near Caen.

A Gutless Bugger

"The plan was to drop this division early on the 13th June in an area South-West of CAEN behind the German line in order to assist in the encirclement of the German Panzer troops in the CAEN area," began the minutes of the special Overlord air conference, convened to discuss Monty's request. The 1st Airborne Division Commander, General Urquhart, was keen to carry out the operation; he wished, however, to land in daylight. Air Vice-Marshal Hollinghurst, commanding the air group responsible, felt a daylight drop was "impossible" over such a heavily defended area; he insisted the operation be conducted at night. The navy, however, would give no guarantee that it would hold its fire if aircraft flew over its ships in darkness. In the circumstances, Leigh-Mallory turned down the request.

Monty, when he heard the news, was beside himself. Leigh-Mallory "should come over and see me and ascertain the true form before he refuses to carry out an operation," he signaled to his chief of staff in England. "He could get here by air in 30 minutes. Meanwhile I want planning to go ahead so that when conditions are favourable the operation can be laid on quickly. Am sending BROWNING [British Airborne Corps commander] to see you tomorrow leaving here by air at 1000 hrs. Inform LM as above."

Monty's signal, however, did nothing to change Leigh-Mallory's mind. As soon as the Prime Minister and his party had departed, Monty therefore wrote a savage letter to de Guingand regarding Leigh-Mallory's "refusal to drop 1 Airborne DIV. The favourable conditions I am working up to are that the DZ [Dropping Zone] would be within range of the artillery of 7 Armd DIV in the VILLERS-BOCAGE area; if we then drop the Airborne DIV in EVRECY area we would be very well placed and might get a big 'scoop.'

"The real point is," Monty ended with exasperation, "that LM sitting in his office cannot possibly know the local battle form over here; and therefore he must not refuse my demands unless he first comes over to see me; he could fly here in a Mosquito in ½ hour, talk for an hour, and be back in England in ½ hour. Obviously he is a gutless bugger, who refuses to take a chance and plays for safety on all occasions."

"My pincer movement to get CAEN is taking good shape," Monty nevertheless reported to Brooke the next morning, "and there are distinct possibilities that the enemy Divisions may not find it too easy to escape; especially Pz LEHR. 21 Pz and 12 S.S. could escape easily, but would have to pull out soon—unless they can hold up the western half of the pincers i.e. 30 Corps swing." At the present moment, he reported, "the Armd Recce Regt of 7 Armd DIV (8H) is moving on NOYERS; there are a lot of enemy, including some TIGER tanks, milling about in the triangle HOTTOT–NOYERS–VILLERS BOCAGE. The situation will clarify later!!"

When it did, eventually, the news was bad. Rommel, with his keen sixth sense based on years of battlefield fighting, had sent in the newly arrived 2nd Panzer Division not to reinforce the three Panzer divisions already in line, but westwards towards the American sector—in defiance of Hitler's order. This division had now smashed into 7th Armoured Division's thrust, with consequences that were to affect the whole fabric of the Normandy operations. "Late last evening (13 June) 2 Pz DIV came into the battle," Monty informed Brooke the next day; "it counterattacked 7 Armd DIV in the VILLERS-BOCAGE area and we took some prisoners. A real good dogfight went on all the evening. The village itself is in low ground and finally 7 Armd DIV withdrew and occupied firmly the high ground immediately to the west—which dominates the village." In fact the heavy artillery of the American 1st Division at Caumont had had to be summoned to halt the German counterattack.

Not only had the British Villers-Bocage thrust failed to make headway, but there were ominous signs of a setback in the American western sector, too—where, according to reports received at 5 P.M. on 13

June, the Germans had recaptured Carentan, the vital junction between 5 and 7 U.S. Corps!

From being on the brink of checkmating the enemy, the Allies
seemed suddenly back at square one.

Hanging On Firmly

As if to underscore the reversing tide of military fortune, the
weather in the Channel now deteriorated—threatening naval
resupply and troop reinforcement. With only limited numbers
of tanks ashore, it was important that the Allies preserve the integrity
of their line—"Bradley's left Corps, 5 US Corps, is getting rather
stretched," Monty signaled to de Guingand, "and he has had to send
some armour over from 2 Armd DIV to lend a hand at CARENTAN."
This now made Gerow's 5 U.S. Corps salient at Caumont vulnerable
to Panzer attack. "So I have told him to hang on firmly to
CAUMONT," Monty explained; indeed he had now told Bradley, if
necessary, to delay his southern offensive towards Brittany "and not to
push the right of the Corps forward to St LO until he feels he can
safely do so. 30 DIV will be coming in through the beaches tomorrow
and then the Corps will be able to move on again."

Overnight, the seemingly ripe fruit of Monty's Anglo-American battle strategy while Collins drove north to Cherbourg—Caen for the
British army, Saint-Lô for the American army—was abandoned.
Monty, however, was far from abashed. As long as Rommel counterattacked, the Allies could destroy his armor on ground of their own
choosing, as at Alamein. "We are very strong now astride the road
CAEN–BAYEUX about junction of 3 Div and 3 Canadian DIV, and if
the enemy attacks he should be seen off," Monty predicted; "I have
400 tanks there. Any such attack here would be good, so long as we
see it off and the right flank of Second Army swings round to
NOYERS and EVRECY."

If 7th Armoured Division remained on the defensive, on high ground, Monty had no fear lest the Allied salient be pinched off by Rommel; but the chance of successfully delivering the British pincer attack around Caen had gone. There would be no surprise; the Germans were installed in depth on the upper Odon, and a costly failure would risk putting Bradley "in the soup" now that his American armor was enmeshed in the fight to hold Carentan, further west.

As at Alamein, when his "crumbling" efforts ran into heavy opposition, Monty now decided to regroup in order to deliver a heavier blow.

Eisenhower, however, was appalled.

Round Two to Rommel

"Last night Ike was concerned that Monty couldn't attack until Saturday," Lieutenant Commander Butcher recorded in his diary the following day. "Ike was anxious that the Germans be kept off balance and that our drive never stop. But apparently Monty wants to tidy up his 'administrative tail' and get plenty of supplies on hand before he makes a general attack. Ike also said that yesterday we had made no gains, which he didn't like."

No commander should be hoisted by the petard of a junior aide, but Eisenhower's response, as recorded by Butcher, did reflect the Supreme Commander's impatient and often shallow grasp of battlefield reality. Rommel's insubordinate counterstroke had in fact put "a different complexion on the problem," Monty explained in a letter to Brooke. "I have got to be very certain of my position, step by step; I must at all costs remain well balanced and able to handle easily any situation that may develop as the enemy reserves come into battle.

"I am now very strong defensively on the left of Second Army, in the CAEN sector; I would be stronger still if I had CAEN itself, but I am quite well positioned as things are at present." His general strategy, however, remained the same: "to pull the Germans on to Second British Army, and fight them there, so that First US Army can carry out its task the easier."

Whatever Eisenhower might imagine in his rear headquarters in England, the situation required careful generalship. At Alamein, Rommel had been unable to call upon reserves, once Eighth Army had smashed a hole in his northern defenses, and had been forced to withdraw tanks and troops from other front-line sectors and to commit them piecemeal to his counterattack—leading to their ultimate annihilation. But in Normandy the situation now favored Rommel, who could call upon vast and hitherto uncommitted Panzer forces, currently held back in case of a cross-Channel invasion in the Pas de Calais area. As the Germans realized that Normandy was the sole Allied invasion target, these Panzer formations would inevitably be committed to battle. The crucial factor was to ensure they be committed to the British front, not the American—allowing Collins free rein to seize Cherbourg without worrying about his rear.

To Monty's relief, the British thrust towards Villers-Bocage had achieved this, even if the envelopment of Caen would have to be postponed. "Enemy reserves look like coming in here—in fact where we broke in," Monty explained to Brooke. "It is here that 2 Pz DIV has come in, and it attacked the Americans at CAUMONT last evening as well as 7 Armd DIV at VILLERS BOCAGE." There were now four German Panzer divisions in line, side by side, facing the British front— and "2 SS Pz (ex TOULOUSE) may appear soon."

Having penned this letter at 9 A.M. on 14 June, Monty spoke by telephone to Bradley. "He is quite happy about CARENTAN and is strongly positioned now, some 2000 and 3000 yards to the west and south of the town." However, "His left Corps (5 Corps under GEROW) is getting rather stretched. So he is putting in 19 Corps (CORLETT) at 1200 hrs today," Monty related to Brooke at 10 A.M., to take over the sector west of Carentan.

Ignored by all too many postwar writers and historians of D-Day and the Normandy invasion, this was the real turning point in the battle. Dempsey's pincer attack to entrap the Panzer divisions had had to be postponed; now, only hours later, the cautious, buttoned-up American army commander, General Bradley, had elected to use his new, incoming corps not to "move on again" to Saint-Lô, but to bolster his line at Carentan and to concentrate entirely on Collins' bid to cut off the Cherbourg Peninsula and the seizure of the vital seaport.

With these British and American postponements the German counterattack had achieved its disruptive aim. Whatever Monty might say, round two of the battle of Normandy had gone to Rommel.

Adjusting the Timetable

In the quiet, assured manner with which Bradley allocated his resources and priorities within First Army, Monty recognized a fellow professional: an admiration that caused Monty to consider Bradley, in the weeks ahead, as far and away the finest all-round field commander produced by the U.S. Army. "Bradley is strongly positioned at CAUMONT. He beat off the attack of 2 Pz DIV there last night, and will hold the area firmly," Monty assured Brooke with complete confidence—a confidence which Bradley reciprocated.

Bradley was watching carefully his supply position. "Worried now on beach situation especially with regard to the unloading of ammo. Short on art[iller]y," his aide noted in his diary. "Had to limit 19 Corps to 25 rds per gun per day. 1st [Division] shoots 200 rds per day. Corlett [19 U.S. Corps Commander] objects. Gen [Bradley]: 'Pete, I hate to do it as much as you—but hell we've got no choice. It's either that or we simply shoot what we've got, pack up and go back home.' "

It was quite clear to Bradley, if not to Eisenhower, that First U.S. Army would have to tackle its two objectives in turn. Like Monty, Bradley felt it was important to conduct American operations logically and relentlessly, while adjusting the timetable so as to ensure that whatever his army undertook, it would achieve. "B. [Bradley] went up to G.3 [Operations] tent to give them his new limited objective line. Fear of overextending himself. . . . 'I don't want involve myself in the V Corps—may hamper my freedom of movement in the VII [Corps] drive on Cherbourg,' " his aide quoted him in his diary. As Bradley told his assistant chief of staff on 14 June, "the corps commanders are all filled with piss and vinegar. They want to go like hell. I've got to stop them, get them solid and dug in. He [the enemy] is going to hit us hard and I don't want a [German] breakthrough."

But if Monty and Bradley, receiving the latest intelligence on the movement of German armored reserves, were completely in accord in this respect, others were not—indeed, the decision to wait while Collins took Cherbourg produced, among the Allied air commanders, consternation.

An Element of Crisis

C ompletely disregarding Dempsey's and Bradley's real situation, the Allied air force commanders now invented an Allied emergency. The German attack at Carentan was fictionalized into a potential disaster, with Monty's chief of plans, Brigadier Richardson, insisting that the town was firmly held by the Americans, and the Allied Air Force Headquarters claiming, as their war diarist recorded, that it was "now probably in the hands of the enemy."

If Leigh-Mallory was proving a "gutless bugger," some of the other air commanders were proving conniving and defeatist. Chief among them was Air Vice-Marshal Sir Arthur ("Mary") Coningham, the New Zealander who held command of all the Allied tactical fighter and fighter-bomber forces for Overlord. "In Air Marshal Coningham's view there was the element of a crisis in the central sector," the Air Historian noted at the time, "the Allied position being worsened by the fact that no fresh Allied formations were due to land today or tomorrow, and those now engaged had been fighting almost continuously for a week and were getting tired."

Coningham was supported by Eisenhower's Deputy Supreme Commander, Air Marshal Tedder, who—like Coningham and Leigh-Mallory—had not yet set foot in France: "Air Chief Marshal Tedder said that the present military situation had the makings of a dangerous crisis."

In his later memoirs, Tedder covered up this monstrous performance, and instead repeated the same Eisenhower allegation that would so infuriate Monty: "When a week had passed since D-Day without the capture of Caen, it became clear to us at SHAEF that the hopes of a rapid breakthrough on the left were now remote." Yet Monty had *never* suggested or intended a "breakthrough on the left": only a battle around Caen that would permit him to bring the main German armor to battle, even surround it—thus establishing and extending an impregnable British shield behind which Bradley could take Cherbourg and break out via Saint-Lô and Avranches to Brittany and the Loire.

In retrospect, however, as his military assistant later recognized, Monty was in part to blame for the misunderstanding. "I think he had given the RAF a totally false impression, at St. Paul's and elsewhere, as to when he was going to get those airfields, south of Caen—a totally false impression," Lieutenant Colonel Dawnay acknowledged. "Because, when we got there [Normandy] we realized quite clearly that he didn't care a damn about those airfields, as long as he could draw all the German armour on to that side and give a chance for his [American] right swing to break out!"

To Brigadier Williams, Monty's chief of Intelligence, what was remarkable was "the speed with which he adjusted" to the situation once ashore: "his recognition that, as long as he represented a threat, a real threat to Caen—as long as he kept that threat, then the enemy armour became magnetised to it, shall we say—and that he must keep that going in order to get Bradley going."

Rommel's reaction, though it denied the Allies certain promised fruits in the form of airfields, had suited Monty, Williams felt, because it accorded with the Commander-in-Chief's overall framework for the development of Anglo-American operations in Normandy. However, it was a framework which, in the inevitable presentations and preparations in England, had gathered "a number of labels that people pin on. And one was Caen, and the other was the airfields at Carpiquet. And these were of course seized on by the people who didn't do land-battle fighting, people who saw things from the sky—these were the things he failed to deliver, from their point of view, [in] their impatience to be on with things."

Had Eisenhower been the battlefield commander he so longed to be, he could have stamped on the premature defeatist rumblings of the air commanders as, at their morning meeting on 14 June 1944, they invented "a state of crisis." But Eisenhower was not. Nor had he, as yet, any real grasp of the Allied air weapon upon the battlefield. Thus he allowed his air barons to rebel, and to manufacture, unchecked, a predicament that did not exist in Normandy—with results that were to sour the greatest Allied victory of World War II.

An Attractive Proposal

So worried was Leigh-Mallory by the atmosphere of doom in the air force war room on the morning of 14 June that he now elected to fly over to France for the first time since 1940. However, when he arrived at 4 P.M. on 14 June at Monty's headquarters, Monty was nonplussed.

Early that morning Monty had, as he had informed Brooke after breakfast, received news that Carentan was back in American hands. He was not in the least worried by the situation, as his note at 11:30 A.M. to Major General Simpson at the War Office demonstrated:

Tac Headquarters 21 Army Group

14-6-4
1130 hrs

My dear Simbo
All quite O.K. and I am very happy about the situation. I had to think again when 2 Pz DIV suddenly appeared last night. I think it had been intended for offensive action against 1 Corps [i.e., north of Caen]. But it had to be used to plug the hole through which we had broken in the area CAUMONT–VILLERS BOCAGE.
So long as Rommel uses his strategic reserves to plug holes—that is good.

Yrs ever
B. L. Montgomery

In the airplane, having picked up de Guingand at Thorney Island airfield on the way from Northolt to France, Leigh-Mallory had meanwhile discussed the situation with Monty's chief of staff. Opinion at Main Headquarters of 21st Army Group (still at Portsmouth) was that, giving the growing armored opposition to Dempsey's forces, it might be better if the whole Anglo-American front went over to the defensive while Collins made his way up to Cherbourg: "On the way across General de Guingand had suggested to the Air C-in-C that it might be sounder for the Army to concentrate on the Cotentin Peninsula and Cherbourg as their first objective, and to hold along the rest of the line."

Monty, however, would have no truck with this idea. To him, as he would put it a day or two later, "Caen is the key to Cherbourg." Rommel *must* be made to believe, like Hitler, that the British were attempting to break out in the eastern sector, so that he would not dare release the four Panzer divisions which had now been put in "to plug holes" there. For the Allies to go on the defensive would in fact give Rommel the initiative, and imperil, not secure, the American thrust to Cherbourg.

Thus, when Leigh-Mallory offered that "an air bombardment might be launched by medium and heavy bombers on a front of say 5,000 yards, behind which the army might advance," Monty was impressed by Leigh-Mallory's newfound willingness to help. "He brisked up a bit when I offered him, in exchange for the operation I was not prepared to carry out [the airborne drop at Evrecy], a much more attractive proposal," Leigh-Mallory recorded that evening. "When I made it he just swallowed it up, though even now I am not sure that he will choose the right area. We shall see."

For Monty, who was acutely aware of the dissension among the senior air force commanders over the proper use of heavy bombers, Leigh-Mallory's sudden offer of medium and heavy bomber support came like a bolt out of the blue. Could he believe it? To make certain, he asked if Leigh-Mallory could send over some of his planning staff the next day to discuss with Dempsey and the staff of 30 Corps "aiming points for such a bombardment." Leigh-Mallory agreed, and the two men parted on much improved terms.

The next morning, 15 June, Monty had arranged to visit Bradley and tour the American sector. Traveling in the front seat of his Humber, with Bradley in a jeep behind and American military police outriders, the Allied Commander-in-Chief and his American army commander set off in a small cavalcade at 11 A.M. "Monty waved to troops as we go along. They recognize him and normally salute the car," Bradley's aide jotted in his diary. "Many of them recognize Brad and smile."

In the afternoon, having visited Isigny and the area where the Germans had broken through, Monty headed back to his headquarters. He was encouraged by all he had seen, and confident the American line was now completely secure. But waiting for him at Creully was another surprise. The day before he had received a sudden visit by Leigh-

Mallory. Now, sitting in his tent at his Tactical Headquarters, he found no less personages than the Supreme Commander and Deputy Supreme Commander—come, as Tedder later put it, "to see whether there really was a crisis."

The Class Is Dismissed

T raveling with Eisenhower was his recently commissioned son, John, who was innocent of the true purpose of the mission. "Dad had missed General Montgomery at his Headquarters, as the latter had gone to visit General Bradley. Our plans were changed in order to meet General Montgomery at 4 o'clock, necessitating our being about one hour later than we had planned in making the trip back."

Eisenhower blamed himself, but Tedder's pride revolted at this snub on his first touchdown on French soil. Moreover, Monty's absence (for he could easily have postponed his visit to Bradley) now proved to be disastrous for army-air cooperation in the Normandy battle—for in Monty's absence the Supreme Commander and his deputy motored over to Dempsey's Second Army Headquarters, where Dempsey was busy planning the first use of heavy bombers in direct support of an Allied land attack: a rolling barrage, paving the way for advancing infantry, but delivered from the air rather than by ground artillery.

"On arrival at General Dempsey's Second Army headquarters," Tedder later recorded in his own version of events, "I found in session a joint Army/Air conference. The purpose was to consider the tactical use of heavy bombers on the lines that Leigh-Mallory had agreed. Neither Spaatz nor Coningham was represented. I was much disturbed at these developments, and found Coningham, who happened to be in Normandy that day, incensed."

Tedder's account, published in 1966, was outrageously deceitful. Coningham did not "happen" to be in Normandy that day. Leigh-

Mallory had spoken to Coningham on the telephone on the night of 14 June to further discuss the project, which had already been discussed at the morning air conference. The telephone call, however, had stirred the conspiratorial and dishonest New Zealander (Coningham was later indicted for war looting and theft) to phone Tedder secretly and arrange to meet him not at the usual Air Force Headquarters meeting at Stanmore the next morning, together with Leigh-Mallory, but privately in France. In short, Tedder and Coningham had deliberately connived to overturn the Leigh-Mallory/Monty scheme by disputing it not at the daily conference of air commanders in England, but in the field of battle. As Solly Zuckerman, the scientific expert on the effects of heavy bombing—who attended the conference of planners in Normandy on behalf of Leigh-Mallory—later described, the airmen were instantly ordered by Eisenhower and Tedder to go back to England. "The class, as it were, [was] dismissed."

Dempsey, in his diary, was blunt: "1030—Discussion with General Eisenhower, Tedder and Coningham disclosed that Leigh-Mallory had not told anyone else of his project for supporting an infantry attack with Bomber Command and 8 USAAF. Both Tedder and Coningham are sure that it cannot be done effectively. For the present we will drop it."

Thus, for the next month of the greatest Allied battle of World War II, the Allies would be condemned to fight with one arm tied behind their backs—primarily because a pipe-smoking, intellectually arrogant Deputy Supreme Commander and a jealous and scheming Tactical Air Forces commander disapproved of close air support to the armies by heavy bombers.

Ike Reverts to "Anvil"

At Creully, when he returned from the American front, Monty sought to defuse the tension by putting the Supreme Commander and his deputy "in the picture." The visitors were impressed—indeed, Tedder, who had the previous day announced "he did not want to panic, [but] the situation in the Eastern Sector was such that it might become critical at any moment," was now forced to admit that, "as for the military crisis, it was apparent to Eisenhower and to me that it was over-emphasized."

Leigh-Mallory had made the same point to the air force commanders in England that morning: "The Air C-in-C said that he had seen General Montgomery in France yesterday and he believed that the appreciation of the military situation given at yesterday's conference by Brigadier Richardson was a truer picture than the more alarming appreciation given by Air Marshal Coningham."

It was important, however, to be clear about the supply problems hampering the Allied effort, Monty felt—and dutifully, like General Alexander in the desert, Eisenhower made notes to take back to Supreme Headquarters with him. Top priority, Monty felt, should be given to speeding up the ferrying of ammunition, as well as the movement to France of fresh fighting divisions, since units that had been fighting continuously since D-Day could not now be expected to undertake offensive operations with the same gusto and willingness to suffer casualties as before.

Eisenhower duly ordered his vast headquarters to look into the matter. However, his disappointment with the lack of "gains" can best be judged by the alacrity with which, instead of seeing his air commanders and exploring the possibility of bomber help to his forces in Normandy, he now shifted his restless attention to his alternative Allied invasion, Anvil—which, he now hoped, could be mounted near Bordeaux, on the Atlantic coast.

To Monty this resurrection of a scheme which had already delayed and disrupted planning for Overlord month upon month between January and March 1944 was absurd. Not only was it a gross distraction from the imperatives of the critical battle in Normandy, but it threatened to produce another Anzio, since the Atlantic seaboard at Bordeaux would be difficult to supply or cover by air. Once again, as so often in 1943, Eisenhower's quick mind was being led astray by bright alternatives to the matter in hand, Monty felt. The situation cried out, in his eyes, for *supreme* command: namely a resolute determination to prosecute the battle in Normandy with all the weapons available in the Allied arsenal: army, air and navy.

Whereas Eisenhower had shown true greatness in the final run-up to the D-Day landings, he now proceeded, in Monty's view, to give his least impressive display of leadership in the war so far.

Hitler Intervenes

The truth was, far from being in a state of crisis, Monty's Normandy strategy was succeeding beyond even Monty's greatest hopes. While Coningham strode into the Allied commanders' meeting at Stanmore on 16 June to announce that "the Army plan has failed," Rommel and von Rundstedt were begging Hitler for an urgent conference in France, before it was too late.

On 15 June, while Tedder sabotaged Leigh-Mallory's bombing program, Rommel had written to his wife: "Was up forward again yesterday, the situation does not improve. We must be prepared for grave events. The troops, SS and Army alike, are fighting with the utmost courage, but the balance of strength tips more heavily against us every day. . . . You can no doubt imagine what difficult decisions we will soon be faced with, and will remember our conversation in November 1942."

The shadow of Alamein was falling across Rommel's furrowed brow. In private conversation with his wife, shortly after Alamein, Rommel had told his wife that, with Monty's victory, the war was lost and that the Axis should best sue for peace. Now, once again, Rommel was faced by his former foe from the desert, and knew in his heart he was doomed. As at Alamein, Montgomery would relentlessly press his advantage till the German cordon snapped, and nothing would stop him.

Hitler, sensing that Rommel's nerve was failing him, flew to France and met his two field marshals at his reserve headquarters at Soissons. According to some accounts, Rommel openly asked Hitler to make peace: but Hitler knew that the time was not yet ripe for negotiation. To secure success in international politics one must argue from strength; to sue for peace now would be tantamount to an admission of defeat in Normandy. For years he had boasted of "secret weapons" that would bring any enemy to his knees: now the time had come, and from 13 June, London had begun to be bombarded by V-1 rocket bombs in an onslaught that soon recalled the height of the Blitz. If Rommel could contain the enemy in Normandy long enough for German reinforcements to move into line, Hitler argued, and if the expected enemy landing in the Pas de Calais could be defeated on the beaches, as it had been at Dieppe in 1942, then the German position would be totally different.

Rommel left the meeting utterly convinced by Hitler's logic—leading Rugge, Rommel's naval aide, to shake his head in disbelief at Hitler's "sheer magnetism" over Rommel. However, it was too late to save the Cherbourg Peninsula, as even Hitler conceded, and a fighting withdrawal was authorized into the fortress, which was instructed to hold out until mid-July. Meanwhile Rommel was to regroup his Panzer divisions for a counterattack upon the British sector.

The lull while Dempsey built up his forces for a renewed pincer attack on Caen, without heavy bomber support, soon caused Rommel to regain his confidence. "A quick enemy break-through to Paris is now hardly a possibility," he wrote to his wife on 18 June. "We've got lots of stuff coming up." He admitted that in many places the battle had been "going badly," but felt that "much of this has now sorted itself out and I am looking forward to the future with less anxiety than I did a week ago."

To regroup his Panzer divisions, however, Rommel needed to pull them out of line. Until reinforcements arrived, this was simply not possible, given the British pressure around Caen. It was, then, a race—but a race which General Eisenhower, unlike Hitler, was ignoring, preferring to concentrate instead upon Anvil.

On 16 June, meanwhile, King George VI visited Monty at Creully. "The King was here on Friday; but you saw that in the papers I have no doubt," Monty wrote to Phyllis Reynolds. "I told the King that I did not think the people of Normandy had any wish to be liberated. When you read in the paper that another town has been 'liberated' it really means that very heavy fighting has taken place around it and that it has been destroyed—that not one house is left standing—and that a good many of the inhabitants have been killed. Such is the price," he remarked, "the French are now paying. When they chucked their hand in 1940 they thought they could avoid all this—but they cannot."

Despite Eisenhower and Tedder's refusal to give him air support, Monty was in good heart. Lieutenant Colonel Dawnay had brought over the remaining portion of Tac Headquarters—"including two Rolls Royce cars!!"—and, in order to stop the Germans from withdrawing their armor from the line, Monty conferred closely with Dempsey over a new plan. Just as he had switched the axis of his offensive by 180 degrees at Alamein, so now he told Dempsey to launch only a mock attack on the British right flank near Caumont. Instead, from the Orne bridgehead, Dempsey was to unleash the newly arrived British 8 Corps in a real blitz attack to try to envelop Caen from the northeast: Operation Epsom.

The Caumont attack by 30 Corps would start immediately, with 8 Corps putting in its surprise attack just when the other thrust was reaching its climax, and in the hope of getting Rommel looking the wrong way. "It is not an easy operation to stage owing to the lack of depth in the 1 Corps [staging] sector, the bottleneck of the bridges over R. ORNE, and the limited space available in the bridgehead itself," Dempsey noted on the afternoon of 17 June. Bad weather and supply difficulties had already delayed operations by forty-eight hours, and "although I very much want 8 Corps to start their attack on 22 June, it is clearly going to be difficult to get it as early as this."

Following Collins' laborious drive on Cherbourg, Bradley was equally realistic about his American effort. "As you know the enemy has built up a much stronger force in the peninsula than we had anticipated. This has made our progress slow," he apologized to Eisenhower. He had already made arrangements for an extra division to be given to Collins when it arrived on 20 June, but meanwhile he had conferred with Monty about the feasibility of bringing a further three divisions in through the Omaha beachhead to "give Gerow and Corlett each an extra infantry division and hold the other infantry division in army reserve."

Given the necessary redisposition of forces, it was important, Monty now began to feel, that there be no misunderstandings about the Allied ground situation in Normandy, nor the logic of his strategy. Phase One of the battle was over. It was time, he decided, to set down in writing, at the risk of seeming pedantic, his appreciation of the current position and his concept of how the second phase of the battle would now develop: a top-secret document which could go to Eisenhower, the British Chiefs of Staff, the War Office and Washington—a sort of Revised Version of the great Presentation of Plans he had organized at his headquarters at St. Paul's School in May, three weeks before the invasion.

Part Eight

THE DOGFIGHT

Monty, Bradley and Dempsey,
Normandy, 10 June 1944.

The Revised Version

"Today is D plus 12," Monty began his report on 18 June 1944, "and we have now been fighting since 6 June." He continued:

During this time we have been working on the original directive issued by me in England, and we have:

a) gained a good lodgement area in Normandy

b) linked up all our different thrusts to form one whole area, and made the area we hold quite secure

c) kept the initiative, forced the enemy to use his reserves to plug holes, and beaten off all his counter-attacks

d) replaced our casualties in personnel and tanks, etc., so that Divisions and armoured units are up to strength again

e) placed ourselves in a sound position administratively.

After "the very great intensity of the initial few days we had to slow down the tempo of the operations," he summarized, so as to "ensure we could meet the enemy counter-attacks without difficulty" and "build up our strength behind the original assault divisions.

"All this is good," Monty commented. "But we are now ready to pass on to other things, and to reap the harvest."

If Rommel was growing more confident in his ability to handle the Allied bridgehead in Normandy, Monty was equally confident he could handle Rommel. Describing the "general situation," Monty noted that even though Rommel could call on reserves from Brittany and else-where, "he still lacks good infantry to release his Panzer divisions so that the latter can be grouped for a full-blooded counter-attack." In the Cherbourg Peninsula his infantry forces were doomed, and he would have to "make a decision as to whether he will continue to fight for Cherbourg." Though Rommel had "never had the initiative" he had nevertheless "been in sufficient strength to stage local counter attacks and these have delayed the full expansion of our plans." However, "once we can snap the enemy 'roping off' policy, he is going to find it very difficult to gather the stuff to stabilise again. The old policy of 'stretch,' which beat him in SICILY, then begins to emerge." At the moment "our own armies are facing in different directions. Once we can capture CAEN and CHERBOURG, and all face in the same direc-tion, the enemy problem becomes enormous. . . . It is then that we have a mighty chance," he prophesied, "to make the German army come to our threat, and to defeat it between the SEINE and the LOIRE."

The Allied aim, then, was to complete the captures of Caen and Cherbourg and line up the two armies facing the same way—"the first step in the full development of our plans. CAEN is really the key to CHERBOURG," he pronounced; "its capture will release forces which are now locked up in ensuring that our left flank holds secure."

As army commanders, Dempsey and Bradley were perfectly clear what Monty meant by the phrase. But General Collins, foreseeing a considerable battle ahead to seize the seaport, is reputed to have said to Bradley: "Brad, let's wire him to send us the key!"

Monty's Luck Runs Out

I f Collins foresaw a tough fight to get Cherbourg, Dempsey saw an even tougher one to get Caen—indeed, pleaded with Monty to al-ter his Epsom plan. "1830—Saw C-in-C at my Headquarters,"

Dempsey recorded in his diary on 18 June. "I told him that I had come to the conclusion that an attack by 8 Corps from the bridgehead EAST of the two rivers is too risky. The bridgehead is too small to form up satisfactorily; there is no room to deploy artillery EAST of the rivers; the L[ines] of C[ommunication] would be dependent on the bridges, and there is always the risk that the enemy, who is very active in this sector, might upset our arrangements just before the start of the attack. The staff had been into the matter very carefully during the morning." Dempsey's answer was to revert to Monty's former strategy of concentrating all his efforts on his right-hand, Caumont sector, leapfrogging 8 Corps through his current 30 Corps operations.

Ought Monty to have resisted Dempsey's suggestion and given him, instead, more time in mounting the left pincer, rather than transferring all his eggs into one basket? It is easy to think so in retrospect, knowing that Dempsey's revised plan failed utterly, and that Caen was ultimately to fall only when a left pincer *did* envelop it from the east, a whole month later. Moreover there is evidence that Monty, still flushed by the success of Overlord to date, did not sufficiently weigh the problems of fighting in the bocage terrain of Normandy, around Caumont. When he wrote, on 19 June, to tell General Simpson at the War Office of the change of plan, he was certainly still thinking in terms of the desert. "It will be a blitz attack supported by all available air power—on the lines of EL HAMMA," he claimed—for at El Hamma, in the great Eighth Army fight for Mareth, Monty had, in the midst of the battle, switched his armored corps over to his inland pincer, with triumphant results.

Normandy, however, was a far cry from the open desert, and even Monty recognized that Dempsey could not match the unique army-air relationship that had made El Hamma such a success. "The trouble in Second Army is that there is no one at Army HQ who knows anything about the practical side of air co-operation in the land battle; so I am lending Charles Richardson to Dempsey as a BGS (Air) to teach them all. I fear that Chilton is not really fit to be Chief of Staff to a large Army; however, we will try and teach him."

In his directive of 18 June, Monty had accepted Bradley's view that his American flank between Caumont and the Cherbourg Peninsula should remain defensive; but soon after he issued his "Revised Version," news came in that Collins had cut off the peninsula. With 700 American tanks at his disposal, Bradley need not wait for the capture of Cherbourg before beginning his breakout towards Brittany, Monty now felt; the bulk of Rommel's armor was tied down at Caen, and he wanted Bradley therefore to start pushing southwards now, while the time was ripe: "It is important that the [First U.S.] Army should not wait till CHERBOURG is actually captured before extending its operations to the south-west. As soon as they can be organised, operations will be developed against LA HAYE DU PUITS and against COUTANCE. Later, as more troops become available, these operations will be extended towards GRANVILLE, AVRANCHES and VIRE." He was even considering landing an airborne division on Saint-Malo so that Patton's Third U.S. Army could be brought into Brittany straight through Saint-Malo—"enabling the whole tempo of the operation to be speeded up, since Third Army would be in close touch with First Army and everything would thus be more simple."

It was at this juncture, however, that luck, which had hitherto so favored the Allies, ran out, and the battle of Normandy became, like Alamein, a relentless, annihilating dogfight, with mounting casualties—and many discordant voices baying in the Allied rear for Monty's blood.

"This Weather Is the Very Devil"

"Yesterday (Monday) was a frightful day, wet and cold, and a high wind, and we could get nothing landed on the beaches," Monty wrote to Phyllis Reynolds of the storm which blew up on 19 June and threatened to disrupt the entire Allied timetable in Normandy. Nevertheless Monty was not downcast, and was well aware of the tribulations people were suffering at home. "The pilotless aircraft seem to be creating rather a sensation in London and to be causing certain casualties. The great point is that people should not panic; they must remain calm and stick it out somehow."

The people of England didn't panic. But the evidence shows that many politicians and rear headquarters staffs did. Night after night Eisenhower now spent in a cramped air-raid shelter, and when he saw Monty's offensive plans in Normandy being postponed *yet again*, he became a prey to doubt. Since 14 June he been reconsidering the launching of Anvil. On 20 June, the day after the Channel gale, he gave way to his anxieties and insisted General Wilson, the Supreme Commander in the Mediterranean theater, be ordered to start Anvil—even though there was no hope of landings being mounted before mid-August.

Monty, knowing that Eisenhower was becoming nervous and impatient, watched with growing despondency as the weather played havoc with his carefully laid plans. "This weather is the very devil," he wrote to Simpson at the War Office on the afternoon of 20 June. "A gale all day yesterday; the same today; nothing can be unloaded. Lying in ships off the beaches is everything I need to resume the offensive with a bang; in particular I must have 43 DIV complete, and more artillery ammunition; if I can unload these by tomorrow night, then I am O.K.; if I cannot do so I shall have to postpone the attack—which would be a great nuisance as every day's delay helps the enemy.

"I am now 5 days behind in my estimated build-up; all due to bad weather. We cannot, in this weather, complete the 'mulberries' [floating harbors]. However," he added with resignation, "one cannot have everything; the movement on Cherbourg is going very well and that port in our hands will help greatly.

"The real point is that the delay imposed on us by the weather is just what the enemy needs i.e. time to get more Divisions over here, and we know some more are on the move. It is all a very great nuisance."

To de Guingand, Monty signaled that evening that Dempsey's "blitz attack" of 8 Corps could not now take place until 25 June, and "each further day of bad weather will mean a further postponement of a day. Inform Eisenhower and D.M.O. at War Office for C.I.G.S."

By the time Eisenhower met General "Jumbo" Wilson's chief of staff from the Mediterranean on 22 June, Eisenhower was in a sorry state. "He said he wanted ANVIL and he wanted it quick," General Gammell signaled to Wilson—despite the fact that it would break up the whole Allied offensive in Italy, and provide no instant relief to Montgomery, whom Eisenhower declined to consult, even though he insisted on Anvil as part of the overall Overlord strategy.

Bradley, meantime, was as chagrined by the weather in Normandy as was Monty. "We've got him [the enemy] on the run and we can't afford to let him stop," he remarked on 19 June as the storm washed away his American floating harbor; "we have the initiative and now we must keep it."

If the Germans were on the run, however, they showed little sign of being out of breath. While the Allies cut down heavy artillery fire to twenty-five rounds per gun per day or less, the Germans began to increase their shelling of both British and American sectors. Hitherto Monty had refused to sleep anywhere but in his accustomed caravan, under the portrait of Rommel; now even he was forced to spend the night in a blanket in a slit trench.

Eisenhower had planned to visit Bradley on 20 June, but the appalling weather prevented this too; and without ammunition or reinforcement supply Bradley once again canceled Monty's instruction regarding the simultaneous thrust southwards to Coutances and Brittany. " 'Let's stick where we are, dig in and hold until we can clean up this [Cherbourg] peninsula,' " his aide quoted him. " 'Urgent that we do so and quickly—get the stuff in from States, directly without transhipment through England.' "

Each day the staff looked anxiously at the barometer; by 23 June ammunition was having to be flown into the American sector and coasters beached rather than wait another day while they bobbed at anchor offshore. "Old man looks morose today," Hansen noted yet again in his diary.

Anxious lest his British generals lose heart, Monty had summoned all corps and divisional commanders to a meeting the day before. "We have been successful in pulling the German reserves to the CAEN, or eastern, sector of our lodgement area," he congratulated them— determined they remain clear about the larger Allied picture. "This has relieved pressure in the American sector, and as a result we now own the whole of the Cherbourg peninsula except the port of Cherbourg itself." After Cherbourg, Bradley would drive southwards to Brittany. "The Americans," Monty predicted confidently, "will do all that quite easily so long as the Second British Army will pull the Germans on to it, and will fight them over this side."

It was, then, an Allied battle, and every British and Canadian life lost was given in an Allied operation, in order to put the American army into Brittany. Once this was achieved, Monty predicted, the enemy would have to make an important decision:

A. To bring the German Army to the south and west of the SEINE and have a big battle there,
or
B. To sit back behind the SEINE.

Personally, Monty believed, as he had always done, that Hitler would never permit a withdrawal to the Seine. He would order his troops to fight tooth and nail in the field, as he had done at Alamein, in Tunisia, in Italy, and in the east at Stalingrad. The next phase of operations would therefore not "be so easy," Monty warned: "The bad weather has put us 5 to 6 days behind and this has given the enemy time to build up against us—and to get three divisions into reserve." East of Caen, Rommel now had three divisions in line; from there to Caumont stretched the four Panzer divisions, "21, 12, Lehr, 2 Pz"; while in line against the Americans the enemy only had "an odd collection of Divisions and bits of pieces," with no less than four infantry divisions cut off in the Cherbourg Peninsula. Unfortunately the Allied supply crisis had given Rommel the chance to bring three divisions in reserve:

1 S.S. Pz SW of EVRECY
2 S.S. Pz South of ST LO
353 Inf About Periers

"He obviously means to hold us in the CAEN sector," Monty considered; "and he will pivot on ST LO and COUTANCE as he is forced southwards by the American thrust towards GRANVILLE and AVRANCHES. . . ."

The Germans, however, were doomed so long as the Allies made no mistakes. "We have now reached the 'show down' stage," Monty announced. "The first rush, inland to secure a good lodgement area, is over. The enemy is 'firming up' and trying to hem us in." The Allies had twenty-three divisions ashore in Normandy, the Germans nineteen, of which seven were elite Panzer or Panzer Grenadier divisions. If Hitler chose to milk all his other sectors along the Atlantic Wall, he could build up a total of sixty-three divisions against the Allies; he would not, of course, dare do so, given the threat of Allied amphibious assaults elsewhere, but it was a measure of what the Allies were up against. If the Allies could continue to draw the German armies in the west into piecemeal battle in Normandy, where they could be destroyed on the ground and from the air, then the outcome of the war was in no doubt; but it would be a tough and demanding battle. "We have thus reached a stage where carefully prepared operations are essential," Monty exhorted. "We must have no set-backs. What we take we must hold."

The establishment of First Canadian Army in the field would now be phased back until mid-July, when Second Army would be able to give it room. This it would achieve by capturing Caen and taking the high ground to the south: the shield behind which Bradley could strike towards Brittany. "The main feature," he summarized Dempsey's forthcoming Epsom operation, "is a strong attack by 8 Corps, delivered through the right Bde front of 3 Canadian DIV. The front is becoming 'glued up' and care must be used to ensure success by great fire power from the ground and air. The attack must not go in till 8 Corps is assembled complete: i.e. 15 DIV, 43 DIV, 11 Armd DIV, 4 Armd Bde, 31 Armd Bde. Then the whole Army front must flare up and the enemy be fought to a standstill."

The generals rose and replaced their caps. There was obviously much fighting ahead.

Holding the Enemy by the Throat

While the officers of British Second Army prepared for an all-out battle with the bulk of Rommel's Panzer divisions, the wreck of the American "mulberry" and the lack of supplies and reinforcements had convinced Bradley that he must not only go on the defensive during his drive on Cherbourg, but even after the port was captured he would require time before switching over to the American offensive aimed at Brittany.

Could the British hold the Panzer divisions so long in the east? Monty decided to see for himself whether Bradley could accelerate the American timetable. "I tried very hard to get First U.S. Army to develop its thrust southwards, towards COUTANCE, at the same time as it was completing the capture of Cherbourg," Monty confided to the CIGS, Sir Alan Brooke, after speaking to Bradley. "I have no doubt myself that it could have been started in a small way, and gradually developed. But Bradley didn't want to take the risk; there was no risk really; quick and skilful re-grouping was all that was required."

Though disappointed, Monty was understanding—and more and more impressed by the performance of his American troops in battle. "I have to take the Americans along quietly and give them time to get ready," Monty explained to Brooke. However, "once they are formed up, then they go like hell. I have got to like them very much indeed, and once you get their confidence they will do anything for you. In the end it will work out all right," he predicted confidently, for the delay might even make Bradley's job on his southern front easier, as German reserves were sucked into Dempsey's fight around Caen.

That Second Army had contained the four German Panzer divisions on its front for the first seventeen days of the battle—longer than Alamein, in fact—was in Monty's eyes a considerable achievement. That it would have to go on doing so—as well as attracting *more* Panzer reserve divisions—for a further two weeks before Bradley could begin his southern breakout was a considerable task for Dempsey, but one which Monty accepted on behalf of his overall Allied plan of battle. "The Americans are doing awfully well," he wrote the next day to his successor at Eighth Army, Sir Oliver Leese. "Bradley is first class as an Army Cmd and is very willing to learn; the same with Bimbo [Dempsey]. Both are very inexperienced, especially on the air side, but both are anxious to learn and are doing so. I have great fears that Harry Crerar [commanding First Canadian Army] will not be too good; however I am keeping him out of the party as long as I can. Georgie Patton," he predicted, "may be a bit of a problem when he comes into it!"

Casualties so far had been "less than half what we had thought was likely," with many wounded but only 2,000 British troops killed so far, and 3,000 Americans. Given that three-quarters of a million Allied soldiers had now been put ashore "over the beaches in under three weeks—not a bad effort," Monty remarked. "Our total will go up to two million!!"

As regards the British divisions, Monty was pleased with the performance of 50th Division under Major General Graham, though he added that "they have had a lot of casualties." The Highlanders of 51st Division had performed less well: "51 DIV have not been so good under Bullen-Smith; but I have no doubt the Division will be all right when it settles down, and when Bullen is more in the saddle. 3 Canadian DIV started well, but then became rather jumpy; the Bosche snipers in our own back areas rather upset them."

To Monty every division had its strengths and foibles, and he still treated each one like a conscientious father, despite his exalted role as Allied Land Forces Commander. To outsiders this often smacked of interference in the proper affairs of the individual army commander—an instance of this being Monty's address to the corps and divisional commanders of Second Army. Yet Dempsey, at any rate, accepted such "interference" because, whatever command protocol might be and whatever jealous tongues might say, it was such palpable evidence of Monty's "grip": his desire to see that his intentions were understood by every subordinate under his command.

The next evening, 25 June, as the troops and tanks of the British Epsom offensive moved into position, Monty signaled to Eisenhower that "blitz attack of 8 Corps goes in tomorrow at 0730 hrs and once it starts I will continue the battle on the eastern flank till one of us cracks and it will NOT be us. If we can pull the enemy on to Second Army," he added, reminding Eisenhower of the overall purpose, "it will make it easier for the First Army when it attacks southwards."

That Eisenhower understood, at the time, is proved by his letter to Bradley that evening: "I most earnestly hope that you get Cherbourg tomorrow [26 June]. As quickly as you have done so we must rush the preparations for the attack to the southward with all speed. The enemy is building up and we must not allow him to seal us up in the northern half of the Peninsula. The Second Army attack this morning and enemy reinforcements should be attracted in that direction. This gives us an opportunity on the West that may not obtain very long," he warned. "I know that you already have General Montgomery's directive on these matters; all I am saying is that I thoroughly agree with him and know that you will carry out your part of the task with resolution and boldness."

To Monty, Eisenhower wrote with equal comprehension: "I am hopeful that Bradley can quickly clean up the Cherbourg mess and turn around to attack southward while you have got the enemy by the throat on the east."

Such sympathetic rapport between Supreme Commander and his Land Forces Commander, unfortunately, was not to last long.

Dirty Business

Late on 26 June, Monty jubilantly reported to Eisenhower: "It can be accepted that CHERBOURG is now in First Army hands and the enemy commander has been captured." Despite "very bad" weather with such low cloud that little air support could be given, Dempsey's blitz attack had meanwhile begun. "Fighting will go on all day and all night and I am prepared to have a show down with the enemy on my eastern flank for as long as he likes."

On 27 June, after a meeting with Bradley "on the tactics or strategy to be employed from this point," Monty sent his military assistant, Lieutenant Colonel Dawnay, to England with a personal letter to Brooke. "It is a pity the weather went bad on us just when we wanted it to be fine," he lamented. "I had planned to get Second Army offensive launched on 20th June, and given fine weather we could have done it—and the Germans would not have had the extra time they have now had to bring up more stuff.

"We got it launched yesterday (Monday); it was a bad day, with rain and low cloud, and our air was grounded; the air plays a big part in the plan and there were attempts to postpone the operation; but the troops were all ready formed up and I ordered it to go, air or no air; and it went—successfully.

"I cannot give Rommel any more time to get himself organised," Monty explained. This brought him to the overall masterplan:

> I think my general broad plan is maturing quite reasonably well. All the decent enemy stuff, and his Pz and Pz S.S. Divisions are coming in on the Second Army front—according to plan. That has made it much easier for the First U.S. Army to do its task.

What worried Monty much more than the delays caused by bad weather and the still cautious approach of General Bradley was, however, the Allied air force problem:

> My main anxiety these days is the possibility that we should not get the full value from our great air power because of jealousies and friction among the air "barons." The real "nigger in the woodpile" is Mary Coningham; I know him well and he is a bad man, not genuine and terribly jealous. There is constant friction between him and L-M [Leigh-Mallory]. L-M does not know much about it; but he is a very genuine chap and will do anything he can to help win the war; he has not got a good staff and he fiddles about himself with a lot of detail he ought to leave alone; but he does play the game.
>
> Mary [Coningham] spends his time in trying to get L-M to "trip-up" and putting spokes in his wheel; he would prefer to do this rather than winning the war quickly; he does know his stuff, but he is a most dangerous chap. The man who ought to keep the whole show on the rails is Tedder; but he is weak and does nothing about it; actually he and Mary are in the same camp, and both of them combine against L-M.
>
> So L-M is fighting hard to hold his own. I myself am determined to keep right clear of the whole dirty business; but I am also determined

not to lose the battle; and the chap who will do anything to help in that respect, and who does not spend time trying to "trip-up" other people, is L-M.

We manage all right so far. But several hours a day are wasted in argument with the opposing camps, and in ensuring that the "air jealousies" do not lost us the battle.

It is a curious world is it not? But I expect you could add very considerably to the above story, as I am sure similar happenings are of daily occurrence in your circles!!!

They were—with Winston Churchill the worst of Brooke's problems: moody, erratic and, with the inability of the Allied air forces to deal with Hitler's V-1 bombing program, a deeply worried man.

Meanwhile, with or without Allied air support, Monty was determined to adhere to his overall design. "The battle is going very well," he continued his account to Brooke.

a) Cherbourg is now definitely captured; the enemy commander was collected yesterday afternoon (26 June) and that ended organised resistance.

b) On Second Army front the 8 Corps has broke[n] through the enemy position on a 400 yard front. . . . On the first day (26 June) it reached the line GRAINVILLE–MOUEN, on the railway line from VILLERS-BOCAGE to CAEN. Today (27 June) 15 DIV is moving forward to the ODON valley, and I hope to see 11 Armd DIV at ESQUAY tomorrow (28 June). . . .

Since the primary object of Dempsey's attack was to force Rommel to commit his main strength—particularly armor—on the eastern flank, Monty was "keeping my eyes very firmly directed to the suspected enemy concentration of three S.S. Pz divisions in the area ALENCON–EVREUX. That may mean dirty work ahead, in the shape of a full-blooded counter stroke. However, we will see. I have got my British strength well built up now, and am prepared to go on fighting on my eastern flank for as long as the Germans like."

With Rommel committed on the eastern sector, Bradley could, in four days' time, begin his belated thrust southwards, having now captured Cherbourg. "On my western flank . . . I am also very strong. First U.S. Army will get cracking southwards on 1st July," Monty estimated. "So the whole situation is now becoming more interesting. It requires all my time and attention, and a close grip on the battle, to ensure that the battle swings the way I want."

That night, 27 June, Monty signaled to Brooke that 8 Corps had reached the river Odon, and, he hoped, Dempsey would put 11th Armoured Division onto the "Esquay feature" next day—the high, defensive ground between the Odon and the river Orne (Hill 112). He certainly showed not the least disappointment or vexation at Dempsey's limited progress—for Rommel seemed to be reacting exactly as intended. "I am trying to procure locally (a) a dog, (b) some canaries," he wrote contentedly to Phyllis Reynolds. "I think pets are a good thing when living a caravan life in the fields as we do." His assistant, who was taking over the long letter to Brooke, would tell Mrs. Reynolds "all about our life in Normandy. We get any amount of fresh milk, and butter, and cheese; this is a rich dairy farming area. But," he lamented, "they will not sell their poultry."

Fierce fighting resumed on 28 June, and, having secured the northern part of the Esquay feature, 8 Corps that evening went over to the defensive. By midday the following day Monty was convinced that his strategy was succeeding, for by then Rommel had thrown in 1st SS and 2nd SS Panzer Divisions in an effort to beat back the British eastern offensive. "Since offensive began on eastern flank on 26 June we have pulled two extra Panzer Divisions in to that flank," Monty reported to Brooke with relish. "Have now six Panzer Divisions involved in trying to hold my advance west and south-west of CAEN. Have since D day worked on the general policy of getting enemy heavily involved on eastern flank so that my affairs on the western flank could proceed the easier. So am well satisfied with present situation."

To the world at large this might seem a strange situation considering the relative lack of "gains" in the blitz attack by the British 8 Corps; but the world at large tended to see Monty as the British commander and all too often failed to recognize his position as overall Allied Land Force Commander-in-Chief. That his strategy was working was not only demonstrated by the Panzer divisions committed piecemeal to plug holes in the British sector, but by Rommel's reports to OKW, the German high command. By 26 June, Rommel recorded that whereas there had been a "slackening of the enemy's fighting acuities" on the American front (excluding Cherbourg), the British had "attacked on both sides of TILLY SUR SEULLES after intense bombardment and corresponding preparation in the air, along a front of 7 km in width and managed to break through to a depth of 5 km. In this fighting the enemy again sustained high and serious losses, as he himself concedes, and since the 6.6 has lost 750 armoured vehicles. Our own losses are, however, also exceedingly great."

The Germans had, in fact, so far suffered 43,070 casualties—including six generals, sixty-three commanders and four general staff officers—equaling those of the Allies, despite being in prepared defensive positions. Above all, Rommel and his chief of staff, General

Speidel, were convinced that, from the distribution of forces and from Intelligence sources, all signs "point to a thrust from the area to the North and North-West of CAEN in the direction of PARIS"—a threat which, combined with the possibility of further Allied amphibious landings between Le Havre and the Somme, completely outweighed the other threat—that once the Cherbourg area was cleaned up, the enemy might "regroup his forces to the south and advance between CARENTAN and PORT BAIL for the thrust south, in order to obtain possession first of all of the St. LO–COUTANCES line," and then with "the possibility of a thrust being made from the area S.E. of CARENTAN to the S.W. with known target [i.e., Brittany]."

The latter was indeed Monty's aim. It was at this juncture, however, on 29 June 1944, that General Bradley regretfully reported to Monty he would have, again, to postpone his American thrust.

Rehearsing the American Breakout

B radley, knowing the significance of another American delay for Dempsey's troops as they battled with six German Panzer divisions, was deeply apologetic. "The storm in the UK has delayed the sailing of VIII Corps troops so that we will be lucky if we have them available by Monday [3 July]," he informed Monty. "I hope to have enough by that time to jump off. In addition, it has taken longer to clean up the Cherbourg peninsula than I had hoped. . . . I am very sorry to have to make this postponement but I feel that we must be set for this next attack so that when we once break his [the enemy's] present defensive lines we will give him no chance to get set, but can keep right on pushing until we get at least to the base of the peninsula. In fact, I would like to keep right on to the [Brittany] corner. I feel that this is entirely feasible," Bradley acknowledged, "due to the fact that he has placed so much of his strength in front of Dempsey."

But could Dempsey, whose troops had now been fighting hard since 25 June against the toughest German armored opposition, without full air support, keep up the tempo of their operations until Bradley "kicked off" on 3 July? By 29 June, Dempsey was aware that *another* two Panzer divisions were entering the fray on his British front: 9th and 10th SS Panzer Divisions, making no less than "eight PANZER Divisions located between CAEN and CAUMONT," as Monty signaled to Churchill and Brooke.

This was a disturbing tally: a veritable Panzer army—in fact, the largest concentration of German Panzer strength assembled in battle, in the West, since Dunkirk.

At 4 P.M. on 30 June, therefore, Monty met his army commanders at his new headquarters above the village at Bray, in the American sector, beyond the Cerisy forest.

"My broad policy, once we had secured a firm lodgement area, has always been to draw the main enemy forces in to the battle on our eastern flank," Monty summarized at the conference.

> We have been very successful in this policy. Cherbourg has fallen without any interference from enemy reserves brought in from other areas; the First US Army is proceeding with its reorganisation and re-grouping, undisturbed by the enemy; the Western flank is quiet. All this is good; it is on the western flank that territorial gains are essential at this stage, as we require space on that side for the development of our administration.
>
> By forcing the enemy to place the bulk of his strength in front of the Second Army [on the eastern flank], we have made easier the acquisition of territory on the western flank.
>
> Our policy has been so successful that the Second Army is now opposed by a formidable army of German Panzer divisions—eight definitely identified, and possibly more to come. . . .
>
> It is not yet clear whether Hitler proposes to concentrate great strength in NW Europe so as to annihilate the Allied forces in Normandy. He may decide that this is a good proposition; and in order to achieve success he may be quite prepared to give ground gradually on the Russian front, and to accept reverses in that theater.
>
> His policy in this respect will emerge in due course.

For the present, Monty remarked, "it is quite clear that he has reinforced the Normandy front strongly, and that a full-blooded counterattack seems imminent"—having just received an Ultra signal relating to 9th SS Panzer Division's intended attack on Cheux, at the center of the British offensive. *"We welcome such action,"* Monty boomed. *"Our* tactics must remain unchanged: a) To retain the initiative. We shall do this only by offensive action. On no account must we remain inactive. Without the initiative we cannot win. b) To have no set-backs. This is very important on the eastern flank; the enemy has concentrated great strength here and he must not be allowed to use it successfully. Any setback on the eastern flank might have direct repercussions on the quick development of our plans for the western flank. . . .

"We must retain such balance and poise in our dispositions that there is never any need to re-act to enemy moves or thrusts; the enemy can do what he likes; we will proceed with our plans."

The "PLAN IN OUTLINE" was to "hold the maximum number of enemy divisions on our eastern flank between CAEN and VILLERS BOCAGE, and to swing the [American] western or right flank of the Army Group southwards and eastwards in a wide sweep so as to threaten the line of withdrawal of such enemy divisions to the south of PARIS.

"The bridges over the SEINE between PARIS and the sea have been destroyed by the Allied air forces, and will be kept out of action; a strong Allied force established in the area LE MANS–ALENCON would threaten seriously the enemy concentration in the CAEN area and its 'get-away' south of PARIS. . . ."

Thus, three weeks after D-Day, Monty began to rehearse the American breakout role that would bring victory in the West—if the British could only keep Rommel's armor committed around Caen. Within this grand design, Monty now assigned the roles which each army commander was to play. Originally, before D-Day, he had intended to push the British Second Army south of Caen to secure space for the airfields and to provide the shield he needed for Bradley's southern thrust to Brittany. Rommel's fierce reaction at Caen had, however, made this unnecessary. Indeed, a British thrust too far from its present sector was not only what Rommel expected, but would open Second Army to a German counterthrust by extending the front to be defended— whereas, although it was greatly congested, the British front was currently almost impregnable. Dempsey's task as Second Army Commander was therefore:

a) To hold the enemy main forces in the area between CAEN and VILLERS BOCAGE

b) To have no set-backs

c) To develop operations for the capture of CAEN as opportunity offers—and the sooner the better.

A full-blooded enemy counter-attack seems likely, put in somewhere between CAEN and VILLERS BOCAGE; the main axis of such an attack
is not yet apparent. In order to provide a mobile reserve in the hands of
the Army Commander, the 7 Armd DIV, now holding the right divisional sector, will be relieved tomorrow by First Army and that divisional
sector will be included in First Army area.

Meanwhile, as Dempsey continued to act in his flypaper role, Bradley
was to uncoil his American spring. With over 1,000 American tanks
and an army of more than 350,000 American troops, he was to start
his southern offensive on 3 July. His first thrust was to be launched
from the right flank, furthest from the Panzer concentration, on that
day. Dempsey, in mortal combat with the Panzer divisions at Caen,
would not be able to provide the deep inland shield that had been
planned in England; therefore the American thrust would have to
hinge on the Caumont salient—"the Army to pivot on its left in the
CAUMONT area, and to swing southwards and eastwards on to the
general line CAUMONT–VIRE–MORTAIN–FOUGERES." From this,
an attack was to be mounted eastwards towards "the important inter-
communication centre of FLERS." This thrust would, like the British
attack at Caen, preoccupy the enemy and, it was to be hoped, draw to
it any incoming German reserves. Behind it Bradley was to sneak down
his westernmost forces: "On reaching the base of the peninsula at
AVRANCHES, the right hand Corps (8 Corps) to be turned westwards into BRITTANY and directed on RENNES and ST MALO."
This corps was to "consist of three infantry divisions and one armoured
division." However, this was not all; for Monty wanted Bradley to start
planning for a *third* thrust, employing the remainder of his army, in a
wide encircling movement eastwards towards Paris:

> Plans will be made to direct a strong right wing in a wide sweep, south
> of the bocage country, towards successive objectives as follows:

> a) LAVAL–MAYENNE
> b) LE MANS–ALENCON

The tactical strategy that would defeat the German armies in the West
had now been given out. Although it entailed Bradley's mounting his
own shield between Caumont and Fougères, Bradley accepted the
plan, for no one could have done more to contain the main German
fighting strength than Dempsey: a thankless but crucial role Dempsey
was committed to keeping up.

The army commanders therefore returned to their headquarters with something of the same excitement they experienced when, in England, the masterplan had been presented at St. Paul's. Only now it was no longer a scheme predicated upon successful landings and an effective Allied buildup. Almost a million troops had been brought ashore in Normandy in less than a month, despite the June gales; even Stalin had said to the American Ambassador in Moscow, Averell Harriman, that the crossing of the Channel and landings in Normandy were " 'an unheard of achievement,' the magnitude of which has never been undertaken in military history," and had spoken of "the remarkable achievement of landing so many men so rapidly."

More, however, was to come. In a manner not even Monty had dreamed possible in England, Rommel had concentrated his armored strength against the British eastern sector. The great port of Cherbourg, the key priority in Monty's Overlord plan, had been captured, and the way now seemed open to fulfil a grandiose design which, only weeks before, had appeared to many but a dream—if the Allies kept their nerve.

Part Nine

JULY PLOTS

Churchill visits Monty in Normandy,
21 July 1944.

Flying Bombs

The month of July 1944 was to herald, in many ways, the greatest struggle of Monty's life.

Though Commander-in-Chief of the largest group of Allied armies in the field, Monty had not seen his Supreme Commander, General Eisenhower, since the latter's visit, with his son, to his headquarters in Normandy on 15 June, soon after the German V-bomb blitz began. Since then, concern over German V-bombing at Supreme Headquarters had verged at times on panic. "Our defensive measures against the flying bombs and attacks against the site have failed to stop the nuisance," Eisenhower's naval aide recorded at the end of the first week. "The total number of casualties [in Britain] is about 500 dead and nearly 1500 seriously wounded. . . . There is considerable uneasiness approaching jitters."

By the second week of the Blitz it was decided to divide up Supreme Headquarters and, for safety's sake, to scatter its personnel to the four winds. By the beginning of July 1944, therefore, an extended camp, or "Advanced Command Post," had been set up for the Supreme Commander at Portsmouth, while other officers were moved elsewhere. Eisenhower himself was embarrassed by the undignified flight. "Ike said that there was considerable reluctance amongst officers, both British and American, to leave Main Headquarters under conditions," Lieutenant Commander Butcher candidly confessed, "which must appear that we are running away from the flying bombs."

The necessity for safer quarters, however, was real; the roof over the corridor between Eisenhower's and his chief of staff's office had been sucked away by one bomb blast, and when Eisenhower arrived at Bradley's headquarters in France on the night of 1 July, he "talked of the flying bombs on London," Major Hansen recorded. "They are dreadful nuisance. Ike now living underground as is everyone else. . . .

Will not win the war for the Germans but it will cause great political pressure to be brought upon the govt to clean them out."

His office life disrupted by the bombing, Eisenhower had been glad to get away for a few days. Apart from Anvil, he had now been studying Monty's suggestion of putting Patton's Third Army straight into Brittany if one of the Brittany ports—Saint-Malo, Brest, Nantes, Rennes "or even Bordeaux"—could be seized: "The whole point is that we must get planning fully coordinated, and drive ahead just as hard as we possibly can," he wrote to Bedell Smith in England.

Remaining in Normandy to watch the delayed American attack, Eisenhower meanwhile arranged to see Monty the next day, 2 July, at 10:30 A.M. at the Commander-in-Chief's new headquarters in the American sector.

A Smoldering Supreme Commander

"It was a typical Sunday morning as the sun was shining and General Montgomery and his officers were just returning from church," Eisenhower's British military assistant, Lieutenant Colonel Gault, recorded. General Bradley had also accompanied Eisenhower—his ADC struck by the almost Cromwellian piety and tidiness of Monty's headquarters:

> CP [Command Post] was remarkable. All the vans and caravans. . . . Monty not there originally, arrives downy, corduroys and sweater with black beret. . . .
>
> Two new puppies playing around his van. . . . Trees green in the valley, tiny church visible on opposite hill to the west and we could hear the ringing of bells mingled with the thunder of cannon down on 1st Div front. Monty's CP is in V [U.S.] Corps sector, at Bray.
>
> Took us out to show us Panther and Tiger tanks which he had in CP. Covered with laminated plastic to prevent stick bomb or magnetic bomb

used by Russians from sticking. Huge tank. Panther had been hit by 75 which simply glanced off it. Tankers are concerned about it. Need a heavier gun. . . .

They retired to van.

Inside his map lorry, away from the aides and photographers, Monty explained once again to Eisenhower his current tactical strategy, as he had summarized it on 30 June (his typewritten copy had not arrived at Supreme Headquarters when the Supreme Commander left the previous day).

Eisenhower was stunned by the clarity and logic of Monty's military design. One of the reasons behind his five-day visit to France was—as Churchill had attempted to do in the desert in 1942—to send a first-hand report to the Combined Chiefs of Staff, and to see if there was any way in which he could accelerate operations. However, like Churchill in Egypt, Eisenhower was totally won over by Monty's professionalism and conviction while in the latter's presence in Normandy—yet almost immediately a prey to other views and exigencies when out of it.

"First reports indicate satisfactory gains," Eisenhower's naval aide Butcher recorded on 4 July. Anxious to feed the veritable posse of newsman at Supreme Headquarters, however, Butcher was baffled by the slow progress of the British and Canadians around Caen—and skeptical about Monty's strategy. "Monty has issued another directive now saying it is his policy to 'contain' German armor around Caen on the left front of the beachhead so that the Americans on the right would not be bothered in taking Cherbourg. Now he wants Bradley to expend [sic] his holdings in the peninsula to give room for 'administration.' In Monty's previous directive he seemed to be all out to capture Caen which he still doesn't have. For purposes of illustration of nimbleness of mind," the naval aide scoffed, "I am incorporating this directive in the diary."

Butcher's insolence, as an untrained, inexperienced noncombatant, was remarkable, for the diary was officially the desk diary of the Supreme Commander of the Allied Expeditionary Force, and regularly checked by Eisenhower himself. But by 7 July even Butcher's tone had altered—for it was clear that, despite all the German armor which Dempsey had pulled over to the British front, American forces were facing the same problems as the British had in their advance, notwithstanding a three-to-one superiority in infantry and *eight-to-one* ratio in tanks in the American sector.

Tanks were, however, of limited value in the bocage country, as General Collins, commanding 7 U.S. Corps, later recalled:

Neither we nor the British were familiar with what real obstacles these growths of trees and dividing lines between small bits of property in France were—they were real obstacles! They gave wonderful cover and frequently they were double. In other words, there was one row of trees between one piece of property marking the boundary, then a little space, and then another row of trees immediately back of them, but with a space in between which could be used just like a communications trench and also as a place to put mortars. And very difficult to determine which one of these combinations held the mortars—which were very effective, those German mortars!

Collins could not recall being held up in any way by concern over American casualties. "I can readily see how the British commanders were more cautious—after all, Britain had been in the war for two or three years before we were even in it, and you had all taken very heavy casualties in North Africa and other places, whereas our casualties were relatively light." Nevertheless, even without such a concern, the fighting in the bocage was gallingly slow for the fiery Collins—as it was to Eisenhower as Supreme Commander. "We began attacking south-ward with the VIII Corps on the 3rd [July] and the VII Corps joined in with one division on July 4th," Eisenhower reported to Marshall. "I was particularly anxious to visit these Corps and their Divisions during actual operations. The going is extremely tough, with three main causes responsible. The first of these, as always, is the fighting quality of the German soldier. The second is the nature of the country. Our whole attack has to fight its way out of very narrow bottlenecks flanked by marshes and against an enemy who had a double hedgerow and an intervening ditch almost every fifty yards as ready made strong-points. The third cause is the weather. . . ."

Monty's patient, repetitive "masterplan," as Commander-in-Chief in Normandy, was of no help. "Ike has been smouldering and today burst out with a letter to Monty which in effect tells him to get busy to avoid having our forces sealed into the bridgehead, take the offensive and Ike would support him in every way, as if it were necessary," Butcher noted in his diary. "Actually Monty is following his character-istic, which is super-cautiousness."

The actual letter which Eisenhower sent was, like his letter to Mar-shall, far more comprehending and profound than ever the Butchers of the world would understand. Yet, in a SHAEF Headquarters which had now dispersed in some panic to escape the V-1 attacks, it reflected the same frustration that overseas onlookers had felt at the height of the battle of Alamein: a growing fear of stalemate.

The Fear of Stalemate

The Supreme Commander's fears were sincere and genuine.
However unruffled Monty might appear at his headquarters in
the field of battle, it was clear to Eisenhower that all was not
as well in Normandy as Monty claimed. Second Army had indeed performed valiantly in the flypaper role Monty had given it on the left
flank of the Allied lodgement area. Yet the fact remained, despite its
superiority in tanks, the British sector had failed to expand, causing
great congestion and leading to a lowering of morale in some divisions.

Already on 25 June Monty had had to close down the extensive network of officers making "Immediate Reports" about the battle. "I have
had to stamp very heavily on reports that began to be circulated about
the inadequate quality of our tanks, equipment, etc., as compared with
the Germans. . . . I enclose a copy of the letter I have sent out on the
subject of alarmist reports," Monty wrote to Brooke. "Such reports are
likely," he had told Dempsey, "to cause a lowering of morale, and a
lack of confidence among the troops. It will generally be found that
when the equipment at our disposal is used properly, and the tactics
are good, we have no difficulty in defeating the Germans. . . . You will
issue orders at once that further reports are forbidden, until I give permission. Alarmist reports, written by officers with no responsibility
and little battle experience, could do a great deal of harm."

But if Monty thought that such a directive—which went also to
General Crerar, who was soon to command First Canadian Army—
would keep the lid on the simmering pot, he was mistaken. Success, as
General Wimberley later observed, stood at the very heart of Monty's
leadership—and since the first, heady days when the British and Canadian forces stormed ashore in Normandy, there had been insufficient
British success to preserve morale at its peak. The Normandy battle
had now raged a whole month; casualties, particularly from artillery

shelling and mortars, were steadily rising and the phrase "we are hold-ing the ring while the Americans expand their sector" began to sound hollow when repeated day after day, week after week.

Although Rommel's Panzer counterattack was easily repulsed around Rauray in the Odon salient, Intelligence began to point on 3 and 4 July to the relief of some of the German Panzer divisions by infantry—a truly ominous sign. The Canadian attack on Carpiquet air-field failed ("the operation was not well handled," Dempsey noted in his diary), and a mood of recrimination, which had been latent for some time, set in—beginning with a letter from the 1 Corps Com-mander, General Crocker, to General Dempsey, who passed it on to Monty.

The story of the Canadian 3rd Division was in many ways the story of the British Second Army in the thankless role to which it had been committed. "The Div. as a whole carried out its D-Day tasks with great enthusiasm and considerable success," Crocker acknowledged.

> Once the excitement of the initial phase passed, however, the Div lapsed into a very nervy state. . . . Exaggerated reports of enemy activity and of their own difficulties were rife; everyone was far too quick on the trigger, and a general attitude of despondency prevailed. Everyone was naturally tired and a bit shaken by the first impact of real war and there was a quite understandable reaction after the pent-up excitement of the as-sault. It was just here and now that the steadying hand of the Com-mander was required. It was totally lacking, indeed the state of the Div was a reflection of the state of its Commander. He was obviously not standing up to the strain and showed signs of fatigue and nervousness (one might almost say fright) which were patent for all to see.

This was a damning indictment of a divisional commander's perform-ance in battle. Although the Canadians had subsequently regained a measure of "poise," the offensive operation at Carpiquet had once more revealed signs of rot:

> In this last day or two 3 Cdn Div has started active operations again. . . . The limited success of this operation I am afraid I can only attribute to a lack of control and leadership from the top. When things started to go not quite right all the signs of lack of calm, balanced judgment and firm command became evident again.

Dempsey, in his covering letter to Monty, "entirely agreed" with Crocker's criticisms, and recommended the removal of the Canadian 3rd Division's commander. Monty passed the two letters on to Crerar, saying, "I have little to add to these letters. I definitely agree with them." The commander "has certain qualities which are assets," Monty acknowledged. "But taken all round I consider he is not good enough to command a Canadian division; the Canadian soldier is such a magnificent chap that he deserves, and should be given, really good generals."

The Canadians may have felt that their division was being made a scapegoat, but other performances, like that of the veteran 51st Highland Division, similarly came under Monty's withering scrutiny. Monty had himself decided to replace the beloved commander, General Wimberley, who had led the re-created division from Alamein to the end in Sicily, by a protégé from the days of 1939–41, Charles Bullen-Smith, a hugely built Lowland Scot. But a week after the reports on 3rd Canadian Division Monty was signaling secretly to Brooke:

> Regret to report that it is the considered opinion of CROCKER DEMPSEY and myself that 51 Div is at present NOT repeat NOT battleworthy. It does not fight with determination and has failed in every operation it has been given to do. It cannot fight the Germans successfully. I consider the Divisional Commander is to blame and I am removing him from command. BULLEN-SMITH has many fine qualities but he has failed to lead the Highland Division and I cannot therefore recommend him to command any other Division. . . .

General Bullen-Smith was secretly sent home, without even being given time to collect his kit.

In a rumor factory such as Supreme Headquarters, it was inevitable that such stories circulated, and were magnified—particularly when set against memories of World War I and haunting recollections, still vivid among older officers, of trench warfare on the Western Front. The "buzz" bombs had added to this sense of foreboding—raising concern among the soldiers, too, about their wives, children and families in England—and it is understandable how, in his impatience to see the Allied armies on the move, the Supreme Commander dreaded the notion of stalemate. "I am familiar with your plan for generally holding firm with your left, attracting thereto all of the enemy armor, while your right pushes down the Peninsula and threatens the rear and flank of the forces facing the Second British Army," Eisenhower wrote in his "hurry-up" letter to Monty on 7 July, after news of Bradley's slow progress, the failure at Carpiquet and the new intelligence regarding the relief of Rommel's Panzer divisions.

"However the [American] advance on the right has been slow and laborious," Eisenhower continued, "due not only to the nature of the country and the impossibility of employing air and artillery with maximum effectiveness, but to the arrival on that front of reinforcements, I believe the 353rd Div. In the meantime, I understand from G-2 [Intelligence] that some infantry has arrived on the front opposite the British Army allowing the enemy to withdraw certain Panzer elements for re-grouping and establishing of a reserve.

"It appears to me," he went on, "that we must use all possible energy in a determined effort to prevent a stalemate or of facing the necessity of fighting a major defensive battle with the slight depth we now have in the bridgehead." Thanks to his decision to resurrect the Anvil landings at Marseilles, however, he had surrendered his airborne-reserve option: "Because of the transfers that we have to make to the Mediterranean to help out in ANVIL, I think we cannot put on a full-scale three or four division [airborne] attack before early September." His alternative, therefore, was either to overrule the planners and mount an amphibious operation at Saint-Malo (with all the attendant risks of another Anzio), or for Monty to try to break out in the east. This was much more to his liking:

> We have not yet attempted a major full-dress attack on the left flank supported by everything we could bring to bear. To do so would require some good weather, so that our air could give maximum assistance. . . .

Eisenhower's letter amounted to a plea to Monty to revise his Normandy strategy, four days after Bradley's "slow and laborious" performance. Monty's grand design was all very well, in Eisenhower's view, but it was *not* working.

Setting Things Alight

When Eisenhower's anxious letter arrived by messenger on 8 July, Monty was perplexed. He had already given orders for a renewed offensive on the British flank, to stop Rommel pulling Panzer divisions into reserve, as he had explained to Brooke the day before:

> I am working quietly on the general plan contained in my Directive M505 dated 30 June. We must keep the initiative and not let the enemy "dig in." The American offensive on my western flank is gathering momentum slowly. When it began on 3 July, the weather was too awful; driving rain, mist, low cloud, no visibility; and since then we have had fine periods only, and no continued spell of good weather. The country over that side is most difficult; it is very thick and approximates to jungle fighting. However the Americans are gaining ground gradually, and will shortly go much quicker I think. At the time of writing this they have got past LA HAYE DU PUITS, and are pushing on southwards.
>
> In order to help the western flank I am going to set things alight on my eastern flank, beginning tomorrow; the enemy is very sensitive to thrusts eastwards in the CAEN sector, and I shall make use of that fact.

Within the next few days Monty hoped to have Caen, or "that part of CAEN which lies north of the river, and I think it might be got by Monday [10 July]." Thereafter he would mount operations "to get that part of CAEN which lies south of the ORNE, and to organise operations to push S.E. on that axis." While this southeastern axis or arm was pushed out from Caen, the gap between it and Caumont would be filled by simultaneous attacks up the Orne. In this way he hoped at last to get the airfield area he had originally promised Leigh-Mallory; though his primary task was still, as he reminded Brooke, to *"draw attention away from my western flank."* By pushing an "armoured force out into the good going to the S.E. of the town" he was confident he could once again magnetize the German Panzer divisions, as well as giving the British lodgement area greater security in the event of a German counteroffensive employing all eight Panzer formations: "Also, we cannot be 100% happy on the eastern flank until we have got CAEN. We have pulled such weight of enemy on to our eastern flank that I want to be 100% happy there!!"

Recalling Eisenhower's impatient letter of 7 July, Monty himself told Wilmot in 1946:

> Yes, I did get a letter like that. The trouble was that *Ike began to lose his nerve*. He didn't understand the battle and there was no one at Shaef [Supreme Headquarters Allied Expeditionary Force] who did.

Whatever the political pressures for a swift advance towards the Pas de Calais area in order to capture the V-1 rocket launching sites, Monty was certain there was no way through the densely defended and echeloned German defenses on the eastern flank. However painfully slow, and whatever accusations of overcautiousness were aimed at him, it was the strategy of swinging Bradley through the less-well-defended western sector that would ultimately defeat the German armies opposing the Allied bridgehead in Normandy, he was certain. He therefore sat down in his office trailer at Bray and wrote as calm a rebuff as he could.

The Best Way to Help First U.S. Army

MY DEAR Ike,

Thank you for your letter of 7 July.

I am, myself, quite happy with the situation. I have been working throughout on a very definite plan, and I now begin to see daylight. . . .

I think we must be quite clear as to what is vital and what is not; if we get our senses of values wrong we may go astray.

There was no question of the British breaking out eastwards; what was wanted was that the Americans should break out from the back of the field and overwhelm as much of the enemy's forces as possible. Brittany was the next objective after the fall of Cherbourg; and despite the bad weather and appalling terrain, Bradley *would* get there. To help him, Monty had already decided to "set my eastern flank alight, and to put the wind up the enemy by seizing CAEN and getting bridgeheads over the ORNE; this action would, indirectly, help the business going on over on the western flank. These operations by Second Army on the eastern flank began today," he assured Eisenhower; "they are going very well; they aim at securing CAEN and at getting our eastern flank on the ORNE river—with bridgeheads over it."

However locally successful Dempsey's attack might, or might not, turn out to be, there was no question of a British breakout to the east,

Monty emphasized. Dempsey's primary job was to help Bradley's army, and this could best be done by extending the current anti-Panzer shield, running southwards from Caen, to denude the Germans in front of Bradley of armor, and shield the American thrust against German flank attack. Dempsey would be ordered either to drive south along the banks of the Orne, or towards Falaise, as originally conceived in the St. Paul's plans. If this proved impossible against fierce Panzer resistance, "it may be best for Second Army to take over all the CAUMONT area—and to the west of it—and thus release some of Bradley's divisions for the southward 'drive' on the western flank. Day to day events in the next few days will show which is best."

Whatever happened, Monty made clear, *great patience* would be required. It was idle to imagine that the battle of the breakout was more than beginning. Monty did not expect Bradley's 8 U.S. Corps to reach the Brittany coast at Avranches for another *three weeks:* "sometime about the first week in August, when I hope 8 U.S. Corps will have turned the corner and be heading for [the Brittany ports] RENNES and ST MALO." He therefore declined Eisenhower's offer of American armor on the British flank:

> I do not need an American armoured division for use on my eastern flank; we really have all the armor we need. The great thing now is to get First and Third U.S. Armies up to a good strength, and to get them cracking on the southward thrust on the western flank, and then turn Patton westwards into the Brittany peninsula.
> To sum up.
> I think the battle is going well.

Later that evening, as British and Canadian troops fought in the outskirts of Caen, Monty informed Brooke that he would opt not for Falaise, but for a shield running from the Orne at Thury-Harcourt back to the American sector at Caumont: "Have decided on this line of advance for Second Army as being *the best way to help First US Army forward.*"

By the evening of 8 July 1944 the city of Caen, save for the southern suburb of Vaucelles, was indeed in British and Canadian hands, and both Eisenhower and Churchill were free to announce the "great" news.

Monty, however, was not concerned with capture celebrations (the battle for Caen had been bloody and, like the earlier towns "liberated" by the Allies, more reminiscent of Ypres in the First World War than the popular image of liberation), but rather with the unfolding of his Normandy strategy over the next three weeks. He therefore quietly assembled his four army commanders, Bradley, Dempsey, Crerar and Patton, at his headquarters at Bray to reiterate, as he had put it in his letter to Eisenhower, "what is vital and what is not."

Patton's Swell Chance

General George S. Patton, who had landed in France on 6 July and lunched with Montgomery on the 7th, could barely contain his impatience to get fighting. Brave, bigoted and determined to prove himself on the field of valor, he was little interested in the patient mechanics of victory *à la* Monty.

"Montgomery went to great length explaining why the British had done nothing," Patton recorded in his diary on 7 July; moreover he hated the idea of waiting until August before smashing into Brittany with his Third Army, and saw Monty's concern not to make Third Army operational until the First U.S. Army had reached the Brittany corner at Avranches as an insult.

Yet even Patton, for all his pathological distrust of his rival Monty, could not fail to be excited by the grander aspect of Monty's Normandy strategy, and his own forthcoming role as Third Army Commander. As soon as the green light was given by Montgomery he was to send one corps of three divisions to clean up the Brest Peninsula and gain the "administrative" space the Allies would need for a thrust into Germany; meanwhile with the remaining ten divisions of Third Army he was to wheel eastwards on the outer (Loire River) flank of Bradley's army group and help roll up the German armies facing Dempsey's Second Army. "When I do start, I will, if current plans hold, have a swell chance," he reported to his wife on 8 July.

Bradley, by contrast, was depressed by his own recent performance. Dempsey recalled, "The American break-out attack was launched on 3rd July, but made small and slow progress, contrary to expectation.

At a conference in Monty's caravan on 10 July Bradley frankly said that he had failed in this effort to break-out."

Monty, Dempsey also related, was singularly understanding:

> Monty quietly replied: "Never mind. Take all the time you need, Brad." Then he went on tactfully to say: "If I were you I think I should concentrate my forces a little more"—putting two fingers together on the map in his characteristic way.
>
> Then Monty turned to me and said: "Go on hitting: drawing the German strength, especially some of the armor, onto yourself—so as to ease the way for Brad."

This was, behind the scenes, the antithesis of the vain, cocky British general beloved by glory-writers. Nor would Monty hear of altering his overall strategy. After the conference Dempsey offered, in private, to try and mount a breakout on the eastern flank if Bradley's thrust remained blunted—"but Monty did not favour," Dempsey confided, "such a change of aim."

"My broad policy remains unchanged," Monty began his new M510 Directive to the four army commanders on 10 July. *"It is to draw the main enemy forces in the battle on our eastern flank, and to fight them there, so that our affairs on the western flank may proceed the easier."* Copies of this directive went not only to the four Allied army commanders but also to Eisenhower, de Guingand, Leigh-Mallory, Coningham, Brooke, Simpson and General Graham, responsible for administration in Normandy. Monty wanted no misunderstanding, and was prepared to repeat his intentions ad nauseam rather than risk confusion in the higher echelons of Allied command—confusion that could so quickly spread to lower levels in the weeks of hard fighting still ahead.

Bradley's news of the failure of his American thrust was, however, a disappointment, and in order to help him, Monty accepted that Second Army must not allow Rommel to withdraw forces from the British front:

> The enemy has been able to bring reinforcements to oppose the advance of the First Army. It is important to speed up our advance on the western flank; the operations of the Second Army must therefore be so staged that they will have a direct influence on the operations of First Army, as well as holding enemy forces on the eastern flank.

To achieve this, Dempsey was now to withdraw his own armor from the battle, grouping it into a corps of three armored divisions; meanwhile he was to push infantry southwards towards Thury-Harcourt and Le Bény-Bocage, securing bridgeheads across the Orne, ready for a concentrated armored attack. Rommel would not be able to ignore the threat of a British armored breakout employing the massed tanks of three British armored divisions, as at Alamein: he would thus be forced into a do-or-die defense of the sector.

Meanwhile, pivoting *behind* Dempsey's southward thrust to Le Bény-Bocage, Bradley would relaunch his drive south to break out of the bocage. Once through, 8 U.S. Corps would turn into Brittany while the remaining American forces were to wheel *eastwards:*

> Plans will be made to direct a strong right wing in a wide sweep, south of the bocage country towards successive objectives as follows:
>
> a) LAVAL–MAYENNE
> b) LE MANS–ALENCON.

The time was inexorably approaching, Monty was confident, when the Allies could harvest the fruits of their laborious struggle: and victory, when it came, would be all the greater for their patience.

No Running Madly Eastwards

17 July 1944 was fixed as the target date for the British attack, code-named "Goodwood," with "Cobra," the relaunched American offensive, beginning the following day, 18 July. As Dempsey recalled, "the primary consideration in the 'Goodwood' plan was necessity of hitting hard; attracting the enemy's armor to the eastern flank; and wearing down his strength there—so as to weaken his capacity to resist a renewed break-out effort on the western [American] flank."

Another consideration, however, was the need to "to gain more room" on the British flank, Dempsey explained later. It was thus necessary to capture the rest of Caen, "which blocked our expansion and was an awkward wedge in our flank. Its capture would loosen the enemy's hinge, and provide us with a firm hinge. . . . There was also an increasing need for new airfields, and the best area for these was around Caen—particularly on the Bourguébus plateau. To gain that airfield area had been a feature of our planning before D-Day."

Aware of the danger that this British offensive might not only convince the enemy that the British were launching a breakout towards Paris but Churchill too, Monty signaled to Brooke on 12 July that he would send over his military assistant, Lieutenant Colonel Dawnay, to brief the War Office in person about the *real* intention behind Dempsey's new attack.

On 14 July, Dawnay duly reported to General Simpson, bearing a secret letter from Monty to Brooke, written after another meeting of the Allied army commanders the day before, and with instructions that he, Dawnay, should personally ensure that Dempsey's Goodwood offensive not be misunderstood at the War Office. Dawnay emphasized to his superiors:

> General Montgomery has to be very careful as to what he does in his Eastern flank because on that flank is the only British Army there is left in this part of the world. On the security and firmness of the Eastern flank depends the security of the whole lodgement area. Therefore, having broken out in country S.E. of CAEN, he has no intention of rushing madly Eastwards, and getting Second Army on the Eastern flank so extended that that flank might cease to be secure.
>
> *All the activities on the Eastern flank are designed to help the force in the West,* while ensuring that a firm bastion is kept in the East. At the same time all is ready to take advantage of any situation which gives reason to think that the enemy is disintegrating.

Dawnay's explanation, on top of Monty's seven-page letter to Brooke, was abundantly clear. Indeed, rarely in military annals can a commander, engaged in a world-historical battle being fought over an anticipated period of three months, have gone to such lengths to ensure that his superiors—political and military—be kept at all times "fully in the picture."

In his diary even Lieutenant Commander Butcher was, despite his growing antipathy to Monty, impressed by the Allied Land Forces Commander-in-Chief's relentless simplification of complex military issues. "I have gotten started inserting in the diary Monty's epistles to his Commanders," Butcher noted on 11 July. "Perhaps it is because I am attracted by the simplicity of Monty's directive. In any event I think the large-scale operations in which our ground troops are about to engage—operations which may be spectacularly decisive—should be backgrounded by at least this order from Monty dated July 10th."

To support Dempsey's Second Army attack Monty had personally asked Eisenhower to put pressure on Air Marshal Harris to provide heavy bomber assistance. This Eisenhower did—but in order to "sell the target," Eisenhower, in his enthusiasm, once again misrepresented Monty's aims, as he had done to Churchill. ("He [Churchill] had lots of questions," Eisenhower had reported to Monty of his latest talk with the prime minister, "most of which I answered by saying we were going to the offensive all along the line and would gain room and kill Germans. I didn't have your letter at the time. . . .")

Such misrepresentation would ensure bomber support for Monty's operations—but would prove almost fatal for Monty's command in Normandy.

First Army Nearly Through

"All senior airmen are in full accord because this operation will be a brilliant stroke which will knock loose our present shackles," Eisenhower excitedly signaled to Monty on 14 July. "Every plane available will be ready for such a purpose." To Bedell Smith, Eisenhower even remarked that if Bomber Command could saturate an area "half a mile in diameter . . . at night, the infantry in a quick attack could then practically walk through."

Considering the manner in which Eisenhower and Tedder had, four weeks before, chased Leigh-Mallory's air force planners back to Britain for attempting to give precisely such help to the army, this was a U-turn indeed.

Eisenhower's euphoric hopes disturbed Monty. To disabuse the Supreme Commander of any idea that "decisiveness" meant a British breakout from the eastern sector, Monty had sent his chief of staff, de

Guingand, to brief Eisenhower in person on 14 July, just as Dawnay had been instructed to do at the War Office. The "plan if successful promises to be decisive," Monty therefore signaled Eisenhower, but it would be decisive in that it would write off the German ability to marshal Panzers and reserves to stop Bradley's southern sweep. "The real object is to muck up and write off enemy troops"; in mounting Dempsey's attack Monty was "aiming at doing the greatest damage to enemy armor." Far from bursting out eastwards, however, "if the proposed plan can be completed, next moves would be *westwards* in order to ring round and eliminate troops in the VILLERS BOCAGE–EVRECY area," thus smashing Rommel's ability to hit Bradley's flank. Certainly there was no prospect of a British advance directly eastwards, along the heavily defended coast, against the bulk of the enemy's Panzer army and without American support. "General Montgomery does not think the capture of HAVRE and ROUEN will be so easy as was originally thought [before D-Day]," Dawnay explained to Brooke. "His present idea is that the Germans will do all they can to prevent him from crossing the SEINE and getting up to the PAS DE CALAIS area because they rely on the latter area for flying bomb and/or rocket activities against ENGLAND. They will want these activities going until the last day of the war in order to hope for better terms. General Montgomery therefore thinks the decisive battles in the West may be fought South of the SEINE and that HAVRE and ROUEN may not be captured before the war is over. If this view is correct, it would have certain repercussions on his administrative layout and plans. He would therefore be glad to know the War Office view on the subject."

It was partly for this reason that Brittany seemed such an important "administrative" prize to Monty. Cherbourg was still not cleared for the unloading of ships, and once the early autumn gales began, beach supply would become even more unreliable. The port of Cherbourg should therefore become a British supply port, he felt, while the Brittany ports supplied the Americans.

Meanwhile, if Dempsey's armor could get out south of Caen on the Caen–Falaise road, they might do the utmost destruction, "and the air would have an absolute field day," Monty wrote to Brooke: a terrific blow "designed to 'write off' and eliminate the bulk of his [the enemy's] holding troops" while Bradley, taking immediate advantage of the conflagration on the British flank, would relaunch his southward attack, now code-named Cobra.

"The First [U.S.] Army has been battling its way since 3 July through very difficult country, thickly wooded and very marshy, and canalised avenues of approach to enemy positions," Monty explained to Brooke.

"The Americans have had very heavy casualties; but they have stuck it well, have killed a great many Germans, and have severely mauled the enemy divisions facing them. *The First Army is nearly through this country.* Once it can get a footing on the road PERIERS–ST LO it will be able to launch a real 'blitz' attack with fresh troops. This attack would break in on a narrow front with great air support, and fresh divisions would pass through the gap. I have discussed problem with Bradley and this operation will be launched on 19 or 20 July."

With Dempsey bringing the main German reserves to battle south of Caen, then Bradley smashing out of the bocage to Avranches, the enemy would be unable, Monty felt, to "collect more troops to rope us off again *in the west* [opposite Bradley], and it is in the west that I want territory, i.e. I want Brittany."

The layout and plans for the British offensive were then described to Brooke, simultaneously as de Guingand was describing it to Eisenhower. "I shall watch over the battle very carefully," Monty emphasized in reviewing Dempsey's plans; "we must be certain that we neglect no chance of inflicting a real heavy defeat on the enemy." The general aim of the Goodwood part of the battle "will be to destroy all possible enemy troops in the area CAEN–MEZIDON–FALAISE–EVRECY, and to see if we can cut off those in the general area between EVRECY and CAUMONT. Whether we can do all this remains to be seen; but we will have a good try."

As with his hopes of surrounding Rommel's three Panzer divisions at Caen after D-Day, however, it was not to be.

Goodwood—a Complete Failure

S ir Ronald Adam, the Adjutant-General at the War Office, had come out to Normandy, "and in a talk in my caravan he warned me that if our infantry casualties continued at the recent rate it would be impossible to replace them, and we should have to 'cannibalise'—to break up some divisions in order to maintain the rest," General Dempsey later recorded. "For we had put almost all our available man-power into Normandy in the first few weeks." There was also a shortage of 25-pounder ammunition, which made extended artillery support impossible.

In mounting Operation Goodwood, Dempsey now decided to avoid a costly infantry offensive in the Odon valley, and instead to use his armor, backed by bombers, in the more open country northeast of Caen, hoping then to strike southwest, roll up the German front line in the southern outskirts of Caen, seize the high ground at Bourguébus, and strike on in the same southwesterly direction: a reverse of his original Odon pincer in June.

Countered by four Panzer divisions, with two further Panzer divisions echeloned behind them, the British armored attack soon ran into trouble, however. The spearhead reached the Caen railway line without difficulty, the Bourguébus Ridge was in British hands by lunchtime, and for a while it looked as if the armor would smash its way through to Falaise—Monty signaling to Eisenhower that "the weight of air power used was very great and its effect was decisive. Second Army has three armoured divisions now operating in the open country to the south and S.E. of CAEN and reg[imen]ts of armoured cars supported by tanks are being directed to the crossings over the DIVES between MEZIDON and FALAISE."

Thereafter, however, the fighting became "sticky." "There is a maximum of 50 enemy tanks around BOURGUEBUS," Dempsey lamented at 4:45 P.M. in his diary. "I told BGS 8 Corps not to let the enemy build up a gun line against us," and he urged the commander to drive on before the Germans could cordon off the assault. As at Alamein, however, it proved impossible to stir the tank commanders into further losses, and Dempsey's exhortations proved futile. Over 400 tanks had been lost, and 5,000 casualties suffered. "Once it was evident that the armor were not going to break out, the operation became an infantry battle—and it was no part of the 'Goodwood' plan to get drawn into a costly struggle of that kind. So I really lost interest in the operation by evening," Dempsey candidly confessed to the American Official Historian, in confidence, "and was ready to call it off—except for trying to get onto the initial objectives, which were necessary if we were to obtain a satisfactory tactical position."

For Monty it was a bitter blow, and one that was doubled that day when news came from General Bradley that he would no longer be able to launch his matrix attack on 19 July or even 20 July, but was postponing it until 21 July, three days away.

To the best of his ability, Monty attempted to paint the British attack, on 19 July, as a tactical success. Such grandiose statements, however, deceived no one. The air barons were livid. Goodwood, in the eyes of both British and American airmen, had been a complete failure—and they were soon baying for Monty's blood.

The Plot to Sack Monty

According to Eisenhower's naval aide, Lieutenant Commander Butcher, the mood at Supreme Headquarters in England turned bleak on the night of 19 July, as reports filtered in of the withdrawal of British armored units from the Goodwood battlefield. Eisenhower's blood pressure had risen; he was listless and suffered from ringing in his ears. "Ike hasn't been feeling so hot these last few days," Butcher noted; indeed, Eisenhower had lain in bed the entire day. "The slowness of the battle, the desire to be more active in it himself, his inward but generally unspoken criticism of Monty for being so cautious: all these pump up his system. It ain't good. He'll have to take care of himself, but his troubles are not from physical exertion, they are from mental strain and worry.

"Around evening Tedder called Ike and said Monty had in effect stopped his armor from going further. Ike was mad," Butcher recorded—adding that Tedder "said that the British Chiefs of Staff would support any recommendation that Ike might care to make, meaning that if Ike wanted to sack Monty for not succeeding in going places with his big three armored division push, he would have no trouble, officially."

The next day the mood grew worse. "The Air people are disgusted with Monty," Butcher recorded, "Tedder telling Ike last night, 'I told you so,' the Air Marshal always having burned inside, and not always succeeding in suppressing this to the air and navy." Soon Eisenhower's British and American aides were openly discussing "who would succeed Monty, if sacked. I thought his chances now are 60–40, in his favor," Butcher considered—though the odds would turn against Monty, Butcher felt certain, once Eisenhower crossed the Channel, as he was planning to do, and found that Monty had deliberately halted his successful advance "until the customary counter-attack of the Germans had been met," at which time Butcher expected Monty to resume the advance, "the worst being over."

Tedder had even begun working out the ramifications of Montgomery's dismissal—to his own advantage. Like Eisenhower, Tedder longed to command actual air force formations instead of chairing Supreme Headquarters committee meetings. With Monty's departure, he had calculated, he would also take Leigh-Mallory's place. But if Tedder replaced Leigh-Mallory, who would replace Montgomery? The name of Alexander was circulated as a possible replacement of Monty in command of 21st Army Group, while Eisenhower was himself encouraged to take overall field command. "Chief Big Wind" (as SHAEF had dubbed Monty) could then "be made a peer and sit in the House of Lords, or even given a Governorship, such as Malta, whose governor is leaving to take over racially-conscious Palestine," Lieutenant Colonel Gault, Eisenhower's British military assistant, suggested.

Yet another proposal was to promote Monty's chief of staff. "After the war," de Guingand later recalled, "Bedell Smith told me, we were talking about that phase, the failure [of Goodwood], and the agitation against Monty. He said, 'Do you know, at one point we were discussing successors, and your name was suggested?' I said, 'Good Christ! Thank God that never happened!'

"I couldn't have done it. There is all the difference in the world being a Chief of Staff and a commander—tremendous difference."

If Eisenhower's staff genuinely believed that the Allied armies in Normandy would have taken their orders from a relatively junior *staff* officer whose office was still in England, then they had clearly lost all contact with battlefield reality.

Field Marshal Brooke was one step ahead of the SHAEF plotters, however. Knowing how much was at stake, Brooke had quietly visited Monty in Normandy on 19 July. There he had counseled Monty to relax his current ban on visitors and to ensure that by personal meetings he kept his masters sweet—indeed, he made Monty write out a personal invitation to Churchill, which he could take back to England with him, as well as issuing a similar invitation to the Supreme Commander.

The rest, Brooke had made clear, would be up to Monty.

Shots in the Arm

Monty's signal to Eisenhower had asked him to visit him the next day: "alone—meaning don't bring Tedder," Butcher noted in his diary, "or other top airmen."

Eisenhower went—and once again was overwhelmed by Monty's patient, logical exposition.

To Butcher's and Gault's astonishment, when Eisenhower returned from Monty's headquarters on the afternoon of 20 July, he became a changed man. He went fishing. He piloted a liaison plane. He threw away the "slow-down potion" given him for his high blood pressure. He even told Butcher to telephone Bedell Smith and "caution him against even hinting at the subject we have been discussing"—in other words, the sacking of Monty!

This "shot in the arm" was repeated the following day, 21 July, when Churchill visited Monty. In Henderson's recollection it was "common knowledge at Tac [Headquarters] that Churchill had come to sack Monty. I mean we all knew it. He came in his blue coat with a blue cap, and in his pocket he had the order, dismissing Monty. There was quite an 'atmosphere.'

"However Monty showed not the least nervousness. He shook hands, took him into the Operations caravan—and when they came out Churchill was beaming. I've no idea what happened to that piece of paper—but we all knew how near 'Master' had come to being sacked. I remember it quite clearly, near the Cerisy forest. . . ."

Whether Churchill really had such an order in his pocket is undocumented, but the very rumor that he did illustrates the blackest chapter in the highest Allied counsels of power—a crisis that would stretch for almost a whole week, as Bradley's Cobra attack was postponed day after day, from 19 to 20, 20 to 21, 21 to 22, 22 to 23, and 23 to 24 July—the weather deemed too bad for the vital heavy bombers.

The Plot to Kill Hitler

Ironically, as certain Allied commanders plotted Monty's downfall, Rommel had reacted throughout the Normandy battle in the way Monty had predicted. On the eve of Goodwood, Rommel's head-quarters still considered that "the well-known operational intentions of Montgomery's Army Group still appear to exist. The British 2nd Army is clearly concentrated in the area of Caen and the south-west, and will carry out the thrust across the Orne *towards Paris.* . . . There are no fresh indications for estimating the aims of the American 1st Army Group." Nor was Rommel able to withdraw his Panzer divisions and replace them with infantry, thanks to Dempsey's pressure at Caen: "The replacement of armoured formations by infantry formations *has not yet succeeded,*" Rommel's headquarters reported to Hitler—indeed, "the reserve groups of the armoured [Panzer] formations had, to a large extent, to be put back in the field."

Rommel's road injury on 17 July, after an aircraft attack, did not alter any of this, for on 18 July the British armored corps had almost breached the Panzer cordon at Caen, and even the two Panzer divisions defending the Caumont area were now recalled. Rommel had warned on 15 July that "the position on the front in Normandy is becoming more difficult daily and is approaching a serious crisis," for his Panzer divisions and their reserves were "tied down by the fighting on the front of the Panzergroup West [facing Dempsey]" and there were "no mobile reserves to defend against a breakthrough. . . . The force is fighting heroically everywhere, but the unequal combat is nearing its end. It is in my opinion necessary to draw the appropriate conclusion from this situation."

Field Marshal von Rundstedt had already been sacked from command of Army Group A. His successor, Field Marshal von Kluge, taking temporary command of Rommel's Army Group B as well as A, agreed with everything Rommel had said. "The views of the Feldmarschall are unfortunately right," von Kluge reported to Hitler on 21 July. "My discussion yesterday with the commanders of the formations near Caen, held immediately after the recent heavy fighting, has, particularly, afforded regrettable evidence that . . . there is no way by which, in the face of the enemy air force's complete command, we can find a strategy which will counter-balance its actually annihilating effect without giving up the field of battle."

Monty's tactics—and the punishing effect of Allied air power—had proved far more effective than even the Allies could know. "I came here with the fixed determination of making effective your order to stand fast at any price," von Kluge apologized to Hitler. "But when one sees by experience that this price must be paid by the slow but sure annihilation of the force . . . anxiety about the immediate future of this front is only too well justified."

By this time, however, dissatisfaction with Hitler's conduct of the war had reached its climax. On 20 July, Count von Stauffenberg's bomb beneath Hitler's conference table in Rastenburg had exploded, intended to be followed by a putsch by the Wehrmacht—which would then arrange to surrender to the Allies.

Von Stauffenberg's bomb, however, failed to kill the Führer. Two hundred conspirators were arrested and executed. It was clear the war, and the killing, would have to go on—to the bitter end.

A Bill of Goods

If the German army feared ultimate annihilation in Normandy, not so Air Marshal Tedder. Furious at being told to keep away from Monty's headquarters, then by the way Monty persuaded Eisenhower and Churchill all would be well, Tedder continued to stalk the corridors of Supreme Headquarters, complaining that Monty had deliberately "restricted" Dempsey's breakout and that SHAEF had been "had for suckers. I do not believe there was the slightest intention to make a clean breakthrough [at Caen]," he remarked with perfect justification—but without the meanest understanding of Monty's patient Normandy strategy. Moreover, in absolute contradiction of the facts, Tedder later pretended that Bradley, "now that it was clear there was going to be no breakthrough on the British Front," had therefore been "urging Eisenhower . . . to plan a break-out on the western flank."

Such conniving deceitfulness would be the saddest aspect of an otherwise extraordinary Allied undertaking. Six thousand British and Canadian soldiers had given their lives, even before Goodwood, to make possible the expansion of the American sector behind them, first to Cherbourg, and now towards Brittany and the Loire. Ten thousand Americans had fallen in fulfilling their part of Monty's strategy—a just balance considering the growing preponderance of American troops in the lodgement area.

Tedder's sedition did the Deputy Supreme Commander no credit. Nor did it work. When Churchill telephoned on the night of 24 July, after his return from Normandy, Eisenhower's first question was "What do your people think about the slowness of the situation over there?"—"meaning," Lieutenant Commander Butcher confided in his diary, "was the P.M. also after Monty's scalp, as Tedder obviously is."

Butcher had gone back to bed after Eisenhower began talking to Churchill. He was therefore astonished when, the following morning, Eisenhower "said he had talked more than a half hour to the P.M. and that during the P.M.'s recent trip Monty obviously had sold Winston 'a bill of goods.' The P.M. was supremely happy with the situation."

With Churchill's firm support for Monty, the wind at last seemed to go from Tedder's sails—though it was not for long.

Monty, meanwhile, hearing from colleagues how near he had come to dismissal in the preceding days, determined to make quite sure that Eisenhower was now kept fully abreast of proceedings. Hitherto he had relied on nightly cables, copies of his directives to the army commanders, and personal liaison through de Guingand. When, on 24 July, Cobra was yet again postponed, he penned a personal letter to Eisenhower:

24–7–44

My dear Ike

The weather here has been quite frightful; we have not seen the blue sky for days on end; there is 10/10ths clouds, and air operations have been practically closed down. The heavy mud turned the area S.E. of CAEN into a complete sea of mud, and everything came to a stop.

Today it is still cloudy and misty, and we could not get Brad's attack launched.

Lest Eisenhower panic, however, Monty went to great pains to reiterate the essential features of the battle. As at Alamein, the enemy had been made to expect the main attack elsewhere, and had no idea what was about to come in the west. "It is a large scale operation and, once we get it launched, I am sure it will go well; it has great possibilities and Collins is a grand leader. The opening gambit is an attack by three divisions west of ST LO, under a great air bombardment. The objective of this 'break-in' is the general line MARIGNY–ST GILLES. Three more divisions then pass through, turn right handed, and make for COUTANCE and GRANVILLE." It would be, in fact, the first full-scale *concentrated* attack mounted by the Americans in the Second World War. Once again, Dempsey's task was to act as decoy by launching yet another British attack in the east:

It is very necessary that, while Third U.S. Army is swinging southwards and eastwards on the *western flank*, Second Army should fight hard on the *eastern flank* so as to draw the enemy attention and strength over to that side—keep the enemy pinned down in the CAEN sector—and constitute the definite and continuous threat of an advance on FALAISE and ARGENTAN.

Dempsey's diversionary attacks would be mounted in four consecutive phases, so that the Germans could not possibly withdraw Panzer divisions in line, or even reserves, to oppose Bradley—beginning with Canadian attack the nest day, 25 July, and building up to a crescendo over the subsequent days. The climax would be an armored drive "by possibly three or four armoured divisions, which I want to launch towards FALAISE. . . . The object would be to create complete chaos in the FALAISE area, and generally to put the wind up the enemy." If this succeeded it would "bring about a major enemy withdrawal from in front of Brad"; at the very least it would stop reinforcements moving west to oppose Bradley's Cobra breakout.

What it all amounted to, Monty wrote in summary, was a "really hard fight" on "both flanks simultaneously." But while the enemy *had* to counter the British offensive—since it threatened an armored breakout to Paris and the Seine—Bradley's attack through the enemy's weaker, western sector remained the Allies' "real business," and was bound to succeed because the Germans could not possibly transfer sufficient forces to stop Bradley in time:

The really big victory is wanted on the western [American] flank, and every thing will be subordinated to trying to make it so.

Such was still the plan. As if to mock these patient hopes, however, the fates had two further reverses in store—for, although Cobra had indeed been canceled at the last minute that day, 300 American bombers, by a tragic mistake in planning and communications, had followed the wrong flight path, had continued their journey over Normandy, and had bombed their own troops, killing, wounding, and shell-shocking many hundreds of Americans.

Amid total confusion, and with heartbroken, accusatory signals sent to the headquarters of the U.S. Eighth Air Force, Bradley's Cobra attack was rescheduled for a seventh consecutive day. But when, on 25 July 1944, it finally kicked off, the American bombing was even worse—killing and wounding over 600 American troops, and shell-shocking still more.

Eisenhower Again Runs Down Monty

Eisenhower, who had flown to Normandy to witness the Cobra kickoff, returned "glum" and full of foreboding. By early afternoon the Americans had advanced only a few thousand yards.

Fearing another stalemate, Eisenhower once again gave in to his worst fears. To his guide at First Army, he remarked that he "does not believe in tactical use of heavies," Bradley's ADC recorded. "I look upon heavies as an instrument for strategic attack on rear installations," Eisenhower declared, reflecting Tedder's view. "I don't believe they can be used in support of ground troops. That's a job for artillery. I gave them the green light on this show but *this is the last one*," he warned—ignoring the shortage of ammunition in the American sector, which had become so critical Bradley was rationing its use. When Churchill phoned late that night, Eisenhower said that, though he still saw "eye to eye" with Montgomery, the battle was "touch and go, with hard fighting under way and much more in prospect."

His spirits sinking, and with Tedder once again complaining about Monty, Eisenhower went to lunch with Churchill the next day, accompanied by Bedell Smith. Bedell Smith would go on record, in a conversation with the American Official Historian after the war, as saying he did not "see how it would be possible to give a correct portrayal of Montgomery without showing him to be a SOB. . . . Monty's trouble was that he never rose to Army Group Commander level. He was a Corps commander or an Army commander. He liked to go off by himself and fight the Corps or the Army himself. That is, he did that in his own area. He tended to let Bradley alone."

As Bedell Smith had not visited Monty a single time in the battle of Normandy, this was a pernicious calumny. Yet it was not said merely in hindsight. On 26 July, Eisenhower and Bedell Smith so decried Montgomery to the Prime Minister that Churchill, in anxiety, summoned Brooke after lunch to inform him of the Supreme Commander's dissatisfaction. "Eisenhower had been lunching with him and had again run down Montgomery," Brooke recorded in his diary, "and described his stickiness and the reaction in the American papers."

Churchill's response to this renewed demand for Monty's scalp was to ask Eisenhower and Bedell Smith to repeat their criticisms the following evening, over dinner, with Brooke present.

Once again, however, Eisenhower and Bedell Smith had miscalculated. From Monty, Brooke had received a very different picture from the defeatist one which Eisenhower and his chief of staff were peddling to the Prime Minister—indeed, Brooke was quite certain Monty's strategy was finally about to pay off.

"I have got to fight very hard on the eastern flank while the Americans are battling on the western flank," Monty had written in a personal letter to Brooke on 26 July, enclosing his new directive to the army commanders. "From one or two things Ike said yesterday when he was here, there is no doubt that public opinion in America is asking why the American casualties are higher than the British—and why they have captured so many more prisoners."

It was clearly impossible to make a public statement, outlining the whole strategy of the battle to the public at home—and consequently to the enemy. The Germans still had no idea of Patton's presence in Normandy, nor of the full buildup of American infantry and armor in the western sector compared with that of the east, where the Germans still believed the primary threat lay. Yet the caviling and miscomprehension in Allied rear headquarters and the British and American press worried Monty, as it threatened to undermine the morale of his British and Canadian troops in their thankless role. "It is not good for the morale of British troops in Normandy to see headlines in the English Newspapers: Set-back in Normandy etc. etc.," he complained. "I wonder if Grigg could have lunch with some leading editors and get this across to them":

> *From the beginning it has been my policy to try and pull the main enemy strength, and especially his main armoured strength, on to the British Second Army on the eastern flank so that our affairs on the western flank could proceed more easily.* After a great deal of hard fighting we got the main enemy armoured strength deployed on the eastern flank when the big American blow was struck in the west on 25 July at 1100 hrs. This was not a bad achievement. Very heavy fighting took place south of CAEN on 25 and 26 July and on the front of 2 Cdn DIV, which was fighting its first battle in Normandy, we were forced back 1000 yds in two places, i.e. at MAY and at TILLY.
>
> *I would give 5 miles on the eastern flank* if I could thereby get the whole of the Cherbourg and Brittany peninsulas!!

No more telling phrase could illustrate Monty's strategy. The next night he sent a similar message to Churchill, rejecting any sensational notion of a Canadian reverse. "I know of no 'serious set-back,' " he protested. "The enemy has massed great strength in area South of CAEN to oppose our advance in that quarter. Very heavy fighting took place yesterday and the day before and as a result the troops of Canadian Corps were forced back 1,000 yards from the furthest position they had reached." This was not serious, since "my policy since the beginning has been to draw the main enemy armoured strength on to my Eastern flank and to fight it there so that our affairs on Western [American] flank could proceed the easier. In this policy I have succeeded; the main enemy armoured strength is repeat is now deployed on my eastern flank to East of the river ODON, and my affairs in the West are repeat are proceeding the easier and the Americans are going great guns."

This was indeed the case, as Collins' troops began to smash through the German line—behind which, thanks to Monty's relentless efforts in the east, there were no German reserves. "It begins to look as if the policy we have been working on for so many weeks is now going to pay a dividend," Monty signaled to Brooke. "When the American attack went in west of St LO at 1100 hrs on 25 July the main enemy armoured strength of six panzer and SS divisions was deployed on the eastern flank opposite Second British Army. That was a good dividend.

The Americans are going well and I think things will now begin to move towards the plan outlined in M512."

When Brooke thus met Eisenhower and Bedell Smith on the evening of 27 July, therefore, he had little difficulty in shaming them. Moreover, if Eisenhower had criticisms of the way his Land Forces Commander-in-Chief was directing the battle, Brooke stated, he should go back to Normandy and put them to Monty, not cavil behind his back. "I told Ike that if he had any feeling that you were not running operations as he wished he should most certainly tell you, and express his views," Brooke explained in a letter the next day to Monty. "That it was far better for him to put all his cards on the table and that he should tell you exactly what he thought. He is evidently a little shy of doing so. I suggested that if I could help him in any way by telling you for him I should be delighted. He said that he might perhaps ask me to accompany him on a visit to you! So if you see me turn up with him," Brooke warned, "you will know what it is all about."

Meanwhile, in his personal diary Brooke noted:

There is no doubt that Ike is all out to do all he can to maintain the best relations between British and Americans. But it is equally clear that Ike knows nothing about strategy. Bedell Smith, on the other hand, has brains but no military education in its true sense. He is certainly one of the best American officers, but still falls far short when it comes to strategic outlook. With that Supreme Command set-up it is no wonder that Monty's real high ability is not always realised. Especially so when "national" spectacles pervert the perspective of the strategic landscape.

The Scent of Victory

In the meantime, in order to allay further criticism in the American press, Brooke urged Monty to ensure Dempsey launched his next attack "at the earliest possible moment on a large scale. We must not allow German forces to move from his front to Bradley's front or we shall give more cause for criticism."

Monty, however, had no intention of allowing the Germans to move over to Bradley's front—indeed, it was now too late for them to do so. Events on the field of battle were at last overtaking the back-room carping. Operation Spring on the Canadian Army's front, due south of Caen, had been designed to keep the principal German armor in the east, and was doing so, despite sacrificial casualties. (Though the press had decried the Canadian lack of "gains," Bradley was grateful, his ADC noting in his diary on 26 July: "The British effort east of CAEN continues with attacks from their positions south and east of Caen. Hoped that German would accept our preliminary Cobra simply as diversionary attack for the Caen operation and thrust his weight over there [in the east] while we got off on the real business in our sector.")

The time was rapidly approaching when Patton's Third Army would be activated, and on the afternoon of 26 July, Hansen recorded, a smiling Monty had arrived "from his hqs to discuss progress of the attack, plan the employment of FUSAG [1st U.S. Army Group] when we reached our objective calling for the employment of both [American] armies. Monty dressed in same peculiar uniform and he sauntered up, greeted cordially by Brad who unfailingly hangs on the sir term of address."

The next day, as Bradley pushed through his armored divisions, the German front began to disintegrate. Patton arrived at Bradley's headquarters "worried for fear the war may end here before he gets in. . . . Patton admits to Bradley that he is anxious to get in: 'I must get in and do something spectacularly successful,' he says, 'if I am to make good.' "

On 28 July, Monty brought Dempsey himself to Bradley's headquarters to discuss the next Allied moves. The mood was now one of gathering excitement. "Brad's welcome to them was warm and refreshing, came out of his truck, wrung their hands and said he was glad to see them. . . . Dempsey is planning to jump off his 30th corps on the left of the V [U.S.] Corps," Hansen recorded, "and protect our flank on that side as we move out."

With the success of Cobra now becoming apparent even to the staff of SHAEF, Eisenhower changed his tune. A cable from Monty reached him on the evening of 28 July, bearing out all that Brooke had predicted. "On west flank the battle is going splendidly and Bradley's troops are in COUTANCE. It begins to look," Monty informed him with undisguised pride, "as if the general plan on which we have been working so long is at last going to pay a dividend." To make certain nothing "leaked" from the German Caen sector to Bradley's salient he had already instructed Dempsey that afternoon to advance the date of the 30 Corps attack from Caumont—in fact the 7th Armoured Division and Guards Armoured Division had been ordered to move fifty miles to their right and attack at dawn on 30 July. "I have ordered DEMPSEY to throw all caution overboard and to take any risks he likes and to accept any casualties and to step on the gas for VIRE," Monty assured Eisenhower. This crossed with a signal from Eisenhower in which the Supreme Commander at last complimented his Commander-in-Chief in the field—"Am delighted that your basic plan has begun brilliantly to unfold with Bradley's initial success"—and in which he begged Monty to speed up Dempsey's Caumont attack.

Such constant post-factum harrying was a trial to Monty, but in view of Brooke's warning Monty patiently answered:

> Expect you have got my M68 saying that attack from CAUMONT area goes in tomorrow Sunday. Two divisions can reach that area by then and others will be thrown in to the battle as they arrive.
>
> BRADLEY DEMPSEY and myself met together yesterday afternoon and drew up agreed plans to complete the dislocation of enemy and on eastern flank CRERAR will play his part. Have great hopes we shall win a great victory and achieve our basic object.

Later that day, elated by the reports he was receiving, Eisenhower boarded his B-25 and flew to Normandy to see Bradley and Monty, taking his personal assistant Kay Summersby on her first trip to France.

Once in Normandy, Eisenhower recognized at first hand that victory was indeed in sight. Back in England the following day, 30 July, as Bradley pushed further south and Dempsey's Caumont attack kicked off, Eisenhower belatedly attempted to make up for his seesawing support of Monty during the preceding weeks. Addressing a telegram to the American military censor, General Surles, he took to task those writers who in America had expressed "sharp criticism" of Montgomery—criticism which he took upon his own shoulders. As Supreme Commander he was, he now claimed, himself responsible "for strategy and major activity" in Normandy; therefore criticism of Montgomery was criticism of him, the Supreme Commander.

Considering that less than forty-eight hours previously Eisenhower had been leveling these same criticisms against Monty in the presence of Churchill and Brooke, this was a trifle hypocritical. Now that he had seen for himself in Normandy that Monty's long-drawn-out strategy was about to produce victory, however, Eisenhower could at last, with sincerity, stand up for his "principal subordinate." The battle of Normandy looked certain to end in triumph.

Enter Patton

***

S oon after Collins' breakthrough, Field Marshal Brooke wrote to congratulate Monty:

> I am delighted that our operations are going so successfully and conform-
> ing so closely to your plans.
>   For the present all the "mischief making tongues" are keeping quiet; I
> have no doubt they will start wagging again and am watching them.

The sudden ripening of Monty's Normandy strategy had transformed the moment. At last the doubters, the belly-achers, grumblers and men of faint heart were silenced, and those armchair strategists who wanted "gains" could mark up their atlases once more. Not only had Monty succeeded in keeping the entire German "Armored Group West" away from the American breakout, but he had kept much of it east of Noyers. When on 30 July Dempsey launched the start of his armored attack from Caumont, von Kluge was therefore wholly misposi-tioned—still certain Monty would "make the thrust towards Paris" from the Caen sector.

Like Rommel, von Kluge was playing straight into Monty's hands. Within hours of the 30 July kickoff, Dempsey had a British armored division nearing Le Bény-Bocage, thus shielding the left flank of Bradley's new salient—which in turn had reached Avranches, at the base of the Cherbourg Peninsula. "On west flank right Corps of First U.S. Army is now fighting in AVRANCHES and I hope to turn it west-wards into BRITTANY tomorrow or Wednesday," Monty signaled Brooke on the evening of 31 July.

Patton's Third U.S. Army Headquarters was now to become operational—though in order to conceal the importance of the American breakout, it was decided (much to Patton's chagrin) not to release his name as Commander of Third U.S. Army.

"I must throw everything into the present battle," Monty wrote in high spirits on 1 August 1944 to General Simpson at the War Office:

> The American armies on the right, and the Second British Army in the centre, are now in process of carrying out the big wheel that will I hope clear Brittany—push the Germans back behind the ORNE—and swing the right [American] flank of the wheel up towards PARIS (possibly).
>
> If the Second Army can progress steadily now, we have the German "roping off" force cut in two. Once we get to VIRE and CONDE, it will be awkward for the Germans—and I am working to that.
>
> On the left, Canadian Army must hold, while the force pivots on that flank. I must take everything I can from the left and put it into the right swing. . . .
>
> Everything is going very well. The full plan, which I have been working to all the time, is now slowly working out as planned. I hope to turn the right Corps of 12 Army Group westwards into Brittany tomorrow.

There was something moving about this long-awaited moment. Had the June storms not forced Bradley to close down his Saint-Lô offensive at the time of the advance on Cherbourg, a month might have been saved—a month in which Dempsey had had to keep up his costly feint on the eastern flank, and Bradley to take the heavy casualties necessitated by a belated southward offensive. Yet these were the fortunes of war. Despite the "real tragedy in delaying build up and deployment of your forces," as Brooke had called it in June, Monty had nevertheless stuck relentlessly to his strategy throughout July: a strategy that was now paying off in the most spectacular way. Thus at one moment Eisenhower's headquarters was openly discussing the dismissal of Monty; hours later the Supreme Commander was agreeing to give tactical command of his imminent new American army group—12th U.S. Army Group, under Bradley—to Montgomery. At twelve noon on 1 August 1944, despite the original agreement that Eisenhower would assume command in the field of all Allied ground forces once two army groups became operational in Normandy, Monty therefore formally took command of both 12 and 21 Army Groups for the final phase of the battle. By the following evening Monty was writing to Simpson:

> The battle goes well and completely according to plan. RENNES is now ours—and ST MALO.
>
> I doubt if there are many Germans in the whole of Brittany, except base wallahs, etc. George Patton should be in BREST in a day or two.

The broad plan remains unchanged.

I shall swing the right [American] flank round, and up towards PARIS. And while this is going on I shall try to hold the enemy to his ground in the CAEN area. Then I hope to put down a large airborne force, including 52 [British] Div, somewhere in the CHARTRES area and cut off the enemy escape through the gap between PARIS and ORLEANS.

The big idea would be to push the enemy up against the Seine—and get a "cop" [big catch].

Not even Monty, however, expected the Germans to stick their heads into his noose as they now did—or Patton to streak away so fast that Monty would not even need to drop an airborne division. The long July was giving way to the greatest Allied victory of the war.

Part Ten

BREAKOUT

Bradley and Patton confer with Monty in
Normandy shortly before Patton's breakout.

Monty's Grip

As in the desert and in Sicily and Italy, Monty spent much of the day visiting his formations and units in the field. What was different now, however, was his deliberate use of a carefully chosen team of young personal liaison officers. These young men, his "eyes and ears," enabled Monty to keep his finger on the pulse of every formation—British, American, Canadian, French or Polish—in the largest group of armies ever fielded by the Allies in the war so far. As the senior operations officer, Major Odgers, explained:

> Time was the essence of the thing—I mean he [Monty] wanted to know, if he could, what the situation was two hours ago in a certain Corps headquarters. And that could very often be achieved.

If Monty could not dictate what was being said in rear headquarters in England, he was in total command of all that went on in the field of battle. No visitor who ever set foot in his Tactical Headquarters in Normandy could doubt the unique aura of authority that informed his military "grip." The special truck which he had had built prior to D-Day contained a vast wall map of Normandy, constantly updated by the latest information from the Tac HQ operations room:

> The master map was in a way ours. We were putting on stuff in very considerable detail—a great big wall, if you can picture the scene. We had a caravan which had a central passage with two sorts of tables, either side, well-lit, and the sides of it, which were solid, would lift up and supports would come down, and you then had two lean-tos. . . .
> The LOs [liaison officers] would come in and—depending entirely on the urgency of the thing I used to favour their coming to me first and collecting themselves and giving us a report, they'd dictate straight out.

The typewriter, in a big operation, was going all the day, like a ticker tape! And copies were held back for historical purposes for Main 21 Army Group, and always a copy went off to the ADC in Monty's caravan. And then, their minds to a degree ordered, they would go in and talk to Monty. And I never allowed the poor chaps to go into a meal or anything until they'd unburdened themselves and we'd got this thing straight from the horse's mouth.

Two of the liaison officers died in the course of their duties, two were wounded; all were decorated for personal bravery. Subordinate commanders might well have felt vexed by such young and relatively junior officers (all were majors) reporting back to the Commander-in-Chief not only the latest military situation as seen in their headquarters, but also the state of morale. Yet few commanders took this unique system amiss, partly because the officers chosen by Monty were sincere, loyal and courageous, and partly because their presence was tangible evidence of Monty's relentless desire to keep in closest touch with his fighting commanders—to feel continuously, like a caring doctor, the heartbeats of his captains.

"Did we ever feel in doubt about the way the battle was shaping? I think one must say—I don't think we ever did," Odgers later reflected. "Because, you see, we had this vast confidence in Monty at the time. I mean, let's face it, it was too plain to us that we were not actually breaking-through. Second Army was butting its nose against the most formidable opposition the whole time. . . . One did feel 'hope we can do it,' but I didn't feel that something was dreadfully wrong, no. But I do remember this long July wait. And realizing the strains that were being created."

Wanted: Generals Who
Will Go Like Hell

No battle in the West had equaled the struggle for Normandy. The battle of France in 1940, up to the Anglo-French evacuation at Dunkirk, had taken barely three weeks. The battle of Alamein, in 1942, only twelve days—and even then, weak hearts had failed. The entire assault and campaign to conquer Sicily had taken only thirty-eight days. Yet, as in Sicily, the astonishing success of the D-Day landings had given rise to hopes of a quick victory in Normandy thereafter, and it had required all Monty's patient guidance to keep his forces working towards his masterplan. To the English military historian Basil Liddell Hart, Dempsey was at pains later to emphasize how "Monty's plan never changed—his design from the start was to break-out from the Western (American) flank of the bridgehead." In the field, on 6 August 1944, even Monty's chief of staff said the same to the BBC correspondent Chester Wilmot: "Monty stuck to his original plan and didn't try altering it to any marked degree, despite everyone's natural impatience."

Time and again, however, within the overall masterplan in Normandy, Monty had hoped Second Army would do more than merely hold the German armor and reserves in the east, while the Americans smashed their way behind the enemy; had hoped Dempsey might envelop Caen in the early days of the invasion, surround the initial German Panzer divisions in the battle, get armored cars way out beyond the Bourgébus Ridge and expand the British flank of the bridgehead. Thus when Major General "Pip" Roberts, plucky veteran of Alamein, smashed his 11th Armoured Division some twelve miles through the German front at Caumont in less than thirty-six hours on 30 July, there arose the chance that, if Dempsey could keep up the British momentum towards Vire, a whole pocket of German troops facing Bradley's left flank could be rolled up. To do this, however, Dempsey must push out enough armor on Roberts' left flank to allow him to swing without hindrance towards Flers, cutting off the Germans in Vire.

To Dempsey's disappointment, such exploitation proved impossible, partly because 7th Armoured Division simply failed to push out its flanking shield in time. By midday on 2 August, Dempsey was aware it was too late, for by then no less than three German Panzer divisions—21st, 10th SS and 9th SS—were shifting westwards to counter the threat. As Monty lamented that evening to Simpson, "these things don't always work out quite as planned! . . . I fear I shall have to remove Erskine from 7 Armd DIV. He will not fight his division and take risks. It was very easy in the desert to get a 'bloody nose,' and a good many people did get one. The old desert divisions are apt to look over their shoulder, and wonder if all is OK behind, or if the flanks are secure, and so on. 7 Armd Div is like that. They want a new General, who will drive them headlong into, and through, gaps torn in the enemy defence—not worrying about flanks or anything." Some 90,000 Germans had surrendered already since D-Day—"the big mass of German soldiery want an opportunity to surrender, and they must be given it; this does not apply to the S.S. troops," Monty remarked. "Great vistas are opening up ahead, and we want Generals now who will put their heads down and go like hell."

Such a man was George S. Patton.

Swinging the Right Flank Round to Paris

In the following weeks Patton was to give perhaps the finest performance of "headlong" mobile operations ever seen in modern military history—certainly on a par with the German armored breakthrough to Boulogne and Calais in 1940. Disregarding his flanks, Patton set about surprising the enemy by sheer speed rather than by fighting, and with stunning results. At 10:30 A.M. on 1 August, Monty had given orders to Bradley that when Third Army "takes up the reins at midday" it was to "pass one Corps through AVRANCHES straight into the BRITTANY Peninsula. Its other two Corps will be directed on LAVAL and ANGERS" on the Loire. Though Bradley and Patton both faltered before committing so large a part of Third Army to the wheel eastwards towards Paris, the lack of German resistance did not prejudice such indecision as it had on Dempsey's front, and over the ensuing days Patton would indeed make the sweep on Paris which Monty wanted.

Patton's giant eastward wheel, however, could only succeed if Crerar, Dempsey and Bradley kept von Kluge's primary forces committed between Caen and Mortain. It was vital therefore to ensure the Germans formed no new defensive line behind which they could withdraw mobile forces to deal with Patton. By attacking the main enemy pivots, Monty felt, he could force the Germans to accept all-out battle on the Fifth Panzer Army/Seventh Army front, for fear of it disintegrating. Meanwhile, General Hodges—who, with the elevation of Bradley to 12th U.S. Army Group, had taken command of First U.S. Army—and General Patton could wheel their two armies eastwards towards Paris. Hodges was to swing around Dempsey's right flank and make for Argentan, while Patton would send two corps racing round in a deep envelopment towards the French capital, pivoting on the Mayenne at Laval. "The broad strategy of the Allied Armies is to swing the right flank round towards PARIS, and to force the enemy back against the SEINE—over which river all the bridges have been destroyed between Paris and the sea," Monty's M516 directive of 4 August laid down.

The battle of Normandy was becoming the battle of France.

The Falaise Pocket

The day before, at 10 A.M. on 3 August 1944, Monty had visited Dempsey at his headquarters. A new shape to the battle seemed to be appearing, as the two men ran their fingers across the Normandy map. With three complete Panzer divisions contesting his advance at Le Bény-Bocage and further divisions fighting hard to deny American access into Vire, there arose a fresh possibility: namely the outflanking of the Germans facing Dempsey and Hodges *from the north*, using the newly formed Canadian army in what would become known as the "Falaise gap."

If General Crerar's Canadian forces could be made to strike southwards from Caen towards Falaise, Monty reasoned, von Kluge's armies in the German salient would be pinched off, with Hodges and Patton barring their escape route on the southern flank. Thus on the evening of 3 August Monty gave telephone instructions for Crerar to "launch a heavy attack from the CAEN sector in the direction of Falaise."

This was possibly the most exciting moment of the war—and Monty was in his element. "My dogs, rabbits, and birds, are all in good health. We are acquiring large areas of France at a rapid rate," he boasted on 6 August to Phyllis Reynolds. He had moved his Tac HQ near to 21st Army Group's Main Headquarters, which had at last come over from England and was established at Le Tronquay. Having drawn up a new directive for his armies—M517—he sent a copy to Brooke with a grateful covering letter:

Tac Headquarters
21 Army Group
6-8-44

My dear CIGS

I am sending Dawnay over with my directive for the advance to the SEINE, and he will take this letter.

All goes well. In fact everything is working out so much according to plan that one wonders, sometimes, whether it isn't a bit too good.

On the other hand we have been through our difficult days, as you know. And if we had faltered in those days we might well not be where we are now.

I would like to thank you for your firm support at all times. It makes a great difference to me to know that you stand like a firm rock behind us, and your faith in what we are trying to achieve is constant.

In his new directive Monty was still unsure whether von Kluge was perhaps pulling back to "some new defensive line; but there is no evidence yet to show exactly what that line is." If the Canadians were successful in reaching Falaise, however, then all von Kluge's forces west of Falaise would be outflanked—indeed, even if von Kluge managed to block the Canadians, Patton could cut the German forces off by moving behind. "If he [the enemy] holds strongly in the north as he may well do, that is the chance for our right [American] flank to swing round and thus cut off his escape. But whatever the enemy may want to do will make no difference to us," Monty declared. "We will proceed relentlessly, and rapidly, with our own plans for his destruction."

No more troops were to be used for the clearing of Brittany "than are necessary, as the main business lies to the east," Monty now laid down. "Plans will be made for the right [American] flank to swing rapidly eastwards, and then north-eastwards towards PARIS; speed in this movement is the basis of the whole plan of operations." By dropping two airborne divisions at Chartres, the Allies would block the Germans retreating southwest of Paris, while the absence of bridges north of Paris would enable the Allies to squeeze the Germans against the Seine. In this case, Monty stated, "We shall have hastened the end of the war."

That night, however, the shift of von Kluge to a "new defensive line" was revealed to be a shift to an *offensive* line—a secret counterattack by four Panzer divisions ordered directly by Hitler to take place at dawn on 7 August, with the object of splitting apart the two Anglo-American army groups at Avranches. Far from trying to escape, the Germans—even *before* the launch of the Canadian offensive—seemed to be putting their head, deliberately, into the Allied trap!

The Jig Is Up

Although Ultra intelligence did not reveal the German Panzer attack in advance, the rapid decrypting of ancillary orders for air support enabled both Monty and Bradley to assess the scale of the enemy offensive almost immediately—and to prepare for it. Thus when Monty reported by signal to Brooke on the evening of 7 August he was delighted by the way things were going:

> Enemy attack in MORTAIN area has been well held by the Americans and all positions intact. . . . When the attack developed three American divs were moving southwards between MORTAIN and AVRANCHES and these were halted this morning to provide additional security in this gap. I have no fears whatever for the security of this part of the front and am proceeding with my offensive plans elsewhere without change.

Forty-five minutes later he was signaling spectacular news of these offensive plans:

> My L.O. has just returned from the LAVAL front and reports that the leading troops of 15 US Corps have reached LOUE which is only about 15 miles from LE MANS. This is very good news and it is quite possible that this Corps will reach LE MANS tomorrow. . . . If only the Germans will go on attacking at MORTAIN for a few more days it seems that they might not be able to get away.

Monty still favored a wide envelopment that would permit Patton to shut off the Orléans escape route, then swing north to the Seine and the Channel. Such a deep envelopment would ensure the least opposition, since the bulk of the German fighting units were inextricably bound up in the fighting from Falaise to Mortain. Bradley, however, fa-

vored a shorter hook, and was supported by Monty's own senior staff
officers, de Guingand and Williams. "Monty was sold on the wide outflanking move—blocking the Orléans Gap with paratroopers etc. and
switching the armor Northwards along the left bank of Seine to form
a big pocket," Brigadier Williams confided to Chester Wilmot after
the battle. "Did not change this," Wilmot noted, "till after Mortain began—and then only on urging of Freddie, Bradley and Bill
[Williams.]"

On Bradley's advice, Monty now went for the short envelopment at
Falaise, not the Seine. Time was of the essence. By 8 August, American
patrols on Hodges' front at Mortain reported von Kluge was withdrawing his armor, following his abortive Panzer attack. If Patton moved
immediately north from Le Mans, as well as continuing with the
planned wider envelopment of the enemy at Chartres and up to Paris,
then there was a chance of bottling up von Kluge's armies between
Mortain and Falaise. "A strong force of four divisions will operate tomorrow northwards from the LE MANS area towards ALENCON,"
Monty therefore signaled to Brooke that evening. "I am trying to get
FALAISE and ALENCON as the first step to closing the ring behind
the enemy."

Monty remained in two minds himself about the short envelopment
at Falaise. "There are great possibilities in the present situation," he signaled to Brooke the next day. "If we can get to ALENCON ARGEN-
TAN and FALAISE fairly quickly we have a good chance of closing the
ring round the main German forces and I am making all plans to drop
an airborne division at GACE about 15 miles east of ARGENTAN in
order to complete the block." But would it work in the confined bocage countryside which so favored defense? Certainly Monty seems to
have been unsure whether the German pocket could be successfully
sealed, for at the end of his 9 August signal he added: "Should the
Germans escape us here I shall proceed quickly with the plan outlined
in M517"—the wider envelopment.

Knowing the terrain, Monty cautioned Brooke not to expect spectacular results. The Canadians ought to reach Falaise, but "they will
not have the easy time they fancied," he warned. "The Germans will
fight hard for FALAISE I think," whereas "I don't think the Americans
will have any difficulty in getting to ALENCON, as there is nothing
there to oppose them. If we can get to FALAISE, and can also hold
ALENCON strongly, we should then be able to close the gap in
between—and that would be very excellent.

"But the Germans will fight hard; it is good defensive country and
we must not expect things to go too rapidly."

"So far the Poles have not displayed that dash we expected, and have been sticky."

General Crerar, in particular, had not impressed Monty as commander of First Canadian Army. At the critical moment on 23 July when Crerar's army headquarters became operational, Crerar had had a stand-up row with his corps commander, Lieutenant General Crocker, whom Crerar immediately sacked. "I have had each of them to see me," Monty had reported to Brooke, "and I now hope I can get on with fighting the Germans—instead of stopping the generals fighting amongst themselves!!" Crerar was now "fighting his first battle and it is the first appearance in history of a Canadian Army H.Q. He is desperately anxious that it should succeed. He is so anxious that he worries himself all day!! I go and see him a lot and calm him down. He will be much better," Monty remarked, "when he realises that battles seldom go completely as planned, that you keep at it until the other chap cracks, and that if you worry you will eventually go mad!! He seemed to have gained the idea that all you want is a good initial fire plan, and then the Germans all run away!!"

Crerar's inexperience was something Monty felt time would cure. The "mischief-making tongues'" at Eisenhower's headquarters were, however, something he could not cure, and when he learned further details of the recent attempts to unsaddle him, he was justifiably annoyed. For the moment, however, he hoped the looming Allied victory would serve to keep the critics at SHAEF silent—for it was vital to ensure Allied coordination if the enemy was to be decisively defeated west of the Seine.

Would the Germans go on fighting to the bitter end in Normandy, however—or would the mobile divisions attempt to flee, like the remnants of the Afrika Korps at Alamein, leaving the infantry to its fate?

As the hours passed it seemed unbelievable that the Germans would risk sacrificing their entire Panzer army group in the Mortain salient: yet as Monty reported to Brooke, there was every indication the Germans were not withdrawing—indeed that they were launching another attack! "The German is either crazy or he doesn't know what's going on," Bradley remarked with incredulity to his ADC on 10 August. "I think he is too smart to do what he is doing. He can't know what's going on in our sector. Surely the professional soldier must know the jig is up."

That day Ultra decrypted von Kluge's suicidal order for a *renewed* German offensive at Mortain—and, given the fanatical way in which many of the German units were fighting, neither Monty nor Bradley really expected the Germans to surrender. On 11 August, Monty therefore issued another directive, M518, in which he congratulated

Bradley's army group for the way it had blunted the German armored bid for Avranches, and considered what would now happen. It was clear that the enemy, in danger of being surrounded, would not surrender, and would attempt to flee. But where to?

An Alleged Disagreement

"The bulk of the enemy forces are west of the general line LE MANS–CAEN," Monty's M518 began. "All their supplies, petrol, etc. must come from the east. But the gap through which this must all come is narrowing; in the north we are approaching FALAISE and in the south we are approaching ALENCON.

"Obviously, if we can close the gap completely we shall have put the enemy in the most awkward predicament."

In Monty's new directive the Canadians were instructed to pivot on Falaise, and close the German escape route by pushing a phalanx of armor down to Argentan; meanwhile Bradley would swing forces up from Le Mans to Alençon and then to a line between Carrouges and Sées, about twenty kilometers south of Argentan, thus depriving the Germans of any roads out of the pocket. In a final rider Monty warned, however, "we must be ready to put into execution the full plan given in M517 [for full envelopment, including an airborne landing at Chartres] should it appear likely that the enemy may escape us here." In his evening telegram to Brooke he added: "I have instructed BRADLEY to collect a fresh Army Corps of three divisions in the LE MANS area and to hold it ready to push quickly through towards CHARTRES if and when we suddenly put M517 into operation."

To capture Falaise, Monty predicted, would take forty-eight hours— but the speed of Patton's maneuver now surprised Monty as much as it did the Germans. At 10 P.M. on 11 August, Patton had not even reached Alençon. By the same time the following evening, when Monty drafted his signal to Brooke, American forces were claiming (falsely) to be in Argentan itself, with reconnaissance elements in the Carrouges–Sées area. "It was this situation," Hansen noted in his diary, "that this evening caused Gen. Patton in a moment of lightheartedness to call Brad and ask, 'We now have elements in Argentain [sic]—shall we continue and drive the British into the sea for another Dunkirk?' "

In truth, Monty preferred to see Patton race towards Paris and the Seine rather than become entangled in the sort of "sticky" fighting the cavalryman had always avoided. Bradley was against this, however. "There is some discussion now concerning an alleged disagreement in strategy between Brad and Monty concerning the timing of this north-ward movement [of Patton's Third Army]," Major Hansen recorded that day, 12 August 1944. "I am told that Monty is anxious that the continued movement toward Paris [be maintained] in seizure of more terrain while Brad is equally insistent that we turn north now at Le Mans and trap the German army containing the hinge of the 1st Army. . . ."

Bradley, by nature more cautious than Monty, vividly remembered Patton's performance in Sicily when he removed his main armored units from the battle in the west and raced east to Palermo, in the wrong direction. Thus Bradley now insisted on keeping Patton back for the short envelopment at Falaise, though even here he wanted no he-roics, he made clear: "We can't risk a loose hinge. . . . German hit us with three divisions there and it'll make us look very foolish. It would be embarrassing to George. George is used to attacks from a single di-vision. He's buttoned up well enough for that. But he's not used to having three or four German divisions hit him. He doesn't know what it means yet."

With Patton's 15 U.S. Corps claiming to be already in Argentan on the evening of 12 August, however, it was essential to coordinate the Allied army and air effort across the Falaise gap. Monty thus asked Bradley to fly to his headquarters for lunch the next day. "Our great object will be to see that whatever part of the enemy forces escapes us here does not get back over the SEINE without being so mangled that it is incapable of further action for many days to come," Monty assured Brooke. "The whole weight of the AEAF [Allied Expeditionary Air Force] is being used tonight, tomorrow and every day and every night in the task of destroying the enemy forces."

However, the destruction or enforced surrender of an entire German army group within a matter of days, Monty was well aware, would be no easy matter.

Heartbreaking Losses

Field Marshal von Paulus' Sixth German Army had been completely surrounded at Stalingrad on 23 November 1942. It had taken a further month before the Russians mounted their final artillery and armored attack, on Christmas Day—and only on 30 January 1943, some five further weeks later, had von Paulus surrendered the 94,000 surviving troops.

The truth was, however much Monty might exhort Crerar to take Falaise and seal off the German salient, it was a tremendous task. Not even the passionate valor of the Poles had enabled the Canadian "Totalize" operation—using cut-down Priest tanks to transport infantry—to reach its objective at Falaise on the evening of 7 July, for once again, after a spectacular initial Canadian breakout, American bombers of Spaatz's Eighth U.S. Air Force had run amuck, bombing their own Allied troops and causing more casualties than on the first day of Cobra. Patton's alleged jest about driving the Canadians back into the sea thus seemed in poor taste, considering the heartbreaking losses suffered by Canadians and Poles in the fierce and bloody battle to "plug" the Falaise gap. Using Panzers, Tigers and 88mm guns, the 12th SS "Hitlerjugend" Panzer Division wrought havoc with Poles and Canadians alike—one armored regiment of the Canadians being so annihilated that for years afterwards the "riddled hulls of the regiment's tanks" could be seen like an involuntary memorial in the fields near Estrées village, eight miles from Falaise.

Both Crerar and Simmonds became convinced that only a second, full-scale assault on the lines of Totalize could propel the Canadian First Army through the powerful German SS forces screening Falaise—and Monty accepted their judgment. Thus when, shortly after noon on 13 August 1944, Monty met Dempsey and Bradley at his headquarters, it was to ensure that the proposed encirclement was properly conducted, and that Patton be prepared for a sort of fighting he had so far merely bypassed.

A Solid Shoulder,
Not a Broken Neck

T he plan agreed upon between Monty, Bradley and Dempsey was that First Canadian Army should deliver a concentrated attack, supported by heavy bombers, within twenty-four hours: a feat which Crerar considered wholly possible. To help Crerar, Dempsey would, under cover of the Canadian assault, seize Falaise itself with British forces and thus allow the Canadians to keep up their momentum towards Trun and Argentan. Hodges was to match this from the southern flank by pushing Collins' 7 U.S. Corps eastwards towards Argentan, and permitting Patton to bring up another corps to act as "long-stop," east of the German salient's neck, at L'Aigle. As Dempsey recorded in his diary:

> 1215—Flew to 21 Army Group and there met C-in-C and General Bradley. We discussed future operations—particularly as regards Army Group and Army boundaries; and the bringing up by Third Army of another Corps directed on LAIGLE.
> *So long as the Northward move of Third Army meets little opposition, the two leading Corps will disregard inter-Army boundaries.* The whole aim is to establish forces across the enemy's lines of communication so as to impede—if not prevent entirely—his withdrawal.

Such was Dempsey's understanding—yet by that same evening Bradley's ADC was noting that the "British [sic] were still short of their objective, apparently unable to drive farther though I know not why. . . . It is suggested in G-3 [Operations staff] that we were ordered to hold at Argentan rather than to continue the drive to Falaise since our capture of that objective would infringe on the prestige of forces driving south and prevent them from securing prestige value in closing the trap."

It was clear that, at this triumphant moment in the battle of Normandy, as the Allied pincers closed around the German armies, nationalistic sentiments were coming to the fore, and that history was in danger of being perverted by ADCs.

Whatever rumors such junior officers might circulate, however, there was no misunderstanding between Monty, Bradley, Dempsey and Crerar. National prestige was simply not involved; it was a matter of military efficiency, *and of men's lives*. With a properly supported attack by the Canadians, involving both medium and heavy bombers, and mindful of the fearful inaccuracy of the latter, it was Bradley himself who was unwilling to allow further Third Army units to take unnecessary casualties in pushing north from Argentan. Therefore when Patton had phoned him shortly before midnight on 12 August to ask it he might continue towards Falaise, Bradley had responded without hesitation: "Nothing doing. You're not to go beyond Argentan. Just stop where you are and build up on that shoulder. Sibert [Bradley's chief of Intelligence] tells me the German is beginning to pull out. You'd better button up and get ready for him."

Patton—whose troops had never actually captured Argentan—later sought to blame Monty for the decision not to push Haislip's virgin 15 U.S. Corps north of Argentan. "I believe that the order," he wrote, "emanated from the 21st Army Group, and was due to jealousy of the Americans or to utter ignorance of the situation or to a combination of the two. It is very regrettable that XV Corps was ordered to halt, because it could have gone on to Falaise and made contact with the Canadians northwest of that point and definitely and positively closed the escape gap."

This judgment was jotted down days later, however. On the evidence available to him at the time—air reconnaissance, Ultra, Phantom (monitoring of own Allied radio signals) and operational reports—Bradley had had no hesitation in stopping Haislip's corps from overextending itself: "I much preferred a solid shoulder at Argentan," he afterwards mused, "to the possibility of a broken [American] neck at Falaise."

In fact, Patton's new order to halt Haislip only reached the 15 U.S. Corps Commander at 11 A.M. on 13 August; he had *still* not actually captured Argentan and, with a *thirty-kilometer gap* between himself and First U.S. Army on his left, cohesion was at this moment vital. To suggest that Monty was to blame, and for reasons of national prestige, was typical of Patton. Bradley, by contrast, willingly shouldered responsibility for the decision to halt Patton at Argentan. "I did not consult with Montgomery," he afterwards recorded. "The decision to stop Patton was mine alone."

To Brooke, meanwhile, Monty signaled on the night of 13 August: "I am continuing operations on the assumption that the bulk of the enemy forces are still inside the ring as stated by my Intelligence staff.

"But in order to head off any who get through the gap 20 U.S. Corps is being directed east of 15 U.S. Corps toward LAIGLE and 12 US Corps is being assembled at LE MANS ready for any action that may be necessary in an easterly or northeasterly direction."

Confident he had the main elements of the German armies in Normandy bottled up, and with further American forces performing a second envelopment further east, to the Seine, Monty went to bed.

It was only on the following day, 14 August 1944, that doubts began to arise over which portion of the German armies was still entrapped in the pocket—and the accusations began.

Eisenhower's Ignorance as to How to Run a War

"I have been watching your battle with enormous interest," Field Marshal Brooke wrote meanwhile on 14 August 1944. "There are wonderful possibilities and I do hope that fortune may favor us, and that you succeed in dealing him [the enemy] a crippling blow S.W. of the Seine.

"You can go on relying on my firm support, my dear old Monty. We have now been working together for a long time, and in some unpleasant places, where we have been able to appreciate each other properly. If I do talk plainly to you at times it is because I know that I can help you by doing so. There are people who don't understand you and I have had some pretty stiff battles on your behalf at times. . . .

"You can go on relying on me to the utmost to watch your rear for you. I have complete confidence in your ability to beat the Bosch. Unfortunately there are a lot of jealous, critical, narrow minded individuals in this world. They can succeed in making the easiest things difficult, & in perverting the truth in a marvellous way. Waging war may well be difficult, but waging war under political control becomes at times almost impossible!!"

To Brooke, when he received this wonderfully supportive letter, Monty replied with relief:

> Things really do seem to be going very well. We have a ring round the enemy forces and the only way out is now between FALAISE and ARGENTAN. What actually is inside the ring one cannot tell. How much has so far got away eastwards, one cannot tell. But I very much doubt if he dare "firm up" again this side of the Seine.
>
> I had a conference yesterday with Bradley, Dempsey, and Crerar, and we have our plans well tied up—for any eventuality. . . .
>
> The present week may well see great happenings.

After so many weeks of trial, Monty was savoring the cup of victory. About the Supreme Commander, who had shown such impatience with his strategy as it unfolded but was now as excited as a child over the prospect of a great victory, Monty was, however, scathing:

> Ike is apt to get very excited and talk wildly—at the top of his voice!!! He is now over here [in Normandy], which is a very great pity. His ignorance as to how to run a war is absolute and complete; he has all the popular cries, but nothing else.

Lest this sound too harsh a judgment on his own Supreme Commander, Monty added the rider: "He is such a decent chap that it is difficult to be angry with him for long. One thing I am firm about; he is never allowed to attend a meeting between me and my Army Commanders and Bradley!" And with this, Monty returned to the battle.

Monty Digs His Professional Grave

W hat Brooke felt when he received this letter, shortly before leaving to visit the Italian front, is not known—but at the thought of Monty shutting Eisenhower out of his command conferences in the field, Brooke must have groaned.

Whether Monty liked it or not—and clearly Monty did *not* like it— Eisenhower was not only his Supreme Commander, but a Supreme Commander determined to take field command of the Allied army groups in France as soon as he had established a working battlefield headquarters. To treat General Eisenhower like a visiting politician, forbidding him even to sit in on meetings with the four Allied fighting army commanders, was therefore not only insulting on Monty's part but horribly, indeed willfully, misguided. In a historical sense it was, in fact, more. By his contemptuous dismissal of Eisenhower's claims to be or to become a battlefield commander, Monty was boxing himself into a corner from which he could never, and never would, escape.

Convinced of his own mastery of the modern European battlefield, Monty had for years scorned incompetent generals such as Lord Gort at Dunkirk or General Auchinleck in the desert. Dwight Eisenhower, however, was not a British general. He was the senior American commander in Europe, responsible for the lives and military fortunes of over a million American troops in France—and with more on their way.

The "insubordinate smile" Monty had once worn when taking premature command of Eighth Army at Alamein was now no good; it was a liability. But with Brooke's attention wholly occupied by Churchill, the Anvil landings near Marseilles on 15 August, the repercussions of Anvil on the fighting in Italy, and the prosecution of the war in the Pacific as well as Southeast Asia, there was no one senior enough to tell Monty so—and thus, unchecked, Monty dug his own professional grave.

Part Eleven

A CROWN OF THORNS

———————————

Eisenhower visits Monty in Normandy during
the battle of the Falaise gap, 19 August 1944.

Palermo All Over Again

B y mid-August 1944 it was clear the German armies in the West were beaten and that, if the Allies capitalized on this great victory, the war against Hitler might soon be over. It was therefore essential, Monty felt, to keep a "grip" on the battle—and not allow overexcitement to masquerade as military judgment.

If the ring around the German armies could not be closed fully between Falaise and Argentan, Monty argued, the Allies must not miss the wider envelopment on the Seine; indeed, it was with this in mind he had ordered Bradley to build up such strength (some three American corps) south of Argentan.

"My dear Brad," Monty dashed off a note to Bradley on 14 August, as the Canadians launched their latest attack, with massive air support, towards Falaise. "It is difficult to say what enemy are inside the ring, and what have got out to the east. A good deal may have escaped. I think your movement of 20 Corps should be N.E. towards DREUX. Also any further stuff you can move round to LE MANS, should go N.E. We want to head off the Germans, and stop them breaking out to the S.E.

"I will get Bimbo [Dempsey] here at 1100 hrs tomorrow and we will all meet and discuss the situation."

That night Monty signaled to Brooke, recording the heavy fighting "against determined resistance" around the pocket, but was pleased Collins had now reached the main road east of Argentan and that the Mayenne "gap" on the southern American flank had now been closed. "In the North, First Canadian Army attacked at 1200 hours today and the last reports were that leading troops had reached ERNES, SASSY and OLENDON and were pushing on towards FALAISE. Considerable chaos was caused to the attack when about twenty per cent of heavy bombers dropped their bombs well inside our lines on attacking divisions. There is no doubt that a good many enemy have managed to escape eastwards out of the ring. I have ordered 12 Army Group to direct 20 U.S. Corps on the axis LA FERTE BARNARD [sic] through NOGENT LE ROTROU on DREUX as it is important to stop the enemy from turning south-east. We want those who have escaped us here to be pushed up against the Seine."

Patton, however, was not interested in the Seine. The truth was, Patton's eyes were already shifting from the German armies fleeing the Falaise pocket to Paris and Metz: the eastern gateway into Germany. By the evening of 15 August, Monty was reporting to Brooke: "The general picture in this part of the front [Third Army] is that PATTON is heading straight for PARIS and is determined to get there and will probably do so."

It was Palermo all over again. As Monty later ruefully remarked to Churchill's military assistant, General Sir Ian Jacob, Patton was a tremendous thruster, without equal in the Allied camp, but he was not a team player. "Patton," Monty shook his head, "could ruin your battle in an afternoon."

Intense Military Confusion

As Patton raced eastwards, he left "a scene of intense military confusion" in the pocket. "We discussed future operations—in particular as regards closing the gap between FALAISE and ARGENTAN, neither of which we hold yet," Dempsey noted in his diary on 15 August. Yet with only an unblooded infantry division and one French armored division left in the Argentan area once Patton had moved towards Paris, Bradley could no longer offer to close the Falaise gap from the south. Thus the task was handed over entirely to Crerar and Dempsey in the north, Falaise being given to Crerar, Argentan to Dempsey. "The general picture in this area," Monty described the situation to Brooke, "is of a full scale withdrawal by the enemy to get eastwards out of the pocket."

Almost 150,000 prisoners had already been taken in Normandy, and perhaps 100,000 Germans—more than von Paulus' remnants at Stalingrad—were believe to be still in the pocket. The bag *must* therefore if humanly possible be sealed, and the neck tied, whether at Falaise or on the Seine. To round up those who had already escaped from the pocket, Bradley must push at least some of Patton's formations north, instead of eastwards to Paris.

After giving the matter further thought, Bradley telephoned Patton on the evening of 16 August and asked him to form a new corps out of the troops left near Argentan, and to drive it northeastwards towards Trun, where he would meet Poles and Canadians advancing from the direction of Falaise. With the British 30 Corps aimed on Argentan, and 5 U.S. Corps thrusting north to Trun, the jaws of the Allied trap would fold behind each other and shut. The matter of larger envelopment Bradley left open, however, not wishing to clip Patton's seemingly golden wings.

From Monty's point of view, this was unfortunate. Patton's headlong race towards Paris now prejudiced even the agreement he had made with Bradley to close the Falaise gap at Trun, since Patton's French field commanders had no wish to take the sort of heavy casualties being suffered by Canadians, Poles and British troops in closing the Falaise pocket, while American and French cavalry forces raced towards Paris virtually without opposition. General Leclerc, commander of the 2nd French Armored Division near Argentan, for instance, seeing Patton move on towards the French capital, simply refused to carry out the Trun attack. Bradley later confided, "While Leclerc was still engaged in the Falaise pocket, to avoid being scooped on the liberation of Paris he secretly despatched his reconnaissance battalion in the direction of that city. Gerow, the Corps Commander, learned of Leclerc's action and immediately ordered Leclerc's troops to 'get the hell back where they belonged.' "

Apart from German infantry, Monty was sure on 16 August "that six Panzer and SS divisions are still inside the pocket and elements of five of these divisions are trying to break out eastwards between ARGENTAN and SEES," but, as at Mortain, Bradley's imperturbable reaction gave him confidence that the Germans would not succeed: "I think the Americans are strong enough in the ARGENTAN area to hold this attack." Between them, Monty was sure that Crerar, Dempsey and Hodges would finish off the pocket. What he was more worried about was where Patton was heading.

It was time now, Monty felt, to ensure Patton did not prejudice the outcome of the great Allied victory in Normandy by an unplanned, unauthorized, and unrehearsed breakaway to the east. It was time, indeed, to consider the next step in the Allied campaign, *beyond* the Seine—and with this in mind he flew, on 17 August, to see Bradley at his headquarters.

A Solid Mass of Forty Divisions

I t was on this same day, 17 August, that Hitler relieved von Kluge of his command, replacing him by General Hausser in the Falaise pocket and by Field Marshal Model outside. But though Model was given orders to form a new defensive line forward of the Seine-Yonne, not only the battle of Normandy but the battle for France was now lost.

Von Kluge died two days later, ostensibly of a heart attack, but actually from potassium cyanide, his pride as a field marshal shattered along with that of his defeated armies. For with the closing of the Falaise gap by the Canadians and Poles the carnage within became a veritable holocaust. The smell of death—it is estimated that 10,000 Germans lost their lives in the pocket—would haunt witnesses for years afterwards. "I should doubt if ever before in the history of this war air forces have had such opportunities or taken such advantage of them," Monty signaled to Brooke. "The whole area is covered with burning tanks and MT [motor transport]. One column of 3,000 plus was caught head to tail and almost totally destroyed. I would say that any German formations or units that escape eastwards over the SEINE will be quite unfit to fight for months to come."

The burning question in Monty's mind, however, was the direction in which the Allied armies should now thrust. After speaking to Bradley on 17 August, Monty sent Brooke a signal that would, in the controversy afterwards, become historic:

M99. TOPSEC. Personal for CIGS from General Montgomery.
Have been thinking ahead about future plans but have NOT yet discussed subject with IKE. My views as follows:

After crossing SEINE 12 and 21 Army Groups should keep together as a solid mass of some 40 divisions which would be so strong that it need fear nothing. The force should move northwards.

21 Army Group should be on the western flank and should clear the Channel coast and PAS DE CALAIS and WEST FLANDERS and secure ANTWERP.

The American armies should move with right flank on the ARDENNES directed on BRUSSELS, AACHEN and COLOGNE. The movement of the American armies would cut the communications of enemy forces on the Channel coast [from Germany] and thus facilitate the task of the British Army Group.

The initial objects of the movement would be to destroy the German forces on the coast and to establish a powerful air force in BELGIUM. A further object would be to get the enemy out of V1 or V2 range of England.

BRADLEY agrees entirely with above conception. Would be glad to know if you agree generally. When I have got your reply will discuss matter with IKE.

It was too late, however. Enciphered at 8:30 on the morning of 18 August, it arrived at the War Office in London just as Field Marshal Brooke was preparing to leave for Italy and the Mediterranean. The Assistant CIGS, General Kennedy, was already a sick man, and the Director of Military Operations, General Simpson, had departed on a fortnight's leave. Churchill was in Italy (having insisted upon watching the Anvil invasion of southern France, renamed "Dragoon," on 15 August from a battleship), and there was thus nobody of sufficient authority to address the matter. It was simply left up to the Supreme Commander.

Preventing the Enemy's Escape

For months the Supreme Commander had swung between high hopes and fears of stalemate, but now that Allied victory seemed assured, it was found he had made no plan of campaign beyond Normandy.

Monty had, in his meeting with Bradley on 17 August, supposed that Bradley was in favor of a cohesive Allied drive to the north. Major Hansen's diary entry the following day, when General Eisenhower came to discuss future strategy, belied this, however:

> Ike arrived with Jim Gaunt [sic] and Kay Summersby this morning for a conference with Brad on the strategy from this point onwards. *Believe he favors the Brad plan of driving eastward to Germany rather than diverting too much strength up over the northern route to the Lowlands and into Germany from that direction.* . . .
>   Ike feeling lighthearted and gay and he is taking active part in determining the strategy—allocating missions to Bradley and Monty. . . .

If Bradley had such an eastward "plan," Monty was as yet unaware of it. The next morning at 10:00, 19 August, Bradley flew to Monty's headquarters "for conference on plan after the Seine," attended by Dempsey and Hodges. It was only now that Monty learned that, according to Bradley, "Ike wants to split the force and send half of it eastward to Nancy." Patton was evidently burning to drive east, and Bradley sympathized, seemingly tantalized by the absence of opposition in front of Third Army. Hearing this, Monty decided not to press the point, but to take it up directly with Eisenhower. In the meantime, whatever the plan of battle beyond the Seine, it was vital to cut off any Germans escaping from the Falaise pocket. Bradley suggested Dempsey bring round two divisions through the American sector to execute this, the long envelopment; Dempsey, however, felt it would waste time, be difficult administratively, and lack punch—for at the heart of Money's northern-thrust concept was a distressing manpower problem in 21st Army Group. The British army was now wasting so fast that whole divisions, both in Normandy and in England, were having to be broken up and their units transferred as reinforcements to other formations. As a result, Bradley loyally agreed to furnish two American corps, one of them under Hodges' First Army command, which would drive immediately northwards towards the mouth of the Seine and cut off all Germans fleeing towards the river.

General Hodges was apparently quite satisfied with this, as his ADC at First U.S. Army Headquarters recorded:

> The conference with General Montgomery was successful in every way. General Hodges' map, with plan, was approved without change. First Army, with its XIX Corps, is to strike north, bypassing Dreux, to Gouches, Evreux, and then on further north to Elbeuf and Le Neubourg. . . . The attack is to capture Elbeuf and prevent escape of the enemy across the Seine.

Patton, however, was mortified.

Violating the German Border

"Bradley has just returned from a visit to Monty and Ike," Patton recorded in his own diary. "He now has a new plan. He thinks there are still Germans east of Argentan and in order to check up on this pocket, he wants me to move the 5th Armoured Division of the XV Corps north along the west bank of the Seine to Louviers, while the XIX Corps of the First [U.S.] Army comes up on its left."

Patton, aware there was no opposition to the east, had no wish to be involved in the methodical destruction of the remnant German forces from Falaise—and, increasingly, Bradley agreed with him. As Major Hansen noted in his diary, Bradley was now "desirous of pursuing a direct route to Metz and the German border. Monty in deference to the political angle involved in the effort is, of course, desirous of taking the rocket coast and relieving London of the terrific burden there. Bradley agrees that reduction of the coast will deprive Germany of one of his primary secondary [sic] weapons now bolstering the German people in the belief of retaliation.

"Ike likewise favours Bradley's desire to drive eastward and violate the German border as quickly as possible. There is evidence that little remains to stop us on the far side of the Seine."

Monty and Bradley both turned to Eisenhower. It was up to the Supreme Commander to decide.

Eisenhower Is Torn

As Eisenhower belatedly grappled with competing scenarios of German defeat, Monty prepared, as one of his final directives as Commander-in-Chief of the Allied land armies in France, a document setting out the situation—sending a copy with a covering letter to the War Office the following day:

> I must impress on all commanders the need for speed in getting on with the business.
> The Allied victory in N.W. Europe will have immense repercussions, it will lead to the end of the German military domination of France; it is the beginning of the end of the war.

In its way, the directive was reminiscent of Haig's great message to his commanders in the autumn of 1918: "risks which a month ago would have been criminal to incur, ought now to be incurred as a duty." For two and a half months, until Bradley's breakout could be effected, the task of 21st Army Group had been to hold the main enemy forces in combat on the eastern sector. With the current destruction of the remaining enemy forces in the Falaise pocket, however, it was vital neither fatigue nor complacency set in:

> If these great events are to be brought about, we must hurl ourselves on the enemy while he is still reeling from the blow; we must deal him more blows and ever more blows; he must be allowed no time to recover.
>
> This is no time to relax, or to sit and congratulate ourselves. I call on all commanders for a great effort. Let us finish off the business in record time.

But how best to finish off the business? And how do so "in record time" if the Supreme Commander could not make up his mind?

Attempting to put the best gloss upon the situation, Monty contented himself with orders concerning the "destruction or capture" of the enemy still "inside the Normandy 'bottle' " as well as the wider envelopment on the Seine by the two appointed American corps under Bradley. But regarding the strategy thereafter, he could say nothing until Eisenhower made a decision:

> *General Policy for Forward Movement*
> As the situation develops, the Supreme Allied Commander will be issuing orders regarding the general movement of the land armies. Meanwhile, we must be so disposed that we can very quickly develop operations in any way he [Eisenhower] requires, and to meet any situations that may suddenly arise.
>
> As a first step we have got to cross the SEINE, and to get so disposed beyond it—tactically and administratively—that we can carry out quickly the orders of the Supreme Allied Commander.

The British Second Army was to be prepared to drive northeast across the Seine, via Beauvais into Belgium, with Antwerp as its target and boundary. Whether 12th Army Group would accompany it, seizing Brussels and then swinging eastwards into Germany at Aachen, was still a matter for the Supreme Commander to decide. For the moment the American armies would "advance on the general area ORLEANS–TROYES–CHALONS–REIMS–LAON–AMIENS." In this way "it will be so disposed in this general area that it retains the ability to operate north-eastwards towards BRUSSELS and AACHEN, while simultaneously a portion of the Army Group operates eastwards towards the SAAR."

The split in Allied strategy that had started to show as Patton raced for Paris, however, was now becoming a tear—worrying Monty. He still hoped Eisenhower would see reason, but without guidance from Churchill or the War Office, Monty was now in the most difficult of positions. Hour by hour came ever more horrifying reports of the carnage in the Falaise pocket. Even on 20 August his Intelligence staff estimated "that the best part of sixteen German divisions are still west of a north and south line through ORBEC," and by 21 August it was estimated that 160,000 German prisoners had been taken in the eleven weeks of battle since D-Day, with many more expected. Not even Stalingrad could match the strategic scale of the German defeat in Normandy, and some of the scenes within the Falaise pocket exceeded in death and destruction the worst memories of the Western Front in World War I. Monty wrote on 21 August to General Sir Oliver Leese, commanding Eighth Army in Italy:

> The campaign in Normandy has been of very great interest. The real gist of the matter is that the German armies in N.W. Europe have had a most terrific hammering, and they have ceased to exist as effective fighting formations. We could capture Paris any time we like; I am holding back from that commitment just at the moment, as the very large population of that city is short of food and fuel.
>
> At the time of writing this we have some four to five SS divisions locked up in the "pocket"; they cannot possibly escape; we are right round the southern flank and I have two corps moving north from the line MANTES–DREUX–VERNEUIL, with their right on the Seine. . . .
>
> My next move is to cross the Seine; clear the Pas de Calais and West Flanders and secure Antwerp; establish a powerful air force in Belgium; and invade the Ruhr—via Aachen and Cologne.
>
> I do not see what there is to oppose us; and provided I can persuade the Americans to put everything into this movement, then it would end the war—and quickly.
>
> But many political cross-currents are now likely to arise; and if these are to be allowed to influence what we do, then the quick end of the German war may be endangered.

In the event, it was to prove an accurate prediction.

Eisenhower Makes Up His Mind

Though Bradley had loyally accepted the need for 15 and 19 U.S. Corps to swing north and envelop the German forces withdrawing towards the Seine, he was, his ADC noted, reluctant to do so, since "he is more particularly desirous of driving eastward to Germany and taking a force into that country for the tremendous psychological effect it would have on the people."

On the evening of 21 August, Bradley addressed a meeting of war correspondents at his headquarters in which he again spoke of "the psychological effect of the capture of Paris" and the "psychological effect of a violation on the German border" as two of the five main considerations in "planning for future operations"—considerations so important that, he told the correspondents, the British would now drive north to take out the V-bomb sites *while we go into Germany.*"

Eisenhower's indecision was now becoming acute, with Monty insisting the Allies stay together and breach the German border *north* of the Ardennes, Bradley arguing that Eisenhower should separate the army groups and permit the Americans to strike eastwards, *south* of the Ardennes, with both First and Third U.S. Armies.

Finally, on 21 July 1944, after several days of argument at his advanced headquarters in Normandy, Eisenhower made up his mind. As Monty later recounted to General Nye, Brooke's deputy at the War Office, Eisenhower decided: "a) to change the system of command on 1st Sept; b) Eisenhower to take personal command of the two Army Groups himself; c) 12 Army Group to be employed towards METZ and the SAAR. . . . A cable was then drafted to be sent to the Combined Chiefs of Staff, and a Directive to be sent to me.

"My chief of staff suggested that it might be as well to consult me in the matter before any action was taken," Monty chronicled. "This was agreed, and my Chief of Staff brought the draft telegram up to my Tac HQ that night [21 August].

"I did not agree with the decisions that had been reached. I sent my Chief of Staff back to see Eisenhower on the morning of 22 August, and I gave him some 'Notes on Future Operations' to take with him; he was to inform Eisenhower that these notes represented my views and that Bradley had expressed to me his agreement with them."

But if Bradley *had* expressed agreement on 17 August, he no longer did—and, in his heart if not his head, Monty knew it. Moreover, as Monty's "Notes" made abundantly clear, Monty's objection was not simply to Eisenhower's splitting of the Allied army groups into two separate thrusts, in different directions. Monty not only wanted the Allies to stay together in a phalanx of forty Allied divisions, he now made clear, but he wanted Eisenhower to abdicate his right to command them.

A Lost Cause

"The quickest way to win this war," Monty's "Notes" declared, "is for the great mass of the Allied armies to advance northwards, clear the coast as far as Antwerp, establish a powerful air force in Belgium, and advance into the Ruhr." As in the invasion of Normandy, the enemy would have to guard against numerous possible Allied thrusts, from different directions; they could not bring all their defenses to bear against one thrust, if it was prosecuted in overwhelming force at one decisive spot.

"The force must operate as one whole, with great cohesion and so strong that it can do the job quickly," Monty laid down. "Single control and direction of the land operations is vital for success. This is a whole time job for one man. The great victory in N.W. France has been won by personal command. Only in this way will future victories be won. . . . To change the system of command now, after having won a great victory, would be to prolong the war."

The force of this argument was as powerful logically as it was politically naïve. On D-Day, 6 June 1944, British troops landing in Normandy had slightly outnumbered American. Now, two and a half months later, American troops in France were almost twice as numerous as British, and with each fresh division arriving from the United States, this numerical superiority grew larger. In such circumstances, it was impossible *not* to change the system of command. "I knew I was arguing a lost cause," de Guingand later confessed. "I remember a long conversation [with Eisenhower] we had in an apple orchard. And at the end of it he said, 'Would you like to see me present a medal to the American Naval Commander?' . . . I couldn't get him to budge."

Monty was distraught. "My Chief of Staff spent two hours on 22nd August trying to persuade Eisenhower on certain basic points of principle," Monty related to Nye. The result had been, from Monty's point of view, procrastination. Eisenhower insisted that he must take field command of the armies as soon as he could establish a proper field headquarters on the Continent, which he thought could be achieved by 1 September; he agreed that Monty must clear the Pas de Calais and make for Antwerp; but about the direction in which he would send Bradley's forces he now wobbled: "The Army Group of the Center [First and Third U.S. Armies] will advance, under General Bradley, to the east and northeast of Paris, from which area it can either strike northeastward, thus assisting in the fall of the Calais area and later advance through the Low Countries, or, if the enemy strength in that region is not greater than I now believe, it can alternatively strike directly eastward . . . passing south of the Ardennes."

This decision—or indecision—was embodied in a signal sent to the Combined Chiefs of Staff at 4:55 P.M. on 22 August, and in a covering letter to the copy he sent Monty, Eisenhower indicated he did not want the British to plan on using any significant American ground forces in their northern thrust: "You may or may not see a need for any U.S. ground units, after the crossings of the Seine have once been secured. . . . Initial estimates of such additional forces should be kept to a minimum, not only because of increased difficulties in maintenance if U.S. lines of communications are stretched too far, but because of the desirability of thrusting quickly eastward and severing almost all of the hostile communications in the major portion of France."

The British and Canadians, in other words, would go north, along the coast; the Americans, in all likelihood, east.

The Military Lincoln

B rooke's deputy, General Nye, was actually present at Montgomery's headquarters when de Guingand relayed the news that the Allied armies would now be split.

Recognizing that one of the crucial decisions of the Allied alliance was being made, and sensing the danger not only of a partition of military forces but of a possible split in the alliance, Nye begged Monty, on Brooke's behalf, not to precipitate an Allied command crisis while both Churchill and Brooke were absent from England. "Montgomery told me," Nye reported to Brooke, "his attitude would be that he would make it abundantly clear that he strongly disagreed with any plan which split the Allied forces and would give his reasons in full" to Eisenhower, whom Monty had now arranged to meet the following day, 23 August. "He would say that if, after having heard these views, Eisenhower still decided to adhere to his plan, he would loyally accept it and carry out whatever orders were issued to him." The alliance, Nye pointed out to Monty, must come first.

Back in England that evening, Nye discussed the subject with the Secretary of State for War, P. J. Grigg, and General Ismay, Churchill's military assistant and Secretary of the Defence Committee, "and we feel it preferable not to send a telegram to Prime Minister," Nye cabled the CIGS in Italy, "but to leave it to your judgement to give information to him whenever you think best."

Undoubtedly Nye, Grigg and Ismay feared that Churchill would make the same protest as he had done over Anvil: a protest which would merely encourage Washington, ironically, to see in the British attitude special pleading of a political nature (since it came from Churchill) while they, the American Chiefs of Staff, were willing to support the tactical military views of the Supreme Commander in the field.

Meanwhile Monty was due to meet Eisenhower at midday on 23 August. Anxious to enlist Bradley's support for the northern thrust, Monty secretly flew first to Bradley's headquarters, as he informed Nye:

> Early on 23 August I flew to LAVAL to see Bradley; I wanted to check up with him again before I saw Eisenhower. I found, to my amazement, that Bradley had changed his views completely; on 17 Aug. he had agreed with me; on 23 August he was a whole-hearted advocate of the total American effort going eastward towards the SAAR.

Monty refused to believe Bradley was telling the truth. "He had obviously been 'got-at' in the interim period. I know Bradley well; my own opinion is that he is not voicing his own views when he advocates the SAAR venture."

But Monty was mistaken. With each passing day following the closing of the Falaise pocket, Bradley had become less and less willing to operate under British field command. The truth was, with Allied victory in Normandy the American army had finally come of age, effacing its failures at Kasserine, Salerno and Anzio. As the British had learned, finally, from their disasters at Dunkirk and in Scandinavia, the Mediterranean and North Africa, so the Americans had become steadily more professional. They had carried out their part in Monty's masterplan in Normandy with tenacity, courage and growing confidence, and in the headlong rush towards Paris it was easy to forget what sacrifices the British had made to keep the real weight of the enemy on the eastern sector. By giving the role of breakout to the American armies in the less-well-defended western sector, Monty had capitalized on American mobility and bravura. Relying on speed and daring, Patton had simply moved faster than the Germans could react, tied down as they were by the fierce fighting on Hodges', Dempsey's and Crerar's fronts; and, if Bradley had wished, he could then have swung Patton right up to the English Channel, along the banks of the Seine, to cut off the survivors of Falaise, and have put Patton on a course towards the Ruhr.

But Bradley *did not wish it so.* He had nothing against Monty's thrust to Antwerp, as his ADC noted after the war: "Bradley always recognized the need for the Allies to drive north. 'There was never any question in anyone's mind but that you had to do that thing to the north.' " But Bradley felt this was a task Monty could tackle on his own with 21st Army Group, with only one American corps to help. " 'I wanted to go due east with all American troops except one corps. I wanted to give Monty one corps to drive to the north. Then take First and Third Armies due east.' "

For Monty, this was to repeat the very same mistake the Allies had been making since Torch: the splitting of Allied offensives into separate undertakings which the Germans, with their shorter lines of communication and rapid redeployment of troops, could defeat or at least contain in detail. It was the story not only of North Africa but of Italy, all over again: of dispersion rather than concentration of Allied effort.

What saddened Monty most was that Bradley, whom he had so patiently "brought on" as an army and then army group commander, should now be lured by the same fantasies as Eisenhower and Patton at their most wishful—especially the belief that, if an area was relatively undefended by the enemy, it was good strategy to rush in, like fools, and seize it; the desire to "bull ahead" while the going was good—but never to face up to the fact that the Germans were masters of defense, and could only be defeated in battle by the inexorable application of concentrated effort at the decisive point.

Bradley, however, was in no mood to listen to Monty's schoolmasterly insistence on cohesive command and "keeping together as one solid mass." Two days before, on 21 August, at the press conference which had been "attended by entire corps of 1st Army correspondents, including Red Knickerbocker, Charles Wertenbach, Don Whitehead, Jack Thompson, Bob Cabba, Clark Lee, Al Dinny, Bert Bryant," Knickerbocker had, Major Hansen noted proudly, "suggested 'Bradley for President Club' and Lee called Bradley *the military Lincoln*. All fantastically pleased with the conference which resulted in several offhand jibes at the BBC to which the BBC representative objected but the innuendo nevertheless struck. The General was buoyant after last night and he conducted himself magnificently."

The following day, 22 August, Bradley had been "off early" to see Eisenhower, "campaigning now on the drive to Germany which everyone now thinks may go quickly with the Bosche falling apart in front of us and still fleeing with small rearguard movements which hamper our progress but do not delay it sufficiently for them. . . . Everyone is confident he will take care of our interests and even Col Conrad says, 'Brad'll look out for us.' Interests himself particularly in the American picture and he is certainly our spokesman here. . . . This may be the turning point and if we do not quickly follow up our advantage to slam through into Germany and end the war on his ground, we may be forced into a longer fight in the lowlands where the terrain is better suited for defense and where he [the enemy] will have time to make a stand and prepare a line. If he does not defend here, he has no intention of defending anywhere."

Like it or not, Bradley was all for the thrust east, south of Ardennes.

The Guts of the Whole Matter

Even to Monty it was clear that times had changed when the two army group commanders met at "Tac Eagle," Bradley's headquarters at Laval, on the morning of 23 August 1944. Buoyed by the absence of opposition on their eastern flank, the American commanders and press correspondents were sold on the idea of eastward penetration into Germany, and did not wish to get bogged down in the "lowlands" of Belgium and Holland.

Should Monty have bowed to the inevitable? Recognizing the desire of most Americans to go for broke and shoot for an Allied invasion of Germany via the Saar and Frankfurt, should he not have simply held his tongue and agreed?

But Monty would not have been Monty if he had been willing to agree to a strategy which, in his view, would not shorten the war but prolong it. The Allies had never in truth broken into Germany in World War I, despite their successes in the summer of 1918. As Hindenburg had in 1918, Hitler still disposed of very considerable military forces in Germany: but his war machine was predicated on the industrial output of the Ruhr. Without that, he would be unable to continue the war. It followed in Monty's view—and this was certainly the view which SHAEF's planning staff had taken hitherto—that, at a moment when the German armies in the field were in disarray, the Allies should advance upon the Ruhr as one mighty fist, and finish the war promptly.

From Bradley's tactical headquarters, Monty, disappointed, returned by air to his own, there to face Eisenhower. When he reached his own headquarters at noon, however, he found Eisenhower already arriving with a retinue of advisers, including his chief of staff, Bedell Smith, and General Gale, chief of administration.

"This was the first time I had seen Bedel [sic] Smith since I left

Portsmouth for Normandy on D day, 6th June," Monty related to Nye, pointedly. "I told Eisenhower that I must see him alone, and get his decision on certain big points of principle; we must do that ourselves, and the staff must not be present. He agreed, and we talked alone for one hour.

"I put to him my views as outlined in M99"—the plan for the Allies to move north in a "solid mass of some 40 divisions which should be so strong that it need fear nothing," the British moving along the coast to Antwerp, the Americans to Brussels, Aachen and Cologne.

But this was not all. Ignoring Nye's injunction, Monty now told Eisenhower he thought it a mistake for him to take command of the Allied armies in the field: "I also said that he, as Supreme Comd., could not descend into the land battle and become a ground C-in-C; the Supreme Comd. has to sit on a very lofty perch and be able to take a detached view of the whole intricate problem—which involves land, sea, air, civil control, political problems, etc., etc., etc. Someone must run the land battle for him; we had won a great victory in Normandy because of unified land control and NOT in spite of it. I said this point was so important that, if public opinion in America was involved, he should let Bradley control the battle and put me under Bradley—this suggestion produced an immediate denial of his intention to do anything of the sort!!!"

Would Monty have served under Bradley? The notion was not unthinkable. Patton, erstwhile superior of Bradley in Sicily, was now serving beneath Bradley—with distinction. But the reality of the problem was that Eisenhower did not, in truth, favor a single thrust to the Ruhr; nor did he see Monty's point about unified command in the field anymore. The German field armies seemed in total confusion; it was time for the Supreme Commander to become generalissimo in the field, *with the flexibility to reinforce whichever thrust might prove the more prosperous.*

But *could* Eisenhower carry out two thrusts simultaneously, waiting to see which one worked best? In his military heart, Monty was convinced neither one would be strong enough—particularly the thrust north to Antwerp. "After some talk, Eisenhower agreed that 21 Army Group was not strong enough to carry out the tasks on the northern thrust, alone and unaided," Monty recorded. It followed then that Eisenhower's letter of 22 August, in which he asked Monty to keep "estimates of such additional forces . . . to the minimum," was unrealistic. "He agreed that whatever American assistance was necessary must be provided."

If this was so, who was to command the thrust?

"He agreed that the task of coordination and general operational direction on the northern thrust must be exercised by one commander; he said he would give that task to me," Monty informed General Nye.

But could he? 21st Army Group would only provide fourteen divisions for the Army Group of the North. The Allied Airborne Army was available, but its three Normandy divisions were refitting. How many extra American divisions would therefore be needed, Eisenhower asked, to help carry out the essential tasks in the north—seizing the Pas de Calais area with its ports, capturing Antwerp, establishing the Allied Air Force in Belgium, and providing sufficient forces to mount, eventually, a thrust towards the Ruhr?

"I said I wanted an American army of at least twelve divisions to advance on the right flank of 21 Army Group," Monty answered without blinking an eyelid.

Eisenhower was stunned.

"He said that if this were done then 12 Army Group would have only one Army in it, and public opinion in the States would object," Monty noted.

It was not an argument that recommended itself to a soldier as professional and logical as Monty. "I asked him why public opinion should make him want to take military decisions which are definitely unsound," Monty went on. "He said that I must understand that it was election year in America; he could take no action which was calculated to sway public opinion against the President and possibly lose him the election.

"That because of this he must now separate the two Army Groups, take command himself of the ground forces, and send the two Army Groups in such different directions that there could be no question of the American Army Group being under the operational control of a British General.

"This is really the guts of the whole matter," Monty ended, dejected.

National Army Groups

B radley, at least, had given Monty a strategic preference. Eisenhower's reasoning, involving the reelection of President Roosevelt, Monty considered an affront to military logic.

The trouble was, in his narrow-minded military mind, Monty could not see it was too late to stand on principle. Positions had already been taken, while Monty fought the finale to the battle of Normandy, from which it was increasingly difficult to withdraw. A veritable and potential tragedy was unfolding. Only by making Eisenhower's task *easier*, not more difficult, could Monty have hoped to convert Eisenhower to the concept of a massive northern thrust. Instead, he had once again insulted the Supreme Commander by suggesting he was incompetent or unfitted to direct the Allied armies in the field. This, not Eisenhower's presidential reasoning, was the true "guts of the matter."

"They [Eisenhower and Bedell Smith] have now both gone off to draft a directive as a result of our conversation," Monty reported in a cable to Brooke that evening. "The draft is to be shown to me before it is issued. It has been a very exhausting day." Flying against all military logic, the Allied ground forces would, at the height of their success, be split in fact into three: an Army Group of the North, an Army Group of the Center, and an Army Group of the South (once the Anvil invasion forces worked their way up from the Mediterranean coast). Eisenhower would become, on 1 September, the Allied ground force generalissimo, in the field. As a result, in Monty's view, the fruits of the greatest Allied victory of World War II would be cast to the four winds.

It was, Monty felt, a wretched business. "I believe that Eisenhower in his heart of hearts knows he is wrong," Monty ended his account to General Nye; "I believe he is being pushed into his present decision by

Bedel [sic] Smith and certain others at SHAEF. I do NOT believe that things in America are really as he says they are."

They were not. But, whatever explanation was given to Monty, the result was an unholy compromise. The northern thrust—given the importance of further ports—must inevitably be the Allies' first priority. However, 21st Army Group was too weak to achieve its objectives without American reinforcement. This reinforcement, though, could not be put under a British general.

With growing preponderance of men and arms, American armies must remain under the tactical command of American generals, Eisenhower reasoned. Bradley would be ordered to send whatever he could spare to shield 21st Army Group's right flank—but under the aegis of the 12th U.S. Army Group. The concept of Army Groups of the North, and of the Center, and of the South, so neatly laid before the Combined Chiefs of Staff the day before, was in all honesty a sham. From now on, in effect, there would be "national" army groups. In the north, Monty would only be empowered to exercise "operational coordination between 21 Army Group and the left wing of 12 Army Group"—a concept so vaguely defined Monty questioned what it would amount to.

Meanwhile the true tragedy of Eisenhower's decision would never be made known to Monty in his lifetime—for, on the very day Monty wrangled with Eisenhower over the splitting of the Allied Overlord armies into two, General George S. Patton himself began to have second thoughts about the matter.

Patton's Momentous Idea

"**M**ark this August 23rd," Patton suddenly declared to his chief of operations, Colonel Muller. "I've just thought up the best strategical idea I've ever had. This may be a momentous day." In great excitement he now flew straight to Bradley's headquarters to tell him of it.

Had Patton conceived his idea a few hours earlier, he could have met both Bradley and Monty at Bradley's headquarters, and the three men could have discussed his brainwave. Moreover Monty would undoubtedly, as in Sicily when Patton put forward his proposals for taking Messina, have welcomed the plan; for, in effect, the idea was that Patton should now rejoin the main Allied thrust to the north, dumping the idea of a drive towards the Saar.

In one of the terrible ironies of military history, however, Patton arrived too late at "Tac Eagle," Bradley's Laval HQ. The birds had flown—literally. Not only had Monty returned to his headquarters for his historic confrontation with Eisenhower, but Bradley too was gone—having traveled to SHAEF advanced headquarters at Tournières to await, on tenterhooks, Eisenhower's decision. Thus Patton was reduced to outlining the "best strategical idea" he'd ever had to the 12th U.S. Army Group's chief of staff: a plan in which Third Army would cross the Seine at Melun, and the Yonne at Sens (southeast of Paris), then swivel *northwards* across the Marne and Oise in a Schlieffen-type operation to cut off the German forces fleeing before Dempsey and Hodges at Beauvais. This meant Patton's Third Army would abandon its Saar thrust in order to participate in Monty's northern thrust.

General Allen took it down in writing. Tersely, he said: "Seems fine to me, General."

Patton was beside himself. "Tell it to Brad when he comes back," he urged. "I'm going back to my CP to have my staff put both plans in writing—the one I told you yesterday about going straight east, and this one going north. If Bradley approves the attack to the north he has only to wire me 'Plan A' by 1000 tomorrow [24 August]. If I don't hear from you fellows by that time, I'll then move east as per my plan 'B.' "

Decisions and Revisions

Patton's proposal would, in the aftermath of Allied failure in the autumn of 1944, be concealed or downplayed by every major military historian: an opportunity so cruelly missed, it was too awful to contemplate. How much easier to pillory Monty as a thorn in Eisenhower's long-suffering hide, and to depict Patton as the unrepentant advocate of the eastern thrust!

In fact, Bradley only received his chief of staff's version of Patton's idea the next day, 24 August, after returning from Eisenhower's headquarters, where he had stayed the night. By then, the die was cast. "At 1200 hours," Patton's chief of staff recorded on 24 August, "instructions went out to the XII and XX Corps to execute Plan 'B' "—the thrust east to the Saar.

The chance of a cohesive, full-blooded Allied drive, combining the forty divisions of the Canadian, British, and American First and Third Armies, had thus been squandered in an extraordinary effort to keep British and American forces apart, each with its own field commanders and separate objectives, and with Eisenhower in field command.

Monty was heartbroken. It seemed as if everything he had ever learned, everything he had ever fought for in his military life, was now being frittered away. "I do not know what the situation is in PARIS," he signaled that night to Brooke. "The order to send troops in to that city was given by Eisenhower direct to Bradley and I was merely informed that it was to be done at the request of General Koenig. I am out of touch by telephone with Bradley at present and it is difficult to find out exactly what is going on. From all reports it looks as if the action taken was premature and may prove an embarrassment and detract from our main business."

The "main business" was the Allied thrust beyond the Seine—and an hour later Monty was signaling to General Nye the sad news that "Ike has now decided on his line of action. His [draft] directive to me is about all that I think I can get him to do at present. He has agreed that we must occupy the Pas de Calais and get possession of the Belgian Airfields and then prepare to move eastwards into the Ruhr and he has given this mission to 21 Army Group." But would the 21st Army Group be strong enough to achieve this?

"He has ordered 12 Army Group to thrust forward its left with what it can spare to assist 21 Army Group in carrying out its tasks and for this some six to eight U.S. Divisions will possibly be available"—a far cry from the great forty-division phalanx that Monty had proposed, and commanded with such patient mastery in Normandy.

"The remainder of the 12 Army Group is to clear up Brittany and then to assemble east of Paris. Eventually the whole of 12 Army Group is to move eastwards from Paris towards METZ and the SAAR. Ike is taking command himself of 12 and 21 Army Groups on 1 September."

To Monty this was all distressingly feeble. "You will see that instead of moving the combined might of the two Army Groups northwards into Belgium and then eastwards into Germany via the Ruhr Ike proposes to split the force and to move the American portion eastwards from Paris and into Germany via the Saar. I do not myself agree with what he proposes to do and have said so quite plainly."

Eisenhower, however, was the Supreme Commander—and like Bradley, Monty had to accept that in the interests of Allied unity he must obey Eisenhower's decision. "I do no[t] propose to continue the argument with Ike. The great thing is that I have been given power to coordinate and control the movement of the left wing northwards towards Antwerp and Belgium."

But Monty was wrong in assuming Eisenhower was sold on the Saar thrust. The more Eisenhower studied the map, the more he realized he did not dare pass up the responsibility of seizing the Channel ports, V-bomb sites and the great port of Antwerp with sufficient Allied forces.

Had Eisenhower summoned a conference of his army and army group commanders at this juncture, many subsequent misunderstandings might have been avoided. Instead, however, each army group commander and each army commander understood something different from the other, since Eisenhower's draft directive not only was vague, but was not officially issued for another five days. Thus the day after Monty's fateful conference with Eisenhower, at a time when Monty understood he would only receive the help of what Bradley could "spare" (i.e., "six to eight U.S. Divisions"), the new commander of First U.S. Army, General Courtney Hodges, *understood the complete opposite*, namely that the entire First U.S. Army would go north along-side Monty's 21 Army Group, as Hodges' ADC recorded in the First U.S. Army War Diary:

> General Bradley had many interesting things to announce: 1—General Eisenhower will assume command on September 1st. 2—First Army's mission, as it is contemplated now, will be to advance northeast from Mantes to Beauvais to Albert to Antwerp. The British will be responsible from there to the sea. . . .
>
> 3—It is contemplated that First Army will be composed in this drive of nine divisions: 1, 4, 9, 28, 30, 79, 2nd, 3rd and 5th Armoured, and that in addition we will get one or two of the divisions which are now completing the mopping up of the Brittany peninsula.

Bradley even ordered that a tenth division, the 4th U.S. Division, cross the Seine on the *north* side of Paris, instead of the south. The following day Hodges' ADC was noting:

> We are to strike northeast with the British taking care of the Crossbow [V-bomb] sites and we are to have temporary XV Corps troops but not the Corps itself. This is not the most direct route to Germany and not a route which General Hodges wished to take, but at the time at least apparently there was nothing else politically to do.

A Terrible Mistake

Ironically the British now believed Eisenhower was opting for sep-arated thrusts, commanded by separate national commanders, for American political (i.e., public opinion) reasons, while the Americans believed the reverse—that Eisenhower was being forced to take the northern route into Germany for British political reasons!

Patton, having seen his "momentous idea" ignored by Bradley, soon blamed Monty for the new wobbling Eisenhower directive, saying it was not the V-bombs but Monty who was the menace, and that if he, Bradley and Hodges all "offered to resign unless we went east, Ike would have to yield."

Patton claimed that if permitted to drive east, he could "cause the end of the war in a very few days," and that the decision to turn Hodges north in support of Monty "is a terrible mistake, and when it comes out" in the after years "it will cause much argument."

It would—though most of those who did the arguing would be unaware of the real course taken by the Allied high command in August 1944, and of the almost incredible misunderstandings between the generals. Though Monty was still in supposed tactical command of the Overlord ground forces, he was, from 23 August, out of telephone communication with Bradley, his fellow army group commander. Distressed by the imminent splitting of the two Allied army groups, he watched the saga of Leclerc's liberation of Paris with a sort of distant cynicism, as he cabled to Brooke on 25 August:

> When the French Armoured Division entered the outskirts of PARIS on 23 August they received such a tumultuous welcome from the population that most of the men became very drunk and nothing happened for the rest of the day.

The Germans had retired to the north side of the city. No Allied forces having appeared, the Germans came back and seized the bridges again. "When the French Armoured Division became sober they went forward into PARIS on 24 August and the Division is now on the left bank of the SEINE in the centre of the city. Fighting is going on for the bridges and desultory fighting continues in the streets. The Americans have had to send 4 US Division into the city to lend a hand.

"The net result is that the report that PARIS has been liberated was premature. I suggest that no celebrations are held in LONDON until I can officially report to you the occupation of the whole city."

Such faintly spinsterish response to the historic liberation of Paris gives a good illustration of Monty's state of mind at this critical juncture in the war. He had won one of the greatest battles in military history, he knew—a battle of incalculable importance in the Allied prosecution of the war. Ten weeks before, the Allies had been spectators, gazing at Hitler's Westwall. Not only had they subsequently landed in strength in Normandy, but the German armies in the West had, in those extraordinary ten weeks, been crushed, and their remnants were in helter-skelter retreat.

This was no time, Monty felt, for dissipation of Allied strength, whether military or moral. In this twilight of his position as Commander-in-Chief of the Allied armies, he could not see the liberation of Paris as anything other than a distraction. Nor could he see Eisenhower's imminent assumption of field command as anything other than inevitable catastrophe. Thus on 26 August he cabled to Brooke to announce that "all resistance in PARIS has ceased and it can now be said that we have occupied and liberated the city." But when, that same evening, the Supreme Commander signaled from Bradley's headquarters and asked Monty, as victorious Allied Land Forces Commander, to accompany him into the city the next morning, Monty's reply was terse:

Eisenhower: If you should like to accompany me will wait until flying conditions permit you to arrive Bradley's headquarters. Request prompt reply to Bradley.

Montgomery: Regret unable to go with you tomorrow. Thank you for asking me.

A Self-made Prison

Monty's intended snub—he had spoken to Eisenhower for only a few minutes the day before, when Eisenhower passed through his headquarters, directing Eisenhower, as he might a tourist, to "the best place to see the results of the battle" at Falaise—was unfortunate. Worse indeed, for it demonstrated Monty's smallness of character at the moment when greatness was required.

Though confusing from a tactical military point of view, Eisenhower's decisions represented those of the military leader of an Allied coalition, wishing to do right by the differing nations of the alliance, in war and upon the field of battle. To snub Eisenhower was therefore to snub the coalition. General Nye had begged Monty to put the alliance first. Monty had put it second—encouraging skeptics at SHAEF and in certain American headquarters to feel Monty was putting himself first.

In this, Monty had, in the end, no one to blame but himself. Ever since his victory at Alamein in 1942 he had become a law unto himself, distancing himself not only from the distracting detail of his Main Headquarters, but also from the give-and-take of discussion of the wider issues among senior staff officers at Main HQ—men who were intimate not only with the members of SHAEF but with American colleagues who now staffed Bradley's 12th U.S. Army Group Headquarters.

This self-isolation on the battlefield had been intentional, and Monty never later regretted or sought to excuse it. His lifelong ambition had been the perfection of the art of modern field command. The great victory in Normandy was his crowning achievement, the product of extraordinary vision and preparation, followed by relentless leadership on the battlefield. Yet the truth was, the more Monty commanded from his small Tactical Headquarters, the less constructive use he made of his Main Headquarters, which became increasingly a rear headquarters, used for administrative purposes rather than being intimately involved in the day-to-day fortunes of the battle. Colonel Bonesteel, for instance, had served at 21st Army Group before becoming deputy G3 in charge of operations at 12th U.S. Army Group. "Let me say here," Colonel Bonesteel remarked after the war to the American Official Historian, "that 21 Army Group was the best I saw in the war from a mechanical standpoint. But Monty sailed off across the Channel and didn't use it. Most unfortunate. Bad hiatus between him and staff."

Bonesteel represented the staff officer's view, however. Charles Richardson, Bonesteel's senior officer at 21st Army Group, felt there was a conundrum here that staff officers—British and American— tended to ignore: the question of battlefield *command*.

Richardson had witnessed Monty's transformation of morale in the desert; he had then witnessed the deplorable failures of morale and command under Mark Clark in Italy. Bonesteel was wrong, Richardson felt, in placing staffwork before command—Richardson felt that this overreliance upon staffwork had resulted in the same degree of American failure in North Africa and Italy as the British had suffered in pre-Monty days, under Generals Gort, Wavell and Auchinleck. As a result, the Germans had simply run rings around their opponents.

A modern battle commander, Monty had insisted, must be prepared to command *from the front*—not from behind as in World War I. But having demonstrated the virtues of his modern system of command, Monty had become, by the summer of 1944, its prisoner, unable to adapt himself to the larger realities and problems of coalition war: an imprisonment that was now vividly demonstrated as the victorious Commander-in-Chief of the D-Day armies refused to attend the liberation of Paris, or even to speak civilly to his Supreme Commander. Insisting that the senior officer must go forward, in battle, to confer with his subordinates, he refused ever to go back to Eisenhower's headquarters, or even to his own Main Headquarters, to discuss the critical decisions that had to be made. "Monty flatly refused to go back to SHAEF, and therefore Freddie had to go back in his place," Richardson frankly recalled. Yet, when Eisenhower *did* come to his field headquarters, Monty refused to permit the Supreme Commander's chief of staff or his chief of administration to be present.

Problems of communication, sympathy and international understanding were, as a result, inevitable. De Guingand was a brilliant staff officer, as well as a conciliator of great talent; but in the evolution of Monty's method of battlefield command, de Guingand could no longer be the watchful alter ego he had been in desert days. "I think Freddie did get increasingly out of touch fully with the nuances of the situation as they were arising." Monty's military assistant, Lieutenant Colonel Dawnay, admitted. "He saw SHAEF and the SHAEF people much more often than he saw Monty. And so he got really quite often a different picture of the situation than he would have got if he had had more regular touch with Monty."

In his determination to *command*, Monty had severed the vital umbilical cord with his Main Headquarters—had kicked out de Guingand's man, Leo Russell, and was now, as Commander-in-Chief of Allied armies totaling two million men, closer to his fighting generals, brigadiers and colonels than to his own staff, let alone the staff of Supreme Headquarters. It was in this sense that Bedell Smith claimed Monty had never grown above corps or at most army commander level—and in this sense Smith was all too right.

In Dawnay's view, such separation between Tac and Main Headquarters was "absolutely deliberate. And planned from his experiences of the desert, planned for Europe—with his liaison officers, his 'eyes and ears,' who sometimes transmitted his orders, which Freddie only got to hear about afterwards, so to speak. Freddie used to get very cross about Monty and his LOs on a number of occasions, because he didn't know what was happening, almost. It was very hard because Monty was giving direct orders right down sometimes to divisions and below! Of course, Freddie initially had Leo Russell in command of Tac Headquarters. . . . Well, Leo was a very abrasive character. He was difficult to get on with, and then came the incident of the pig [when Russell arrested two of Monty's liaison officers for stealing a loose pig]—and Monty kicked him out! Which was an unfortunate thing, for he wouldn't have anyone in his place. Freddie suggested several other people he could send out in Russell's place—and Monty wouldn't have it.

"So Freddie was cut off from that source of information. Paul Odgers, I mean, he was only GSO 2 and a major then—I was thirty-three, that sort of thing—we weren't any of us proper [i.e., Regular Army] soldiers, and it was very difficult for Freddie. I did my best to keep Freddie in the picture as far as I could, but then very often *I* didn't know what was happening! I mean, Monty went out, he went out every day somewhere, wherever the battle was hottest, and he sent his LOs to other places to report back to him wherever he might be, forward, what was happening in this section of the front, in that section, and so on; and it was only when Monty got back in the evening that I could gather up a bit of information and find out what had happened myself! And then Monty had these meetings with the LOs in the caravan, when they marked up the map and told him the whole thing. And then Monty would talk to Freddie on the telephone. But they got further and further apart as time went on. And it was very unfortunate, really. Twice when they were flying up to see him the weather closed in, they couldn't get down and had to go back—never saw him!

"It was a great pity, that.

"Freddie, needless to say, was rather jealous that he wasn't in the picture, wasn't put in the picture properly by Monty—particularly when he was then expected to argue on Monty's behalf. He wasn't sufficiently in Monty's mind to be able to argue those things—especially with high-powered Americans who'd also got their own point of view and their own political point of view, strategic point of view, which Monty didn't appreciate. I mean, there is no doubt about it, he [Monty] thought winning the war was the only thing that mattered and he could do it best—and why couldn't people come to him and understand that!

"If only de Guingand had been closer to Monty," Dawnay lamented in retrospect, much distressing misunderstanding could have been avoided. "Freddie was the only person who could say, 'Really, sir, you *can't*—it's very unwise.'

"It was a terrible pity. . . . And of course, once we did break out, the thing went so fast that we were moving Monty's headquarters about every second or third day—we were always on the move," Dawnay recalled—a situation that made communication between Tac and Main Headquarters even more difficult. "We were off the air from say eight or nine in the morning till five o'clock in the evening, when you'd got everything set up again, lines through, and you could talk on the telephone again. And it was very hard to keep people informed for that reason. It went tremendously fast. Tremendously exciting too! It was astonishing, the control he kept of his troops during that period."

This was indeed the nub. If Monty was able to demonstrate, in contrast to Lord Gort's ineptness in 1940, how a modern battle commander should exercise command in the field, it was a demonstration that carried incontrovertible penalties.

"His conception of the battle, and the way he fought it, were exceptionally clear in his own mind," Dawnay reflected. "But there were doubts in a lot of other people's minds whom he hadn't seen enough or talked to enough to explain exactly what he was doing. . . . And there ought to have been somebody considerably senior to me, representing Freddie at Tac Headquarters. If only there had been, not Leo because he was so abrasive, but some other individual who could have found out what was going on and really kept Freddie fully in the picture, it would have been a good thing—no doubt about that.

"Monty looked at it solely through military eyes. There's no doubt that he never paid any attention to the political or other, national concerns at all. He said: 'I've proved myself militarily, I have shown them that their doubts in Normandy, that if you fight it my way, you [win]. The results of winning a battle like that are tremendous. And surely by now they must understand that if we want to win the war quickly, this is the only way to do it.'

"But of course it's a matter of national pride as well as what is militarily best! And Monty could not have been given command of the Americans at that stage, there's no question about it—it was not possible with the Americans, because they were supplying three-quarters of the soldiers! And the air too!"

Defects of Character

It was now, more than at any time during the war so far, that
Monty's grave defects of character prevented him showing
a greatness of spirit to match his generalship. His letters to Phyllis
Reynolds—who had increasingly become a form of surrogate wife and
mother—betray the strains and limitations to which he became prey.
Once again the gremlin that urged him to reject his family resurfaced;
once again it centered on possession of his son, David. "The idea that
David should come out to see me here is quite ridiculous," he had
snapped on 17 August, "and I cannot think who started such an idea.
I quite agree with you; he needs to be kept quiet and to mature gradually; he should not see too much of Jocelyn [David's half brother's
wife, who had allowed David to drink sherry]; the more time he
spends quietly at home [i.e., the Reynoldses' school], the better."

Once again Jocelyn Carver was made—largely through Phyllis Reynolds' maneuverings—the butt of Monty's almost manic suspicions. By
1 September, Monty was writing: "I always said that he [David] should
never be allowed to go to Jocelyn, or any of her friends; and I still say
so"—and he supported Phyllis Reynolds' embargo on visits by David to
his half-brother's home.

To say that Monty thereby demeaned himself is not the point, for
his consideration for the lives and welfare of his men never weakened.
When General Horrocks, only recently returned to command of 30
Corps, fell sick with fever on the Normandy battlefield, Horrocks tried
to hide himself and his disability. "I told [my ADC] to send a message
to ask [Monty] to postpone his visit as I would be very busy away from
my headquarters during the next few days. A couple of hours later the
caravan door opened again and to my horror in came Monty. 'Ah,
Horrocks,' he said. 'I thought that something odd was happening so I
came up to see for myself.' Monty immediately had Horrocks' caravan

placed alongside his own at 21 Army Group Tac HQ, and the best medical specialists in the army to see him. "Each day Monty paid me a visit, and these talks proved more than usually interesting because this was the time when the big argument about the future conduct of the war was going on between Monty and Eisenhower."

Had the Allies been stalemated in Normandy, or even suffered a defeat such as that of the British and French forces in 1940, the strain upon the Allied alliance would have been understandable. What was ironic was that the issue had arisen at the moment of the greatest Allied victory of the war, with British and American troops now racing pell-mell north across the Seine and through eastern France. Yet the issue was not, as Monty claimed, one of military logic and sensible command; it was the shift of power within the "grand alliance," as the United States, not Britain, became, finally and irrevocably, a superpower.

The days when Britain was the preponderant or even equal military contributor in the struggle for Europe were over. The great muscle of the United States was being flexed—and instead of again visiting Bradley, his imminent "opposite number," Monty talked to his ailing British corps commander. "I have no news today from the American front," he signaled to Brooke on the night of 27 August—and there is no record that between 22 August and 3 September Monty made any attempt to see Bradley.

Not only was this a mistake in terms of Allied unity, but it was self-defeating. In Monty's absence from the "councils of war," Bradley began to take a more and more "American" line, egged on particularly by the jingoistic Patton. Thus Eisenhower's agreement that Monty assume operational control and co-ordination of the Allied armies in the north was frankly rejected by Bradley on 25 August. "Brad renegs strenuously," his aide Major Hansen recorded in his diary. " 'I get along with Monty fine enough,' he said. 'But we've got to make it clear *to the American public* that we are no longer under any control of Monty's.' People back home are needling Marshall on this issue now."

It was in this way that Monty lost even the chance of operational control of Hodges' First U.S. Army which Eisenhower was initially disposed to grant Monty—and all because Monty remained in his ivory tower, scorning the chance to share with Bradley, Patton and Hodges the celebrations in Paris, trying from a frosty distance to bend Eisenhower to his will. It was in these circumstances that, at last, on 29 August 1944, Field Marshal Brooke arrived at Monty's headquarters, shortly after his return from the Mediterranean.

A Staggering Allied Achievement

A t a British Chiefs of Staff meeting in London on 28 August, Eisenhower's proposals for the continuation of the war in northwest Europe had been discussed. "This plan," Brooke noted with prophetic resignation in his diary, "is likely to add another three to six months to the war." Eisenhower "straight away wants to split his force, sending an American contingent towards Nancy, whilst the British Army Group moves along the coast. If the Germans were not as beat as they are this would be a fatal move; as it is, it may not do too much harm. In any case I am off to France tomorrow to see Monty and to discuss the situation with him. . . . The Germans cannot last very much longer."

Monty disagreed. In the same way as he had done the year before, when he had cautioned General Alexander not to assume that the Italian surrender would mean automatic victory for the Allies invading Italy, he warned Brooke that the Germans, though down, were not out. It was vital, Monty felt, to act immediately and in unison. "The enemy has now been driven north of the SEINE except in a few places," he had declared in his M520 directive to 21st Army Group on 26 August,

> and our troops have entered PARIS. The enemy forces are very stretched and disorganised; they are in no fit condition to stand and fight us. This, then, is our opportunity to achieve our further objects quickly, and to deal the enemy further blows which will cripple his power to continue in the war. The tasks now confronting 21 Army Group are:
> a) to operate northwards and to destroy the enemy forces in N.E. France and Belgium.
> b) to secure the PAS DE CALAIS area and the airfields in Belgium.
> c) to secure ANTWERP as a base. Having completed these tasks, the

eventual mission of the Army Group will be to advance eastwards on the RUHR. Speed of action and of movement is now vital. I cannot emphasize this too strongly; what we have to do must be done quickly. Every officer and man must understand that by a stupendous effort now we shall not only hasten the end of the war; we shall also bring quick relief to our families and friends in England by over-running the flying bomb launching sites in the PAS DE CALAIS. . . .

The enemy has not the troops to hold any strong position. The proper tactics now are for armoured and mobile columns to by-pass enemy centres of resistance and to push boldly ahead, creating alarm and despondency in enemy rear areas.

Enemy centres of resistance thus by-passed should be dealt with by infantry columns coming on later.

I rely on commanders of every rank and grade to "drive" ahead with the utmost energy; any tendency to be "sticky" or cautious must be stamped on ruthlessly.

But could 21st Army Group achieve all this with First U.S. Army only temporarily assigned to guard Dempsey's right flank between Paris and Brussels? What would happen if one or other thrust—Monty's or Patton's—prospered? Which would Eisenhower reinforce? "It remains to be seen what political pressure is put on Eisenhower to move Americans on separate axis from the British," Brooke noted in his diary after leaving Monty.

Certainly, all previous calculations by the staffs were cast to the wind. British armored formations were now moving faster than Patton's—indeed, by 30 August, British armored columns were beyond Beauvais and the projected airborne operations in the Pas de Calais area were dropped in favor of another at Tournai, in Belgium, to secure the Escaut River line, so familiar to Monty from his retreat towards Dunkirk in 1940. "For the first time in this campaign I can now report that the total prisoners captured by the Allied Armies exceed the total casualties suffered," Monty reported to Brooke. "The prisoners since D day now amount to 210,000 and our casualties are less than that by some thousands." This was more than twice the number of prisoners taken by the Russians at Stalingrad, and all were German. The following day, Horrocks' 30 Corps alone captured 5,000 men—including "the complete Tac HQ of German 7th Army with the Army Commander of German 15th Army who presumably had been sent up to take command of 7th Army. The whole HQ was surprised while having breakfast and was captured complete with all documents, maps and so on."

The very speed of the northern thrust, however, was wrenching the

Allied armies apart, and fulfilling Monty's every fear. He cabled to Brooke that night:

> I have every hope that we shall have a strong armoured force astride the SOMME at AMIENS tomorrow [31 August]. The right hand corps of First U.S. Army has reached LAON.
>
> Third U.S. Army has been told to go to FRANKFURT and the leading troops of 20 US Corps are now half-way between RHEIMS and VERDUN.
>
> I am not at all happy about this eastward thrust into the SAAR and over the RHINE. The northward thrust is now proceeding very fast and we are going to be strained administratively and will require all available resources.
>
> It is my opinion that administratively we cannot develop two strong thrusts simultaneously and all resources should be allotted to the northern thrust as being the really important one.
>
> This is an example of how we may get into difficulties by not having a C-in-C for the land armies. . . .

But the Allies *did* have a C-in-C for the land armies: General Eisenhower.

Like it or not, Monty's last day as commander of the Overlord armies had arrived. Dieppe fell to the Canadians almost intact, and Saint-Valéry to the 51st Highland Division. The "Great Adventure" which had begun at dawn on 6 June 1944 had resulted, thanks to Monty's generalship, in one of the outstanding military victories of all human history. In three months the British took 215,611 German prisoners, the Americans 207,153. Counting dead and wounded, the German armies had suffered losses of more than half a million soldiers: a staggering Allied achievement. However, it was a victory which, thanks to Eisenhower's failings as a field commander and Monty's intransigent personality, would quickly turn to tears and terrible casualties in the bitter months ahead.

Part Twelve

THE RACE TO THE RHINE

British tanks cross the Seine
late August 1944.

Missing a Great Opportunity

C ould World War II have been won in 1944?

Most senior German commanders felt that with Montgomery's triumph in Normandy, the Allies could have ended the war within weeks. "All the [German] generals to whom I talked were of the opinion that the Allied Supreme Command had missed a great opportunity of ending the war in the autumn of 1944," wrote the military historian Basil Liddell Hart. "They agreed with Montgomery's view that this could best have been achieved by concentrating all possible resources in a thrust in the north, towards Berlin."

The chief of staff to von Rundstedt confirmed Liddell Hart's account. "The best course of the Allies would have been to concentrate a really strong striking force with which to break through past Aachen to the Ruhr area," General Blumentritt stated. "Strategically and politically, Berlin was the target. Germany's strength is in the north.

"He who holds northern Germany holds Germany. Such a breakthrough, coupled with air domination, would have torn in pieces the weak German front and ended the war. Berlin and Prague would have been occupied ahead of the Russians. There were no German forces behind the Rhine, and at the end of August our front was wide open."

General Kurt von Manteuffel, who later commanded the Fifth Panzer Army in the Battle of the Bulge, agreed. "I am in full agreement with Montgomery," he later recorded. "I believe General Eisenhower's insistence on spreading the Allied forces out for a broader advance was wrong. The acceptance of Montgomery's plan would have shortened the war considerably."

Birth of the Broad-Front Strategy

Ironically, Eisenhower had not originally intended a "broader advance"—he wanted a full-blooded American thrust to the Saar, south of the Ardennes, while the British and Canadian armies "cleared up" the northern coast of France and the Low Countries. To this end he had on 24 August instructed Bradley to send only sufficient American forces into Belgium to enable Monty to carry out his coastal mission. Thereafter Bradley was to carry out an American "advance eastward from the Paris area. . . . I cannot tell you how anxious I am," he signaled to General Marshall in Washington, "to get the forces accumulated for starting the thrust eastward from Paris."

It was in the euphoric days thereafter, with the capture of Paris and the disintegration of the German front, that Eisenhower became ever more, not less, optimistic. Nor was he alone. So confident was Bradley that the Germans would shortly surrender that he now began making tentative plans for an American "army of occupation of Germany." Planning for the Allied occupation of Berlin had already begun at Supreme Headquarters, with an Allied Control Commission "called upon to make itself ready to operate in Berlin by 1st November." "The August battles have done it and the enemy in the West has had it," Eisenhower's Intelligence chief reported. "Two and a half months of bitter fighting have brought the end of the war in Europe within sight, almost within reach."

Churchill was equally ecstatic. The Prime Minister's private secretary noted in his diary at the end of August 1944: "Our Armies are racing to the Belgian frontier, faster by far than went the Panzers in 1940. There is a feeling of elation, of expectancy and almost bewilderment, and it may well be that the end is now very close."

The signs "are not wanting that he [the enemy] is nearing collapse," Eisenhower himself stated in his first Message to Commanders on 29

August, shortly before taking over as Allied Land Forces Commander. Following the successful landings in the south of France, the Seventh U.S. Army was "rapidly advancing on Dijon from the South." In an interview with over a hundred Allied war correspondents in London on 31 August, Eisenhower explained his new strategy: "General Montgomery's forces were expected to beat the Germans on the north; General Bradley's to defeat them in the center, and the Mediterranean forces, under General Devers, to press from the south." The erstwhile single-thrust strategy—first by the British to Antwerp, then by the Americans to Metz and Frankfurt—was becoming, in expectation of total German collapse, a policy of simultaneous thrusts on all fronts: leading inexorably to the label "broad-front."

Eisenhower's Press Conference

Meanwhile, however, Monty's reduced role after Normandy had to be explained to the public. For almost three months Monty had commanded the American, Canadian and British armies. Now, in the moment of Allied triumph, Eisenhower was taking Monty's place in the field—giving rise to speculation that Eisenhower was dissatisfied by Monty's performance.

At his press conference on 31 August, therefore, Eisenhower loyally defended Monty from the jibes of those commentators who saw the slowness of the British forces at Caen in marked contrast to American mobility under Patton. "The Germans had thrown in every Panzer division available to hold that region," Eisenhower explained. "Every piece of dust on the Caen front was more than a diamond." By holding the German armor at Caen, the British had made it possible for the Americans to "break through westward from Saint-Lô and start the end run which eventually dislodged the Germans west of the Seine." As his naval ADC and PR executive noted in his diary, Eisenhower "praised Monty and said that anyone who misinterpreted the transition of command as a demotion for General Montgomery simply did not look facts in the face. He said Montgomery is one of the great soldiers of this or any other war and he would now have the job of handling the battles on his side of the front. It would be most unfortunate if this plan of campaign, which had developed as it was conceived from the start, should be interpreted as a demotion or a slap at anybody. . . . He made clear that when the initial beachhead was established, it was very restricted, and since there was only one tactical battle to be conducted, he had put General Montgomery in tactical control of the American land force. Montgomery's control was to exist until we could break out of the base of the Cherbourg Peninsula. The time had come when they had broken out, and General Bradley was taking over part of the job and reporting directly to SHAEF. Ike described Monty as a 'great and personal friend' and emphasized that he had a great admiration for him."

Eisenhower's press conference was nobly conceived and ably conducted—a tribute to his statesmanlike talents as a coalition leader. It certainly did much to dispel inter-Allied rivalry—though the rivalry itself worried Eisenhower. "As signs of victory appear in the air," Eisenhower wrote sadly to Marshall after the conference, "I note little instances that seem to indicate that the Allies cannot hang so effectively in prosperity as they can in adversity."

This was to be an understatement.

Field Marshal Montgomery

As Eisenhower gave his press conference, meantime, Monty raced on with his British and Canadian armies towards Belgium. On 1 September 1944, Tac Headquarters 21st Army Group crossed the Seine and set up camp in the grounds of the Château of Dangu. The owner's wife later recalled:

My eldest son in the morning noticed a private [GI] with khaki sweater and black beret walking in one of the alleys; later a cousin of ours came across the same private. After discussion they agreed this could only be Montgomery.

The figure *was* Montgomery; and in the same simple gray sweater, corduroy trousers and black beret Monty now sat for the portrait which James Gunn had been painting each day for the past fortnight, in five different locations. Gunn's canvas depicted Monty seated on a simple mahogany armchair, beneath the camouflaged awning of one of his famous caravans—much as a medieval English king might have sat after Crécy or Agincourt. Indeed, King George VI had already written to commend Monty on the magnitude of the Allied victory: "Ever since you explained to me your masterly plan for your part in the campaign in western France, I have followed with admiration its day to day development. I congratulate you most heartily on its overwhelming success."

Further congratulations now poured in—for on 1 September 1944 it was announced that General Sir Bernard Montgomery had been promoted to the rank of field marshal "in circumstances that are certainly unique in the history of such things," the King's private secretary wrote. "Done on the Field of Battle at the moment of your greatest triumph enhances its value a hundred-fold," signaled Field Marshal Sir John Dill, British military representative to the Combined Chiefs of Staff. Even General Marshall, Chairman of the Combined Chiefs of Staff in Washington, cabled to congratulate Monty "on this latest acknowledgment of the magnificent fighting service you have rendered the Allied cause."

With the extent of Montgomery's victory now apparent, moreover, the world's press joined in the jubilation. The *News Chronicle* prefaced its front-page headline on 1 September 1944: "Eisenhower gives the facts of victory: 400,000 German casualties, including 47 divisions destroyed, mauled or trapped; in material the enemy has lost 1,300 tanks, 2,000 guns, and 3,500 planes. . . ."

These, however, were statistics. It was the headline itself which, after three months of battle since D-Day, affixed the seal to Allied victory in France:

ALLIES CROSS THE MEUSE AND SOMME
The British are over the Somme; the Americans are over the Meuse and driving on Sedan and Charleville.
    The German front, it was stated in despatches from the war fronts last

night, is completely broken and the battle of France is rapidly drawing to a close.

Robert Reuben, Reuters' special correspondent with the First American Army, cabling last night, said: The German front has completely broken, and the battle has turned into a rout. The Germans are fleeing so fast that it is becoming most difficult for the American forces to maintain contact. "It has turned into a pursuit instead of a battle," said a military official. . . .

Recording that General O'Connor's armored troops had driven "60 miles in 48 hours to seize Amiens," Reuben announced that "the British left flank was advancing as fast or faster than Patton. Amiens is ours. Last night we had three bridges over the Somme. It now seems impossible for the enemy to hold on to a line anywhere, and it looks as though it may not be long before the Channel coast with the flying bomb sites will fall to us."

In the adjacent column, carrying a photograph of Monty in beret, battle dress and flying jacket, there ran the simple headline "FIELD MARSHAL MONTGOMERY."

The Duke of Dangu, anxious lest his own sympathies as a Frenchman be considered suspect—his château had been occupied by the German Luftwaffe since 1940—attempted to assemble as many members of the local resistance as possible for Monty's inspection. But Monty, sitting for his portrait, refused to see them. His promotion did little to mollify him. His gnarled hands were clenched. His steel-blue eyes stared; and to his military assistant he dictated an acid letter addressed to his chief of staff.

It was not the letter of a newly promoted field marshal, but tart and vexed. However enthralled the world's press might be by the sprawling onrush of the Allied armies from the coast of France to the "iron and steel centres of Lorraine at the southern end of the line," Monty was appalled. By failing to impose a clear strategic plan upon the battlefield, weighed down by the civil, political and military responsibilities of a Supreme Commander, Eisenhower was, in Monty's narrow view, squandering a great and decisive Allied victory.

How Eisenhower proposed to exercise field command of the Allied armies from his new SHAEF Headquarters at Granville, on the *Atlantic* side of the Cherbourg Peninsula, many hundreds of miles behind the front lines, Monty was at a loss to understand. As he put it later to Chester Wilmot, Eisenhower would have been in closer touch with his field commanders had he stayed in London, across the English Channel. Thus, in response to de Guingand's message that Eisenhower "was trying to get you on the 'phone in order to congratulate you" on being promoted to field marshal, but had "not been successful so far," Monty replied testily, "I do not suppose that IKE or anyone else will be able to telephone me for months."

A Bad Omen

―――――――――

I f Monty was contemptuous of the Supreme Commander's wish to become, overnight, a great field commander, it was as nothing beside his feelings about his "lesser" Allies. He had already given orders to General Crerar, he wrote in his letter to de Guingand, "to transfer the Belgian detachment to Second Army at once. They will be the first troops to enter BRUSSELS. They will all get tight in BRUSSELS, and I hope that is the last we shall see of them."

Nor was Monty more respectful of Free Dutch troops. "The Dutch contingent I am leaving with the Canadian Army as there is a bit of HOLLAND just beyond BRUGES," he sneered, "and they can frig about in that."

Such unbridled sarcasm betrayed the frustration Monty felt at this critical juncture of the war. With Dempsey's Second British Army and Hodges' First U.S. Army steaming across the Belgian border, north of the Ardennes, Monty felt the American target *must* be the Aachen gap, which, in the view of Monty's planning staff, offered "the most satisfactory approach to the Ruhr and being on high ground is likely to be best in Autumn and Winter." To this end Monty was willing even to sacrifice Eisenhower's offer of airborne assistance in seizing the coastal ports and V-bomb launching sites. The existing 21st Army Group plan to drop an entire airborne corps in the Pas de Calais was thus canceled. Instead, General Browning was now told to drop with three Allied airborne divisions at Tournai on the left flank of Hodges' First U.S. Army. In this way Dempsey's Second Army would be able to take over a front some seventy kilometers east of Antwerp—freeing

Hodges' entire First U.S. Army to head straight for Aachen instead of the great Belgian seaport.

This airborne drop (Operation Linnet Two), to help catapult an American army across the Rhine to the Ruhr, was fixed for 3 September 1944. However, at midday on 2 September, General Dempsey noted in his diary that the operation "looks unlikely . . . owing to the weather."

It was a bad omen. The sands of time, for the Allies, were now running out. After days of glorious summer sunshine, the skies darkened. Heavy rain began to fall, making airborne operations impossible.

The difficulties of an autumn campaign, conducted with too few resources, were now, at the very height of Allied elation, about to become painfully, tragically apparent.

Changes in Direction

B y the afternoon of 2 September, de Guingand was signaling to Monty:

In view of delay and uncertain weather feel we should dispense with LINNET if possible and prepare similar operation to suit your future plans. Please signal your decision most immediate.

Monty agreed. With 21st Army Group's armored spearheads already approaching Brussels and Antwerp—the immediate objectives laid down in Eisenhower's current directive—airborne landings at Tournai were indeed redundant. It was vital, Monty felt, to make a new plan. But Eisenhower, the supposed new Land Forces Commander, was out of touch. Monty therefore did the only thing he could: he asked the Commander of the Army Group of the Center, General Bradley, for an urgent meeting.

Headquarters of 12th U.S. Army Group was near Chartres—where, ironically, Eisenhower was visiting Bradley to discuss the future, in the presence of Patton and Hodges.

Patton, determined to reach Metz and the Saar before the Germans organized a defensive line, was dismayed by Eisenhower's caution, which made him—as well as Bradley and Hodges, he claimed—"quite ill." Since 23 August Bradley had "vigorously" disputed Eisenhower's decision "to give Montgomery all three Corps of 1st Army. One, I insisted, would have been enough." On 1 September he had told his ADC, Major Hansen, that he was "going to sell Ike on the possibility of turnhing [sic] his effort to the East and head for the German border, break through the Siegfried Line while the enemy is disorganized and before he can plug it, make for the Rhine and drop paratroops to protect the Bridge crossings." He had already told Eisenhower on the occasion of the Supreme Commander's last visit "that Monty didn't need anything to help him in his effort; that what he had was plenty and that he wouldn't find any opposition going up there—that we should turn east, through [throw] everything we've got into Germany and now by Krist we can . . . Give me 8,000 tons east of Paris and we'll get going. I'll stop effort over on [21st Army Group] flank almost altogether [i.e., north of the Ardennes] and turn everything toward Germany. We can start nine divisions almost immediately. Six should certainly get to the Rhine and very quickly." According to Hansen, "General [Bradley] expects to be on the Rhine a week on Sunday [10 September] if Ike will give him the go ahead sign on the movement he wants to make. Had we been able to go [before], perhaps we should have been there today."

Unaware of the impending cancellation of Browning's airborne landings in Belgium, however, Eisenhower ordered Hodges to "curl up both VII and XIX Corps short of Tournai and Mons respectively," lest they were required to move northwards into Ghent and Antwerp if Monty's Linnet operation at Tournai met serious resistance. However, if Brussels and Antwerp fell to Monty without difficulty, Eisenhower agreed that Hodges' 5 U.S. Corps need not be directed towards Aachen, but would be diverted across the tail of 7 U.S. Corps and race east to the Rhine to guard the left flank of Patton's thrust into Germany via the Saar, south of the Ardennes.

Hodges was understandably confused—uncertain whether he was to drive on Antwerp, make for the Aachen gap, or support Patton's thrust into Germany south of the Ardennes, or all three. "There have been so many changes in the First Army direction," his aide, Captain Sylvan, noted in his diary, "that indeed there seems at times as if those on top did not have an altogether clear and consistent conception of the direction from which they wish to cross the German frontier."

This was an understatement.

A Council of War

As Bradley and Hodges journeyed to Dempsey's headquarters at Lailly, near Amiens, Brussels was falling to British armored spearheads. The capture of Antwerp was expected within the next twenty-four hours. The question at the conference, therefore, was: Where next? First U.S. Army was no longer needed to support 21 Army Group's coastal tasks. Did Bradley now intend to push First U.S. Army to the Rhine via Aachen, north of the Ardennes, as well as Third U.S. Army south of the Ardennes? If so, would Bradley need the First Allied Airborne Army?

"I had a meeting today with Bradley and it is quite clear to me that the Americans are planning to make their main effort via METZ and NANCY directed on FRANKFURT and the First U.S. Army on my flank will be depleted accordingly," Monty lamented to Brooke on the evening of 3 September—referring to the switch of Hodges' 5 U.S. Corps to Patton's flank, south of the Ardennes.

Bradley, had, however, turned down the offer of airborne assistance. "Have consulted Bradley and he does NOT require airborne drop on LIEGE line," Monty signaled to de Guingand after the conference broke up. "We both consider that all available aircraft should go on to transport work so that we can maintain momentum of advance." But what was to be the direction of the British advance?

In Eisenhower's absence, and with Bradley intent upon making his main effort south of the Ardennes, Monty decided to concord his own strategy beyond Antwerp, as he reported to Brooke:

I have not seen Eisenhower since 26 August and have had no orders from him, so I am getting my own plans for advancing against the RUHR and am getting Bradley to lend a hand.

Such was Monty's cable—one of the most fateful and extraordinary telegrams of World War II.

Isolating the Ruhr

The tragedy of Monty's council of war on 3 September 1944 was that, in Eisenhower's absence (Eisenhower had flown back on 2 September to Granville, where he had injured his knee attempting to pull his plane to safety in high winds), each Allied field commander understood a different Allied strategy to be pursued. In his diary General Dempsey recorded:

> C-in-C [21st Army Group], General Bradley and General Hodges came to my headquarters. We discussed future plans and agreed the inter-Army Group boundary, which will be the boundary between Second Army and First American Army. It will run just SOUTH of a line BRUSSELS–DUSSELDORF, *which gives the whole of the RHUR* [sic] *to me.* We will, if possible, by-pass the RHUR to the NORTH and come in behind it near HAMM.

Such a plan, giving the "whole of the Rhur" to Dempsey's Second British Army, made nonsense of Monty's original notion of a forty-division Allied thrust "so strong that it need fear nothing." With the Canadian army still stuck on the Seine and the Somme, hundreds of miles behind Second Army, it was inconceivable Dempsey would have enough British troops to secure the Antwerp approaches *and* turn northeast to attack the Ruhr from the north, without significant American help. Yet this is what, in Eisenhower's absence, Dempsey undertook.

General Hodges, released from his orders to wait and see whether Dempsey required help in taking Brussels and Antwerp, went back to his maps of Germany. "He [Hodges] returned at four o'clock with news," Hodges' ADC noted, "that we are to push on East as settled previously and not drive north."

Bradley, paradoxically, seems to have undergone a change of heart as a result of the meeting. His initial preference had been for an American single thrust: an all-out American race to the Saar and a quick bridgehead across the Rhine, with Patton aimed at Frankfurt, reinforced by Hodges' First U.S. Army, once Antwerp was secured. After meeting Monty at Lailly, however, Bradley decided to hedge his bets, and split his thrusts into two *simultaneous* thrusts to the Rhine, south *and* north of the Ardennes. His ADC, Major Hansen, recorded in his diary on 4 September: "Gen's original plan called for supply schedule [sic] that would assign supply to [Patton's] Third Army, hold [Hodges'] First in place until Third got on the Rhine." Now, however, "it is planned to shoot both armies on to the Rhine in force and for that reason it has been necessary to hold them up for supply. When both are up to the Rhine, the force of the effort will go to the First Army which will then gain a bridgehead and together with the British Army plan to cut off an[d] isolate the Rhur [sic] from the rest of Germany, the British fr.[om] the north and we from the south. If possible, we shall extend a bridgehead on the far side of the Rhine as a base for future operations in the Third Army sector."

Bradley was thus indeed attempting to "lend a hand" to Monty, by conforming to Monty's idea of a pincer attack on the Ruhr, while pushing Patton, as in Normandy, around the German flank, ready to outmaneuver the enemy from Frankfurt.

Meanwhile, to conduct this pincer attack upon the Ruhr a single tactical commander was urgently required, Monty felt, as in Normandy. Instead, "I have powers only of coordination and not of operational direction," Monty lamented to Brooke.

This was not the way to beat the Germans in battle, Monty knew. But what could be done?

It was in this anarchic atmosphere, in the absence of Eisenhower, that Monty now addressed the military ramifications of the British part of the Ruhr plan.

A Considerable Airborne Drop

On both Monty's and Dempsey's large-scale maps the line of Second Army's next advance was now marked in red, running directly northeast from Antwerp through Eindhoven, Goch, Cleves, Emmerich and Bocholt, then swinging around the north face of the Ruhr short of Osnabrück.

As Monty began to study more detailed maps of Holland and western Germany, however, it became apparent that the river Meuse (or Maas) presented a considerable obstacle, with only one tiny crossing between Venlo and Grave; similarly, between Wesel, on the Ruhr perimeter, and Arnhem far to the north, there was only a single bridge across the Rhine, at Emmerich. With 21st Army Group's bridging material and engineers fully stretched from the Seine to the Somme, the capture of existing bridges was vital—bridges which could not be seized by advancing ground troops, as the retreating Germans would inevitably destroy them. Despite his agreement with Bradley about not employing airborne forces, Monty was thus soon signaling urgently to de Guingand:

> Consider we may want considerable airborne drop to make certain of getting over MEUSE and RHINE. Order BROWNING [Corps Commander, First Allied Airborne Army] to come to see me tomorrow and you come too.

Thus began the inexorable chain of events leading to the disaster at Arnhem—for de Guingand's 21st Army Group Headquarters staff did not favor such a northerly winter thrust line, nor had planned for it.

Monty's Ultimatum

W hile Monty, Dempsey and Browning pored over their maps
of the Ruhr region, there were still 21 Army Group's
coastal tasks to be carried out. Antwerp city fell on 4 September, but the approaches to Antwerp harbor from the North Sea, on
either side of the Scheldt estuary, had yet to be captured, and there
was a whole German army retreating along the coast—as Monty was
well aware. "It is estimated that there are some 150,000 Germans
north of the general line ANTWERP LILLE BETHUNE HESDIN but
the bottle is now corked," he maintained in his next nightly telegram
to the CIGS, "and they will not be able to get out. A great many prisoners are being taken every day by every unit and one Corps today
took 10,000."

All this would take time and troops, however.

With such important military obligations to be met on the coast,
why then did Monty become obsessed by the notion of a unilateral
British thrust through the lowlands, at a time when Bradley's interest
in the Ruhr was, at best, halfhearted?

The truth is, Monty found it impossible to step down in rank and
busy himself with limited Allied objectives at the very moment the
Allies should, in his view, be harvesting the fruits of their great victory
in Normandy. Without the Ruhr, the Germans were finished. "You will
have got my M523 giving my plans for future action," he signaled to
Brooke. "The only addition to that is that I am planning a big airborne
drop to secure the bridges over the RHINE and MEUSE ahead of my
thrust." Apart from planning to detach "one division, or if necessary a
Corps, to turn northwards towards ROTTERDAM and AMSTER-
DAM," he was not planning on giving any extra support to his coastal responsibility. His eyes remained glued to the German industrial
heartland.

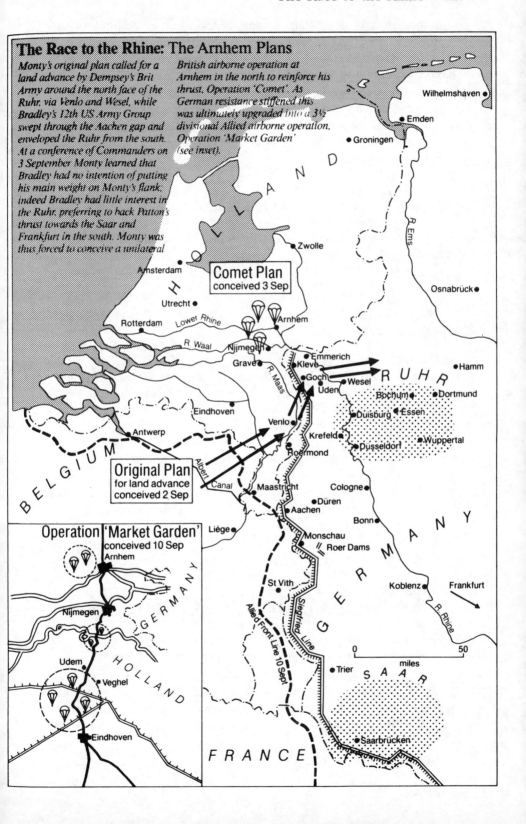

The Race to the Rhine: The Arnhem Plans

Monty's original plan called for a land advance by Dempsey's Brit Army around the north face of the Ruhr, via Venlo and Wesel, while Bradley's 12th US Army Group swept through the Aachen gap and enveloped the Ruhr from the south. At a conference of Commanders on 3 September Monty learned that Bradley had no intention of putting his main weight on Monty's flank; indeed Bradley had little interest in the Ruhr, preferring to back Patton's thrust towards the Saar and Frankfurt in the south. Monty was thus forced to conceive a unilateral

British airborne operation at Arnhem in the north to reinforce his thrust, Operation 'Comet'. As German resistance stiffened this was ultimately upgraded into a 3½ divisional Allied airborne operation, Operation 'Market Garden' (see inset).

Wilhelmshaven

Emden

Groningen

HOLLAND

R. Ems

Osnabrück

Zwolle

Comet Plan
conceived 3 Sep

Amsterdam

Utrecht

Arnhem

Lower Rhine

Rotterdam

R. Waal

Nijmegen

Emmerich

Hamm

Grave

Kleve

R. Maas

Goch

Wesel

RUHR

Uden

Bochum

Dortmund

Eindhoven

Duisburg Essen

Venlo

Krefeld

Wuppertal

Antwerp

Roermond

Düsseldorf

BELGIUM

Albert

Original Plan
for land advance
conceived 2 Sep

Canal

Maastricht

Cologne

Düren

Liège

Aachen

Bonn

Operation 'Market Garden'
conceived 10 Sep

Monschau

Roer Dams

Arnhem

GERMANY

St Vith

Siegfried Line

Koblenz

Frankfurt

Nijmegen

R. Rhine

Udem

HOLLAND

Veghel

0   50

miles

Trier

SAAR

Allied Front Line 10 Sept

Eindhoven

Saarbrücken

FRANCE

The breach between Monty's Tactical and Main Headquarters now became a chasm. Main Headquarters, Monty claimed, was out of touch with the operational picture. The Antwerp approaches and the Channel ports would in any case take weeks to open, even when captured. If the Germans were to be defeated and the Ruhr seized in 1944, there was not a moment to lose. Indeed, anxious lest the last chance of quick success be prejudiced by lack of supplies, Monty next day signaled an historic ultimatum to Eisenhower, his new field Commander-in-Chief:

I consider we have now reached a stage where one really powerful and full blooded thrust toward BERLIN is likely to get there and thus end the German war.

We have not enough maintenance resources for two full blooded thrusts.

The selected thrust must have all the maintenance resources it needs without any qualification and any other operation must do the best it can with what is left over.

There are only two possible thrusts, one via the RUHR and the other via METZ and the SAAR.

In my opinion the thrust likely to give the best and quickest results is the northern one via the RUHR.

Time is vital and the decision regarding the selected thrust must be made at once. . . . If we attempt a compromise solution and split our maintenance resources so that neither thrust is full blooded we will prolong the war.

An Uncomfortable Quandary

What Monty did *not* explain to the Supreme Commander was that he was no longer intending to smash his way to the Ruhr and Berlin via the Aachen gap, as had been the stated axis of his forty-division plan on 17 August. His new thrust was projected way to the north of Aachen, routed on a lowland axis which, though it promised to bypass the enemy's Siegfried Line (which ended at Wesel), had already been rejected as unsuitable by Monty's own planners: a route, in the words of Monty's chief planner in his August report, bisected by "numerous rivers" and beset by a "maze of inundatable areas."

In the urgency of the moment, however, such autumnal considerations were considered irrelevant. Despite the fact that he had made no effort to speak to Eisenhower since 19 August, Monty now wanted a lightning decision—and suggested they meet the next day, 5 September.

General Eisenhower had no wish to meet Monty, however. Since visiting Bradley in the field he had had to make a broadcast to the "peoples of Northwest Europe," consider the next way in which the Italian campaign could assist the Overlord forces, and hold a conference with General Devers to discuss operational control of the Franco-American forces coming up through southern France. He also had to consider a request that one hundred transport planes be sent to the Mediterranean theater for an operation in Greece.

It was in the midst of such discussions that Monty's urgent cable arrived—and placed the Commander-in-Chief in an uncomfortable quandary.

Weighing the Political Aspects

E isenhower was frankly torn over what to do. According to Major Peter Earle, a member of Brooke's staff who dined with Strong a few days later, when Monty's telegram was received by Eisenhower "it was read out by Bedell Smith to a small meeting consisting of Freddy Morgan, Humphrey Gale (P [supply planning]), Strong (I[ntelligence]), Jock Whiteley (O[perations]). Each in turn was asked to comment on it."

Despite what would later be concocted in the memoirs and accounts of the various senior officers concerned, Major Earle's diary entry was hauntingly clear: "Strong voted strongly for one army to go with 21 Army Group to make a strong thrust through Belgium to the Rhine."

Strong, though a reputed coward, was no fool. According to Earle's diary, Eisenhower had then closeted himself with Strong for an hour, during which "Ike showed him a telegram from Stimson [U.S. Secretary of State for War] urging him to take control.

" 'What can you do in the face of this?' he [Eisenhower] said."

Like it or not, Eisenhower *had* to take into account the political ramifications of every decision he made—"Ike has to weigh the political aspects"—but was now cornered. To give top priority to Monty's northern thrust—and to put Monty in charge of both British and American contingents—would, Eisenhower feared, incur the wrath of Stimson in Washington, as well as Bradley and Patton. His only answer, therefore, was to proceed with *both* thrusts, keeping them apart, north and south of the Ardennes, and himself in command. "He wants both armies to strike Germany together," Earle summarized.

Fearing Monty's response, however, Eisenhower ignored Monty's invitation to meet on 5 September. Instead he told Bedell Smith to draft a written reply to Monty. This Bedell Smith did, and after Eisenhower had gone over it carefully, it was sent by secret cipher to Monty's Tactical Headquarters later that day.

Vital to Stop Monty

E quivocal and statesmanlike, the new signal began by saying that, although Eisenhower liked Monty's conception of a "powerful and full blooded thrust towards Berlin," he did not agree that it should be initiated at this moment "to the exclusion of all other maneuver." Eisenhower's official SHAEF policy had been formally set out in a directive the day before. Both the Ruhr and the Saar were considered the chief targets of the Allied advance—but until Le Havre and Antwerp harbors were operating there was "no question," he emphasized, "of a thrust to Berlin."

Nevertheless, Eisenhower did attempt to soften the blow. Ultimate priority had always been given to the Ruhr thrust, he now claimed. Not only was the new First Allied Airborne Army instructed to operate in support of Monty's Army Group of the North, but "locomotives and rolling stock are today being allocated on the basis of this priority to maintain the momentum of the advance of your forces, and those of Bradley northwest of the Ardennes [towards Aachen]."

Had Monty met Eisenhower in person that day, and had Monty's relationship with Eisenhower been different, the tragedy of Arnhem might never have occurred, for it is clear from the diary of Eisenhower's aide, Lieutenant Commander Butcher, that Eisenhower was impressed by the positive response of his senior advisers to Monty's suggested marriage of British and American armies in advancing upon the Ruhr, north of the Ardennes, even though he was loath to hold back Patton. Not having attended Monty's council of war on 3 September, however, Eisenhower was still under the impression—as most of the staff at SHAEF and even Monty's Main Headquarters had been—that the major axis of advance upon the Ruhr would be *via Aachen*, and *could perhaps be tied in with Patton's thrust to Metz*. In an office memorandum on 5 September, in fact, Eisenhower noted that "from the beginning of this campaign I have always visualized that as soon as substantial destruction of the enemy forces in France could be accomplished, we should advance rapidly on the Rhine by pushing through the Aachen gap in the north and the Metz gap in the south. The virtue of this movement is that it takes advantage of all existing lines of communication in the advance towards Germany and brings the southern force on the Rhine at Coblenz, practically on the flank of the forces that would advance straight eastward through Aachen."

If Eisenhower had "always visualized" such an advance, however, he had failed to convey it to his field commanders. The week before, such a strategy might well have recommended itself to all parties, British and American. Now, however, it was now almost too late. The field commanders had made up their minds to go their separate ways—and Monty's new way was off around the north side of the Ruhr, beyond the Siegfried Line, across "innumerable water obstacles."

It was vital to stop Monty. But Eisenhower couldn't: not only was he unaware of Monty's new axis, but he was afraid to meet Monty in person and be insulted by the new field marshal.

History, military history, was being subverted by Monty's unfortunate character.

Berlin in Three Weeks

Incarcerated in his ironically named Villa Montgomery by the Atlantic near Granville, Eisenhower thus attempted, like a juggler, to keep all his torches in the air—without realizing the Allied offensive towards Germany was now being split into *three*, apart from the numerous subsidiary attacks, from Brest to the Channel ports, and with Devers' army group still making its way northwards up the Rhône valley.

Could any one of the three main Allied thrusts into Germany now succeed, though, given the critical resupply position in the first week of September 1944? Monty, with his ruthless battlefield realism and experience, felt they were in danger of failing, as they had failed the previous year in Italy, under Eisenhower's overall command.

Order must be restored to the battlefield, Monty reasoned. Bradley's 8 U.S. Corps investing Brest, for instance, had been issued with almost a million gallons of petrol in the first days of September—while Patton's recce columns were starved, and Monty was grounding whole divisions in both Second British and First Canadian Armies for lack of fuel. To King George VI, Monty reiterated his belief that only one thrust could prosper.

> Our great Allies are very "nationally minded," and it is election year in the States; the Supreme Commander is an American; I fear we may take the wrong decision. I am throwing all my weight and influence into the contest; but fear of American public opinion may cause us to take the wrong decision.

Certainly, without airborne help Monty could not hope to reach and cross the Rhine north of the Ruhr in the immediate future. However, it was proving impossible to drop those airborne troops close to the Ruhr, since the RAF, as Monty later confided to Chester Wilmot, was worried by the density of German antiaircraft fire in the vicinity of the Ruhr. Thus if Second Army attempted to seize a Rhine crossing at Wesel, as planned, the unarmed troop-carrying planes would be easy prey to the Ruhr batteries (Wesel was a bare fifteen miles from Essen). General Browning had therefore argued it would be best to strike further north, following the main road network via Grave and Nijmegen and seizing Arnhem itself—thus taking the operation out of reach of German antiaircraft artillery and putting it within supporting distance of fighters and fighter-bombers based in England.

Having still not heard from Eisenhower's headquarters, Monty therefore signaled his interim plan to the CIGS on the night of 5 September:

The advance of Second Army northeastwards towards the Rhine will begin on 7 September from LOUVAIN and ANTWERP in cooperation with airborne forces which will be dropped that evening to secure the RHINE bridges. A very limiting factor in the progress of this thrust is going to be maintenance and transport. I have as yet no reply from Eisenhower to my telegram yesterday regarding allotting all available resources to one selected thrust.

Eisenhower's silence was worrying. To Major General "Simbo" Simpson, the Director of Military Operations at the War Office, Monty wrote the same day: "We have reached a vital moment in the war and if we now take the right decision we could be in Berlin in 3 weeks and the German war would be over." In a postscript he added: "I fear very much that we shall have a compromise, and so prolong the war."

Already the momentum of the great race from Normandy was petering out. Although 11th Armoured Division had captured Antwerp intact, all bridges across the Albert Canal were blown, and the small bridgehead established by the Guards Armoured Division was being resolutely counterattacked. The tide of victory had taken the Allies almost within reach of the Rhine—but with three competing thrust lines and a new Allied Commander-in-Chief in the field, Monty could not conceal his growing feeling that Eisenhower would make the "wrong decision."

In the event, Eisenhower did—though it would be Monty's thrust he backed!

A Sense of Foreboding

That Monty was driven to the brink of despair in these first days of September is well illustrated by the story of his treatment of his subordinate General Crerar. Crerar had arrived at Dempsey's headquarters too late for the crucial conference of Allied army and army group commanders on 3 September, and was subsequently driven to Monty's nearby Tactical Headquarters at Conty, near Amiens, for one of the most abrasive interviews Monty ever conducted in the field. As Crerar noted in his diary, "the Field Marshal addressed me abruptly, asking me why I had not turned up at the meeting, in accordance with his instructions." When Crerar attempted to explain about a memorial parade in Dieppe, to remember the Canadian soldiers killed in the abortive raid of 1942, Monty cut him short. "The C-in-C intimated that he was not interested in my explanation," Crerar recorded in his diary, adding Monty's statement that "the Canadian aspect of the Dieppe ceremonial was of no importance compared to getting on with the war."

Vain, boastful, proud, but every inch a soldier, Monty was trying, by supreme effort of will, to control himself. Nevertheless his frustration at the lack of decisive command from above was driving him to the point at which—like Patton—he was capable of impetuous and potentially damaging acts.

To Crerar, Monty soon sent a note of apology. But at heart he was full of anxiety: a sense of foreboding that grew the worse when, on 7 September, he heard from Major Bigland, his liaison officer with 12th Army Group, that General Bradley planned to site his next headquarters not on the route to the Ruhr, but well to the south, at Metz: the route to the Saar.

Canceling the Party

Monty's isolation at his new Tactical Headquarters near the Dutch border was compounded by the fact that, as in August, there was no one to advise him from London. Once again Churchill and his Army, Navy and Air Force Chiefs of Staff were traveling abroad: this time to a summit conference with their American counterparts in Quebec.

Like Monty, Eisenhower had to conduct the northwest Europe campaign without guidance from above. Torn between personalities and priorities, he procrastinated. Had he now unequivocally ordered Monty to secure, as first priority, the Channel ports and the surrender of the 150,000 estimated enemy soldiers ringed by the First Canadian and Second British Armies, Monty would without doubt have obeyed. Instead, Eisenhower sent his cable of 5 September calling for seizure of the Ruhr *and* the Saar *and* Brest *and* Le Havre *and* Antwerp port (a long signal which arrived in two parts at Monty's headquarters on 7 and 9 September)—and then ignored the issue for a further five days!

If this was great battlefield leadership, Monty could only shake his head in disbelief. Each day he became more perplexed. Given the current supply crisis, he had agreed with Bradley it would be better to use Allied troop-carrying air transport to maintain the momentum of advance. This advance was, however, now beginning to meet fierce resistance. Those Germans compressed against the coast were far from surrendering. "It looks as if the Germans will hold on the line BRUGES–GHENT," Monty reported to the CIGS in his nightly telegram on 7 September, adding that "on Second Army front the enemy is offering very determined resistance in the northern outskirts of ANTWERP and along the general line of the ALBERT CANAL from ANTWERP to MAASTRICHT." To Eisenhower he therefore appealed for increased supply allocation: "my maintenance is stretched to the limit . . . my transport is based on operating 150 miles from my ports and at present I am over 300 miles from BAYEUX. . . . It is clear therefore that based as I am at present I cannot capture the RUHR." Once again he asked whether "it be possible for you to come and see me."

Because of an Allied victory parade in Paris in which he wished to participate on 8 September, however, Eisenhower felt unable to obige. Moreover the following day he traveled in the opposite direction, to Brittany, to visit 8 U.S. Corps headquarters outside Brest, subsequently staying overnight with General Bradley, at the latter's rear headquarters at Versailles.

In growing frustration Monty therefore shelved the British airborne drop at Arnhem—to the chagrin of Browning and the parachute troops of 1st British Airborne Division and the Polish Air Brigade. It was the *seventeenth* operation planned by 1st British Airborne Division—and the tempers of the men were becoming distinctly frayed, as a divisional ditty, circulated at the time, well illustrated:

> Come stand to your glasses steady
> Here's a toast to the men of the sky.
> To the First (British) Airborne Division
> Past masters at how to stand by.
> (Theirs not to reason for why!)

> The number of bum operations
> For which they've prepared since D-Day
> Would require a mathematician
> With Slide-rule, Slidex and maphy.
> (A month of brain storms anyway!)
> . . .

> *Conclusion*
> And now that the whole thing is over,
> Now that the party is cancelled once more,
> Signal "Finis" from Tarrant to Dover,
> Then collapse in a heap on the floor,
> (Cursing blindly the whole Airborne Corps.)

Arnhem—or Cologne?

W hile the paratroopers cursed, imagining the war would shortly be won without them, the prospect of a successful strike into Germany was in fact becoming hourly less certain. Impotently, Monty watched while Bradley transferred further First U.S. Army troops south for his Metz thrust, and divided his supply fifty-fifty between his two American thrusts, as Monty learned from Major Bigland.

Short of transport and troops, facing growing enemy resistance, and with a Commander-in-Chief who refused either to meet or command him, Monty was tempted to abandon his notion of a unilateral thrust to the Ruhr via Arnhem. On 9 September, not having seen Eisenhower now for fifteen days (and that "only for 10 minutes"), Monty put off his airborne drop on Arnhem for the foreseeable future. "Second Army are meeting with very determined resistance on the ALBERT CANAL line and rapid progress here cannot now be expected," he cabled to the CIGS. "The airborne drop in the ARNHEM area on the RHINE has now been postponed for the present."

Dempsey, in his diary that night, certainly wondered whether the whole notion of a British northern pincer should be shut down, putting instead all British effort alongside Hodges' Aachen axis:

> Owing to our maintenance situation, we will not be in a position to fight a real battle for perhaps ten days or a fortnight. Are we right to direct Second Army to ARNHEM, or would it be better to hold a LEFT flank along the ALBERT canal, and strike due EAST, towards COLOGNE [south of the Ruhr] in conjunction with First Army?

This was a profound and penetrating question. Meanwhile, the port of Le Havre was still not in Canadian hands. Boulogne, Calais and Dun-

kirk were also uncaptured, and would probably "require to be methodically reduced," as Monty explained to Brooke. The surrounded Germans on the Bruges–Ghent coast were even counterattacking. It
seemed—particularly after hearing "the left two corps of First U.S.
Army have very little opposition but they cannot get on as they are
short of petrol"—that Monty might indeed be better to cancel the
Ruhr thrust altogether and concentrate upon the Belgian and
Dutch coast—particularly in view of Germany's latest secret weapon: the V-2.

Eisenhower—Completely out of Touch

On the afternoon of 9 September a special cable arrived from
the War Office, sent by the VCIGS, General Nye, in the absence of Field Marshal Brooke. Its text ran:

> Two rockets so called V.2 landed in England yesterday. Believed to have
> been fired from areas near ROTTERDAM and AMSTERDAM.
>   Will you please report most urgently by what approximate date you
> consider you can rope off the Coastal area contained by ANTWERP–
> UTRECHT–ROTTERDAM. When this area is in our hands the threat
> from this weapon will probably have disappeared.

The V-2, a German ballistic missile fired from mobile—and thus
undetectable—rocket launchers, had long been expected. Now it was
a reality.

Rotterdam and Amsterdam lay due north of Antwerp. Again, Monty
and Dempsey returned to their maps. By striking north from Eindhoven to Arnhem, and then to the Zuider Zee, 21st Army Group would
be in a position to "rope off" the whole of Holland, including the
150,000 fleeing German troops *and* the crucial V-2 bomb sites. But
could 21 Army Group—with one corps still stranded on the Seine for

lack of fuel—hope to reach Rotterdam *and* strike north of the Ruhr without more troops and priority in Allied resupply? To Nye Monty thus signaled back:

> As things stand at present it may take up to two weeks but very difficult to give accurate estimate. There are aspects of the present situation which cause me grave concern and these are first the present system of command of the land battle and secondly the admin situation. My letter being sent by DAWNAY will give you all the facts. These matters affect the time we will take to do what you want.

Monty's letter, when it arrived in London, was starkly realistic. "The situation is NOT good," Monty admitted; "the Bosch is firming up on the Albert Canal; Second Army will now have to bring 8 Corps up from the Seine; we shall change over from a petrol war to an ammunition war, involving more delay.

"I have no power of operational direction or control over the U.S. Army on my right; the whole Northern thrust should really be under MY COMMAND. The U.S. Troops on my right have no resistance in front of them but they cannot get on because they have no petrol!! The whole show is lamentable. . . . I shall go on hammering at it myself—until I go mad."

Meanwhile, to Field Marshal Sir Alan Brooke Monty also penned a long and bitter letter, which vividly encapsulated his frustration:

> My dear CIGS,
>   When you visited me on Tuesday 29 August you asked me if I was quite happy about the general war situation, and the future possibilities. I said that I had managed to reach a compromise solution with Eisenhower; an American Army of nine divisions was to move forward on my right flank, and I was to have the power of operational control and co-ordination of the whole northern thrust.

Such control had never been given, however—and Monty listed, day by day, the disagreements that had arisen, and the signals sent between the protagonists. As in Italy in 1943 there had been no "grip":

> It became clear during the advance northwards that a very tight grip was necessary over the general battle that was going on.
>   There was no such grip.
>   Bradley's HQ moved eastwards.
>   My HQ moved northwards.
>   Bradley's left Army (First US Army under Hodges) was moving on my

right flank. But I had to effect coordination through Bradley, and had no communication with him except W/T.

Eisenhower's HQ were at Granville, on the west coast of the Cherbourg peninsula.

At the Lailly conference on 3 September, Bradley had insisted that three of Hodges' nine American divisions should advance south of the Ardennes, flanking Patton. If he seriously wished to seize the Ruhr, Monty had had, therefore, to conceive his own plan for the advance to the Rhine. This he had done, as part of a supposed British-American pincer attack—but even this seemed doomed to failure when SHAEF did not allot overall priority to the Ruhr thrust in terms of supplies, and Bradley decided to transfer all further troops to Patton for the Metz attack. Monty concluded wearily:

> Eisenhower has apparently decided to capture the RUHR and the SAAR, and then develop one or both thrusts to Berlin. He keeps saying that he has ordered that the northern thrust to the RUHR is to have priority; but he has NOT ordered this.
>
> The staff at SHAEF, and all the Americans generally, want to scale down the RUHR thrust and give more impetus to the SAAR thrust; and this they are doing whatever Eisenhower may say.

If the proposed British northern pincer around the Ruhr was being starved, so too was the American southern pincer, he lamented. "On my right flank the two Corps of First U.S. Army that are north of the ARDENNES (7 and 19 Corps) were stopped yesterday as they had no petrol; today they have been given enough to move one B[riga]de Group forward a few miles; there are very few enemy in front of them and this is where we want to push on hard," he remarked with feeling, adding two further emphasis strokes in the margin. For if Hodges could penetrate to the Ruhr via the Aachen gap, the success of the northern pincer seemed assured, since the Germans had not the troops currently to defend both the north and south faces of their industrial heartland.

"Meanwhile, away in the east," Monty reported, "Third U.S. Army under Patton is meeting heavy resistance and has been pushed back in some places."

The situation cried out for robust and energetic leadership in the field. But this, thanks to Monty's prickly and insulting character, was not forthcoming:

> Eisenhower has taken personal command of the land armies; he sits back at GRANVILLE and has no communication to his commanders except W/T, and this takes over 24 hours to reach him!

He would be closer to the battle in flying distance if he was in London; and he would have better communications.

He is completely out of touch with what is going on; he tries to win the war by issuing long telegraphic directives.

Eisenhower himself does not really know anything about the business of fighting the Germans; he has not got the right sort of chaps on his staff for the job, and no one there understands the matter.

No C-in-C of the Land Armies

Monty's condemnation of his commanding officer in the field was, of course, reprehensible (though Eisenhower did much the same about Monty in his private letters and signals to Marshall, and in the memoranda he dictated to be included in Lieutenant Commander Butcher's desk diary at Granville). It certainly smacked of disloyalty—yet the force of Monty's military logic was undeniable:

> I very much fear that we shall NOT get either the RUHR or the SAAR quickly. In fact if things go drifting along much longer like this, then we shall not get them in time to finish this war off quickly.
>
> I am definitely convinced that if this show had been gripped tightly all the time, and a firm grip had been kept on the operational conduct of the war, we could have followed up our advantage.
>
> We could have thrust quickly and with great strength to the RUHR. We should have put everything we had into one terrific blow, and smashed right through.
>
> Just when a firm grip was needed, there was no grip.

"The 'command' factor has broken down," Monty concluded. It marked the end of any hopes of the war ending before winter:

In the Battle of Normandy, and up to the Seine, the operational command of the land war was vested in one commander. Now there is no C-in-C of the land armies, the Supreme Commander acts in this capacity, in addition to his other duties.

I do not know what he does in actual fact, but he seems to have no time to spare for the land battle; this is not surprising, as it is a whole time job for one man.

In fact unless something can be done about it pretty quickly, I do not see this war ending as soon as one had hoped. It may well now go on into the winter.

I hope the above will put you fully into what is going on.

Thus Monty ended his letter—adding: "I do not know if you can do anything but I thought you should know the facts."

Major Earle, Brooke's military assistant, noted in his diary on 10 September: "The most poignant thing today was a long letter to the CIGS from Monty. . . . By and large it says that he is at the limit of his maintenance and no-one seems to be helping. He has no command over I U.S. Army except through 12 Army Gp which is only just in W/T [radio] range. I U.S. Army has nothing in front of it north of the Ardennes but has no petrol. Patton has got a bloody nose at Metz. Ike insists that he has the maintenance resources to push on to the Saar and Ruhr simultaneously. Monty says the results of this decision will be that we will take ages to get either and the length of the war will be prolonged into the winter."

It was a most able summary. But whether Monty liked it or not, he was no longer running the war. Eisenhower was.

Brooke's Vision

What Monty, as a battlefield commander, could not see was that coalition warfare *necessitated* compromise and lack of grip at the top, since those leaders most suited to coalition command were of necessity conciliators, such as Eisenhower and Alexander.

Monty certainly recognized how important were Eisenhower's conciliatory talents. As Supreme Commander, Eisenhower possessed powers of leadership and inspiration that Monty genuinely admired. But as Commander-in-Chief in the field of battle General Eisenhower was, Monty felt, proving as disastrous as Lord Gort had been in 1940: both men incapable of higher combat command not from lack of integrity or valor, but by their inability to dominate the battlefield, as well as their failure to operate from first-class mobile headquarters with first-class communications. That Eisenhower believed he could effectively command his armies in the field from headquarters on the Atlantic seaboard of France, barely thirty miles from the Channel Islands, was to Monty the ultimate example of Eisenhower's battlefield incompetence. But what could be done? Field Marshal Brooke was still aboard the *Queen Mary* on his way, with Churchill, to Quebec. Passing on to Brooke a summary of Monty's letter, General Nye remarked presciently: "I suspect Eisenhower doesn't know what his maintenance resources will do and hopes he will be able to bring off both thrusts. If he fails to do so, the war may be prolonged into the Spring."

To Monty, meanwhile, Nye could only declare the impotence of the War Office in Whitehall:

I fully sympathize with you in these difficulties which must seem exasperating. Unfortunately we are NOT fully informed in the WAR OFFICE on the total maintenance resources available to SHAEF and how the remainder of resources are allocated as between the Army GROUPS yourself and BRADLEY. But even if we had full facts about this it would be difficult to intervene with Eisenhower at COS [Chiefs of Staff] level. Indeed it would probably do more harm than good. However much we would like to help therefore there does NOT seem much we can do from here.

Brooke, by contrast, when he received the gist of Monty's letter by special cipher at Quebec, immediately spread out his maps of Belgium, Holland and Germany. He had battled with Churchill in the darkest days of the war, and was battling now with coalition partners whose full cooperation would be essential in first bringing the war against Germany to a successful conclusion, then vanquishing the Japanese, and finally ensuring the Russians did not become too powerful in Europe. Speed, from a strictly soldierly point of view, was being compromised by Eisenhower's failure to command armies as well as he led allies. But speed, in terms of the Anglo-American alliance, was not the critical factor now. The alliance was.

If Eisenhower's inability to exercise decisive field command threatened to prolong the war in Europe by three or even six months, Brooke reasoned, then so be it. Better, he felt, to concentrate upon the ramifications of a long-term campaign: namely the supply factor.

The depth of Brooke's penetrating vision can be gauged by the signal he now sent to Monty via the War Office:

Personal for Field Marshal Montgomery from CIGS:
Looking at operations from this distance it seems to me that early opening of Antwerp and clearance of river Scheldt is likely to be of great importance. Now that Operation COMET [the British airborne drop at Arnhem] is postponed have you considered possibility using your airborne forces or part of these in Walcheren area? This would have further advantage of cutting off further withdrawal 15 [German] Army from their present bridgehead.

Brooke's signal arrived early on the morning of 12 September 1944. But by then, alas, the vacuum left by the postponement of Comet and increasing enemy resistance had been filled.

A Most Important Meeting

Owing to a 9 A.M. conference with Dempsey, Monty had asked Eisenhower to fly to Brussels rather than to Amiens, and it was at the airfield there, on 10 September 1944, that the two Allied commanders met for the first time that month.

Monty had by this time discarded any notion of getting to Berlin in the immediate future. As he said after the war to Chester Wilmot, "I knew now that we could not hope to get much more than a bridgehead beyond the Rhine before the winter, and be nicely poised for breaking out in the New Year."

Tedder confirmed this, when interviewed just after the war by the American Official Historian, Dr. Pogue:

> Monty had no idea of getting on to Berlin from here [Arnhem]. By this time he was ready to settle for a position across the Rhine.

Moreover, in a signal to the British Chief of Air Staff (Air Marshal Portal) immediately after the 10 September meeting, Tedder stated that "the advance to Berlin was not discussed as a serious issue."

What *was* the issue then? As at Lailly, no minutes were kept of the meeting, and Monty even refused to allow General Gale to sit in on the proceedings. To the end of his life Monty remained touchy about it. "This obviously was a most important meeting," Wilmot noted after a talk with Monty in 1946, "for as soon as I mentioned it and asked what took place and mentioned some points that had been discussed, he [Monty] said: 'No one else was there—only Eisenhower and myself.' "

Why should Monty have been so sensitive about the meeting?

The simple reason was that Monty had decided to present Eisenhower with a *fait accompli*. As Monty put it to Wilmot, "we discussed the big picture, the administrative problems . . . the broad strategy . . . not much about Arnhem. That was decided upon *already*."

It was. But, unknown to Eisenhower, the ink on the revised Arnhem operation was but a few hours old.

A Mad Suggestion

T he previous night the sky had been cloudless but cold: weather ideal for the use of airborne forces. In Monty's map lorry, at 9:00 that morning, both Monty and Dempsey had therefore agreed that, as Dempsey recorded in his diary, "in view of increasing strength in the ARNHEM–NIJMEGEN area the employment of one airborne division in this area will not be sufficient. I got from C-in-C his agreement to the use of three airborne divisions."

Thus, instead of redirecting his British forces towards Cologne alongside Hodges' First U.S. Army, as Dempsey had mused the night before, Monty authorized a revival of the air drop on Arnhem; only now, rather than a one-divisional affair, the operation would employ all three Allied parachute divisions currently ready for battle—1st British, 82nd U.S. and 101st U.S. Airborne Divisions. Dempsey left immediately to start planning.

Monty evidently intended to present Eisenhower not with a plan, but with an operation. The midday meeting at Brussels airfield, however, did not start well. Monty, waving a batch of Eisenhower's most recent telegraphic directives, decried the lack of supplies and support for 21st Army Group and referred scathingly to Eisenhower's dispersal of Allied effort.

"Steady Monty, you can't speak to me like that," Eisenhower warned, putting his hand on Monty's knee. *"I'm your boss."*

Monty was forced to apologize.

Like Patton, Monty was in a sense overbidding his hand. By involving the entire Anglo-American airborne army he had hoped to persuade Eisenhower to throw all his weight behind the Ruhr thrust—which Monty insisted should be commanded by one man.

Eisenhower, abashed by Monty's peremptory tone, did not intend to be browbeaten, however. He had come well prepared, knowing that German resistance was stiffening on all combat fronts. Though he authorized the use of First Airborne Army he resolutely refused to give Monty overall command in the north or, indeed, priority of supplies over Patton's attempt to reach the Saar. Logistically Eisenhower now saw no hope of deep incursions into Germany until further Allied ports were opened; it was meanwhile important to get bridgeheads across the Rhine both north *and* south of the Ardennes, he felt. "We must fight with both hands at present, and the moment for the left hook had not come yet," Tedder recorded, "and could not come until Northern Army Group maintenance was based securely on the Channel ports."

It was Monty who thus felt defeated. Only hours previously he had decided to involve the whole of First Allied Airborne Army in a bid to win Eisenhower over to the Ruhr offensive. Instead, while agreeing to a massive Allied air drop at Arnhem, Eisenhower had refused to give complete logistical priority to the Ruhr offensive. "Monty made great play over word 'priority' and insisted that his interpretation of the word implies absolute priority, if necessary to the exclusion of all other operations. Argument on such a basis futile," Tedder commented in his message to Air Marshal Portal. Eisenhower's personal assistant at Granville, Kay Summersby, was more biting: "Monty's suggestion is simple, 'give him everything,' which is mad."

Getting No Further

———————————

Mad or not, Monty signaled despondently to General Nye that evening:

Ike came to see me today at BRUSSELS airport. He is lame and cannot walk and we talked in his plane. I said it was essential he should know my views and the action to be taken was then for him to decide. I gave him my opinion on the need to concentrate on one selected thrust vide my M160 of 4 Sep. He did NOT repeat NOT agree. I said that in para 4 of Part 4 of his 13889 of 5 Sep he stated he had always given and still did give priority to the RUHR and the northern route of advance. He then said that he did not mean priority as absolute priority and could not scale down the SAAR thrust in any way. He said he had not meant what was in the telegram as regards priority for the RUHR thrust.

Everything was very friendly and amicable. But we have got no further. I foresee considerable delay before I can build up enough strength to develop operations northwards with Second Army towards ARNHEM and UTRECHT as I have not the transport to get forward any maintenance and bridging. A great deal of bridging will be required.

No mention was made of the increased Anglo-American scale of the proposed air drop at Arnhem. In fact the whole operation, in the wake of Eisenhower's meeting with Monty, looked like being postponed for weeks—if indeed it took place at all.

The Die Is Cast

"The trouble was that Eisenhower did not know what he should do," Monty later told Chester Wilmot. "He had no experience and no philosophy of battle by which to judge the rival plans. His method was to talk to everyone and then try to work out a compromise solution which would please everyone. He had no plan of his own. He was a sociable chap who liked talking, and he used to go from one HQ to another finding out what his various subordinates thought, instead of going to them and saying—here is the plan, you will do this, and so and so will do that. Eisenhower held conferences to collect ideas; I held conferences to issue orders."

This was the crux of the matter. For good or bad, however, Eisenhower was now the Allied Land Forces Commander-in Chief as well as Supreme Commander, and by failing to adapt himself to this reality, Monty did his cause no good.

Although Monty felt he had failed to convince Eisenhower about the necessity of selecting one thrust and backing it fully, he was in fact mistaken, for his presentation had had far more impact on Eisenhower than Monty believed. Tedder cabled to Portal:

> I feel the discussion cleared the air, though Montgomery will, of course, be dissatisfied in not getting a blank cheque. It will help ensure that the Ruhr thrust does get the proper priority which we all feel it should have.

With Monty in such a demanding mood, no one seems to have dared raise Dempsey's question: should not Second Army support Hodges in an Anglo-American thrust via Aachen and Cologne? Such a proposition would once again have entailed discussion of who should command such a thrust, however, and this Eisenhower was loath to do. Bradley was known not to favor the Ruhr thrust over Patton's to the

Saar; better then, Eisenhower felt, to continue to keep the various Allied armies separate, as he had laid down in August, than risk personal confrontations over command.

Thus the Arnhem die that Monty had cast went unchallenged. Unwittingly, Eisenhower had given the green light to a strategic blunder.

Last Hope of a Quick Bridgehead

Meanwhile, if Eisenhower and his deputy were unwilling to question Monty's ambitious new airborne operation, their staffs were.

Bedell Smith, Eisenhower's chief of staff, expressed deep concern at the implications relating to Antwerp—"restriction of air lift for freight would be very serious, and the airborne operation did not give them a new port, which was an urgent need. This was the fourth time that air lift had been diverted for an operation which so far had not materialised," the minutes of the next day's conference of senior Allied air force commanders recorded. Even Tedder himself concurred, believing that the chance quickly to open the port of Antwerp might already have been "thrown away"—and that there was much to be said for an airborne drop to seize the island of Walcheren, which guarded the Scheldt estuary approach to Antwerp, and "for which the Navy had been pressing."

The wild hopes engendered by the spectacular advance of the armies in the first days of September were now tempered by a realization that the Germans, though fighting on three fronts, were by no means beaten. Military Intelligence pointed to the increasing quality and number of German divisions facing Patton. Though Patton boasted he would break through, the way to the Saar seemed blocked—and on Hodges' front, too, German opposition was stiffening.

Backwards and forwards, the ball was tossed. Monty's Arnhem thrust, though it promised no new port, did at least offer a quick

Rhine bridgehead, bypassing Hitler's recently reinforced Siegfried Line. "After further discussion," the minutes ran, "it was agreed that Operation 'COMET,' if it succeeded in its objective of putting the Army across the Rhine [at Arnhem] and turning the Siegfried Line, would make the most valuable contribution at the present juncture."

It was in this somewhat doleful context that Monty's latest signal was received at Eisenhower's headquarters, announcing the postponement of the revised Allied airborne drop across the Rhine, owing to lack of supplies, for another twelve days.

Instead of seeing in this a sign from the Almighty, Eisenhower caved in. Dispatching his chief of staff for only the second time in the entire campaign since D-Day to see Monty, he told Bedell Smith to give Monty all he asked. Everything. The race to the Rhine was on again.

A Pyrrhic Victory

As Monty excitedly explained to Brooke on the evening of 12 September, his telegram of postponement to Eisenhower had produced "ELECTRIC results":

IKE has given way and he sent BEDELL to see me today.

The SAAR thrust is to be stopped.

Three American divisions are to be grounded and their transport used to give extra maintenance to 21 Army Group.

The whole of the maintenance of 12 Army Group is to be given to First U.S. Army on my right and that army is to cooperate closely with me and I am to be allowed to deal directly with HODGES.

Airborne Army H.Q. had refused my demand for airborne troops to help capture WALCHEREN as not being a suitable job for airborne troops and they are now going to be ordered by IKE to do what I ask.

As a result of these changed conditions I have now fixed D day for operation MARKET previously known as COMET for next Sunday 17 Sept.

So we have gained a great victory. I feel somewhat exhausted by it all but hope we shall now win the war reasonably quickly.

The "electric" results, however, were all to prove illusory. Monty's "great victory" was pyrrhic. The war, far from being won more quickly, would now be won more slowly—and with more loss of life.

The Tail Wagging the Dog

B radley flew to meet Monty the next afternoon, 13 September. What disturbed him now was that the revised plan, employing almost the entire First Allied Airborne Army, threatened to halt the massive airlift of supplies he was receiving. "Opposed to use of airborne effort on Monty's front," his ADC noted that night, "since he feels it will accomplish little that the ground troops could not do."

Whatever Eisenhower might agree with Monty, Bradley remained opposed to a concentrated Allied attack on the Ruhr north of the Ardennes—British or American, or both. His eyes were still on the Saar. His ADC also noted after Bradley's meeting with Monty that Eisenhower was now "anxious that Brad put the main effort with the first [U.S.] army and push on to the north . . . concentrating the bulk of his effort on the left flank of the [12 U.S. Army] group.

"Brad is opposed to this, sensing the possibility of a breakthrough in the V corps sector [south of the Ardennes] where sharp penetrations have already been made, or in the area of the 3rd Army which may then pinch the Ruhr from the south and plunge through to the Rhine. *Ike, however, has his heart set with Monty on main effort to the Rhine.*"

Bradley's response to Monty's northern thrust was thus far from enthusiastic—especially when Monty asked that, to help Dempsey strike faster overland to Arnhem, Hodges' left-hand boundary be moved thirty miles north. "Had I known this gap was going to be created," Bradley reported to Eisenhower, "I would have left 79th Division [moved to Patton's Third Army in the first week of September] with Hodges."

This was unfair, since Monty had objected strongly to the removal of 79th Division at the time. The truth, as Bradley knew, was that Patton's appeals to be allowed to push on to the Rhine via Metz had been too seductive for him to reject—and would not be rejected now.

Whether Monty realized he was being deceived—that Bradley could not resist the temptation to put his weight behind Patton's southern thrust, and that Eisenhower could not resist the temptation to support Bradley, his senior American subordinate—is difficult to know for certain. On 14 September, two days after his "electric" promises of support for Monty's Arnhem thrust, Eisenhower also approved Patton's latest attack towards the Saar. "There is no reason why Patton should not keep acting offensively if the conditions for offensive action are right," he signaled to Bradley—striving to make each of his army group commanders believe he, Eisenhower, was behind his conception of advance.

Monty cannot have been unaware of this. Not only did his liaison officer, Major Bigland, report daily on American plans, order of battle and current fighting, but Bradley himself made no secret of the fact that he was not going to halt Patton in mid-battle. Rather, he assured Monty, he would begin to swing Patton's thrust northwards, once across the Moselle, to reinforce Hodges' assault on the Ruhr:

> As I told you yesterday, he [Patton] will either advance northeast from the vicinity of Metz or I will have him shift one Corps north of the Moselle River.

Patton, of course, did neither. Nor would Bradley permit Monty to deal directly with Hodges—"I will not have the tail wagging the dog," he quipped to Eisenhower's chief of American operations, General Bull, who had come from SHAEF "to discuss the effort of our armies in conjunction with the effort of Montgomery."

In such circumstances it was hardly surprising that Monty's Ruhr thrust became hour by hour a British rather than an Allied one. "Goddamit Brad," remarked Patton, "you kept the [American] flag waving; I'm proud of you."

It was clear that Bradley's long "honeymoon" with Monty was now over. Bradley's ADC noted in his diary of 15 September:

> Brad represents Amerk viewpoint. . . . Monty hopes to control all of effort. Ike apparently unable to say "go to hell" for diplomatic reasons

which are involved. Monty is the darling of the British public, irascible and difficult to work with. . . .

Bull has difficult time trying to get Ike's plan across, everyone worries for fear Ike favors the Brit. too much. . . . Brad and Patton agree neither will be too surprised if we [12th Army Group] are on the Rhine in a week.

When Patton received news, during the Bull conference, that Nancy had fallen to Third U.S. Army, he was cock-a-hoop. " 'Damn! How do you like that. Better congratulate me!' Pleased as punch with effort," Hansen recorded.

As a result, Bradley decided then and there to rescind his order that Patton must halt if by Thursday he was not across the Moselle— "Patton now across the Moselle in force and an earlier decision of the general [Bradley] to call off his effort by Thursday [14 September] evening if he did not force a crossing is now revoked."

Casualties in Third U.S. Army, however, were increasing—indeed had now risen above 30,000 men. Whatever Patton might promise, the hope of Third Army reaching the Rhine within the week would prove as illusory as Monty's hopes in the north.

Part Thirteen

ARNHEM

Tanks cross the Nijmegen bridge, leading to Arnhem, September 1944.

Too Late

M any books would be written about the "epic" of Arnhem. Preparations and operational mistakes would, as in every failure, be exhaustively analyzed and debated. If the presence of two refitting German armored divisions had been properly taken into account in the planning; if ground-to-air radio communications had been better; if the landing grounds had been closer to Arnhem; if troops had been landed on both sides of the Arnhem bridge; if close support by 21 Army Group fighter-bombers from Belgium instead of Britain had been permitted; if the men of General Horrocks' 30 Corps had only got up faster, perhaps . . .

Such speculations are the stuff of military history. Many important historical lessons *were* learned—in fact, Second Army and 21st Army Group were sponsoring reports on the lessons of the battle within days of its end: lessons which were soon assimilated and which affected the mounting of all airborne operations conducted thereafter. Yet the failings in the planning and execution of the battle of Arnhem ought not to blind us to the larger, uncomfortable truth.

The revised airborne landings between Zon and Arnhem, as ordered by Monty on 10 September 1944, did not fail because of the unrecognized presence of German Panzer divisions, or poor radio communications, or bad operational planning, or lack of zeal among the ground formations. It failed because, as in the case of resistance on Patton's front at Metz and Hodges' front at Aachen, it was too late. And, worst of all, in his heart of hearts, Monty knew it.

Getting into Further Difficulties

On 17 September, Monty had received Eisenhower's latest directive, airily reciting the possible thrusts to the German capital that would be mounted once the Allies were "soon" in possession of "the RUHR, the SAAR and the FRANKFURT areas. . . . There is no doubt whatsoever, in my mind, that we should concentrate all our energies and resources on a rapid thrust to Berlin."

Monty was appalled both by Eisenhower's failure to back the northern thrust, as he had promised, to the exclusion of all else, and his evident naïveté about imminent possession of the Ruhr *and* the Saar, let alone Berlin. In a tone of utter resignation Monty had therefore offered to abandon his Ruhr thrust altogether: "If you consider that . . . the proper axis of advance is by FRANKFURT and central Germany, then I suggest that 12 Army Group of three Armies would be used," Monty signaled on 18 September. "21 Army Group would do the best it could with what was left over; or possibly the Second British Army would be wanted in a Secondary role on the left flank of the [American] movement."

Like Patton's "momentous" offer of an end run to the Channel on 23 August, Monty's proposition was sent, however, twenty-four hours too late. The previous morning two columns of aircraft the equivalent of 350 miles long, protected by 1,500 fighters, had made their way across the Channel, and had swung northwards towards the Lower Rhine.

What made the Arnhem operation even more tragic was that Monty's own staff were largely against it. Monty's chief of operations, Brigadier Belchem, disliked the narrowness of the thrust to Arnhem, along the low, polder ground in which all advance was necessarily canalized by the Dutch waterways. Like Dempsey's own staff, Belchem would have preferred a thrust towards Wesel—if necessary without airborne forces if the airmen would not "play." Monty's chief of plans, Brigadier Richardson, did not even know of the revised Arnhem drop until several days after it had been agreed on; his recommendation had *always* been for a concerted Allied drive through the Aachen gap, not through the lowlands of Holland, with their "maze of inundatable areas" and "numerous rivers." Monty's chief of Intelligence, Brigadier Williams, was disturbed by increasing indications of German Panzer divisions refitting in the area—an area already known to have been put under the command of the German Parachute Army, under the redoubtable General Kurt Student, airborne conqueror of Crete. Colonel Poole, deputy chief of administration and supplies, was worried by the lack of port capacity to nourish such an ambitious British thrust. Finally, Monty's chief of staff, Freddie de Guingand, was so worried he telephoned from his hospital bed in England to warn Monty that increasing enemy resistance and logistical dependence on the winning of more deep-water ports made such a unilateral thrust a very doubtful proposition, even if it succeeded in reaching Arnhem.

Isolated at his forward Tactical Headquarters, however, Monty had refused to listen to the protests of his Main Headquarters staff. The atmosphere at Tac HQ was best described by Major Odgers, the officer in charge of the operations staff, in the brief chronicle he wrote shortly after the war:

> The speed of events ever since the crossing of the SEINE had given an almost unreal quality to life in which nothing now seemed impossible. This fantastic quality still persisted as the Dakotas and gliders roared ceaselessly overhead and reports came back of Eindhoven's capture and the great river bridges secured.

On the night of 18 September, with news of the capture of Eindhoven, Monty still had no idea that his plan was in jeopardy—though a note of realism did begin to temper his signals:

> Guards Armoured Division have now joined up with the 101 Airborne Division who extend from EINDHOVEN as far north as VEGHEL. . . .
> This advance is being made on a single road and movement by wheeled and tracked vehicles off the road is extremely difficult owing to the low lying nature of the country which is intersected by ditches and dykes and which has been made very wet by the recent heavy rain.

The rain in fact had sundered the planned second lift of troops and supplies to 1st British Airborne and 82nd U.S. Airborne Divisions. From the former, at Arnhem, there was, ominously, no news at all;

from 82nd Airborne, on the Maas and Waal, there was reassuring information that the crossing at Grave was in Allied hands, and the bridge at Nijmegen, though not yet captured, was intact. "Operations are going well on the front of Second Army," Monty overconfidently reported to Brooke—but given the fierce German resistance and the narrowness of the corridor General Horrocks had achieved, it was too early to crow.

The following evening (19 September), as Allied ground troops penetrated as far as the Waal at Nijmegen and radio contact was finally established with 1st Airborne Division west of Arnhem, Monty turned his attention to the flanks of his thrust: "Second Army is engaged in widening the corridor beginning at the south end and good progress is being made in this task by 8 Corps on the eastern flank and 12 Corps on the western flank."

Such progress was, however, increasingly hard-won—and by the fourth day of the offensive Monty's optimism regarding a breakthrough began to fade. True, his forces were across the southern fork of the Rhine, the Waal, after 82nd Airborne Division's brilliant capture of Nijmegen bridge; true, the Polish Parachute Brigade had dropped at Driel, south of the lower Rhine at Arnhem, and it looked as though there was "a good sporting chance of getting the bridge at ARNHEM" itself. But the bridges, however luring, were not the true objectives of the battle. The target remained the Ruhr. 30 Corps had assembled some 2,300 vehicles and some 9,000 engineers to transport and erect bridges if the airborne divisions were unable to secure the existing bridges intact. "The corridor running northwards through Eindhoven is still a bit narrow and is not yet very secure and has been twice broken today by the enemy a few miles north of Eindhoven. But this situation will improve as 8 Corps and 12 Corps make progress northwards on the flanks of the corridor," Monty assured the CIGS. But would the two flanking corps make such progress? And if opposition at Arnhem was so great, would it not be wiser to start swinging eastwards towards the Ruhr at Wesel, without bothering about Arnhem?

Dempsey's diary at Second Army recorded his apparent satisfaction with the advance of his flanking corps at this stage of the battle. Monty, writing to his son's guardians, again boasted of the "superb new portrait by James Gunn" which the artist had recently painted at his headquarters and which would undoubtedly "create a tremendous sensation at next year's Academy." Dispatching largess in the form of Brussels lace for Mrs. Reynolds, cigarettes for Major Reynolds, and chocolate for his son, David, Monty also referred to the way his "latest operations" were "developing very satisfactorily."

Yet at the back of Monty's mind was the nagging fear that, even if he reached Arnhem, the necessary resources to exploit the bridgehead and seize the Ruhr would not materialize. "My administrative situation is beginning to cause me some concern and the tonnage promised by rail has not so far been forthcoming," he informed Brooke on 20 September. He had already summoned Eisenhower's chief administrative officer to come and see him. When Gale arrived on 21 September bearing Eisenhower's response to Monty's letter of 18 September recommending that either the Saar or the Ruhr thrust be pursued, but not both, Monty's doubts became feverish. For Eisenhower was still referring to an Anglo-American drive to Berlin, to be mounted by Second British Army and First U.S. Army, while insisting that Patton's Third U.S. Army, reinforced by Simpson's Ninth U.S. Army (from Brest), continue its Metz advance in order to reinforce the Berlin drive after taking the Saar.

To Monty the soldier, this notion of a 250-mile-wide Allied offensive was anathema, as he signaled back to the Supreme Commander's new headquarters at Versailles:

> I cannot agree that our concepts are the same and I am sure you would wish me to be quite frank.
>
> I have always said stop the right and go on with the left but the right has been allowed to go on so far that it has outstripped its maintenance and we have lost flexibility. In your letter you still want to go on further with your right and you state in your para 6 that ALL of BRADLEY's Army Group will move forward sufficiently etc. I would say that the right flank of 12 Army Group should be given a very direct order to halt and if this order is not obeyed we shall get into further difficulties.

By "further difficulties" Monty meant the rapidly darkening operational picture.

All Ranks Exhausted

B y 23 September, Monty was aware of the perilous condition of
1st British Airborne Division—for General Urquhart's chief of
staff had managed to get back across the lower Rhine and had
reported the division's plight to Browning's staff in person. Although
one brigade had been forced to surrender in Arnhem itself, the rest of
the division held a bridgehead on the north bank of the river at
Oosterbeck. To Brooke, therefore, Monty declared his aims that night
as twofold: to cross the river with Horrocks' 30 Corps at Oosterbeck
to reinforce Urquhart's bridgehead *as if threatening to seize Arnhem;*
meanwhile to turn O'Connor's 8 Corps *eastwards towards the Ruhr*
while the Germans dealt with Horrocks' Arnhem threat in the north.

Although a few hundred gallant Poles of the Polish Parachute Brigade did get across the river to reinforce Urquhart, the crossing was
overlooked by German gun positions. "Last night reinforcements from
the Polish Para Bde were passed across the river but suffered considerable casualties in so doing as the river is swept by machine gun fire
from both flanks," Monty sadly explained to Brooke. "A further attempt is being made tonight to get an infantry brigade of 43 Div over
the river but it is a very tricky business as we have not sufficient troops
up there on a wide front. If we suffer heavy casualties tonight in trying
to get across the Neder Rijn I shall probably give it up and withdraw
1 Airborne Div south of the river. This decision will be taken tomorrow morning."

It was the beginning of the end of a ferocious battle, waged behind
enemy lines with extraordinary courage. Many writers have questioned
why Monty, so strict in his insistence on remaining on the field of battle rather than attending SHAEF meetings way back in France, should
have failed to visit General Horrocks during the battle for Arnhem, or
to put personal "ginger" into the forces struggling to relieve Urquhart.

Certainly Monty was distracted by the plethora of messages and signals incurred by his dispute over strategy with Eisenhower; but the real reason why he did not personally go up to Nijmegen was straightforward. He sent his planning chief to visit the front personally and report back to him; for thirty-six hours Brigadier Richardson was cut off by a German counterattack, which severed the road to Arnhem. Similarly, General Dempsey's chief of staff also flew in; his aircraft was shot down and he signaled to Dempsey on 22 September that Horrocks considered a bridgehead west of Arnhem "will be difficult with present resources. . . . Was shot down today. Do NOT you fly tomorrow."

Given Horrocks' worrying signals from the bridgehead all day on 22 September, Dempsey had had in fact no other recourse but to give O'Connor's 8 Corps the task of holding open Horrocks' lines of communication. Yet this was the very corps intended to drive eastwards to the Ruhr at Wesel! Worse still, if Horrocks did manage to cross the Neder Rijn and relieve 1st Airborne Division, he would need, as he signaled urgently on 23 September, a further infantry division "for subsequent exploitation"—a division Dempsey simply did not have. The only reserve which could be fed in was 52nd Air-Landing Brigade—but Browning reported that Grave airfield could only take thirty-six aircraft per hour, and the division required some 2,000 lifts. At a moment when Browning needed vital air resupply for his existing airborne forces, this was clearly impossible.

Later that evening Browning found a clearing which could be made into an airfield. Dempsey approved—but the sands were running out. Strong enemy resistance on the west flank of the Arnhem corridor was making the task of Dempsey's third corps—Lieutenant General Ritchie's 12 Corps—as difficult as that of the other two. Whatever Monty—who lunched with Bradley on 24 September—might agree about sidestepping Hodges' First U.S. Army to relieve 8 Corps in the field for a British thrust eastwards to the Ruhr, it was impossible for Dempsey to disengage O'Connor's divisions from the battle for such an offensive until the corridor up to Nijmegen was secure.

Bradley left Monty in the afternoon—"We have arranged everything satisfactorily," Monty cabled to Brooke—but by 5 P.M. Dempsey was again recording in his diary that the Nijmegen corridor had been cut between St. Oedenrode and Vegel: an interdiction that this time was to last two critical days.

At 9 P.M. on 24 September, Monty's Tac Headquarters received a despairing signal from Urquhart, still holding out in a small bridgehead north of the Neder Rijn. "All ranks exhausted. Lack of rations, water, ammunition and weapons, with high officer casualty rate." At 11 A.M.

the next day, when Dempsey met Monty at the headquarters of 50th Division, it was agreed enough life had been lost; the remnants of 1st Airborne Division would be withdrawn under cover of darkness, that night.

A Brave Face

Meanwhile, how close to victory Monty came was proved by the German Commander-in-Chief's pessimistic message to Hitler on 24 September, requesting permission for a phased withdrawal of all German forces in Holland to the line of the Maas, Waal and subsequently the extended Siegfried Line.

Hitler, however, refused—ordering instead that von Rundstedt counterattack and annihilate Montgomery's threat to the Ruhr. Thus, to the astonishment of those Allied staff officers hurriedly making plans for the occupation of Germany and the disarming of the German armed forces, there arose the spectacle of a beaten enemy rising up and assailing the victor.

If this was difficult for Allied military and civilian planners to believe, it was doubly so for the battlefield commanders who had mounted the great Ruhr offensive. Even the decimation of 1st Airborne Division at Arnhem was still not appreciated as the ebbing of the victorious Allied tide. On the contrary, by containing the bulk of the 2nd Panzer Corps so far north at Arnhem, General Urquhart's 1st Airborne Division had, it was believed, permitted the Allies to establish a firm left flank on the Waal for a subsequent thrust eastwards across the Rhine at Wesel, thence to the Ruhr. To the CIGS Monty put on a brave face: "The fact that we shall not now have a crossing over the NEDER RIJN will not affect the operations eastwards against the RUHR. In fact by giving up that bridgehead we shall now be able to keep more within ourselves and be less stretched. I shall hold a very strong bridgehead across the RHINE at NIJMEGEN." Even General

Horrocks remained certain, having reached the Lower Rhine, he could quickly reestablish a bridgehead across the river, west of Arnhem, and "mop up" Holland by striking north towards Amsterdam and the Zuider Zee. "After tonight's ops completed [retrieving the survivors of 1st Airborne Division from across the Neder Rijn]," Horrocks signaled to Dempsey at 7 P.M. on 25 September, "great opportunities of developing vigorous offensive in NORTH and NORTH EAST direction when time is ripe. . . . Hope to discuss future with you tomorrow afternoon if rd is open."

But it wasn't.

Sideshow Artist

General Kurt Student, in a statement after the war, considered the thrust to Arnhem a "great success. The Allied Airborne action completely surprised us," he admitted. "The operation hit my army nearly in the centre and split it into two parts. . . . In spite of all precautions, all bridges fell intact into the hands of the Allied airborne forces—another proof of the paralysing effect of surprise by airborne forces!"

Student was expressing the professional admiration of a distinguished airborne commander. "At one stroke it brought the British 2nd Army into the possession of vital bridges and valuable territory," he went on. "The conquest of the Nijmegen area meant the creation of a good jumping board for the offensive which contributed to the end of the war."

Such praise, however, could not conceal the fact that, with the lucky discovery of the entire Allied plan of maneuver on the body of an American parachute officer, Student had been able, with his Commander-in-Chief, Field Marshal Model, to mastermind one of the finest defensive battles of the war, first wiping out the Allied bridgehead at Arnhem and then subjecting the Allied lines of communication—the "wasp's waist" as he called it—to a series of such virulent and often successful attacks that Monty's entire Second Army was gradually sucked into the fighting, leaving nothing with which to mount the *real* offensive task behind the operation: the thrust towards the Ruhr.

Hour by hour, as Hitler now ordered up 2nd and 116th Panzer Divisions and more infantry to the Nijmegen bridgehead, Monty's room for maneuver decreased. Day by day, the candle he had lit by his bold thrust through Holland was extinguished by the blast of German artillery, mortars, machine-gun fire and even air attack. From fighting for a foothold on the Ruhr or even Amsterdam, Monty now found himself fighting for his life, as he sought to retain the very bridgehead at Nijmegen he had so dramatically established. Huffing and puffing he had, in his recent 21st Army Group directive, threatened to blow Hitler's house down. But with his own jumping-off area now under heavy German attack, and with First U.S. Army failing to make headway in its southern pincer attack towards Aachen, the British threat began to ring very thin. The race to the Ruhr was, in truth, over.

On 5 October 1944, Eisenhower held a new conference of commanders. To ensure Monty came, and to ensure the British tail was no longer permitted to wag the top American dog, Eisenhower invited Field Marshal Brooke—who had returned from Quebec—to attend.

It was a masterstroke. In his diary Brooke confided not only his admiration for the way Eisenhower ran the conference, but his feeling that "Monty's strategy for once is at fault. Instead of carrying out the advance on Arnhem he ought to have made certain of Antwerp in the first place. [Admiral] Ramsay brought this out well in the discussion and criticized Monty freely. Ike nobly took all blame on himself as he had approved Monty's suggestion to operate on Arnhem."

Thus, from the ashes of Arnhem, General Eisenhower emerged, in the councils of the Allied high command, the only victor: a military statesman of such obvious personal stature his battlefield failings could easily be forgiven. Whereas Monty, the outstanding Allied battlefield commander of the war, was, as a result of his defeat at Arnhem, reduced to the status of a sideshow artist.

For the eclipse of such a professional battlefield commander, however, the Allies would, in the bitter days ahead, pay a further, far more terrible price: the Ardennes.

Part Fourteen

THE BATTLE OF THE BULGE

Monty in the Ardennes with his four army
commanders, Generals Dempsey, Hodges,
Simpson and Crerar, December 1944.

Completely and Utterly Useless

Monty did not react well to obscurity. Fame had fanned the flames of an ebullient ego; humility had become arrogance; inspirational professionalism had turned to self-righteousness. He had overplayed his hand, assuming that victory in Normandy had made him invincible, both in battle against the Germans and with his masters at SHAEF. Now, in the fall of 1944, he had to accept that he had been doubly defeated: by the enemy at Arnhem, and by "the Americans," his allies, in the struggle for a common, concentrated tactical strategy.

Obediently, he turned his belated attention to the opening of Antwerp by clearing the Scheldt estuary (completed by the end of October 1944); but, disobediently, he watched and commented with scorn as Eisenhower and Bradley attempted to show the world the effect of American military might and the efficacy of Eisenhower's "stretch" strategy.

"As a commander in charge of the land operations, Eisenhower is quite useless. There must be no misconception on this matter; he is completely and utterly useless," Monty told Brooke in confidence in late November. "First Army is struggling forward slowly but here again there are no reserves," he reported on 23 November. "The whole business is a first class example of the futile doctrine of everybody attacking everywhere with no reserves anywhere."

In vain, Monty proposed Patton's Third U.S. Army be shifted north for the Ruhr offensive; that Bradley be made the Allied Land Forces C-in-C to relieve Eisenhower of a responsibility he was simply not carrying out; or that Bradley be made at the very least Commander-in-Chief of all Allied forces north of the Ardennes.

But Bradley himself demurred, sticking to his notion of separate, national army groups with himself the commander of the American "steamroller." A a conference of senior commanders at Maastricht on 7 December, Monty's final, despairing call for concentration of Allied effort under unified field command was shot down. Bradley was triumphant.

Bradley had set up his headquarters in Luxembourg, south of the Ardennes, and considered that the Sixth SS Panzer Army—reportedly assembling behind the German lines—was being readied only to plug gaps when Hodges and Patton relaunched their stalled Ruhr and Saar offensives. Patton's new thrust was designed to kick off on 19 December.

But the Germans had a quite different purpose in mind.

Drake's Bowls

B efore dawn on 16 December 1944, three German armies assaulted a narrow, sixty-mile sector in the Ardennes defended by four American divisions.

General Hodges, upon whose 8 U.S. Corps front the main German blow fell, had done no reconnaissance and was initially undisturbed by virulence of the attack. "At first it appeared that these counter attacks of the Boche were only what the General called 'spoiling attacks,' " his ADC, Captain Sylvan, recorded, "to take pressure off the important V Corps drive towards the ROER river dams. But by eleven o'clock it became more evident that the enemy was staking all on this drive and that he was putting his maximum strength against the 106th Div and in the general area bordering the boundary between V and VIII Corps. General Hodges immediately put the 1st Div resting in AUBEL, on a six hour alert and not long afterward in a call to General Bradley he was given the 7th Armd Div of the Ninth Army and the 10th Armd Div of the 3rd Army." A captured enemy document "spoke of a counter-offensive order signed by von Rundstedt and on which the enemy was gambling his life. According to von Rundstedt the fate of the

German nation depends upon the success or failure of this savage blow directed at the VIII Corps. According to PW's captured, who were more precise, the counter-offensive is a pincer-movement on AA-CHEN, and an attack is apparently about to begin in the Ninth Army area [north of Hodges' First Army] to join up with those troops who have attacked to the south."

The Germans, however, had not assembled twenty-eight divisions in the utmost secrecy merely to retake Aachen. Their objective was, if possible, to smash through the weak American forces in the Ardennes, cross the Meuse and seize Antwerp, cutting off the British and Canadian armies as they had done in 1940.

Bradley, having finished breakfast at Luxembourg, got into his car. Instead of driving or flying to Spa, however, to see his First Army Commander, he journeyed in the opposite direction, to Paris. There he lunched leisurely at the Ritz, then drove on to join Eisenhower, the Allied Land Forces Commander, at Versailles. Bradley's aide, Major Hansen, left him there, returning to a boozy evening in Paris in the company of Ernest Hemingway, which ended at the Lido, "where we saw bare-breasted girls do the hootchy kootchie until it was late."

While Hansen watched naked girls in Paris, Bradley drank and played five rubbers of bridge with Eisenhower: a scene of almost surreal symbolism as, in the palatial luxury of the Trianon Palace Hotel, the two most senior American battlefield commanders played cards, like Louis XVI with his courtiers (complete with Eisenhower's British lover, Kay Summersby, in the background), cracked open a special bottle of champagne to celebrate Eisenhower's promotion to five-star general, and refused to credit the incoming reports from the Ardennes as more than a German spoiling attack. Other than authorizing Hodges to take the 7th and 10th Armored Divisions, Bradley refused to alter or call off his plans for the offensive in Patton's southern sector.

The game of bridge, like Drake's bowls at the approach of the Spanish Armada, went on.

"Pardon My French"

E arly the following morning, 17 December, Bradley revealed to his ADC the first signs of anxiety. He had gone to bed at midnight but "had not slept well. He lay awake, thinking of the problem posed by the German attack. While it was threatening, it is not yet dangerous or critical. The main force is aimed towards Liège in an effort to cut off our supply line while the feint was aimed towards Luxembourg, both attacks being made in those sectors only lightly held by our troops while we massed the strength before the logical approaches to Germany."

Bradley was still convinced von Rundstedt was trying to delay the forthcoming American offensives—particularly Patton's thrust toward the Saar. "He [the enemy] is getting worried about the Third [U.S. Army] which is up against the wall and threatening to break through," Bradley told his ADC. "Of course, if he can force us to pull our strength out of there to stop his counter attack, he will achieve his primary purpose."

Bradley thus assumed the Germans were reacting to Patton's threat—though neither then nor later was there any evidence to show the Germans were anxious about a breakthrough by Patton.

Finally, during midafternoon on 17 December, *thirty-six hours* after the German attack had begun, Bradley arrived back at his Luxembourg headquarters. Like Rommel at Alamein and in Normandy, he had been absent from his command post when the enemy's blow was struck—and as Monty had always argued, it is hard to recover from a faulty plan or dispositions. So certain was Bradley that von Rundstedt would use his Panzer army reserve in a fire-fighting role that he had failed to echelon his forces in the Ardennes for possible German counterattack. "Our lines have not been built in depth," Bradley's ADC acknowledged that day, owing to the "offensive mindedness of our command. Our reserves existed in moderate strength but it is difficult to estimate how much of a drive they might be able to contain."

The American strategy of "bulling ahead" on too many fronts, without reserves, was being embarrassingly exposed. In his diary, Field Marshal Brooke had predicted on 7 November that "after they see the results of dispersing their strength all along their front it may become easier to convince them that some drastic change is desireable." Mounting American casualties in November and December had, however, only made Bradley more obstinate. "Although the present [broad-front] plan has failed," Monty lamented to Brooke after the Maastricht conference, "we are to continue to consider it has not failed and are to work on it."

Worried about the Ardennes sector, Monty had warned Eisenhower the front was dangerously lightly held. Eisenhower had passed on the warning, but Bradley had responded with a polite but firm request that Monty mind his own military business. His continuous attacks, he was certain, were, as in Normandy, stretching the German line to breaking point.

Far from stretching the German forces to breaking point, however, they merely enabled Hitler to regroup and form a striking reserve of two complete Panzer armies. Bradley, once he finally acknowledged the severity of the situation, was stunned. "Pardon my French," he exclaimed as he surveyed his maps in Luxembourg, "but where in hell has this son of a bitch gotten all his strength?"

No Idea How to Deal with the Problem

Bradley himself never lost his composure—indeed, his stature as a soldier is well illustrated by the remark he made to his ADC when warned by the Commander of the 4th U.S. Infantry Division, on the second morning of the battle, that he might have to evacuate his Luxembourg headquarters, together with American fighter squadrons that were retreating to safer airfields in the rear. Bradley was adamant. "I will never move backwards with a headquarters," he declared loftily. "There is too much prestige at stake."

Bradley's refusal to move his headquarters, however, was to be his downfall—for once American telephone landlines were cut in the Ardennes, Bradley could only communicate with Hodges and Simpson, his Ninth U.S. Army Commander north of Aachen, by radio.

Meanwhile, exasperated by Eisenhower's pitiful performance as Commander-in-Chief, Monty had warned Eisenhower's deputy chief of staff on 16 December that the Allies were in for trouble. The Allies had built up no strategic reserve; different commanders were launching separate, uncoordinated attacks all along the Allied front; there was no masterplan. Eisenhower had issued no directive as Allied battlefield Commander-in-Chief since 28 October, almost eight weeks past. "Unless IKE could make up his mind quickly as to what he wanted to do and would issue definite orders," Monty made clear to General Whiteley at his Main Headquarters in Brussels, "we were quite likely to drift into a unfavourable situation vis-à-vis the enemy."

Receiving reports of a German attack in the Ardennes, Monty rushed back to his Tactical Headquarters at Zonhoven, certain, from the start, that this was no ordinary affair. Keeping in close touch with the American front by means of his team of young liaison officers—trained to report back in person without the use of telephones or signals equipment—he signaled to Brooke on the night of 17 December:

> My LO has just returned from First US Army HQ at SPA. It seems clear that the enemy gained surprise. The Americans have practically all their troops in the front line from LINNICH to KARLSRUHE and have no reserves immediately available to hold the enemy penetration. Two divisions [sic] are being sent south from Ninth Army and one from the DUREN sector of First Army. One division has been sent north from Third Army. BRADLEY's HQ are at LUXEMBOURG. The Americans are definitely tactically unbalanced and First Army at 1700 hrs had no idea as to how they could deal with the problem.

This was, sadly, no exaggeration.

The Price of Drift

The danger to 21st Army Group if twenty-eight German divisions sliced through Hodges' front and crossed the Meuse was real. Monty therefore immediately ordered three British divisions—43rd, 53rd and the Guards Armoured Division—to move south towards the Meuse, ready to defend 21st Army Group's southern flank should the need arise.

"It looks as if we may now have to pay the price for the policy of drift and lack of proper control of the operations which has been a marked feature of the last three months," Monty signaled to Field Marshal Brooke. "Also the present enemy offensive is likely to show up our faulty command set up. The Americans have had to react at once and are now milking their northern flank to get troops to restore the situation." This meant, however, that the seizing of the Roer dams and the crossing of the Rhine in the north would be put back by months. "If this happens we shall have to admit that we have suffered a bad setback," Monty warned—having begged General Whiteley at SHAEF to "draw on their south flank for troops" instead.

Bradley disagreed, however—indeed, he only consented, in consultation with Eisenhower, to send up the 10th U.S. Armored Division from Patton's army with great misgivings, knowing that Patton would protest.

Patton did—recording in his diary that Bradley was taking "counsel of his fears" and was contemptibly "timid." Indeed, far from wondering whether the American policy of "stretchout" was appropriate, in view of the German counteroffensive, Patton blamed Hodges' four divisions in the Ardennes for not having been "more aggressive." "One must never sit still," he opined with typical bravado—ignoring the fact that it was his own Metz-Saar thrust which had so weakened the rest of

Bradley's front that Hodges was naturally unable, on his own, to stem the concentrated assault by three German armies.

Bradley, meanwhile, had obtained, on the evening of 17 September, Eisenhower's consent to use SHAEF's airborne reserves, the 82nd and 101st U.S. Airborne Divisions, in a ground-defense role at Bastogne and further north, and declared his intention to fly north to Spa the next day to meet Hodges in person at First U.S. Army Headquarters and discuss the role of the airborne troops. However, news of a German parachute operation behind Allied lines on 16 December, with German troops dressed in American uniforms, as well as the report, the next day, that SS units had machine-gunned 200 American prisoners in cold blood, had helped create a sense of fear, bordering on panic, which intensified as the rolling German advance destroyed American communications. Hodges' ADC therefore called Bradley to suggest the army group commander fly to Liège instead, and be escorted from there by car. The news at First Army, Captain Sylvan warned, was not good.

The next morning, before leaving, Bradley consulted his staff and studied the latest reports of the German advance. It was now 18 December 1944, and the Germans had been attacking for two days and nights. Patton's latest offensive was due to kick off in the south the following day. Should he cancel it, as Monty was begging SHAEF to force him to do?

Bradley's pride revolted at the idea—particularly the likely response of General Patton. However, Bradley was nothing if not a soldier. Recognizing that he might have already waited too long, he telephoned Patton at Nancy at 10:30 A.M. and told him to drive straight to Luxembourg with his senior Intelligence, operations and supply officers. "What he was going to suggest," Patton recorded, "would be unacceptable to me, but he wanted to see me."

The Flight of Hodges

A t Luxembourg, Bradley asked how many units Patton could immediately switch north. Patton, knowing his Saar offensive was at least temporarily doomed, replied three, to be ready to move in twenty-four hours. Even as Patton drove back to Nancy, though, Bradley was phoning Patton's chief of staff to state that the situation was getting worse every hour, and to ask if one combat command could move that night.

Despite his conference with Patton, Bradley hoped to contain the German offensive without taking too many forces from the Saar thrust—a thrust Bradley *still* believed, according to his ADC's diary on 18 December, was "the logical one for us to take into Germany," and one which threatened the Germans with a "crack through" that would justify Bradley's long-standing belief in the southern advance route into Germany. In fact, Major Hansen assumed that a new conference at Verdun, convened by Eisenhower for 19 December, "will probably determine our ability to launch an all out offensive on the southern effort of Patton's, enable us to rush the Siegfried Line and hurry our way to the Rhine down in the sector of the Saar"—where "the German," according to Bradley, was "desperately afraid of our strength there."

It was Bradley's obsession—it cannot be termed less—with this Saar thrust that was to be his and Eisenhower's undoing, just as Monty's fixation with his northern thrust at Arnhem had led to his downfall in September. Thus, instead of flying north to see his First Army Commander in the field, Bradley now canceled his plans and remained in Luxembourg all day—leaving Hodges to fight three German armies, two of them Panzer armies, on his own.

In the evening Bradley went home to his hotel for dinner, then returned to his office "in good spirits despite the situation—which he obviously did not view as seriously as most of the others," Major Hansen recorded.

This was precisely what worried Hodges. "The situation is rapidly deteriorating," Hodges' ADC noted. "It is not yet known whether Twelfth Army Group fully appreciates the seriousness of the situation though both General Hodges and General Kean [chief of staff] talked with General Bradley half a dozen times during the day."

By 4 P.M. on 18 December, German Panzers were in fact reported in Stavelot, heading northwards towards Spa itself—and the entire First Army Headquarters staff had to turn out to man a roadblock! In considerable agitation the chief of Intelligence counseled that Hodges should fly, literally: "a Cub plane was waiting . . . to take him away."

With over four million gallons of petrol at the Spa storage depot, the Germans were within an ace of getting the very fuel they required for a drive on Antwerp. However, by "one of the fortunes of war that can never be explained" (as Hodges' ADC afterwards recorded in his diary) the Germans decided to plunge on westwards, instead of striking further north.

Hodges, however, decided it was high time to move his headquarters. In pitch dark, the staff burned their secret files, abandoned the buildings, and drove through the night to First U.S. Army's rear headquarters at Chaudfontaine—but having neglected to inform anyone of their departure.

A Very Confused Situation

Monty, hearing nothing of the battlefield situation directly from Eisenhower, or Bradley, or Hodges, was justifiably concerned. A German breakthrough, across the Meuse, and aimed at Antwerp, was of enormous significance to 21st Army Group—yet 21st Army Group was being kept in the dark.

This was scarcely an example of Allied cooperation, let alone of military tidiness: so little so, in fact, that Monty had decided earlier that day to dispatch his entire liaison officer team south to assemble a true picture of the German penetration—even sending them to American corps commanders in the field.

"A very confused situation exists in First Army area and the HQ of higher formations do not really know what is going on," Monty signaled frankly at 10 P.M. on 18 December to Brooke.

> I have had to send down to the HQ of Corps to ascertain the picture.
>
> The main enemy thrust has now penetrated some 20 miles and reached STAVELOT and the road centre at TROIS PONTS and VIELSAM. . . . There is much confusion in the area of 5 and 8 [U.S.] Corps where hospitals and administrative echelons are being moved back and divisions are being moved in. Incoming divisions are being thrown at these two Corps, each of which has now seven divisions and neither Corps can handle so many.
>
> The two American airborne divisions 82 and 101 have been sent for use in a ground role. I think the Americans ought to be able to hold the enemy if they take a proper control at Army and Corps HQ level but a strong enemy thrust north of MONSCHAU if successful would be most awkward for them.
>
> I have been urging for two days that the whole southern front should close down and become defensive under PATCH [Commander, Seventh U.S. Army] and that Patton's army should be moved northward to put in a strong attack on the axis PRUM–BONN.
>
> I have heard tonight that IKE has now agreed to do this but we have had to enlist the help of the Germans to make him do so. . . .
>
> I had hoped to come home and spend a quiet Xmas at HINDHEAD but unless the situation improves I shall not leave here.

Monty's cancellation of his Christmas plans proved wise. Although his personal liaison officer to Bradley's headquarters reported that Bradley's staff in Luxembourg were not overly worried by the situation, Monty's military intuition suggested otherwise. From his liaison officers that evening, it became obvious the situation was getting worse, not better—and that Monty himself would soon have to take a hand, if the Germans were to be stopped.

A Conference at Verdun

Bradley, in truth, was so removed from the reality of Hodges' predicament on the evening of 18 December that, according to his ADC's diary, he still believed that Hodges' headquarters at Spa was "not planning to move out."

The following morning, after telephone communication with Hodges had been completely cut, Bradley was even more ignorant of what was happening in his First U.S. Army sector. "Bastogne is in enemy hands," Bradley's ADC recorded, while "in the center area of the principal breakthrough in the situation remains obscure." Nevertheless Bradley remained "apparently unworried even though the situation continued to become more aggravated with the commitment of additional enemy reserves in the breakthrough near Bastogne."

The truth was, Bradley's eyes were not focusing on the enemy, but on the fight he felt he was going to have at Eisenhower's conference later that day at Verdun—for the SHAEF staff had indeed, as Monty had signaled, prepared a draft order to be issued "after the meeting," a directive which ordered Devers to close down all offensive operations in the south and to relieve Patton's Third U.S. Army so that this could be shifted north. Once having restored the situation on Hodges' First U.S. Army front, Bradley's 12th U.S. Army Group was then to mount the single northern offensive Monty had proposed at the Maastricht conference on 7 December, employing all of its three American constituent armies "North of the Moselle. Attacks comprising this counter offensive will converge on the general area Bonn–Cologne."

Bradley was determined to challenge this change of strategy—but arrived at Verdun to find Eisenhower, as Allied Land Forces Commander-in-Chief, far more worried about the current German offensive than about future Allied plans. The atmosphere at the conference was tense. Eisenhower was tempted to take field command himself, but instead turned to Patton. "Said he wanted me to get to Luxembourg and take command of the battle and make a strong counter attack with at least six divisions. The fact that three of these divisions [overrun by the German advance] exist only on paper," Patton recorded contemptuously, "did not enter his head."

Patton's counteroffer was to attack in three days' time, employing three divisions. Patton's biographer and Official American Historian, Martin Blumenson, considered that this was "the sublime moment" of Patton's career, requiring him to "reorient his entire army from an eastward direction to the north, a 90-degree turn. . . . Altogether, it was an operation that only a master could think of executing."

In reality, Patton, like Monty, had been alerted the previous night about Eisenhower's intention to move Third U.S. Army north of the Moselle. What stunned Eisenhower was not the speed with which Patton reoriented his divisions, but the alacrity with which, once offered command of the American forces in the southern sector of the Ardennes, Patton abandoned his planned Saar offensive. Eisenhower was bewildered. Was this the same commander who had railed against Monty's call for concentration of the main Allied land forces since August, and had made it a matter of American honor that his Saar offensive *not* be closed down? "I do not see how they stand such conversation," Patton had noted a bare five days before, when discussion took place of Monty's continuing call for the Saar thrust to be canceled—certain that it was "up to me to make a breakthrough [to the Saar], and I feel that, God helping, it will come about."

Without complaint, Patton now moved his headquarters to Luxembourg, alongside Bradley's. But even as, three months too late, Third U.S. Army began to move north, the cocoon in which Eisenhower, Bradley and the SHAEF staff were living was finally shattered—for, returning from Versailles, Major General Strong received Intelligence reports which, at last, confounded the complacent SHAEF view that the Germans were engaged only in a spoiling attack.

Finding the Cupboard Bare

From fatal optimism ("This situation might develop very favourably for the Allies," Strong's deputy, Brigadier General Betts, had remarked at the daily staff conference at Versailles on the morning of 19 December) the SHAEF staff now became distraught, as Monty's chief of Intelligence confided to the American Official Historian after the war. "Bedell [Smith] told a direct lie when he said there was no flap at SHAEF over the Ardennes," Brigadier Williams related. "They kept calling us until we thought we would go crazy. Strong . . . got hysterical over the Ardennes."

Major General Strong himself later admitted to the American Official Historian that it was not "until on Tuesday [19 December] when he came back from conference at Verdun and found evidence of parts of 10 [enemy] divs around Bastogne" that he became "worried." He also allowed that, although Eisenhower was "completely right in insisting on Allied drive in north and south," he himself was in retrospect unsure "that the administrative situation was in proper touch with strategy. Couldn't maintain two front attacks at the time."

Monty, meanwhile, had still heard nothing direct from Eisenhower, his supposed Allied Commander-in-Chief in the field, as he reported with contempt in a telephone call to General Simpson at the War Office. "What he had found out," Simpson recalled "was that neither General Hodges [First U.S. Army] nor General Simpson [Ninth U.S. Army] had had any communication whatever from General Bradley, at 12th Army Group HQ, and he did not see how they *could* have had any communication, with Bradley positioned as far south as Luxembourg. Monty asked me to tell the CIGS that he was still watching the situation very carefully. He was uneasy about his southern flank, and he could make available at short notice a corps of four divisions to look after that flank and indeed help the Americans if they wanted it—the HQ of [Horrocks'] 30 Corps."

Up until this point Monty had been confident that, despite the confusion and lack of up-to-date information, the Americans would be able to run their own battle in the Ardennes. Just as Allied Intelligence belatedly began to recognize the magnitude of the German offensive, however, Monty received an even more vivid indication of the breakdown in American command. Two of his liaison officers had driven on the morning of 19 December to General Hodges' First U.S. Army headquarters at Spa—and had found the cupboard bare!

As Major Tom Bigland, Monty's special liaison officer to Bradley, recorded in his diary: "Find HQ deserted & b'fast laid!" In a letter to the American author Ralph Ingersoll after the war, Bigland described his arrival in greater detail:

> Another of the Field Marshal's Liaison Officers came with me so that he could report back to him while I went on to Eagle Tac [Bradley's headquarters in Luxembourg] with details of his [Monty's] plans. We found no Army M.P.s in Spa and walked into the H.Q. to find literally *not one single person* there except a German woman.
>
> Breakfast was laid and the Christmas tree was decorated in the dining room, telephones were in all the offices, papers were all over the place—but there was no one left to tell visitors where they had gone to! Germans in the town said that they had gone suddenly and quickly down the road at 3 a.m. I found them again at their rear H.Q. and here they had even less control of the battle than the day before.

When he heard this, Monty was shocked. The Americans, he recognized, had now lost control of the battle.

Strengthening the Meuse

H odges had not impressed Monty as an army commander in Normandy. At 5 P.M. on 19 December, Monty telephoned Dempsey. Irrespective of American intentions, Monty had decided to transfer Horrocks' 30 Corps HQ from the Canadian army to Dempsey's Second British Army; it would become Dempsey's reserve corps on the west bank of the Meuse in case the Germans *did* break through First U.S. Army. The 51st Highland Division was also being transferred forthwith from the Canadian army, so that from dawn the next morning Dempsey would have four full-blooded British divisions ready to halt any German attempt to cross the Meuse.

Meanwhile, having heard from his LOs that there were no American garrisons on the Meuse bridges in the First U.S. Army sector, Monty transferred to Dempsey the 2nd Battalion of the Household Cavalry Regiment and ordered tank patrols to fan out along the river from Liège to Givet, on the French border.

To send such British patrols fifty miles into the American sectors of the First and Ninth U.S. Armies in darkness was perhaps foolhardy, at a time when German parachute troops were known to be operating behind the lines in Allied uniforms; nevertheless the British regiment was safely "disposed on the river line shortly after first light" the next day, as Dempsey recorded in his diary. The victor of the classic defensive battles of Alam Halfa and Medenine was taking no chances. His diarist, Kit Dawnay, noted:

> As soon as the Field-Marshal saw what was happening, although he had received no orders or requests of any kind from General Eisenhower, he took certain precautionary measures to ensure that, if the Germans got to the MEUSE, they would certainly not get over that river. It was nec-

essary for these steps to be carried out quickly, as otherwise the British area might be in grave danger, and a threat might develop to BRUSSELS and even to ANTWERP.

As Monty reported to the CIGS that night, he was assembling a reserve corps of four divisions ready to meet von Rundstedt "with under command 43 DIV, 51 DIV, 53 DIV, Guards Armoured DIV, and three independent armoured brigades. . . . I can add 4 C'dn Armd DIV to 30 Corps in 48 hrs time making it five divisions in all. I shall then direct 30 Corps under Second Army to operate to maintain intact the line of the MEUSE from LIEGE to NAMUR and DINANT."

It was from this moment, on the evening of 19 December 1944, as the staff of Eisenhower's headquarters at Versailles gave way to panic, that the chances of a German breakthrough to Antwerp were in fact terminated, whatever happened in the Ardennes.

The Front Cut in Two

Meanwhile the confusion that existed in the various American headquarters, the lack of reliable information, and the absence of unified and coherent Allied command in the face of the German counteroffensive affronted Monty's professional dignity as a soldier. "The command set up has always been very faulty," he signaled to Brooke, "and now is quite futile with BRADLEY at LUXEMBOURG and the front cut into two."

There was only one sensible solution, Monty reasoned. "I have told WHITELEY [at SHAEF] that IKE ought to place me in operational charge of all troops on the northern half of the front," he informed Brooke. "I consider he should be given a direct order by someone to do so. This situation needs to be handled very firmly and with a tight grip."

But who could *compel* Eisenhower to take such action, other than the Combined Chiefs of Staff? Certainly Brooke could not do so, any more than he had been able to force Eisenhower to concentrate his Allied forces after Normandy. Moreover, if Eisenhower had balked at the political/press ramifications of placing a British general in command of all American troops in the advance to the Rhine, following triumphant Allied victory in Normandy, how could he do so *at a time of impending American defeat?*

The notion seemed preposterous. But in the context of the battlefield it was far from being so. Monty was not exaggerating when he told "Simbo" Simpson at the War Office that he had found it "impossible to get any information" out of Eisenhower's headquarters. Although the Combined Chiefs of Staff, President Roosevelt and Prime Minister Churchill were supposed to obtain their battlefront information from SHAEF, there was no such information to be had from that source. Both the War Office and Churchill therefore turned to Monty as the only Allied commander capable of giving a realistic picture of the battlefield. Indeed, as General Simpson, the Director of Military Operations at the War Office, informed Monty, the Prime Minister had begun to use Monty's personal signals to Brooke in his Cabinet war room to mark up his maps—and to begin fantasizing about a British counterstroke! Thus the next day, Brooke noted in his diary, the Prime Minister emerged "very much the worse for wear having evidently consumed several glasses of sherry for lunch. It was not very easy to ensure that he was absorbing the seriousness of the situation. We had many references to Marlborough and other irrelevant matters!"

Churchill was all for instantly hurling Horrocks' 30 Corps into battle, regardless of future plans, command sectors, fronts, or lines of communication. "Winston had worked himself up into a considerable state of excitement and was preparing a telegraphic order to Monty instructing him to take action at once with 30 Corps on some thrust line or other," "Simbo" Simpson recalled. "In effect Winston was trying to get down to ordering formations put under Monty. The CIGS was appalled at the possibility and pointed out to the Prime Minister that any order to Monty could only come from Ike; also it was quite impossible for anyone in London to say at that time how Monty should act seeing that circumstances on the spot were not known in London."

In fact, the only information that *was* known came from Monty! Finally, Simpson recalled, "the Prime Minister admitted the force of [Brooke's] argument very reluctantly and gave up the attempt to telegraph to Monty. He then asked the CIGS what he could do to help. The CIGS suggested that he should telephone to Ike, ask him about

the situation, and then put the suggestion that the whole of the northern half of the front should be put under one general, preferably
Monty. That call was put through at 5 P.M. [20 December]."

By then, however, Eisenhower's own staff had forced him to act.

Strong and Whiteley Are Dismissed

"By midnight [19 December] the news from the front had become so bad that I felt it absolutely essential to inform Bedell
Smith about my growing doubts whether the Allies were
matching up to the situation," Major General Strong later recounted.
"Some German units had penetrated well beyond Bastogne and were
getting far too near the Meuse for my liking. So together with General
Whiteley . . . I went to the Chief of Staff's quarters, next to his office
and got him [Bedell Smith] out of bed."

Strong now begged that Monty be given command at least of the
Allied troops north of the penetration. "General Whiteley added some
operational details, saying that, to his sure knowledge, there had been
no contact between General Bradley and the headquarters of his First
Army in the north for two days. He had also received a report from an
officer who had carried out an extensive personal reconnaissance in
the rear of the American troops and found considerable confusion and
disorganization."

Accounts differ about what happened next. Bradley recorded in
1948 that Bedell Smith telephoned that night to ask if he would object to Monty taking over the whole of his front north of Bastogne—
and that he, Bradley, advanced no objection.

According to General Strong, Bradley was not, however, telling the
truth. "Bedell Smith telephoned Bradley in our presence [on the night
of 19 December] and told him what we had said," Major General
Strong later chronicled. "Bradley replied that he doubted whether the
situation was serious enough to warrant such a fundamental change of

command, especially considering the effect it might have on opinion in America."

Embarrassed and ashamed at having questioned Bradley's ability to handle the battle, Bedell Smith then rounded upon his British colleagues, calling Strong and Whiteley "sons of bitches" and "Limey bastards"—and announcing they were sacked! "Because of the view we had taken of the situation, neither Whiteley nor I could any longer be accepted as staff officers to General Eisenhower," Strong narrated. "Next day instructions would be issued relieving us of our appointments and returning us to the United Kingdom."

Whether Whiteley telephoned Monty to inform him of this extraordinary development is unknown; but at 4:15 A.M. (Strong recalled that his meeting with Bedell Smith ended at 3 A.M.) on 20 December 1944, Major General Simpson was awakened at the United Services Club in London. "I went down to the telephone to find Monty in a state of quite high excitement," Simpson later recalled. "He said he had just sent a telegram to the CIGS saying that really somebody must take charge of the whole northern flank at least, nobody was getting any orders, and there would be a major disaster if something was not done. . . . He asked me to go down to the War Office immediately, to get hold of his telegram from the signals people then to wake the CIGS and ask him to do something immediately. So I dressed at once and went to the War Office, and there was the telegram."

Simpson read it carefully, aware of the critical situation on the main Allied front—a crisis that affected the very future of the war in Europe.

"Well, the fact is I did nothing," Simpson afterwards confessed. "It was no good waking up the CIGS; there was nothing he could do— there was nothing he could even get the other Chiefs-of-Staff to do. They would have to take the matter up with Washington, and the few hours remaining before the CIGS came to the office at nine o'clock meant that no time was really lost. So I went back and had breakfast. I then returned to carry on the day's work.

"I told the CIGS when he came in exactly what had happened. He said I was quite right. There was nothing I could do and nothing he was going to do now. He would tell the other Chiefs of Staff but they could not possibly give orders to Eisenhower, however dangerous the situation."

A Prisoner in His Own
Headquarters

T he impotence and incoherence of a democratic Allied high command in war against a dictatorship was perhaps never better illustrated than the scene in Brooke's office in London early on the morning of 20 December 1944, as the German Panzer armies swept on towards the Meuse.

As Brooke declared his powerlessness to help, however, Major General Strong addressed the daily chiefs of staff conference at SHAEF, Versailles, for what he understood would be his last time. "I gave my briefing of the enemy situation," Strong remembered nearly twenty-five years later. "Bedell Smith, who presided, was glum and scarcely spoke. But as Whiteley and I started to walk across to Eisenhower's office after the briefing, he quietly joined us and took hold of my arm. He intended, he said, to put our proposals to General Eisenhower as his own; he would recommend giving Montgomery charge of the northern attack against the [German] salient. Above all, he asked us to remain silent when he was speaking to Eisenhower since such a proposal would come much better from an American."

The truth was, the German counteroffensive in the Ardennes had reached the point at which, it seemed, it might bring down the entire Allied house of cards in Europe. Colonel Lash of the operations staff had reported at the 9 A.M. SHAEF meeting that "the two armoured thrusts that had pierced our front north of the Luxembourg frontier had made further progress and may now have joined up. . . . General Strong said that two further divisions of 6th Panzer Army were now committed, but two Panzer Grenadier Divisions were still unlocated. . . . It was appreciated that the Germans might be prepared to give ground on the Eastern Front and in ITALY in order to reinforce the counter offensive in the West, and there are rumours that two Panzer Corps that were last heard of in RUSSIA were now in the Black

Forest area. General Spaatz asked whether the Germans had picked up much gasoline in the area which they had overrun. General Smith said that small local dumps might have been overrun, but orders had immediately been given that big dumps were to be evacuated or destroyed. General Spaatz said that American supplies of gasoline were so liberal that what was regarded as a Company supply for the U.S. Army could run a German division for several weeks."

The picture, like the weather, looked bleak. Visibility was so poor, with fog, subzero temperatures and snow, that Allied aircraft were still unable to operate.

Worse still, the German paratroopers operating behind the Allied lines were now thought to be out to assassinate senior Allied commanders. Eisenhower's personal assistant, Kay Summersby, anxiously recorded in her diary "that an attempt is to be made on E's life. 60 Germans are supposed to be on their way to Paris for this purpose, they will be in Allied uniforms and will stop at nothing. E. is urged by all his senior staff members to stay in the office and not go home at all."

Eisenhower questioned the necessity, but then meekly agreed.

From that moment, on 20 December 1944, General Dwight D. Eisenhower, five-star General of the United States Armies, Supreme Commander of the Allied Expeditionary Force and Commander-in-Chief of the Allied armies in the field in northwest Europe, thus became a prisoner in his own headquarters office in the Trianon Palace Hotel in Versailles.

It was also there, at 10:00 on the morning of 20 December, that Eisenhower listened in astonishment to his chief of staff's latest recommendation that Monty be given command of two of Bradley's three armies. Like Bradley, Eisenhower objected—concerned not with the tens of thousands of American soldiers struggling against impossible odds in the Ardennes, but with the likely reaction of the American press.

An Open-and-Shut Case

Had the American press known the extent of the catastrophe in the Ardennes, however, and of Eisenhower's meek decision to secrete himself in his rear headquarters at Versailles, there would in all likelihood have been demands for a congressional inquiry. The press, however, were kept at bay, muzzled by wartime censorship rules—and later by a monumental cover-up. As Colonel J. O. Curtis, one of Eisenhower's senior operational Intelligence officers, later confided to the American Official Historian: "Ardennes business much bigger than believed. Will never have all the story."

Meanwhile, shocked by Bedell Smith's recommendation, Eisenhower went over the situation, calling in Generals Strong and Whiteley to give him the latest Intelligence and operational picture.

The Germans, Whiteley reported, had now bypassed Bastogne; they were sweeping through a broken American front, virtually unchallenged, towards the Meuse. No Allied strategic reserve existed to stop them there, save those which Monty had assembled behind the river. Patton might make a small dent on the southern flank of the German salient with his three divisions—but it would be a pinprick in the side of upwards of thirty German divisions.

In mounting concern, Bedell Smith had already sent Monty a cipher message in the early hours of the morning of 20 December, asking for advice: his first message since the battle had begun, four full days before. "Please let me have your personal appreciation of the situation on the northern flank of the penetration particularly with reference to the possibility of giving up, if necessary, some ground on the front of First Army and to the north thereof," Bedell Smith pleaded, "in order to shorten our line and collect a strong reserve for the purpose of destroying the enemy in Belgium."

By the time Lash and Strong gave their morning briefing a few hours

later, however, at 9 A.M., and with the new concern about the Supreme Commander's life, Bedell Smith recognized neither Bradley nor
his own boss could ever handle the battle, even with Monty's fatherly
guidance. "What made me really mad was that I knew you were right,"
he confessed to Strong afterwards. "But my American feelings got the
better of me because I also knew of the outcry there would be in the
United States about your proposal, if it was put into effect."

Having heard out his closest advisers, Eisenhower finally caved in.

There was no alternative, whatever the press might make of it in the
United States. According to Major General Strong's version in 1946,
Eisenhower telephoned Monty first, then Bradley. Air Vice-Marshal
Robb, who was present and who kept a diary, gave no hint of dissent
on Bradley's part—"Supreme Commander discussed this [the change
in command] with General Bradley, who agreed." But other accounts
have suggested that Bradley at first objected, only to be overruled by
Eisenhower, who said it was an order and put down the phone. "A long
conversation ensued of which we naturally could hear only one end,
but General Bradley was obviously protesting strongly," Strong himself
recalled, "for the conversation ended with Eisenhower saying, 'Well,
Brad, those are my orders.' "

Bradley certainly gave no hint of such protest in his 1948 version of
events—but, as Bedell Smith later confided to the American Official
Historian, the order shattered the 12th Army Group Commander. "I
thought Bradley could handle the armies, and so flared up when
Strong and Whiteley came to me with the suggestion that Montgomery take over," Bedell Smith confessed. "However, we traced our roads
communications and noted directions the enemy was coming. I called
Bradley's Headquarters and found he had not contacted First Army for
2–3 days. It was an open and shut case, so I agreed to recommend to
Ike the change. He accepted it and called up Bradley and Montgomery.
It hurt Bradley."

Bedell Smith was right. Relieved of command of two of his three
great American armies in the midst of battle, Bradley was mortified.
But there was worse, much worse, to follow.

The Fear of Assassination

I n fact, Bradley had lost telephone contact not only with his army commanders, but with his air commanders too. Therefore not only did Eisenhower give Monty command of all American troops north of Bastogne, but Monty's chief tactical air support commander, Air Marshal Coningham, was given direct command of all American supporting air forces. As Air Vice-Marshal Robb recorded in his SHAEF diary, it was "agreed that Coningham will take over the 9th and 29th Tactical Commands (Quesada and Nugent). They are reported as saying they are glad, because have had no word from Bradley for some time."

Bradley, in Luxembourg, had meanwhile also allowed himself, like Eisenhower, to become a victim of the German assassination scare. Major Hansen confided to his diary:

> The threat of enemy attack on the person of the General has grown more real. Reports indicate that an enemy sabotage b[attalio]n has now filtered between our lines. Paratroopers dressed in American uniforms, equipped with our weapons, driving our jeeps are supposed to be behind our lines: 40 of them are detailed to sabotage and assassin duties directing their efforts particularly toward high ranking officers. . . .
>
> All this has led to increased security precautions in the headquarters. We have removed the plates from the General's jeep—he rides in nothing else, no more sedans.

The Cadillac which Eisenhower had given Bradley on the eve of the fateful Maastricht conference was now locked away in a garage. Not only did Bradley ride in an open jeep without markings in subzero temperatures, but he was even persuaded to cover the three general's stars on his helmet and uniform, and to use only the back entrance of the hotel, through the kitchen. Even these "entrances and exits from the hotel" were henceforth to be "hurried. . . . The general looks on all this with a mild skepticism," Hansen noted. "When we suggested he sleep in another room, he looked slightly askance at first; realized the feasibility of it afterwards, however, and has agreed to use another room."

Bradley had thus surrendered control not only of his armies, but of his bedroom. It was the nadir of his fortunes—fortunes which, after the formal acceptance of his strategy at the Maastricht conference a fortnight before, had seemed to place him on the threshold of military greatness, with the prospect of almost sixty American divisions under his command.

For Monty, however, it was the reverse.

The Call to Battle

"To achieve success, the tactical battle will require very tight control and very careful handling. I recommend that the Supreme Commander hands the job over to me, and gives me powers of operational control over First U.S. Army."

Monty's request, made to Lieutenant General Bedell Smith, had been dated 21 September 1944—three months before the Battle of the Bulge!

When Eisenhower's call finally came through to Monty's Tactical Headquarters at Zonhoven at 10:30 A.M. on 20 December 1944, Monty was relieved. Since being forced to hand over tactical command of the American armies of 12th U.S. Army Group at the end of August, he had been considered by some to be verging on madness in his campaign for unified command in a single Allied thrust via the Ruhr. General Crerar had, for instance, written to a colleague on 5 September: "Monty . . . is very upset at the loss of operational command over the U.S. Armies and his nomination to Field-Marshal's rank has accentuated rather than eased his mental disturbance. It is a pity he cannot see that his importance to Allied Governments, based essentially on the fact that he is a great field commander, tends to diminish as final victory comes even more assured."

Victory, however, was no longer assured—and the Allies once again required not a great conciliator or international cooperator, but a great field commander.

"He [Eisenhower] was very excited and it was difficult to understand what he was talking about," Monty recounted of his call to battle a few days later; "he roared into the telephone, speaking very fast. The only point I really grasped was that 'it seems to me we now have two fronts' and that I was to assume command of the northern front. This was all I wanted to know. He then went on talking wildly about other things; I could not hear, and said so; at last the line cut out before he had finished."

Words, Monty felt, were now redundant. Four critical days had already been lost since the Germans had begun their offensive. According to Dawnay, who was on duty and answered the telephone, Monty deliberately exaggerated the indistinctness of the line. Shouting, "I can't hear you properly. I shall take command straight away," Monty put the phone down on his "boss."

Then, turning to Dawnay, Monty said: "Kit, I want the largest Union Jack that will go on the bonnet of the car. Also eight motor-cycle outriders."

Thinking of His Next Battle

What the American commanders in the field needed, Monty recognized, was a boost to their self-confidence, after four days' continuous fighting in subzero temperatures against three massed German armies. "Monty was a showman," Colonel

Dawnay acknowledged—"but, my goodness, he understood the nature of morale!"

First, however, Monty wished to speak personally with his Canadian and British army commanders, whom he had summoned for a conference at Zonhoven at 11 A.M. Announcing that Eisenhower had just given him command of First and Ninth U.S. Armies, he outlined to them the situation as he saw it. German Panzer units seemed to have reached Marche—less than thirty miles from Namur. Three American divisions had been substantially "written off"—the 7th, 28th and 106th. On the other hand, no German forces had yet reached the Meuse, and "along the northern flank of the breakthrough" American units had " 'firmed up' fairly definitely." Under his own personal command as Commander-in-Chief, 21st Army Group, Monty had already placed an *ad hoc* British armored force to "cover and hold the R. MEUSE crossings NAMUR–GIVET." Antiaircraft artillery was being moved up from Brussels to be used in an antitank ground role, similar to the famed German 88s. Dempsey was straightaway to assume responsibility for all Meuse crossings east of Namur. For the moment, however, 30 British Corps under General Horrocks would come under Monty's personal command, ready to take part in the battle in the Ardennes—if required.

As Monty confided to Crerar and Dempsey, he hoped he would *not* have to commit Horrocks' corps to the battle in the Ardennes. Already, as at Alam Halfa, Monty was thinking of his *next* battle: a fresh Allied offensive to seize the Ruhr. If possible, therefore, he favored the assembling of a counterattack force from within the American armies, to deal with the German salient: "It was the C-in-C's intention to organize, if at all possible, a strategic reserve for this purpose from U.S. forces in First and Ninth US Armies," Crerar recorded in his diary, and "in order to accomplish this latter purpose, he was quite prepared to give up certain ground presently held by U.S. Forces to the East, South East and South of AACHEN."

Monty's willingness to give up American-held ground was to prove one of the most controversial aspects of his command of American forces in the Ardennes. Time and again American writers would portray Monty as overcautious in comparison with the swashbuckling George S. Patton, who was all for instant counterattack in the Ardennes. Yet the Ardennes, Monty made clear to Crerar and Dempsey, was *no place for a major Allied offensive*. It most certainly would *not* lead the Allies to the Rhine, since its thick forests and hilly countryside were perfect for defense, and the Germans were now positioned there in immense depth. Better by far to *outflank* the Germans by holding their attack in the Ardennes with American troops, and if necessary giving ground and assembling the necessary reserves for a well-conducted defensive battle—while all the time proceeding with plans for the Allied thrust to the Ruhr, *further north:*

> The C-in-C intimated that it was possible that the situation confronting the Allied armies would improve materially within the next few days. If such turned out to be the case and 30 British Corps was not required for counter-offensive purposes on the right flank, then it was quite probable that HQ 30 Corps and several Divisions would be returned to First Cdn Army, in order to proceed on Operation "VERITABLE" [a preliminary operation to capture the necessary ground for a crossing of the Rhine and the seizure of the Ruhr in the north]. With that in view, the work of improving the communications in First Cdn Army area, leading to the NIJMEGEN salient would vigorously proceed. . . .

Monty's confidence that there were ample American troops to ensure an American defensive victory in the Ardennes, and his intention to form an American strategic reserve, were thus evident even *before* he went to visit his new American subordinates. "The C-in-C was proceeding to a further conference with Generals Hodges and Simpson of First and Ninth U.S. Armies, as soon as he had finished his discussion with General Dempsey and myself," Crerar concluded his account of the meeting. "The conference ended at 12.05 hrs."

Dempsey and Crerar were heartened by Monty's spirited presentation of his future plans. As in Normandy, with four Allied armies once again under his command, he was obviously in his element.

"Like Christ Come to Cleanse the Temple"

An hour and a half later, with the Union Jack flying on the hood of his Rolls-Royce and a cavalcade of outriders, Monty arrived at First U.S. Army's new Verviers headquarters, "like Christ come to cleanse the Temple," as his ADC recalled.

Hodges and General Simpson, commander of the Ninth U.S. Army, were waiting. "Neither army commander had seen BRADLEY or any of his staff since this battle began," Monty cabled the CIGS that night. "Ninth Army had three divisions and First Army fifteen divisions," he recorded, "and there were no reserves anywhere behind the front. Morale was very low. They seemed delighted to have someone to give them firm orders."

Simpson's Ninth U.S. Army, Monty instructed, would immediately assume responsibility for the sector north of the German penetration above Monschau, taking under command "the divisions now in it" and inserting a new corps headquarters (19 Corps). Next, as Hodges' ADC noted in his diary, Monty wanted to form a tactical reserve corps of at least three divisions to mount an eventual counterattack; for this attack "he told General Hodges he wanted the most aggressive fighting Corps Commander": General "Lightning Joe" Collins, who had captured Cherbourg under Monty's overall command three weeks after D-Day.

Collins would be given the 84th Division from Simpson's Ninth Army, the newly arrived 75th Division, and 3rd U.S. Armored Division. "This Corps is to assemble in the general area about DURBUY and MARCHE and is not to be used offensively until it is all assembled and ready for battle," Monty informed Eisenhower that night.

"I think I can deal with the situation south of the MEUSE with the American troops already there," Monty reported to Brooke. "There are plenty of American troops available and they merely wanted sorting

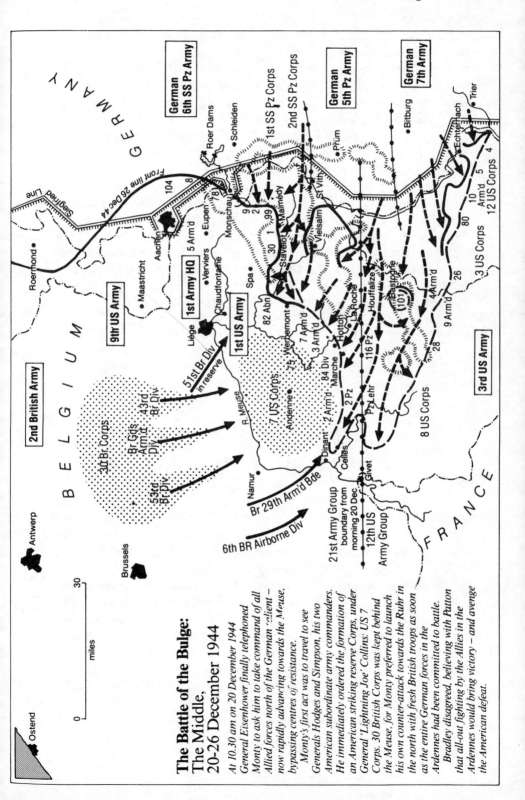

**The Battle of the Bulge:
The Middle,
20–26 December 1944**

*At 10.30 am on 20 December 1944
General Eisenhower finally telephoned
Monty to ask him to take command of all
Allied forces north of the German salient –
now rapidly advancing towards the Meuse,
bypassing centres of resistance.*

*Monty's first act was to travel to see
Generals Hodges and Simpson, his two
American subordinate army commanders.
He immediately ordered the formation of
an American striking reserve Corps, under
General 'Lightning Joe' Collins: US 7
Corps. 30 British Corps was kept behind
the Meuse, for Monty preferred to launch
his own counter-attack towards the Ruhr in
the north with fresh British troops as soon
as the entire German forces in the
Ardennes had been committed to battle.*

*Bradley disagreed, believing with Patton
that all-out fighting by the Allies in the
Ardennes would bring victory – and avenge
the American defeat.*

out." Hodges' First U.S. Army "shoulder" ran from Elsenborn westwards through Malmédy, Stavelot, Durbuy and Hotton to Marche; it
was from Marche southwards to Bastogne that the Allied line was
broken—"there is a gap between MARCHE and BASTOGNE from
which place the [Allied] line runs SE to ECHTERNACH." Would the
Germans reinforce their success by pushing westwards through this
gap? "All the bridges over the MEUSE from excl LIEGE to incl
GIVET are now held by British garrisons," Monty reassured the CIGS.
"In rear of this screen I shall have 30 Corps assembled and ready by tomorrow night 21 Dec."

"I have every hope that the situation can be put right now that we
have a properly organised set up for command and that a proper supervision and control can be kept over the battle," Monty summarized.
As he wrote a few days later to "Simbo" Simpson: "By 20 Dec I was
sitting very pretty, I did not much mind what happened on my right
so long as the Germans did not get over the MEUSE, and I was pretty
certain I could stop that."

The battle was at last "under control"—his control.

A Word of Warning

Monty's first biographer, Alan Moorehead, told the American
Official Historian after the war that, in his estimation, this
was Monty's "finest hour" as a battlefield commander,
eclipsing even his distinguished performance as Allied Land Forces
Commander-in-Chief for D-Day and the invasion of Normandy.

But by the time Moorehead was writing his biography, in 1946, it
was already a battlefield performance unacceptable to punctured
American self-esteem—and it had been made all the more unacceptable by Monty's own worst enemy: his boastful, cocksure, irrepressible
vanity.

Brooke, as usual, had foreseen the problem. "I would like to give you a word of warning," he warned Monty by secret cipher on 21 December. "Events and enemy action have forced on Eisenhower the setting up of a more satisfactory system of command. I *feel it is most important that you should not even in the slightest degree appear to rub this undoubted fact in to anyone at SHAEF or elsewhere.* Any remarks you may make are bound to come to Eisenhower's ears sooner or later and that may make it more difficult to ensure that this new set-up for command remains even after the present emergency has passed."

Brooke's warning was particularly prescient because, as "Simbo" Simpson recalled, even on 21 December Eisenhower seemed to be going back on the decisions he had made the day before. He duly confirmed in a cable to the War Office that Monty had formally been given command of "all units of Central [Bradley's] Group of Armies north of the boundary . . . Givet–St Vith–Cologne." But he reneged on the assurance he had given Churchill that the whole Western Front would now be divided into two, with General Bradley being given command of all forces south of the German penetration—i.e., the rump of 12th Army Group *and* Devers' 6th Army Group. "Simbo" Simpson therefore wrote to Monty to inquire whether Monty knew what was happening. "I asked," Simpson later explained, "because we were not clear about it, whether General Bradley was in command of the *whole* of the southern half of the front, from Prum to the Swiss border. We had thought that he had been given all that, but then re-reading all the directives that were coming out thick and fast from Supreme HQ we could not find that they established definitely that Bradley had been put in command of the 6th Army Group."

This was ominous—for with an army "group" containing merely one army (Patton's Third U.S. Army, now that Ninth and First U.S. Armies had passed to Monty's command), Bradley would be bound to press for the eventual return of his American forces, once Monty had restored the situation.

More important, without command of the 6th Army Group, Bradley could not do what Monty was doing in the north: namely, thin out that part of the Allied line unaffected by the German attack, and thus create tactical reserves. As the War Office feared, the 6th Army Group Commander, General Devers, proved reluctant to surrender formations for use in another army group. Moreover Patton, who disliked Devers, was equally unwilling to surrender Third U.S. Army territory to 6th Army Group, since Patton still dreamed of continuing his Saar offensive once the Ardennes business was over.

Had Bradley been named the overall commander between the Ardennes and Switzerland, coherent military decisions could have been made in the south. Instead, however, Eisenhower clung to his instinctive policy of "divide and rule"—though incapable of military rule himself, penned as he was for eight crucial days and nights of the battle in his office in the Trianon Palace Hotel, Versailles.

Thus, even as Monty set about restoring order to the battlefield, the seeds of yet more misunderstanding and ill will were sown.

Tidying Up the Mess

G eneral Collins was all for instant combat in the Patton style—"General Collins is full of his usual fighting Irish vigor. He is confident that with the 2nd and 3rd Armd Divs he can beat any collection that the Boche want to throw at him," Hodges' ADC noted.

Monty applauded such "vigor," but refused to surrender his nascent reserve corps by impetuous involvement that would deprive him of the tactical initiative if—as he suspected from his Intelligence staff—the Germans were themselves keeping reserve formations in order to exploit whatever gaps they could engineer. All day on 20 December, General Ridgway, who now commanded 18 U.S. Corps (made up of 30th, 82nd and what remained of 7th U.S. Armored Division), had telephoned Hodges "to say that he is being attacked in strength by an estimated two or three armoured divisions." There were definitely Germans in Marche, but Hodges was unsure whether 7th U.S. Armored Division still held Saint-Vith, or what was the true fate of the 106th U.S. Infantry Division south of Saint-Vith. "It is impossible to tell where we stand at this point," Hodges' ADC recorded in summary of the First Army Headquarters view on the evening of 21 December.

Monty was determined to find out.

"This was a very confused battle and it was under these circumstances that Monty's liaison officers, or gallopers, really came into their own," Horrocks later stated. "They consisted of hand-picked, intelligent, tough young staff officers who lived at his tactical headquarters.

Every day they were dispatched to the different formations fighting the battle. In the evening after dinner each in turn would report to Monty on what he had seen and heard. As a result of their reports Monty was probably the only man who had a completely up-to-date picture of the whole battle front. The only way I could keep touch with what was going on was to send my intelligence officer daily to study Monty's own operational map."

Monty himself summarized his approach: "My policy in the north is to get the show tidied up and to ensure absolute security before passing over to offensive action"; moreover offensive action "will be taken by 7 [U.S.] Corps only when that Corps is fully assembled and ready to deal a hard blow."

It was all very well Patton boasting to SHAEF he would be launching his counterattack "with six divisions" in the south in less than twenty-four hours; according to Monty's "gallopers" the three divisions of General Middleton's 8 U.S. Corps were in chaos. "I sent a LO down that way yesterday and he returned tonight with a picture of a very disorganised front with divisions in bits and pieces all over the place," Monty informed Brooke on 21 December. His forecast of the result of Patton's counterthrust was therefore pessimistic. "My information about the situation on the southern front about BASTOGNE is somewhat alarming and it looks to me as if the enemy columns are moving westwards having passed that place."

Whatever Patton might proclaim, Monty was frankly doubtful that Patton's premature attack would do anything to halt the enemy's main westward drive. Indeed, not even SHAEF believed Patton in this respect—as Air Vice-Marshal Robb noted in his diary on 21 December 1944: "Concern was expressed by the Deputy Supreme Commander and others that the counter attack being mounted by Bradley might be a piecemeal affair similar to the German counter-attacks in Normandy. This might happen if the two divisions that were on their way were put in without awaiting build-up of greater strength."

Even Eisenhower was skeptical. "The Supreme Commander mentioned that what he was afraid of was that the impetuous Patton would talk Bradley round into allowing him to attack at once with the object of going right through and not awaiting a fully coordinated counter-offensive," Robb chronicled. As a result, Bradley was ordered to relieve Bastogne, but not to let the attack "spread" until a "firm stepping off point" had been established, with sufficient reserves to sustain a genuine "main counter-offensive."

But the "main counter-offensive" was, in truth, all hot air.

Living in a Fool's Paradise

How Eisenhower imagined he could fight, like Hitler, the land battle of the Ardennes by telephone from his locked and shuttered office at Versailles is difficult in retrospect to credit. In truth all he could do was monitor events and issue exhortations, hundreds of miles in the rear. Even his own staff admitted that as the battle developed, information at SHAEF became scarcer and more and more out of date—sometimes a day and a half to two days late.

Afraid to leave his office building, night or day, Eisenhower could not really hope to dictate effective orders to Devers or to Bradley—whose staff, as Monty explained to Brooke on 21 December with disdain, "consider the attack north of Third U.S. Army is going to finish the Germans completely."

Monty, a professional soldier to his fingertips, was less sanguine. "12 Army Group attack began today before it was really ready," he reported. "From the limited information at my disposal I am not happy about the southern front and I have a definite feeling that Third U.S. Army will get involved with 7 German Army [the force protecting the southern flank of the German counteroffensive] and will be stopped from thrusting northwards to interfere with 5 Pz Army.

"I do not think Third U.S. Army will be strong enough to do what is needed. If my forecast proves true then I shall have to deal unaided with both 5 and 6 Panzer Armies. I think I can probably manage this but it will be a bit of a party."

Admiral Ramsay, attending the daily SHAEF conference at Versailles at 9 A.M. the following day, felt the same concern about Patton: "Weather prevented air forces taking any part in the battle. Patton launching a counter attack on the southern flank with three divisions that seems to have made little progress."

Nevertheless, the fact that Monty was now in charge north of

Bastogne seems to have reassured SHAEF that the German offensive would be contained. As Ramsay put it, "Monty having taken over the northern half of the battle gives one confidence that this part will soon be stabilized. I am less sure of the southern half."

Bradley's failure either to visit his field commanders or even to send staff officers to see them was a sign, meanwhile, of bewildering complacency. American newspapermen and even leading baseball players were touring the front. Yet because of the assassination scare Bradley remained secluded in his office, or at night in his hotel. Moreover he seemed to have little idea and even less concern about the fate of his former two armies north of Bastogne. When confronted by the prospect of the Germans reaching the Meuse bridges, he declared that he had "been expecting it for several days. SHAEF is terribly worried about this," he continued. "I'm not. If they get up to the river, there aren't many bridges he [the enemy] can use." "The prospect that advance elements of the German penetration may soon reach the Meuse does not seem to worry him a bit," his ADC recorded on 23 December!

Confined in Luxembourg, Bradley was living in a fool's paradise, fostered largely by ignorance of the true battle situation on Hodges' front, and the presence now of the swashbuckling Patton, who had moved into Bradley's hotel alongside him. "Patton has been living with the general, scurrying quickly to his headquarters each morning. . . . He and Brad get long famously with their 'Brad' and 'George' adlibbing. 'Don't come in George, if you're not bringing good news,' and Brad would laugh."

There was little to laugh about, however. On 24 December Bradley gave a press briefing in which he announced that he had foreseen the possibility of the enemy's attack in the Ardennes six weeks before the battle, and that for this reason had sited no American dumps of ammunition or petrol east of the Meuse! This, as Bradley well knew, was patently false. The unpublishable truth was, the whole area east of the Meuse around Liège was *littered* with supply and fuel depots—much of which had to be destroyed lest they fall into German hands. It was nothing short of a miracle that the German onslaught had missed major American arsenals—as Bradley's staff privately confessed ("General Moses, our G-4, tells me the enemy could not have chosen a more fortunate route of advance as far as the movement of supplies is concerned," Hansen noted in his diary).

Fueling Bradley's complacency, sadly, had been the reports of his 12 Army Group chief of Intelligence, Brigadier General Sibert, who on 22 December had calculated that the bulk of the German reserves were now committed—an estimate he came to rue in the days thereafter, as he did his complete failure to recognize the German buildup in the Ardennes throughout November and December. Two days later, on 24 December, General Sibert was "revising upwards" all his estimates of German strength, adding not only 25,000 more men to the enemy total (now reckoned to number 335,000 troops, or twice the number of troops the Allies had landed on D-Day), but almost three times the originally estimated number of Panzers—some 905 heavy tanks now, as opposed to the 345 he had first indicated.

Though Sibert's latest news did not visibly upset General Bradley's demeanor, it evidently affected his digestive system—"a light recurrent attack of those stomach troubles that aggravated his condition last week," his ADC recorded.

The failure of Patton's piecemeal attacks, moreover, did not help. As the Germans simply brushed them aside and swept on toward the Meuse, both Bradley and his 12 Army Group staff became more and more shamed and uncomfortable. It was in this situation, indeed, watching with impotence while the German "juggernaut" drove on, that they became more and more concerned by Monty's refusal to counterattack before he was ready—ridiculing Monty's concern for the security of the Meuse bridges and his "characteristic caution" in "building a conventional line of defence."

But, whatever Bradley might think in the ivory tower of his Luxembourg hotel, reality was very different in the field of battle—where, as Monty learned for himself, American infantry soldiers were still fighting with great courage, often against overwhelming odds, and still without Allied air support.

Honoring the Fighting Man

B earing the brunt of the German armored offensive, General Hodges had become increasingly anxious on 21 December lest the Germans make an all-out drive on Liège through Ridgway's

18 Corps sector at Malmédy. The following morning, 22 December, General Collins became alarmed that the Germans would attempt to drive west through his 7 Corps assembly area and across the Meuse, and asked Hodges' chief engineer "to find out what bridges in that area had been prepared for demolition. . . ."

"There was, however, no need for him to worry about this," Hodges' ADC noted with relief on the evening of 22 December, "as Monty arrived shortly after 1.45 and brought the General the good news that an Armoured Brigade with 50 tanks at NAMUR, 50 at GIVET and 50 at a point equi-distant between those two towns, had sent its reconnaissance elements forward to the VII assembly area and would methodically clean up any small pockets of Germans if such existed. . . . Monty was chipper and confident as usual. The employment of this Armoured Brigade to screen in back of VII Corps area lifted a tremendous load off the General's mind. Obviously we had no troops to do it," Captain Sylvan candidly confessed.

What Sylvan did not relate was a further "load" Monty had taken off General Hodges' mind. Hodges was intending to move his headquarters again that day, this time west of the Meuse. He was not in touch with all his First U.S. Army formations and units, and still had made no attempt to go forward to see them in person or give heart to their commanders. Moreover, despite his own move to the rear, he refused to authorize any withdrawal on the battlefront. Thus when General Gerow, the experienced 5 U.S. Corps commander, asked permission to pull back to a better defensive line from Monschau to Elsenborn, Hodges would only give unofficial approval, thus forcing Gerow to take formal and personal responsibility for the American retreat. Similarly, when Major General Hasbrouck requested permission to withdraw 7th U.S. Armored Division from the American salient at Saint-Vith while there was still time, Hodges refused.

Monty's style was radically different. Ever since taking command of First U.S. Army on 20 December he been determined to obtain his own picture of Hodges' front, both from his own visits and from the reports of his liaison officers. He reported to Brooke on the night of 22 December:

My own personal team of LOs has now gained for me a very complete picture of the situation of First Army. Many stray combat teams were discovered in strange and unexpected places. . . .

The most curious discovery was the situation S.E. of VIELSALM. 7 US Armd Div stretches in a sausage shape area from incl VIELSALM through PETIT THIER and POTEAU to ST VITH. Then in the general area NEUNDOR THOMMEN ALDRINGEN BOUIGNY are three combat teams one each of 28 DIV, 106 DIV, 9 ARMD DIV and two task forces of stragglers. The whole party to the S.E. of VIELSALM consisting of 7 Armd Div and other stray units was heavily attacked this morning by SS troops and was in grave danger of being done in. I was at HQ First US Army at the time and I gave orders at once that the whole party was to be withdrawn at once into reserve in the BRA area 5793 and this is being done. This reserve will be very useful in that area where before there was none.

Monty's decisiveness was viewed with disbelief at 12 Army Group Headquarters, where Bradley, as his ADC described, now spent his time poring over colored charts:

I found the general on his knees before the map, peering through his bifocals at the road net in the Luxembourg area used by the Germans to support his effort. The general marked them in carefully with a brown crayon pencil. Figured that the XII Corps offensive [under Patton] would cut one, permit the other to be interdicted by art[iller]y fire. He figured similarly on road cuts and interdictions from the St Vith sector, turned about and pointed to the road—"if we cut this and cover this with arty fire," he said, "this fellow will begin to sweat."

The sweating, however, was being done by American troops, such as the survivors of 7 U.S. Armored Division. Bradley's paper courage bore no relation to the trials and tribulations of such men in combat. Far from being in a position to make "road cuts and interdictions" from the Saint-Vith sector, the unhappy Major General Hasbrouck was aware on 22 December that his hours were numbered. Monty's LO arrived in the morning; having given the young British captain a briefing on the situation in Saint-Vith, Hasbrouck declared that he was prepared to fight on in his present positions if the stand was considered vital, but that he personally favored withdrawal to a cohesive defensive line. By 11 A.M. he was predicting to General Ridgway, his 18 Corps Commander, that he would be unable to "prevent a complete breakthrough if another all-out attack comes tonight," and in a postscript, as the next German attack by Fifth Panzer Army came, added: "In my opinion if we don't get out of here and up north of the 82nd before night, we will not have a 7th Armoured Division left."

Monty's decision to overrule Hodges, however, was final. "They can come back with all honour. They come back to more secure positions. They put up a wonderful fight," Monty declared. As the American Official Historian remarked, Monty's decision "here showed the ability to honor the fighting man which had endeared him to the hearts of the Desert Rats in North Africa." Hodges, "tired and worried from the strain under which he had lived since 16 December, agreed to the withdrawal."

Whatever happened in the south, Monty was adamant that no more American lives be sacrificed than necessary. For this he would become a hero to the men in the field—but be excoriated by Bradley's outraged staff.

Eisenhower—Pinned in the Office

B oth Bradley and Patton refused to think of anything but counterattack—leading Eisenhower to underestimate, in Monty's view, the seriousness of the Allied position.

Monty's own appreciation was that both Fifth and Sixth Panzer Armies were bypassing Bastogne and sweeping westwards and northwards against First U.S. Army, with the motorized infantry of Seventh German Army "attacking S.W. towards ARLON with the intention of widening the gap and keeping Third US Army in the south away from 5 Pz Army," as he described in his nightly cable to Brooke on 22 December. As a soldier and a general he took his hat off to the German Commander-in-Chief: "RUNDSTEDT is fighting a good battle."

Monty felt supremely confident he could handle Rundstedt, now that he had "tidied up the mess and have got the two American armies properly organised." By judicious rearrangement, on the field of battle, he now held a reserve corps of four American divisions, two of them armored, under General Collins, "which will make a very powerful force." But with Patton failing to "interfere with 5 Pz Army," Collins' corps would probably have to do the job: "5 Pz Army will have to deal with my 7 Corps positioned as in Para 4 [Barvaux–Marche–Nettenne–Terwagne area] and that Corps will not be easy to by pass or to shift."

Where Monty "saw rocks ahead" was in the "optimism that IKE seems to feel" at SHAEF. For with the enemy fighting such a good battle, the Americans were in for considerable further casualties as well as much disappointment if they truly considered Patton's attack was going to "finish the Germans completely."

Eisenhower had directed that a Special Order of the Day be prepared—one which was "not to be a Backs to the Wall Order but, on the contrary, an order of encouragement and pointing out that this is the opportunity," the chief of staff, air operations, at SHAEF recorded. The order, when drafted, ended with the stirring slogan: "United in this determination and with unshakeable faith in the cause for which we fight, we will, with God's help, go forward to our greatest victory."

Such paper messages about "greatest victory" reinforced Monty's conviction that Eisenhower, like Bradley, was living in cloud-cuckoo land in Versailles—though Eisenhower was himself more anxious than Monty perhaps knew. His personal assistant, Kay Summersby, recorded frankly in her diary:

> Our attack [by Patton's 3 U.S. Corps] got off. It now appears that the German forces in the North are stronger than we had antisipated [sic], they are still attacking, the weather has been bad, for the last 3 days it has been impossible to use our air. Long sessions for E[isenhower]. with Strong, Bull [chief of American operations]. Strong is uneasy regarding the Russians, we do not know what they are going to do, the German is withdrawing Divs from the R[ussian] front. E. is going to send a cable to the CCS [Combined Chiefs of Staff] re the Russians. G2 [Intelligence staff] have no new reports re E's life, the [assassination] "party" is supposed to be in Paris.

This was the aspect of Allied military history which no one, in the aftermath, wished to acknowledge. Eisenhower's biographer Stephen Ambrose even went so far as to write that "Eisenhower's confidence in himself had grown tremendously during the crisis. . . . Whatever Brooke and Montgomery might say about his lack of experience, he had taken control of the battle and made it his."

This, unfortunately, was moonshine—as all the participants knew. By 23 December, Mrs. Summersby was recording: "Patton is still attacking, going is slow on account of demolitions, munes [sic] etc. . . . *E. is still pinned up in the office.*"

Admiral Ramsay, in his own diary, was less charitable. While the Supreme Commander/Land Forces C-in-C had remained locked away for four days and nights during a critical Allied battle, seemingly every journalist and entertainer in northwest Europe appeared at liberty to move where he wished. Nor did Ramsay have much faith in the Bradley-Patton counteroffensive, launched on 22 December: "the centre of the breakthrough is still unsealed. Three divisions are on their way to close it, but two of these have never been in action before," he remarked caustically. The following day he was even more forthright. "Very little news, gap still open. It is most disturbing," he added, "that Supreme HQ should be without information later than about 36–48 hours."

Ramsay had, after a distinguished performance in the Mediterranean, masterminded the Allied naval role in the D-Day landings. He had deplored Monty's failure to open Antwerp quickly in September, but his opinion of Eisenhower as the Allied Land Forces Commander was, after four months, utterly damning:

> It is only too clear that there is no Supreme Operational Command in existence. No master-mind and therefore no staff of one.

Such frank commentary even by Eisenhower's own colleagues would be, as far as possible, erased from the official record, once the battle was over and the Allies moved forward to their ultimate victory. In the dire postwar need for American political and military presence in Europe, Eisenhower's reputation as the personification of inter-Allied cooperation would be lauded to the skies—whereas Monty's prickly, boastful arrogance was abhorred, for all his battlefield virtues. As Monty once said of his nemesis, Eisenhower's British deputy chief of staff, General Morgan, he "considered Eisenhower was a god . . . he placed me at the other end of the celestial ladder."

Difficult, dictatorial, often impossibly small-minded, Monty had never been nor would ever be the personification of cooperation. "Cooperation, my dear chap?" he had once responded when, during his prewar military invasion rehearsal he had been asked how he got the other services, air and navy, to cooperate. "No problem there. *I tell them what to do and they do it.*"

Such a man, in a coalition war, could be a menace. However, in a tight corner he could be a saving grace—and behind the historical curtain that would be rung down on the Allied catastrophe in the Ardennes, Monty's simple battlefield genius inspired his commanders—American and British—to renewed confidence in their ability to meet and defeat the German onslaught.

A Shortage of Manpower

From this point in the Battle of the Bulge, Churchill gave up relying on SHAEF for information. On the basis of Monty's unexpurgated telegrams of 22, 23 and 24 December, Churchill soon felt content to leave the Ardennes battle in Monty's hands, deciding to fly out instead to Greece to harden the British garrison in Athens.

Monty was now by far and away the senior Allied army group commander in the field, commanding some four Allied armies; Bradley and Devers each commanded only four corps. General Collins, the "piss and vinegar" commander chosen to marshal the reserve corps in the north, later concluded: "Eisenhower was right in my judgement in placing Montgomery . . . in command of all troops on the north side. . . . A dangerous front had been opened, which would have made it difficult if not impossible for Bradley to have controlled operations north of the Bulge from his headquarters in Luxembourg. For the Army's part of this success [driving the enemy back to the West Wall] Monty deserves much credit, though the same results could have been achieved sooner and with more devastating losses to the enemy if [Montgomery] had acted boldly and with greater confidence in the ability of the American troops and their combat leaders."

Collins felt that Monty ought to have counterattacked towards Saint-Vith, so as to hit the enemy salient at its neck; Lieutenant General Horrocks, Collins' counterpart, commanding the British 30 Corps in reserve west of the Meuse, was, by contrast, convinced Monty ought to have withheld all American counterattacks, allowing, instead, the German Panzer armies to penetrate as far west as Waterloo, thirty miles west of Namur; whereupon he, Horrocks, would have seen to their destruction in a grand tribute to Wellington.

Monty himself spurned both suggestions. Hitler was not to be given the honor of crossing the Meuse; equally, an offensive towards Saint-

Vith, where the Germans were strongest and nearest to their supplies, would entail senseless loss of American life. From the beginning he had chosen Bastogne as the target of his counterattack; but even this axis was likely to be more difficult than Collins presumed, as Monty explained to Brooke on the evening of 23 December. The answer, Monty felt, was to let the combined Panzer offensive run on against his own reorganized defensive line, as at Alam Halfa and Medenine: forcing the enemy to lose heavy casualties by having to assault prepared defenses. Then "when the time comes to pass over to the offensive with [Collins'] 7 Corps my present idea is to direct it southeastwards towards the road centre of HOUFFALIZE about eight miles north of BASTOGNE. I am not clear yet as to when I shall be able to begin this movement and hope to be able to let you know further on this point tomorrow night by which time the intention of 6 and 5 Panzer Armies may have become clearer."

For the moment, two enemy Panzer divisions from Fifth Panzer Army were "tapping in against 7 US Corps and trying to overlap to the west," while Sixth Panzer Army, despairing of a breakthrough at the northern shoulder of the salient, seemed also to be moving west and "may possibly try again in a north-westerly direction" on Ridgway's 18 Corps front. This was all to the good, Monty reported. What caused him to question the likelihood of effective Allied counterattack was the lack of infantry troops in the American divisions:

> A disturbing factor which is coming to light as I visit American formations is the weak state of most divisions. I visited HQ 5 Corps at EUPEN today and found that the four divisions of that corps in the line are together deficient of 7,000 men mostly infantry and that 5 Armd Div in reserve is only sixty per cent of its strength.

One of Monty's LOs, visiting 29th U.S. Division, found it 2,000 men below strength, mainly in infantry. "I fear it is much the same in all divisions and I am told that there are no replacements in sight in Europe. This shortage of manpower in American divisions is a new one on me," Monty confessed—and it cast a deep shadow over Bradley's claims to have been inflicting, in his abortive November offensive and south of the Ardennes, unbearable losses upon the enemy.

As Monty visited his corps and divisional commanders, directing his familiar razor-sharp questions, it became increasingly clear that it was the Americans, not the Germans, who had failed to replace their autumn losses.

Collins, eager to "have a crack" at the Boches, was not interested in such realities, however. Indeed, all too often commanders were indifferent to the importance of the welfare of their own men, as General Horrocks discovered when he took Collins' 84th U.S. Division under command, a few weeks prior to the Ardennes battle:

> The thing that worried me most was the initial failure of the Americans to get a hot meal through to their forward troops. This is where battle experience counts. It may be necessary to make the most elaborate plans many hours beforehand; but if troops are to go on fighting in winter, somehow or other they must get hot food. Every day my first question to the 84th was: "How many units have had a hot meal during the night?"
>
> The first day the answer was—none. The second day—fifty per cent, and the third day—100 per cent. The great thing about the Americans was that they were very quick to learn.

As Monty toured his northern flank, however, he was less and less convinced that the Americans *had* learned about soldier welfare. Many troops had not had a hot meal since the beginning of the battle on 16 December. The chances of a "great victory" in such bitter December weather, with divisions so short in infantry, struck Monty as unlikely. He might be criticized behind his back for being overcautious, but his loyalty was to the lives of the men fighting the German penetration— and such lives ought not, he felt, to be squandered in uncoordinated and expensive counterattacks against Germans in possession of ground of their own choosing.

By Christmas Eve the enemy, unhindered by Patton's much-trumpeted offensive, was "now attacking 7 US Corps in the area about HOTTON and MARCHE," with further elements striking east to the Meuse. The German 2nd Panzer Division had even come within striking distance of the river, leading to the first confrontation between German and British tanks, as Monty cabled Brooke:

> Between CINEY and DINANT is a gap and 3 R[oyal] Tanks from the DINANT bridgehead has been engaged with 2 Pz Div today in this gap and has destroyed four TIGER tanks without loss.

Monty's plan was, if necessary, to lure the German spearhead northwards from the Marche area up to the Meuse between Namur and Huy. The Germans would not be able to cross the Meuse, since the river was defended by the Guards Armoured Division; between Namur and Huy the German spearhead could be hammered by artillery from both sides—Horrocks' 30 British Corps firing from the west, Collins' 7 U.S. Corps from the east—as well as from the air, now the skies were clear and the RAF and American air forces were once again beginning to operate. For this reason Monty had given orders that Collins should *not* commit his reserve corps to battle yet, but should swing back his right flank to the Meuse at Ardennes and Huy if attacked in strength.

When Collins received the order, by telephone, he misunderstood it, however. Hodges' chief of staff dared not spell out the names Ardennes and Huy, so referred to them as "A" and "H." Collins, who already had his 2nd U.S. Armored Division positioned between the villages of Achène and Houisse, was dumbfounded when, that evening, he was told by a special messenger from Hodges of the true meaning of the initials. To him, the idea of withdrawal was tinged with defeatism, and by locking 2nd U.S. Armored Division in combat against German reconnaissance elements he was able to get Hodges to rescind the order.

Monty was dumbfounded by Collins' disobedience. As he lamented to Brooke, he "had hoped that 7 Corps would be able to remain concentrated and available for offensive action but it is now getting involved with 5 Panzer Army." He had therefore given orders to pull Ridgway's 18 Corps back from the Vielsalm salient to the "general line GRANDMENIL–TROIS PONTS. This will give it a short front and some useful reserves."

Such orders, when heard at Bradley's headquarters, gave rise to rumors that Monty was being unnecessarily defensive—ignoring the fact that, the previous day, Monty had ordered all demolition charges to be removed from the Meuse bridges, so confident did he now feel about being able to hold the line of the river. With Collins becoming involved, however, Monty's hopes of a really powerful counterattack by the American forces in the Ardennes dwindled, as he explained to Brooke:

> I cannot pass over to any large offensive action just at present as I am very stretched and the American divisions are all weak and below establishment. I shall hold firm on my present line and I do not think the enemy will be able to break it or to get over the MEUSE at GIVET. I shall aim at getting the enemy very stretched and shall harry and jab him all the time. The main offensive action just at present must be from the air and given a spell of fine weather we should make his life intolerable by air action. While this air action is going on I shall form another striking force.

He would have to start over again.

The Last Great Defensive Battle

As at Alam Halfa and in Normandy the effectiveness of Monty's strategy—however misunderstood then and later—was proved by the actions of the enemy. Field Marshal Model, commanding the three German armies attacking the Ardennes, was unhappy about Patton's thrust to relieve Bastogne; but Field Marshal von Rundstedt, as the C-in-C West, overruled him, arguing on 24 December that, from his Intelligence and planning staff, he was certain the Allies could not assemble a force strong enough to defend the Meuse before 30 December. The German Panzer armies were thus given six days in which to reinforce their successful advance, now only six miles from the river.

Apart from one combat group peeled from 15th Panzer Grenadier Division, *no* German forces were switched to the siege of Bastogne, and *no* further forces whatever were assigned to meet Patton's piecemeal thrust from the south. As in an aggressive game of chess, the Germans simply ignored the threat on one side of the board in order to concentrate their offensive strength upon their primary objective: the Meuse.

With 30 British and 7 U.S. Corps already assembled by 23 December, however, Monty confounded German expectations by some seven days. Patient and secure in the knowledge that time was on his side, Monty was in his element, once again leading four great armies in the field, in the last great defensive battle of the war.

Unfortunately Bradley, responsible only for a single army—and that commanded by Patton—was surrounded by staff officers increasingly critical of the Briton who had supplanted their "chief." Thus, as in Normandy, the stage was set for misunderstandings and intrigue, at the very moment that the fate of the German armies was sealed.

A Change in Inter-Allied Feelings

U naware of the true state of his former American troops in the Ardennes, and unwilling to interfere with Patton's conduct of Third U.S. Army, Bradley meanwhile began to formulate plans for a 12th Army Group offensive through the Eifel area of the Ardennes, once the current battle was over and Ninth and First U.S. Armies were restored to his command. He blamed Monty, not Collins, for having "dissipated the VII Corps by committing them on a defense line that runs west to Givet and the river." Moreover, despite the slow, costly and still ineffective advance made by Patton, Bradley considered that "we have been making good progress from the south," his ADC recorded. "He is anxious for a closing movement from the north."

Bradley's misreading of Monty's performance in the north was perhaps inevitable given the setback he had suffered, his lack of communications, the failure of Patton's counteroffensive ("They seem unable to get through," Bradley's ADC, Major Hansen, noted, puzzled, on 24 December) and the loss of two-thirds of his army group. Certainly his ADC, once so respectful of Monty's patient leadership in Normandy, now gave way to derisive comments about Monty's "stagnating conservatism of tactics," accusations that Monty had become "quite panicky initially," and remarks such as "Monty's contributions in the Sicilian campaign were negligible. His part in the battle of France and the Lowlands have always been subordinated to ours. . . ."

Since Hansen was later to ghost Bradley's memoirs, this was an ominous change in attitude. It would become, indeed, a symbol of the abrupt change in inter-Allied feelings in the winter of 1944–45, confirming Monty's subsequent impression that whatever he said of the battle, he was bound to be misunderstood. The humiliation of the Ardennes had been too much for American pride; thereafter he himself would inevitably become the scapegoat of senior officers shamed by their misfortune.

What Monty conveniently overlooked, however, was the humiliation he had personally administered to Bradley. For on Christmas Day 1944, nine days after the Battle of the Bulge began, Bradley had finally ventured out from his headquarters at Luxembourg for a meeting with Monty: a meeting which all major historians of the battle would neglect, yet one which the participants themselves could *never* forget and which Bradley—essentially a simple, gentle, shy soul—could also never forgive.

"What a Life!!"

Monty's letter to his son's guardian told all:

Tac Headquarters:
21 Army Group
Xmas Day 25–12–44

My dear Phyllis

My plans for coming home for a few days at Christmas did not mature; events, and the enemy, decreed otherwise. The Americans have taken a 1st Class bloody nose; I have taken over command of the First and Ninth American armies and all troops in the northern part of the front, and I am busy sorting out the mess. I hope you will all have a very happy time.

What a life!!

My love to you all.

Monty

Brooke, as we have seen, had specifically warned Monty not to crow about the American catastrophe. Such cautioning from the War Office world of London did not, however, take sufficient account of Monty's vengefulness. His demolition from command of the Allied Land Forces on 1 September 1944, and Eisenhower's subsequent refusal to concentrate his forces, had offended his professional pride as a soldier in a way he had found difficult to control. Now, with the demise of Eisenhower's policy of separated thrusts, and Bradley's being relieved of his command of First and Ninth U.S. armies, Monty exulted.

To Admiral Mountbatten, Supreme Allied Commander in Southeast Asia, Monty wrote on the same day, in almost the same triumphant words, purportedly restraining himself, but making quite clear his contempt for his allies:

> I won't add my comments on the war. The Americans have taken the most awful "bloody nose" and have been cut clean in half. I now once more find myself commander of two American armies as well as 21 Army Group, and am trying to clean up the mess.
>
> Personally I always enjoy a good battle. But this thing should never have happened; one ought really to burst into tears. It has prolonged the war by months.

To General Sir Oliver Leese, Mountbatten's new Land Forces Commander-in-Chief, Monty wrote in identical vein, ending with the ominous words:

> I won't add my comment on the war. There is no ink that I know would stand up to what I would like to say.

Bradley, meanwhile, arrived at Monty's headquarters at 3 P.M. Fearing German fighter interception, Bradley's chief of Intelligence had insisted he fly from Etain, almost fifty miles from Luxembourg; but when Bradley reached Etain it was to find that his aircrew was still waiting for him at Luxembourg! By the time he had been given an aircraft with a makeshift crew, and had had to line up with dozens of transport aircraft awaiting takeoff at 1 P.M., Bradley became more and more impatient. "Another 10 minutes," he told his ADC, "and I would have called the damned thing off."

Accompanied by an escort of American fighters, however, Bradley finally flew to Saint-Trond. There, by the runway, he could see no car to greet him. "If there's no transportation," he said, "we'll climb in the plane and go back."

Bradley had not seen Hodges since before the battle of the Ardennes had begun; Monty he had not seen since the Maastricht conference on 7 December. Then he had held his head high, his strategy in the ascendant, his forces outnumbering those of Monty almost three to one. Now, however, he came in shame, his victory at Maastricht having turned disastrously sour in only a week. Part of him, indeed, had no wish to see Monty at all. So distracted was he that while riding to Monty's headquarters in the staff car provided by General Hodges, he expressed astonishment at the way the people in the villages were all wearing their Sunday clothes. He was then reminded it was Christmas Day!

Dressed in a simple, loose-hanging arctic coat, his three general's stars still concealed beneath white tape, Bradley entered Monty's headquarters with understandable apprehension. "Hqs were located in a small house near the road front," Hansen recorded in his diary, "and the officers there had celebrated Christmas, smoked pipes over port in the lower room where all of Monty's Christmas cards were tacked to a wall in exhibition. They came from everyone and from almost all of his regiments. Quite different from the Amerks where many of our people busily engaged in heavy fighting, neglected to send their cards this year."

For Christmas lunch Bradley had munched an apple and a pear, given him by the chief of U.S. supplies. He had only dared to walk from his headquarters to his hotel for the first time the previous day. "I felt suddenly conscious for my old combat jacket and patched GI trousers," Hansen confessed, as his revered general mounted the stairs alone with Monty "for a conference."

Monty, leading Bradley up to his study, had chosen to wear regulation uniform, with a tailored battle blouse bearing his many rows of medal ribbons, knife-edged trousers, and shining leather shoes. Bradley, wrapped in his arctic coat, "looked thin, and worn, and ill at ease," Monty described in a letter to "Simbo" Simpson at the War Office. "He was obviously tired. I explained my situation, and made certain he understood."

The enemy, Monty summarized for Simpson in the same terms that he used with Bradley, "has the initiative. He is using his left to hold off Bradley and with his right—two Panzer Armies—he is attacking me.

"I shall hold him.

"But the American divisions are all very weak, and any major offensive action from the north against the right flank of the enemy penetrations is definitely not possible at present. The 5 Panzer Army is now engaged with the garrison of the DINANT bridgehead.

"In the south, Bradley is trying hard to get to BASTOGNE to relieve 101 Airborne Div. He may possibly get that place, but he admits himself that he is not strong enough to get any further.

"The enemy is in such strength that, neither from the north nor from the south, can we develop offensive action in sufficient strength to cause him to react.

"All we can do is to attack him ceaselessly from the air; for this we require good weather, which we have now had for two days.

"The enemy will get very stretched and this, combined with our air attack, may cause him to wonder if he should not pull back a bit: having given us a real 'bloody nose.'

"This is all we can hope for as things are at present. And we can hope for that much, only if we get good weather.

"We are holding the two enemy Panzer Armies off from infiltrating the First U.S. Army area only because for the last two days it has been good flying weather and we have been able to hit the enemy hard from the air. If the weather goes bad on us, then we may have difficulty in holding him. This is a very important point to bear in mind."

According to Monty's account, Bradley "agreed with my summary of the situation. I then asked him what Eisenhower proposed to do."

This question, perhaps more than any other feature of the Ardennes, was the most extraordinary: the final Allied indignity, since, incarcerated still at the Trianon Palace Hotel, the Allied Land Forces Commander-in-Chief had not spoken to Monty since giving him command of the main battle in the Ardennes.

The Humiliation of Bradley

B radley was nonplussed. "He said he had not seen Eisenhower recently," Monty recorded, almost in disbelief, "and did not know."

Monty's own strategic view was clear. The German onslaught should blunt itself against a firm Allied line, employing corps artillery and Allied air attack. But as far as counteroffensive operations in the Ardennes were concerned, Monty was now convinced that without more troops, the Americans were unlikely to quickly regain the initiative, let alone win a great victory against a German army group of more than a third of a million men, in ideal defensive country that made the Normandy bocage seem straightforward:

> I said it was quite clear that neither of us could do anything without more troops.
>
> We must shorten our front somewhere and thus save divisions; this can be done only by withdrawing back our right flank [between the Ardennes and Switzerland].
>
> I was absolutely frank with Bradley. I said the Germans had given us a real "bloody nose"; it was useless trying to pretend that we were going to turn this quickly into a great victory; it was a proper defeat, and we had much better admit it, and it would take time to put right.
>
> I then said it was entirely our fault; we had gone much too far with our right; we had tried to develop two thrusts [against the Ruhr and the Saar] at the same time, and neither had been strong enough to gain decisive results.
>
> The enemy saw his chance and took it.
>
> Now we were in a proper muddle. We must admit all this, and then someone must make a big decision as regards withdrawal on the right.
>
> For the future we must at all costs hang on to our present bridgehead area beyond the MEUSE in the north; if we lost that then any advance against the RUHR would be off. The enemy knows this well.
>
> Therefore there must be no withdrawal in the north; we might be driven back, but we must not withdraw.
>
> But there is no objective in the south, and I have never understood what we were after down there.
>
> A withdrawal to the line of the SAAR river, running south from SAARBRUCKEN and linking with the COLMAR pocket, would "iron out" the STRASBOURG salient and save four divisions. A big withdrawal, back to the line of the MEUSE from CHARLEVILLE southwards to TOUL and thence down the MOSELLE, would save possibly 12 divisions.
>
> We talk about passing over to the offensive, but it must be clearly understood that we had not now got the troops for the offensive.
>
> We should never have gone so far with our right; we must now come back with our right and thus collect divisions for offensive action. I said I had always advised against the right going so far: I said I knew that he (Bradley) had advised in favour of it; Eisenhower had decided to take his (Bradley's) advice.
>
> Bradley agreed entirely with all I said. Poor chap; he is such a decent fellow and the whole thing is a bitter pill for him. But he is man enough to admit it, and he did.

A Poisoned Heart

D id Bradley admit his error?

Bradley dictated no memorandum of the meeting. However, it is improbable he would have admitted to Monty his entire tactical strategy since the autumn had been wanting, nor that his American armies had, through his negligence, been "defeated." He wrote to General Marshall a few days afterwards, "As a matter of fact, I do not blame my staff, my commanders, nor myself for the fact that the Germans were able to launch this attack against us and gain ground."

To Monty, such excuses were "fudging" the issue. Far better, in Monty's simplistic mind, to acknowledge the fact manfully, pull oneself together, and to seek diligently to learn the lessons, as after Dunkirk.

Whatever was said during the interview, however, there can be little doubt that it was this personal and deliberate humiliation, not the much-publicized press conference later in the battle, that really poisoned Bradley's heart against Monty. He had been humbled, like a pupil before his headmaster.

Just as Monty hated to be told that Arnhem was a major defeat or "bloody nose," so Bradley responded poorly to this criticism of his leadership—and would return the compliment by disparaging Monty to later historians and chroniclers of the battle, including the American Official Historian in 1946. To the latter Bradley claimed that at Eisenhower's meeting at Verdun on 19 December, "much of the later dispositions" of First and Ninth Armies were made, and that Monty's subsequent "selection" as commander of the two American armies therefore "came as a surprise." "General Bradley said he knew of nothing particularly brilliant about Montgomery's tactics," when asked; he claimed that Monty planned a withdrawal of American forces that "was opposed by all American commanders"; and that Monty had been given charge of the two American armies not because of any break "in communications between my Headquarters and the northern forces" but "because it was the only way to get Monty to use British forces to help."

Such charges, given the true manner and circumstances in which Monty was authorized to take command of the American armies in the Ardennes, were preposterous. Yet the fact remains that Monty himself incited such a response by his total lack of sensitivity towards a shamed colleague: a hitherto loyal and sincere ally.

Monty's detractors would later consider this an example of his failure to "get on" with Americans; but Monty's relations with Hodges and Simpson and the American corps and divisional commanders during the critical days of the German offensive contradict this. The fact is, had Monty wished, he could easily have ensured Bradley's lasting loyalty and friendship by a display of gentle magnanimity, of understanding and goodwill. Instead, Monty chose to humiliate the shyest and most professional of American generals in his hour of shame—not, it would seem, from personal spite but simply because Monty was, at heart, as he had always been and always would be, a bully.

Eisenhower—A Bit Low in His Mind

Monty had not been speaking only for himself, however, when telling Bradley that no immediate and effective American counterattack was on the cards.

At considerable risk (for there were reports of enemy troops massing at Monschau for renewed attacks on the Ninth/First U.S. Army boundary) he had ordered General Simpson to thin out his Ninth U.S. Army front in order to send reserves to First U.S. Army; yet even on Christmas Day 1944, Hodges was appealing to Monty urgently for *more* troops to meet the continuing German offensive, and expressing grave anxieties about enemy infiltration on his 150-mile front, as his ADC's diary recorded. So anxious did Hodges become, indeed, that on Christmas Eve he had actually prepared "plans for the movement to the rear of all heavy equipment of V Corps divisions, in order that, if it becomes necessary for these troops to withdraw, the roads would not be clogged with this heavy material," Sylvan noted, "and it would be necessary to hand it over to the enemy."

"Despite the air's magnificent performance today things tonight look, if anything, worse than before," Sylvan added. "Indications from G2 [Intelligence] are that the Boche will attempt to drive north with everything he possesses towards VERVIERS and LIEGE. . . . We are doing our best to organize a defence in depth and only time can make that possible."

The following morning Sylvan recorded that "the situation looked bad; strong enemy pressure being directed due north from MANNAY and also in the CELLES area." Several American units were overrun and "forced to destroy their equipment."

If this was an army Bradley thought should be "slammed through on a pincer movement," as he told his ADC, then Bradley was not living in the real world. That evening a V-1 rocket landed outside First U.S. Army Headquarters, injuring sixty-five men and shaking the rest, but the American front held firm. "Tonight it can be said that the enemy is temporarily at least halted," Sylvan noted. "No more gains were chalked up by him today. This does not mean, as both the General and General Kean realise, that he is going to stop attacking. . . . General Kean impressed most forcibly on Field Marshal Montgomery this afternoon, in a telephone conversation that he wished to obtain at once an infantry division preferably the 102nd which could be replaced by a British division. We have the 51st Highlanders backing up our line [with 17,800 men] but the general would prefer to stick in the 102nd to strengthen the front of the XVIII and VII Corps."

Sadly, such diary entries would be rigorously excluded from both official and unofficial American narratives of the battle. Bradley, wishing to be home before dark, had not even taken the time to see Hodges in Verviers. His view of the battle was thus prejudiced not only by his humiliation at Monty's insensitive hands, but by continuing ignorance of conditions on the American northern flank; he never once met either Hodges or Simpson during the entire thirty-three-day battle.

Bradley, after 20 December, was, of course, no longer Hodges' or Simpson's commander. Eisenhower, however, remained Allied Land Forces Commander, and had no excuse to neglect his armies in the field, save timidity. Every day since assuming command of the First and Ninth U.S. Armies, Monty had loyally dispatched a telegram to Eisenhower reporting on events. Between 21 and 26 December, however, Monty received only one communication in return—a cable authorizing him on 22 December to recommend dismissal of Hodges or Simpson "if any change needs to be made on United States side"! ("Hodges was a bit shaken early on and needed moral support and was very tired," Monty responded. "He is doing better now and I see him and Simpson every day.") However, the absence of significant word from Eisenhower irritated Monty—and when, by Boxing Day, 26 December 1944, he had still heard nothing, he wrote with barely concealed contempt to the Director of Military Operations, "Simbo" Simpson:

> An interesting feature of the present situation is that I have no idea where IKE is.
> I asked Bradley yesterday; he did not know.
> I told Freddie [de Guingand] to ask Bedell [Smith].
> Bedell's reply was that IKE is locked up whatever that may mean.
> It may mean that they are frightened of his being shot up by enemy agents sent over here to kill him and me.
> Or it may mean that Bedell is fed up with the way IKE is quite unable to make up his mind about things, and he has persuaded him to stay at home and leave it to me and Bradley. Freddie thinks this is it. Bedell I know is very fed up with the whole affair.

Bedell Smith was certainly embarrassed by Eisenhower's immurement in the Trianon Palace Hotel. "E. is a bit low in his mind," Mrs. Summersby confided in her diary on 25 December—for with Monty's latest message decoded that morning, Eisenhower was near despair. Monty had already signaled to Eisenhower the deficiency of infantrymen in the American divisions, as well as his view that the two German Panzer armies would ignore Patton's hastily mounted counterattack and continue to concentrate their assault upon First U.S. Army. Now Monty was reporting he "could not at present pass over to offensive actions"—and nor could Bradley, even when Bastogne had been relieved: "BRADLEY said he hoped to get BASTOGNE but doubted his ability to get any further without more troops."

Where were such troops to come from? Two further divisions—6th British Airborne and 17th U.S. Airborne Divisions—were on their way from England for use in a ground role; 11th U.S. Armored Division was moving up from France. Beyond that the Allied cupboard was bare. Eisenhower would therefore *have* to thin out Devers' 6th Army Group, as Monty had suggested six days before, and was requesting yet again: "I consider if we are to wrest the initiative from the Germans we shall need more troops and we can get these only by withdrawing from salients and holding shorter fronts. I suggest that this aspect of the problem might be examined on the Southern front."

Eisenhower's heart undoubtedly sank upon receiving this cable. So preoccupied with the crisis had he and his staff been that Christmas Day had been forgotten entirely. He dreaded having to act decisively as Supreme Allied Commander by ordering Devers to shorten his front and to provide reinforcement for counterattack in the Ardennes; indeed, in his anxiety he had unwisely sent a message direct to Stalin asking if a senior SHAEF officer might be allowed to fly to Moscow to discuss *Russian* offensive plans! As Major General Strong later wrote, this was bound to smack of supplication in the midst of the Ardennes battle. Nevertheless Stalin's positive reply arrived on 26 December and Eisenhower ordered his deputy, Air Marshal Tedder, his chief of operations staff, Major General Bull, and a senior Intelligence officer to fly to Russia to find out more, as soon as weather permitted.

To Monty it seemed utterly extraordinary that Eisenhower could send his deputy and his most senior staff officers halfway across the world to discuss Russian military operations, but did not dare send them to 21 Army Group!

Eisenhower's fear of leaving his office and visiting his own commanders in the field also struck Monty as weird. Indeed, something of Monty's annoyance must have reached Eisenhower's ears (possibly via Bedell Smith), for on the night of 26 December Eisenhower finally ordered that a special train be got ready for a night journey to Brussels. He would, eleven days after the start of the Battle of the Bulge, finally go and see Monty, his senior commander in the field.

Planning the Next Battle

Eisenhower's ghosted memoirs, *Crusade in Europe*, published in 1948, later gave the impression that he had been the decisive, unwavering mind directing the efforts of the Allied armies in the winter of 1944–45. His decision to appoint Montgomery to command all Allied forces north of Givet was described as if Eisenhower were an exemplary battlefield commander—"I telephoned Bradley to inform him of this decision and then called Field Marshal Montgomery and gave him his orders."

Monty, however, knew the truth: knew that Eisenhower had been caught completely unawares by the German counteroffensive, had locked himself day and night in his office suite in fear of assassination, had appealed to the Russians for help; and, since the brief and garbled telephone call he'd made when asking Monty to take command of the American forces in the Ardennes, had issued *no orders whatsoever* regarding the battle!

To Monty, Eisenhower had proved a broken reed as supposed Land Forces Commander—a veritable mockery of the role; a performance that surpassed in incompetence even that of Lord Gort, when commander of the ill-fated British Expeditionary Force before Dunkirk. And with every day's silence, Monty's estimation of Eisenhower as a field general declined further—particularly when Eisenhower postponed his visit. (Eisenhower's train was caught in a German bombing raid. Weather conditions on 27 December then made it impossible for him to fly instead. At 10:30 that evening Monty signaled to Brooke: "EISENHOWER could not get here by air today and is coming up tonight by train.")

Unable to wait any longer, Monty decided to go ahead with his own strategic masterplan. The next morning, 28 December 1944, the roads were dangerously icy and often impassable. Nevertheless Hodges,

Dempsey, Crerar and Simpson all managed to motor to Monty's Zonhoven headquarters for a crucial conference at 9:45 A.M.—for it was now, in the presence of all four of his army commanders, that Monty gave out his plan.

Since Ultra intelligence indicated one final German attack in the Ardennes salient, Monty proposed to lure it onto the Allies' prepared positions, as at Alam Halfa. However, although he wished Collins to counterattack towards Houffalize thereafter, the attack was to be, in essence, a feint, forcing the Germans to keep their main Panzer and infantry reserves committed in the Ardennes, while Monty struck from the far north at the true Allied strategic target: the Ruhr. VERITABLE, Crerar noted of his operation to close up to the Rhine in the north, "would be mounted *just as soon as the Bosche became thoroughly involved in the counter-offensive which would shortly be launched by First U.S. and Third U.S. Armies* [author's italics]."

This stipulation has been italicized, for it was to become a cardinal misunderstanding among contemporary American critics and later military historians who found it hard to credit Monty's caution in the Ardennes. Yet whatever others might say or claim, Monty had not been put in charge of two American armies in the north merely to see them decimated in a hasty Allied counteroffensive, in appalling winter conditions, without full air support, and without training, preparation or rehearsal. He had, it was true, moved 30 Corps Headquarters from the Canadian army on 19 December to the Meuse; but he had *never* intended its British troops should be wasted in local fighting unless there were an unexpected German breakthrough. "From the point of view of the future mounting of Operation VERITABLE by First Canadian Army, he wished to keep H.Q. 30 Brit Corps, Corps troops and several British Divisions, earmarked for that operation, uncommitted to any active, exhausting operations," Crerar noted—for the primary role of 30 Corps was to be the backbone of Operation Veritable: a northern flank attack down the west bank of the Rhine, under the aegis of Crerar's Canadian army, that would enable Dempsey's British Second Army to vault the Rhine at Wesel and ultimately seize the Ruhr. "As soon, therefore, as 12 and 21 Army Groups' counter-offensives developed favourably," Crerar summarized Monty's orders, "it was his intention to transfer 30 Brit Corps, and the several Brit formations previously planned to be under its command, to Cdn Army and launch Operation 'VERITABLE' as speedily and forcefully as possible." 30 Corps would thus be in a "protective, rather than in an operational role" in the Ardennes, in order to retain maximum strength for its *real* offensive, roughly a fortnight after being released from the Ardennes.

General Hodges and Simpson clearly understood this strategy. So

did Crerar and Dempsey. But Eisenhower, as in Normandy, did not—
leading to decades of loyalist but irresponsible historiography.

Comply—or Fail

I t was early in the afternoon of Thursday, 28 December 1944,
when Eisenhower's train finally pulled into Hasselt station.
Monty was somewhat surprised by Eisenhower's presidential
arrival—as he told "Simbo" Simpson when the latter flew over to
Monty's headquarters the following day. "He said it was most impressive. The train drew into the station and immediately teams of
machine-gunners leapt out, placed their machine guns on both plat-
forms at each end of the train, and guards leapt out and took up every
possible vantage point. No question of letting any German assassination troops get at the Supreme Commander. Monty commented that
he himself felt rather naked just arriving with an armoured car behind
him, and he felt much safer with this enormous American guard before he met Ike."

Eisenhower was, however, embarrassed and somewhat ashamed—
even instituting an official investigation after the battle to determine
whether there had been due cause for such exaggerated security
measures.

Monty, meanwhile, immediately asked to get down to business—in
private. At Maastricht, on 7 December, Eisenhower had insisted that
his chief of staff, Bedell Smith, be present. As a result, Monty felt, the
American policy of dissipating Allied strength into two separate and
unrelated thrusts had prevailed, and he had lost the day. This time,
however, the situation was different. Bedell Smith had not accompanied Eisenhower, Tedder had flown to Moscow, and Monty refused to
let his own chief of staff, de Guingand, be present for the tête-à-tête.
The two men thus moved into Eisenhower's study on the train, without witnesses—both de Guingand and Monty's intelligence chief, Brig-

adier Williams, being asked like schoolboys to wait outside, in the unheated corridor.

Did Monty tell Eisenhower why he would not be using the British 30 Corps in an offensive role in the Ardennes? The previous day Eisenhower had heard from 21 Army Group that the northern counterattack would, when assembled, comprise two Allied corps, 7th U.S. and 30th British—indeed, so relieved was Eisenhower that he was heard to exclaim, at his daily conference in the Trianon Palace Hotel: "Praise God from whom all blessings flow." With Bradley declaring that afternoon, on a personal visit to Versailles, he had "immediate plans for strengthening up the southern flank of the salient and then attacking," Eisenhower had cast off his Christmas depression and was undoubtedly hoping for light at the end of his traumatic tunnel. How soon would Monty counterattack the northern face of the German salient, he wanted to know, and in what strength?

Monty's refusal to discuss the timing of his own operations, and the cold water he poured on the Supreme Commander's newfound optimism for the battle in the Ardennes, came as a rude shock to Eisenhower. From desperation and personal fear—some might say cowardice, given the bravery of so many ordinary GIs fighting the German armored onslaught in the field—Eisenhower had switched to sudden and fantastical hopes of a great Allied victory in the Ardennes. It was Normandy all over again.

Meantime, Monty went on to give his masterplan for invading Germany after the Ardennes battle was over. Patiently he outlined to Eisenhower his plans for Operation Veritable in the north, while the German Panzer divisions were still locked in combat *in the Ardennes*, to be followed by "Grenade," an Anglo-American pincer attack from British Second Army and Ninth Army's sector.

However, to ensure a clear tactical link between current operations and the resumption of the real Allied counteroffensive towards the Ruhr, Monty insisted that Allied operations north of the Moselle be permanently handed over to one commander:

> I then said it was vital to decide now on the master plan for the future conduct of the war so that all concerned could equate their present action with the future plan. In making this plan he [Eisenhower] must satisfy two basic conditions.

> First. All available offensive power must be allotted to the northern front.

Second. One man must have powers of operational control and coordination of the whole northern thrust which would be from
about PRUM northwards.

I then said that he must clearly understand beyond any possibility of
doubt what was my opinion on this matter of the master plan. My opinion was that if he did not comply with the two basic conditions . . . then
he would fail.

Air Vice-Marshal Robb's notes, made the following day upon Eisenhower's return to Versailles, bear out this account of the Hasselt
meeting. "Monty firmly believes that unless he has control up to the
Moselle everything will fall flat," Robb reported, summarizing Eisenhower's verbal report to his staff at SHAEF. Robb then added: "Monty
considers that Bradley has made a mess of the situation"—a statement
that caused the American members of Eisenhower's staff and even his
British subordinates to bristle with indignation.

As in the case of Monty's interview with Bradley, however, Monty
was certain Eisenhower had agreed with him. "He [Eisenhower] agreed
at once to the first condition," Monty informed Brooke on the night of
28 December, "and said he realised now that he had been wrong before. But BRADLEY and PATTON and DEVERS had all wanted the
FRANKFURT thrust and he had given way to them."

Monty's signal, only hours after his meeting, certainly gave the impression of candor and honesty at the meeting. Moreover, contemporary records indicate Eisenhower had, indeed, undergone a change of
heart concerning his overall Allied strategy. The previous day, from
Versailles, he had dispatched his chief of operations to see Devers,
bearing an order that 6th Army Group was to withdraw to the Vosges
and begin thinning out its line in order to provide vital SHAEF reserves. Tedder had objected, but Eisenhower—though not daring to
speak to Devers himself—had been adamant. Air Marshal Robb
quoted Eisenhower's exact words in his diary: " 'Pink, you'd better go
and see Devers today. I think your best line is this.' (S[upreme] A[llied]
C[ommander] thereupon outlined his view on the map on the line
down the Vosges to join up with the French forces north of Col-
mar.) . . . 'See Devers and give him this line.' He finished: 'It will be
a great disappointment giving up ground but this area is not where I
told Devers to put his weight.' "

Eisenhower had thus, apparently, seen the strategic light: that the
Allies *must* cease attacking in different directions and form sufficient
reserves to concentrate their major effort *on one particular target*.

But what of the command aspect? Even Monty saw how difficult
this would be for Eisenhower:

He said there would be difficulties about the second condition [that one man must command the whole northern thrust] and it would be particularly difficult to explain the situation to the American public. I said he would probably find it somewhat difficult to explain away the true reasons for the "bloody nose" we had just received from the Germans but this would be as nothing compared to the difficulty he would have in explaining away another failure to reach the RHINE. I again gave it as my definite opinion that if he did not comply with the second condition he would fail. It was not enough to comply with only one of the basic conditions. He must comply with both or fail.

This was Monty at his worst: bullying, disrespectful and threatening—to his superior officer. According to "Simbo" Simpson, who arrived at Monty's headquarters on 29 December, Monty was certain "General Eisenhower agreed to do what F. M. Montgomery wanted." But did Eisenhower really agree?

Too Much "I Told You So"

O nce again, Monty had overplayed his hand, imagining that the American defeat in the Ardennes would miraculously restore to him the proud command he had assumed exactly a year before, as Allied Land Forces Commander-in-Chief for the invasion of France.

Monty's obtuseness, in this respect, was as unfortunate as it had been after his victory in Normandy—failing completely to see the political ramifications when the United States was contributing almost three-quarters of the land forces in northwest Europe.

Monty had, it was true, once again offered to serve under General Bradley, if Eisenhower so wished. But Eisenhower did *not* wish it ("General Eisenhower had replied that he had no intention of giving Bradley such a command, nor was there any likelihood of his changing his mind on this point," Simpson reported back to the War Office). Not only had Bradley failed in battle, in the Ardennes, but Eisenhower still, at heart, disputed the necessity for a single commander. "General Eisenhower thought that it would be possible to devise a formula giving F. M. Montgomery power of co-ordinating where co-ordination is necessary," Simpson explained to Brooke. Nevertheless, according to Monty's understanding, as he informed Brooke, "Eisenhower finally agreed to comply with both conditions and he gave me powers of operational control and coordination over the two Army Groups employed for the northern thrust." Monty was certain that Eisenhower would this time stand by his word: "We have reached agreement on these matters before and then he has run out. But I have a feeling that this time he will stick to the agreement. He was very pleasant and the meeting was most friendly but he was definitely in a somewhat humble frame of mind and clearly realises that the present trouble would not have occurred if he had accepted British advice and not that of American generals. There will be no trouble over the first basic condition [concentration upon the major Allied offensive targeted on the Ruhr]. I am taking steps to ensure he does not run out over the second."

Far from being pleased, Brooke was alarmed. "Monty has had another interview with Ike," he noted with anxiety in his personal diary. "I do not like the account of it. It looks to me as if Monty with his usual lack of tact has been rubbing into Ike the results of not having listened to Monty's advice!! Too much 'I told you so' to assist in producing the required friendly relations between them. According to Monty, Ike argues that the front should now be divided into two and that only one major offensive is possible. But I suspect that whoever meets Ike next may swing him to any point of view. He [Eisenhower] is a hopeless commander."

Getting Inside the Salient

B rooke's doubts were soon confirmed—indeed, when Eisenhower returned from Hasselt to Versailles on 29 December, the atmosphere at SHAEF was one of mounting rebellion—against Monty!

Eisenhower may have been a hopeless battlefield commander, in Brooke's view, but he was a peerless coalition leader, and a beloved "boss" to his huge, international SHAEF staff. Mrs. Summersby noted in her diary: "E. and Monty had a long talk, Monty wouldn't let his C/S [chief of staff] be present. Monty still tries to convince E. that there should be one commander of the entire battle front, left no doubt as to who should be that commander. From all accounts he was not very co-operative. E. has a conference with his staff. They are all mad at Minty [sic], especially Whiteley."

The problem, as in Normandy, was one of tactical strategy: of patience versus impatience, cautious "stage management" of the battle versus pragmatic opportunism. In the first days of the German attack in the Ardennes, General Whiteley had actually prepared plans for a massive Allied retreat in the north, as Major General McLean confided to the American Official Historian shortly after the war ("We drew up a plan for withdrawal to protect Liège and Antwerp. . . . Whiteley used me instead of [Major General] Nevins"). McLean, no friend of Monty's, considered that "Monty was right in holding his forces back and letting Germans come in. Patton got his whole force committed and couldn't move elsewhere."

McLean's view was not shared by his colleagues, however. In Patton's counterattack all too many desk soldiers now saw a chance to avenge the American setback in the Ardennes. Frustrated by their paper-shuffling role at SHAEF, Eisenhower's courtiers were uninterested in Monty's plans for attacking Germany *after* the Ardennes; they desired victory *now*—and Monty's caution, and his insistent call for a single commander in the north, they found infuriating. The gratitude all had felt for Monty's prompt action in restoring order in the north thus quickly turned to derision. Air Vice-Marshal Robb noted in his diary, "It was agreed that while Monty had quickly restored the situation in the U.S. Army area on the north flank and got this army straightened out by bringing order out of disorder, when it came to the necessity for rapid offensive action he was far behind Bradley and that his inherent overcarefulness was going to cause us to miss the opportunity of inflicting a severe defeat on the enemy in the immediate future. The above view was stated by Bedell Smith and confirmed by the other three present [Eisenhower, Strong and Whiteley]."

A short while previously, surprised and stunned by the severity of the German counterattack, Eisenhower and his staff had locked themselves up in their offices and left the battle to the soldiers at the front. Now, as the steam appeared to be going from the German onrush, the staff spread their maps upon carpeted floors and planned counteroffensive operations in the bitter winter terrain of the Ardennes as though playing with tin soldiers:

> Offensive measures were reviewed after which Eisenhower stated that our one object must be to break through the enemy, get inside the salient and move East along the enemy's supply lines—lines he obviously could not demolish or obstruct as he has done other roads. Also that when Patton's attack from the Bastogne area converged with Collins' attack from the northern part of the salient, then Bradley should resume command of the First Army.

To Monty, schooled by a lifetime's experience and study of battlefield command, this was a wanton, criminal foolery with brave American, and British, lives. The answer to the "bloody nose" in the Ardennes was not to dream of breaking through inside the German salient, in ideal defensive territory that posed no strategic threat to the Germans, but to focus instead upon a well-planned Allied assault at the industrial heartland of the crumbling Third Reich: the Ruhr.

It was in the midst of this disagreement on 30 December that Freddie de Guingand, Monty's chief of staff, arrived in Versailles, bearing further "bad" news. Monty now refused, de Guingand reported, to commit his forces in the Ardennes to counterattack before 4 January 1945.

A Collision of Military Philosophies

"Y ou cannot switch suddenly from defensive positions to the offensive without careful preparations," de Guingand explained to the "gang of four" at Versailles. Besides, the Allies now had the German salient ringed tight, a prey to air and artillery attack. As Air Marshall Robb summarized de Guingand's version of Monty's tactical thinking: "We had got the enemy on the run like a wet hen from one side of the salient to the other, that time was on our side and that we should let him [the enemy] exhaust himself and [then] come back with a riposte, and that there is nothing worse than laying on a half-baked attack. That the fire-plan for an attack must be worked out carefully and reserves collected and disposed."

De Guingand was not only speaking for Monty; he was voicing his own experience from Alamein to Tunisia, from Sicily to Italy, from the shores of Normandy to the frontiers of Germany. But neither Eisenhower nor Bedell Smith nor Strong had ever commanded troops in battle, or even served on the staff of a commander in battle. Bedell Smith countered by declaring that Monty had promised Eisenhower he would counterattack by January at the latest—in two days' time.

Bedell Smith now ordered a search of the files, hoping to turn up a signal from Monty confirming the date, but de Guingand scoffed. "De Guingand said, knowing Monty the last thing he would do is commit himself on paper. . . . De Guingand pointed out the basic difference in offensive policy between 21 and 12th Army Groups is that normally all U.S. divisions attacked whereas in 21 Army Group the attack is on a narrow concentrated front."

The whole issue of Operation Veritable and post-Ardennes offensive strategy was left unraised—the "gang of four" seemingly besotted by the notion that they could suddenly reverse their humiliation since 16 December by a great Allied counterstroke in the Ardennes, mounted without preparation or forethought, and in appalling weather, merely because Bradley had already begun his own attack.

"There appears to be a complete lack of coordination between 21 and 12 Army Groups," Air Vice-Marshal Robb noted after the meeting at Versailles. "Bradley has in fact launched his attack from the Bastogne area on the full understanding that Monty was going to attack from the north on or before the 1st. What happened is that no German attack on the north [as predicted by Ultra intelligence, and for which Monty wished to wait before launching his own offensive] has taken place but that one of the Panzer Divs being held for this attack has been switched south to hold up Bradley. It appears that if Monty does not attack soon the enemy may be able to hold off Bradley and switch his strength back to the north—in effect retaining the initiative which he would lose at once if we put in a coordinated attack. Far from being on the run like a wet hen the enemy is making use of his interior lines on a small scale."

Robb, an airman, was expressing the same anxieties and frustrations that had characterized SHAEF all through the Normandy campaign— when Eisenhower's headquarters became more and more myopic, hindering a battle they did not and could not, by reason of their battlefield ignorance and distance, understand. Thus, while Monty calmly saw the Germans running "like a wet hen," bombarded by air and artillery, and counterattacked in force where and when it suited the Allies—thus preserving Allied strength for the *real* Allied offensive to seize the Ruhr, beginning with Operation Veritable—Eisenhower's staff dreamed, as they had each time operations were undertaken in Normandy, of instant and decisive breakthrough, attainable in their eyes only by speed and simultaneous "stretchout" combat by all divisions, on all fronts.

In Monty's and de Guingand's experience, such tactics had not worked in Tunisia. Nor had they in Sicily. Nor had they in Italy. Even in Normandy, Patton's great armored breakout—Operation Lucky Strike, which had first been planned at 21st Army Group Headquarters on 14 June, less than a fortnight after D-Day—had had to be postponed until the main German forces in western France had been locked, as at Alamein, in annihilating battle and so weakened that the American breakout prospered, *more than a month later.* Such a favorable battlefield situation, Monty and de Guingand felt, had *not* been reached in the Ardennes—indeed, without fair weather for flying it would be criminal to risk so many Allied soldiers' lives.

It was clear that two wholly different approaches to modern war were in conflict—with neither side able to see the merits of the other.

Faced with this stalemate, Eisenhower now read out to his staff the personal letter which de Guingand had brought with him from Monty, stating categorically that unless operational control of the combined Allied thrust to seize the Ruhr was put into his, Monty's, hands, the Allies would fail.

Seeing the outraged reaction of his colleagues, Eisenhower realized that his credibility as Supreme Commander/Land Forces Commander was at stake; that he could not allow himself to be barracked and bullied by one of his subordinate commanders in this way. As Mrs. Summersby recorded: "E['s] one aim is to keep the staff together."

It was in this atmosphere, then, that Eisenhower decided he had, after first losing control of his American armies, now lost control over Monty. Spurred on by his nobles, he ordered Bedell Smith to prepare a cable to General Marshall and the Combined Chiefs of Staff—stating that it was "Monty or me."

A Cable from Marshall

Monty's intransigence—his lack of faith in the prospect of a great Allied victory to be won in the Ardennes and his insistence that Eisenhower concentrate Allied reserves on the real strategic target, the Ruhr, under a single field commander—was a cross Eisenhower felt he simply could bear no longer.

At this very moment, however, a cable arrived from Marshall which put a somewhat different complexion on the matter. Marshall had seen British press reports, which worried him. Eisenhower's staff "may or may not have brought to your attention," Marshall telegraphed, "articles in certain London papers proposing a British Deputy Commander for all your ground forces and implying that you have undertaken too much of a task yourself. My feeling is this: Under no circumstances make any concessions of any kind whatsoever. You not only have our complete confidence but there would be a terrific resentment in this country following such action. I am not assuming that you had in mind such a concession. I just wish to be certain of our attitude on this side. You are doing a grand job and go and give them hell."

Marshall's new signal, once deciphered, altered the wavering balance of power in the Allied high command in the West. Monty's star, in the early days of the battle in the Ardennes, had risen, while those of Eisenhower and Bradley plummeted. Now, however, with the German offensive parried, the Chairman of the Combined Chiefs of Staff had sent a vote of full confidence in Eisenhower, together with a veto on any plans he might have to give Monty—or any other British or indeed American general—ground command as his deputy. If Eisenhower went ahead with his intention to make command a resignation issue, it was obvious to de Guingand who, in fact, would be the one to go.

A Cloak of Loneliness

Alert to the threat to his commander, de Guingand now wisely begged Eisenhower not to send his draft cable but to wait a few hours until he, de Guingand, had had a chance to speak to Monty in Zonhoven, in person.

That day, however, there was thick fog, and it was only at 3 P.M. on 31 December that de Guingand finally reached Monty's headquarters, landing at an advanced airstrip nearby. Tea was being served in the mess, but "before I had been there very long, he [Montgomery] realized that I had something on my mind and that something must be wrong. As he left the table he said, 'I'm going upstairs to my office, Freddie. Please come up when you have finished your tea.' " In Monty's study de Guingand then related what had happened in Versailles.

At first Monty refused to believe the seriousness of the situation. Besides, if it came to a showdown, why did de Guingand believe that

Eisenhower would win? De Guingand thereupon instanced the ratio of war effort between Britain and the United States, which made it difficult, if not impossible, for Churchill to make the Americans do anything against their wishes. Monty acknowledged the force of this argument. But if Eisenhower sacked him, who was there who could take his place?

It was at this juncture that de Guingand mentioned Alexander. "During my interview with the Supreme Commander," de Guingand related, "he had actually hinted at this very solution. In fact I seem to recall that Alexander's name was mentioned in the [draft] signal [to Marshall]."

Monty was, for once in his life, completely floored. He considered he now held the tactical initiative on the northern flank of the Ardennes, having moved 30 Corps into position between Marche and Givet to enable Collins' 7 U.S. Corps to bring "three complete divisions in reserve," as Monty had cabled the CIGS the night before. He planned to sidestep 30 Corps still further eastwards, swelling Collins' counterattack force into a reserve of four complete American divisions, ready to strike southwards to Houffalize with its right flank on the Ourthe River and left flank on the Grandmenil–Hotton road, whenever Monty so ordered. Monty's target date was 4 January for this attack, "but as to whether I shall actually launch it then will depend on general situation and particularly on what happens on southern front," he had informed Brooke—for his aim was to make von Rundstedt shift further forces south to counter Patton, then punch the Germans hard with Collins' four divisions, in the back. To this end he had, already on 29 December, recommended that Bradley push hard from Bastogne: "It is from the south that our offensive operations should now be developed in as great strength as possible and I have urged SHAEF to give Third Army [Patton] all the reserve divisions that can be made available."

Monty's object, however, had been no more than to punish the Panzer armies for their ambitious offensive by jabbing attacks that kept the German forces guessing. Against twenty-eight or even thirty concentrated German divisions, he did not, however, anticipate any grand Allied breakthrough, or even a "severe defeat" for the enemy. Better by far to keep the Germans tied down in the Ardennes while delivering the real Allied offensive where the Germans were weaker and the sector strategically more valuable: namely the gateway to the Ruhr, in the north. It was for this reason, not caution, he reminded de Guingand, he had been adamant 30 British Corps should not be thrown into the battle and become inextricably involved, since it could not then play its planned role in operation Veritable.

Looking at de Guingand's perplexed face, however, Monty knew it was no good. Such long-term military strategy was suddenly redundant. His very command was on the line. De Guingand recorded, "I felt terribly sorry for my Chief, for he now looked completely nonplussed—I don't think I had ever seen him so deflated. It was as if a cloak of loneliness had descended on him."

Eating Humble Pie

T he thought of Alexander usurping his role as Commander-in-Chief, 21st Army Group, was a factor Monty had never considered. "ALEXANDER is a very great friend of mine," he had written in his diary twelve months before, "and I am very fond of him. But I am under no delusion whatsoever as to his ability to conduct large scale operations in the field; he knows nothing about it; he is not a strong commander and he is incapable of giving firm and clear decisions as to what he wants. In fact no one ever knows what he does want, least of all his own staff; in fact he does not know himself." Increasingly, in Tunisia, Sicily and Italy, Alexander's loose-reined, uncoordinated conduct of command had irritated and finally exasperated Monty. Though Churchill's ideal figure of a soldier—brave, charming and imperturbable—Alexander would, Monty felt, prove a disaster in northwest Europe.

The combination of Eisenhower, Bradley and Alexander combating on all fronts and laying themselves open yet again to the sort of defeat they had suffered in the Ardennes . . . it was too awful to contemplate. The German offensive had already put back the end of the war many months. With Eisenhower and Alexander at the helm, it might be prolonged even further, as had happened in Tunisia and again in Italy.

That his command should be offered to a general as ineffective as Alexander seemed ridiculous to Monty. Moreover it was completely untrue that he, Monty, was agitating for command of all ground forces in northwest Europe—he merely wished, as he had pleaded for four months, to see the thrust to seize the Ruhr put under a single commander: a man who would relentlessly ensure the operation's success. Yet Marshall's telegram, with its categorical insistence that Eisenhower not give way over the command issue, left little doubt that Monty was on a "bad wicket."

It was Monty's ruthless adherence to his own principles of command that had made him the outstanding Allied battlefield general of the war. Yet such ruthlessness was founded upon profound military realism. Again and again, when his battles did not go according to his prescribed plan, he had turned tactical reverse to advantage by altering his battle scheme. Such tactical flexibility permitted him to adhere to his larger strategy, by which he retained the ultimate initiative. In writing to Eisenhower he had sought to "thump the table," dictating the new Allied strategic objective and the terms by which it should be achieved: his masterplan. But it was clear that he had misjudged the moment—and no one would thank him for engineering such a crisis in the Allied high command.

"What shall I do, Freddie?" he now asked.

From his battle-dress pocket de Guingand pulled a piece of paper—the draft of an apologetic message to Eisenhower. It seemed the only solution, and it is to Monty's credit that for all his vanity and self-assurance he was able at this moment to swallow his pride and recant. Six days previously he had humiliated Bradley in his study; three days previously he had put the Supreme Commander in his place on board *Alive*, Eisenhower's heavily guarded train at Hasselt. Now it was Monty's turn to undergo humiliation.

"Dear IKE," he began.

> Have seen Freddie and understand you are greatly worried by many considerations in these difficult days. I have given you my frank views because I have felt you like this. I am sure there are many factors which may have a bearing quite beyond anything I realize. Whatever your decision may be you can rely on me one hundred percent to make it work and I know BRAD will do the same. Very distressed that my letter may have upset you and I would ask you to tear it up.
>
> Your very devoted subordinate,
> MONTY

The cable was enciphered at 3:55 P.M.

This was not all. When Hodges arrived early that evening with his final plans for the First U.S. Army offensive, Monty advanced the timing by twenty-four hours. "After consultation with HODGES I am putting forward the attack of VII Corps towards HOUFFALIZE by one day and it will now be launched at first light on 3 January," with 30 Corps taking over the Allied front as far east as Hotton by 2 January, Monty signaled to Eisenhower. De Guingand meanwhile returned to Brussels, having asked for an urgent meeting of British war correspondents.

In Normandy Monty had fought the finest Western Allied offensive battle of the war; in the Ardennes the finest defensive battle. But from being the "savior" of the Allies, able to thump the table, Monty was now back to square one: a British know-all in a predominantly American pond.

Bradley's Disappointment

The irony behind Eisenhower's threat to seek Monty's replacement was that Eisenhower had in fact abandoned the idea of an American advance towards Frankfurt, and had finally accepted Monty's case for a concentrated Allied effort, after the battle in the Ardennes was over, to seize the Ruhr. In fact, as de Guingand flew up to Zonhoven on the afternoon of New Year's Eve, Eisenhower was already drawing up new orders.

Ninth U.S. Army would remain under Monty's command in 21 Army Group. "The main effort" was now to be "north of the Ruhr," while all forces south of the Moselle were "to be strictly defensive." Patton was to move up *north of the Moselle*, under Bradley; Patton and Hodges were then to fight their way around the south face of the Ruhr on the line Prum–Bonn, while Monty's 21st Army Group first cleared the west bank of the Rhine (operations Veritable and Grenade), then crossed the river and swung around the north face of the Ruhr. To this end Bradley was ordered to move his headquarters north to be nearer Montgomery, and "from now on, any detailed or emergency coordination required along Army Group boundaries in the north will be effected by the two Army Group Commanders with power of decision vested in C[ommanding] G[eneral] 21st Army Group."

This was, short of actually giving Monty command of both north and south pincers in the Ruhr offensive, all that Monty had been asking for since the previous autumn—and Monty was delighted. "You can rely on me and all under my command to go all out 100% to implement your plans," Monty cabled back—having assured Eisenhower in a New Year's message that he wished "to assure you of the personal devotion and loyalty of myself and all those under my command. We will follow you anywhere."

Deluged by such professions of apology and loyalty, Eisenhower now assured Marshall that there was no need to worry. "You need have no fear as to my contemplating the establishment of a ground deputy," he cabled. To Monty he signaled his thanks for "your very fine telegram [of apology]. . . . I truly appreciate the understanding attitude it indicates"; moreover he was grateful that Monty had "found it possible to speed up your re-grouping arrangements" for the attack southwards to Houffalize.

General Bradley, however, was less pleased. "When General Eisenhower informed me that he was leaving the Ninth Army under command of the 21 Army Group, I protested and stated that if nothing else, all American forces should be returned to Twelfth Army Group even if it were only for a few days," Bradley recorded in a memorandum several weeks later. "In my opinion, the failure to return all American troops to the command of Twelfth Army Group might be interpreted as a lack of confidence in the American command."

The humiliating Christmas Day interview at Zonhoven; the failure to return Ninth U.S. Army to 12 U.S. Army Group; the orders to leave Luxembourg and move his headquarters north, nearer to Monty; the decision to adopt Monty's masterplan; and the decree allowing Monty "power of decision" in coordinating the Ruhr offensive—these were all knocks that Bradley found hard to stomach, as did his staff, who were desolated.

"SHAEF has issued its new directive on the Army Group effort and it now appears that we are committed to a principal effort in the north after the bulge has been eliminated," Bradley's ADC recorded on 2 January. "I expressed some surprise and disappointment at this." Hansen was not alone—and in high dudgeon Bradley now drove to Etain airfield to go and protest in person to Eisenhower.

Reproductive Tanks

Bradley had been busy preparing plans not only for Patton to thrust southeast to the Saar, but for a breakthrough in the Eifel area by First and Ninth U.S. Armies that would put them on the Rhine at Cologne. These plans were now redundant. Eisenhower, arriving in a C-47, attempted to sugar his bitter pill by saying that Bradley's "estimate was the only correct one he had of the situation on the breakthrough. His [Eisenhower's] staff leaned first one way and then the other."

Bradley could not, however, be exonerated. The truth was, the Americans had, as a result of Bradley's faulty dispositions, suffered a substantial defeat. Nor did Bradley's paper plans for a great victory in the aftermath sound very convincing. Eisenhower had cabled to Marshall that Bradley had "been making only slow and laborious progress from the south," and even Bradley had to admit that he had "as yet been unable to punch a hole we can pour through quickly." Monty had warned Eisenhower on 2 January that "tactical victory within the salient is going to take some little time to achieve and that there will be heavy fighting"; nevertheless both Patton and Bradley had felt the time was propitious to give their own press conferences—Patton even boasting to reporters on 1 January 1945 that he knew "of no [feat] equal to it in military history" (the move of his three divisions from their sector on 22 December), and claiming "we can lick the Germans any place . . . I don't care where he fights. We'll find him and kick his teeth in." The defense of Bastogne was "as important as the Battle of Gettysburg." Bradley gave his own conference three days later—but by then even he was beginning to realize that "our operation in the closing of the gap was apt to be a long one," as Patton's divisions began to tire and the true extent of American casualties became clear. Patton blamed Bradley for not permitting him to attack through the shoulder of the German salient. But behind Patton's bombast was a Third U.S. Army racked with contradictions, misunderstandings, and lack of competence—as the unpublished diary kept for Patton's chief of staff, General "Hap" Gay, recorded.

Certainly General Middleton, charged by Patton with the main 8 U.S. Corps offensive northwards from Bastogne, had little faith in it. On Friday, 29 December, Middleton begged "that the Army Commander [Patton] come to see him. General Gay told him that the Army Commander was sick and could not go out on a long trip. General Middleton then . . . asked for permission to launch his attack to the left [of Bastogne, owing to congestion in the town]. General Gay stated that the Army Commander said he didn't care how General Middleton made the attack but he must make it, and he must take the objective." When the next day Middleton launched the attack—which Generals Patton, Bradley and Eisenhower all felt should be matched by a similar, unprepared attack from Monty's northern flank—Gay recorded:

> While history may prove that the launching of an attack on this line was necessary, at present it indicates a complete misunderstanding of the problem involved, on the part of the Commanding General, VIII Corps.

Middleton's attack failed. American Eighth Air Force bombers bombed their own 4th Armored and 4th Infantry Divisions, while American antiaircraft gunners shot down American fighters. General Gay lambasted the incompetence of inexperienced American divisions and General Middleton's lack of aggressiveness. Middleton had been ordered to capture Monty's target, Houffalize, while 3 U.S. Corps "killed or captured some 8,000 Germans" who would be caught in a salient southwest of Bastogne, according to Patton's reckoning. Instead, Middleton was himself attacked by German forces. 17th U.S. Airborne Division, moreover, failed to attack at all, since the American Communications Zone did not bring up the necessary trucks in time.

Middleton, bracing himself for the German counterattack, wished to take up defensive positions. Patton overruled him:

> The Army Commander refused this request and directed that the VIII Corps launch its attack on the morning of 4 January. During the last two years this "seance," so to speak, has repeated itself many times and in each and every case the Army Commander has been correct. He has continuously held that once an attack is set to be launched, it should be launched; that our main mission is to destroy the German Army, and we

can do it better by attacking them than we can by waiting for them to attack.

Here indeed the difference between Monty's and Patton's attitude to modern warfare against a well-trained, indoctrinated, well-equipped and well-led enemy: Monty welcoming the chance to meet German attacks in Alam Halfa style, Patton hating ever to be defensive at all.

Bradley, dining with his Third Army Commander that night, approved Patton's orders. As a result, one entire regiment of 17th Airborne Division was wiped out the following day, as its commander confided a few weeks later to an American combat historian:

> When we arrived at NEUFCHATEAU, our destination had been changed and we were told to go 9 miles farther along and relieve 11 A[rmoured Division] again. That division in the meantime had moved up and taken a crack at the line, but the fighting had been heavy and 11 A had failed to make any dent on the enemy. It was felt infantry was needed for this situation.
>
> We started our move on 2 January. On 3 January we were ordered to make a night relief of 11 A and to attack the next day at daylight. But we couldn't do it because we couldn't get up there in time. We were still having truck troubles. When daylight came only 50 per cent of 17th [Division] was closed on the line. The assignment—to relieve and then attack at once—was a large order for a new division. But the high command was insistent at this time that there was nothing in front of us. By high command, I mean that Third Army was presenting this view to VIII Corps. . . .

Patton had claimed to the newspapermen that he wanted "to catch as many Germans as possible, but he [the enemy] is pulling out"; moreover, he had boasted that "unless they have reproductive tanks" the Germans had "damn little armor left."

This was not what the virgin U.S. paratroopers of 17th Airborne Division found on 4 January 1945, however. Fighting in subzero temperatures, charging with their bayonets, "they did one hell of a fine job" in clearing the woods at Flamizoulle, their divisional commander recorded, but then met German armor coming down the Saint-Hubert–Bastogne road. The same happened at Maude. Because of the fog there was no possibility of artillery observation; within hours the men were back on their start line.

When the 87th U.S. Division attempted to attack to reach the beleaguered paratroopers, they likewise were counterattacked by the Germans and made no headway. The Germans did not have reproductive tanks, but were feeding them into the Ardennes from the Eastern

Front, where Stalin's offensive had failed to materialize. By 5 January 1945, when Gay finally went forward in person to see Middleton, he realized that it was futile to pursue attack for attack's sake:

> The Commanding General of the VIII Corps was quite depressed and felt that he could not attack, and also questioned if he could hold against the enemy's attacks. General Gay, feeling that for him to attack in this mood would result in a half-hearted attack and would probably gain nothing, told him that he would take the responsibility for calling off the attack on that date.

Patton's much-trumpeted offensive by 8 U.S. Corps, upon which Eisenhower had set such store, was thus shut down. Monty was unsurprised—indeed, in his nightly cable of 1 January 1945 he had warned Brooke not to expect too much of the attacks in the north either. "I do not think we must expect any spectacular results from this [Collins'] attack but it should certainly serve to relieve pressure on the southern front about BASTOGNE."

The following day, on the eve of Collins' attack, Monty expanded on this—for he had heard that Brooke and Churchill were planning a visit to Eisenhower's headquarters. He had already informed Brooke of the momentous fracas over the command issue and its result ("I am now going to withdraw from the contest. It is clear to me that we have got all we can and that we shall get no more"). Now he gave his most professional military opinion on the forthcoming operations in the Ardennes.

Under the Control of One Man

"It is gradually becoming clear to me that we may not have sufficient strength to push the Germans out of the penetration area and obtain what IKE calls 'tactical victory in the salient,' " Monty began. "The Germans are in great strength. The American divisions are either weak or inexperienced and there has been a tendency in the south to throw them in piecemeal and on wide fronts as they become available. . . .

"The general tendency at SHAEF and among the American high command is one of considerable optimism. It is considered that very shortly the First and Third Armies will join hands and that the Germans will then soon be pushed back to where they started from. I must confess I cannot share this optimism. I foresee a very great deal of hard and bitter fighting in the penetration area and I doubt if the Americans have the reserves to keep it up and I have given these views to SHAEF."

In order to help Bradley and to show his willingness to cooperate with Eisenhower, Monty had agreed to accelerate Collins' attack—but he was under ̀no illusions. As he had cabled to Eisenhower right at the start of the battle, only by ruthlessly withdrawing their overextended line south of the Moselle could the Allies hope to produce the reserves necessary if they genuinely wished to gain victory in counterattack. Eisenhower had declared he would do this—but apart from verbal directives passed on by SHAEF staff officers no action had been taken in almost two weeks. "I give you these ideas of mine before your visit to IKE," Monty meanwhile added to his message to Brooke on 2 January. "I wonder if you could discreetly explore the situation in the light of the above ideas before you come on to me and possibly find out the form? At the back of my mind is the thought that it may be necessary to make a considerable withdrawal in the south and come on to a shorter line so as to produce troops to deal with the Germans in the penetration area. I put this to IKE in his train on 28 Dec but have not referred to the subject again as I am completely in the dark as to what total forces the Americans can produce."

In his nightly situation report to the War Office on the evening of 2 January, Monty commented on the way the Germans seemed to be withdrawing their Panzer and SS divisions *into reserve*, indicating that the enemy was not, as Patton supposed, pulling out, but intended "to hold on to everything he has gained until he is pushed out." Although Collins' attack might make initial progress against positional infantry, Collins was thus bound to be counterattacked in strength "by the SS divisions in reserve north of HOUFFALIZE."

Monty was right. On the evening of the first day of Collins' attack, in fact, Monty's predictions were confirmed, and 30 Corps was therefore ordered to advance on Collins' flank. By 4 January 1945 the snow was "three feet deep and nowhere less than about six inches and visibility on the battlefront has been almost nil." Collins later recorded how fierce the fighting against the SS divisions became: "Under such conditions progress against the veteran SS divisions was slow and costly, especially on the front of the 2nd [U.S.] Armoured Division, and for the first and only time I had to put some pressure on my great friend and good fighter, Ernie Harmon, to keep his 'Hell on Wheels' division moving." Even the British 30 Corps, which Monty was determined to keep fresh for his Veritable operation further north, became embroiled as it pushed its left flank forward alongside Collins' Houffalize thrust—both 29th Armoured Brigade and 6th British Airborne Division becoming fiercely engaged with 2nd Panzer Division.

Disappointed but determined to back up Collins' energetic thrust, Monty now ordered that 53rd British Division, adjoining Collins' right flank, "be put into the battle to fight until it is exhausted when I will pull it out immediately and replace it by 51 [Highland] Div[ision] and thus keep up the tempo of the operation on the right flank of 7 US Corps"—but he remained quite clear about the heavy fighting that lay ahead. "From the operations today it would seem that the Germans at present have no intention of withdrawing from any part of their salient and as to whether they will decide later to do so this may well depend on the progress we can make in the north in the next few days," he signaled on 5 January.

Even Eisenhower's headquarters acknowledged "the fanaticism of the fighting"—though they ascribed this "to the CASABLANCA declaration that unconditional surrender would be demanded. B[edell] S[mith] thought that this declaration by the President was to influence the JEWISH vote in his forthcoming election but he did not understand why the Prime Minister subscribed to it."

SHAEF's shallow answer to the fanatical German fighting reflected their utter frustration. Toward the end of December 1944 it had looked to them as though swift and energetic Allied counterattacks north and south of the German salient might miraculously restore the Allied initiative. But with the fierceness of German resistance in the Ardennes, and the growing threat from German attacks on Devers' front in the south, Eisenhower and his staff became frantic at their loss of initiative. "We must seize the initiative," Eisenhower's chief of staff declared, and Eisenhower agreed: "We must get the initiative quickly."

Quickness was not, however, a commodity that could be miraculously procured like a rabbit from a SHAEF hat.

It was in this situation that Eisenhower, full of anxiety about Devers' performance in the south, returned to the agreement he had made with Monty at Hasselt on 28 December: that one man take over the northern sector and by coordinated offensive operations wrest back the Allied initiative. "He considers it essential that operations," after the Ardennes salient had been cleared up, "from then on be under the control of one man. S[upreme] A[llied] C[ommander]: 'There is going to be a twilight period in there and I don't give a damn who is in command so long as it is under one man,' " Robb recorded, quoting the Supreme Commander's exact words, on 8 January 1945.

For a moment it seemed possible that Field Marshal Bernard Montgomery would be that man. But, thanks to Monty's press conference, it was not for long.

Churchill's Visit

P rime Minister Winston Churchill had appeared at Monty's head-quarters on 5 January, traveling on Eisenhower's train as the weather, once again, precluded flying.

Arriving at Kermpt station, near Zonhoven, Churchill was struck by the change in Monty's attitude towards Eisenhower. Only days before Monty had harped, in his telegrams, on the "bloody nose" the Americans had received. Now, since the fracas with Eisenhower, Monty seemed a changed man. He had sent his American ADC, Dick Harden, back to Amesbury for a rest—and to spare him some of the ragging inevitable at Tac HQ. "It is good of you to have him for so long," he thanked Mrs. Reynolds; "he is a very decent chap and it is not always too easy for him in my mess—where he is the sole American. . . . Occasionally he hears things about the Americans' point of view which must upset him."

To Churchill's surprise, Monty now declared his wholehearted allegiance to Eisenhower, despite the débâcle in the Ardennes. Monty was particularly touched that Eisenhower had instantly sent him a new C-47 when his own was destroyed in the Luftwaffe's brilliant New Year's Day "dawn raid" on British airfields at Saint-Trond and Brussels; likewise, Monty had ordered 200 British tanks to be handed over to Hodges' First Army for the Houffalize thrust. Three and a half British divisions were now fighting alongside American forces in the salient. The moral was clear: despite differences in tactical strategy the Allies' greatest strength lay in their unity.

That night Churchill prepared a cable to Roosevelt, expressing His Majesty's Government's "complete confidence in General Eisenhower. . . . He and Montgomery are very closely knit, and also Bradley and Patton, and it would be disaster which broke up this combination, which has in 1944 yielded us results beyond the dreams of military avarice. Montgomery said to me to-day that the [German] break-through would have been most serious to the whole front but for the solidarity of the Anglo-American Army."

This was not mere Churchillian rhetoric. Monty had told him of the gallantry shown by American units when cut off in the early days of the German advance, and the punishing treatment meted out to 2nd Panzer Division by Collins at the extreme tip of the salient. This Churchill passed on to Roosevelt, together with a plea for American infantry reinforcements—"I have not found a trace of discord at the British and American headquarters; but, Mr. President, there is this brute fact: we need more fighting troops to make things move."

Whether Monty felt guilty at his recent disparagement of Eisenhower is difficult to know for certain. Within Monty the ruthlessly professional tactician existed a surprisingly emotional heart. Hearing Churchill's account of Eisenhower's difficulties with de Gaulle (Eisenhower had been forced by de Gaulle to drop his plans to pull back to the Vosges on his southern front, and instead was compelled to help the French defend Strasbourg, thus ending all hope of gathering the reserves necessary for a "full-blooded" Allied counteroffensive in the Ardennes), Monty was filled with an almost childlike desire to atone for his own misbehavior. He thus implored Churchill to help counter the current British press campaign that was casting doubt on Eisenhower's fitness to command the Allied armies on the continent of Europe; and in an excess of zeal asked Churchill if he, Monty, might set the matter straight in a frank talk to the press.

Churchill—who should have given the conference himself, given the delicacy of the situation—agreed.

It was thus on the next day, 6 January, as his Anglo-American forces conducted their northern offensive in the Ardennes in "the most appalling mud and slush" and snow, that Monty made arrangements for a press conference that would be his downfall.

The Press Talk

T hough Bradley would later claim "Montgomery had not cleared his [press] interview with Eisenhower," this was not true.

In a secret signal to Churchill on 6 January 1945, Monty took up the matter of the press conference he'd discussed with Churchill, reporting:

In my talk tomorrow to British and American press correspondents I propose to deal with the following points:

1. The story of the battle which followed the German onslaught on First U.S. Army, being careful not to compromise security.

2. I shall explain how the Germans were first "headed off," then "seen off," and are now being "written off."

3. I shall show how the whole Allied team rallied to the call and how national considerations were thrown overboard; team work saved a somewhat awkward situation.

4. I shall put in a strong plea for Allied solidarity. Nothing must be done by anyone that tends to break down the team spirit; it is team work that pulls you through dangerous times; it is team work that wins battles; it is victories in battle that wins wars. Anyone that tries to break up our team spirit is definitely helping the enemy.

I shall stress the great friendship between myself and IKE and tell them that I myself have an American identity card and am identified in the Army of the United States, my finger prints being registered in the War Department at Washington.

Churchill signaled by return: "What you propose would be invaluable. I am not broadcasting till a few days later as the President himself will be putting out his message to Congress. Thank you very much."

First reports of Monty's press conference, held on 7 January 1945, were good—American newspapers in particular quoting Monty's generous tribute to the fighting performance of U.S. troops in the salient. Such reporters had heard Patton's talk to the press, Bradley's thereafter, and on 5 January Bedell Smith's at SHAEF. Monty's long, prepared statement, charting the events leading up to his assumption of command of First and Ninth U.S. Armies and the battle since then, was soldierly, sober and certainly a great deal less bombastic than Patton's. "He clarified much that was obscure about this great conflict in the Ardennes, revealing how a broken line is mended bit by bit, stabilized and finally flung once more into offensive action," *The New York Times* commented admiringly in an editorial, also stating: "No handsomer tribute was ever paid to the American soldier than that of Field-Marshal Montgomery in the midst of combat."

Thus when Churchill received word on 8 January that General Bradley had taken great umbrage at Monty's words, the Prime Minister was puzzled. What could Monty have said that so distressed him?

A Crisis in Allied Relationships

That Bradley would be hurt was, perhaps, inevitable. Eisenhower had, despite the catastrophe in the Ardennes, kept his job. Bradley had not—and was bound to be hurt by newspaper accounts, now that press restrictions had been lifted. In fact, as Bradley's ADC's diary chronicled, the crisis had been triggered two days before Monty met the press by Bedell Smith's official SHAEF statement.

"The SHAEF announcement on January 5th that operational control of the First and Ninth Armies had passed to 21 Group of Field Marshal Montgomery has precipitated a crisis in our allied relationships," Hansen recorded portentously. "In the announcement it was explained that command of these armies passed from Bradley to Monty because communications had been cut between our headquarters and that of

Hodges. For that reason it became necessary that the control revert as it did. However the effect has been a cataclysmic Roman holiday in the British press which has exulted over the announcement, and hailed it as an increase in the Montgomery command."

Patton and Bradley's recent press conferences had given the impression that Bradley still commanded First and Ninth U.S. Armies—indeed, as Hansen noted, even "the anti-American *Daily Mail* ran a picture of von Rundstedt and Bradley, called them the rivals in this great battle."

With Bedell Smith's SHAEF announcement, the press had learned that not Bradley but Montgomery had been in command of all forces in the main battle of the Ardennes, since 20 December. "Now the First Army of Hodges has suddenly lost its identity and Monty emerges as the commander," Hansen lamented. "In all press releases the troops are referred to as 'Monty's' troops in a palavering gibberish that indicates a slavish hero devotion on the part of the British press.

"The issue, however, goes deeper than that," Hansen continued. "Monty is the symbol of the British effort on the Western front. He is regarded as such by the British press and by the quasi official BBC and London Times. . . . He is the symbol of success, the highly overrated and normally distorted picture of the British effort on our front."

Behind all this, Major Hansen suspected "a popular British campaign affot [sic] to have Monty named Eisenhower's field deputy and thereupon assume supreme command of all the ground forces while Ike devotes his time to policy matters. The implication in such demands is simple. The German breakthrough would not have resulted had Monty been in command to prevent it."

This was true. But it did not stop there, Hansen lamented guiltily, for "the current inference of all news stories now is that the German attack succeeded because of the negligence of the American commander—Bradley."

Even the American newspaper *Stars and Stripes* added insult to injury, on 6 January, "by describing the [American] troops as Monty's troops," Hansen recorded with fury. "Furthermore in their story they committed the grievous sin of speculating on Bradley's command and . . . said '*it is presumed that Bradley continues to command the Twelfth Army Group which now consists of only the Third Army.*' This infuriated everyone. Bradley said Patton told him that he believes The Stars and Stripes has lengthened the war six months in its editorial policy and release of information to our units."

Bradley's agony was thus plain to those around him—well before Monty spoke to the press. "If I become the [American] Theater Com-

mander," Bradley threatened ominously, "the Stars and Stripes will undergo a major readjustment."

In such circumstances, however, anything Monty was likely to say in
his press conference on 7 January was bound to exacerbate Bradley's
bleeding wound—and it did.

A Storm of Resentment

I f Churchill and Montgomery were both oblivious to Bradley's pain,
Monty's own staff were not. Monty's chief of Intelligence, Brigadier Williams, later recalled of Monty's statement to the press on
7 January:

> The text in a sense was innocuous; the presentation quite appalling. It
> was meant to be a tribute to the American troops; that is what he had
> *meant* it to be. The idea was okayed with Churchill. But when I read [the
> script] I tried to stop him doing it because it seemed to me that it
> was—he said of course that he wanted to pay a tribute to the American
> soldier and so on—but it came across as if he was, *as if he had rescued the
> Americans*—"of course they were jolly brave," and so on and so forth—
> but he used that awful phrase *"a very interesting little battle,"* or words to
> that effect.
>
> I think Chester Wilmot was actually at that Press conference. Alan
> Moorehead certainly was, because I remember him saying afterwards,
> "Oh God, why didn't you stop him?" and I said, "Look, I couldn't"; and
> he said, "It was so *awful*." Monty appeared in a new Airborne Corps be-
> ret with a double badge on it and sort of said, "How do you like my new
> hat?" so to speak—and the whole sort of business of *preening* made one
> feel extremely uncomfortable.

In the already strained context of relations between Monty and
Bradley, Monty's press conference was the last straw. "The British presentation on Montgomery's command," Hansen expostulated in his

diary—driven almost to incoherence by the British newspaper accounts—"whether deliberate or not would indicate that the Field Marshal was calling in preponderantly British strength in a desperate last ditch effort to retrieve from the chaos of American command some semblance of a better mind and stop a powerful moving offensive towards Antwerp and Paris."

The "storm of resentment" caused already by the SHAEF announcement of 5 January now became a hurricane. Bradley, seeing the morale of his staff breaking, was justly tormented. As Allied Supreme Commander, Eisenhower could not be expected to champion purely American considerations. Bradley himself would have to champion them. "We urged the General to remember that the U.S. has no spokesman on the Western Front," Hansen candidly recorded in his diary. "Montgomery can speak as a Briton while Eisenhower must speak as an Allied Commander. . . . Because Eisenhower is, nevertheless, the senior American in this Theater, Bradley has consistently reiterated that he cannot speak for the American Command and has refused time and again to do so. *This crisis, however, forces us to adopt such change in policy and it now becomes unavoidably necessary that some spokesman present the American viewpoint of our co-ordinated Twelfth Army Group effort on this front.*

"The General admitted this readily," Hansen noted. "We urged a release for publication of a statement of fact that would accurately state the issues involved in the transfer of command and correct such inaccuracies as were evident in the British newspapers and in the BBC broadcasts." Tom Bigland, Monty's liaison officer, was temporarily banished from 12th Army Group Headquarters to spare his feelings; Hansen and Ingersoll thereupon spent the entire night of 8 January concocting a new, completely unauthorized statement for Bradley to issue to the press the next afternoon.

At first Bradley was reluctant—"I can't do it. The army is my life, Ingersoll," he explained. "A direct order [by SHAEF not to give a press conference] is a direct order and I cannot break it." At Ingersoll's repeated urging, however, Bradley consented. "Tell Chet [Hansen] to get the press up here tomorrow morning—without informing Paris."

The Price of the Ardennes

ews of Bradley's unauthorized, outspoken and anti-Monty press conference soon sped across the Channel, where it was greeted with disbelief, since the first American newspaper cuttings had given such a very favorable impression of Monty's address. Without delay, however, Churchill had to pour oil on troubled waters, sending a special congratulatory signal to Bradley on his magnificent performance in the Ardennes, while President Roosevelt awarded Bradley the Bronze Star, and Eisenhower recommended (vainly) that Bradley be promoted to four-star general, to comfort him. Monty, hearing from his liaison officer how upset Bradley was, immediately dispatched his own congratulations on Bradley's Bronze Star.

It was too late, however. Medals and congratulations notwithstanding, Bradley had made the historic decision, on behalf of his shamed and furious staff, to overcome his innate shyness, and to blow the American trumpet as loudly as he could. From now on he would have photographers escort him everywhere he went, as well as some fifteen "resident" newspaper reporters attached to his headquarters.

Thanks to Monty, the Germans had failed in their bold bid to reach the Meuse and Antwerp. But, thanks also to Monty, the split between 12th Army Group Headquarters and 21st Army Group had now become a chasm, wrecking the very thing Monty had said he wanted, in his press conference, to bolster: Anglo-American solidarity.

Such would, in addition to almost 100,000 American casualties, be the saddest price of the Ardennes.

Part Fifteen

THE RACE TO BERLIN

Monty, Eisenhower and Bradley at Rheinberg
on 25 March 1945 discussing Monty's plans
to advance to the Elbe—and Berlin.

A Tragedy

T he story of the final Allied campaign in 1945 would be the story of 1944, repeated over and over again. In the absence of decisive battlefield leadership from Eisenhower, the three Allied army group commanders would wage separate battles, often with each other—and with dire results for the ending of the war in Europe.

Monty, having lost his struggle for tactical command in the battle for the Ruhr, now learned the cost of having treated Bradley like a poor relation. Though Monty's Ruhr plans were approved by Eisenhower in January 1945, so were Bradley's new plans, in the Ardennes! Combating simultaneously on all fronts was, despite the manifest failure of such strategy, back in business—not because the Allied high command really believed in such a military strategy, but because Eisenhower could not bring himself to choose between the different plans proposed by his army group commanders.

"I very much regret that since 17 Jan we have lost all the ground we had gained," Monty lamented to King George IV on 24 January; "infirmity of purpose, indecision, and national pride are all becoming apparent; the agreed plan is fading into the distance; instead of regaining the strategical initiative it remains with the enemy on this front; and we are losing the opportunity created by the Russian offensive. . . . It is a tragedy."

Assuaging Bradley's Bitterness

Monty had, in the end, only himself to blame. In his address to the press on 7 January he had spoken of the value of teamwork. But the truth was, unless he himself was in charge, Monty had not the faintest idea of how to play in a team. As the Prime Minister made clear on 26 January, when Monty flew to London to complain of Eisenhower's continuing conduct of the war, Monty should consult a mirror. Thanks to his "cock-a-doodle" crowing after the Ardennes, the American generals had declared "their troops would never again be put under an English general."

By the American generals, Churchill meant Bradley. "While we are fighting our own war, we are certainly helping the British very materially, and our own interests should come first," Bradley recorded in a January memorandum, pleading with Eisenhower to return Ninth U.S. Army to his command. Eisenhower countered by stating "that he had fought the propaganda to put Marshal Montgomery in command so long it was wearing him out; that we had all agreed that eventually the Ninth Army should be under the 21 Army Group for the attack north of the Ruhr, and that by putting it under 21 Army Group at the present time, he might be able to shut up the element that was trying to put everything under Marshal Montgomery."

Eisenhower's diplomacy certainly worked in that Bradley eventually accepted Eisenhower's decision regarding Ninth U.S. Army, which remained in 21 Army Group; but it did not assuage Bradley's bitterness. "Bradley is badly upset over E.'s decision to leave 9th Army under Monty," Mrs. Summersby noted at Versailles. "He sees the logistics [sic] of E's decision, but the real trouble fates [sic] back to Dec and Jan. when Monty got so much publicity in the press."

From now on, Bradley chose to see in Monty a power-hungry Briton rather than a professional, tactical commander fighting Germans. "In considering any of Montgomery's plans," Bradley would write in a confidential note after the war, "it was necessary to consider how such plans affected Montgomery personally. His plans were most always designed to further his own aggrandizement."

Thus the situation, early in 1945, once again resembled that of the fall of 1944. There was, however, one crucial difference. After Normandy, Eisenhower's policy of dispersed thrusts on a very wide front had given Hitler the opportunity both to build up and launch the most concentrated single counteroffensive attack of the war. Monty's blunting of that attack and the subsequent Russian offensive which opened on 12 January 1945 now made the chances of German exploitation very slim.

The danger was thus no longer German counterattack. Rather, it was the unnecessary prolongation of the war, with concomitant casualties—and the likelihood that, in the end, not the Western Allies but the Soviets would win.

Keeping Bradley Employed Offensively

A merican casualties in the Ardennes were meanwhile reaching almost the same level as those of the *entire* Normandy battle, from D-Day to Paris—yet with no sign of success. Still Bradley fought on, resuming command of Hodges' First U.S. Army on 16 January, but refusing to give to General Simpson's Ninth U.S. Army the divisions needed to take part in Monty's pincer plan to cross the Roer, outflank the German defenses in the north, and prepare a launchpad for the crossing of the Rhine—Operations Veritable and Grenade.

By 22 January, Monty was in despair, writing to Brooke: "So far as I can see the Ardennes battle is being continued *for the sole reason of keeping Bradley employed offensively.*"

Brooke agreed—as did the Germans. Allied Intelligence now showed that Hitler was moving his Sixth Panzer Army to the Eastern Front.

"Although we are attacking in the Ardennes the German is moving troops away," Eisenhower's assistant noted on 30 January. "E. says we are not hurting the German very much."

At a "stormy" conference convened the next day, Eisenhower and his staff argued with General Bradley, with "some very violent speaking on all sides." Finally, at lunchtime on 1 February, Monty's telephone rang. It was General Whiteley, with news that, after the matter had been raised at Combined Chiefs of Staff level, Eisenhower had, in the end, decided to end the Ardennes offensive and transfer his weight to the north, under Monty. Bradley must immediately close down his operations in the Ardennes and shift his strength to Monty's flank to capture the vital Roer dams, if Grenade was to be launched in tandem with Veritable on February 8.

Lending Bradley his personal aircraft, Eisenhower meantime asked Bradley to return at once to his new headquarters at Namur and get working on the new plan. Bradley took off at 1:45 P.M., in high dudgeon. For the second time he had lost the battle of the Ardennes.

Expunged from Memory

In conversations with visiting dignitaries and journalists, Bradley and his courtiers now began to spin the myths that would dominate subsequent American writing about World War II. The Normandy campaign had only been rescued from British stalemate by bold American opportunism, they now claimed. In the Ardennes, Bradley had foreseen the German intentions and given all necessary corrective orders to forestall the German drive to the Meuse, even before Monty took charge, as Hansen quoted his revered general saying at dinner, in his diary:

> In recalling the staff organization during the Ardennes attack the General remembered that not a written order had been planned for the

movement of troops. He stated that everything depended upon the essential movement of men and material to the Third and First Armies and they were tremendous. Bradley's decision to engage the forces immediately is probably his biggest and quickest of the war. Within five minutes after he ascertained the extent of the German drive, he had ordered armored divisions in the south to reinforce the Luxembourg front. It was this quick decision that permitted us to save the Duchy and at the same time provide the 101st with armored strength and permit them to hold Bastogne. General Bradley admits the decision was the quickest he had ever made—and incidentally one of the most crucial.

Bradley's refusal to credit the strength of the German attack in the Ardennes was thus expunged from memory—and with it the confusion, complacency and breakdown in communications between Bradley and his commanders. From now on the publicity accent would center upon opportunistic American exploitation of circumstances as opposed to British rigidity, deliberately drawing attention away from the hard, unromantic aspect of Allied success in battle: the business of careful planning, of detailed training and rehearsal, and the necessity for relentless will in the execution of an Allied masterplan against a professional German foe.

Such revised self-portraiture was unfortunate, since it had been Bradley's quiet professionalism in command of 2 U.S. Corps in Tunisia, then in Sicily, and above all as First U.S. Army Commander and 12th U.S. Army Group Commander in Normandy that had demonstrated his real virtue: he was a soldier's soldier, intelligent, shy and undemonstrative. Now, in the wake of his two defeats in the Ardennes, he allowed his staff not only to concoct ever wilder press statements and disseminate ever more misleading versions of American tactics, but even to invent complete lies—such as Ralph Ingersoll's latest plan to "plant" a rumor that Bradley had deliberately enticed the Germans to attack in the Ardennes to draw off German reserves from the Eastern Front, prior to the Russian offensive!

Lamentable though such attitudes might be, however, they reflected not only the shame of the Ardennes but the unfortunate fact that, as Bradley put it, the new Allied Rhineland battle in February 1945 "was a 21 Army Group show."

In these circumstances, the success of operations Veritable and Grenade could only rub salt in American wounds—and did.

Success in the North

The early spring thaw, followed by German flooding of the Roer dams, did nothing to dampen Monty's spirits. As before D-Day, Monty was determined to visit as many of his commanders and men as possible before they went into battle, and he was well aware of the conditions in which they would have to fight. "I visited the VERITABLE area today. The ground is very wet and roads and tracks are breaking up and these factors are likely to make progress somewhat slow after the operation is launched," he warned the CIGS on 6 February, two days before Veritable began. "I am visiting the GRENADE area tomorrow."

Simpson's Grenade area was no better. "The Roer River is very flooded," Monty reported to the CIGS on 7 February. "I met and talked to all the Corps and Divisional Commanders. All ten American Divisions are now assembled in 9th Army area and they are all in good shape and ready for battle. I have ordered that GRENADE will be launched on 10th Feb."

Fought over four fateful weeks in February and early March 1945, Monty's two pincer operations, Veritable and Grenade, proved triumphant. By 1 March, Monty was signaling excitedly to Brooke that "the enemy seems to have lost all grip on the battle in this area and his command organisation seems to have broken down. We have captured static back area units who are quite unaware of the situation and in one area we captured a complete armoured column of tanks moving westwards from NEUSS towards MUNCHEN GLADBACH which was very astonished at being captured.

"I am unable to say how many prisoners have been captured today but the number is considerable and divisions are finding them an embarrassment in the fast moving battle.

"All headquarters are moving forward and the distances for liaison are becoming great and I shall be on the move myself very shortly and back to the caravan life in the fields."

For the first time since Normandy the operations of three major Allied armies—Canadian, British and American—were married to a single tactical purpose, under a single commander. As in Normandy, the result confounded all Bradley's and Eisenhower's staffs' predictions of doom or stalemate, netting 100,000 German prisoners, and putting Simpson's Ninth U.S. Army on the Rhine in five days—indeed, in a domino effect, German resistance west of the Rhine thereupon began everywhere to collapse, even enabling Collins' 7 U.S. Corps, on Simpson's right flank, to obtain a small bridgehead across the Rhine at Remagen.

At last, the Ruhr was within striking distance of the Allies—so much so that Eisenhower announced that if Monty's plans to cross the Rhine (Operation Plunder, set for 23 March) proved successful, he intended to shift Bradley—currently dissatisfied by his subsidiary role—north and to put him in command of Ninth and First U.S. Armies once again, alongside Monty's Second British and First Canadian Armies, for the dénouement of the campaign in Germany.

This, ignored by virtually all military historians, was the last chance to weld the Anglo-American armies together at the climax of the campaign to defeat Nazi Germany—and it failed, *tout court*, because Monty simply could no longer bring himself to work alongside Bradley, or to abandon the theories of clear-cut battlefield command that had brought him, save at Arnhem, such a string of victories.

Plunder

As he had before D-Day, Monty now assembled the senior officers of his three armies on 21 and 22 March to sum up the enemy's strategic situation, and then outline the main features of Plunder.

The Germans, Monty began, had made three great military blunders—accepting decisive battle south of the Seine in the summer of 1944, then launching their Ardennes offensive without adequate air support and reserves, and finally "fighting it out" west of the Rhine, where some 200,000 German casualties had recently been suffered. The only German strategic reserve, Sixth Panzer Army, had now been drawn off into combat on the Eastern Front in Hungary; the Ruhr had been paralyzed by Allied air interdiction, and the Saar and Palatinate industrial belts had been overrun. The Rhine was now the last major barrier to the march of the Western Allies.

Operation Plunder, mounted between Wesel and the Ruhr, was opposed only by five enemy divisions, with two in reserve. "Thereafter, apart from odd battle groups, the enemy had no further reserves capable of opposing our advance. By D + 4 we should have established twelve divisions east of the RHINE which would be opposed by eight German divisions. It was essential to go all out in the early stages and seize quickly a large bridgehead within which the enemy would be unable to pin us down."

Those who had attended Monty's great D-Day conferences the year before at St. Paul's School were aware of the same sense of historical moment. The weather was fine, the troops were confident. As in the Normandy landings, the airborne drop would help guarantee the amphibious assault, even if the latter met stiff opposition. Thereafter it would be up to the armor to strike out, if necessary being resupplied by air.

"The enemy has been driven into a corner," Monty declared in the last "Personal Message from the C-in-C to be read out to all Troops" he would issue during World War II. "Events are moving rapidly. The complete and decisive defeat of the Germans is certain; there is no possibility of doubt on this matter. 21 ARMY GROUP WILL NOW CROSS THE RHINE. The enemy thinks he is safe behind this great river obstacle . . . but we will show the enemy that he is far from safe behind it. . . . And having crossed the RHINE, we will crack about in the plains of Northern Germany, chasing the enemy from pillar to post. . . . May the 'Lord Mighty in battle' give us the victory in this, our latest undertaking, as He has done in all our battles since we landed in Normandy."

Not all were so confident. The commander of the famed 51st Highland Division, Lieutenant General Rennie, had a premonition of death; there were anxieties about the strength of German antiaircraft fire in relation to the daylight airborne drop. General "Bill" Simpson would have preferred an earlier, unplanned assault, as at Remagen. But Monty himself exuded optimism. It had been the most striking feature of his military campaigning since Alamein to face an enemy on the defensive, whether across minefields, wadis, mountains, seas or, as now, the greatest river in Europe, some 1,500 feet wide. As Monty had found before Dunkirk and thereafter in Home Forces in England, the lessons of World War I were redundant in modern battle, where no defensive line could be made safe against invasion. The defender had to spread his forces throughout the front. Given ruthless leadership, tactical surprise, great concentration of men and firepower, and a violent and relentless prosecution of the assault, offensive success was assured. Moreover, once having drawn the enemy into all-out combat in a particular area, the Allies could then exploit their advantages of superior air and artillery firepower to gain decisive victory—in this case smashing their way to Berlin without fear of enemy counterattack.

Monty was now more confident than he had ever been. The Germans did not have the mobile reserves to prevent a relentlessly mounted breakthrough, and the plan for the assault, beginning at dusk on 23 March and rising to a crescendo the following morning as the two Allied airborne divisions were dropped, was in Monty's eyes so good that he was quite prepared to postpone the operation if bad weather prevented the airborne drop. Thus in the early afternoon of 23 March he wrote a final word to his son David's guardians:

My dear Phyllis,
    We are off over the Rhine. I send you two copies of my message to the soldiers; give one to David. . . .
    The weather is lovely, and if it keeps fine we should have a very good operation. The P.M. arrives this evening to stay the weekend. . . .
    In haste

                                    Yrs ever
                                    Monty

A Momentous Moment

C hurchill had insisted, against all advice, on coming to watch the Rhine crossing. "I didn't want him but he was determined to come; so I have invited him in order to keep the peace," Monty explained to the Minister of War, Sir James Grigg. The Prime Minister would be "difficult to manage and has no business to be going," Brooke himself noted in his diary on 22 March. "All he will do is to endanger life unnecessarily. However, nothing on earth will stop him."

The august party landed near Monty's new Straelen headquarters at 5 P.M. on 23 March, and after tea Monty gave Brooke and Churchill a personal briefing in his map lorry. "The whole plan of our deployment and attack was easily comprehended," Churchill later recalled with typically romantic grasp of the great drama to which he was privy. "We were to force a passage over the river at ten points on a twenty-mile front from Rheinberg to Rees. All our resources were to be used. Eighty thousand men, the advance guard of armies a million strong, were to be hurled forward. Masses of boats and pontoons lay ready. On the far side stood the Germans, entrenched and organised in all the strength of modern fire power."

Punctually at 9:30 P.M., Monty retired to his bed. But for Brooke it was a "momentous moment," and one to be savored. For all his austerity and reserve, Brooke was a sentimental man, and when Churchill asked him to walk outside in the moonlight, he complied. Churchill's reminiscences, harking back to the desert days of August 1942 and the long but triumphant years since then, were especially moving for Brooke, since Churchill for the first time chose to thank his CIGS for his unfailingly wise counsel, his refusal to be intimidated, and his ability to choose good men and delegate responsibility. But when they returned to Churchill's "wagon," the mood of quiet pride in their mutual achievement was disrupted by a new signal from Stalin, accusing Churchill of duplicity in trying to make a separate peace with the Germans. Once again Brooke witnessed the daily burden the Prime Minister carried.

Only fifteen miles away, meanwhile, the battle to cross the Rhine in massive force was under way. Marveling at Monty's mixture of sangfroid and self-confidence, Brooke was unaware of the latest machinations over what was to happen *after* the Rhine crossing.

"One man must be in general command north of the Ruhr," Monty had stated emphatically in a letter three days before to "Simbo" Simpson—determined *not* to share command in the north with Bradley once the Allies were across the Rhine. "I shall be interested to see what comes next. Jock Whiteley is coming to stay here tomorrow night and he will get my view in no uncertain voice."

A New Plan

To General Whiteley, in "no uncertain voice," Monty had duly put forward an alternative plan. Eisenhower's current directive that two army groups—his own and Bradley's—operate north of the Ruhr should be abandoned. Instead, the nascent Fifteenth U.S. Army headquarters under General Gerow should, Monty recommended, take over and hold a defensive front across the west face of the Ruhr. Instead of moving north, Bradley should remain south, launching an attack from the existing First U.S. Army Remagen bridgehead as a pincer movement to encircle the Ruhr, as Monty had first counseled in September 1944: "12 Army Group should get a good large bridgehead from BONN to MAINZ and then strike northeast; joining me east of the RUHR." Devers' 6th Army Group would then be responsible for the front south of Mainz.

For two days Monty had heard nothing. Eisenhower was vacationing on the Riviera with Kay Summersby, and no decision could be given

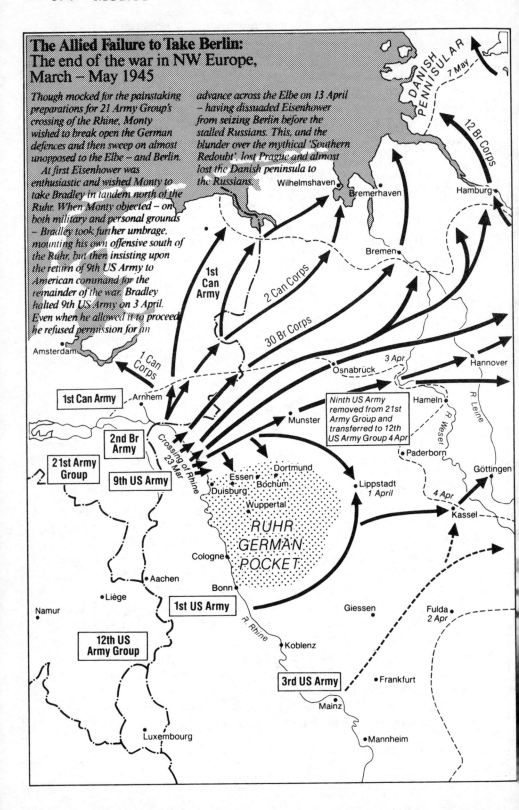

The Allied Failure to Take Berlin:
The end of the war in NW Europe,
March – May 1945

Though mocked for the painstaking
preparations for 21 Army Group's
crossing of the Rhine, Monty
wished to break open the German
defences and then sweep on almost
unopposed to the Elbe – and Berlin.
At first Eisenhower was
enthusiastic and wished Monty to
take Bradley in tandem north of the
Ruhr. When Monty objected – on
both military and personal grounds
– Bradley took further umbrage,
mounting his own offensive south of
the Ruhr, but then insisting upon
the return of 9th US Army to
American command for the
remainder of the war. Bradley
halted 9th US Army on 3 April.
Even when he allowed it to proceed
he refused permission for an

advance across the Elbe on 13 April
– having dissuaded Eisenhower
from seizing Berlin before the
stalled Russians. This, and the
blunder over the mythical 'Southern
Redoubt', lost Prague and almost
lost the Danish peninsula to
the Russians.

DANISH PENINSULAR

7 May

12 Br Corps

Wilhelmshaven

Bremerhaven

Hamburg

Bremen

1st Can Army

2 Can Corps

30 Br Corps

3 Apr

Osnabrück

Hannover

Amsterdam

1 Can Corps

1st Can Army

Arnhem

2nd Br Army

21st Army Group

9th US Army

Crossing of the Rhine 23 Mar

Munster

Ninth US Army
removed from 21st
Army Group and
transferred to 12th
US Army Group 4 Apr

Hameln

R Weser

R Leine

Paderborn

Göttingen

Essen   Dortmund

Duisburg   Bochum

Wuppertal

Lippstadt
1 April

4 Apr

Kassel

RUHR
GERMAN
POCKET

Cologne

1st US Army

Aachen

Bonn

Liège

Namur

12th US Army Group

R Rhine

Koblenz

Giessen

Fulda
2 Apr

Frankfurt

3rd US Army

Mainz

Mannheim

Luxembourg

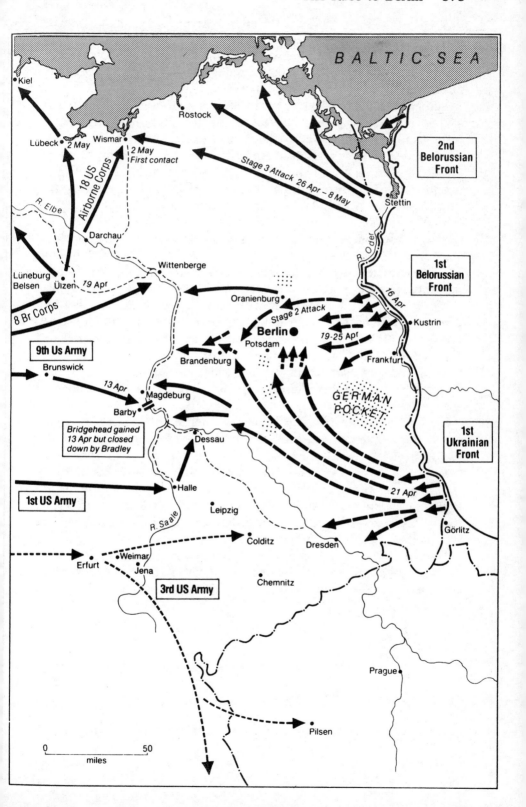

BALTIC SEA

Kiel

Rostock

Lübeck 2 May   Wismar
2 May   2 May
First contact

18 US Airborne Corps

Stage 3 Attack 26 Apr – 8 May

2nd Belorussian Front

R. Elbe

Darchau

Stettin

R. Oder

1st Belorussian Front

Lüneburg Belsen   Ülzen   19 Apr   Wittenberge
8 Br Corps

16 Apr

Oranienburg

Stage 2 Attack

Kustrin

9th US Army

Berlin

Potsdam

19-25 Apr

Brunswick

Brandenburg

Frankfurt

13 Apr   Magdeburg

GERMAN POCKET

Barby

1st Ukrainian Front

Bridgehead gained 13 Apr but closed down by Bradley

Dessau

1st US Army

Halle

21 Apr

R. Saale

Leipzig

Colditz   Dresden   Görlitz

Erfurt   Weimar
Jena

3rd US Army

Chemnitz

Prague

0   50
miles

Pilsen

in his absence. However, on 23 March, anxious like Churchill to witness the historic Rhine crossing north of the Ruhr, Eisenhower flew from Cannes to General Simpson's Ninth U.S. Army Headquarters at Maastricht—and it was there that Eisenhower was given Monty's new plan, dressed up as a SHAEF proposal.

Surprised, Eisenhower telephoned Bradley, who was—so Monty was told—"very pleased with it." Instead of waiting until mid-April to take command of First and Ninth U.S. Armies north of the Ruhr, Bradley could under the new plan push straight ahead into Germany, south of the Ruhr, with First and Third U.S. Armies—of which the latter had, unknown to Monty, erected that morning a pontoon bridge across the Rhine, north of Worms. With General Marshall cabling that same day from Washington to complain about "the overdose of Montgomery which is now coming into the country," Eisenhower not only immediately approved on the telephone the gist of Whiteley's new plan, but asked Bradley to throw an immediate press conference that day to obtain better coverage in America of 12th U.S. Army Group operations.

Monty heard the "good" news about his plan shortly before Churchill arrived on 23 March. The next morning Churchill and Brooke set off with a hamper to watch the airborne operation from a nearby hill. Monty, however, drove to his Ninth U.S. Army Assault Corps Headquarters at Rheinberg to see his field commanders, General Simpson and General Anderson, the 16th U.S. Corps Commander— and Eisenhower.

Simpson reported that the Rhine crossing in the sector was going excellently—indeed, some thirteen battalions of U.S. infantry were already across the river. But it was in a side office alone with Eisenhower that Monty "fixed" the matter of strategy and command. Eisenhower confirmed he was agreeable to the new plan for enveloping the Ruhr from north *and* south, and it was arranged they would return for a formal conference the next day, together with Bradley, to go over the concomitant details and boundaries.

Eisenhower's erstwhile directive for Bradley to share Monty's breakout north of the Ruhr was now dead—and with it, unknown to Monty, any hopes that he would keep Ninth U.S. Army after the seizure of the Ruhr.

American Suspicions

A s in Normandy, Monty was too energized by command in battle to pay attention to the feelings of staff officers in rear headquarters or press opinion. With Ninth U.S. Army under his command he was confident he could now smash his way across northern Germany. Speed, moreover, was essential, for the Soviets were already on the Oder, only thirty-five miles from Berlin.

Ruthless and clear-cut command would win the day for the Western Allies, Monty was certain, and he returned to his headquarters at Straelen well satisfied by the verbal deal he had struck with Eisenhower.

Eisenhower was less sure—sensing that Monty might be intending to finish off the war himself, leaving Bradley and Devers only subsidiary roles. However, provided Bradley did not take exception to his new, pincer task south of the Ruhr, Monty's plan promised flexibility at a time when anything was possible—with secret surrender negotiations already being requested by Himmler, Westphal (chief of staff to Rundstedt), Blaskowitz (commanding German Army Group H) and von Zangen (commanding the German Fifteenth Army), Kesselring (C-in-C South) and Wolff (C-in-C in Italy). Eisenhower had therefore given his provisional blessing to Monty's proposal, flying that afternoon to Namur to discuss it in person with Bradley, prior to the "Big Three" conference the next day.

Bradley's enthusiasm for the new plan was genuine. In reality he had no more desire to move his headquarters north of the Ruhr and join Monty there than Monty had—especially since the original plan entailed relinquishing Patton's Third U.S. Army to Devers in the south. By launching his First and Third U.S. Armies eastwards towards Giessen he could, instead, surround the German troops east of the Rhine between Remagen and Worms; then direct, if necessary, *both* armies north to outflank the Ruhr, or send one to Frankfurt. Thus "we were delighted to get the 'go-ahead' signal on our plans," Bradley later chronicled, considering that this was in fact "superior to Montgomery's [earlier] plan."

But was it? Superior or not, the latest plan also aroused Bradley's suspicions. What was Monty really up to?

Whereas Eisenhower suspected Monty's strategic-egoistic ambitions—to win the war by himself—Bradley remained haunted by the shame of the Ardennes. Simpson's Ninth U.S. Army had never been returned to 12 U.S. Army Group, and its loss rankled. Monty's motives must be possessive, Bradley remained certain—"I got the very definite impression," he confided after the war, "that Montgomery was more interested in commanding as many American troops as possible than he was in having a large number of divisions attack north of the Ruhr."

Bradley was not alone in this. Back at Reims, Eisenhower's personal assistant recorded the same SHAEF feeling that Monty was primarily interested in feathering his own nest by keeping command of the maximum number of American troops. Eisenhower, she noted, saw Monty, "who is very satisfied. . . . The attack is going well. . . . He now says that he does not want any more American troops. Monty really wants to retain command of the 9th Army. He knows very well that if another American Army is committed in his area he will loose [sic] co[n]trol of the 9th. E[isenhower] would be forced to put Bradley in comans [sic] of American troops."

In Marlborough's Footsteps

U naware of such suspicions, Monty's eyes remained fixed upon the Elbe. At his headquarters that evening, with Churchill and Brooke in attendance, he listened to the glowing reports of his liaison officers—and dictated his nightly telegram to the War Office.

Once again Churchill was mesmerized by Montgomery's "methods of conducting a battle on this gigantic scale. For nearly two hours a succession of young officers, of about the rank of major, presented themselves. Each had come back from a different sector of the front. They were the direct personal representatives of the Commander-in-Chief, and could go anywhere and see anything and ask any questions they liked of any commander, whether at the divisional headquarters or with the forward troops. As in turn they made their reports and were searchingly questioned by their chief the whole story of the day's battle was unfolded. . . . This process having finished, Montgomery gave a series of directions to de Guingand, which were turned into immediate action by the Staff machine. And so to bed."

There can be no doubt that Monty's grip on the day-to-day performance of such vast forces in the field was made possible by the courage and tenacity of his team of personal liaison officers, some of whom traveled between 200 and 400 miles each day on their missions, using jeeps and Auster aircraft. Joining Monty's team that spring, after serving almost two years as military assistant to the CIGS in Whitehall, Major Peter Earle had first met Monty during the Normandy campaign, when he had been repulsed by Monty's behavior at table: his cocksure vanity, schoolboy jokes and bumptious bad taste. But working for Monty in the field of battle, Earle was soon astonished by Monty's continual concern for his staff, as well as his extraordinary brand of battlefield leadership: "a bounder, a complete egoist, a very kind man," he noted, perplexed, "very thoughtful to his subordinates, a lucid tactician, a great commander."

Churchill, meanwhile, pondering Monty's qualities as a commander, began to cast his mind back to his ancestor the Duke of Marlborough, whose life and campaigns he had once studied in four volumes, and which, bound in leather, he now presented to Monty. On their way to meet Eisenhower—for Churchill insisted on accompanying Monty—Churchill began to expound on the parallels between Monty's system of liaison officers and Marlborough's use of strategically stationed lieutenant generals watching the battle.

Monty affected to listen. But in reality his own mind was on the plains of northern Germany, "His [Churchill's] visit was very amusing," Monty confided to the Reynoldses; "but it is difficult to attend properly to the battle while he is here." At Rheinberg, Monty once again learned the latest "score" on Ninth U.S. Army's front, where German resistance was rapidly becoming a rout. However, it was in a private tête-à-tête with Eisenhower and Bradley that the real meat of the remaining campaign was to be decided: decisions that would affect the history of Europe for the next generation.

Eyes on the Elbe—and Berlin

Amazingly, given its importance, no record of the Rheinberg meeting on 24 March 1945 was kept. According to Monty, however, the new strategy of enveloping the Ruhr from north and south was discussed, in order that Eisenhower might issue a formal Supreme Commander's directive. As the three senior Allied commanders pored over the map of Germany Monty had brought with him, Monty outlined his plan for racing on to the Elbe. "I explained my plan of moving up to the ELBE line," Monty recorded a fortnight later, "and drew on the map the right boundary that I suggested for 21 Army Group i.e. between me and Bradley. The only comment made by IKE was that he thought MAGDEBURG (on the ELBE) should be inclusive to Bradley; it [sic] had drawn it as inclusive to me. I at once agreed, and Bradley agreed also. No other comment was made."

Elated by his "blitzkrieg" success in crossing the Rhine, Monty's focus was on the Elbe—and Berlin. The last thing Monty wanted at this stage was a Stalingrad-like battle to mop up the Ruhr. Without reserves, fuel or air support, Field Marshal Model's Army Group B could not do much offensive damage once surrounded in the Ruhr, and would probably surrender without heavy Allied casualties being incurred in house-to-house fighting. It was time, Monty felt, to cast caution aside and strike deep into Germany with Allied armor and close air support: and Eisenhower's lack of comment, save for the assignation of Magdeburg to Bradley, Monty construed as agreement.

It was—but not for long.

Completely Wrong

M onty was not the only person to misjudge Eisenhower's new mood. Field Marshal Brooke had monitored Eisenhower's changes of mind over the past fortnight with wry humor. The war in western Europe was now virtually won. If Eisenhower wanted Bradley to command an army group north of the Ruhr—as de Guingand had informed Brooke on 16 March—then, however administratively congested it would make the campaign, so be it. When on 19 March de Guingand had telephoned to say the idea was "off," only to learn via "Simbo" Simpson that it was "on" according to Eisenhower's latest letter to Monty, Brooke "laughed" and declined to fret. "He did not feel the Operations Staff at SHAEF were being very firm in any view of theirs," Simpson informed Monty; but provided Eisenhower did not actually withdraw forces *away* from Monty's three armies in the north, Brooke agreed with Monty that events should dictate "the tactical strategy to be employed."

Thus when Brooke, accompanying Churchill and Monty, met Eisenhower at Rheinberg on 25 March, he saw no danger in Eisenhower's latest plan not only to surround the Ruhr from the north *and* south, but to thrust also to Frankfurt. In his diary that night Brooke recorded:

He [Eisenhower] also wanted to know whether I agreed with his present plan of pushing in the south for Frankfurt and Kassel. I told him that, with the Germans crumbling as they are, the whole situation is now altered from the lines of our previous discussions. Evidently the Boche is cracking and what we want now is to push him relentlessly, wherever we can, until he crumbles. In his present condition we certainly have the necessary strength for a double envelopment strategy, which I did not consider applicable when he [the enemy] was still in a position to resist seriously.

The failures that had beset the Allies since September 1944, culminating in the disaster in the Ardennes, were now forgotten. Eisenhower telegraphed to his mentor, General Marshall: "Naturally I am immensely pleased that the campaign west of the Rhine that Bradley and I planned last summer and insisted upon as a necessary preliminary to a deep penetration of the Rhine, has been carried out so closely in accordance with conception. You possibly know that at one time the C.I.G.S. thought I was wrong in what I was trying to do and argued heatedly upon the matter [on the eve of the Ardennes catastrophe]. Yesterday I saw him on the banks of the Rhine and he was gracious enough to say I was right, and that my current plan operations are well calculated to meet the current situation. . . . I hope this does not sound boastful, but I must admit to a great satisfaction that the things that Bradley and I have believed in from the beginning and have carried out in the face of some opposition both from within and without, have matured so splendidly."

Brooke was enraged when Eisenhower repeated this travesty in his memoirs of the campaign, *Crusade in Europe*, in 1948, but waited some eleven years before authorizing Arthur Bryant to publish his diary entry, contradicting Eisenhower's account—adding, "I am quite certain that I never said to him 'You were completely right,' as I am still convinced that he was completely wrong!"

Brooke was clear that Eisenhower's "broad-front" strategy had, in fact, prolonged the war by six months—but that, in the wake of the Rhine crossing, it no longer mattered. As Monty's diarist innocently recorded:

> The great successes all along the front which followed as a natural result of the successful battle in the north, made everyone happy; all was well, the end of the war in Europe was clearly in sight and success had united the Allied commanders in a way that nothing else could.

But in this assumption, Monty's diarist was now to be proved spectacularly mistaken.

The Blind Optic

Meanwhile, even Winston Churchill was surprised by Monty's wild good humor now that it was clear Operation Plunder was a triumph and the Allies were about to sweep across Germany. Expecting to be rebuffed, Churchill suggested going across the Rhine after Eisenhower's and Bradley's departure from Ninth U.S. Army Headquarters. "Why not?" Monty replied.

To General "Bill" Simpson's consternation the three most important British figures of the war—Brooke, Churchill and Montgomery—thus squeezed into a tank landing craft, crossed the Rhine, and walked for about half an hour on the east bank. Monty then asked the craft's captain to motor downriver to the town of Wesel. When the captain refused, owing to the danger of floating mines, Monty packed the party into jeeps and drove them there, along the west bank. Soon Churchill was seen scrambling across the twisted wreckage of Wesel's iron-girder railway bridge. As German shells began to land uncomfortably close, raising great plumes of white spray from the dark river, General Simpson finally appealed to Churchill's good sense: "Prime Minister, there are snipers in front of you; they are shelling both sides of the bridge and now they have started shelling the road behind you. I cannot accept the responsibility for your being here and must ask you to come away." Brooke noted in his diary, "We decided it was time to remove the P.M., who was thrilled with the situation and very reluctant to leave!"

That evening Monty's liaison officers reported on the latest situation. Though the airborne drop had resulted in considerably higher casualties than at first thought—"30% in personnel" in 6th British Airborne Division, as Monty recorded sadly in his nightly cable to the War Office—its effect had been to destroy the last vestiges of German morale. Thus on the left flank of the assault, where there had been no airborne drop, progress was still poor, with fierce hand-to-hand fighting, whereas in front of 12 British Corps and 16 U.S. Corps, where Allied airborne troops had landed, resistance had melted. Simpson already had three Class 40 bridges across the Rhine in 16 U.S. Corps area, and had taken 3,500 prisoners; 12 Corps also had three bridges across. Prisoners in 21 Army Group exceeded 10,500. The gateway to the plains of north Germany seemed at last unbarred. With six bridges up and more being constructed by the hour, the time was approaching when the Allied tank divisions could be fed across the Rhine. "I shall exploit to the full the good progress made on the right flank by 16 US Corps," Monty signaled to the War Office, "and on 12 Corps front will drive eastwards toward BRUNEN and RAESFELD and northwards towards BOCHOLT."

Monty explained later in a letter to "Simbo" Simpson (now Assistant CIGS):

> My dear Simbo,
> I managed to get rid of the P.M. on Monday afternoon. . . . It was difficult to get down to the battle properly till he had gone.
> It was then clear to me that there was not very much in front of me between DORSTEN and BOCHOLT, and I then decided to burst through between these two places and to repeat the PAS DE CALAIS tactics [i.e., masking centres of resistance while pushing ahead with armored columns]: and to make for the ELBE. This was on the evening of 26 March.
> I ordered Army Commanders to come to my Tac HQ at 10 a.m. 27 March, and gave out my orders; I had given them the gist of my intentions on evening 26 March by telephone.

Monty was quite aware that in ordering his army commanders to race straight to the Elbe, he was contravening Eisenhower's latest directive, issued after the Rheinberg conference the day before, in which it was clearly laid down that the Ruhr was to be surrounded and mopped up *before* an advance further east took place:

> You will note that I have ignored completely SCAF 247; there are moments in war when you take risks and act boldly; and use the [Nelson] doctrine of the "blind optic"!!

Nevertheless, elated by the way German resistance was crumbling, Monty felt "certain that SHAEF will be delighted," and after meeting his three army commanders the next morning he sent the following signal to Eisenhower:

> Today I issued orders to Army Commanders for the operations eastwards which are now about to begin. My general plan is as outlined in follow-

ing para. My intention is to drive hard for the line of the ELBE using Ninth Army and Second Army. The right of the Ninth Army will be directed on MAGDEBURG and the left of the Second Army on HAM-BURG. . . . The operation will be similar in design to those when we crossed the SEINE and drove hard across the rear of the PAS DE CALAIS with Canadian Army mopping up the coastal belt of the PAS DE CALAIS later. I have ordered Ninth and Second Armies to move their armoured and mobile forces forward at once and to get through to the ELBE with the utmost speed and drive. The situation looks good and events should begin to move rapidly in a few days.

Had this been all, it would have been enough. But in a last paragraph Monty added, with typical Monty flourish:

My Tactical Headquarters move to an area 1033 Northwest of BONNINGHARDT on Thursday 29th March. Thereafter the axis on which my Tactical Headquarters move will be WESSELMUNSTER–WIEDENBRUCK–HERFORD–HANNOVER—thence via the Autobahn to BERLIN I hope.

Eisenhower's Peach

Monty's assumption that SHAEF would be "delighted" was overoptimistic. His nagging insistence that Eisenhower adhere to his, Monty's, tactical strategy for winning the war had more than once brought Eisenhower to the brink of despair. Now, pepped up by his recent holiday and the spectacular Allied successes not only in the north but then in First and Third U.S. Army sectors too, Eisenhower had traveled to Bradley's headquarters in Namur on 25 March. The following day he crossed the Rhine at Remagen together with Bradley, Hodges and Patton. From Remagen he returned on the morning of 27 March to his forward headquarters at Reims, and in the afternoon drove to Paris for a major press conference—a performance which his ADC-cum-PR officer, Lieutenant Commander Butcher, considered "a peach." Thereafter he watched a preview of a SHAEF D-Day film in the Champs-Elysées, and spent the night incognito at the Raphael Hotel with his assistant, Mrs. Summersby. It was thus only on his return to Reims the next morning, 28 March, that he finally saw Monty's cable about advancing to the Elbe—and Berlin.

Only days before, in an official message to the Combined Chiefs of Staff, Eisenhower had declared: "While we are continuing to plan for army to be ready to meet strong resistance, it is my personal belief that the enemy strength on the western front is becoming so stretched that penetrations and advances will soon be limited only by our own maintenance. . . . *I intend to reinforce every success with the utmost speed.*"

Why, then, did Eisenhower now decide, without reference to the Chiefs of Staff, to stop Monty and the Allied advance?

No biographer or historian would ever adequately explain Eisenhower's strange and sudden metamorphosis in the last days of March 1945. Certainly Monty never understood the decision to halt him in his tracks and wreck the logical conclusion of the campaign—though his shrewd suspicion was that Bradley had had a significant hand in what was to him SHAEF's "skulduggery."

Abandoning Berlin to the Russians

For Field Marshal Montgomery's eyes only from Eisenhower. Top secret.
I agree in general with your plans up to the point of gaining contact with Bradley east of the Ruhr. However thereafter my present plans being co-ordinated with Stalin are as outlined in following paragraphs. . . .

E isenhower's cable on the night of 28 March 1945 was for Monty the biggest shock of the war—with the mention of Stalin the phrase that most stunned him. He had spent three days in the company of Churchill and Brooke, from 23 to 25 March, and no reference had ever been made to an arrangement with Stalin regarding coordination of the end of the war; nor had Eisenhower mentioned such a plan when conferring with Monty and Bradley at Rheinberg on 25 March. What then could such a plan possibly entail?

Eisenhower's signal duly spelled out the core of the new strategy:

> As soon as you have joined hands with Bradley in the Kassel-Padderborn area *Ninth United States Army will revert to Bradley's command.*
>
> Bradley will be responsible for mopping up and occupying the Ruhr and with the minimum delay will deliver his main thrust on the axis Erfurt–Leipzig–Dresden to join hands with the Russians.
>
> The mission of your army group will be to protect Bradley's northern flank.

There was no mention of Berlin. Only *after* Bradley had laboriously mopped up the Ruhr would the Western Allies advance to meet the Russians—and then in *southeast Germany.*

Far from ending the war on equal terms with the Soviets, joining hands in the conquered capital of the Third Reich, Eisenhower had sold out. Why?

Very Dirty Work

"**O**n 28 March I issued M563, my written directive [to 21 Army Group commanders]," Monty wrote in renewed despair to "Simbo" Simpson. "On this same day I received the blow from IKE in which he disagrees with my plan and removes Ninth Army from me; a very good counter-attack!! All very dirty work, I fear."

Monty, fuming with anger and disappointment, even enclosed with his letter a photograph taken of himself with Eisenhower and Bradley on 25 March at Rheinberg, three days before the blow. "From the look on Bradley's face there is obviously trouble ahead!" he remarked with disgust—for thinking back, Monty felt Eisenhower and Bradley must have been planning to revise the Allied plan, but had deliberately kept silent until Churchill and Brooke were out of the way. Apart from commenting that he thought Magdeburg should be inclusive to Bradley, Eisenhower had made no objection to Monty's explanation "round the map" of his next moves to the Elbe, nor of his continuing command of Ninth U.S. Army: "No other comment was made. Yet on that day IKE must have known that he was going to take Ninth Army away from me, and that he intended the main thrust to be southeast towards DRESDEN so as to join up with the Russians in that area."

As Monty saw it, it had all been planned in advance, to scotch his advance by giving the Russians the pearl of the campaign: Berlin.

Spiking Monty's Guns

Was Monty right?

No record was kept by Eisenhower or Bradley of their 25 March discussion, nor did either of them ever record the exact genesis of the momentous decision not to advance to Berlin. However, the historical evidence does not support Monty's view that it was premeditated. As late as 29 March, Bradley's own ADC, Major Hansen, for instance, assumed—as he noted in his diary—that the Allied target was Berlin ("In the Third Army sector the 4th Armoured Division is continuing its smashing penetrations eastward and is now being turned north toward Kassel to complete our *first phase of the battle for Berlin*" [author's italics]).

How, then, did Eisenhower come to his decision? Did it derive from SHAEF Intelligence officers, who feared a last-ditch German stand in the south German mountains: the so-called Southern Redoubt?

Intelligence information about such a stand had begun to circulate in the second week of March 1945, though Monty certainly did not take the notion seriously when asked by Churchill for his opinion. Bradley's appreciation, by contrast, was very different. Far from mounting a token rearguard struggle, Bradley believed "and is convinced that we shall have to fight the German in to the mountain fortresses of southern Germany and there destroy the core of his SS units which are determined to carry on the battle," Major Hansen had recorded as early as 9 March: a battle that might go on for *a further year,* Bradley cautioned!

This concern with the "Southern Redoubt" seems, sadly, to have grown like a tumor at SHAEF, fueled by Eisenhower's British chief of Intelligence, Major General Strong. By 27 March, as both 21st Army Group and 12th Army Group began to cut armored swathes into the German interior, Eisenhower was openly warning at his Paris press conference that "the German would probably make a stand in the mountains." The next day, having seen Monty's cable about advancing to the Elbe and Berlin, Eisenhower then had lunch with General Bradley at Reims.

Bradley's personal visit to Reims may well have played the decisive role, as Monty suspected, in Eisenhower's sudden decision to abandon Berlin to the Russians. Certainly Eisenhower asked Bradley, at the luncheon, how many casualties the seizure of Berlin from the west might entail. Without thinking, Bradley gave the first number that came into his head, namely the casualties he had suffered in the Ardennes: 100,000.

That Eisenhower did not ask Monty, in command of the Allied forces racing to the Elbe, the same question spoke volumes. "Had Bradley been on the northern flank, Eisenhower might well have sent him to Berlin," Eisenhower's biographer, Stephen Ambrose, later admitted. But Bradley was *not* on the northern flank—thanks to Monty. Nor did Bradley wish to advance on Berlin. To allow Monty to seize the city, however, was to Bradley unthinkable after the business of the Ardennes.

Thus, over lunch in Reims, a small city in northern France, over 300 miles in the rear, Eisenhower and Bradley now decided to spike Monty's guns.

A Message to Stalin

E isenhower's orders were emphatic. Monty was to halt in his tracks and hand back Ninth U.S. Army to Bradley's command. 12 Army Group would methodically "mop up" the Ruhr, then make for Dresden in the southeast, and Regensburg in the south, to prevent the establishment of Hitler's "Redoubt." Eisenhower cabled that afternoon directly to the Allied Military Mission in Moscow for immediate transmission to the Russian dictator:

> *Personal Message to Marshal Stalin from General Eisenhower.*
> My immediate operations are designed to encircle and destroy the enemy forces defending the Ruhr, and to isolate that area from the rest of Germany. This will be accomplished by developing offensives around the north of the Ruhr and from Frankfurt through Kassel, until the ring is closed. The enemy enclosed in this ring will then be mopped up.
> I estimate that this phase of operations will terminate in late April [i.e., in *four weeks'* time] or even earlier, and my next task will be to divide the enemy's remaining forces by joining hands with your forces.
> For my forces the best axis on which to effect this junction would be Erfurt–Leipzig–Dresden; moreover, I believe, this is the area to which the main German governmental departments are being moved. It is along this axis that I propose to place my main effort. In addition, as soon as the situation allows, a secondary advance will be made to effect a junction with your forces in the Regensburg–Linz area, thereby preventing the consolidation of German resistance in a redoubt in southern Germany.

That Eisenhower could have cabled to tell the Russian dictator—unasked—of a new Allied plan he had neither placed before his own superiors (the Combined Chiefs of Staff) nor his own army group commanders save Bradley was one of Eisenhower's most astonishing acts in World War II. Air Marshal Tedder, the Deputy Supreme Commander, was not present at Eisenhower's luncheon—and was not even consulted in the drafting of the new plan!

Understandably, Monty could scarcely believe his eyes when, early the following morning, he was shown Eisenhower's decrypted message. Not knowing what Eisenhower was transacting with Stalin, he felt "that complete silence is the best line of country at the moment"—though convinced Eisenhower's decision had nothing to do with military reality but was designed as a sop to Bradley, as he reported to "Simbo" Simpson:

> I hear privately that there has been great pressure from the staff at SHAEF, and from BRADLEY, to get Ninth Army back from 21 Army Group. Ninth Army has done very well in 21 Army Group; the better it does, the greater is the pull to get it back: and BRADLEY shoves very hard at the back of the scrum. With victory in sight the violent pro-American element at SHAEF is pressing for a set-up which will clip the wings of the British Group of Armies, and relegate it to an unimportant role on the flank; the Americans then finish off the business alone.

"I am making no change in my plans and orders," Monty confided to Simpson—in the desperate hope that with Brooke's help he might get Eisenhower's order rescinded without having to close down his thrust to the Elbe. He had, after all, managed to get withdrawal of Eisenhower's plan for Bradley's army group to be moved north of the Ruhr only a few days previously. There was a strong chance that if his British and American armies looked like breaking out for the Elbe without hindrance and with only nominal casualties, the very force of circumstance would suffice. To Eisenhower he therefore signaled a brief and poignant "holding" plea:

> I note from FWD 18272 that you intend to change the command set-up. If you feel this is necessary I pray you not to do so until we reach the ELBE as such action would not help the great movement which is now beginning to develop.

Brooke, equally shocked by Eisenhower's unauthorized message to Stalin, quickly forwarded copies of Monty's supplicatory telegram, together with Eisenhower's directives, to the Prime Minister—hoping against hope it was not too late.

Churchill's Remonstration

C hurchill was already suspicious, even before Brooke's message. He had seen a copy of Monty's signal of 27 March heralding a great Anglo-American advance to the Elbe; when a copy of Eisenhower's message to Stalin arrived in London on the evening of 28 March, concerning the "main" Allied effort in the Dresden area, but not mentioning Berlin, northern Germany, the North Sea ports or Denmark, Churchill was nonplussed. "This seems to differ from last night's Montgomery, who spoke of the Elbe," he minuted General Ismay, his military secretary. "Please explain."

Ismay could not. By the morning of Thursday, 29 March 1945, "a fair gale" had started to blow in Whitehall—in fact, Churchill telephoned SHAEF on the "scrambler" at 6:45 P.M. to protest to Eisenhower personally. "He does not agree with E's future operational plans," Mrs. Summersby noted, "and wants our forces to turn North instead of East. In other words he wants to keep a large force under Monty."

Besotted by the figure of Monty, Eisenhower's staff could not at first see the strategic point behind Churchill's vexation. They therefore insisted upon treating it as a protest against the removal of Ninth U.S. Army from Monty's command, instead of an appeal to seize Berlin while the Western Allies still could—whether under Bradley *or* Montgomery.

Churchill, however, was demonstrating once again the genius of his political, diplomatic and military perception. Britain was only contributing a "quarter of the forces invading Germany," he warned the British Chiefs of Staff as they prepared protesting signals to send to the American Chiefs of Staff; though the latest Allied successes might owe their genesis to Monty's great battle in the Rhineland, the fact remained that Eisenhower's policy of closing the Rhine throughout its whole length had been enacted, enabling the Allies to mount a double advance now, rather than the single one originally insisted upon by the British Chiefs of Staff at Malta. Eisenhower's stock thus stood very high in Washington—and accusations that he was not considering "issues which have a wider import than the destruction of the main enemy force in Germany" sounded very odd coming from men who had for so long sought to teach their American cousins to concentrate their forces on defeating the enemy, rather than on territorial or political gain. To argue that Montgomery ought to be given sufficient American strength to help clear up the North Sea ports, Denmark and the Baltic *before* Eisenhower had dealt with the "main enemy forces" was inconsistent with previous British military policy; moreover, their argument about U-boat bases was unsound, since the current U-boat meance was far less damaging than had been anticipated.

What Churchill correctly perceived, after seeing a copy of Monty's signal to the CIGS about the imminent removal of Ninth U.S. Army from 21st Army Group, was that Britain was being relegated to an almost "static role in the North," condemned to wait until an "altogether later stage in the operations" in the Ruhr before it could advance across the Elbe in the north. Moreover, it ruled out the prospect of "the British entering Berlin with the Americans"—if the Americans fought their way to Berlin. The gravity of Eisenhower's telegram to Stalin, however, was that the Americans did *not* now intend to go to Berlin—and it was *this* strategic decision the British government and the British Chiefs of Staff must combat while they still could. "I do not know why it would be an advantage not to cross the Elbe," Churchill signaled to Eisenhower. "I do *not* consider that Berlin has yet lost its military and political significance."

To his Chiefs of Staff, Churchill meanwhile minuted: "The idea of neglecting Berlin and leaving it to the Russians to take at a later stage does not appear to me correct. As long as Berlin holds out and withstands a siege in the ruins, as it may easily do, German resistance will be stimulated. The fall of Berlin might cause nearly all Germans to despair"—and he instructed them, instead of chiding the Americans, to do everything in their power to make Washington see the importance of reaching Berlin, not Dresden, and of ensuring the Russians were not permitted to enter the Danish peninsula before the Western Allies, irrespective of who was in command of whom.

A Terrible Mistake

N ot even Churchill, however, could gauge the extent of "American" feeling at Reims and Namur. Bradley had wanted Ninth U.S. Army returned to him after the humiliation of the battle of the Ardennes; Eisenhower had then courageously refused, regardless of Bradley's injured pride. Now, however, the tables were turned; the American armies were enjoying great success, and nothing that Churchill or the British Chiefs of Staff might say could alter Eisenhower's determination to do right by Bradley. Thus, on 31 March 1945, Eisenhower formally rejected Monty's plea to be allowed to continue to the Elbe.

The Ruhr, Eisenhower directed, must first be "brought under control." Thereafter "the axis KASSEL–LEIPZIG" seemed to the Supreme Commander "the most direct line of advance" to divide and destroy the German forces opposing the Allies, and the best way to join hands "with the RED ARMY." Beyond that, Eisenhower was unsure whether to go north "to seize the important naval, political and shipping objectives across the ELBE or to the south to destroy any effective concentration of forces which the enemy may succeed in creating [the "Southern Redoubt"]. The course I shall adopt," Eisenhower explained, "must depend upon the development of a very fluid situation."

Without Ninth U.S. Army, however, Monty would be marginalized, leaving General Bradley in sole charge of the Ruhr operation. Only when the Ruhr was actually captured would the Western Allies proceed—and Bradley would be "in the position to judge" when the best moment came to strike east to Leipzig—with Ninth U.S. Army under command. Later, if operations across the Elbe were required, "an American formation" could be furnished to 21st Army Group. "You will note that in none of this do I mention BERLIN. That place has become, so far as I am concerned, nothing but a geographical location, and I have never been interested in these," Eisenhower added, untruthfully. "My purpose is to destroy the enemy's forces and his powers to resist."

Once again Monty was shattered. In his soldierly view, it was futile to waste time mopping up the Ruhr when the "main business" lay to the east and the north; it would be enough, he considered, to turn one corps of Ninth U.S. Army around the north face of the Ruhr; the rest, he felt, should be directed alongside Dempsey's Second Army to the Elbe. Now, with Eisenhower's unequivocal signal of 31 March, the advance to the Elbe was off: "The gist of his [Eisenhower's] reply is that he intends halting the present movements whilst 12th Army Group cleans up the Ruhr," Monty lamented to Brooke the next day. "After that 12th Army Group will develop a thrust on Axis LEIPZIG–DRESDEN to join up with Red Army. For all these operations he intends that 9th Army will return to Bradley and he adheres to this decision and this alone is quite enough to halt the present movement. . . . I consider we are about to make a terrible mistake. The great point now is speed of action so that we can finish off German war in shortest possible time. We must keep going and NOT give enemy time to recover and especially we must not let his troops in Holland and northern Germany get down to the south.

"It seems doctrine that public opinion wins wars is coming to the fore again," Monty added, knowing that Bradley was behind the pull to get Ninth U.S. Army transferred, for American public consumption. "I have many times told Ike that this is a dangerous doctrine and in my opinion it is victories in battle that win wars. The Germans have had a great defeat and are in a state when if we act correctly we can finish the business quickly."

In reporting this to the CIGS, Monty promised to "maintain complete silence." But Monty was not one to surrender without a fight, whatever Brooke's advice. Summoning his chief of staff, Freddie de Guingand, Monty urged him now to put pressure on his friend Bedell Smith, who was recovering from his recent illness.

This, according to Monty, de Guingand did—and Bedell Smith at first assented to Monty's strategy, as Monty excitedly reported to "Simbo" Simpson on 2 April:

I got Freddie to put over to Bedell the plan outlined in para 5 of M564; this was done and Bedell agreed. Conference took place at SHAEF last night and this morning, to try and reach a sound decision.

But it was, in the end, in vain.

As after Normandy, Eisenhower was in another world, buoyed by the success of his armies in the field, flattered by sycophantic courtiers, and for the moment oblivious to the magnitude of his, and Bradley's, historic miscalculation.

Standing Fast

That very morning, 2 April 1945, Monty was ordered to hand over Simpson's Ninth U.S. Army at midnight the following day. As Monty pointed out, this meant that "12 Army Group stands fast and cleans up the Ruhr pocket"; only weeks later, with Ninth U.S. Army under command, would it then set off in "a S.E. direction towards DRESDEN." Meanwhile 21st Army Group would, with its Canadian and British armies, be left to undertake its coastal tasks alone. No 12th U.S. Army Group forces would be available to support or even flank Dempsey beyond Hannover: "21 Army Group effort is secondary and it does what it can, looking after its own flanks; it is not visualized that it will go beyond the line BREMEN–HANNOVER."

As Monty protested, without Ninth U.S. Army he could no longer carry out his advance to the Elbe between Hamburg and Magdeburg, "unless of course the Germans all run away. I shall go on to the WESER on the general line MINDEN–BREMEN [halfway to the Elbe] and there I may have to stop; even this may take some time," he warned, for experience in the aftermath of Normandy had shown that both in Brittany and in the Pas de Calais it took far longer and far more troops to mask or reduce enemy-held ports than was anticipated. Yet the North Sea ports were vital not only to the effective overrunning of Germany but to its administration thereafter; and with Russian forces on the Oder, the Red Army had only *half* the distance to advance to reach the east bank of the Elbe—giving it free access to the Danish peninsula and Kiel Canal: an alarming prospect.

"I have always fought for being strong on the left i.e. in the north," Monty summarized, looking back over the campaign. "From September 44 to January 45 we were never strong enough in the north to get decisive results. Then in February 45 I was given the Ninth Army and for the first time we were really strong in the north; the results were terrific and everything else was 'added unto us.' Now we are to be weak again in the north, and no good will come of it," he prophesied. "A strong effort in north Germany is the correct strategy in this campaign; it is vital from the naval point of view.

"Nothing could have stopped us getting to the ELBE, and then we hamstring the whole enemy naval and submarine campaign. Now, it is not even contemplated that we should get there; the north is to play a secondary role while the main effort goes off to the S.E. I have a feeling that this new plan of IKE'S will prolong the war. I hope the P.M. understands this."

Meanwhile, Monty reported to Simpson, "these alarms" had caused de Guingand to have another breakdown—"he is not sleeping and has to take drugs again; his brain races along and gets no rest. If he gets no better I shall send him home for a few days rest.

"All work would be so much easier if the 'captain of the ship' would handle his ship properly; we spend so much time rushing from one side of the ship to the other side, trying to keep it on an even keel."

Having Ninth Army for a Bit

That Eisenhower, for so long a champion of pragmatic, broad-front advance, should suddenly halt his armies and limit their tasks to methodical, step-by-step operations seemed an irony indeed. De Guingand, sensitive, warmhearted, and a model of inter-Allied harmony, was indeed rendered sleepless and ill by the tensions and misunderstandings surfacing now, at the very moment when the war seemed won. Again and again he attempted to make SHAEF see that without Ninth U.S. Army, Monty could not be expected to liberate Holland, seize Bremen and the north German seaports, cross the

Elbe in the east and forestall the Russians from reaching the Danish peninsula. However, at Supreme Headquarters in Reims, possession of the Ninth U.S. Army had now become an emotive, indeed patriotic issue—as "Simbo" Simpson also discovered on 2 April.

Like de Guingand, Simpson had pleaded by telephone with "Jock" Whiteley, Eisenhower's deputy chief of operations, but without avail, as he reported to Monty: "I said, 'Can you not imagine Monty's feelings when he finds that his most promising plan has been whittled down. Have you had any communication with him and do you know whether he is happy about it?' Jock then made a most illuminating remark in reply: 'Oh! Simbo, do try and be fair. Bradley has feelings too; *and he must be allowed to have the Ninth Army for a bit.*' "

For Simpson this was "the matter in a nutshell."

All historical evidence would sadly point to the same conclusion: namely, that it was Bradley's desire, as the senior American battlefield commander, to regain command of his three U.S. armies at the conclusion of the European campaign—and in so doing erase the stains of the Ardennes disaster—that precluded Eisenhower from accepting Monty's or even Churchill's logic over Berlin and the North Sea ports.

For this, in the end, Monty had only himself to blame. Not only had he humiliated Bradley in the preceding months; he had himself rejected Eisenhower's proposal to insert Bradley's army group headquarters north of the Ruhr and thereby ensure overwhelming Allied strength in northern Germany—the very policy Monty now criticized Eisenhower for relinquishing.

But as Brooke warned Monty, there was nothing to be done. Thanks to Monty's treatment of Bradley, the Second World War in Europe would end not with a *coup de grâce*, but with a terrible *bêtise*.

Part Sixteen

SURRENDER AT LÜNEBURG

Admiral von Friedburg and his German
delegation sue for peace, Lüneburg,
1 May 1945.

The War Between the Allies

"When I review the campaign as a whole I am amazed at the mistakes we made," Monty wrote after the German capitulation.

"The organisation for command was always faulty. The Supreme Commander (Eisenhower) had no firm ideas as to how to conduct the war, and was 'blown about by the wind' all over the place; at that particular business [i.e., commanding the Allied armies] he was quite useless. . . .

"The staff at SHAEF were completely out of their depth all the time."

By then Eisenhower's decision—despite appeals from Monty, Churchill and even General Marshall—to halt the Allied armies until the Ruhr was "mopped up"; his insistence on the "main" Allied thrust thereafter being southeast, to meet the Russians in Leipzig or Dresden; his belief in a mythical "Southern Redoubt"; and his two weeks of refusal to seize Berlin from the west, culminating in the decision not to allow General Simpson's Ninth U.S. Army to race the sixty miles to Berlin from its Elbe bridgehead at Barby on 13 April, had ensured, behind the scenes, a disastrous finale to the war in Europe.

Had Eisenhower left Simpson's Ninth U.S. Army under 21st Army Group command, or even ordered it to cooperate with Monty, under Bradley's command, the situation would have been the reverse. Instead, forced to spend weeks masking the Ruhr and forbidden to operate across the Elbe, the potential power of an entire American army operating on Dempsey's right flank had been squandered. Berlin had not been taken or even reached by the Allies, the Elbe had not been bridged in the north, and it now looked as though the Russians, stalled for so many weeks on the Oder, might actually reach Denmark and the islands before the Allies.

To an almost unbelievable extent, however, the reasons for such tactical and strategic myopia could be traced back to Monty's caravan door. "Montgomery had become so personal in his efforts to make sure that the Americans—and me, in particular—got no credit," Eisenhower later confided to Cornelius Ryan, "that I finally stopped talking to him."

Bradley's feelings were even more pronounced—indeed, a sort of Anglophobic paranoia seems to have infected 12 Army Group Headquarters in the final weeks of the war, blinding even senior officers to the ease of taking Berlin from the west ("I think we could have ploughed across there and been in Berlin in twenty-four to forty-eight hours *easily*," General Simpson later confided), let alone the politico-military necessity of taking the city. Instead, such officers so exaggerated the importance of the mythical "Southern Redoubt" that, according to Major Hansen, they actually became fearful lest Monty's British troops sneak south and take the redoubt before Bradley's forces!

Thus the war between the democracies and the Nazis deteriorated, at its moment of triumph, into a war between the Allies.

Stiff Opposition

F ar from being able to send forces south, Monty found himself completely hamstrung in the north. The chance of a rapid crossing of the Elbe had been lost when Ninth U.S. Army was removed from 21st Army Group Command and halted, on 3 April. However, with German resistance thereafter firming up on the Elbe and all British bridging and engineering equipment concentrated upon the vital seizure of Bremen, the advance of Dempsey's right flank at Lauenburg, near Hamburg, was stalled. "The Elbe is a big river similar to the RHINE and to cross it in the face of stiff opposition is a major operation," Monty warned Brooke on 21 April. The next day Dempsey dolefully confirmed the strength of German opposition, as a consequence of which he would be unable to force a crossing before 1 May, in the wake of the capture—he hoped—of Bremen.

It was in this unprepossessing situation that two of Monty's liaison officers—John Poston and Peter Earle—went missing "I think it likely that they have been captured," Monty cabled optimistically to Brooke on 22 April, for a large pocket of Germans, between Munster and Soltau, close by Tac Headquarters of 21st Army Group, was holding out in the woods; "if so we shall recover them because they cannot be got away."

Monty was, however, wrong. John Poston, the "apple of his eye" and former ADC from the time of Alamein, was dead.

The Death of John Poston

Poston, the youngest of Monty's LOs, had already twice been awarded the Military Cross for gallantry. Between Soltau and General Barker's 8 Corps Headquarters at Lüneburg there were known to be enemy troops (some 2,000 German prisoners were eventually taken, including SS, marines and ten tanks), but given the need for up-to-date information, Major Earle, the LO detailed to drive up to see Barker on 21 April, decided to take the shortest, uncleared route north of the Lüneburg Forest—and took Poston with him. The two men reached General Barker without mishap and obtained his plan for crossing the Elbe with 53rd Division. On the way back, however, traveling at forty-five miles an hour along a route that ran closer to the Lüneburg Forest than the one they had taken (it was 6 P.M. and the officers wished to report back by nightfall), they ran into a German ambush.

Wounded in the arm and temple, their ammunition exhausted, Earle drove the jeep straight at the German machine-gunner in front of him, killing the gunner. Poston and Earle, however, were thrown from the jeep and soon surrounded. As Earle attempted to wipe clean his chinagraph location map of 8 Corps dispositions he was shot again from the back, and fell to the ground. Poston, his Sten gun empty, "was lying some three yards on my right," Earle recalled. "I heard John cry out in an urgent and desperate voice, 'N—No—stop—stop.' These were his last words and were spoken as a bayonet thrust above the heart killed him instantaneously. At the time he was lying on the ground, unarmed and with his hands above his head. He was [left on] the spot, having been stripped of his watch and other valuables. . . . He was the most determined character for his age [twenty-five] I have ever met and, I should say, knew no fear. He was simple, ruthless and absolutely self-contained, a greater lover of animals than of his fellow beings. He would certainly have sailed with Drake."

That night a further two Reconnaissance Corps officers were ambushed and killed on the same small road, as well as a cartload of innocent Russian and Belgian refugees.

Monty's Breakdown

E arle, left wounded with a nearby farmer, survived in a German field hospital to be freed the following evening, 22 April, and was moved to 212 Field Ambulance Station. From there he sent an urgent signal to be sent to Monty's military assistant, "Kit" Dawnay: "Regret to report JOHN POSTON killed at 1800 hrs Saturday 21 April."

Monty's physician, Dr. Robert Hunter, was sent to check Earle's condition in hospital—and recover Poston's body. "It wasn't buried, I found it still lying in the ditch where he'd died," Hunter later recalled. "There was no mark on it save where a bayonet had been plunged through his chest.

"And for the first time I was tempted to tell Monty a lie—to say he'd been killed by a bullet or something during the skirmish. I . . . I knew Monty would be upset.

"When I told him, he just nodded, turned on his heel, and went into his caravan.

"Joe Ewart [Monty's Intelligence officer at Tac Headquarters] said that for a day they could get nothing out of him at all."

Monty was heartbroken. "I regret that JOHN POSTON was killed and we have recovered his body," Monty signaled sadly to Brooke on 23 April. "I would be grateful if you would inform the Prime Minister about these casualties to my LO's as he knew them all and takes a keen interest in their work."

The loss of John Poston, with his "steely blue eyes" and "furious hawk-like face," hit Monty in some ways as harshly as the death of his beloved wife, Betty, eight years before.

Forty years later, Lord Hunter reflected on the event, struggling to explain Monty's quasi-breakdown:

> The LOs were a wild bunch. John Poston was created or thrown up by the war. He'd been with Monty a long time, was devoted to him. And Monty had a sort of paternal affection. . . . Poston was always "up to" something, there were tens of occasions where Monty could or should have hauled him over the coals but didn't—though he knew very well what John was up to.
>
> Monty . . . it was as though John Poston represented something Monty couldn't himself be—because Monty was so disciplined and kept himself on such a tight rein.

Poston's body, meanwhile, was buried "with full military honours in a meadow on the forest edge." He had been, the senior ops room officer recorded, "the most vivid officer we ever had amongst us and his energy ran like a current through all our doings."

Monty, standing by the open grave, wept openly. Poston's death was like the death of a son. This boy, an intrepid liaison officer from Normandy onwards, had now given his life in the service of the uniquely well-informed nexus of operations at Monty's mobile headquarters. Churchill sent a moving telegram: "I share your grief at the death of John Poston and the wounding of Peter Earle. Will you kindly convey to their gallant comrades the sympathy which I feel for them and you. This marvellous service of Liaison Officers, whose eyes you know and whose judgements you can exactly measure, will be one of the characteristic features of the manner in which you exercise your superb command of great Armies."

But not even Churchill's measured compassion could solace Monty.

"For a few days he was like that—would see nobody," Lord Hunter remembered. "Then suddenly he seemed to snap out of it, after the funeral at Soltau when he and his chosen padre, a Scottish Presbyterian Minister called Tindale, buried Poston."

There was a more compelling reason for Monty to snap out of his melancholy, however—for soon after Poston was buried, Monty received a phone call from SHAEF at Reims "to say they hoped I realised the urgent need to get LUBECK before the Russians," Monty reported to the War Office. "This," he expostulated, remembering Eisenhower's deaf ears to his entreaties for the past *month* regarding Ninth U.S. Army, "is adding insult to injury." Barely controlling his spleen, Monty asked de Guingand "to get on to Whiteley and inform him as follows:

1. I have always been very well aware of the urgent need to reach and cross the ELBE quickly. See M563 dated 28 *March*.

2. It was SHAEF that prevented this plan being implemented. They removed the Ninth Army from me and left 21 Army Group so weak that the tempo of the operations became slowed down.

3. If the Russians should get to LUBECK, and on up to KIEL and DENMARK, before we can do so, I would suggest that SHAEF should accept the full blame.
I trust I shall have no more enquiries on that line!

Crossing the Elbe

Monty did, however, have further inquiries—for that evening a cable arrived from Eisenhower himself, reminding him of the important of Lübeck and the Danish peninsula, and belatedly promising Monty that "this HQ will do anything at all that is possible to help you insure the speed and success of the operation."

At a moment when no less than "7 Allied armies are closing on Hitler's 'last stand' redoubt in the mountains of Austria and Bavaria" (as was being openly reported in the press), the assignment of only two armies to clear the whole of Holland, all of northern Germany and all the North Sea ports, and also to seal the Danish peninsula before the arrival of the Russians—who had crossed the Oder in the north on 26 April—had been, for Monty, a sad reflection of Eisenhower's military incompetence. However, too much depended on the outcome, and so, swallowing Eisenhower's affront, Monty advanced the timing of Dempsey's Elbe crossing, writing to "Simbo" Simpson the next day, 28 April, that all was ready for the assault:

> We go over the ELBE tonight; the technique is the same as in the Rhine crossing, and the Commando Bde crosses first (at 0200 hrs) and secures LAUENBURG. 15 Div then goes over. . . . After a spell of lovely weather, it is now cold and wet and altogether very unpleasant. I hope it will clear up before tonight.

That night, the crossing of the Elbe at Lauenburg duly took place. Some 200 men were killed or wounded in the operation, but the bridge was secured and further pontoon bridges soon began to span the river in the wake of the commandos, in readiness for the race to the Baltic.

By the morning of 29 April, Monty was thus confident he could still outstrip the Russians—who were now beginning to break out of their own bridgehead around Stettin, as Monty cabled to Brooke:

> I have just returned from 8 Corps HQ where I met DEMPSEY and BARKER and RIDGWAY commander 18 US Airborne Corps and examined the situation. . . .
>
> I have now given orders as [follows]:
>
> 18 US Corps make an assault crossing over the ELBE in the BLECKEDE area at 0300 hours tomorrow and this will be done with 82 [U.S.] Airborne Div. A further crossing to be made in the DARCHAU area if this is found suitable and possible. 18 US Corps to then operate towards SCHWERIN and WISMAR and it will be joined by 6 British Airborne Div which will be passed over at LAUENBURG. . . . II Armd Div of 8 Corps to be moved forward and to start crossing the ELBE at ARTLENBURG at 1200 hours tomorrow and this division to be directed straight to LUBECK.

The 82nd U.S. Airborne Division's crossing at Bleckede, advanced to 1 A.M. that night, "took the Germans completely by surprise," though the German artillery barrage was, the division's commander later recorded, the greatest the division had ever faced, as the Wehrmacht expended its last stocks of ammunition—including even magnetic sea mines.

Recovering gradually from Poston's death and his funeral, Monty felt sure he could reach Lübeck in good time: "In the Lauenburg area all is ready for rapid exploitation northwards towards LUBECK by armoured columns and this begins tomorrow. I have every hope that we shall reach the LUBECK area in two days time," he cabled Brooke.

As General "Pip" Roberts' 11th Armoured Division raced north, Monty's own "tribe" meanwhile collapsed its tents and began its final move of the war, leaving behind it the flower-decked grave of Major John Poston, MC and bar, in the quiet meadow at Soltau—and the horrors of the nearby concentration camp at Belsen.

Belsen

"The concentration camp at BELSEN is only a few miles from my present HQ," Monty wrote to Phyllis Reynolds on 29 April. "You have actually to see the camp to realise fully the things that went on." For news purposes and for historical evidence, he had immediately ordered photographers and film cameramen to record the extent of German bestiality. "The [enclosed] photographs were all taken by a photographer from my HQ. The SS Commandant is a nice looking specimen!" he added sardonically—having given instructions that the people of the neighboring villages be forced to parade in the camp and see for themselves what their fellow countrymen had done to their fellow human beings.

Through the empty forests and across the Panzer training grounds the vehicles of Monty's Tactical Headquarters meantime wound their way westwards.

"And so we came to the LUNEBURG HEATH—on a windswept site on the bluff above the village of DEUTSCH EVERN with a great view across the barren heath to Southward," wrote the senior operations officer, Major Odgers, a few weeks later. The nomad-like caravan, which had boasted on D-Day twenty-seven officers and 150 men, had grown ever larger. "By now the Headquarters numbered nearly 50 officers and 600 other ranks with over 200 vehicles," Odgers chronicled, "and had travelled over 1,000 miles from the NORMANDY beaches." As the nerve center of some four Allied armies in Normandy and the Ardennes, and three Allied armies until the removal of Ninth U.S. Army three weeks before, Tac Headquarters 21st Army Group had performed outstandingly.

One by one, on 1 May 1945, the vehicles of Monty's Tac HQ drew into the familiar laager formation, with Monty's own vehicles at the center, beneath a cluster of birch trees: his sleeping caravan, his office caravan, and his map lorry, all screened by a vast camouflage net stretched across the three of them. "About 25 feet in front of the caravans was a small portable flag pole," Monty's Canadian assistant, Lieutenant Colonel Warren, recalled, "where the Union Jack was always flown."

"I think we are approaching the moment when the Germans will give up the unequal contest," Monty had written to the Reynoldses on 29 April. "They are hard pressed; they keep on fighting only because every German soldier has taken a personal oath to Hitler and so long as he is alive they must keep on fighting. Once it is known that he is dead, or has cleared out, there will be a big scale collapse."

The Russians were now, finally, in the suburbs of Berlin, and German formations were beginning to surrender to the Allies without further fighting. By 1 May, Russian troops were only a few hundred yards from Hitler's bunker—whereupon, from his temporary headquarters in Lübeck, Admiral Dönitz announced the Führer's death and his own succession as new Führer of the Third Reich, broadcast by Hamburg radio. That same evening, 11th Armoured Division had reached the outskirts of Lübeck, with 6th British Airborne Division being fed across the Lauenburg bridges and into Ridgway's 18 Corps bridgehead north of Bleckede, ready for Ridgway's race to Wismar.

The Russians too were racing forward. By 1 May they had reached Rostock, a bare thirty-five miles from Wismar. The following day, however, patrols of 6th Airborne Division entered Wismar—"our arrival at WISMAR was very unexpected and there were in the harbour nine destroyers and five submarines but our paratroops had no means of shooting up these vessels and they all escaped," Monty cabled the CIGS. The old Hanseatic port of Lübeck fell too, to 11th Armoured Division—forcing Dönitz to move to Plön, and then Flensburg. Monty reported to Brooke on the evening of 2 May:

> There is no doubt that the very rapid movement from the ELBE bridge-heads northwards to the BALTIC was a very fine performance on the part of the troops concerned. There is also no doubt that we only just beat the Russians by about 12 hours. Alls well that ends well and the whole of the SCHLESWIG peninsula and DENMARK is now effectively sealed off and we shall keep it so.
>
> The flood of German troops and civilians fleeing from the approaching Russians is a spectacle that can seldom have been seen before and it will be interesting to see how it sorts itself out tomorrow.

Meanwhile, during the day there had been two indications that the Germans were now ready to surrender, at least in the north. The Commander of the German Twenty-first Army had come into Ridgway's 18 U.S. Corps Headquarters to offer the surrender of his army, facing the Russians. This had been refused. Meanwhile, however, there were indications that General Blumentritt, commanding "the forces facing us between the BALTIC and the WESER river," was willing to throw in the towel. "He is coming in tomorrow at 1100 hours to offer the surrender of his forces," Monty explained to Brooke. "It may well be that he is plenipotentiary for some bigger commander and we shall not know this until tomorrow." As Monty had headed his telegram, "We have had a remarkable day today and tomorrow may be even more so."

The war was finally coming to its appointed end.

The Plenipotentiaries Arrive

The plenipotentiary did indeed represent bigger fish than Blumentritt's forces, as Lieutenant Colonel Warren later recalled:

At 0800 hours on 3 May Colonel Dawnay, the M.A., received a 'phone call from Colonel Murphy, who was General Dempsey's Intelligence Officer, to say that he had received a delegation of four officers, and although General Dempsey had not spoken to them it was thought that they wanted to try and compromise a surrender if they could get certain terms for Germany.

Dawnay went immediately to the C-in-C—whom we called "the Chief"—and reported this to him. He told Dawnay to have Dempsey send them to his Headquarters and when this was done to report back to him. He then pushed the buzzer in his caravan, sending for me. Very quickly he told both of us to get the Union Jack put up; that when they [the four German officers] arrived they were to be lined up under the Union Jack, facing his office caravan; that we were to get everyone else out of sight; the two of us were to put on our side arms, stand at ease to the side about 25 feet between his caravan and the Union Jack, and under no circumstances were we to make a move until he told us; also to get Colonel Ewart, his Intelligence Officer and interpreter.

We expected them to arrive in about twenty minutes. In due course they arrived, escorted by military police, who were immediately dismissed. These four [German] officers were lined up under the Union Jack and being proper officers they stood to attention; two were Navy and two were Army. The Navy officers were dressed in long black leather greatcoats and the Army wore grey greatcoats and the General had the most beautiful red lapels.

On the right of this little line was the Senior Officer, General Admiral von Friedeburg, Commander-in-Chief of the Fleet. Next was General Kinsel, Chief of Staff of the German Army, North. He was a magnificent looking officer about 6' 5", in his late 40's, complete with monocle—a real professional Prussian. Next was Rear Admiral Wagner, Flag Officer to the Admiral of the Fleet. Last was Major Friedl. This chap was really something! He was at least 6' 2" and had the cruellest face of any man I have ever seen—he was 28 years old. . . .

They stood to attention under the Union Jack with great-coats on early in May and it was getting quite warm. They faced the three caravans with the doors all closed. How long they stood there I do not know but it seemed like ages—it was probably four or five minutes and they never moved.

Quietly the door of the centre caravan opened and there stood a rather short Anglo-Irishman, wearing khaki trousers and battle dress, a black beret (which he was not entitled to wear) with two badges, one of the Royal Tank Regiment and the other a hat badge of a general; his hands behind his back.

Monty, as so often in his dealings with dignitaries in the past, deliberately intended to humble the delegation.

The minute they saw him, they saluted. It is interesting to know that in the German Army the Junior Officer's hand comes up and his arm remains there until the Senior Officer has completed his salute—and it just so happened that Montgomery took a hell of a long time to complete his salute! With his hands behind his back he walked very slowly down the five steps to the ground and then the 25 feet so that he was directly in front of the Germans and all the time they remained at the salute. He then very casually put his right hand to his beret in a most slovenly manner and they dropped their arms.

He then looked at the first officer and in a very sharp, austere voice bellowed out: "Who are you?"—and the answer came back, "General Admiral von Friedeburg, Commander-in-Chief the German Navy, Sir." As quick as a flash, and in a loud voice Montgomery shouted back at him: "I have never heard of you." [Von Friedeburg had in fact only been appointed C-in-C of the Navy that day by the new Reichsführer, Admiral Dönitz.]

He then turned to the next fellow and said: "Who are you?" and the same procedure followed until the last officer, who announced that he was "Major Friedl." The Chief barked back, "Major! How dare you bring a major into my Headquarters!"

I whispered to Dawnay the Chief was putting on a pretty good act.

Dawnay whispered back, "Shut up, you S.O.B., he has been rehearsing this all his life!"

Unconditional Surrender

A nd so it seemed. The long road from appeasement and disastrous British performance in war had led inexorably, under Monty's command, from the sands of Egypt, close by the pyramids that marked the boundaries of Napoleon's bid for military supremacy, to the windswept, sandy heath at Lüneburg—and Monty intended to savor the cup of victory to the fullest.

Behind Monty's exercise in personal triumph there was, however, a simpler motive. The German officers had come to discuss a truce. If Monty wished to obtain unconditional surrender, it was important the delegation be made to bow to Monty's personal authority—to credit the power of his command and his absolute determination to go on prosecuting the war to its final, bitter end unless they obeyed him. Without further American troops, Monty did not, in fact, possess the forces necessary to crush quickly the German armies now hemmed into the Danish peninsula if they resisted.

"What do you want?" Monty now barked.

Von Friedeburg answered on behalf of his delegation, saying they had come from Field Marshal Busch, the Commander-in-Chief North, to offer the surrender of the German armies facing the Russians in Mecklenburg—"to ask me to accept the surrender of the three German armies that were withdrawing in front of the Russians between ROSTOCK and BERLIN," as Monty cabled Brooke.

"Certainly not! The armies concerned are fighting the Russians. If they surrender to anybody it must be to the Russians," Monty snapped. "Nothing to do with me."

Then, to soften the blow, Monty added the rider that he would "naturally take prisoner all German soldiers who came in to my area with their hands up."

It was time for Monty to put forward his own demand: that von

Friedeburg and Busch "surrender to me all German forces on my west-ern and northern flanks. These to include the following. All forces in west HOLLAND. All forces in FRIESLAND including the FRISIAN ISLANDS and HELIGOLAND. All forces in SCHLESWIG HOL-STEIN. All forces in DENMARK."

The delegation "refused to agree. But they said they were anxious about the civil population in those areas and wished to come to some agreement with me about looking after them. If I would agree to this, they would arrange some plan by which they withdrew their forces as my forces advanced."

For Monty, this newfound concern with civilian life cut no ice—as Colonel Warren recalled:

> Montgomery replied to this by saying: "Do you remember a little town in England called Coventry, which six years ago was blown off the face of the earth by your bombers? The people who took the brunt of it were the women, children, and old men.
>
> "Your women and children get no sympathy from me—you should have thought of all this six years ago."
>
> He then proceeded to tongue-lash them for some minutes, explaining in great detail some of the concentration camps he had seen and bringing home as best he could, and he was a master of it, the horrors of the war and suffering that they had caused.

Concluding his harangue, Monty rejected agreement with regard to civilians—and warned the delegation that unless they surrendered im-mediately and unconditionally, he would order the fighting and bomb-ing to continue, with the inevitable loss of German civilian as well as soldiers' lives.

"By this time I reckoned that I would not have much difficulty in getting them to accept my demands," Monty later chronicled. "But I thought that an interval for lunch might be desirable so that they could reflect on what I had said."

Drawing to a Close

The German delegation saluted as Monty turned about and walked slowly over to Lieutenant Colonels Dawnay and Warren, out of German earshot. "He told us to put the best possible luncheon on we could in the Visitors' Mess and to supply them with all the drink they wanted," Warren recalled.

"Quickly we got hold of the Mess Sergeant and told him to shoot the works. He used bed-sheets for table cloths. The Officer in charge of the visitor's set-up could speak German and he was instructed to act as Mess Sergeant. Somebody produced, and I don't know where it came from, a white Mess Sergeant's tunic that fitted pretty well, after which we did a job with a number of safety pins. Half-way through their lunch, in which they were given really good food, a bottle of red wine and a bottle of Cognac with their coffee, the supposed Mess Sergeant went in and apologized for the poor meal and explained that the day's rations had not yet arrived. One of them said, 'We have not eaten food like this for months,' and the Mess Sergeant came back with the remark, 'Our Private Soldiers won't touch this muck!'

"In our own mess at lunch, the Chief knew exactly what he was going to do and how he was going to do it. He told us to put our two Mess tables together, to cover them with army blankets and to put one chair, that he would sit at, at one end and four chairs as close as they could be put at the other end; to put two maps on the table, one marked in red, which was to be our front line, and one marked in blue, which was to be their front line. He told Dawnay and me to sit at a table to the side and that we should be armed but to be sure our revolvers were not noticeable; the interpreter [Colonel Ewart] was to stand behind him. The rest was to be left up to him."

All Monty's most competitive, domineering qualities seemed to merge into an absolute clarity about the way he should conduct the meeting. It was certainly an act—but an act upon which, as the final hours of the war ticked away, the lives of many Allied soldiers, airmen and seamen depended. Having given Dawnay and Warren their instructions, Monty walked to his caravan. Warren remembered:

> In due course, after the Germans had had a really good whack at their coffee and brandy, they were asked to come into the C-in-C's mess.
> This time Monty did not keep them waiting.
> Immediately following them, the C-in-C came in, with his tunic on, showing his [field marshal's] rank and decorations. He was abrupt, to the point, and very quick.

Monty put three points before them. "First. They must surrender to me unconditionally all forces as in para three," Monty telegraphed to Brooke. "Second. Once they did this I would discuss with them the best way of occupying the areas and dealing with civilians and so on. Third. If they refused to agree as above then I would go on fighting and a great many German soldiers and civilians would be killed. I then showed them a map of the situation of the western front."

As the German delegation stared at the map, Monty "told them that we had tremendous strength pouring into Germany on the ground," Warren recalled, "and that we had sufficient aircraft for 10,000 bombers, day and night."

The "tremendous strength" was an exaggeration. In truth, *no* new formations were available to reinforce 21st Army Group, the Secretary of State, Sir James Grigg, had just announced, to Monty's consternation. The threat of further devastation from the air, however, was real enough. Hamburg, obliterated by Allied bombers, was only a taste of the air weapon the Allies could now wield—and *would* wield, Monty warned, unless the Germans surrendered. "They had no idea of this situation," Monty cabled to Brooke, "and when they saw the map they at once gave in."

Monty had won—as was clear from the faces of the delegation. But von Friedeburg and Kinsel still needed to obtain formal permission. "They explained that they had no power to agree with my demands," Monty related in his cable to the CIGS, "as they had come solely to get me to agree as in para two above."

When SHAEF was informed in a similar manner that afternoon, Major General Strong completely misunderstood, assuming that formal surrender would emerge through different channels. But Strong was being obtuse—as both Monty and the War Office knew. Von Friedeburg, staring at the special maps displayed on the blanket-covered tables in Monty's mess tent, had lost all hope of prolonging the struggle and was now prepared to recommend to Dönitz as well as to the German Chief of Staff at OKW, Field Marshal Keitel, that they offer unconditional surrender to Montgomery in the north to save further loss of life. As Monty reported to Brooke: "They were now prepared to recommend to KEITEL that he should accept my first point [re unconditional surrender]. Von Friedeburg has gone back to see KEITEL and has taken FRIEDL with him. KINSEL and WAGNER are staying at my Tac HQ until they return."

Von Friedeburg had asked for forty-eight hours; Monty gave him twenty-four—promising to unleash the Allied bombers if no surrender was forthcoming. Von Friedeburg was also asked to question Keitel about "the surrender of other areas e.g. NORWAY. If so I would send him on to SHAEF."

To conclude the discussion, Monty had drawn up an account of their meeting, which von Friedeburg signed, taking one copy with him to Keitel. "There is no doubt that the party came in to study the form generally," Monty summarized in his signal to Brooke, "and to try and get some compromise plan out of me. I think they will agree to surrender unconditionally all forces, as they are now quite clear as to the hopelessness of their situation."

To the Reynoldses, Monty wrote:

I really do think the German war is drawing to a close. Now that Hitler is dead we shall have large scale surrenders—in Denmark, Norway, and in fact everywhere. We took one million prisoners in April, and the total since D day is over three million.

My love to you both

Yrs ever
Monty

Bradley's Fixation

D own at his new headquarters at Wiesbaden, meanwhile, General Bradley was still obsessed by the "Southern Redoubt"—*"We may be fighting one month from now and we may be fighting a year from now,"* Bradley's ADC had quoted him on 24 April. "He is convinced the German is fleeing to the redoubt area with what he can salvage to carry the fight on from there."

Bradley's fixation with the Southern Redoubt would be one of the sadder errors of the end of World War II in Europe. But for Monty that war was now almost over. "Thank you very much for telephoning to me," "Simbo" Simpson wrote from the War Office. "I know that S[ecretary] of S[tate], CIGS and VCIGS are all very grateful for your taking so much trouble, whenever anything big is going on, in letting us know what you think about it personally. I don't think we in the War Office have ever been so completely in the mind of a Commander-in-Chief in the field!

"These are great days to live in. You must have felt a very fine triumph when the Germans came to see you to-day. I wish I could have been present at the interview."

Von Friedeburg felt the opposite. As the two German parleyers were escorted back through the front lines, Monty's staff began to prepare for the possible surrender on the morrow. A marquee was erected for the occasion and Allied war correspondents were summoned, together with the BBC and film cameramen.

In the quiet of his office caravan, Monty now drafted the bleak surrender document he would make the delegation sign, five years after the triumphant German invasions of Norway, Denmark, Holland, France, Belgium and Luxembourg.

The document was brief. It allowed of no misunderstanding. Monty handed it to his ADC for typing, and retired to his sleeping caravan.

Surrender at Lüneburg

A s Monty slept, the signals personnel of Tac HQ, 21st Army Group, tapped out the C-in-C's nightly report to Field Marshal Sir Alan Brooke. On the eastern flank, from the Elbe town of Dömitz to Wismar in the north, "we are now in contact with the Russians and everything is very friendly and it has been agreed that we remain in the positions we now hold," Monty's message ran. From Wismar his northwestern flank then ran across the Danish peninsula via Bad Segeberg down to Hamburg, "and I have given orders that there is to be no further advance beyond this line for the present. . . . We entered HAMBURG this afternoon and are now in full possession of the city with all the bridges intact between that place and HARBURG and in the city itself.

"Between the two flanks there is still much congestion and this will be fully realised when I tell you that the prisoners taken yesterday and today probably total half a million and most of them are still in this area wandering about by themselves."

But would von Friedeburg persuade Dönitz and Keitel to surrender unconditionally straightaway? Monty's Canadian assistant, Lieutenant Colonel Warren, had been detailed to accompany von Friedeburg back to the German lines. "We started out immediately," Warren later recalled. "We had their car, with their driver, and an orderly. In front of this I had my own jeep with my driver and two British Provosts. Behind their car I had another jeep with four British Provosts. We put a small flag pole on each windshield with a white bed sheet which would be visible for some miles and we set out. . . .

"We then drove through Hamburg. . . . There was hardly a building left standing. We had to go down back alleys and the like to get around the debris on the main streets and we were driving quite slowly hoping, of course, nobody would take a shot at us. It took us well over an hour to go through Hamburg . . . and in that whole period we never saw one living thing—not even a cat.

"After we had gone about 12 miles north of Hamburg we turned a corner and drove right into the muzzles of two guns mounted on two German tanks. A young-looking officer, with one arm, was standing by the side of the road in command of these tanks and when he saw the German vehicle he gave the Heil Hitler sign. Major Friedl got out, spoke to him in German, got in the car and left with great speed. I was left facing this officer and I said out loud to my men 'Get in your jeeps, turn around, and let's get the hell out of here as quickly as we can.' Before they left it had been arranged that I would pick them up at this spot at 1400 hours the next day and that I would wait there for two hours only."

The next day, 4 May 1945, Warren returned. The two hours elapsed, but there was no sign of the delegation. Warren told his men, however, to wait, for Monty was quite certain the Germans would sign, as he had explained to Brooke:

> You will now have received my M577 giving you details of the meeting at my Tac HQ today which is almost certain to lead to the surrender of all the remaining troops between West HOLLAND and DENMARK. General KINSEL who is at my Headquarters tonight has had talks with my Intelligence Staff Officer and he states that the forces to be surrendered will total over one million men. He also states that there are four hundred thousand Russian prisoners of war in SCHLESWIG-HOLSTEIN. He further states that there has been an influx of two million civilians into SCHLESWIG-HOLSTEIN which came from the eastern counties as the Russians advanced and that the food situation in the area is such that there will be nothing for them to eat in about ten days time. He added that it is almost certain that KEITEL will surrender tomorrow because it is not possible to get the German soldiers to fight any more and they cannot cope with the frightful civil problem.
>
> You can well imagine from all this that there are some nice problems to solve. . . .

Half an hour after the deadline, vehicles began approaching Warren's party, as Warren vividly recalled: "We got out to meet them and discovered that they had brought another officer with them—it turned out to be a Colonel Pollok."

Pollok carried, in his briefcase, the German army and navy wireless codes, as well as locations of all German naval minefields in the North Sea, Frisian Islands, Heligoland Bight and the Baltic. "We arrived back at our headquarters shortly after 1700 hours and were told to take the Germans to the Visitors' Mess where there was hot coffee and cognac available for them," Warren recounted, "and the two that were left behind met them there. This, then, gave them an opportunity to have a private meeting amongst themselves. While this was going on, Ewart went straight to see the C-in-C, where he advised the Chief that they [the Germans] were authorized to sign."

This was the news that Monty wanted. He had been addressing the Allied war correspondents on the background to the surrender, in fact, when Ewart appeared. "The General-Admiral will be back about five," Monty had just explained. "Ha! He is back!" he remarked, seeing Warren's party arrive. "He was to come back with the doings. Now we shall see what the form is!"

In Monty's caravan, Ewart explained "the form," while the correspondents gathered around the "surrender tent." War correspondent R. W. Thompson described the moment in his dispatch:

> There was complete stillness. The dark woods . . . seemed to enclose a kind of vacuum in which we waited. The rain was driving in the wind and it was bitterly cold.
>
> Fighter planes roaring overhead emphasized the stark bluntness of the ultimatum, and the might of the Allies. . . .
>
> And then they came. Through the woodland, over the crisp brown heather, over the path we had traversed five minutes earlier, the delegates owning the utter defeat of Nazi Germany. . . .
>
> They came slowly, the Admirals in blackish-grey rain-coats, the soldiers in their long grey coats, tight-belted at the high waists, the skirts swinging round their black jack-boots. Only the bright scarlet of General Kinsel's lapels relieved the drabness of their appearance, this solitary little procession bringing with it the submission of a once mighty nation. So they walked, General Kinsel, thick-set, tall, monocled, and the shorter, more thick-set naval officers, to the steps of the Field-Marshal's caravan. General-Admiral von Friedeburg climbed the steps alone, and entered. The others waited, as we all waited. And above these four figures the Union Jack fluttered, the flap of its bunting almost the only sound in this quiet woodland setting.

Monty had only one question, as he recorded later: "I asked him if he would sign the full surrender terms as I had demanded; he said he would do so. He was very dejected and I told him to rejoin the others outside."

Monty now gave orders that the surrender would be signed immediately. "The German delegation went across to the tent, watched by groups of soldiers, war correspondents, photographers, and others—all very excited. They knew it was the end of the war.

"I had the surrender document all ready. The arrangements in the tent were very simple—a trestle table covered with an army blanket, an inkpot, an ordinary army pen that you could buy in a shop for two pence. There were two BBC microphones on the table."

The business, as Colonel Warren recalled, was brisk and to the point. It was clear that Monty was no longer treating the Germans as emissaries, but as men defeated in battle:

> This time they saluted Montgomery and he returned the salute properly and quickly; in fact he was most regimental. The senior members of the Press were then allowed in and stood round the tent wall.

Seated at the head of the table, Monty then read out the "Instrument of Surrender" he had prepared:

> The German Command agrees to the surrender of all German armed forces in HOLLAND, in Northwest GERMANY including the FRISIAN ISLANDS and HELIGOLAND and all other islands, in SCHLESWIG-HOLSTEIN, and in DENMARK, to the C-in-C. 21 Army Group. . . .

It was thus a surrender personally to Montgomery—the climax of a career as an army officer begun so inauspiciously at Sandhurst almost forty years before. Yet, as he read aloud the terms of the surrender with his lisping "R," the simple, tortoiseshell-rimmed reading spectacles set upon the sharp, foxy nose, the five rows of decorations below his lapel, the small gold chain linking the breast pockets of his battle blouse, the bony, sinewy hands resting upon the table on either side of the document, seated with the representatives of a vanquished army, giving that characteristic occasional emphasis to a point—the slightly gnarled knuckles which the artist James Gunn had captured in Monty's tent the summer before—it was evident that the once reprobate cadet had become a master of his profession.

At the press conference at 5 P.M. he had displayed the schoolboyish bumptiousness that so surprised those who did not know him, at one moment relating matter-of-factly the events of the past twenty-four hours, at the next gloating. "My intention is that they shall sign a piece of paper I have prepared," R. W. Thompson reported him saying. "No doubt that if the piece of paper is signed, forces to be surrendered total over a million chaps. Not so bad, a million chaps! Good egg!"

An hour later, however, before the microphones that would broadcast his voice across the Western world, a quite different Monty was in evidence—the ruthless army group commander who brooked no disobedience or vagueness, whose life had been devoted to the study and practice of the art of war. Having read out the "Instrument of Surrender," Monty announced that, unless the German delegation signed the document in front of him, he would order hostilities to resume immediately.

There was a pause, while Colonel Ewart translated the threat into German. The German delegates nodded their assent. Then, rising from his chair, Monty announced that the German officers would sign in order of seniority—and handed General-Admiral von Friedeburg the two-penny pen. Von Friedeburg dejectedly rose, took the pen, and signed. General Kinsel followed, then Rear Admiral Wagner, then Colonel Pollok—each one adding his signature beneath its predecessor. "And Major Friedl will sign last," Monty rasped.

There was silence in the tent, save for the clicking of cameras.

"Now I will sign on behalf of the Supreme Allied Commander, General Eisenhower," Monty declared, signing and dating the "Instrument" to the left of the German signatures, together with his rank: "B. L. Montgomery, Field-Marshal."

"His lips were firm, and as he finished signing he sighed faintly, sat back, and removed his tortoiseshell rims, relaxed. 'That concludes the surrender,' he said. The tent flaps were let down," Thompson recorded, "and we walked away over the brown heather."

Monty's battles were finally over.

Epilogue

Monty in old age, 1968.

In the aftermath of World War II, Field Marshal Sir Bernard Montgomery was made a Knight of the Garter and created 1st Viscount Montgomery of Alamein. Meanwhile, from May 1945 to April 1946, he commanded the British sector of occupied Germany as Military Governor and British Control Commissioner for Berlin.

On 1 May 1946, Monty became head of the British army—CIGS. In a difficult period of postwar austerity, imperial retreat, and increasing confrontation with the Soviets in Europe, he was charged with the transfer of military power to India and Pakistan, the withdrawal of British troops from Palestine, and the crisis of the Berlin airlift. In 1948 he was then asked to become the first military commander of the defense forces of the Western Union, as a demonstration of the intent of the Western democracies to challenge Stalinist expansion in Europe.

In 1951, the United States took over the Western Union military organization, transforming it into the North Atlantic Treaty Organization. General Eisenhower became NATO's first Supreme Commander in Europe, with Monty his deputy.

Seven years later—having loyally served Generals Eisenhower, Ridgway, Gruenther and Lemnitzer as Deputy Supreme Commander, Allied Powers in Europe—Monty retired to his converted mill at Isington, in Hampshire, England. That year his controversial *Memoirs* sold millions of copies worldwide, but sundered his long and difficult friendship with President Eisenhower—for, released from military service, Monty had been determined to tell his side of the World War II story, at whatever cost.

Lonely, venerated by some and disliked by others, Monty traveled, wrote books on leadership and warfare, worked for charitable causes and, on 24 March 1976, died in his bed at the age of eighty-eight. "History will in time deliver its verdict on Montgomery the soldier," stated *The Times* of London; "until it does, he will be mourned not only as a national figure, but, even by those far removed in spirit or sympathy from the profession of arms, as the last of the great battle-field commanders."

Acknowledgments and Sources

G iven the purpose of this book—to condense the three volumes of my official life of Field Marshal Montgomery into a single, more accessible work for the general reader—I have had to dispense with a vast amount of military detail, as well as rich biographical, historical and background material. For this, I hope the more specialized reader and student of World War II will forgive me, and will turn, rather, to the original volumes, published in the 1980s, where footnotes, source notes, further maps, photographs, full acknowledgments and bibliographies may also be found.

The original text and notes for the Prelude and for Parts One through Four of this volume may thus be found in *Monty: The Making of a General* (London: Hamish Hamilton, 1981); for Parts Five through Eleven in *Monty: Master of the Battlefield* (London: Hamish Hamilton, 1983); and for Parts Twelve through Sixteen in *Monty: The Field-Marshal* (London: Hamish Hamilton, 1986). To the original publishers of the *Monty* trilogy, Hamish Hamilton in London and McGraw-Hill in New York, I am particularly indebted, as I shall always be to the director and staff of the Imperial War Museum, where Monty's papers and my own research materials are all now housed.

This single-volume condensation was much harder to achieve than I at first imagined—indeed, without the patient editorial skills of my American and British editors, Robert D. Loomis in New York and Richard Cohen in London, it could not have been accomplished. To both of them I owe a very great debt of gratitude.

Likewise my thanks to my agents Bruce Hunter in London and Claire Smith in New York, who first encouraged the project and arranged for transatlantic publication.

Working on my original text, however, I was reminded how much help and encouragement I derived from Monty's son, David, 2nd Viscount Montgomery of Alamein, and from my father, the late Sir Denis Hamilton, who acted as Monty's literary executor on behalf of the Thomson Organisation, which had purchased Field Marshal Montgomery's papers in 1962. No attempt was ever made to inhibit or proscribe my biographical investigation, nor to influence my version of Monty's struggles with others—and himself. As a result I was able, I hope, to present a candid yet not unsympathetic account of an extraordinary military career, as well as advancing, as far as possible, our understanding not only of Monty the man and soldier, but of the pressures and realities of the battlefields on which he fought.

To the many hundreds of interviewees who contributed to my account, I shall always be in debt—most particularly to Sir Edgar Williams and Sir Charles Richardson, who guarded the innocent author against many an error of military comprehension, as well as of judgment. The staffs of many great institutions in America and Britain cooperated in my undertaking, as recorded and footnoted in my original publication, but let me again record my thanks to them—especially the Eisenhower Library, the Military History Institute at Carlisle, the National Archives in Washington, the Public Record Office at Kew, the Liddell Hart Centre for Military Archives at King's College, London, and the Imperial War Museum at Lambeth.

Finally, let me acknowledge my greatest debt of all: namely to Field Marshal Montgomery himself. Peremptory, vain, bullying to a degree, yet to the end of his life anxious to further the careers and happiness of younger people, he became a surrogate father in my youth. His clarity of mind and purpose, as well as his abiding affection, were, and remain, an inspiration to me.

NIGEL HAMILTON

Index

ABOUT THE AUTHOR

NIGEL HAMILTON was born in 1944 and took an honors degree in history at Cambridge University. His first major biography, *The Brothers Mann*, was critically acclaimed in both Britain and the United States, as was *Monty*, his three-volume official biography of the legendary World War II commander Field Marshal Bernard Montgomery, which won the Whitbread Prize and the Templer Medal.

For four years, while researching the best-selling first volume of his biography of John F. Kennedy, *JFK: Reckless Youth*, Nigel Hamilton has been the John F. Kennedy Scholar and Visiting Professor in the John W. McCormack Institute of Public Affairs, University of Massachusetts, at Boston. He lives with his wife and children in the Boston area, where he is now preparing the second volume of *JFK*.